COMMUNICATION
AND THE
LAW

Communication and the Law
2024 Edition
Communication Law Writers Group
W. Wat Hopkins, Editor

ISBN 978-1-885219-95-4

Vision Press
307 Hoagtown Loop
Sylvan Springs, AL 35118

On the cover: *Scene at the Signing of the Constitution of the United States*, by Howard Chandler Christy (1940), depicts the signing of the U.S. Constitution at Independence Hall in Philadelphia. The painting hangs in the House wing of the Capitol building in Washington.

Printed in the United States of America

Communication Law Writers Group

COMMUNICATION
AND THE
LAW

2024 Edition

W. Wat Hopkins, Editor

VISION PRESS

Preface

The law is ever-changing.

While the guarantees of the First Amendment are provided in clear, succinct language, jurists, attorneys and free-speech advocates have come to learn that interpreting that language is often complicated. Communication law draws upon virtually every type and source of the law — from regulations to statutes, from contract law to constitutional law, from administrative law to the common law. In addition, each year Congress, regulatory agencies, state governments and the U.S. Supreme Court provide a wealth of information that those who follow communication law must locate, digest and come to understand.

So the law — and the interpretation of the law — continues to change.

The publication of the first edition of Communication and the Law in 1998 marked the beginning of an effort to keep up with that change in a concise, readable way. Sixteen authors — among them some of the leading communication law scholars in the country — agreed to update the text annually and to work for its continued improvement.

While authorship has changed — indeed, the number of authors has increased from sixteen to nineteen — the commitment to the comprehensive review of the law and to the continuing improvement of the textbook has not changed, as this, the twenty-first edition of *Communication and the Law*, reflects.

In addition to its comprehensive overview of communication law, this edition of the text discusses some significant events that have had an impact on communication law over the past year. And it continues to follow the evolution of changes that occurred in recent years.

For example, the Supreme Court delivered several important cases during its 2022-23 term, some of which came down late in the term. *Andy Warhol Foundation for the Visual Arts v. Goldsmith*, a copyright case dealing with copyright ownership and transformativeness, is discussed as is *Counterman v. Colorado*, a case involving Internet harassment. In addition, artificial intelligence is discussed for the first time in the copyright chapter, in what is likely to be a continuing discussion. *Dominion Voting Systems v. Fox News*, though not a Supreme Court case, is an important libel case discussed in this edition of the book.

Important new developments are also discussed in the advertising, cable, public relations and confidential sources chapters.

This edition of the textbook is better than the first, but it can be better still. We continue to need the help of our readers. This edition was barely in the mail to the publisher before we began planning the 2025 edition. If you have comments or if there are changes you would like to see, don't wait — let us know now. Our goal is to provide a comprehensive, readable text that is concise but complete. The e-mail address of each author accompanies that author's biography at the end of the book. If you have comments, please let us know.

A number of people played a big part in making *Communication and the Law* possible. I would like to thank longtime friend and colleague David Sloan of the University of Alabama and Joanne Sloan of Vision Press for suggesting the project to me, for encouraging its completion and for their continued support. The eighteen people who, with me, make up the Communication Law Writers Group have been a pleasure to work with. I thank them for their willingness to engage in this venture and for their willingness to work hard to see it through.

As always, I am thankful for my colleagues in the Department of Communication at Virginia Tech, a wonderfully supportive group that makes it a pleasure to go to work each day. Finally, I owe special thanks to the members of my family, especially to my wife, Roselynn, for continued love and support. They make it a pleasure to go home each day.

W. Wat Hopkins
September 2023
Blacksburg, Virginia
whopkins@vt.edu

Table of Contents

Expanded Table of Contents

The Law in Modern Society

By Cayce Myers

☑ **Headnote Questions**

- What is law?
- What are the sources of U.S. law?
- What is the difference between a trial court and an appellate court?
- What are the basic steps in a court case?
- How are judges chosen?

To understand communication law or any other area of the law, students need a general introduction. That is the purpose of this chapter. Although the law is a complex subject, its basics will be presented here so readers will have a framework within which to put any particular aspect of communication law. Like the society it serves, law is dynamic. It is important to come to terms with the fundamentals of communication law, but it is also important to understand the forces that create and sustain the law – forces that inevitably will change the law – and how legal change comes about.

THE NATURE OF LAW

"Law" has a number of meanings. It is usually defined as the rules of conduct established and enforced by authority in a society. The law of a society is one of its most fundamental characteristics; the kind and amount of behavior a society prescribes and proscribes for its members reveal much about the nature of that society. It is the recognition of the law's authority that allows society to function.

The term "law" is also frequently used to refer to a variety of types of law including statutes, court decisions, administrative rulings or private contracts. When people say, "It's the law," they are referring to any sort of official policy. When they use the word "law," people may also mean jurisprudence, the theory of law. Law in this sense refers to a variety of legal philosophies including private ownership, civil liberties, government redress and human rights.

THE SOURCES OF LAW

All American law can be organized according to its sources. Any particular policy affecting communication may be categorized, roughly in the order in which the categories evolved, as common law, equity law, statutory law, constitutional law, administrative law, international law or contract law. These sources work together to inform what is "the law" in the American legal system. Virtually every law examined in this book can be categorized into one of these seven sources of law. When thinking about any particular law, you should consider where it fits in the larger scheme of the law.

Common Law

One of the most important and complex areas of law is "case law." In the American legal system case law is a body of law in which courts have applied the principles established in previous court decisions. These previous decisions are commonly referred to as "precedent." The use of these previous court decisions, or precedents, is the basis for common law.

The roots of common law are found in twelfth-century England, where local courts created a system for resolving disputes between common people. Judges assigned to these courts were charged to determine and apply local customs and values to resolve the conflicts. Consistency became a prized feature of the common law. In the name of fairness, a kind of conflict resolved one day naturally should be resolved the same way the next day, the next year and, perhaps, indefinitely. For a community to be stable, law should be stable, too.

Thus developed the powerful common law principle known as *stare decisis*, part of a Latin phrase meaning that once established, a legal decision should not easily be changed. When a common law court makes a decision, it sets a precedent. Courts within the same jurisdiction are required to apply that precedent in deciding similar cases. Today, one of the main functions of courts is to decide which precedents are applicable. Lawyers find precedent and argue that it should be construed in favor of their clients. Judges must analyze precedent and decide how it applies to particular cases. In a common law system there is a strong preference for following precedent. In fact, when lower courts fail to follow precedent, appellate courts frequently overturn the decisions. It is not a given that *stare decisis* will always govern a court's decision. Sometimes appellate courts may decide to overturn their previous decisions because the court thinks the legal rationale for the decision was wrong.

Colonial America was subject to English common law, and a reformed system continues in modern American courts. Many American judicial precedents are rooted in older British interpretations of law. Today, several areas of law are controlled principally by common law or "judge made" law. Other branches of government generally leave the development of this law, obviously very important in society, to the courts. Other sources of law usually are not specific enough to handle each aspect of every dispute that arises in courts. Thus, judges have to make law to fill in the gaps.

The decisions and accompanying opinions — written rationales for court decisions — are recorded and maintained chronologically. The reports of some trial courts and almost all appellate courts are continuously published according to jurisdiction in consecutive volumes of books called "reports" or "reporters." These bound volumes constitute the seemingly endless rows of books on shelves in law libraries, law offices and courtrooms.

A number of these important analyses of English common law were performed near the turn of the eighteenth century. For instance, Sir William Blackstone, the first professor of law at Oxford University, collated English common law. The resulting set of volumes, which became known as *Blackstone's Commentaries*, organized the law according to subject matter, including the law of freedom of speech and the press. These scholarly collections and analyses of the law for use by lawyers and judges are referred to as legal "treatises" – authoritative books on a particular legal subject. Certain treatises, notably the American Law Institute's *Restatements*, are highly influential on lawmakers and judges, and assist them in defining what the law should be in a particular area.

Equity Law

The United States inherited the law of equity from England, where equity courts were established as early as the fourteenth century. Judges in equity courts, unlike common law judges, were empowered to use general principles of fairness, rather than cus-tom or precedent, in resolving problems. Equity solutions to problems brought to these courts, however, were to be supplemental to the common law, not to supersede it.

It is from these equity laws that we get what is commonly referred to as court orders or "writs." The best known is the writ of *habeus corpus*, provided for in Article I of the U.S. Constitution. Extraordinary writs, most commonly in the forms of temporary or permanent injunctions or restraining orders, are judicial orders requiring people to do something that they do not want to do or stopping them from doing something that they want to do. Violation of a court order would be a serious matter that can result in severe punishment.

The term "writ" has largely been removed from the vocabulary of federal American jurisprudence. The *Federal Rules of Civil Procedure* has done away with the term. However, the writ of *certiorari* (the petition used to ask the U.S. Supreme Court to hear a case) and the writ of *habeas corpus* (a prisoner's petition to be released from illegal imprisonment) remain in use. And some state systems still use the term "writ" for a few specific areas of law.

Statutory Law

The United States is a republican democracy. A pure democracy, frequently called a "direct democracy," is a political system where citizens vote in regular elections on all governmental issues. The United States is a republican democracy in which the majority rules through officials whom the voters elect to represent them in political institutions. Representatives at the municipal, county, state and national levels meet regularly to enact legislation that reflects the will of the electorate. This legislation is called "statutory law."

Legislative bodies, city councils, county commissions, state assemblies and Congress, for example, tend to follow strict procedures to create statutory law. Students of politics have a good sense of how ideas typically become laws. In Congress, a representative or senator may propose a law in the form of a bill, which congressional leadership may refer to an appropriate committee for consideration. The committee may refer the bill to a subcommittee. The subcommittee examines the bill, perhaps by holding hearings or undertaking other studies. After this review, the subcommittee may vote on whether to recommend to the full committee that the bill be amended or not be enacted as a statute. If the majority of the subcommittee members vote in favor of the bill, the committee may conduct additional deliberations before voting on whether to recommend the bill to the full chamber of Congress.

The full chamber may have additional discussion of the bill before voting on whether to enact it as law. In a bicameral legislature, such as Congress, a similar bill has usually followed a similar process in the other chamber. If the legislation is approved in the other chamber but in a different form, representatives of each chamber meet to work out the differences in a conference committee. Both the House of Representatives and the Senate must approve any compromises made in the conference committee. Upon adoption of these changes, a bill is referred to the president, who has the power to veto it. Article 1, section 7, clause 3 of the U.S. Constitution states that Congress can override the veto by a two-thirds vote of each chamber. Rescinding laws requires the same process. All states except Nebraska have bicameral legislatures, while local governments tend to have unicameral councils or commissions.

Other sources of law are apt to be deferential to statutory law because it is seen as the will of the people in a democracy. Statutory law, however, must be consistent with the Constitution and applied, enforced and interpreted by the executive and judicial branches of government. Statutory law sometimes leaves room for interpretation. Sometimes courts give legal interpretations of statutory law in case law. In these situations case law and statutory law work together to constitute "the law" on a particular issue. A state statute applies only to people in the state where it was adopted and must be consistent with both the federal and the state's constitutions; a federal statute applies to all people in the United States and must be consistent with the federal Constitution.

Constitutional Law

The United States' most important contribution to thought about law in society is the written constitution. From 1781 to 1789 the colonies operated under the Articles of Confederation, which placed the colonies in a loose confederation with a weak centralized government. After the American Revolution, each of the thirteen states wrote and ratified a document that was intended to be a kind of powerful contract between the people and government. Carrying the idea of democracy to a new and original extreme, the state constitutions vested sovereignty in the people through the constitutions and designated public officials and government bodies as public servants.

Based on the model of the early state constitutions and the desire for a stronger central government, the U.S. Constitution — written in 1787 and ratified in 1789 — became a model for constitutions of other nations and for states that subsequently joined the union. The Constitution is made up of the Preamble, seven articles and twenty-seven amendments. The most important parts are the first three articles and the Bill of Rights — the first ten amendments.

Important to understanding American constitutional law is the concept of "limited government." The colonial experience with Great Britain taught America's constitutional framers not to trust centralized power. They intended to create governments that would be explicitly excluded from almost all aspects of an individual citizen's life. Governments would be assigned only those functions in society that citizens could not perform for themselves. The Constitution was the device for assigning specific powers to government. The assumption was that govern-

ment was powerless to do anything that it was not entitled to do in the Constitution.

Article I of the Constitution establishes Congress and enumerates its powers, including the powers to tax and mint money, declare war and regulate interstate commerce. Article II establishes the presidency and enumerates its powers, including leading the military, establishing foreign policy and appointing government officers. Article III establishes the federal judiciary and enumerates its powers, including hearing cases involving federal and international matters and disputes between states and between citizens of different states. According to the theory of limited government, the states retain all other powers, or no government can exercise those powers.

FEDERAL JUDICIAL POWER

Article III, Section 2 of the Constitution provides that "the judicial Power shall extend to all Cases ... and Controversies":

1. "arising under this Constitution, the Laws of the United States, and Treaties made, ..."
2. "affecting Ambassadors, other public Ministers and Consuls, ..."
3. "of admiralty and maritime jurisdiction, ..."
4. "to which the United States shall be a Party, ..."
5. "between two or more States, ..."
6. "between a State and Citizens of another State, ..."
7. "between Citizens of different States" [also known as "diversity-of-citizenship" cases], ...
8. "between Citizens of the same State claiming Lands under the Grants of different States, ..."
9. "between a State, or Citizens thereof, and foreign States, Citizens or Subjects, ..."

All other matters are reserved for state courts. Most cases in federal courts involve items 1, 4 and 7.

The framers, particularly Alexander Hamilton and James Madison, believed the federal government could not exercise any powers not enumerated in the Constitution, so they rejected efforts to include a listing of individual rights and liberties, including freedom of speech and of the press, that the government should be forbidden to abridge. Including such provisions in the Constitution was politically popular. In its first session, Congress approved twelve constitutional amendments, the first two of which were not ratified. The remaining ten became the Bill of Rights, including the First Amendment provisions for freedom of religion and expression. Madison clearly changed his mind on the protection of individual rights because he was the congressman who introduced the original bill of rights.

The Constitution, according to Article VI, is "the supreme Law of the Land," which has come to mean that any conflicting source of law must yield to constitutional law. Because the Constitution is brief and often ambiguous, however, its provisions are subject to multiple interpretations. What one person considers an exercise of First Amendment protected "freedom of speech" may not be to another person.

Through their assertion of the power to declare statutory law inconsistent with constitutional law, the courts, especially the U.S. Supreme Court, are decisive in explaining and applying the Constitution. Perhaps the most famous decision in U.S. constitutional history is *Marbury v. Madison* (1803). In his opinion for the Court, Chief Justice John Marshall asserted the power of the U.S. Supreme Court to deem congressional enactments unconstitutional. At best, Article III of the Constitution is ambiguous as to whether the framers meant that the Court should have such power. When reviewing a challenge to the constitutionality of a government action, the Court explains what the Constitution means, thus producing constitutional law.

The Constitution details how it can be amended under the process set out under Article V. It allows the Constitution to be amended either by calling a new constitutional convention, which has never happened, or by a vote of two-thirds of each house of Congress and three-fourths of the state legislatures. Constitutional law, of course, provides the theoretical umbrella for all law. Virtually every law affecting communication is ultimately answerable in some form to constitutional law.

Administrative Law

The nature of American life changed dramatically during the Industrial Revolution. In the decades following the Civil War, the national economy became dependent less on agriculture and more on manufacturing. Business saw the introduction of large-scale manufacturing, corporations and market speculation. Large cities now had to provide public services for growing populations of workers who left farms for factory jobs. These changes occurred in tandem with increased public consumption of manufactured goods, and technological innovations in mass communication and transportation.

As the economy became centralized, industrialists and financiers came to dominate society. They amassed great wealth and used their money to influence politics and government. Farmers, small business owners and workers became increasingly agitated over monopolies that dictated wages and prices. A wealthy few seemed to control markets and governments. Political groups calling themselves "Populists" and "Progressives" emerged near the end of the nineteenth century to seek political change. Frustrated in its appeals to corrupt legislatures, executives and courts, the reform movement pushed the concept of administrative law for reforming government.

The reformers reasoned that if unregulated capitalism resulted in reduced competition in the marketplace of goods and services, then the government should regulate the economy to ensure free enterprise. Some midwestern states first experimented with the idea of administrative law by regulating aspects of intrastate commerce. Then, in 1887, Congress created the first federal administrative agency, the Interstate Commerce Commission, to regulate commerce between states. Beginning in the 1910s, Congress created dozens of so-called "independent" agencies to regulate specific aspects of commerce. Among these agencies are the Federal Communications Commission, the Federal Trade Commission and the Securities and Exchange Commission.

Framers of federal administrative law meant for commissioners to be apolitical experts in the fields they regulate. Instead of being elected in a political process that the regulated industries might control, a commissioner is appointed by the president to a fixed term, although the Senate can veto appointments. Congressional legislation attempts to restrict politics in the appointment process by limiting the number of members of one political party on a commission. Administrative law was to be created by people trained and experienced in the frequently complex issues of finance and technology that the appointees would address. These administrative agencies proliferated during the twentieth century at both the federal and state levels.

Administrative law is a creature of administrative agencies, most of which, unlike other political institutions, have quasi-legislative, quasi-executive and quasi-judicial powers. In short, an administrative agency can pass its own laws, execute those laws and adjudicate disputes over enforcement, unrestricted by considerations of the separation of powers that limit Congress, the president and the courts. The sum total of the rules, regulations, decisions and other policy-making of these agencies make up the body of administrative law.

Also important is how Congress, the president and the courts affect administrative law. Congress empowers the agencies through enabling statutes. An agency can exercise only the power the enabling statute grants. Federal agencies also are governed by the Administrative Procedures Act of 1946, codified in 5 U.S.C. § 551 (1994), which requires that agencies be fair and reasonable. In addition, congressional legislation funds the agencies, and Congress sometimes threatens what it considers agency misbehavior with budget cuts. The agencies are accountable to the president most directly through the appointment of agency members. Decisions of the agencies can be appealed to federal courts, which usually are deferential to the expertise of the agencies but also can rule agency actions to be unconstitutional. This deference to administrative agencies is found in the Supreme Court's decision in *Chevron USA. Inc. v. Natural Resources Defense Council, Inc.* (1984). In that case, the Court held that federal courts should give great deference to an agency's interpretation of its own rules and regulations. The practical result from this decision is federal courts rarely overturn agency rules or regulations. However, at the time of this writing *Chevron* deference is at issue in the U.S. Supreme Court case *Loper Bright Enterprises v. Raimondo* (2023). The deference standard established in *Chevron* has been criticized, particularly by some conservatives, as too deferential to agencies. Its elimination would allow courts greater latitude in interpreting agency rules.

International Law

Beginning in the nineteenth century there was a movement toward creating a comprehensive international law. At the end of World War II, the United Nations was formed, and new international laws were created, such as those governing human rights. However, for centuries treaties have governed formal relationships between independent nations. Treaties are agreements that establish policies for how societies interact politically and economically. Designated the Commander in Chief and head of state by Article II of the U.S. Constitution, the president has much unilateral authority to conduct American relations with other nations, but Article I empowers Congress to fund transnational initiatives, declare war and approve treaties. Article III grants federal courts exclusive jurisdiction to hear cases involving U.S. foreign affairs.

The United States has entered into numerous world and regional covenants subjecting it and its citizens to policies of various multinational organizations, the most important of which is the United Nations. The U.N. Charter commits member nations to participate in efforts to foster peace and prosperity throughout the world. The Universal Declaration of Human Rights, International Covenant on Civil and Political Rights, European Convention for the Protection of Human Rights, and American Convention on Human Rights are examples of international and regional agreements that governments should protect human rights such as freedom of expression.

Treaties such as the United States-Mexico-Canada Agreement (which governs trade among the three nations) have important implications for both the amount and kind of communication between nations and the protection of freedom of expression in each nation. Agreements such as the Berne Convention for the Protection of Literary and Artistic Works and the Agreement on Trade-Related Aspects of Intellectual Property Rights attempt to establish harmonious policies for the international treatment of intellectual and creative property. (Intellectual property is discussed in Chapter 13.)

Contract Law

One of the most common sources of law that affects both individuals and businesses is contract law, sometimes referred to as "private law." Since ancient times, contracts have been present in almost every legal system. Contracts include a variety of agreements between parties such as purchase agreements, employment contracts and the transfer of ownership. In the American legal system, case laws and statutes have regulations that dictate what constitutes a legal contract. These laws prohibit contracts made for illegal purposes, disallow contracts that unjustly enrich one party at the expense of another and require that both contracting parties willingly enter the contract.

Modern American contract law requires three essential elements of all contracts: an offer, acceptance and consideration.

Basically this means that during the formation of a contract there must be a meeting of the minds between all of the contracting parties in which one party pays the other for a good or service. Under most state laws, contracts can be written or oral; some states, however, require contracts over a certain amount, usually $500, to be written. This written requirement is commonly known as the statute of frauds.

While states have general regulations about contracts, the parties involved usually have unfettered discretion in selecting the terms of their contract. A contract can contain provisions that do not follow a specific state or federal law. In fact, contract terms can even include an election of laws that will govern any future contract disputes. Courts only become involved in contract terms when one party breaches his or her part of the contract. In that situation, the wronged party can sue the breaching party in court. Absent a breach, courts occasionally become involved with regulating or interpreting contracts.

When courts become involved in contract disputes, they are frequently asked to interpret vague components of contracts. Over the years, legal conventions have developed that assist courts in determining the meaning of a contract in dispute. Courts usually resolve disputes by first examining what is written in a contract. This process is sometimes referred to as examining the "four corners" of the contract. In cases where the contract is vague or a meaning cannot be determined by the "four corners," most courts resolve the ambiguity in favor of the party with the fewest financial resources. In addition to interpreting contracts, courts sometimes are asked to issue orders requiring parties to fulfill their contractual obligation or pay the non-breaching party money damages.

In communication law, contracts are frequently at issue because they are a part of daily management governing the sale of goods, employment and other obligations between private parties. Contract issues emerge in a variety of laws including intellectual property ownership, licensing agreements and employment contracts for journalists and public relations practitioners. When examining a contract issue, a student needs to know the terms of the contract, how the contract is to be interpreted and what remedies the law provides if there is a breach.

COURTS

Courts are at the center of the study of U.S. law for many reasons. Unlike judges of almost every other nation, American judges are vested with wide political authority. Through the power of judicial review and the ability to rule laws unconstitutional (and to have their decisions taken seriously), courts are the ultimate forums for the resolution of disputes, whether between private or public parties. In theory at least, even the most powerful must answer to the least powerful in courts. Congress, the president and the states have largely acceded to the courts the ability to square other laws with the Constitution. As primary guardians of the Bill of Rights, the courts are protectors of individual rights

THE AMERICAN JUDICIAL SYSTEM

FEDERAL COURTS		STATE COURTS
	Courts of Last Resort	
Supreme Court		Supreme Court*
	Intermediate Appellate Courts	
Courts of Appeals		Courts of Appeal**
	Trial Courts of General Jurisdiction	
District Courts		Circuit Courts***
	Trial Courts of Limited Jurisdiction	
Court of Federal Claims		*Examples:*
Court of International Trade		Family Court
Court of Appeals for Veterans Claims		Juvenile Court
Rail Reorganization Court		Small Claims Court
Tax Court		Traffic Court

* In Maryland and New York, this court is called the Court of Appeals, and in Maine and Massachusetts, the Supreme Judicial Court. Texas and Oklahoma have both supreme courts and courts of criminal appeals as courts of last resort. State supreme court decisions can be appealed to the U.S. Supreme Court. However, as with any other appeal to the U.S. Supreme Court, the court first must grant a writ of *certiorari.*
** Eleven states do not have intermediate courts of appeal. Twelve states call these courts by variations on this name, e.g., the Maryland Court of Special Appeals, the Florida District Court of Appeals and the Pennsylvania Superior Court.
*** Names of state trial courts include Circuit Court (18 states), District Court (16 states), Superior Court (13 states), Court of Common Pleas (Ohio and Pennsylvania), Supreme Court (New York) and Trial Court (Massachusetts). Vermont has both a District Court and a Superior Court.

and liberties, perforce an anti-majoritarian responsibility. The courts, however, tend to be cautious in exercising judicial review. In its history, the Supreme Court has declared unconstitutional only about 170 acts of Congress and 1,200 acts of state and local governments. The courts seem sensitive to the undemocratic image of an un-elected body invalidating a law passed by elected representatives. Judges may also be aware, at least subconsciously, that their existence and funding depend on legislatures. The power of the courts is sometimes called "the judicial myth" because courts actually have few resources to require obedience to their decisions. They generally have only public esteem as political capital.

A court hearing a case is supposed to resolve a carefully framed question in a genuine dispute between two or more parties. The court should be apolitical, fair and principled in making a decision. The court is expected to follow strict legal procedure to ensure impartiality for all parties and to explain fully the rationale for the decision in a public document called the court's opinion. These decisions and opinions of American courts are not only important sources of law guiding everyday life but also of authoritative American political philosophy.

Jurisdiction

Perhaps the most important way to distinguish between courts is by their jurisdiction, that is, their power to hear and rule in a case. "Jurisdiction" usually refers to the subject matter (the kinds

of legal issues) on which a court is entitled to rule, or to geography, places or types of parties over whom a court has authority.

There are two ingredients in a court case: the facts and the law. Trial courts find facts and apply the law. An appellate court reviews only the trial court's application of the law; the appeals court is generally powerless to seek new evidence or directly apply the law to the case under review. Appeals courts affirm or reverse trial court verdicts; they do not issue new verdicts. Most American court systems consist of trial courts ("law-applying and fact-finding" courts), intermediate appellate courts ("law-reviewing" courts) and courts of last resort.

Courts will have either general or limited subject-matter jurisdiction. A general jurisdiction court handles a wide array of criminal and civil matters. A limited-jurisdiction court may be created to handle only, for example, tax issues, bankruptcy issues or juvenile issues.

Federal Courts

Article III of the Constitution says little about the number and sorts of federal courts, mentioning "one supreme Court" and "such inferior courts as the Congress may from time to time ordain and establish." With the Judiciary Act of 1789, as amended, and other legislation, however, Congress has developed an elaborate federal judiciary.

When Congress creates a court under Article III, that court is called an "Article III court." When a federal court is created by

THE U.S. COURT CIRCUITS AND DISTRICTS

FIRST CIRCUIT — The districts of Maine, Massachusetts, New Hampshire, Rhode Island and Puerto Rico

SECOND CIRCUIT — The districts of Connecticut, Eastern New York, Northern New York, Southern New York, Western New York and Vermont

THIRD CIRCUIT — The districts of Delaware, New Jersey, Eastern Pennsylvania, Middle Pennsylvania, Western Pennsylvania and Virgin Islands

FOURTH CIRCUIT — The districts of Maryland, Eastern North Carolina, Middle North Carolina, Western North Carolina, South Carolina, Eastern Virginia, Western Virginia, Northern West Virginia and Southern West Virginia

FIFTH CIRCUIT — The districts of Eastern Louisiana, Middle Louisiana, Western Louisiana, Northern Mississippi, Southern Mississippi, Eastern Texas, Northern Texas, Southern Texas and Western Texas

SIXTH CIRCUIT — The districts of Eastern Kentucky, Western Kentucky, Eastern Michigan, Western Michigan, Northern Ohio, Southern Ohio, Eastern Tennessee, Middle Tennessee and Western Tennessee

SEVENTH CIRCUIT — The districts of Central Illinois, Northern Illinois, Southern Illinois, Northern Indiana, Southern Indiana, Eastern Wisconsin and Western Wisconsin

EIGHTH CIRCUIT — The districts of Eastern Arkansas, Western Arkansas, Northern Iowa, Southern Iowa, Minnesota, Eastern Missouri, Western Missouri, Nebraska, North Dakota and South Dakota

NINTH CIRCUIT — The districts of Alaska, Arizona, Central California, Eastern California, Northern California, Southern California, Hawaii, Idaho, Montana, Nevada, Oregon, Eastern Washington, Western Washington, Guam and Northern Mariana Islands

TENTH CIRCUIT — The districts of Colorado, Kansas, New Mexico, Eastern Oklahoma, Northern Oklahoma, Western Oklahoma, Utah and Wyoming

ELEVENTH CIRCUIT — The districts of Middle Alabama, Northern Alabama, Southern Alabama, Middle Florida, Northern Florida, Southern Florida, Middle Georgia, Northern Georgia and Southern Georgia

DISTRICT OF COLUMBIA CIRCUIT — District of Columbia

FEDERAL CIRCUIT — National jurisdiction in certain cases in administrative law, intellectual property and monetary claims against the U.S. government

---

way of other constitutional provisions, it is called a "non-Article III court." Article III provides that judges assigned to Article III courts have lifetime tenure, meaning they hold office until they die, are impeached and convicted, or choose to retire (at age 65 with at least fifteen years of service or age 70 after at least ten years of service). A non-Article III judge may serve a term specified in the law that established the judge's court. Examples of non-Article III courts are the Court of Federal Claims, the Court of Appeals for the Armed Forces and Administrative Law Judges. These courts have specific jurisdiction suggested by their names. Article III courts include the district courts, courts of appeals and U.S. Supreme Court.

U.S. District Courts

The ninety-four district courts are the federal courts of original jurisdiction. At least one is located in each state, Puerto Rico, the Virgin Islands, Guam and the District of Columbia. As many as four are located in each of the most populous states. The number of judges assigned to each court ranges from two to twenty-eight, depending on the amount of work in the court. Normally, one judge presides in a case, with or without a jury, but a three-judge panel may be assigned to decide a case in special circumstances.

There are more than 670 district court judgeships in the fifty states and territories and fifteen in the District of Columbia. Each district also is assigned at least one magistrate, bankruptcy judge, marshal, clerk, U.S. attorney (federal prosecutor), probation officer and reporter. One of the judges in each district is appointed the chief judge to handle administrative matters. The district court judge is nominated by the president and confirmed by the Senate. Other judges in federal districts, such as magistrate and bankruptcy judges, are appointed by appellate and district court judges. Federal magistrate judges are appointed by a majority of the district court judges in a particular district. Bankruptcy judges are appointed for each circuit by the circuit judges. In 2022, there were more than 309,000 civil filings in the district courts and more than 71,000 for criminal cases.

U.S. Courts of Appeals

Congress established the current system of federal courts of appeal in the Everts Act of 1891. These courts take appeals of decisions of the district courts and federal agencies. Except when the Supreme Court agrees to review decisions of appeals courts, the decisions are final. Because the Supreme Court in recent years has been granting full review to fewer than 100 of about 9,000 petitions it gets each term, the courts of appeals are, as a practical matter, the courts of last resort in the federal judiciary.

There are 179 judgeships in eleven numbered multi-state circuits, the Federal Circuit, and the District of Columbia Circuit. Each circuit has one appeals court with six to twenty-nine permanent judgeships, depending on the docket size. All federal appeals court judges are nominated by the president and confirmed by the Senate.

Rather than involve all of the judges in every decision, an appeals court normally assigns a case to a three-judge subcommittee, called a "panel." When the entire court assembles to decide a case, it is said to act *en banc. En banc* hearings are rare. They usually are reserved for special appeals cases. While an attorney may request an *en banc* hearing, holding such a hearing is ultimately a federal appellate court's decision.

Federal appellate courts received 42,900 appeals in 2022. That included more than 22,000 civil appeals, more than 10,000 criminal appeals, and more then 5600 are administrative appeals.

A chief judge is assigned in each appeals court to handle administrative work. In addition, a Supreme Court justice is chosen to be the supervising "circuit justice" for each circuit.

U.S. Supreme Court

The Supreme Court of the United States, the federal court of last resort, is the only court specifically mentioned in Article III of the Constitution, and the Constitution says little else about how it was to be structured or how it was to conduct its work. Through legislation, Congress established the office of the Chief Justice of the United States and determined the number of justices, which was set at nine in 1869. In recent years the politicization of the Supreme Court has resulted in calls, mainly by Democrats, for expanding the number of justices. However, the history of expanding the number Supreme Court justices has been politically difficult with the last earnest attempt being in 1937 when President Franklin Roosevelt attempted what was later called his "court packing" plan to expand the court to 15 justices. That attempt failed marking one of the biggest political setbacks of the Roosevelt administration.

A Supreme Court term opens on the first Monday in October, according to statute, and usually concludes at the end of June.

In the past thirty years, the annual number of petitions reaching the Court has grown from about 1,000 to about 10,000. The Court gave full-dress treatment to a peak of 174 cases in each of the 1982 and 1983 terms, but in recent terms it has decided fewer than 100 cases per term this way.

Notice that the title of the federal judiciary's chief administrative officer is the "Chief Justice of the United States," not the "Chief Justice of the U.S. Supreme Court." The associate justices do not regard the chief justice as their boss. Rather, the chief justice is head of the federal judiciary, chair of the Federal Judicial Conference (the policy-making body for the federal courts), and in charge of administrative matters for the Supreme Court, including its building. The chief justice chairs the conferences of the justices in deciding cases and presides at public hearings for the Court.

State Courts

Article III gives broad authority to the federal courts to handle legal issues, but the vast majority of American judicial work is done in the state courts. Federal jurisdiction is actually limited, leaving most matters of civil and criminal law to states. Although the most important constitutional issues seem eventually to reach the federal courts, state courts actually produce the law most directly affecting citizens on a day-to-day basis.

State court systems are generally organized like the federal court system, with trial and intermediate appellate courts and courts of last resort. Names of these courts vary in the states. Sixteen states call their general jurisdiction trial court the "district court," but New York calls it the "supreme court." Most intermediate appellate courts are called "appeals courts," but in Pennsylvania, this court is called the "superior court." Most courts of last resort are "supreme courts," but in Maryland it is called the "court of appeals."

Each state court system is independent of other state court systems and the federal system. A state supreme court is the ultimate authority on that state's law. Just as a state court cannot correct the U.S. Supreme Court in its interpretation of federal law, federal courts cannot correct a state supreme court in its interpretation of state law. The U.S. Supreme Court can overrule a state supreme court on a state law question only when the two courts disagree over whether state law violates federal law. The U.S. Constitution, as the supreme law of the land, prevails whenever a law, even a state constitution, violates it. On the other hand, a state constitution can provide more and different rights than the federal constitution can.

State court systems have created a large number of courts in special subject-matter jurisdiction. Probate, traffic, domestic relations and juvenile courts are common, as are courts dealing in only minor crimes, such as justice of the peace courts, and in minor civil matters, such as small-claims courts.

LEGAL PROCEDURE

Law is either substantive or procedural. Most of what this book describes is the substance of communication law, for instance, whether a particular communication is defamatory or obscene.

Procedural law, on the other hand, includes the rules for how substantive law is created, administered and adjudicated. In essence these laws enumerate the procedures used in the practice of law. To protect against governmental abuse, the federal and state constitutions require that authorities treat individuals fairly, equally and decisively. Mandating that a criminal suspect be represented by legal counsel and be given an impartial trial by peers are examples of procedural law. In federal courts, the *Rules of Civil Procedure* and *Rules of Criminal Procedure* establish details as specific as the cost of filing records and the dimensions of the paper permitted to be submitted as court documents. States have similar procedural laws. A case that is likely to be won on the merits may be lost for failure to follow procedure. If a plaintiff's lawyer does not file an action within the statute of limitations, the legal deadline that procedural law establishes, the court will probably dismiss the action. That may be cause for the client to sue the lawyer for malpractice.

The procedure for a legal action depends on many factors, the most fundamental of which are whether the action is civil, criminal or administrative and where the action is brought. A civil action generally involves a dispute between private parties usually over money damages. Civil due process applies; the standard of proof is a "preponderance of the evidence"; and remedies in equity, such as an injunction, or in law, such as monetary damages, are available.

An administrative action is also a type of civil lawsuit. It typically involves a case over compliance or lack thereof with an administrative rule or regulation. An administrative agency's decision can be appealed through the agency's appeals process. Rules of administrative procedure are applied. Decisions by an agency's bureaucracy on fines and orders may be upheld, adjusted or dismissed by an agency's judges or by the agency's policy-making commissioners, acting as a kind of internal court of appeals. The administrative process is also subject to external judicial review only when all agency appeals are exhausted.

A criminal action is brought by the federal or state government against an individual for committing a crime designated in legislation. Criminal due process applies, the standard of proof is "beyond a reasonable doubt," and remedies include fines and imprisonment.

Legal procedure also depends on where an action is brought. Although procedural rules in different systems resemble each other, each state has its own specific procedures for its courts and agencies. Federal courts and agencies have separate sets of procedures. Procedures will also differ depending on whether the action is in a trial court or appellate court.

Trial Court Procedure

Courts are in the business of remedying or punishing social wrongs. Civil law was established to correct civil wrongs, such as torts or breaches of contracts, but has also become a way to achieve constitutional rights. Civil courts are intended to be

places where civilized people will resolve their disputes rather than through violence or other inappropriate behavior. Criminal law was established to punish criminal wrongs, such as arson or larceny, although a major part of criminal law is devoted to protecting the constitutional rights of suspects.

Civil Procedures

The victim of a civil wrong will first consult an attorney who may specialize in a particular area of law, such as torts or contract disputes. The attorney tries to determine whether the client has a cause for action based on the facts and the law and, if so, whether the law provides a remedy in equity or damages. The two major branches of civil law are torts and contracts. A tort is a non-criminal wrong committed by one party against another. Libel and invasion of privacy are torts. However, tort law covers many different scenarios including medical malpractice, defective products and personal injuries. A contract is an agreement between two parties. If one party violates the agreement, the other may seek a remedy for breach of contract.

A typical civil case seeks monetary damages to help the plaintiff recover from various kinds of losses, for example, harm to reputation, shame and ridicule resulting from defamation. A plaintiff has to present evidence that the defendant was at fault for causing the harm to the plaintiff and that the plaintiff suffered as a result. The defendant can prevail by contradicting the plaintiff's evidence or introducing other evidence. The judge and jury decide on whether the plaintiff succeeds in the action by proving a claim by a "preponderance of the evidence."

The plaintiff's attorney, once satisfied that a client has a case, may begin to collect evidence to support the claim. An example of evidence would be affidavits — sworn statements by potential witnesses. The attorney will also conduct legal research. One initial decision will be deciding in which court to bring the case. If the case involves state law and both parties are in the state, then the case should be filed in a court in that state. If the case involves federal law, then the case should be filed in the federal district of the legal wrong. If the parties are in different states and the case involves a controversy in excess of $75,000, the case may be brought in a court in either state or in a federal district court. If the case involves state law, the law of the state in which the case is brought prevails, including in a federal court. The law in one state might be more favorable to the plaintiff than the law in another state. These variables figure into "forum shopping," the process of picking a court for an action. The parties must have at least some connection to the court district where the case is brought.

Other initial legal issues for the plaintiff's attorney are the statute of limitations and standing to sue. The statute of limitations is the deadline for initiating a suit. A plaintiff must also establish "standing" – the right to bring the action; that is, does the plaintiff have a legally established interest in the litigation? For example, survivors of a libel plaintiff who dies generally do not have standing to sue on behalf of the deceased.

The legal system tries to encourage litigants to settle the case out of court. After the initial investigation, the plaintiff's attorney may ask the defendants for an amount of money to settle the case before legal action is filed. A defendant may also volunteer to settle at any stage of the process. Settlements account for a much larger proportion of the dispositions of civil actions than do trials. Part of the reason for this is the expense of a trial. As attorney's fees, expert witness fees, and the length of time it takes to prepare for trial have increased, settlement in civil cases sometimes is the most cost-efficient option.

The pre-trial process consists of two stages: pleadings and discovery. The basic pleadings are the complaint and answer. The first formal document filed in a case is the complaint, in which the plaintiff states the grounds for the action and jurisdiction of the court and demands judgment. Upon receipt of the complaint and a filing fee, the clerk of the court puts the case on the docket. The clerk issues a summons to be served on the defendant, notifying the defendant of the action. This step is called "service of process." The defendant is given a deadline within which to respond to the summons.

The defense attorney analyzes the complaint and researches other facts and law that may be relevant. If the defense does not challenge the complaint on the grounds of lack of jurisdiction or specificity, a document called an "answer" is prepared. The defendant's answer can admit, deny or neither admit nor deny the facts in the complaint. The defendant's attorney strategically selects these possible answers to the complaint. The answer may deny the allegations in the complaint and establish the defense, even if the defendant denies the plaintiff has a cause of action. The answer is delivered to the clerk of court and sent to the plaintiff. At this stage and in subsequent pre-trial stages, the defendant can ask the court summarily to dismiss the case on the grounds that the plaintiff's case is insufficient as a matter of law.

The next stage of the civil process is discovery, during which each side of a case obtains information from the other side. In civil discovery, the parties have wide latitude in seeking this information. Refusal to cooperate can result in a citation for contempt of court. Discovery includes interrogatories, depositions and requests for documents or other evidence.

An interrogatory is a list of written questions by one party of the other party. The answers are admissible as evidence in court. A deposition is a transcript of a formal interview by an attorney of a witness who answers questions under oath. The transcript is prepared by a court reporter, and the deponent is allowed to read it before signing it as an accurate account of the interview. A deponent, as a potential witness in a case, is served a subpoena, a court order that the person appear at a time and place to give evidence. A subpoena *duces tecum* requires that the person also produce any documents or other evidence relevant to the issues in the case. All of this evidence, filed at court, is available to both parties.

After completion of the discovery stage, the attorneys for both sides meet to discuss where the case stands and whether a settlement is possible. If a settlement isn't possible, they will try to produce a stipulation, an agreement on which facts both sides consider settled and which facts are still at issue. After requesting a trial, the attorneys meet with the judge in the case. The judge may review the record of the case, encourage settlement and request that the attorneys file briefs on legal issues. A trial date is scheduled.

The first step in the trial stage of civil procedure is *voir dire*, the selection of the jury, assuming a jury is used. In certain kinds of cases, a jury may not be used, perhaps at the request of the parties to the case. A case without a jury is called a "bench trial." When used, a civil jury's job is to determine the facts, that is, to determine from the competing versions of the events exactly what happened. If a jury is not used, the judge determines the facts as well as applies the law. Otherwise, the function of the judge is solely to apply the law to ensure a fair trial.

Juror selection usually follows a standard procedure. Court clerks select potential jurors from drivers' registration or voter lists. Failure to report for a call for jury duty can result in a citation for contempt of court. In *voir dire,* the judge and attorneys may question the members of the preliminary *venire,* seeking information that might prevent them from being fair and effective. After this questioning, the attorneys can ask the judge to remove some of the jurors "for cause," that is, for a reason that the judge finds acceptable. In addition, the attorneys are given an opportunity to remove a set number of jurors through "peremptory challenges," or without justifying the removals.

After the jury is impaneled, the trial begins. The judge normally gives preliminary instructions to the jury about the conduct of the trial. The plaintiff's opening statement and then the defendant's opening statement follow. They are presentations by the attorneys of what they intend to show.

Next is the presentation of evidence, first by the plaintiff and then by the defendant. The lawyer who calls the witnesses conducts direct examination. The opposing lawyer conducts cross-examination. Throughout the presentation of evidence, the attorneys may invoke various rules of evidence. Arguments over these rules are directed at the judge, not the jury, because they are questions of law, not facts. One side may object that the other side is violating some rule of evidence. For example, lawyers are not allowed to ask leading questions during direct examination (although they can on cross-examination) — that is, to frame questions in such a way as to encourage specific answers. A lawyer also may not use hearsay evidence — evidence of a statement made out of court and, therefore, of questionable validity. In determining the proper application of the rule, the judge may sustain or overrule an objection. The side that loses the arguments may use them as bases for an appeal that the judge misapplied the law.

At the conclusion of the plaintiff's presentation of the evidence, the defense may move that the judge dismiss the case on the grounds that the plaintiff failed to show with sufficient evidence a *prima facie* case, that is, a case that would likely prevail before a reasonable jury. This is called a "directed verdict" because the case ends at that point and does not go to the jury. Assuming the plaintiff has not failed to present a *prima facie* case, the defense presents its evidence and witnesses, subject to cross-examination by the plaintiff. Since the burden of proof is on the plaintiff, the defendant is not required to produce evidence but generally will do so. When the defense rests, the plaintiff's attorney presents closing arguments, followed by the defense attorney's closing arguments. Like the opening statements, closing arguments do not include presentation of evidence but are summaries of the evidence and arguments as to how the evidence should be interpreted.

After the closing arguments, the judge orally instructs the jury on the law as it applies to the case. These instructions to the jury are carefully written, sometimes in consultation with the attorneys in the case. The judge explains how a jury is supposed to use evidence, the plaintiff's burden of proof, the requirements necessary for the defense and any other law applicable to the jury's deliberations.

The jury retires to the jury room, selects a chairperson (often called a "foreman" or "foreperson") and deliberates until reaching a verdict in favor of one of the parties. In civil actions, depending on the jurisdiction, a party to the case sometimes can request that the jurors be unanimous in their decision. Sometimes only a majority vote is necessary for one side to prevail. The jury is usually asked not only to rule for one side of a civil action but also to determine how much in damages should be given to the plaintiff if the plaintiff wins. A jury is not expected to explain its decision.

After the jury decision is announced, the losing side is normally given a deadline within which to file a petition arguing that the jury's verdict should be set aside as a matter of law. In most jurisdictions, a judge has the power to order a judgment as a matter of law. The judge is expected to explain any decision that contradicts a jury's determination.

Criminal Procedure

The legal system sees crimes as wrongs committed against society, not just against the victims of those crimes. As a result, an elaborate criminal justice system, including police, prosecutors, defense attorneys, judges and jailers, has been constructed with tax money to deal with crime. Crimes are usually categorized as felonies or misdemeanors. Felonies are serious crimes — such as treason, murder and rape — with penalties of capital punishment, lengthy prison terms and large fines. Misdemeanors are less serious crimes — such as reckless driving, marijuana possession and disorderly conduct — that carry penalties of lower fines and shorter jail terms.

Some assumptions of criminal law procedure resemble those in civil law procedure, but because the liberty and perhaps life of the criminal defendant may be at stake, criminal law procedure tends to be much more strict and specific than those of civil law.

Criminal rights in the Fourth, Fifth, Sixth and Eighth amendments of the U.S. Constitution have been the subject of great interest to the Supreme Court and other courts whose decisions on criminal procedure have had a great impact on the work of police, prosecutors, courts and prisons.

Criminal law procedure includes a police investigation, arrest, complaint, initial appearance, preliminary hearing, prosecutorial investigation, indictment, arraignment, plea, defense investigation, discovery, trial, verdict, sentencing and punishment.

Police must follow certain procedures when investigating a crime. They must find and preserve physical evidence and question witnesses and others with information relevant to the crime. They are restricted by the Fourth Amendment prohibition against unreasonable search and seizure. They can obtain a search warrant by satisfying a judge that they have probable cause to believe that evidence related to a specific crime can be obtained at a location specified in the warrant. Before an interrogation police must be careful to "Mirandize" suspects, that is, to advise them of their rights to have attorneys and not to speak to the police. (The applicable case is *Miranda v. Arizona* (1966)). Police must know when to discontinue custodial interrogation and arrest a suspect.

An arrest occurs when a person suspected of a crime is taken into custody. An arrest is usually made with an arrest warrant, which is based on reasonable evidence that the suspect committed a crime. The suspect is taken before a judge for an initial appearance and further advised of his or her rights. The suspect, who is legally presumed innocent until proven guilty, may ask to be released from custody until required to appear at subsequent proceedings. The judge considers whether to grant bail and, if so, how much the bail should be, based on the seriousness of the charge and the likelihood the suspect will appear at future court proceedings.

A criminal defendant has the right to an attorney. If the defendant is indigent, the court will assign one, probably a public defender. The defense attorney represents the defendant at the preliminary hearing before a judge to determine whether there is probable cause to believe the suspect committed a crime. Depending on evidence presented, a judge can dismiss the case or "bind it over" for further proceedings. Note there is no right to an attorney in civil lawsuits.

Next, the prosecution is expected to file an accusation or seek a grand jury indictment. An accusation, normally used in a less serious case, is a document read at a public hearing outlining the charges and evidence. Accusations do not require the presentation in front of a grand jury. More commonly, especially in serious cases, an indictment is issued by a grand jury, a panel of citizens assembled in secret to determine whether there is sufficient evidence to support further prosecution. Accusations are typically used to charge defendants with misdemeanor crimes. A grand jury indictment is used to charge defendants with felonies.

The arraignment is another court hearing at which the defendant is expected to enter a plea to the charges filed by the prosecutor, generally guilty or not guilty. A suspect may also plead *nolo contendere,* which essentially means that the defendant will not contest the charges. If the defendant pleads guilty, the judge will set a date for sentencing. If the defendant pleads not guilty, the judge will set a date for trial.

The criminal discovery process differs from that of a civil case. Depositions are rare in criminal discovery; they are used only when a witness is unable to appear at a trial. Defendants have the Fifth Amendment right not to make any statements to law enforcement officers or prosecutors, but if they do, they probably will be required to respond under oath at the trial to a cross-examination by the prosecutor. In addition, the criminal record of a defendant may be suppressed as evidence against the defendant if it would unnecessarily prejudice the jury against the defendant. The police and prosecutor are required to share evidence they obtain that may help the defendant. Each side is free to ask the other for evidence, but not all evidence is required to be presented before trial. Each side is required to reveal to the other a list of witnesses expected to be called and exhibits to be presented.

The prosecutor will develop a theory about the criminal case and explain how the crime was committed. In response, the defendant develops a defense strategy. To have enough time to gather evidence and otherwise develop a sound strategy, the defense may ask for additional time through a motion for a continuance. Other pretrial motions might include a motion to suppress evidence illegally obtained, a motion to change the place of the trial because of adverse publicity and a motion to remove the judge because of prejudice.

Prosecution and defense strategies are often dependent on what are called "aggravating" and "mitigating" circumstances. Aggravating circumstances are often named and defined in legislation as factors that must be shown in order to convict a defendant of a certain crime. In a death penalty case, for example, the prosecutor might be required by state law to show that the defendant killed a police officer or a minor, had previously been convicted of a violent crime or was unusually cruel in committing the murder. Mitigating circumstances may be argued by the defense attorney to convince the jury to convict a guilty defendant of a lesser crime or to decide on less punishment than the prosecutor seeks. For example, evidence may show that the defendant played a small role as an accomplice to the principal perpetrator of the crime, that the victim consented to the conduct leading to the murder or that the defendant felt the murder was morally justified.

Voir dire in criminal cases works the same as with civil cases. In trials involving felonies, twelve jurors are typically empaneled. In an attempt to avoid mistrials, additional jurors may be chosen as alternates in the event regular jurors, once seated, become sick or are disqualified. Lawyers usually get more peremptory challenges in criminal cases than in civil cases. Jury selection in criminal cases can be lengthy and complicated. Behavioral experts may be hired as consultants to the lawyers in choosing jurors.

At trial, the prosecutor makes an opening statement, followed by one by the defense attorney. The prosecutor presents the evidence with cross-examination by the defense. When the prosecution rests, the defense may ask the judge to dismiss the case on the grounds that as a matter of law, the prosecution failed to present evidence that the defendant was guilty "beyond a reasonable doubt." If the motion fails, the defense may present evidence, attempting to raise serious doubts about the defendant's guilt. The prosecutor and defense attorney then give closing statement. Who goes last is determined by the circumstances of the case and the jurisdiction.

TYPICAL STAGES OF LEGAL PROCEDURE

CIVIL CASE
Complaint filed • Answer • Discovery • Hearings and motions • Settlement conference • Trial • Appeal

CRIMINAL CASE
Investigation • Arrest • Arraignment • Complaint • Preliminary hearing • Grand jury indictment • Hearings and motions • Trial • Sentencing • Appeal

After the judge gives the jury instructions, the jurors retire to the jury room and, in almost all jurisdictions, must reach a unanimous vote on a verdict of guilty or not guilty. If a unanimous vote cannot be achieved, the judge generally declares a mistrial. The jury forewoman or foreman announces the verdict in court. The defendant is free of custody from the moment of a verdict of not guilty. If found guilty, the defendant will be held for sentencing, which is normally a separate proceeding, sometimes involving the jury. The judge may request a report from a probation officer on the defendant's background and seek recommendations on sentencing from witnesses, the prosecution and the defense. Ranges of possible sentences for convictions of crimes are established in legislation. Once sentenced, a convict is turned over to law enforcement and later prison authorities.

Plea bargaining in criminal procedure is important because the vast majority of the dispositions of prosecutions end when deals are reached between the defense and prosecutor. Plea bargaining is used in about 95 percent of cases in pretrial stages. In exchange for pleading guilty to a crime, a defendant may be charged with a lesser offense or be offered a lesser punishment than if the defendant pleads not guilty and is found guilty at a trial. A judge must approve a plea bargain.

Appellate Court Procedure

New Hampshire, West Virginia and Virginia are the only states where appellate courts have virtually complete discretion over the kinds of cases they accept. In most states, appellate courts are required to consider appeals in some kinds of cases and have discretion in accepting appeals in other kinds of cases.

In most jurisdictions, a notice of appeal must be filed within thirty days of a trial court's decision. The appellant, the party bringing the appeal, must take responsibility for providing the appeals court with the entire record of the lower court case. The appellant must also satisfy the appeals court that the case contains a legal issue that can be appealed. The appellant can raise only questions of law, not fact, and must show not only that the trial court erred in applying the law but also that the error was prejudicial, that is, an error that actually harmed the appellant's ability to win the trial.

An appeals court will require that the appellant file its argument, called a "brief," within thirty to sixty days after the appellant delivers the trial court record. The brief of the appellee is due thirty to sixty days after the appellant's brief is filed. Since an appeals court cannot overturn a jury's determination of the facts, the goal of the appellant is often to convince the appeals court that the record on which the jury based its decision was inadequate or unfair.

Appeals courts do not re-try cases but sometimes conduct oral arguments, allowing the parties to the case to supplement their briefs with public presentations before the judges. The judges usually ask questions of the attorneys during the arguments.

The appeals court can affirm or reverse the lower court decision. If ruling in favor of the appellant, an appeals court may nevertheless find that the error was not serious enough to have altered the outcome of the case. Further, an appeals court ruling in favor of an appellant is less likely to reverse the lower court than to remand the case to the lower court with directions on how to handle the legal issue that was appealed. This may require a new trial.

In most state systems and in the federal system, losers of court decisions get a second opportunity to appeal to a court of last resort, usually called a supreme court. Cases may arrive in the form of what are called appeals, but often they are technically petitions to the court to have the court review the lower court decision. As a result, many parties bringing the cases are called petitioners rather than appellants and those responding to the petitions are called respondents rather than appellees.

Appellate jurisdiction is sometimes subdivided into categories of mandatory and discretionary jurisdiction. Mandatory jurisdiction means the constitution or legislation requires the court to take cases, either all cases brought to the court or cases addressing certain matters. Discretionary jurisdiction means the court can make the decision itself about whether to take a case.

U.S. Supreme Court Procedure

A brief overview of procedure at the U.S. Supreme Court can foster understanding of the law for three reasons: (1) the Court is an example of a court of last resort, (2) the Court's procedures are models for lower appellate courts, and (3) the Court is the most important of all courts in shaping law in the United States. Although the Court does not enact or carry out laws, it is an im-

portant national policy maker through its interpretation of law. The Supreme Court has been the most influential source of constitutional law.

The Court receives more than 7,000 petitions a year granting and hearing oral argument for approximately eighty cases. There are a number of different ways of obtaining permission to have the Court review a lower court decision. One famous way, though it is rarely accepted by the Court, is through an *in forma pauperis* affidavit, a "pauper's petition." Even when an individual may not be able to afford a lawyer or use a formal process to get the Court's attention, the petitioner might be able to bring the case forward with a simple letter to the Court and no filing fee.

The Court is also required by Article III of the Constitution and by congressional legislation to hear certain cases. For example, when state or federal laws are declared by lower courts to be unconstitutional, the Court has mandatory jurisdiction. Over time, however, the justices have successfully sought more and more discretion over what cases are put on the docket. Almost every case the Court decides is accepted by grant of a petition for a writ of *certiorari*, an order to a lower court requiring that the records of the case be brought to the Supreme Court.

The clerk, using guidelines established by the Court, sorts the petitions into groups called "frivolous" and "nonfrivolous." Both groups are transmitted to the office of the chief justice, whose law clerks screen the petitions, agreeing or disagreeing with the clerk. Petitions deemed frivolous by the chief justice are "deadlisted." Nonfrivolous petitions are put on the agenda for discussion by the justices and a vote on acceptance. Clerks for all the justices review all the petitions, even those deadlisted.

Members of the Court have established criteria for granting or denying *certiorari*. For example, the Court will reject a petition unless the petitioner has exhausted all other legal remedies. In short, if it is possible to take the case to another court, the petitioner must do so before the Supreme Court will consider hearing the case. Unlike some state supreme courts, the U.S. Supreme Court will not give advisory opinions to anyone, including other branches of government. It deals in only *bona fide* disputes between real parties, not hypothetical situations or moot cases. The Court, however, has an exception to its mootness doctrine: When an important issue repeatedly arrives before the Court but cannot be decided because of mootness, the Court may agree to hear the case. The Court also rejects what it calls political questions, that is, issues presented in the form of cases when they should be resolved in the political branches of government. Some issues are not resolvable in the courts. Many disputes between branches of government and between the federal and state governments, according to the Court, should be solved in the political process, not the legal process.

Also influential in shaping the Court's docket is the Office of the Solicitor General in the U.S. Department of Justice. The solicitor general, representing the federal government when it is a litigant before the Supreme Court, is given considerable independence by the president and attorney general in deciding which cases the government should ask the Court to review. Since the federal government — the most frequent and important litigant in the federal courts — loses dozens of cases in U.S. appeals courts each year, the solicitor general has recently asked the Court to hear only about thirty cases. The Court, respecting this advice and the restraint shown by the solicitor general, usually grants review to most of these cases.

Only about 10 percent of all of the petitions survive to be formally presented by the chief justice at regular meetings of the nine justices in the conference room of the Supreme Court building. At this conference, the justices may agree that some cases can be decided summarily, for example, simply affirming or reversing a lower court decision with a brief explanation or with no explanation. Most of the cases are dismissed without explanation. The justices may agree to decide a case without an oral hearing. This is usually done when the justices are unanimous or nearly so on what they see as a fairly straightforward question. Normally, a short unsigned opinion — called a *per curiam* — accompanies such a decision.

If at the conference four of the nine justices agree that a case should be heard, then the case is accepted for review. Commonly referred to as the "rule of four," granting certiorari in only about eighty cases a year. Written briefs by each side addressing the merits of the case are submitted to the Court within forty-five days. The Court may also accept briefs from other parties interested in the case — *amici curiae*, or "friends of the court." Political scientists call these parties "judicial lobbies." State governments, corporations and political organizations frequently file *amici* briefs.

The Court also holds a public oral argument for each case. Before the justices hear a case, they meet in the cloak room adjacent to the hearing room. In a ceremonial tradition, they help each other don their robes, shake hands with each other, line up in order of seniority and walk into the courtroom. At the raised bench in the courtroom, the chief justice — who is always considered the senior-most justice, no matter how long his tenure — sits in the middle. The senior-most justice sits to the chief justice's right, the next most senior justice sits to the chief justice's left and so forth, so that the junior-most justices are sitting at the outer wings of the bench.

The chief justice presides at the hearing, calling the cases for argument and controlling a red light that, when lit, means a lawyer representing one side may speak. When the light is shut off, the lawyer's time has ended. Each side is normally allocated thirty minutes to present arguments. Soon after a lawyer's presentation begins, however, the justices start asking questions, which are often pointed and difficult. Most of the hearing is an exchange between the lawyer and the justices. After one side finishes, the other side presents. After one case is argued, the next case is called. When the scheduled cases have been heard, the chief justice adjourns the hearing, and the justices rise and leave the courtroom, again in order of seniority.

The private conferences of the justices are held not only to decide on which cases the Court ought to accept for review but also to discuss and vote on the cases that have been heard. The chief justice brings up each case, beginning the discussion and indicating his vote. In order of seniority, the justices offer their perspectives on the case and vote, although any justice may change her or his mind anytime between the conference and the time the decision is announced to the public. The chief justice keeps track of the votes. After the conference vote on a case, one member of the prevailing side is assigned to write the Court's opinion, explaining the decision. The senior-most member of the majority either writes the Court's opinion or assigns the authorship. Since the chief justice tends to vote with the majority in most cases, the chief justice makes the assignments much more often than do associate justices. This is considered the most significant power of the chief justice because writing the Court's opinion and explaining the law, especially in important cases, is a prized assignment among the justices.

Once assigned, a justice will draft an opinion and circulate it among the justices who react with comments. The author is under pressure to be responsive to these comments because, if not, the author risks losing the support of other justices. Besides having a vote in each case, a justice has the option of writing a separate opinion and/or joining other opinions.

Members of the prevailing side in a case resulting in a split vote among the justices realize that the strength of the Court's decision and opinion depends on the size of the majority. If a justice, however, agrees with the outcome of the case but disagrees with the rationale in the opinion of the Court, the justice can choose not to join the opinion and write what is called an opinion "concurring in judgment" or result, explaining why the justice disagrees. The ethic of the justices is to strive for unanimous opinions, but the cases often produce split votes and separate opinions. A majority opinion of the Court is one with which at least five justices concur. A plurality opinion is an opinion of the Court that attracts more agreement than any other opinion written by the justices in the absence of a majority. Obviously a majority opinion is stronger than a plurality opinion. In some instances, such as with the sudden death of a justice or if a justice recuses him or herself, the Supreme Court can be evenly deadlocked 4-4. When this situation occurs, Court procedure states that the court's decision affirms the lower court's ruling, but does not set any precedent.

Concurring and dissenting justices have a number of options regarding the writing and joining of opinions. If in agreement with the opinion of the Court, a concurring justice can simply join that opinion. The justice may join the opinion of the Court and write a concurring opinion to clarify certain points the justice thinks necessary. Or, as indicated, the justice can write an opinion concurring in the judgment. These separate writings may or may not be joined by other justices.

Dissenting justices are less systematic than majority justices in the opinion process. Dissenters do not normally try to produce a single opinion that they then "sign." To make matters more complicated, justices sometimes write opinions concurring in part and dissenting in part. Once the justices have settled their votes and opinions, the record of the case is given to the branch of the Government Printing Office located in the basement of the Supreme Court building. Because Court decisions might have undue influence for some people if the decisions are leaked, the decisions and opinions are kept under tight security until the Court is ready to announce them to the public. At separate public proceedings, the justices again parade into the hearing room, and, with the chief justice presiding, announce the outcome of each case and summarize its opinions. At the same time, the printed versions of the judgments and opinions are distributed to the parties to the cases and journalists covering the court.

JUDGES

Judges, through their decisions and opinions, are important in the creation of law affecting communication. The interpretations of the free speech and press clauses by the Supreme Court are especially crucial to understanding the system of freedom of expression in America. A sense of who these decision-makers are and how their decisions are affected by less formal influences is important to a complete understanding of communication law.

States commonly require that a judge have a law degree and legal experience, but neither Article III of the Constitution nor federal statute requires that federal judges have either. There never has been a federal judge, however, who has not been trained in the law (although prior to the early twentieth century some did not have law degrees). State systems for choosing judges vary considerably. A plurality of states use what is called the "Missouri Plan." When a judicial seat becomes vacant, a judicial commission — usually made up of representatives of the legislature, judiciary, bar association and other constituencies — creates a short slate of candidates. The governor fills the seat with one of the candidates on the slate. After a substantial period in office, perhaps ten years, the judge runs not against another candidate, but in a retention election in which the voters are asked whether the judge should return to office for another term. Given the low visibility of judicial elections, it is highly likely that, unless the judge's performance has been extraordinarily poor, the judge will remain in office indefinitely. Proponents of the Missouri Plan argue that it protects honest judges from partisan politics and other electoral influences but provides voters with some opportunity to make judges accountable.

Next most common among state judicial selection systems are elections. Eight states hold partisan elections. Judges, like candidates for non-judicial offices, campaign for election for terms with endorsements of political parties. Fourteen states hold nonpartisan elections, forbidding party labels of judicial candidates on voter ballots. Four states provide for gubernatorial appointments of judges, usually requiring legislative approval of those appointments.

The framers of the Constitution intended to insulate federal

judges from political influences by providing for nominations of judges by the president in Article II, section 2, clause 2, "with the Advice and Consent of the Senate," which has come to mean essentially that the president appoints them, but the Senate can veto the appointments. Article III, section 1 further distances federal judges from political considerations by giving them lifetime tenure and protecting their salaries from being reduced. Under Article II, section 4 federal judges can be removed from office only by impeachment in the House of Representatives and conviction in the Senate.

SYSTEMS FOR THE SELECTION OF JURISTS IN STATE COURTS OF LAST RESORT

MERIT SELECTION
Alaska, Arizona, Colorado, Connecticut, Delaware, District of Columbia, Florida, Hawaii, Indiana, Iowa, Kansas, Maryland, Massachusetts, Missouri, Nebraska, New Hampshire, New Mexico, New York, Oklahoma, Rhode Island, South Dakota, Tennessee, Utah, Vermont, Wyoming

NONPARTISAN ELECTIONS
Arkansas, Georgia, Idaho, Kentucky, Michigan (but with partisan nominations), Minnesota, Mississippi, Montana, Nevada, North Carolina, North Dakota, Ohio (but with partisan primaries), Oregon, Washington, Wisconsin

PARTISAN ELECTIONS
Alabama, Illinois, Louisiana, Pennsylvania, Texas, West Virginia

GUBERNATORIAL APPOINTMENT
California, Maine, New Jersey

LEGISLATIVE APPOINTMENT
South Carolina, Virginia

Set terms for these jurists range from six to fifteen years. The term in Massachusetts and New Hampshire is until the age of 70. In South Carolina and federal courts, a justice has lifetime tenure. The number of jurists on each of these courts is five (nineteen courts), seven (twenty-five courts), eight (only Louisiana) or nine (eight courts).

The countervailing forces that create judicial selection systems that range from partisan elections to executive appointments are the concerns for judicial accountability to the public, on the one hand, and judicial independence from undue influences, on the other hand. The results of comparisons of the quality of the judiciary resulting from these different selection systems are mixed.

How divorced federal judges are from politics may depend at least in part on how they are chosen for nomination by the president for approval by the Senate. When a district court judge retires or dies, the president normally consults with the highest ranking members of Congress in the president's party from the state that contains the district court. Members of Congress consult with party leaders in the state on the person who should be recommended to the president. If the president nominates this candidate, the nomination is unlikely to meet resistance from other members because they will want similar support when they make recommendations to the president. In the Senate, this norm is called "senatorial courtesy." The Senate Judiciary Committee makes recommendations to the Senate concerning judicial appointments. This process is frustrated, however, when the Senate is controlled by the party opposite of the president's party, as was the case for parts of the administrations of George Bush and Barack Obama.

A similar kind of politics plays a role in the filling of U.S. appeals court seats. Members of Congress from states in a federal circuit expect to be able to place an equitable share of judges from each of those states on the appeals court.

Presidents tend overwhelmingly to appoint judges from their own political parties. This is not surprising because state party leaders ultimately choose most judges. Recently presidents have attempted to increase the number of minorities and women on the federal bench. A nominee is subject to an official FBI background check and lobbying by a variety of special interest groups. In addition, a president is not likely to recommend a candidate whose credentials are poor. Political litmus tests of federal nominees are seen as an overt politicization of the federal bench, and presidential candidates often campaign for election by promising that, through judicial appointments, they will remake federal courts that produce unpopular decisions.

There are stories of presidents being sorely disappointed in their nominations to the Supreme Court. President Dwight Eisenhower, a conservative Republican, said his biggest mistake as president was naming Earl Warren the chief justice. Warren, also a Republican, led what historians consider to be a constitutional revolution at the Supreme Court by aggressively taking cases and pronouncing decisions to advance civil liberties and other liberal causes. Nevertheless, most judges, because of their political histories and perhaps interests in advancing to higher courts, perform predictably once on the bench.

Discussion of judicial ideology tends to dwell not only on whether judges develop voting patterns consistent with conservative or liberal perspectives on the issues but also on their attitudes toward the role the courts should play in the political system. Judges called "activists" believe the courts have an active role to play in the political system. Judicial restraintists believe the courts should play a modest role.

Most of the 112 justices in Supreme Court history would be properly labeled "conservative restraintists." Only during the Warren Court era of the 1950s and 1960s did liberal activists become a majority. In recent years, the court has frequently been split 5-4, and liberals have accused the majority of the William Rehnquist and John Roberts Courts of being conservative activists. The conservatives favor limited government, including a modest role for the Court in the political system. In short, the idea of judicial politics should be kept in mind when trying to understand the law, including communication law.

The Senate's role in confirmation has evolved over the last two centuries. Since 1789 there have been 164 nominations to the Supreme Court submitted to the Senate, with 127 of these being confirmed as associate or chief justice. Of the 164 nominations, twelve were rejected, twelve were withdrawn, and ten did not have any action taken by the Senate. Of the 127 nominees who were confirmed, seven declined to serve.

Although the Senate Judiciary Committee was formed in 1816, it was not until 1916, with President Woodrow Wilson's selection of Louis Brandeis, that the committee held a public hearing on a nominee. The first nominee to appear for questioning was Harlan Fiske Stone in 1925, and since 1955, with the nomination of John Marshall Harlan II, nearly all nominees have appeared before the committee. The exception to having hearings since 1955 have been Harriet Miers, who was nominated and then withdrew as a nominee in 2005, and Chief Justice John Roberts, who was originally nominated to replace Sandra Day O'Connor. His nomination was withdrawn pre-hearing, and he was then nominated as chief justice to replace Chief Justice Rehnquist, who died in 2005.

The Senate rules for holding a full vote on a Supreme Court nominee have changed as confirmations have increasingly become hyper-partisan. Because senators have increasingly voted on party lines, Senate Majority Leader Harry Reid, a Democrat, effectively eliminated the filibuster in 2013 for presidential nominations except for the Supreme Court by making the cloture vote on a filibuster a simple majority of fifty-one votes instead of sixty traditionally needed to end debate. This new rule was implemented in order to hold votes on President Obama's nominees to the U.S. Court of Appeals for the D.C. Circuit. This action, popularly referred to as the "nuclear option," in a practical sense means a filibuster could not keep a nominee who had at least fifty-one votes from receiving a confirmation vote. With the death of Justice Antonin Scalia in 2016, President Obama nominated Judge Merrick Garland to the court. Citing the fact there was an ongoing presidential election, Senator Mitch McConnell said the Senate would not hold hearings on Judge Garland because a new president was to be elected in November. This approach, sometimes called the "Biden Rule," meant Judge Garland would not receive a hearing or vote on his nomination and ultimately ended his chance to be an associate justice. The term "Biden Rule" refers to a 1992 speech given by then chairman of the Senate Judiciary Committee Senator Joe Biden. When Senator Biden, a Democrat, made the speech he was speaking about the hypothetical situation if a vacancy occurred on the Supreme Court during a presidential election year. In 1992 there was no vacancy on the court. After the 2016 election, President Donald Trump nominated Judge Neil Gorsuch to fill Justice Scalia's vacancy. Because of the threats of a Democratic filibuster for Judge Gorsuch's nomination, Senator McConnell extended the nuclear option to apply to Supreme Court nominees. This change allowed Gorsuch to be confirmed with a vote of 54-45. With the retirement of Justice Anthony Kennedy in July 2018, President Trump nominated Judge Brett Kavanaugh of the U.S. Court of Appeals for the Dis-

THE JUSTICES OF THE SUPREME COURT OF THE UNITED STATES

NAME	BORN	APPOINTED	IDEOLOGY
Clarence Thomas	1948	1991 by Bush I	Conservative

Born in Pinpoint, G.A., Associate Justice Thomas is a former chairman of the U.S. Equal Employment Opportunity Commission and judge on the U.S. Court of Appeals for the District of Columbia Circuit. Yale Law School, 1974.

John G. Roberts, Jr.	1955	2005 by Bush II	Conservative

Born in Buffalo, N.Y., Chief Justice Roberts is a former private practitioner, lawyer in the Reagan and Bush I administrations, and judge on the U.S. Court of Appeals for the District of Columbia Circuit. Harvard Law School, 1979.

Samuel A. Alito, Jr.	1950	2006 by Bush II	Conservative

Born in Trenton, N.J., Associate Justice Alito is a former lawyer in the Justice Department of the Reagan and Bush I administrations, U.S. attorney for New Jersey and associate judge for the U.S. Courts of Appeals for the Third Circuit. Yale Law School, 1975.

Sonia M. Sotomayor	1954	2009 by Obama	Moderate

Born in New York City, N.Y., Associate Justice Sotomayor is a former assistant district attorney in New York and judge on the U.S. District Court for the Southern District of New York and U.S. Court of Appeals for the Second Circuit. Yale Law School, 1979.

Elena Kagan	1960	2010 by Obama	Moderate

Born in New York City, N.Y., Associate Justice Kagan is a former law professor at the University of Chicago, former professor and dean at Harvard Law School, former associate White House counsel in the Clinton Administration, and former Solicitor General in the Obama Administration. Harvard Law School, 1986.

Neil Gorsuch	1967	2017 by Trump	Conservative

Born in Denver, C.O. Associate Justice Gorsuch is a former private practitioner, lawyer in the Justice Department of the George W. Bush administration, and judge on the U.S. Court of Appeals for the 10th Circuit. Harvard Law School, 1991.

Brett Kavanaugh	1965	2018 by Trump	Conservative

Born in Washington D.C., Associate Justice Brett Kavanaugh is a former lawyer for Office of Independent Counsel, private practitioner, lawyer for the George W. Bush administration, and judge on the U.S. Court of Appeals for the D.C. Circuit. Yale Law School, 1990.

Amy Coney Barrett	1972	2020 by Trump	Conservative

Born in New Orleans, L.A., Associate Justice Amy Coney Barrett is a former private practitioner, law professor at Notre Dame Law School, and judge on the U.S. Court of Appeals for the Seventh Circuit. Notre Dame Law School, 1997.

Ketanji Brown Jackson	1970	2022 by Biden	Moderate

Born in Washington D.C., Associate Justice Jackson is a former private practitioner, Vice Chair of the U.S. Sentencing Commission, federal public defender, judge of the U.S. District Court for the District of Columbia, and judge on the U.S. Court of Appeals for the D.C. Circuit. Harvard Law School, 1996.

Roberts is the 17th Chief Justice. Jackson is the 116th justice to serve on the Court. The Judiciary Act of 1789 provided for a Chief Justice and five associate justices. The number of seats at the Court varied from five to ten until 1869 when Congress established the present number of nine.

The reference to justices as "moderate" is used here to distinguish their views from such 1950s-1970s liberals as William Douglas, Thurgood Marshall and Abe Fortas. Generally, in First Amendment cases, a "conservative" justice gives more weight to the government's interest, and a "liberal" justice favors claimants' interests. A "moderate" justice has a mixed voting record. In the media the justices are sometimes termed either liberal or conservative with some justices identified as "swing votes." A popular characterization of the current court is Chief Justice Roberts and Justices Alito, Gorsuch, Kavanaugh, Thomas and Barrett as "conservatives" with Justices, Sotomayor, Kagan, and Jackson as "liberal." However, it is important to note that justices do not always vote on conservative-liberal basis, and in some cases the Court's decisions are unanimous.

trict of Columbia Circuit. Because this nomination was made prior to a midterm election, many Democrats, citing McConnell's refusal to hold hearings on Garland's nomination, argued that the confirmation vote should be delayed until after the 2018 midterm election. Despite spirited attacks on Judge Kavanaugh, he was confirmed by a 50-48 Senate vote. Justice Ruth Bader Ginsberg died in 2020, creating another vacancy on the court during an election year. President Trump nominated Amy Coney Barrett, a conservative, to the court. Her confirmation was also very

slim, 52-48, with no Democrats voting to confirm. In 2022 President Biden nominated Ketanji Brown Jackson to replace retiring Justice Stephen Breyer. Her confirmation was equally close to Barrett's, with the final vote being 53-47, with all Democrats and three Republican Senators voting to confirm.

ALTERNATIVE DISPUTE RESOLUTION

Between 00 and 05 percent of all civil law disputes are settled out of court before trial but often not until years after the disputes arose. In the meantime, parties to the cases suffer prolonged delays and mounting legal costs that perhaps force unsatisfactory resolutions of the disputes. As dissatisfaction with the clogged courts has risen, some legislatures, courts, attorneys' groups, business leaders, and other reformers have been encouraging, with considerable success, alternatives to courts for the resolution of disputes.

Alternative dispute resolution is a broad term encompassing a number of ways that litigants can avoid courts: negotiation, mediation, arbitration, private judging, expert fact-finding, mini-trials and summary jury trials.

Mediation is a formal version of negotiation. A third party is engaged by the disputants to facilitate communication and reach a solution. The mediator need not be legally trained but should be knowledgeable in the area of dispute and effective at helping identify the problem and creating a resolution for the conflict. Mediation has been used in labor disputes for many years and has also become popular in the commercial world. A mediator may meet with the parties separately before bringing them together. The parties may stipulate that the proceedings are secret, not to be used as evidence in litigation should that follow the attempt to mediate. Mediators may charge hourly fees, but sometimes communities offer trained mediators at neighborhood dispute centers for free or at low cost. Mediation is strictly voluntary and does not foreclose the possibility of litigation if one or both parties are unhappy with the outcome.

Arbitration is more formal than mediation. A neutral third party, called the arbitrator, is chosen by the parties, called disputants. The arbitrator acts with the authority of a judge, issuing a decision that is legally binding on the disputants. Arbitrators often are lawyers, sometimes retired judges, who charge fees. Arbitration is common in resolving contractual disputes between businesses, even at the international level. Contracts increasingly include provisions for arbitration should contractual disputes arise.

Although state law may prescribe procedures for arbitration, often the procedures of the American Arbitration Association are used. The disputants, likely to be represented by lawyers, may also agree to their own procedures. In any case, the procedures normally are more relaxed than those used in courts.

Generally, an arbitration case proceeds like a court case, and the arbitrator issues a decision, called an award, within thirty days after the proceeding ends. Arbitration has many advantages over courts. Cases can be conducted in secret, avoiding exposure of information that the parties would rather keep out of public court documents. Arbitration is speedier than court procedure. Finally, it is less expensive than a court case.

Variations on arbitration include issue arbitration, non-binding arbitration and court-annexed arbitration. Issue arbitration means the disputants agree that an arbitrator will handle only a specific part of their dispute, not all of it. Non-binding arbitration, as its name suggests, is used when the disputants want the formality of arbitration but also want to reserve the right to take their dispute to court. Court-annexed arbitration is when a part of a court proceeding is referred to an arbitrator, either with the consent of the parties or as a state law requirement that certain kinds of civil actions go to arbitration before they are permitted to enter the courts. Courts have the power to enforce arbitration awards. Losers in arbitration can appeal the awards in courts, but judges tend to be deferential to the arbitration decisions.

Private judging is another ADR trend. Parties to a dispute, invoking state law, may hire a retired judge whose decision in what amounts to a private court is as final as that of a judge in a public court. Some states have provisions for rent-a-juries as well. Decisions in some states can be appealed to state appellate courts. Unlike other ADR choices, private judging is likely to be more expensive than regular court proceedings.

Expert fact-finding may be used when the parties to a case want to resolve only factual conflicts in a dispute. The expert investigates and produces a report attempting to establish the truth. This determination is not binding on the parties but can obviously influence their decisions about litigation.

Short of going to court, other ways for potential litigants to try to sort out their arguments over who is right about the nature of their dispute is to conduct a "mini-trial" or a "summary jury trial." Sometimes businesses will conduct an informal mini-trial with corporate officers from both companies acting as the jury. Parties in a summary jury trial, unlike in a mini-trial, will hire private citizens as potentially typical jurors to act as mock petit jurors. Lawyers can present as much of a case as they wish and allow the mock jury to reach a verdict. The lawyers may interview the mock jury to anticipate how an actual jury might react to their arguments. Whether mini-trials or summary jury trials are binding on the parties depends on whether they agree to it.

ADR has no application in the criminal justice system, but there is no doubt that it has helped reduce the number of civil cases in court dockets.

LEGAL RESEARCH

Law is highly codified and organized in surprisingly sophisticated ways. Law libraries at major universities require considerable physical space for the vast published collections of all the sources of laws at the international, federal and state levels. Online access to the law is helping to ease the strain of the ever increasing size of legal collections.

Most law libraries are organized consistent with the structure of government. The national collection will include the primary legal materials generated by the federal legislative, executive and judicial branches of government. Using similar systems of organization, parallel materials from each of the states, in alphabetical order, are stacked behind the national materials. Separate from these primary materials of research are the secondary materials — for example, legal dictionaries, encyclopedias, treatises and law journals.

Legislation is maintained in multi-volume sets of books, called "codes" or "revised statutes," according to topics, usually named "titles" or "chapters." Congressional legislation is officially published in the *United States Code*, organized in alphabetical order of fifty titles. Each enactment of Congress is assigned a title, and each part of the legislation is given a section number. When Congress enacts new legislation, it is assigned to the appropriate title and given new section numbers. If Congress amends statutes, it can specify exactly which sections are affected. If Congress rescinds legislation, the section numbers and text are removed.

In legal research, a citation to the *United States Code* looks like this: Federal Freedom of Information Act of 1976, 5 U.S.C. 552 (1994). The name of the act, which usually includes the year in which the act was passed, is followed by a series of numbers and abbreviations. This act is located in Title 5 of the *United States Code* beginning at section 552. The year "1994" was when the Code book was published. Private publishers issue annotated versions of the *United States Code*, including not only all that is in the *Code* but also citations to court decisions that have interpreted provisions in it. Sets of codes and revised statutes usually have elaborate indexes to help users find laws.

Court decisions are maintained in continually published volumes of books called "reports" or "reporters." Official reports of court decisions are organized by jurisdiction, and the decisions and opinions of the court are reported in chronological order. For example, the U.S. Government Printing Office prints and publishes the official reports of the U.S. Supreme Court as *United States Reports*. The citation to a Supreme Court case looks like this: *Chaplinsky v. New Hampshire*, 315 U.S. 568 (1942). The case name contains the names of the parties to the case. In almost all jurisdictions, the first-named party is the party initiating the action, and the second-named party is the party against whom the first-named party initiated the action. At the trial court level, the action initiator is called the "plaintiff," and the reactor is called the "defendant." In an appellate case, they are, respectively, the "appellant" and the "appellee." When an appellate court, usually a court of last resort, takes the case, in the form of a petition, the parties are called the "petitioner" and "respondent." The "v." is an abbreviation common in law for the word "versus." The legal community has assigned the abbreviation "U.S." to *United States Reports*. The first number refers to the number of the volume of *U.S.* in which the case appears. The second number is the first page of the report of the case in that volume. The parenthetical is the year in which the court made this decision. Thus, the case of *Chaplinsky v. New Hampshire*, decided in 1942, begins on page 568 in volume 315 of *United States Reports*. All reports of other courts also have been assigned unique abbreviations.

Administrative law is organized in several ways. Rules, decisions and other documents may be published officially or by private publishers in reports resembling court reports. For example, the Federal Communications Commission officially publishes its materials in *Federal Communications Commission Reports*. Cita-

tions to an agency's reports follow the format of a citation to a court case. To promulgate formal rules affecting the public or subjects of regulation, however, an agency must publish notice of its intention to do so and invite the public to participate in the process in the *Federal Register*, an official daily public accounting of the activities of the agencies. If a rule is approved, it must be published in the *Federal Register* and then in the *Code of Federal Regulations*. Each agency is assigned a title like a title in the *United States Code*. Each part of a regulation is assigned a section number. Citations to the *C.F.R.* resemble citations to the *U.S.C.* Like the *U.S.C.*, the *C.F.R.* has detailed indexes to facilitate finding regulations.

Although legal research emphasizes using original primary sources of law, comprehensive banks of legal materials are increasingly accessible online. Highly useful organizations of the law online are those provided by LEXIS-NEXIS and WESTLAW. These services are extremely expensive, designed for researchers in law offices and government. However, many university libraries have a subscription to one or both of these databases, and students can gain access to them for research projects. If a student is looking for law review articles, another major database is Hein Online, which is an online database that contains historical legal documents, law review articles and other secondary source material. Hein Online also has a relationship with Fastcase, which is another source for case law and statutes. Even though many legal search engines require a subscription there are many sources that are free to users. For instance, state and federal codes, constitutions, and model codes are available at the Cornell Information Institute, which is an open access legal source. Other cases from the United States Supreme Court can be found using Google Scholar. To search these materials in Google Scholar users need to use the case law function on the search engine.

It is important to note that when conducting research it may be a good first step to consult a secondary source, such as a legal treatise or hornbook, to get a general idea of what the law is on a particular subject. From that beginning researchers can conduct online research in a legal search engine to find material. Sometimes it is best to begin research inquiries using broad search terms. However, to narrow a search a researcher can use connectors (AND/OR), connecting operators (/s for in the same sentence or /p for in the same paragraph, and root expanders (such as the exclamation point on the end of a word to find variations). For example, if a researcher wanted to search student speech rights in context with colleges and universities, a search could look like this: "student speech" /s college! OR university!. What this search means is the phrase "student speech" will be searched in cases where it is in the same sentence with colleges or universities. The exclamation points at the end of college and university means that the terms college, colleges, university, and universities will be included in the search.

SUMMARY

Law is a system of rules established and enforced by authority in a society. Law can be organized according to its sources: (1) common law, which is made by judges in deciding cases; (2) equity law, which consists of orders by courts to resolve legal problems expeditiously; (3) statutory law, which is enacted by legislative bodies; (4) constitutional law, which is documents containing the supreme rules for a society and the interpretation of the documents by courts; (5) administrative law, which is the rules and decisions of administrative agencies; (6) international law, which is mainly treaties between nations; and (7) contract law, which is the law created between individuals in a contract.

Trial courts find facts and apply the law. Appellate courts review the application of the law by trial courts. Civil and criminal legal procedure differs at both the trial and appellate court levels. A civil case usually consists of the complaint, the answer, discovery, hearings and motions, the settlement conference, the trial and appeals. A criminal case usually consists of an investigation, the arrest, an arraignment, the complaint, a preliminary hearing, a grand jury indictment, hearings and motions, the trial, sentencing and appeals.

Federal judges are nominated by the president with the "advice and consent" of the Senate in order to protect the judiciary from politics, but the process of choosing a federal judge is political. States use variations on the appointive and electoral systems to choose state judges.

BIBLIOGRAPHY

Article

Bomboy, Scott. "Early Supreme Court Hearings Little Resembled Their Early Counterparts," *Constitution Daily*, March 13, 2017, https://constitutioncenter.org/blog%20/early-supreme-court-hearings-little-resembled-their-modern-counterparts.

Books

Barkan, Steven M., Roy M. Mersky & Donald J. Dunn. *Fundamentals of Legal Research*, 9th ed. Eagan, Minn.: Westlaw, 2009.

Berch, Michael A., Rebecca White Berch & Ralph S. Spritzer. *Introduction to Legal Method and Process: Cases and Materials*, 5th ed. St. Paul, Eagan, Minn.: Westlaw, 2010.

Greenburg, Jan Crawford. *Supreme Conflict: The Inside Story of the Struggle for Control of the United States Supreme Court.* New York: Penguin Press, 2007.

Harr, J. Scott, & Karen M. Hess. *Constitutional Law and the Criminal Justice System*, 5th ed. Independence, Ky.: Cengage Learning, 2012.

Kerwin, Cornelius M., & Scott R. Furlong. *Rulemaking: How Government Agencies Write Law and Make Policy*, 4th ed. Washington, D.C.: CQ Press, 2010.

O'Brien, David. *Storm Center: The Supreme Court in American Politics*, 11th ed. New York: W.W. Norton and Company, 2017.

Rehnquist, William H. *The Supreme Court.* New York: Knopf, 2001.

Scheb, John M., & John M. Scheb II. *An Introduction to the American Legal System,* 2nd ed. Albany, N.Y.: West/Thompson Learning, 2009.

Segal, Jeffrey, & Harold Spaeth. *The Supreme Court and the Attitudinal Model Revisited.* Cambridge: Cambridge University Press, 2002.

Cases

Chevron USA, Inc. v. Natural Resources Defense Council, Inc., 467 U.S. 837 (1984).

Marbury v. Madison, 5 U.S. (1 Cranch) 137 (1803).

Miranda v. Arizona, 384 U.S. 436 (1966).

Web Sites

Constitution of the United States of America, https://www.archives.gov/founding-docs/constitution-transcripthttps://www.archives.gov/founding-docs/constitution-transcript includes text, analysis and annotations of court interpretations.

CSPAN America and the Courts, https://www.c-span.org/series/?AmericaCourts, includes thoughtful television reports and documents on issues concerning courts and law.

SCOTUSblog, http://www.scotusblog.com, blogging on the Supreme Court, including commentary and analysis; new orders, filings and opinions; multimedia; and stories from major and legal news media.

U.S. House of Representatives, https://www.house.gov, is a site especially useful for following current activity in the House of Representatives.

U.S. Senate, https://www.senate.gov, contains useful information about Senate actions and committees.

U.S. Supreme Court, www.supremecourt.gov, includes the dockets, journal, calendar, oral argument transcripts, rules, *U.S. Reports,* maps and photographs of the Supreme Court building and related links.

2

The First Amendment in Theory and Practice

By Jared Schroeder

☑ Headnote Questions

- Why can't we agree on what the First Amendment means?
- What does history tell us about our free-expression rights?
- What are the prominent theories of the First Amendment?
- What does Europe's approach to free expression tell us about the U.S. system?

Congress shall make no law respecting an establishment of religion, or prohibiting the free exercise thereof; or abridging the freedom of speech, or of the press; or the right of the people peaceably to assemble, and to petition the Government for a redress of grievances.

U.S. CONST. amend. 1

Forty-five words. That's it. The First Amendment provides a short, clear statement that guarantees citizens five crucial freedoms. The amendment is made even clearer by the absence of any qualifying language. It is written as an absolute statement: There shall be no government limitations regarding speech, press, assembly, or petition. The government also cannot favor one religion or limit people's religious practices. Yet, there must be some confusion. If the amendment is so short and clear, with no footnotes, asterisks, or fine print, why is this chapter so long and this textbook so thick? Why can't we say the First Amendment promises government can't limit expression and that's that? The First Amendment, after all, seems pretty clear on the matter.

The answer, which is influenced by history and theory, is complicated. On a practical level, we must ask ourselves: Do we really want to live in a society with no limitations on expression? Perhaps a student at a public high school wants to protest a government policy by marching and chanting through classrooms all day; should administrators have the power to limit that expression so other students can learn? Also, criminalizing child pornography is a government restriction on expression, but one society has agreed is necessary. A limitless interpretation of the First Amendment would not allow the government to halt this type of communication. What about threats to harm others? If someone

threatens to murder people, outlining the time, place and means for committing the act, should law enforcement have to wait until people have been harmed before they can act? The U.S. Supreme Court has reasoned, if there is a threat of imminent, lawless action, the government can limit dangerous, threatening expression. These are just a few of the difficult problems that arise when we consider how to interpret the First Amendment's seemingly clear, simple language. Faced with these types of questions, lawmakers and the courts have agreed the First Amendment's seemingly unlimited promise of free expression has limitations — though there are very few.

These limitations complicate the First Amendment's otherwise simple forty-five-word guarantee. The shift from the clear-and-simple absolute understanding of the First Amendment to an approach that allows some limitations, has fueled a never-ending discussion about what the First Amendment means. Communication law is not a history class. Instead, students in these courses are joining a conversation that started before the First Amendment was written and will persist indefinitely. The debate about how expansive the First Amendment's promises should be changes as society and technology shift. We must remember, for example, those who wrote the First Amendment were all white men. Many of them were slave owners. Society has shifted mightily since such a homogenous group was left to build a government and construct rights for citizens. Those who authored the First Amendment also had no knowledge of radio, television, photography or social media. They could not have dreamed of artificial intelligence and the powerful algorithms social media firms use. TikTok would stun and confuse them — as would airplanes and plastic. Shifts in society and technology do not make the First

Amendment irrelevant, but they contribute to our search for how to understand those seemingly simple forty-five words. Should we attempt to interpret the more than 230-year-old amendment's forty-five words based on our guesses about the original intent of its's eighteenth-century authors or consider the amendment a living document, one that can be adjusted as society and technology change? This chapter introduces readers to the conversation they have joined about free expression, providing three distinct lines of thought to catch them up on what they've missed so far. The chapter explores First Amendment history and theory, as well as comparisons with the European Union's free-expression system, all with the goal of informing students about the meaning of those seemingly simple forty-five words.

HISTORY — THE FREE-EXPRESSION CONVERSATION

The first state constitutions seldom mentioned freedom of speech. Freedom of the press, however, was among the authors' greatest concerns. Months before the Declaration of Independence was signed in 1776, Virginia lawmakers created the commonwealth's revolutionary declaration of rights, which emphasized, "[F]reedom of the press is one of the greatest bulwarks of liberty and can never be restrained by despotic governments." Massachusetts's declaration of rights, passed in 1780, reasoned, "The liberty of the press is essential to the security of freedom in a state: It ought not, therefore, to be restrained in this commonwealth." All but two of the original state constitutions explicitly mentioned protections for the press. Speech was mentioned in only one of the early state constitutions. Nine years later, when James Madison read his initial draft of the Bill of Rights to Congress, he included two amendments that mentioned the press, one of which was later combined with other rights to create the First Amendment. The other, which promised, "No state shall violate the equal rights of conscience, or freedom of the press," was not supported. Certainly, over time, speech became the star of the First Amendment, ultimately coming to mean almost any type of communicative act, but it is noteworthy that the press, as the primary form of communication to audiences in the era the Bill of Rights was authored, was the focus.

The First Amendment, along with the rest of the original ten amendments that make up the Bill of Rights, was ratified in 1791. Then we forgot about it. The crucial rights many Americans demanded, and some states required before they would ratify the Constitution, had taken years to draft and garner state lawmakers' approval. Then they were placed on a shelf and left to collect dust, like a long-awaited gift that, after its reception, is quickly forgotten. The Alien and Sedition Acts, passed in 1798, illustrate the level of forgetfulness. The laws, enacted less than seven years after the Bill of Rights' ratification, gave the federal government power to prosecute and imprison those who criticized the government. Many were jailed for their views, including Rep. Matthew Lyon of Vermont. Lyon, a Revolutionary War veteran who was once attacked by another congressman on the House floor for spitting tobacco juice on him, accused President John Adams of being ridiculously lavish. He was convicted of violating the Alien and Sedition Acts and imprisoned — where he was re-elected to the U.S. House of Representatives.

The laws, by today's standards, seem flagrantly unconstitutional, but the work of interpreting the forty-five words of the First Amendment had yet to begin. The Alien and Sedition Acts never reached the Supreme Court, and therefore never provided a reason for the nation's highest court to interpret the First Amendment and create a judicial precedent regarding its meaning. Crucially, judicial review, the power of jurists to overturn laws or presidential acts because they conflict with the Constitution, was not created until 1803. While the laws expired in 1800, after Thomas Jefferson was elected president, the free-expression-stifling acts illustrate how quickly the First Amendment was forgotten.

The lack of judicial review wasn't the only roadblock that stood in the way of realizing the First Amendment's powerful role in protecting the flow of ideas in democracy. The First Amendment did not apply to state regulations until *Gitlow v. New York* in 1925, when the Court interpreted the Fourteenth Amendment as extending free-expression safeguards to the states. Thus, states could willfully limit free expression without any concern of violating the First Amendment until then. Also, few people who faced legal repercussions for their expression claimed First Amendment protections, which meant jurists were less likely to address its meaning. These problems started to fade away in the years that led up to 1919 — the year we remembered the First Amendment.

The Significance of 1919

The start of the twentieth century created a perfect storm for free-expression concerns. The women's suffrage movement was reaching a boiling point as suffragists risked violence and injury in their fight for voting rights. Suffragists marched on Washington and traveled the nation gathering signatures on a petition for voting rights in 1913. Alice Paul, who was arrested during a protest and ultimately imprisoned, refused to eat, beginning a nationally publicized hunger strike. Women finally garnered the right to vote in 1920. At the same time, Margaret Sanger, who later founded Planned Parenthood, was facing government censorship of her publications admonishing women to take control of their bodies and use birth control.

As women fought for the right to vote and access to contraception, tens of millions of immigrants, who had come to the United States seeking opportunity, found poverty and xenophobia. Anarchist and socialist groups' numbers swelled as disenchanted workers began to give up on capitalism. The groups started to organize and protest for labor rights, contributing to growing questions about free expression and the right to protest. Seven police officers and several protesters were killed in the Haymarket Riot in Chicago in 1889. The protestors sought an eight-hour workday and rejected police brutality. In 1905, the United Brotherhood of Teamsters joined the United Garment Workers' union in a strike that led to riots and conflicts with police. Twenty-one people were killed and more than 400 were injured. Four years earlier, anarchist Leon Czolgosz shot and killed President William McKinley. Upon confessing his crime, he credited anarchist Emma Goldman's influence. Goldman, who published *Mother Earth* magazine, was arrested, but never charged for having anything to do with the murder. Goldman, who newspapers sometimes referred to as "Red Emma," was arrested repeatedly during speeches and rallies in the early 1900s. The Free Speech League, a predecessor to the American Civil Liberties Union, was founded in 1902, providing legal support for people like Sanger and Goldman. The Industrial Workers of the World was founded in 1905 by a group that included American socialist leader Eugene Debs. The fights for voting, contraception, and labor rights were escalating tensions between their advocates and the government. Then the United States entered World War I, turning the already high volume of protest to its highest possible setting.

The United States entered World War I in 1917. Lawmakers quickly passed the Selective Service Act, creating compelled military service, in May. Goldman and others rallied against the draft, holding meetings and organizing protests. U.S. lawmakers responded by passing the Espionage Act in June. The law criminalized expression that interfered with the U.S. war effort. Thousands were arrested and convicted for speaking against the war. Goldman's New York offices were raided in June 1917, and she was placed in federal custody. Twenty-seven farmers from South Dakota were convicted under the act for sending a letter to the governor arguing against the war. Socialists Charles Schenck and Elizabeth Baer were quickly arrested and convicted of violating the Espionage Act after they distributed 15,000 leaflets encouraging men who were drafted not to report for service. Debs, who ran for president as a socialist five times, was convicted of violating the Espionage Act after he spoke against the war, particularly the draft, during a speech in Canton, Ohio. Jacob Frohwerk, a Missouri newspaper publisher, was convicted of violating the act when he published articles that questioned United States involvement in the war.

Suddenly, at the outbreak of an unpopular war, as women were already fighting for suffrage and workers sought labor rights, thousands of Americans were being silenced from speaking against the war by one massive federal law — the Espionage Act. The law was just the catalyst the nation needed to remember the First Amendment. Almost overnight, the courts were flooded with First Amendment-based appeals from people who were convicted of violating the Espionage Act. The law, and the government's actions, had awakened a sleeping giant. The United States would not forget the First Amendment again. Goldman's case reached the Supreme Court first, since she was arrested the very day the Espionage Act became law. Justices upheld her conviction in 1918, never mentioning the First Amendment. Hers was the last case from the era in which the Supreme Court faced a

clear free-expression question and evaded answering it. Justices upheld her conviction without ever addressing the clear First Amendment questions associated with imprisoning a person for speaking against government policies.

By 1919, as Goldman neared completion of her sentence in a federal prison in Missouri, three new Espionage Act cases reached the Supreme Court, including Schenck's, Frohwerk's and Debs'. The decisions in all three were announced on the same day in March. The Court upheld the convictions, reasoning that the Espionage Act did not violate the First Amendment. The decisions, which were all unanimous and written by Justice Oliver Wendell Holmes, were not a very auspicious beginning for the First Amendment's interpretation. The Framers crafted a clearly written promise that the government cannot limit expression and forgets about it. Then, 128 years later, when the First Amendment finally had a day in court, justices unanimously agreed it didn't mean what it said.

The decisions were a starting point. Remember, free expression rights are characterized by an ongoing conversation, not a monolith-like meaning that emerged from the very beginning. While the Court announced three Espionage Act decisions in March 1919, Holmes's reasoning in Schenck's case was the most complete. The decision provided three massive firsts when it comes to understanding the forty-five words of the First Amendment:

- *Schenck v. United States* represents the first time the Supreme Court squarely addressed and rationalized what the First Amendment's promise of free expression means.
- The case also, by default, was the first to qualify the First Amendment. Remember, the amendment's forty-five words are written in absolute terms, leaving no room for limitations on the rights that are promised. Yet in the first case in which justices focused on what the First Amendment means, they ruled expression can be limited.
- Finally, Holmes created the clear and present danger test in the decision. In doing so, he produced the first tool or guide for how jurists can limit expression. The test essentially reasons that free expression is protected, but if the ideas represent a clear and present danger to the government or the well-being of society, the expression can be halted.

Holmes's opinions were not well received, an outcome he was not accustomed to. He had succeeded at everything in life.

Tall and rail-thin, Holmes wasn't a nameless judge in black robes when he wrote these groundbreaking opinions. He was a nationally known war hero, having fought with distinction for the United States during the Civil War. He survived three bullet wounds, and a near-deadly case of dysentery, while part of a unit that lost so many soldiers that, when Holmes healed from his third bullet wound, the regiment's numbers were too decimated to remain active and he was assigned to a new unit. He was born into an elite Boston family and grew up with Ralph Waldo Emerson, Henry Wordsworth Longfellow and James Russell Lowell in

his living room. His father penned the famous poem "Old Iron-
sides" to save the U.S.S. Constitution and helped create The Atlantic magazine. Holmes was one of Harvard Law School's most
successful graduates and a well-published author. Yet, in the first
free-expression decision, Holmes's reasoning drew little ap-
plause. American thinker and free-expression advocate Alexander Meiklejohn, who met Holmes five years later, in 1924, later
explained, "The Magnificent Yankee was one of the very great
teachers of political freedom. And yet the thinking of Mr. Holmes
about the First Amendment had no such excellence."

After *Schenck v. U.S.* and the other to initial First Amendment
decisions were announced in March 1919, the Court recessed.
Holmes hopped on a train from Washington to his beloved ocean-
side retreat in Beverly Farms, Massachusetts. On the train, he
encountered Learned Hand, a respected federal district judge
who greatly admired Holmes. Hand politely expressed to Holmes
that he disagreed with his reasoning from Schenck. Hand explained the clear and present danger test limited too much expression. Hand offered a 1917 decision he had written as an alternative. Holmes brushed him off. In a letter that followed their
discussion, he explained to Hand, "I am afraid I do not know exactly what history you have in mind, but I don't see how you differ
from the test as stated by me in *Schenck v. U.S.*" Respected Harvard Law professor Zechariah Chafee knew exactly what Hand
was talking about. Chafee published an article in the *Harvard
Law Review* in July 1919 concluding that the Supreme Court got
freedom of expression wrong in its March 1919 decisions. In the
influential article, Chafee celebrated Hand's reasoning and critiqued Holmes's.

When justices returned from their recess in fall 1919, *Abrams
v. United States* was waiting for them. Much like Schenck's case,
Jacob Abrams and four others were convicted of violating the Espionage Act after they distributed leaflets that criticized U.S. foreign policy. The Court, using its precedent from *Schenck*, particularly Holmes's clear and present danger test, upheld the convictions against Abrams and the others. Surprisingly, Holmes dissented. He rejected how the Court used the test he had created
fewer than six months ago in a nearly identical case, choosing
instead to write a separate opinion.

His dissent is crucial. It represents the first opinion in which
a justice argued that a law should be struck down because it violated the First Amendment. The case also introduced the marketplace-of-ideas theory of the First Amendment, which is examined later in this chapter. Holmes reasoned society benefits from
a free exchange of ideas. He explained, "We should be eternally
vigilant against attempts to check the expression of opinions that
we loathe and believe to be fraught with death, unless they so
imminently threaten immediate interference with the lawful and
pressing purposes of the law that an immediate check is required
to save the country." After nearly 130 years, 1919 provided the
first interpretations of what the forty-five words of the First
Amendment mean. These interpretations, however, were far
from complete.

The Enlightenment Shows Up

The 1919 cases provided building blocks for the First Amendment's meaning, but when the Court first sought to overturn a
law because it conflicted with the First Amendment, in *Near v.
Minnesota* in 1931, it ran into another problem — how would it
explain its reasoning? It's no small thing for a group of nine une-
lected justices in Washington, D.C., to overturn a law that was
passed by state lawmakers and signed by a governor, all of whom
were elected by democratic majorities. The Court had few precedents it could use in the *Near* case — which dealt with government censorship of a scandalous, unpopular newspaper — because a law had never been struck down because it stood in the
way of the First Amendment's promise of freedom of expression.
Justices could not simply reason: "The First Amendment says so."
The forty-five words didn't have a clear meaning. To conjure an
argument to support their conclusions, justices drew from history, calling upon Madison, who drafted the amendment, and
John Dickinson. Dickinson is sometimes called the "Penman of
the Revolution," because of the many influential documents, including *Olive Branch Petition*, he wrote in the years leading up
to Declaration of Independence. Crucially, both authors, as well
as most of those who constructed the nation's founding documents, were devoted to Enlightenment thinking. To understand
the forty-five words of the First Amendment, and what they have
come to mean, we must outline the foundations of Enlightenment
thought.

Enlightenment thinking came as a response to the Copernican
Revolution, which unleashed a devastating wave of uncertainty
in the sixteenth century. Nicolaus Copernicus's discoveries about
the nature of the universe proved centuries of human knowledge
were wrong. The human senses had failed to explain fundamental phenomena. The earth was not the center of the universe. The
sun did not orbit earth. The doubt these revelations created led
to a search for certainty. How can we know anything is true, especially after misunderstanding the universe for so long? The
outcome was the Enlightenment Era, where thinkers developed
the scientific method to ensure all phenomena could be measured
and discerned in ways that created certainty. These methods, to
Enlightenment thinkers, empowered people to use their inherent
rationality to discern truth from falsity. These scientific ideas,
developed by Isaac Newton, Francis Bacon, and other thinkers,
crept into political thought in the seventeenth and eighteenth
centuries. Thinkers such as John Milton, John Locke, Jean-
Jacques Rousseau, Thomas Hobbes and David Hume began to
contend people have certain natural rights. These rights emphasized the rights of individuals over those of the state or government. These thinkers' influences about individual rights, particularly human rationality and ability to discern truth, were written into the wet cement of the United States' foundational documents. Jefferson borrowed, at times nearly word-for-word, from
Locke's *Second Treatise of Government* when writing the Declaration of Independence. He referenced Locke's ideas about "laws

of nature" and the right of each individual to "Life, Liberty and the pursuit of Happiness." Declaration signers Richard Henry Lee and John Adams found the similarities between Locke's and Jefferson's prose so similar they accused Jefferson of plagiarism. The Declaration is, in many ways, Jefferson's love letter to Locke's ideas. Similarly, Adams and Benjamin Franklin celebrated Milton's ideas in their writing. Franklin wrote in the *Pennsylvania Gazette*, "When men differ in Opinion, both Sides ought equally to have the Advantage of being heard by the Publick; and that when Truth and Err have fair Play, the former is always an overmatch for the latter." The passage tracks very closely to Milton's contention from *Areopagitica* that argues, "Truth be in the field…Let her and Falsehood grapple; who ever knew Truth put to the worse in a free and open encounter?" Adams celebrated Milton's work in his diary, emphasizing, "His Genius was great beyond Conception, and his Learning without Bounds. I can only gaze at him with astonishment, without comprehending the vast Compass of his Capacity."

When it comes to what the forty-five words of the First Amendment mean, the Enlightenment assumptions that truth is universal — meaning it is generally the same for all — and discoverable, and that people share the same or similar abilities to make rational evaluations of the world around them, are crucial building blocks. The Court has used these assumptions to conclude that the government generally can't limit the flow of ideas because Enlightenment thought puts immense trust in each rational citizens' ability to discern truth from falsity. The process of adopting this set of assumptions started in *Near*. When it came to explaining why the Court found the Minnesota law in *Near* must be struck down because it violated the First Amendment, justices dipped into this well of Enlightenment thought. The Court quoted Dickinson's reasoning about a free press from his 1774 Letter to the Inhabitants of the Province of Quebec,

[B]esides the advancement of truth, science, morality, and arts in general, in its diffusion of liberal sentiments on the administration of Government, its ready communication of thoughts between subjects, and its consequential promotion of union among them, whereby oppressive officers are shamed or intimidated, into more honourable and just modes of conducting affairs.

The Court followed Dickinson's Enlightenment-influenced ideas with a 230-word quote from Madison, in which he celebrated the crucial role of the press: "Can the wisdom of this policy be doubted by any who reflect that to the press alone, checkered as it is with abuses, the world is indebted for all the triumphs which have been gained by reason and humanity over error and oppression." Crucially, these Enlightenment ideas were stitched into the fabric of free expression in *Near*. That stitching continued as the Enlightenment-based building blocks of shared, same-for-all human rationality, and truth that awaits discovery and is generally same for all, became a crucial part of what the forty-

five words of the First Amendment mean.

The Enlightenment assumptions that started to take root in the Court's construction of what the First Amendment means expanded in the decisions that followed. In the 1940 *Thornhill v. Alabama* case, in which justices struck down an Alabama law that limited picketing rights, the Court reasoned, "Those who won our independence had confidence in the power of free and fearless reasoning and communication of ideas to discover and spread political and economic truth." Thirteen years later, Justice Hugo Black, in a dissent in *Dennis v. United States*, which was about whether the government could imprison Communist leaders who taught and advocated for the overthrow of the government, explained, "Full and free discussion has indeed been the first article of our faith…[W]e have trusted the common sense of our people to choose the doctrine true to our genius and to reject the rest." Similarly, in the 1953 *United States v. Rumely* case about whether the government could force a bookseller to provide a list of those who purchased his books, Justice William O. Douglas reasoned, the First Amendment "expresses the confidence that the safety of society depends on the tolerance of government for hostile as well as friendly criticism, that in a community where men's minds are free, there must be room for the unorthodox as well as the orthodox views." Each of these examples illustrates the Court's Enlightenment-founded assumptions that free expression should be protected because people share common rationality and that using that rationality, they will identify truth.

The Supreme Court's decision in the landmark *New York Times Co. v. Sullivan* defamation case provides one of the most explicit connections between Enlightenment thought and how the forty-five words of the First Amendment are interpreted. In a case credited as the "rebirth" of the First Amendment, justices reasoned a public official could not win defamation damages simply because a publisher made factual errors. Justices reasoned that siding with L.B. Sullivan, a government official, would endanger the flow of ideas. The Court emphasized, the First Amendment, "was fashioned to assure unfettered interchange of ideas for the bringing about of political and social changes desired by the people." In the same passages, justices characterized free expression as part of "a profound national commitment to the principle that debate on public issues should be uninhibited, robust, and wide-open." The Court's opinion connects these ideas directly to Enlightenment thought, referencing Milton's *Areopagitica*, a crucial seventeenth-century argument for freedom of expression, and John Stuart Mill's *On Liberty*.

Five years later, in the crucial *Red Lion v. Federal Communications Commission* broadcast-regulation case, justices were even more direct and succinct regarding the connection between the First Amendment's meaning and Enlightenment thought. The Court explained, "It is the purpose of the First Amendment to preserve an uninhibited marketplace of ideas in which truth will ultimately prevail." This conclusion goes a long way toward answers what those forty-five words of the First Amendment mean. The Court has conveyed that the First Amendment protects an expansive space for the exchange of ideas, under the assumption that when government has a generally limited role, rational citizens will identify truth and reject falsity.

First Amendment Sprawl

One of the primary reasons the First Amendment's meaning is best framed as a conversation is because there is no clear end to the discussion. Decisions such as *Times v. Sullivan* in the 1960s, and some that followed in the early 1970s, provided a clear connection between the First Amendment's promise of free expression and Enlightenment-based assumptions about truth and human rationality. But what happened next?

Beginning in the 1970s, the Court started adding more and more weight on to the Enlightenment-composed foundations. Justices expanded First Amendment safeguards to advertising in 1976, reasoning people require information to make informed economic decisions. In *Virginia State Board v. Virginia Citizens Consumer Council*, the Court reasoned, "The relationship of speech to the marketplace of products or of services does not make it valueless in the marketplace of ideas." Two years later, in *First National Bank v. Bellotti*, justices struck down a Massachusetts law that barred corporations from seeking to influence certain political issues. In striking down the law, justices essentially reasoned corporations have the same or similar First Amendment rights as people. Justices reinforced this thinking in *Citizens United v. FEC* in 2010. Crucially, the losing parties in these cases argued free expression would be better served if the First Amendment did not protect the rights of advertisers and corporations. They reasoned expanding the First Amendment to these extremes would harm free expression.

Justices, however, continued to use Enlightenment-based reasoning to expand the boundaries of First Amendment safeguards. In 1998, they struck down government restrictions on indecent content on the Internet in *Reno v. ACLU*, extending the highest level of free-expression safeguards to online communication. Five years later, the Court concluded in the *Virginia v. Black* cross-burning case that hate speech is generally protected by the First Amendment. Once again, in both instances, justices used Enlightenment-based assumptions to expand the boundaries of the First Amendment's meaning. Justices continued their work expanding the boundaries of what the forty-five words mean in *Brown v. Entertainment Merchants Association* in 2011, establishing First Amendment safeguards for video games. A year later, the Court struck down a law that criminalized lying about having earned military honors in *United States v. Alvarez*. In 2017, justices overturned a North Carolina law that criminalized registered sex offenders' use of social media in *Packingham v. United States*. Crucially, in each of these examples, justices broadened, rather than limited, the boundaries of what the forty-five words of the First Amendment mean.

THEORY — DIFFERENT WAYS TO UNDERSTAND THE FIRST AMENDMENT

If this chapter has not already made it clear, the First Amendment's forty-five words are deceptively complicated. They have been so vexing that surveying key moments in the Court's efforts to interpret the amendment does not fully explain their meaning. Perhaps nothing illustrates the slippery, elusive nature of the amendment's meaning than the fact that, after more than 230 years, we have several theories — rather than one meaning — of the First Amendment. It's a little mind-blowing to think that a simple forty-five-word statement could create so much confusion.

There are five primary theories of the First Amendment. Before examining them one at a time, let's define what we mean by "theory." A theory is an educated guess. We don't have theories regarding matters we are certain of. Isaac Newton, for example, created the law of gravitation. His proposal is considered a law because it's understood as a fact rather than a guess. His law of gravitation clearly and accurately describes a phenomenon. When a subject is defined by theories, it signals that scholars or researchers in the field cannot express with certainty that they have a complete, agreed upon understanding on the matter. The presences of several actively used theories of the First Amendment indicate we are nowhere near agreeing on a single meaning of the amendment, a fact that has substantial ramifications for freedom of expression.

The differing theories can be understood as lenses through which we can understand the amendment's meaning. Each theory approaches free expression and the meaning of the First Amendment differently. Finally, the building blocks of a theory are called assumptions. Each theory is made of certain assumptions that distinguish it from others and color the lens it provides to the First Amendment's enigmatic meaning.

Absolutism

Absolutism is the most protective lens through which to understand the First Amendment. It is also the simplest. Those who subscribe to absolutist theory reason the amendment's promise that "Congress shall make no law" regarding free expression means exactly what it says — the government can never limit free expression. Few justices and thinkers have adopted this theory, but Justice Black, who played a crucial role in developing the First Amendment's meaning during his thirty-four years on the Court, was a strong proponent of the absolutist approach. When the Supreme Court ruled unanimously in the landmark *Times v. Sullivan* case in 1964, which established government officials can only win a defamation case if they prove the publisher knew the information was false and published it anyway or acted with a blatant disregard for the truth, Justice Black wrote a separate opinion, lamenting the Supreme Court did not go far enough protecting free expression. He emphasized there should never be a time when a government official can win a defamation case. Similarly, five years earlier, the Court struck down a Los Angeles ordinance that criminalized possession of obscene and indecent books. Black agreed with the outcome, but wrote separately to emphasize,

[T]he First Amendment's language leaves no room for inference that abridgments of speech and press can be made just because they are slight. That Amendment provides, in simple words, that "Congress shall make no law. . . abridging the freedom of speech, or of the press." I read "no law. . . abridging" to mean no law abridging.

Absolutism is the simplest and most protective theory of the First Amendment, but it raises questions about the type of information environment society will tolerate. As noted earlier, an absolutist approach means false and reputation-damaging expression is protected. Dangerous speech that threatens to harm others cannot be limited. Child pornography cannot be criminalized. Thus, absolutism's weakness is associated with its strength. It contends the government generally cannot limit expression, protecting rights and freedoms, but its extreme position can expose society to dangerous and harmful expression.

Balancing

Balancing is on the other side of the First Amendment theory spectrum. It is the least protective lens through which to interpret the amendment. The theory, as its name indicates, reasons that when free expression concerns compete with other crucial matters, such as national security or the right to a fair trial, the value of First Amendment safeguards should be balanced with those other concerns. The theory essentially constructs a set of scales, with the First Amendment on one side and the competing concerns on the other. The Court is left to interpret which of the two sides of the scale carries the most weight. The theory provides far more flexibility than absolutism because the First Amendment is, in many ways, rebalanced in each case. While more flexible, the theory undermines the concept of precedent. If free-expression rights are subject to a weighing process with other values in each First Amendment case, it becomes difficult for people to know what their rights are. Perhaps, for this reason, few justices have subscribed to this theory.

It's not an accident that Justice Black's nemesis on the Court, Justice Felix Frankfurter, was one of the leading proponents of the balancing approach. Black was nominated by Franklin Roosevelt, joining the Court in 1937. He was from rural Alabama and built his career through stops as a city judge, practicing lawyer, and U.S. Senator. Frankfurter, who was a close friend and adviser to Roosevelt, joined the Court in 1939 after a decades-long career at Harvard Law School. Frankfurter was mentored by Justices Louis Brandeis and Holmes and was a powerful, well-known, and influential thinker for decades before joining the

Court. For many of his years at Harvard Law, he decided which law students would be assigned highly competitive clerkships with justices. When Frankfurter joined the Court, all expectations were that he would lead Roosevelt's New Deal Court. Black, however, became a more influential leader. His experience as a senator taught him how to work with others to get the votes he needed and his experiences in city court made him a quick, no-frills decision-maker and writer. Their clashing personalities helped articulate the two most extreme theories of the First Amendment. Justice Frankfurter, for example, referenced "striking a wise balance between liberty and order" in *Kovacs v. Cooper*, a 1949 case about whether a city could halt sound trucks from communicating in certain spaces. Justice Black, of course, dissented, reasoning, "The right to freedom of expression should be protected from absolute censorship for persons without, as for persons with, wealth and power. At least, such is the theory of our society." Two years later, in *Dennis v. United States*, which challenged the Court to resolve whether a law that criminalized organizing, teaching, and advocating the overthrow of the government violated the First Amendment, Frankfurter reasoned, reconciling "competing interests is the business of legislatures, and the balance they strike is a judgment not to be displaced by ours, but to be respected unless outside the pale of fair judgment." Frankfurter used 11,000 words, not including an extensive appendix, to construct his argument. Black responded with a simple 725-word dissent. He explained, "No matter how it is worded, this is a virulent form of prior censorship of speech and press, which I believe the First Amendment forbids." Their disagreement in the case provides, in one place, their polarized understandings of free expression. Ultimately, balancing provides more flexibility for courts to consider several factors when making difficult decisions about free expression and other social concerns, but does so at the expansive of strong, clear, and precedent-supported First Amendment safeguards.

Preferred Position

The preferred position approach is more moderate than absolutism and more structured and protective of freedom of expression than balancing. It is in many ways, absolutism-light. If we imagine each of the people who are lined up to board a plane at an airport gate represents legal rights or societal concerns, preferred position assumes the First Amendment gets on the plane first. It has a first-class ticket that makes it more important than the rest of the passengers. The approach recognizes the fundamentally important role of freedom of expression in a democracy but acknowledges these freedoms don't automatically vanquish all other societal concerns. The scales discussed in the balancing approach can be helpful here as well. In the preferred-position approach, the Supreme Court puts its finger on the First Amendment side of the scale, giving it extra weight. If the concern on the other side of the scale can overcome the extra weight the Court gives the First Amendment, then it is possible free expression can be limited.

The theory is popular with most justices. Douglas, Frankfurter's other nemesis on the Court, was most explicit in his use of the preferred-position lens. In the *Roth v. United States* obscenity case, he reasoned, "The First Amendment puts free speech in the preferred position. Freedom of expression can be suppressed if, and to the extent that, it is so closely brigaded with illegal action as to be an inseparable part of it." Similarly, in the 1953 *United States v. Rumely* case, in which justices ruled an author did not have to disclose the list of those who purchased his books to a congressional committee, Douglas listed several instances when the Court had favored free expression over other concerns. He explained, "These are illustrative of the preferred position granted speech and the press by the First Amendment." Ultimately, preferred position draws assumptions from the Enlightenment-based foundations discussed earlier in the chapter. Free expression is valued above most other concerns because justices assume generally rational citizens will be able to identify truth from falsity and make the right decisions.

Meiklejohnian

Alexander Meiklejohn had just completed an eleven-year stint as the president of Amherst College when he visited Justice Holmes in his Washington office in 1924. Holmes was in his eighties, Meiklejohn was fifty-two. After their visit, Holmes described the professor and free-expression advocate as a "dear." He noted, in a letter to Frankfurter, that he was embarrassed by how much he spoke during Meiklejohn's visit. He lamented failing to offer Meiklejohn tea. Meiklejohn, for his part, remained an admirer of Holmes throughout his life, but was critical of one crucial matter: Holmes's understanding of free expression. Twenty-four years after their meeting, and thirteen years after Holmes's death, Meiklejohn critiqued Holmes's approach, offering his own theory of the First Amendment. Meiklejohn's interpretation of the First Amendment is distinguished by its emphasis on democratic self-government. He reasoned the First Amendment was created with one purpose — to protect individual citizens' abilities to encounter information and make decisions about their rights and liberties. Thus, he reasoned, any expression that fostered self-government should be absolutely protected. Expression that was unrelated to self-government, however, could be regulated or restricted without concern. In his book *Free Speech and Its Relation to Self-Government*, he explained, "There are, then, in the theory of the Constitution, two radically different kinds of utterances." He continued,

> The constitutional status of a merchant advertising his wares, of a paid lobbyist fighting for the advantage of his client, is utterly different from that of a citizen who is planning for the general welfare. And from this it follows that the Constitution provides differently for two kinds of "freedom of speech."

Meiklejohn's approach created a two-tiered system for free expression:

- Tier I: Speech that contributes to democratic self-governance. This speech cannot be regulated.
- Tier II: Speech that does not contribute to self-governance. This speech can be regulated.

On the surface, the tiered system makes a lot of sense. Problematically, however, the boundary lines between the tiers were never made clear. What qualifies as self-government-related expression? Do news-related jokes on *Saturday Night Live's* "Weekend Update" count? Burning a flag in protest? A TikTok that critiques politicians' fashion choices? The theory has never been clear regarding what constitutes absolutely protected expression that fosters self-government and lesser ideas that can be regulated without concern. The tiers create gray areas, rather than clear dividing lines.

The theory has flourished despite its lack of clarity. Supreme Court justices have referenced Meiklejohn's work in dozens of opinions, particularly in landmark cases in defamation, commercial speech, corporate speech, broadcast, and press-rights cases. Justices Black and Douglas referenced Meiklejohnian theory in their concurring opinion in *New York Times v. Sullivan*. Ten years after Sullivan, in the crucial *Gertz v. Robert Welch Inc.* defamation case, justices included a 139-word quote from Meiklejohn's book Political Freedom in their reasoning. Justices called upon his theory in the *First National Bank v. Bellotti* and *Citizens United v. FEC* corporate-speech cases. In *Bellotti*, the Court's reference to his work came in the crucial passage in which justices emphasized the priority must be to protect democratic self-government by ensuring people have access to the full range of ideas, even if some of the ideas come from corporations rather than people. Crucially, Meiklejohn's ideas are not merely referenced alongside other works. Justices, in seeking to rationalize arguments, ideas, and decisions in major opinions about the meaning of the First Amendment's forty-five words, have consistently called upon his theory and its self-government-focused assumptions.

Marketplace of Ideas

The marketplace of ideas approach is the most important of the five theories in this chapter. The theory reasons we should have free expression because truth will vanquish falsity in a free exchange of ideas. Justices have consistently used the theory to rationalize an expansive free-expression environment. The theory, in other words, creates a protected space for the exchange of ideas. To safeguard this space, justices have generally reasoned most government limitations on expression are unconstitutional because they limit or distort the free exchange of ideas. The theory ultimately places as much power as possible in the hands of each citizen to evaluate ideas and to discern truth from falsity.

Justice Holmes, in his famous dissent in *Abrams v. United States*, in 1919, reasoned such an exchange of ideas is "the theory of our Constitution."

Fifty years later, the Court was even more explicit in its enshrinement of the marketplace approach as the primary lens through which to understand the First Amendment's free-expression promises. The Court reasoned in *Red Lion v. FCC*, "It is the purpose of the First Amendment to preserve an uninhibited marketplace of ideas in which truth will ultimately prevail." These are powerful, explicit words about the meaning of the First Amendment. Justices essentially reasoned the First Amendment exists to create this imagined space for the exchange of ideas. Other decisions tell us the space generally welcomes any idea or speaker, human or not. The theory also emphasizes government can communicate ideas in the space, along with other speakers, but it generally cannot limit expression.

Why would justices and legal thinkers create such an open, unregulated space for the exchange of ideas? After all, absent government regulation, the marketplace becomes crowded and confusing, full of deception and distortion. How can we trust truth will succeed amidst a sea of falsities and dangerous ideas? The theory places an enormous amount of weight on each citizen to sift through haystacks upon haystacks of ideas to find needles of truth. Why would justices believe truth will win and falsity will fail in a free exchange of ideas? We can thank the Founders' love of Enlightenment ideas for that.

Marketplace theory uses Enlightenment-based assumptions about truth and human rationality to explain why we should assume truth will win and falsity will fail in a generally unregulated exchange of ideas. Think about it. Marketplace theory only makes sense if truth is understood as something that is generally constant and discoverable and people are assumed to share a similar type of rationality. If we don't believe truth has an inherently recognizable and discoverable nature, marketplace theory is simply an invitation for chaos. Similarly, if we don't accept people are rational and capable of making sense of the world around them, marketplace theory would only lead to disaster. The Enlightenment-based assumptions about truth and rationality are the foundational building blocks. The theory only makes sense if we understand truth and rationality in the same ways as Enlightenment thinkers. This line of thinking creates a series of strong arguments for why the government should have almost no role in the flow of ideas. In this regard, the First Amendment protects expression so rational citizens will identify truth from falsity in a generally unregulated exchange. The metaphor's assumptions are influenced by the political and economic theory from the Enlightenment period. It is no accident, for example, that Enlightenment thinker Adam Smith's *The Wealth of Nations* was published only months before the Declaration of Independence was signed, or that the Framers of the Constitution (and the Bill of Rights that followed) read Milton's truth and human rationality claims with zeal.

The Enlightenment-based marketplace approach's power and influence over the shape and contour of the free-expression landscape in the United States was not automatic. The philosophical Enlightenment ideas needed an entry point into First Amendment precedent. Justice Holmes planted those seeds in his dissenting opinion in *Abrams v. United States* in 1919. Holmes, in the first opinion by a justice that argued a law should be struck down because it conflicted with the First Amendment, reasoned, "[T]he best test of truth is the power of the thought to get itself accepted in the competition of the market, and that truth is the only ground upon which their wishes safely can be carried out." Thus, one of the nation's most famous jurists and thinkers introduced the marketplace concept into the Court's vocabulary at the very beginning of justices' efforts to interpret the First Amendment's meaning. His introduction started a century-long process as justices slowly installed Enlightenment assumptions into the foundations of marketplace theory.

No matter how much power and influence the theory has on the meaning of the First Amendment, it cannot escape several crucial problems. First, the Enlightenment-based foundations of the theory might not work. Many scholars have concluded truth is not universal and the same for all, as the Enlightenment basis of the theory assumes. Similarly, Enlightenment assumptions about human rationality tend to treat society as a single homogenous mass. It would seem more reasonable to assume people come to different conclusions about what is true because they share different types of rationality, which are based on individual experiences and influences. Race, religion, and political beliefs, for example, can cause people to come to widely different conclusions about what is true. These questions about the natures of truth and human rationality undermine the assumptions of marketplace theory.

These concerns also lead to questions about whether truth really has a certain inherent quality that allows it to vanquish falsity in a free exchange of ideas. What if falsity wins some of the time? Many of those who voted for Donald Trump in the 2020 presidential election, for example, believe he won the election, and it was stolen by Joe Biden. We have vote totals that objectively represent a reality. Similarly, a Pew Research Center survey found 25 percent of Americans believe the conspiracy theory that COVID-19 was planned by powerful people and purposely released on the population. Some groups were more likely to accept the conspiracy theory as true, such as those with lower education levels and politically conservative respondents. How does marketplace theory reconcile when people come to different conclusions about the truth, even when provided with considerable reliable evidence.

The marketplace concept also suffers from inequalities in the space for discourse. As with certain products, such as shoes or cars, some communicators have more resources and power to get their product or ideas into the space and to ensure people encounter them. Wouldn't the marketplace favor the ideas of those who have the most resources? Elon Musk, who owns Twitter, and Mark Zuckerberg, who controls Facebook and Instagram, likely have far more power to influence the exchange of ideas than most people. On the other side of the coin, some have more access to receiving ideas than others and not everyone encounters the same ideas in their information environments. Wouldn't these access-and-information-flow problems distort the marketplace of ideas and its quest to identify discovered truths? The emergence of algorithms, social media, chat bots and the metaverse have not helped sure up the marketplace approach's sketchy Enlightenment foundations.

Algorithms, complex computer programs that leverage the personal information companies have collected about users to connect them with ideas, people and products they might engage with, preempt many of the assumptions at the heart of the marketplace approach. Algorithms, in many ways, limit the free exchange of ideas. They predetermine the ideas each individual sees, separating people from a shared marketplace of ideas and replacing it with a personal-shopper experience. The marketplace approach assumes people shop for themselves by engaging with a range of ideas in the space. When algorithms predetermine what people encounter, the result is much like a personal shopper's work. The personal shopper picks out only the items on the list and ignores everything else. Customers the shopper is helping don't roam the aisles, stopping when they see unexpected deals or products. They receive only the products (or ideas) they asked for. When algorithms channel ideas to people based on what the program thinks they like or are interested in, people are more likely to only engage with matters that reinforce what they already know or believe. They are also likely to become less tolerant of others' ideas. Algorithms, of course, can be helpful. Online spaces are filled with endless amounts of information, which the algorithms help people navigate. It is only an unintended consequence, though a crucial one, that they undermine the marketplace concept.

Algorithms aren't the only problem. Once they sort people based on corporately motivated processes, we sort ourselves even further. Virtual spaces are choice-rich spaces, meaning there is so much information, we must make decisions about the ideas and people we wish to engage with. Scholars have found, when given a choice, people create online communities with people who are like them. The algorithms and personal choices users make narrow the scope of ideas, which limit the products or ideas in the free exchange of ideas. These twenty-first-century problems raise questions about whether the marketplace approach's underlying assumptions remain viable. AI communicators, generally in the form of bots, represent another massive challenge to the marketplace approach's assumptions.

Virtual spaces, for the first time, have created places where people and AI entities communicate seamlessly with one another. These types of human-AI interactions were not possible in other types of communication. In virtual spaces, however, no physical form is needed. This allows AI entities to influence the exchange of ideas. This is particularly concerning because AI communicators do not share the same characteristics as people. Bots do not

become tired or emotional. They do not vote or have any stake in political issues. They can also post thousands of messages in a short time. These features allow AI entities to distort the marketplace. These messages effectively push human communicators out of the exchange of ideas by overwhelming the marketplace with a certain idea. At the same time, bots can make it appear as if truth has already emerged and falsity has failed by filling the marketplace with a single conclusion. The Enlightenment thinkers who influenced the marketplace's foundational ideas did not account for armies of non-human speakers fundamentally altering the space, yet the marketplace approach remains the Court's dominant tool for defining what the First Amendment's forty-five words mean.

FREE EXPRESSION AND THE COUNCIL OF EUROPE

Much like the First Amendment in the United States, the forty-six-member Council of Europe's organizing conventions promise citizens freedom of expression. The catch, however, is the two promises of freedom of expression have markedly different meanings. The existence of two very different definitions of freedom of expression, both of which represent hundreds of millions of people, helps characterize and frame First Amendment theory and practice as unique. The U.S. system, in other words, isn't the only way to go about freedom of expression. Comparing the United States' safeguards for free expression to how Europe approaches such freedoms, can enhance how we understand the First Amendment and the elusive meaning of its forty-five-word promise.

The Council is governed by the European Convention on Human Rights, a document that was written in the late 1940s as Europe sought to rise from the ashes of World War II. The document, which was modeled after the United Nation's Universal Declaration on Human Rights, sets up the European Court of Human Rights, which holds all member states accountable for respecting the Convention's promises. Article 10 of the Convention provides a two-paragraph promise of free expression. Much like the First Amendment, it begins with an unqualified statement: "Everyone has the right to freedom of expression." Article 10, however, has something the First Amendment does not — a second paragraph that outlines limitations on expression. The paragraph emphasizes free expression carries "duties and responsibilities" and outlines reasons why the government can limit the exchange of ideas. The reasons include public safety, national security, public health, and morals. These initial differences are crucial. While the First Amendment is written in absolute terms that there shall be no limitations on expression, leaving jurists and lawmakers very few conditions under which they can limit the flow of ideas, Article 10 provides a relatively expansive list of instances when expression can be halted, empowering lawmakers and courts in Europe to limit expression for a variety of reasons.

The Council's approach is no more an accident than is the First Amendment's absolute wording. While the First Amendment was written at the end of the eighteenth century, after a wave of Enlightenment thought traveled across the Atlantic Ocean and crashed on the thirteen colonies' shores, the ECHR was written in the aftermath of World War II. Essentially, the two promises of free expression are defined by the context under which they were written. As Europe sought to come to grips with the systematic genocide of groups of people because of their faiths and heritages, as well as the losses of the millions who died fighting, those who wrote the ECHR emphasized human dignity. One of the goals of the documents, according to the United Nations, was to ensure what had just happened in Europe, and to the world, would never happen again. Thus, the authors sought to create a system of free expression that allowed everyone to participate by limiting expression that would threaten, degrade or otherwise push people from discourse. Such limitations also work to safeguard the bloc from the informational and ideological tools that helped create the Nazi's wave of terror.

The ECHR's emphasis on human dignity, tolerance, and pluralistic society requires that some entity curate the space for discourse. The solution has been the government. While the Enlightenment-influenced First Amendment makes government intrusion in the marketplace of ideas abhorrent, the ECHR relies upon on government official to act like gardeners who trim dead branches and remove weeds so a garden can grow. The government, in this approach, acts as a curator for the space for discourse, removing potentially dangerous, misleading or harmful information in order to protect the space for discourse. The Court explained how it understood the role government in the landmark *Handyside v. United Kingdom* decision in 1976. Richard Handyside had distributed his *Little Red Schoolbook*, which included dozens of pages about sex, to students between eight and twelve years old. Government officials seized more than a thousand copies of the book and charged him with violating obscenity laws. He claimed Article 10 protected his expression. The Court sided with the government. Most importantly, the jurists emphasized that free expression must be balanced with a responsibility to use those rights properly. The Court explained, "Whoever exercises his freedom of expression undertakes 'duties and responsibilities' the scope of which depends on his situation and the technical means he uses."

While the U.S. system is characterized by freedom from government limitations, the European system focuses on a preserving careful tension between freedom and responsibility. The tension between the two is meant to both protect expression and safeguard society from a long list of harms. In *Animal Defenders v. United Kingdom* in 2008, for example, an animal-rights group claimed the government's decision to halt the group's twenty-second advertisements from airing on television violated their free-expression rights under Article 10. The Court sided with the government, emphasizing, "The general measure was necessary to prevent the distortion of crucial public interest debates and, thereby, the undermining of the democratic process." Crucially, the Court reasoned the advertisements must be blocked to

protect the exchange of ideas. This approach does not mean government has unchecked power to limit expression. The courts expect the government, according to the ECHR, to justify limitations on expression as being "necessary in a democratic society." When they fail to justify limitations, courts will overturn the government's efforts. In *Magyar Helsinki Bizottság v. Hungary* in 2016, for example, several Hungarian police departments refused to comply with an open records request filed by a legal-rights group. When the group challenged the government's refusals, the ECtHR concluded the government was wrong to bar access to the documents. The Court explained, "[B]y denying it access to the requested information. . . the domestic authorities impaired the applicant NGO's exercise of its freedom to receive and impart information, in a manner striking at the very substance of its Article 10 rights." The Court, once again balanced the government's efforts to limit the flow of ideas but, this time, found the police officials went too far.

The case also emphasized Article 10 expectations that free expression be balanced with responsibility include reasoning that people use their rights for the public good. That expectation worked in the legal-rights group's favor in *Magyar Helsinki Bizottság*. In *Delfi v. Estonia* in 2015, however, that expectation worked against the publisher. In the case, a news portal was found liable for damages after users posted hateful and false comments. Delfi had acted quickly to remove the comments, but the Court still found the company did not do enough to safeguard the public from harmful information. The Court's decision is representative of a careful balance European courts seek to strike between freedom and responsibility. The approach means the Council's system compares most closely with balancing theory discussed earlier in this chapter. Free expression, to European lawmakers and jurists, must be balanced against other crucial societal concerns. This means expression that is hateful, misleading, or found to lack a valid contribution to society, for example, can be regulated.

Article 10's expectations that expression be balanced with other concerns makes free expression protections more flexible and adaptable to change than the U.S. system. The generally rigid, Enlightenment-based interpretation that the First Amendment forbids most limitations on expression, which generally means it is difficult for free-expression safeguards to adapt to changes in society and technology. The emergence of the networked, AI era, for example, has fundamentally changed the shape and contour of free expression, but courts continue to evaluate laws based on Enlightenment ideas that were developed in the seventeenth century. At the same time, European lawmakers continue to experiment with ways to limit harmful expression. The Digital Services Act, which was approved in 2022, requires social media firms to remove hateful, extremist, and terroristic content, as well as misinformation and disinformation. The bloc is also drafting the Artificial Intelligence Act, which seeks to protect citizens from harms caused by AI. The European approach provides boundaries that lawmakers must follow, but they were written to ensure a different type of space for the flow of ideas and to allow more flexibility when new challenges emerge.

SUMMARY

The First Amendment's forty-five words seem straight forward. Their history and our theories of the First Amendment tell us otherwise. We know the First Amendment's promise of free expression is crucial to democracy. In fact, the amendment's history tells us those who wrote the nation's founding documents were particularly concerned about free expression — even before the Bill of Rights was written. The amendment's history also shows that the founders' concerns about free expression were associated with Enlightenment ideas, which were fundamentally influential to them. Enlightenment thought emphasizes individual liberty and assumes truth is generally universal and discoverable and that people are generally rational.

This combination of assumptions can be found at the heart of the First Amendment's history. When the Supreme Court first examined the meaning and boundaries of the amendment's free-expression promises in 1919, these Enlightenment ideas bubbled to the surface in Justice Holmes's dissent in *Abrams v. United States*. They were also at hand in the first case in which justices struck down a law because it conflicted with the First Amendment in *Near v. Minnesota* in 1931. Though they are not the only thread, these Enlightenment ideas form a common thread throughout the nation's conversation about what the First Amendment's forty-five words promise. The Enlightenment thread has not moved in a straight line and it hasn't been tied off at an end point. The conversation about the forty-five words mean continues.

Much of that conversation can be seen in the theories of the First Amendment. Our two extreme ends of the spectrum include absolutism, which is based on a literal meaning of the amendment's absolute wording, and balancing, which seeks to weigh free-expression concerns alongside other important social concerns. Absolutism assumes there can be almost no limitations on expression, while balancing's assumptions often place First Amendment protections on even footing with other concerns. The preferred position approach provides a compromise position between the two extremes. The approach gives greater weight to free expression, but allows that it can be limited when other societal concerns are so compelling that they outweigh the First Amendment's preferred position in democracy.

The Meiklejohnian and marketplace theories provide more nuanced lenses through which to understand the First Amendment. Meiklejohn's theory focuses on self-government. Expression that contributes to citizens' abilities to govern themselves is absolutely protected. Expression that does not aid in self-government can be regulated without concern for the First Amendment. Meiklejohn was a bit unclear about how the two tiers he created would be defined, but that has not stopped justices from using his theory. We spent the most time on the marketplace of ideas, a

theory that is directly associated with the Enlightenment-based foundations of the First Amendment. The marketplace approach assumes that when ideas can generally flow without the government limited expression, truth will succeed, and falsity will fail. The theory places extensive weight on each person to identify truth and eschew falsity. These truth and human rationality assumptions have led many to question whether the theory is valid at all. Whatever criticisms scholars have had of the marketplace approach, the Supreme Court has continued to rely upon it as its dominant tool for explaining why we should have free expression and what the First Amendment's forty-five words mean.

BIBLIOGRAPHY

Article

Chafee, Zechariah. "Freedom of Speech in War Time," 32 *Harvard Law Review* 932 (1919).

Books

Hobbes, Thomas. *Leviathan.* Oxford: Oxford University Press, 1998.

Locke, John. *The Second Treatise of Government and a Letter Concerning Toleration.* New York: Dover Publications, 2002.

Meiklejohn, Alexander. *Free Speech and its Relation to Self-Government.* New York: Harper & Brothers Publishers, 1948.

Meiklejohn, Alexander. *Political Freedom.* New York: Harper & Brothers, 1960.

Mill, John Stuart. *On Liberty.* New York: Dover Publications, 2002.

Milton, John. *Areopagitica.* Arlington Heights, Ill.: Harlan Davidson, 1951.

Newman, Roger K. *Hugo Black: A Biography.* New York: Pantheon Books, 1994.

Posner, Richard A. *The Essential Holmes.* Chicago: University of Chicago Press, 1992.

Powe, Lucas A. *The Fourth Estate and the Constitution.* Berkeley: University of California Press.

Pribanic-Smith, Erika, & Jared Schroeder. *Emma Goldman's No-Conscription League and the First Amendment.* New York: Routledge, 2019.

Rabban, David. *Free Speech in the Forgotten Years.* Cambridge, Mass.: Cambridge University Press, 1997.

Cases

Abrams v. United States, 250 U.S. 616 (1919).

Animal Defenders v. United Kingdom, no. 48876/08, 22 April 2013, https://hudoc.echr.coe.int/eng?i=001-119244.

Brown v. Entertainment Merchants Association, 564 U.S. 786 (2011).

Citizens United v. FEC, 558 U.S. 310 (2010).

Debs v. United States, 249 U.S. 211 (1919).

Delfi v. Estonia, no. 64569/09, 16 June 2015, https://hudoc.echr.coe.int/eng?i=001-155105.

Dennis v. United States, 341 U.S. 494 (1951).

First National Bank v. Bellotti, 435 U.S. 765 (1978).

Frohwerk v. United States, 249 U.S. 204 (1919).

Gertz v. Welch, 418 U.S. 323 (1974).

Gitlow v. New York, 268 U.S. 652 (1925).

Handyside v. United Kingdom, no. 5493/72, 7 December 1976, https://hudoc.echr.coe.int/eng?i=001-57499.

Kovacs v. Cooper, 336 U.S. 77 (1949).

Magyar Helsinki Bizottság v. Hungary, no. 18030/11, 8 November 2016, https://hudoc.echr.coe.int/eng?i=001-167828.

Near v. Minnesota, 283 U.S. 697 (1931).

New York Times Co. v. Sullivan, 376 U.S. 254 (1964).

Packingham v. North Carolina, 137 S. Ct. 1730 (2017).

Red Lion v. FCC, 395 U.S. 367 (1969).

Reno v. ACLU, 521 U.S. 844 (1997).

Schenck v. United States, 249 U.S. 47 (1919).

Smith v. California, 361 U.S. 147 (1959).

Thornhill v. Alabama, 310 U.S. 88 (1940).

United States v. Alvarez, 567 U.S. 709 (2012).

United States v. Rumely, 345 U.S. 41 (1953).

Virginia v. Black, 538 U.S. 343 (2003).

Virginia State Pharmacy Board v. Virginia Citizens Consumer Council, 425 U.S. 748 (1976).

Documents & Tracts

"A European Approach to Artificial Intelligence," European Commission, https://digital-strategy.ec.europa.eu/en/policies/european-approach-artificial-intelligence

"Digital Services Act," European Commission, https://digital-strategy.ec.europa.eu/en/policies/digital-services-act-package.

European Declaration on Human Rights, https://www.echr.coe.int /documents/convention_eng.pdf.

"Of Debates in Congress: Amendments to the Constitution," Library of Congress, https://memory.loc.gov/cgi-bin/ampage?collId=llac&fileName=001/llac001.db&recNum=227

"Universal Declaration of Human Rights," United Nations, https://www.un.org/en/about-us/universal-declaration-of-human-rights.

3

Conduct and Speech

By W. Wat Hopkins

☑ **Headnote Questions**
- How does the Supreme Court determine whether conduct is expressive?
- How does the Supreme Court determine whether expressive conduct is constitutionally protected?
- What are the intermediate and strict scrutiny tests?
- What is the constitutional status of threatening speech, fighting words and intimidating speech?

As readers of this book will no doubt learn — if they haven't already — much First Amendment jurisprudence depends upon interpretation and, beyond that, degrees of interpretation. One man's art is another's obscenity; one woman's opinion is another's libel; one author's fair use is another's copyright infringement.

One of the best examples of the divergence of attitudes toward free speech is the battle waged in the 1960s and '70s between Justice Hugo Black and some of his brethren on the U.S. Supreme Court. Justice Black took the position that the government cannot restrict the distribution of material because it is obscene, defamatory, indecent, or even because it might harm the national security. "I read 'no law ... abridging'" freedom of speech and press, Justice Black wrote in *Smith v. California*, "to mean *no law* abridging." Speech, he maintained, was absolutely protected.

The great free-speech advocate, however, had a very narrow definition of "speech." Just as "no law" meant "no law," in Justice Black's view, "speech" meant "speech" and nothing more. He disagreed, therefore, when the Court ruled that students could not be punished for wearing black armbands to school, or that a protester could not be punished for wearing a jacket with an offensive slogan on the back. These cases, Justice Black contended, involved conduct and did not implicate the First Amendment; no "speech" was involved.

Fortunately for picketers, flag-burners and dozens of others who have chosen over the years to express their views by doing rather than saying, a majority of the Supreme Court has never agreed with Justice Black's definition of "speech." Indeed, a majority of the Court has always recognized that "speech" is more than talking. Justice Abe Fortas, for example, wrote in *Tinker. v. Des Moines Independent School District* that those students

who wore black armbands to school to protest the Vietnam War were participating in activity that was "closely akin to 'pure speech.'" Justice Fortas's characterization was momentous. If something that was so clearly an action could be considered "pure speech," many other types of conduct could be recognized as speech as well and, therefore, eligible for First Amendment protection. Under such a construction, expression, which is not mentioned in the First Amendment, is protected alongside "speech" and "press."

That has long been the case in First Amendment jurisprudence. Indeed, the Court has recognized a variety of activities as being speech: carrying or displaying a flag; marching or picketing; burning a flag, cross or draft card. The Court has also said that a sit-in is a form of expression, as is the "silent, reproachful presence" of a group of African Americans who refused to leave an all-white library. In fact, in some circumstances, even sleeping could be described as "speech."

This is not to say, however, that the First Amendment protects all expressive or symbolic conduct. Conduct, after all, may intrude on individual rights more than other forms of speech. It may literally do what a 1980s advertisement for a long-distance telephone company once suggested consumers figuratively do: Reach out and touch someone. The Court has said, therefore, that there must be some balance between the rights of the actor and the rights of others present when conduct is used as a means of expression. This tension between rights has been at the heart of expressive conduct cases since the 1960s, when the Court's first substantive analysis in this area of the law began.[1]

---

[1] Some cases involving expressive conduct are Barnes v. Glen Theatre (Nude dancing, though expressive, may be regulated.); Brown v. Louisiana (A protest in a public library is protected speech.); Clark v. Cmty. for Creative Non-Violence (Sleeping in some instances is expressive conduct.); Stromberg v. California (A regulation prohib-

CONDUCT AS SPEECH

For First Amendment purposes, there are three kinds of conduct: (1) conduct that has no communicative value, (2) conduct that is purely communicative, and (3) conduct that has a mix of communicative and non-communicative elements.

Sometimes it's easy to tell the difference. One spring, for example, a homeowner noticed that his U.S. flag had become frayed and moth-eaten. He decided to replace the flag and learned from the *United States Code* that the preferred way of disposing of a damaged flag is by burning. He took the flag into the back yard, dropped it into the grill, doused it with lighter fluid and set it ablaze. No one saw the action, and the flag burner later disposed of the cold ashes by spreading them in the flower bed. The act had no communicative value. Its purpose was solely to dispose of a damaged U.S. flag as suggested by the *Code*.

Come summer, the homeowner replaced the damaged flag and, on July 4, put it on a flag pole attached to the garage. The act is purely communicative: The homeowner displayed the flag to demonstrate patriotism on Independence Day.

But when fall arrived, the homeowner became dismayed. An incumbent president had taken actions with which the homeowner bitterly disagreed. He had a series of arguments with a neighbor, who happened to be the local chairman of the president's political party. The homeowner's irritation was inflamed even more because the president was using hundreds of flags in his re-election campaign, even using the flag as a background on campaign posters, bumper stickers and other paraphernalia. To demonstrate his distaste, the homeowner doused his recently purchased flag with lighter fluid, set it ablaze and tossed it on the neighbor's front porch. The burning flag destroyed a "Welcome" mat and left a large, sooty spot, requiring the porch to be repainted.

The homeowner's action contains both communicative and non-communicative elements. He communicated displeasure with presidential politics but also caused property damage.

Under Supreme Court rulings, the government may regulate purely communicative conduct only in extremely rare circumstances. Conduct that has both speech and non-speech elements, however, may be regulated more readily. Courts must balance the rights of an individual to express viewpoints through action against the rights of individuals who may be impacted by the action. The balancing is complex and often controversial.

Over the years, the Supreme Court has developed a series of tests it applies in adjudicating cases in which individuals or

groups claim constitutional protection for symbolic speech. First, the Court asks, is the conduct expressive? If not, the First Amendment is not implicated, the inquiry ends, and the government may regulate the conduct. If the conduct *is* expressive, however, the Court then asks the more difficult question: Is the expressive conduct protected by the First Amendment?

Is the Conduct Expressive?

If conduct is expressive, it is "speech." The expressive nature of the conduct is the element that moves action from simply doing to communicating. The homeowner is no longer burning a damaged flag in his grill; he is burning it in public for the express purpose of communicating a message.

To determine whether conduct is purely utilitarian or has some communicative elements, the Court asks two questions: (1) Is there an intent to express a message? (2) Is there a likelihood the message will be understood by a witness? If there is no intent to express a message, or if it is not likely that a witness will understand the intended message, the conduct is not expressive, and the First Amendment does not apply. Figure 1 demonstrates the flow of this inquiry.

The Court does not require that a viewer of expressive conduct understand the exact message the actor intends; only a general understanding is necessary. For example, when spectators watched in 1984 as Gregory Lee Johnson burned an American flag outside the meeting place of the Republican National Convention in Dallas, it was unnecessary that they knew Johnson was demonstrating his distaste for President Ronald Reagan, who was seeking re-nomination. It was sufficient that the spectators understood that Johnson was dissatisfied with some aspect of the United States or of the U.S. government — those entities symbolized by the flag.

Even though Johnson's action could be interpreted as a demonstration of disgust with President Reagan, the Republican Party, the U.S. government *or* the United States itself, Justice William Brennan, upholding Johnson's right to burn the flag, wrote in *Texas v. Johnson*, "The expressive, overtly political nature of this conduct was both intentional and overwhelmingly apparent."

The Court has recognized a wide array of conduct to be expressive: burning a cross, nude dancing, displaying a license plate, burning a draft card, saluting a flag, displaying a flag.[2]

Not all these activities, however, are constitutionally protected. Once an action has been determined to be expressive, the Court must determine whether the First Amendment protects the expressive conduct. Cases involving expressive conduct date to the early twentieth century, but the Court's first substantive treatment of it was in 1968. In *United States v. O'Brien*, the Court recognized that burning a draft card as a means of pro-

---

iting the display of a red flag is not constitutional.); Virginia v. Black (Cross burning, in many instances, is intimidating speech.); West Virginia Bd. of Educ. v. Barnette (Students cannot be forced to salute the flag.); Wooley v. Maynard (A person cannot be forced to display a license plate that contains an ideological message with which the person disagrees.); United States v. O'Brien (Burning a draft card is not constitutionally protected.). Citations for these cases appear in the bibliography at the end of this chapter.

---

[2] See the cases listed in footnote 1.

testing the Selective Service System and U.S. involvement in Vietnam was expressive conduct, but ruled that other concerns outweighed David Paul O'Brien's right to burn the card. In *O'Brien,* the Court, for the first time, delineated the test for determining whether expressive conduct is protected by the First Amendment.

Court must determine whether the regulation is directed at the suppression of speech or at some other goal. If the purpose of the regulation is to restrict speech, the Court applies what it calls the "strict scrutiny test" to determine whether the regulation is constitutional; if the regulation is not directed at the suppression of speech, but at some other goal, the Court applies a test of intermediate scrutiny. Figure 2 demonstrates the flow of this inquiry.

Figure 1

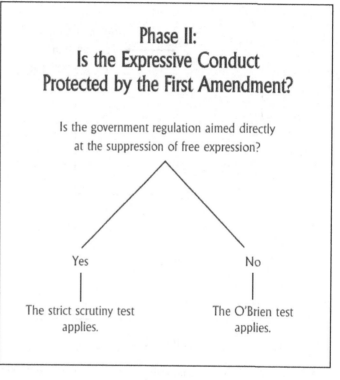

Figure 2

Is the Expressive Conduct Protected?

At first glance, O'Brien's burning of his draft card is remarkably similar to Johnson's burning of a U.S. flag: Both men had audiences, both were expressing distaste with political agendas, and both were using an age-old method of destruction to demonstrate that distaste. In both cases, there was an intent to express a message, and there was a likelihood that the message would be understood by witnesses.

But the Court found significant differences in the two acts. Ironically, the differences were based primarily upon the intent of the government rather than the intent of the speakers.

After the Court finds conduct to be expressive, it determines whether the conduct may be regulated by examining the rationale behind the government regulation being applied. The

Strict Scrutiny. Attorneys for Texas argued to the Texas and U.S. supreme courts that the state's purpose in adopting its flag desecration act was to protect the U.S. flag as a symbol of patriotism and unity. And, the attorneys argued, the state had the right to do so. The Supreme Court agreed that protecting the flag is a noble cause. The method used to protect the flag, however, was directed at the suppression of free speech; the statute would allow expression supporting the state's goals, but would not allow expression contrary to those goals. Because the statute was directly related to the suppression of speech, therefore, strict scrutiny was required to determine whether the statute was constitutional. Figure 3 demonstrates the flow of the strict scrutiny test, which requires the resolution of two questions:

• *Is there a compelling government interest for the regulation?* The government interest advocated by the regulation must be more than a passing interest; it must be vitally important to governmental operations. In *Texas v. Johnson,* Justice Brennan recognized that there may be a compelling government interest in protecting the flag as a symbol of national unity. National unity is important, Justice Brennan wrote, and the flag may be the single best symbol of the United States and that unity.

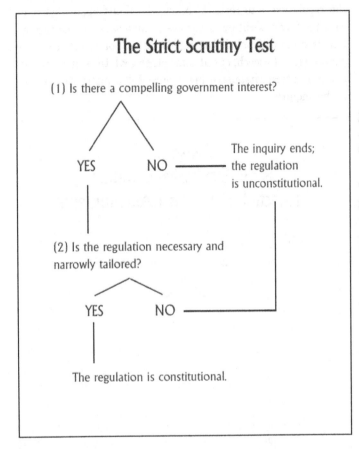

The Strict Scrutiny Test

(1) Is there a compelling government interest?

YES   NO ————— The inquiry ends;
                              the regulation
                              is unconstitutional.

(2) Is the regulation necessary and
narrowly tailored?

YES   NO —————

The regulation is constitutional.

Figure 3

• *Is the regulation necessary and narrowly tailored to advance the government interest?* A necessary regulation is one that is essential, rather than optional, for the advancement of the government's interest. To survive strict scrutiny, a regulation must be necessary; but it also must be narrowly tailored. Being narrowly tailored means that the regulation goes as far as necessary to advance the government interest but does not overstep its bounds. In the area of speech, a narrowly tailored regulation is one that does not encompass protected speech in its prohibitions. Justice Brennan said the Texas act was not narrowly tailored. Even though protecting the flag is a compelling government interest, an individual's right to criticize the government is powerful. The government may promote the flag, Brennan wrote, but may not control messages critical of the government simply because the flag is the medium of that criticism. "If there is a bedrock principle underlying the First Amendment," he wrote, "it is that the government may not prohibit the expression of an idea simply because society finds the idea itself offensive or disagreeable."

Intermediate Scrutiny: The O'Brien Test. The Court came to a different conclusion in *United States v. O'Brien.*

When David Paul O'Brien burned his draft card, he was, like Johnson, expressing his discontent with government policy, specifically, with Selective Service. At the time, federal law required all men in the United States who were 18 or older to carry draft cards until they surrendered them to government officials upon induction into the armed forces or until they were no longer eligible for the draft.

O'Brien did not deny burning his draft card but contended that the law prohibiting the destruction or mutilation of the card was unconstitutional because it inhibited free speech and served no legitimate legislative purpose. A federal district court in Massachusetts found him guilty of violating the law. The First U.S. Circuit Court of Appeals found the statute unconstitutional but affirmed the conviction on grounds that O'Brien should have been convicted of the less serious offense of not having possession of the draft card. Both the government and O'Brien appealed to the Supreme Court.

Chief Justice Earl Warren, writing for a seven-member majority, did not dispute O'Brien's contention that the burning of a draft card was expressive conduct. Instead, based upon the assumption that the conduct was sufficient to implicate the First Amendment, he took issue with O'Brien's argument that freedom of expression includes all modes of "communication of ideas by conduct." Wrote Warren: "We cannot accept the view that an apparently limitless variety of conduct can be labeled 'speech' whenever the person engaging in the conduct intends thereby to express an idea." When speech and non-speech elements combine in some form of expression, Chief Justice Warren wrote, a sufficiently important governmental interest in regulating the non-speech element of the communication can justify incidental limitations of First Amendment freedoms. Warren delineated a four-part test for determining when the government regulation is justified:

• *Is the regulation within the constitutional power of the government?* The government has a right to raise and support armies, the Court noted, and to make all necessary and proper laws to that end; therefore, the Selective Service Act was within the power of the government.

• *Does the regulation further an important or substantial government interest?* Because the draft card and other Selective Service documents further the smooth and proper functioning of the system, Congress has a legitimate and substantial interest in preventing their wanton and unrestrained destruction and assuring their continuing availability by punishing people who knowingly and willfully destroy them.

• *Is the governmental interest unrelated to the suppression of free expression?* The non-destruction requirements of the law were aimed at the continued smooth operation of the Selective Service System, the Court held. That is, they were aimed at the non-communicative aspects of O'Brien's conduct and nothing else.

• *Is the incidental restriction of free expression no greater than is essential to the furtherance of the stated governmental inter-*

est? The Court noted that the restriction O'Brien violated was narrowly drawn.

O'Brien's conviction was upheld, therefore. More importantly, however, the Court established a test to be applied in cases involving expressive conduct. The flow of the O'Brien Test is demonstrated in Figure 4.

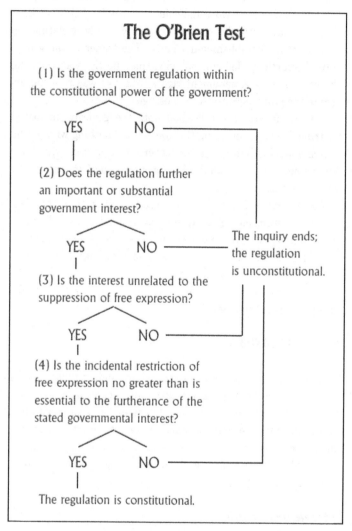

The O'Brien Test

(1) Is the government regulation within the constitutional power of the government?

YES   NO ————————

(2) Does the regulation further an important or substantial government interest?

YES   NO ————————

The inquiry ends; the regulation is unconstitutional.

(3) Is the interest unrelated to the suppression of free expression?

YES   NO ————————

(4) Is the incidental restriction of free expression no greater than is essential to the furtherance of the stated governmental interest?

YES   NO ————————

The regulation is constitutional.

Figure 4

PROTECTED OR NOT: SPECIAL CASES

A variety of external issues may impact how or whether the First Amendment applies to conduct, as demonstrated here.

Private Businesses & Regulating Expressive Conduct

Kneeling is often seen as a form of expressive conduct. Many people kneel — publicly and privately — to show deference to a higher being when they pray. Christians often kneel when they receive the elements of Holy Communion. Some people kneel to show deference to persons in positions of authority or to pay respect during funeral services.

Rarely in the United States, however, has kneeling drawn the attention it did between 2016 and 2018 when Colin Kaepernick, then a quarterback for the San Francisco 49ers, knelt during the pre-game playing of the National Anthem.[3]

The result was a firestorm of controversy that included condemnations and threats by the President of the United States. The owners of the NFL teams added to the controversy when, in 2018, they adopted a policy requiring all players and league personnel to stand and "show respect for the flag and the anthem." The policy allows players to remain in the locker room during the playing of the anthem — a change from an earlier policy — but, if they are on the field, they are required to stand. If they do not, their teams will be fined and the league's commissioner may impose discipline.

Critics attacked the owners for violating the First Amendment rights of the players, but, on the surface, this is not a First Amendment issue. As pointed out in Chapter 1, the First Amendment only protects speakers from unwarranted government intervention in their expressive activities. That is, the First Amendment does not prevent private entities from squelching speech. The NFL is not an arm of the government, so the First Amendment, one would think, does not apply.

But the meddling of the president into the business operations of the NFL and the speech activities of NFL players could have made a difference.

The Trump Administration actively joined in the debate over the actions of Kaepernick and players who joined him. President Donald Trump referred to Kaepernick with vulgar language, called on fans to boycott games, and threatened to use the tax code to punish the NFL if action was not taken to halt the protests or punish the players. In an effort to emphasize the administration's position, Vice President Mike Pence attended an NFL game apparently for the sole purpose of walking out when some players kneeled.

Legal scholars have called the ban illegal for a variety of reasons, most significantly because it may violate labor laws that require such issues to be discussed with unions before implementation. They have also argued that the ban violated the First Amendment because of the intersection of the government and private entities. That is, the NFL owners may be acting to restrict players' speech rights because they are afraid of action by the Trump Administration that may harm their business.

Other observers have suggested that the First Amendment is implicated because of another intersection of government and private business — the fact that many stadiums in which professional football games are played are subsidized by the political jurisdictions in which they are located. That is, cities give

---

[3] For the first four pre-season games of 2016, Kaepernick sat during the playing of the anthem. Then, after consulting with a former Green Beret and professional football player, he began kneeling. *See Ex-Green Beret Nate Boyer Writes Open Letter to Trump, Kaepernick, NFL and America,* ESPN, Oct. 13, 2017, http://www.espn.com/nfl/story/_/id/21003968-2017-ex-green-beret-nate-boyer=writes-open-letter-president-donald-trump-colin-kaepernick-nfl-united-states-america.

tax breaks and other benefits in order to lure NFL franchises and the added income they draw. Such intersections could be tantamount to the NFL taking on the role of government when it restricts speech on matters of public concern by the players.

The Strange Case of Nude Dancing

Dancing, most people will agree, is a form of expression, at least in those contexts in which professionals perform for audiences. And it would seem just as obvious that whether a professional dances with or without clothing is irrelevant to whether the dancer is attempting to express a message, and the message is apparent to an observer. The Supreme Court, however, has reached such conclusions begrudgingly and remains unwilling to grant constitutional protection to nude dancing.

The Court most recently faced the issue in 2000 in *Erie v. Pap's A.M.* The case began when the operator of a nightclub featuring nude dancing challenged an Erie, Pennsylvania, ordinance that prohibited public nudity. The nightclub owner claimed that the ordinance infringed his First Amendment free expression rights by prohibiting expressive conduct in the form of nude dancing. The Pennsylvania Supreme Court agreed, but the U.S. Supreme Court overturned that opinion, ruling that the ordinance was constitutional. The Court was splintered in its rationale.

Writing for four justices, Sandra Day O'Connor found that, since the ordinance prohibited all nudity, not just nude dancing, it was not a content-based restriction and was constitutional under the four-part O'Brien Test. Justice O'Connor admitted that nude dancing is expressive conduct — though "it falls only within the outer ambit of the First Amendment's protection." Two justices concurred in the judgment, thereby allowing the ordinance to stand, but were not willing to go as far as Justice O'Connor. Antonin Scalia, joined by Clarence Thomas, wrote that nude dancing could be regulated as conduct, unless there was evidence that an ordinance aimed at the dancing was aimed specifically at the "communicative character" of the dancing rather than the nudity itself.

Only Justices John Paul Stevens and Ruth Bader Ginsburg recognized that nude dancing is, indeed, expressive conduct, and regulations such as those enacted in Erie must face strict scrutiny. Discounting the Court's argument that the ban was aimed at the secondary effects of nude dancing — increased sex crimes, for example — Justice Stevens wrote that the Court held, for the first time, that such effects "may justify the total suppression of protected speech."

What seems clear from the Court's opinion in *Erie* — as well as earlier nude dancing cases — is that the justices are willing to allow certain types of expressive conduct to be regulated, not because the conduct is not expressive, but because they don't like the message the conduct is communicating.

Government Speech v. Public Forums

Three flagpoles stand in Boston's City Hall Plaza. On one, the city flies the U.S. flag; on a second, it flies the flag of the Commonwealth of Massachusetts; on the third, it usually flies Boston's flag. Sometimes, however, Boston allows private groups to fly their flags on the third flagpole. But it didn't allow a Christian organization to do so, afraid that it would be violating the Constitution's Establishment Clause. The leader of the group, Harold Shurtleff, filed suit, alleging that the city was violating the group's First Amendment rights. The city was refusing access to the group because of its message.

A lower federal court latched onto the government-speech doctrine, however, in ruling that Boston did nothing wrong. The doctrine holds that when the government speaks, the First Amendment is not implicated — a government is free to say what it wants.

The Supreme Court did not agree, finding that the flag-raising program does not express government speech. In addition, "When the government encourages diverse expression. . . the First Amendment prevents it from discriminating against speakers based on their viewpoint,"

That's what Boston did, the Court held, by denying Shurtleff's group access to the flagpole.

SPEECH AS CONDUCT

Thus far, this discussion has centered on conduct that takes on the role of speech, that is, conduct that is expressive. Another area of law with which the Court has wrestled is the regulation of speech that takes on additional characteristics, that is, when the speech takes on the role of conduct. This occurs with fighting words, threatening speech, intimidating speech and, to a lesser degree, picketing.

Threatening Speech

Fighting words are words that are so vile or obnoxious that they are likely to prompt a physical reaction. For example, what might happen if, during a hotly contested football game between two bitter rivals — say the University of Virginia and Virginia Tech — a Tech fan wandered into the U.Va. student section wearing a sweatshirt that read "F*** the Cavaliers"?

The result might seem obvious, and the example is not as far-fetched as it might first appear. In 1968, Paul Robert Cohen walked into the Los Angeles County Courthouse wearing a jacket bearing the slogan "F*** the draft." He was arrested and convicted of violating that portion of the California Penal Code that prohibited maliciously and willfully disturbing the peace or quiet of any neighborhood or person by offensive conduct.

The Supreme Court, however, found that the conduct was speech and was protected. Three justices disagreed. Harry

Blackmun, Warren Burger and Hugo Black argued, in a dissent drafted by Blackmun, that "Cohen's absurd and immature antic ... was mainly conduct and little speech." They said Cohen should have found another way of expressing his opinion.

In the majority opinion, however, Justice John Marshall Harlan pointed out the importance of the emotive as well as the cognitive force of speech:

> We cannot overlook the fact, because it is well illustrated by the episode involved here, that much linguistic expression serves a dual communicative function: it conveys not only ideas capable of relatively precise, detached explication, but otherwise inexpressible emotions as well. In fact, words are often chosen as much for their emotive as their cognitive force. We cannot sanction the view that the Constitution, while solicitous of the cognitive content of individual speech, has little or no regard for the emotive function which, practically speaking, may often be the more important element of the overall message sought to be communicated.

Even though the Court found Cohen's "absurd and immature antic" to be protected speech, the antic demonstrates the type of speech that can take on the role of conduct: The words become like actions. A person willing to respond to the words with physical violence could have confronted either Cohen or the reckless Virginia Tech football fan.

The Court first recognized the so-called "fighting words" doctrine in 1942 in *Chaplinsky v. New Hampshire.* A Jehovah's Witness was arrested for calling a police officer a "damned fascist" and a "God damned racketeer." The Court upheld the conviction, calling the verbal assault an attack of fighting words, that is, words "which by their very utterance inflict injury or tend to incite an immediate breach of the peace." Such utterances, the Court said, "are no essential part of any expression of ideas, and are of such slight social value as a step to truth that any benefit that may be derived from them is clearly outweighed by the social interests in order and morality."

Not only must the words be particularly violent or obnoxious, they must be aimed directly at an individual for the fighting-words doctrine to apply, as the Court demonstrated seven years later in *Terminiello v. Chicago.* A well-publicized speech by a right-wing anti-Semite was met by a crowd of protesters, some of whom were able to break into the meeting hall where the speech was held. The speaker, Arthur Terminiello, repeatedly referred to the protesters as "scum" or "slimy scum." The speech so stirred members of the crowd that police feared unrest. Like Walter Chaplinsky, Terminiello was convicted of breaching the peace by using language that would stir the public to anger. In Terminiello's case, however, the Court reversed. Justice William O. Douglas, in one of his few free-speech majority opinions, wrote that free speech is designed to invoke dispute:

> It may indeed best serve its high purpose when it induces a condition of unrest, creates dissatisfaction with conditions as they are, or even stirs people to anger. Speech is often provocative and challenging. It may strike at prejudices and preconceptions and have profound unsettling effects as it presses for acceptance of an idea. That is why freedom of speech, though not absolute ... is nevertheless protected against censorship or punishment, unless shown likely to produce a clear and present danger of a serious substantive evil that rises far above public inconvenience, annoyance, or unrest. There is no room under our Constitution for a more restrictive view.

What's the difference in the two cases? Among other things, *Terminiello* did not involve a face-to-face confrontation. In an important lower court case, the Illinois Supreme Court upheld the rights of neo-Nazis to march in Skokie, Illinois, displaying the swastika, which an appellate court ordered removed because of the fighting-words doctrine. The state supreme court recognized, however, that the march removed the speech from that one-on-one dialogue to a more abstract insult. Ironically, after winning the right to march in Skokie, the neo-Nazis never did.

The confrontational nature of language has been important to the Supreme Court as well. The Court has consistently struck down as vague and overbroad state laws prohibiting the use of abusive, menacing, insulting or profane language, if those statutes had not been narrowed by state courts to focus on fighting words. Though the Court has upheld convictions for the use of abusive language when there was a threat of a riot, the threat must be relatively direct. A speaker's shout that "We'll take the f***ing streets," for example, was found not to be fighting words, nor did it tend to incite a riot, because the speaker was obviously not referring to an imminent action, but, rather, to some possible future action.

The Court has faced few fighting words cases, but did so in 1992. In *R.A.V. v. St. Paul,* it held that a conviction for burning a cross in the yard of an African-American couple who had moved into a predominantly white neighborhood could not stand under the fighting-words doctrine. The cross that the juvenile burned didn't cause much of a fire — it was made from broken chair legs — but the Minnesota Supreme Court said the act amounted to fighting words. It upheld the conviction for violating a city ordinance prohibiting the burning of a cross, the placing of a Nazi swastika, or other similar action for the purpose of arousing anger, alarm or resentment "on the basis of race, color, creed, religion or gender."

The Supreme Court reversed. It said St. Paul could prohibit fighting words but that the ordinance allowed fighting words unless they were aimed at a member of one of the specified classes. It would be acceptable under the ordinance, the Court ruled, to use fighting words against someone based on political affiliation, union or non-union membership or sexual preference: "The First Amendment does not permit St. Paul to impose special prohibitions on those speakers who express views on disfavored subjects." The Court recognized that the conduct was reprehensible but ruled that the subject was being unconstitutionally punished under an ordinance that advanced what amounted to viewpoint discrimination.

Revisiting the issue of cross burning during its 2002-03 term, the Supreme Court carved out a new category of speech that is not protected by the First Amendment — intimidation. In *Virginia v. Black*, it held that when cross burning achieves the status of intimidating speech, it can be proscribed and punished, but the Court also held that not all instances of cross burning are intimidating. It found a Virginia state law to be unconstitutional because, in addition to banning cross burning that is designed to intimidate "any person or group," the law stated that the act of burning a cross was *prima facie* evidence of an intent to intimidate. The clause making cross burning automatically intimidating, the Court held, also made the law unconstitutional. While cross burning can be "a particularly virulent form of intimidation," Justice Sandra Day O'Connor wrote for the majority, and it always can be considered "a symbol of hate," it has also been used to communicate "messages of shared ideology." Therefore, to be proscribed, cross burning must cross the line from being a symbol representing some ideology, celebration or ritual and must become intimidating.

The Court had previously indicated that, in addition to fighting words, speech that constituted what it called a "true threat" could be proscribed. Some scholars and advocates had argued that cross burning constituted threatening speech. The Court in *Virginia v. Black* agreed and held that intimidating speech as a type of threat could be proscribed and punished. Wrote Justice O'Connor: "Intimidation in the constitutionally proscribable sense of the word is a type of true threat, where a speaker directs a threat to a person or group of persons with the intent of placing the victim in fear of bodily harm or death."

The Court did not elaborate on what kinds of speech might be intimidating, what the distinctions are between intimidating speech and true threats or how lower courts can make such determinations. But that is the way of the Court. Because it only answers questions put to it, the process of establishing tests can be long and arduous. The Court, for example, held in 1957 that the First Amendment does not protect obscenity, but it was 1973 before a majority of the Court agreed upon a test for obscenity. The Court has taken similar paths in the area of expressive conduct[4] and commercial speech.

It may be years, however, before the Court develops a test for determining when speech in general and cross burning in particular become intimidating, if it ever does. Indeed the Court has already turned down one request to expand the scope of so-called intimidating speech. The Seventh U.S. Circuit Court of Appeals cited *Virginia v. Black* in denying First Amendment protection to a prison inmate's statements that he planned to bomb a federal office building in Milwaukee. The court, however, rather than recognizing that Justice O'Connor was recasting intimidating speech as unprotected, reported that she had established a new definition of "true threats." It rejected the government's argument that the inmate's discussion of a potential bombing of a federal building was either a true threat or intimidating speech under *Virginia v. Black*, and the Supreme Court refused to hear the case.

Picketing

The Court has recognized that picketing is a time-honored method of expressing a message, particularly among people who cannot afford to publish their complaints or are focused on narrow problems. Therefore, the Court has granted picketers broad protection, still balancing their rights against those of other individuals and against public peace and safety. It has held that peaceful picketing cannot be licensed, that restrictions on picketing must be content-neutral, and that picketing cannot be banned from public property.

One of the Court's most important rulings on picketing came near the middle of the twentieth century in *Thornhill v. Alabama*. In striking down Alabama's statute prohibiting picketing a place of business, the Court noted that freedom of speech and press "are among the fundamental personal rights and liberties which are secured to all persons" by the Constitution and that picketing is one of the activities that "may enlighten the public on the nature and causes" of public debate.

The rights of individuals to picket or distribute information often depend upon where the picketing occurs and the rationale behind government regulations restricting the picketing. Picketing in an area designated a public forum — like a park or sidewalk — is almost always protected, if the picketing is peaceful and if it does not interfere with other valid uses of the public forum. Even in the absence of a public forum, the Court has held that absolute bans on First Amendment activity — including picketing — may be unconstitutional because the government cannot justify such bans.

The Court reaffirmed the constitutional protections for picketing on public property in 2011. *Snyder v. Phelps* involved intentional infliction of emotional distress, but the Court did not decide the case on that issue. Instead, it held that members of the Westboro Baptist Church of Topeka, Kansas, had a constitutional right to protest at the funeral of a serviceman killed in the line of duty because their speech involved matters of public concern and because the protest took place on public property. "Simply put," Chief Justice John Roberts wrote for the Court, "the church members had the right to be where they were." Under the Court's ruling, the right to picket on public property trumped the right of a private person to be free from verbal attacks that cause severe emotional distress.

The Court, however, let stand a ruling that limited picketing activities near Saint John's Church in the Wilderness, in Den-

[4] *See* the cases listed in footnote 1.

ver. The church was successful in seeking an injunction that prohibited anti-abortion picketing that inhibited worship services. In addition to their shouting, picketers displayed placards that contained pictures of aborted fetuses. The Colorado Court of Appeals distinguished the case from *Snyder* because, the court found, the disturbance caused by the picketers interfered with the church's worship services. The court upheld most of the restrictions, and the Supreme Court denied certiorari.

Politics have often intruded upon the Supreme Court's adjudications related to picketing. Some examples are:

• *Picketing the Supreme Court building.* While the Court has ruled that picketing on the public sidewalks around the Court building is constitutionally protected, that protection does not apply to the adjacent plaza and grounds. The Court held in *United States v. Grace*, a 1983 case, that restrictions on picketing on the public sidewalks are unconstitutional. In 2013, however, the Marshal of the Court, with the approval of Chief Justice Roberts, banned picketing on the grounds. A federal circuit court upheld the restriction in order to maintain a tranquil environment around the Supreme Court building and to preserve the appearance of a judiciary immune to public pressure.

• *Picketing abortion clinics.* The Court has balanced the free-speech rights of persons who picket abortion clinics with the rights of women who want abortions to have free access to the clinics. The Court upheld the use of zones in which picketing could be banned but held that 300-foot buffer zones were unreasonable and burdened more speech than necessary to serve the government's interest in guaranteeing the free flow of traffic. It also held that a so-called "floating buffer zone" requiring picketers to stay at least fifteen feet from people or vehicles entering or leaving the clinics violated the First Amendment because it overburdened speech. In 2014, the Court continued that balancing approach. In *McCullen v. Coakley*, it struck down as overbroad a thirty-five-foot buffer zone around abortion clinics from which individuals were categorically excluded unless they were traveling through those zones to reach an abortion clinic or some other establishment. The Court ruled that the law establishing the zone failed the intermediate scrutiny test and unconstitutionally restricted the speech rights of persons who wanted to communicate with potential patients.

• *Picketing military bases.* The Court has allowed the military to restrict picketing and the distribution of literature on military bases — even those portions of the bases open to the public.

• *Picketing the homes of Supreme Court Justices.* In May 2022, an opinion apparently written by Justice Samuel Alito condemning abortion and the Court's holding in *Roe v. Wade* was leaked to the media. While the holding in the draft was unsurprising, the almost virulent language of Justice Alito's opinion was. The protest against the Court that followed included picketers showing up outside the homes of Justice Alito and two of the four justices who joined the draft opinion, John Roberts

and Brett Kavanaugh. (Neil Gorsuch and Amy Coney Barrett were the other two joiners.) The pickets caused a mini-debate over whether such activity is proper. The federal government and Virginia, where Justice Alito lives, have statutes prohibiting such picketing, though their constitutionality is questionable. Indeed, the Court, in *Snyder v. Phelps*, upheld protests at a funeral because, it held, the protesters were focused on matters of public concern and were not involved in activity that violated the law — they were where they had a right to be. The streets and sidewalks have long been held to be public forums. If the picketers crossed onto private property, that is more problematic. Often, however, even the private property rights of individuals and corporations must give way when individuals choose to express themselves by picketing. While the Court has recognized that owners have certain rights over their property, when the property is used for a public purpose and when it's obvious that the picketers are expressing their own viewpoints and are not speaking for the property owners, the Court has allowed picketing on private property.

The Court has also held that towns may not restrict access to private homes to disseminate information. The Village of Stratton prohibited persons from distributing information door-to-door without first receiving a "Solicitation Permit." Apparently the issuance of the permit was *pro forma*, but the Jehovah's Witnesses of New York complained that the application process infringed their First Amendment rights. The Court agreed, ruling in 2002 that persons engaging in door-to-door advocacy could not be required to identify themselves through an application and permit procedure.

Inciting Violent Action

If speech can be punished for taking on the role of action, it follows that speech that incites violent action can also be punished. And it can. The Court has established a high hurdle, however, that has rarely been cleared. For example, the Court held that a passionate speech in which a civil rights leader promised Blacks who patronized white-owned businesses that "we're gonna break your damn necks" was insufficient for liability in a legal action. Similarly, a promise by the leader of a group of civil rights protesters being dispersed from downtown streets that they would return and "take the f***ing streets later" did not amount to inciting imminent lawless action.

To determine whether those speeches incited violent action, the Court applied a test it established in 1969 in *Brandenburg v. Ohio*. The test has three parts: (1) whether a speaker intended to incite violence, (2) whether such violence was imminent, and (3) whether resulting violence was likely.

Very few speeches have met the Brandenburg Test.

On January 6, 2021, however, Donald Trump delivered a speech to a crowd of protestors who minutes later stormed the U.S. Capitol. The riot caused property damage, injury and death. Application of the Brandenburg Test to Trump's speech demonstrates that it might be a textbook example of speech that did, in fact, incite a riot.

(1) To demand that a group take violent action is clear evidence of intent to incite, but courts have recognized other ways intent can be demonstrated. Trump claimed some fifteen times that the presidential election was rigged and some six times wondered whether Vice President Mike Pence would act to save the election; he said that "we're going to fight like hell" to ensure that the rigged election would be overturned; he encouraged the crowd to walk down Pennsylvania to the Capitol. All this, and more, was directed at an already riled crowd. For weeks, the language of insurrection had been used on social media to encourage participation in the rally. Many persons who attended the rally said they were there because Trump wanted them to show up to take action. In such a volatile environment, even neutral-sounding words could prompt violence, demonstrating intent. The Court has held that context in such situations "is all important," and that intent can be determined by a "rational inference from the import of the language."

(2) Trump's exhortation that the crowd walk to the Capitol, and his promise that he would join them, though he didn't, satisfies the imminence requirement of the Brandenburg Test. In addition, violent mayhem erupted shortly after Trump's speech.

(3) The likelihood element of *Brandenburg* is satisfied because there was, indeed, a violent response to the speech. The Court held that without lawless action, appeals for violence "must be regarded as protected speech." There are dozens of examples of rioters saying they were acting at then-President Trump's direction. Playing into that atmosphere is clear evidence of likelihood.

Application of the Brandenburg Test to Trump's speech, therefore, indicates that Trump intended a violent insurrection and that was, indeed, the result of the speech. Whether he will ever be held accountable is another question.

RECENT CASES

Some recent Supreme Court cases demonstrate the complexities of expressive conduct.

Campaign Paraphernalia & Polling Places

The Supreme Court recently expanded the expressive rights voters have in and around polling places. In 1992, the Court upheld a Tennessee law prohibiting the display of campaign materials within 100 feet of polling places.

In 2018, however, the Court struck down a Minnesota law that prohibited anyone, including voters, from wearing political buttons or other campaign paraphernalia inside polling places. A state, the Court held in *Minnesota Voters Alliance et al. v. Mahsky et al.,* may prohibit certain apparel in polling places, but "must draw a reasonable line," and the Minnesota law doesn't

do so. It fails to define the word "political" in the statute and has provided only "haphazard interpretations" of what may or may not be acceptable. The statue, therefore, is not "capable of reasoned application."

License Plates and Symbolic Speech

The Supreme Court determined Paul Robert Cohen's display of words to be a form of conduct. Similarly, other courts have determined the obscuring of words also to be a form of conduct.

In 1974, George Maynard, a Jehovah's Witness living in New Hampshire, was charged under state law with obscuring the words "Live Free or Die" on his license plate. Maynard said he found the slogan violated his faith, and, therefore, he objected to being forced to advocate that message. A federal three-judge district court found Maynard's action to be symbolic speech. The Supreme Court did not resolve the symbolic speech question, but found that Maynard could not be required by the government to advocate a message with which he disagreed.

Speech by means of license plate returned to the Supreme Court — in a different context — in its 2015 term.

When the Texas Division of the Sons of Confederate Veterans was refused its request for a specialty license plate displaying the Confederate Battle Flag, it filed suit claiming its First Amendment free speech rights had been violated. Members of the group argued that the license plate would constitute private speech — the speech of those who purchased and displayed it — and the refusal by the state amounted to constitutionally forbidden viewpoint discrimination. The Court, however, ruled that the issuance of specialty license plates constituted government speech and ruled for the state. "When government speaks, it is not barred by the Free Speech Clause from determining the content of what it says," the Court held in a 5-4 opinion.

The cases are very different. One involves speech a private individual is required — or not required — to display. The other involves the murky area of government speech. They demonstrate, however, the continuing complexity of the issue of speech as conduct.

SUMMARY

The speech/conduct conundrum consists of parallel issues: conduct that takes on the role of speech and speech that takes on the role of conduct.

Based on *United States v. O'Brien, Texas v. Johnson* and other Supreme Court cases, the Court has established a carefully delineated course in dealing with expressive conduct. That course is described in Figure 5.

In traveling that course, the Court must answer some specific questions.

Is the conduct expressive? The conduct is expressive if there is an intent to express a message and if there is a likelihood the message will be understood. If there is either no intent or no likelihood of understanding, the conduct is not expressive, the First Amendment is not implicated, and the inquiry is over. If the conduct is expressive, however, the inquiry continues.

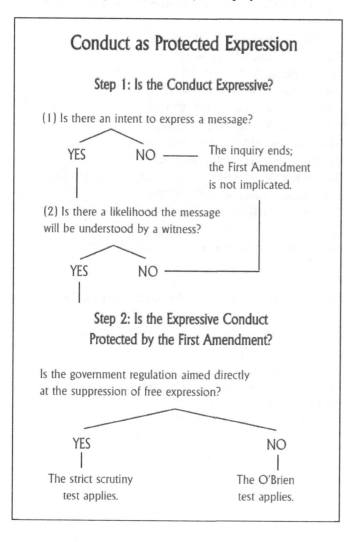

Figure 5

Is the expressive conduct protected? The path to determining whether conduct is protected begins with the rationale behind the government regulation. The Court first determines whether the regulation is aimed directly at speech. If it is, the Court applies a strict scrutiny test by asking two questions: (1) Does the regulation advance a compelling government interest? and (2) Is the regulation necessary and narrowly tailored? If the answer to either question is no, the regulation is unconstitutional. If the answer to both questions is yes, the regulation is constitutional.

If the Court finds that the regulation is not aimed specifically at speech, it applies a test of intermediate scrutiny, called the "O'Brien Test," to determine whether the regulation is constitutional. Under the test, a regulation is required to meet four points: (1) The activity regulated must be within the constitutional power of the government; (2) the regulation must advance an important government interest; (3) the government interest

must be unrelated to the suppression of free expression; and (4) the incidental restriction on speech must be no greater than necessary to advance the government interest.

Just as conduct can take on the role of speech, speech can sometimes become like conduct. Words can be so vile or obnoxious that they prompt a physical response. Courts allow such words to be regulated but take care to ensure that governments don't trammel free expression in their efforts to protect other individual rights. Statutes prohibiting offensive or abusive language, for example, have routinely been held to be unconstitutional unless they have been narrowed so they only prohibit fighting words. In addition, the Supreme Court has ruled that intimidation is a category of what it calls "true threats" and may be banned.

Finally, courts have recognized the value of picketing and have allowed individuals to picket on both private and public property. Picketing in areas traditionally held to be a public forum is almost always allowed. Picketing on private property is more problematic, but the Supreme Court has often allowed such picketing.

BIBLIOGRAPPHY

Articles

Belmas, Genelle I. "Pushing Patriotism: Why Flag Encouragement Doesn't Fly," 14 *Communication Law and Policy* 341 (2009).

DeSiato, Nick. "Silencing the Crowd: Regulating Free Speech in Professional Sports Facilities," 20 *Marquette Sports Law Review* 411 (2010).

Hopkins, W. Wat. "Cross Burning Revisited: What the Supreme Court Should Have Done in *Virginia v. Black* and Why it Didn't," 26 *Hastings Communication and Entertainment Law Journal (COMM/ENT)* 269 (2004).

Hopkins, W. Wat. "*Snyder v. Phelps* and the Unfortunate Death of Intentional Infliction of Emotional Distress as a Speech-Based Tort," 3 *Journal of Media Law & Ethics* 1 (2012).

Hopkins, W. Wat. "Trump's Address at the January 6, 2021, 'Save America' Rally: Inciting Insurrection or Protected Speech," in *The 2020 Post-Election "Campaign": A Communication Perspective* (Robert E. Denton Jr., ed., 2021).

Sachs, Benjamin. "The NFL's 'Take a Knee' Ban is Flatly Illegal, *Vox*, May 24, 2018, https://www.vox.com/the-big-idea/2018/5/25/17394422/nfl-knee-kneeling-labor-law-kaepernick-free-speech-protest-owners.

Books

Goldstein, R.J. *Saving "Old Glory": The History of the American Flag Desecration Controversy.* Boulder, Colo.: Westview Press, 1996.

Haiman, Franklyn S. *Speech and Law in a Free Society.* Chicago: University of Chicago Press, 1981.

Katsh, M. Ethan, ed. *Taking Sides — Clashing Views of Controversial Legal Issues.* Guilford, Conn.: Dushkin, 1995.

Russomanno, Joseph. *Defending the First.* Mahwah, N.J.: Lawrence Erlbaum Associates, 2005.

Smolla, Rodney A. *Free Speech in an Open Society.* New York Vintage, 1993.

Cases

Barnes v. Glen Theatre, 501 U.S. 560 (1991).

Board of Airport Commissioners v. Jews for Jesus, 482 U.S. 569 (1987).

Briskman v. Akima, LLC, No. 2018-5335 (Va. Cir. Ct. Apr. 4, 2018), *available at* 2018 WL 1896070.

Brown v. Louisiana, 383 U.S. 131 (1966).

Chaplinsky v. New Hampshire, 315 U.S. 568 (1942).

Clark v. Community for Creative Non-Violence, 468 U.S. 288 (1984).

Cohen v. California, 403 U.S. 15 (1971).

Cox v. Louisiana, 379 US 536 (1965).

Erie v. Pap's A.M., 529 U.S. 277 (2000).

Greer v. Spock, 424 U.S. 828 (1976).

Gregory v. Chicago, 394 U.S. 111 (1969).

Hess v. Indiana, 414 U.S. 105 (1973).

Madsen v. Women's Health Clinic, Inc., 512 U.S. 753 (1994).

McCullen v. Coakley, 134 S. Ct. 1518 (2014).

Minnesota Voters Alliance et al. v. Mahsky et al., 138 S. Ct. 1876 (2018).

Pruneyard Shopping Center v. Robins, 447 U.S. 74 (1974).

R.A.V. v. St. Paul, 305 U.S. 377 (1992).

Renton v. Playtime Theatres, 475 U.S. 41 (1986).

Saint John's Church in the Wilderness v. Scott, 296 F.3d 273 (Colo. App. 2012).

Schenck v Pro-Choice Network of Western New York, 519 U.S 357 (1997).

Shurtleff v. Boston, 142 S. Ct. 1583 (2022).

Smith v. California, 361 U.S. 147 (1959).

Snyder v. Phelps, 562 U.S. 443 (2011).

Spence v. Washington, 418 U.S. 405 (1974).

Stromberg v. California, 283 U.S. 359 (1931).

Terminiello v. Chicago, 337 U.S. 1 (1949).

Texas v. Johnson, 491 U.S. 397 (1989).

Thornhill v. Alabama, 310 U.S. 88 (1940).

Tinker v. Des Moines Independent School District, 393 U.S. 503 (1969).

United States v. Grace, 461 U.S. 171 (1983).

United States v. O'Brien, 391 U.S. 367 (1968).

United States v. Parr, 545 F.3d 491 (7th Cir. 2009).

Village of Skokie v. National Socialist Party of America, 373 N.E.2d 21 (Ill. 1978).

Virginia v. Black, 538 U.S. 343 (2003).

Walker v. Texas Division, Sons of Confederate Veterans, 576 U.S. 200 (2015).

Watchtower Bible and Tract Society of New York v. Village of Stratton, 536 U.S. 150 (2002).

Watts v. United States, 394 U.S 705 (1969).

West Virginia Board of Education v. Barnette, 319 U.S. 624 (1943).

Wood v. Moss, 572 U.S. 744 (2014).

Wooley v. Maynard, 430 U.S. 705 (1977).

4

Prior Restraint

By Steven Helle

☑ **Headnote Questions**

- What is the origin of the doctrine against prior restraint?
- Did the framers of the First Amendment intend for the amendment to ban only prior restraint, or did they intend something more?
- What are the characteristics of prior restraint, historically and currently?
- Why is a doctrine against prior restraint important?
- How do you distinguish between prior restraint and subsequent punishment?
- What are the critical principles that courts consider in applying the doctrine?

"Censorship" is a word casually used in editorials or angry speeches to denounce everything from postal rate increases, to obscenity prosecutions, to thefts of campus newspapers. But the term meant something specific in historical usage, and it is rarely what writers or speakers mean today. Those who denounce contemporary attempts to control speech, however, are taking advantage of the considerable distaste that became associated with the historical form of censorship.

Therein lies the dilemma that runs throughout this chapter. The battles against the historical form of censorship have been won, and an extensive body of law seems to have extinguished the prospect of future censorship as long as the First Amendment retains any vitality. But is it advisable to expand the notion of censorship and the extent of protection available under the First Amendment in order to combat innovative forms of regulation that accomplish much the same thing as historical censorship? Or would stretching the First Amendment to offer the same degree of protection against more types of control ultimately dilute and weaken the protection, just as a balloon that expands becomes thinner — and more susceptible to breaking?

HISTORICAL BACKGROUND

Much of U.S. law has its roots in English law. England, of course, imposed its law on its American colonies. But even after the American Revolution, twelve of the thirteen states expressly adopted England's common law as their own. Lawyers on this side of the Atlantic educated themselves primarily by reading Sir William Blackstone's *Commentaries on the Law of England.*

"In the first century of American independence, the *Commentaries* were not merely an approach to the study of law; for most lawyers they constituted all there was of the law," wrote Daniel J. Boorstin, librarian of Congress emeritus. Because English law influenced not only U.S. law, but the framers of the U.S. Constitution as well, it is important to trace the English experience with censorship to better understand how and why U.S. law on the subject evolved the way it did.

English Censorship

Printing on a press was introduced to England in 1476, and not long afterward the Roman Catholic Church attempted to impose controls. It wanted to suppress what it considered heretical opinions. In 1501, Pope Alexander VI attempted to require printing to be licensed. In 1517, Martin Luther posted his *95 Theses* on the door of the Castle Church in Wittenberg, Germany, questioning the practice of contributing to the church as a means of buying forgiveness for sins. The Church burned the writings of Luther and others who questioned its authority, dismissed them from the Church, prohibited the faithful from reading their works, and issued rebuttals. But the demand — and profit — for publishing the works only grew.

King Henry VIII of England, at the request of the Church, used this religious debate as the impetus for asserting the Crown's control over printing. Henry, in fact, secretly encouraged the reformers while publicly condemning them, even publishing his own response to Luther. By appearing to lead the effort to defeat the heretics, he hoped to win the favor of Rome and the pope's blessing for his divorce from Queen Catherine.

When the clergy was unable to control the heretics' speech, Henry issued his first list of prohibited books in 1529, and several booksellers and others who possessed the banned books were executed. In 1530, he issued a proclamation establishing a licensing system, the first such system outside the Church. He decreed that no person could print any religious book until it was examined and approved by the clergy, and every printer would obey or "answere to the kinges highnes, at his uttermost peryll." Executions, fines and imprisonment followed. When Henry did not get the dispensation he desired from Rome, he switched sides and began executing the Catholic faithful.

As historian Fredrick Siebert noted, Henry was fully aware of the influence of the printing press in easing his break with Rome. He was an early and excellent master of manipulating public opinion by controlling the press, and he certainly had the tools and will to exercise that control to its fullest. "His policy henceforth was not only to eliminate undesirable reading matter but to stimulate the circulation of that which would strengthen his cause," Siebert wrote in his landmark book, *Freedom of the Press in England, 1470-1776.*

Thus, the Proclamation of 1538 extended the king's censorship to all printing, not just religious writings, including "errors and seditious opinions." Sedition, or criticism of government, had no ecclesiastical foundation. The matter is muddled because Henry had made himself the head of the Church of England. Therefore, an attack on the church could be considered an attack on the state, or vice versa. But for the first time, speech that was expressly political was subject to censorship through a licensing system; and Henry's political appointees, not the Church, would decide what violated the regulations and deserved the king's displeasure. As Siebert noted: "The shift in the administration of the licensing regulations from the clergy to state officers was one of Henry's contributions to the regulation of the press. The method was subsequently adopted on the continent, even in Catholic countries."

Henry also instituted the practice of requiring printers to post bonds, which would be forfeited if their publications offended him. He offered printers "privileges" — or copyrights — in certain works, which protected them from piracy. And the Tudor sovereigns who followed him engaged in a brilliant maneuver by recognizing a Stationer's Company, or organization of officially sanctioned printers. Just as broadcasters in this country did in the 1920s, these early printers actually sought government regulation. In the same way that the broadcasters favored by the U.S. government gained monopolies on the use of radio frequencies, the favored English printers obtained monopolies on the printing of certain works, such as the *Bible*, which were very profitable.

But the monopolies served the interests of the government as well, because the economic interests of the printers ensured that they would do nothing to alienate the government and risk losing their monopolies. Furthermore, the government gained an ally in controlling unlicensed printing. The members of the Stationer's Company were given broad powers of search and seizure to protect their monopolies from renegade printers. Their zealousness in exercising these powers led directly to the enactment of the Fourth Amendment to the U.S. Constitution, prohibiting unreasonable searches and seizures and requiring warrants based on probable cause.

Henry's licensing system endured until the close of the seventeenth century; and it was more or less successful, depending on how aggressively it was enforced or evaded at any given time. It took a brave printer to risk forfeiture of property, fines, imprisonment, torture, amputation and execution for flouting the system. The Stationer's Company sniffed out the trail of a press in 1589 that had been secretly moved all over England to avoid capture. John Hodgkins was finally arrested and charged with printing unlicensed Puritan tracts critical of the Church of England. He refused to confess, was tortured, jailed for a year and then put on the rack. There is no record of his fate after that.

Ingenious printers and authors attempted to circumvent the regulations — forging censors' signatures, changing manuscripts after they had been approved or writing ostensibly fictional dramas whose characters everybody understood to represent real people. But the stakes, depending on the political temper of the times and one's choice of patrons, could be high.

Parliament took control of the licensing system from the crown in 1643, but the structure of censorship remained essentially what it had been in 1538. Publication came to be subject to other forms of governmental regulation, primarily prosecutions for seditious libel and taxation, and the penalties associated with those forms of regulation could be just as severe. The licensing system was distinctive not only because it was first; but, because it applied to every publication, it gave the government complete discretion regarding the content of each publication, and it occurred in advance of publication. This latter feature indicates why this censorship was called "prior restraint."

Understandably, members of the Stationer's Company did not object to licensing (unless, as sometimes happened, some members obtained licenses that others did not). Objections came from those without licenses — and the philosophy and value of freedom of the press began to take shape. Two Puritans who wrote an unlicensed religious pamphlet in 1572 argued that they had presented the tract to Parliament and, in doing so, they should have the privilege of "writing and speaking freely." This, according to Siebert, was the first time that the ancient right of Englishmen to petition Parliament was translated into an argument for a free press. The pair, however, was sentenced to a year in prison.

Milton and Areopagitica

In 1644, John Milton presented in *Areopagitica*, which was itself unlicensed, what law professor Vincent Blasi has labeled the classic attack on prior restraint. Ironically, the impetus for this great treatise arose from Milton's having been cited for an earlier unlicensed tract on divorce, which was no easier for him to obtain than it had been for King Henry VIII. Milton framed his argument broadly:

> And though all the windes of doctrin were let loose to play upon the earth, so Truth be in the field, we do injuriously by licencing and prohibiting to misdoubt her strenth. Let her and Falshood grapple; who ever knew Truth put to the wors, in a free and open encounter.... [I]t is not possible for man to sever the wheat from the tares, the good fish from the other frie; that must be the Angels Ministery at the end of all mortall things. Yet if all cannot be of one mind, as who looks they should be? This doubtles is more wholsome, more prudent, and more Christian that many be tolerated, rather than all compell'd.

Although it is an eloquent tribute to diverse expression without government suppression or endorsement of any one opinion, there is the view that Milton really was more interested in his divorce than in freedom of expression because he became a government censor just seven years after *Areopagitica*. In his defense, however, Professor Jeffery Smith noted that Milton's role as censor primarily involved overseeing publication of the government's own newsletter — and, as censor, he had to recall his arguments from *Areopagitica* when he was questioned for approving a catechism that Parliament afterward condemned. Smith noted that, although Milton's arguments showed up in a few other tracts in his time, he probably had more impact in later centuries as philosophers, statesmen and jurists crafted libertarian theory.

An abridged version of *Areopagitica* was published in 1693, but when the Licensing Act came up for renewal in 1694, the treatise apparently had no influence on the House of Commons' decision to let the act lapse. A list of eighteen reasons for not renewing the act was presented in the House of Commons. The reasons, thought to be written by John Locke, had to do with the vagueness of the licensing standards, the impediments to free trade, the ineffectiveness of the system, and other objections unrelated to the philosophy of freedom of the press.

Under the two-party political system that had evolved, censors risked offending somebody important regardless of whether they licensed a publication. Important people did not want to undertake the task of censoring, and they did not trust unimportant people to do it. As Thomas Macaulay wrote in his *History of England* nearly two centuries later, "On the great question of principle, on the question whether the liberty of unlicensed printing be, on the whole, a blessing or a curse to society, not a

word is said."[1] After more than a century and a half, licensing was dead in England.

The American Experience

Licensing continued in the American colonies until the 1720s. In 1723, the Massachusetts General Court (the colony's legislative body), stung by constant criticism from James Franklin, publisher of the *New England Courant,* ordered him never to publish the *Courant* or any other publication, "Except it be first Supervised, by the Secretary of this Province." Franklin published a new, unlicensed edition but identified his brother Benjamin as publisher. The General Court had not prohibited his soon-to-be-famous brother from publishing without a license.

James was eventually arrested, and the General Court sought an indictment from the grand jury, which historian Leonard Levy described as a mistake. The grand jury refused to indict, "probably motivated by a detestation of the licensing system which had ended a generation earlier in England.... Thus, Franklin went luckily free, and prior restraint of the press was at an end in Massachusetts," Levy wrote.

Blackstone accurately summarized the law on both sides of the Atlantic when, in the late 1760s, he wrote in his *Commentaries* perhaps the most famous lines regarding the prior restraint doctrine:

> The *liberty of the press* is indeed essential to the nature of a free state; but this consists in laying no *previous* restraints upon publications, and not in freedom from censure for criminal matter when published. Every freeman has an undoubted right to lay what sentiments he pleases before the public: to forbid this is to destroy the freedom of the press: but if he publishes what is improper, mischievous, or illegal, he must take the consequences of his own temerity.

Freedom from prior restraint seemed great when measured against the lack of any freedom at all just a few generations before. If subsequent punishment remained an option, that may only seem to be meager progress when viewed from the vantage point of today. But there were voices, even as Blackstone wrote, who argued that freedom *did* mean more, that subsequent punishments such as seditious libel prosecutions were also inconsistent with the notion of freedom of the press.

---

[1] Macaulay observed that the event produced no excitement and was little noted, probably because Parliament was preoccupied with the funeral for Queen Mary. But the vote by the House of Commons not to renew the Licensing Act did "more for liberty and for civilisation than the Great Charter or the Bill of Rights." The House of Lords did not object, probably because it assumed a different bill for regulating the press would be introduced — and, indeed, one was, but it did not clear committee before the session ended. Macaulay noted that "petty grievances did what Milton's *Areopagitica* failed to do."

The Framers' Intent

What did the framers intend in 1791 — a little more than two decades after Blackstone's pronouncement — with the drafting of the First Amendment? Did they intend just to prohibit prior restraint, or did they mean to ban subsequent punishment as well? Professors Smith and Levy lead the opposing camps on this question. The arguments of Levy and the narrow constructionists — those who think the framers were only thinking of banning prior restraint — can be summarized this way:

• Blackstone's definition of the law was the notion of free speech and press commonly accepted at the time; so it must be what the framers were contemplating. If they were departing from the common understanding or common law of the time, they presumably would have said something.

• If the framers thought they were banning subsequent punishment such as seditious libel prosecutions, then how could many of those same members of Congress, just seven years later, enact the Alien and Sedition Acts of 1798 with the express intent of punishing people who criticized government?

• Prosecutions for seditious libel may have ended with the John Peter Zenger trial in 1735, but state legislatures brought citizens up on contempt charges for criticizing government at least twenty times after that date and before passage of the First Amendment, thus indicating endorsement of subsequent punishment as an alternative to prior restraint.

The broad constructionists, who think the First Amendment went beyond banning prior restraint, counter:

• Blackstone may have summarized the English common law that had been practiced up to his time, but he was not summarizing U.S. law, and, indeed, why have a First Amendment at all if it was only intended to commemorate the common law supposedly already in place?

• The American experience with free press far exceeded the English common law. Not only were there no prosecutions for seditious libel after 1735 and no legislative contempt charges after independence in 1776, but politicians, printers and others exercised considerable freedom and espoused a distinctly libertarian theory of a free press in the century before the First Amendment. In short, how could there be so much freedom in practice if the law was so repressive?

• James Madison, an author of the First Amendment, passionately proclaimed that the Sedition Act violated the First Amendment and criticized the Federalist party members of Congress for returning America to "ancient ignorance and barbarism." The act expired by its own terms three years later, which was also the time that Republican Thomas Jefferson became president and pardoned the twenty-five or so Republican printers and journalists convicted under the act. Thus, it can be argued that Congress, as it has demonstrated many times since, was not invoking constitutional principles in enacting the Sedition Act, but petty party politics.

• Why was a Sedition Act necessary if the common law already contemplated prosecution for seditious libel?

• Finally, the theme of the entire Constitution, not just the Bill of Rights, concerns limiting the power of government — in the words of Madison, "fortify[ing] the rights of the people against the encroachments of the government." A broad conception of freedom of speech and press is fundamental to limiting government and placing power in the people, and a narrow conception of the First Amendment would be inconsistent with the rest of the document. A freedom to criticize government without fear of subsequent prosecution is implicit in self-governing; so the First Amendment must have encompassed more than mere freedom from prior restraint.

It is impossible to provide a definitive answer to the question of whether the framers intended the First Amendment to go beyond freedom from prior restraint. Not only was there little debate on the question at the time, but the very issue of "framers' intent" is chimerical because there is no single way to gauge that intent. Whose intent? Do you look to Madison because he wrote the First Amendment, or to a poll of the legislators who voted on the measure, or to the sentiment in the states that ratified it? At what moment is the intent assessed? When proposed, when voted on, or when the framers first spoke on the meaning, which may be many years later? Does it matter if their understanding may be a bit different, more refined, or even contrary a few years later?

It may even be that the legislators actually had no "intent" in mind at the time of passage. They may have deliberately left the First Amendment — and the rest of the Bill of Rights — vague to reduce controversy and facilitate passage. Who can be opposed to freedom of speech and press at that level of abstraction? The legislators may even have been forward-thinking enough to want to leave the interpretation to later generations, which would face problems the framers could not anticipate.

The answer is relevant because interpretation of the Constitution often begins with an inquiry into the framers' intent, and several Supreme Court justices seemingly would end the inquiry there. But most jurists and scholars believe that the framers' intent is only one factor and that the Constitution is an evolving document that must take into account changing circumstances. So, even if we could determine what the framers intended regarding the First Amendment, and even if they only meant it to prohibit prior restraint, that would not necessarily bind current interpretation. Of course, once you break free from the historical intent, current interpretation could yield less as well as more freedom than the framers had in mind.

The strength of the doctrine against prior restraint, dating as it does to well before the First Amendment, is that it carries a certain cachet, a reminder of the baseline of freedom. The historical record of press suppression and manipulation by governments eager to promote their self-interest serves as evidence of what can happen in the absence of a prior restraint doctrine. The doctrine was created to serve two needs: individual freedom and limited government. At a minimum, the First Amendment was created to serve the same needs, with the same doctrine.

Historical Prior Restraint Defined

A number of other conclusions can be drawn regarding the historical record. The nature of prior restraint that Blackstone, Milton and Henry VIII had in mind involved a licensing system. Prior restraint, historically understood, involved (1) submitting *all* proposed publications (2) to government censors (3) who exercised considerable discretion regarding the content to be approved for publication, and it was (4) imposed in advance of publication.

Prior restraint did not refer to isolated efforts by government officials to suppress speech – a judge's order not to print a libelous tract, for example. Historically, the all-inclusiveness of the regulatory system, the fact that *every* proposed publication must be reviewed and approved, defined prior restraint. Therefore, even the works ultimately approved would still have been subject to prior restraint. "Prior review" is a phrase synonymous with "prior restraint."

Prior restraint meant suppression only by the government, although employers, parents and others obviously suppress speech regularly. Indeed, the historical system of prior restraint did not apply to speech at all, because licensing was a reaction to the introduction of the printing press, although speech in the form of parades or theatrical productions, for example, could conceivably be subjected to licensing or a permit system. But any interference with publication, even if it entirely precluded publication, did not constitute prior restraint if undertaken by individuals or institutions not associated with government.

If the standards for what could be published could ever be delineated clearly enough, then a censor's discretion would have been unnecessary, because the violations could be handled easily through subsequent punishment of individual violators. The considerable discretion exercised by censors is a critical objection to a system of prior restraint.

Of course, the aspects of prior restraint most commonly associated with it had to do with its narrow focus on controlling the actual publication, in advance of publication. Other government restrictions that might have the effect of inhibiting or entirely foreclosing publication would still not be included within the scope of prior restraint, even if they occurred in advance of publication. Restrictions on news gathering, for example, or punishment for not revealing a journalist's confidential source would not qualify as prior restraint because they were not directed specifically at stopping publication.

Consider the 1664 case of printer John Twyn. He was caught with proofs for a book claiming the government was accountable to the people and the people were entitled to revolt. Setting the standard for current journalists, Twyn refused to name the author. For his temerity he was hanged, drawn and quartered — a penalty that certainly precluded his publication. Technically, however, it was not prior restraint because the government did not specifically target publication.

Distinguishing Prior Restraint and Subsequent Punishment Currently

A more recent U.S. Supreme Court case is less brutal in its outcome but just as illustrative in its narrow conception of what constitutes prior restraint. In *Alexander v. United States,* the government had prosecuted the owner of more than a dozen stores and theaters dealing in sexually explicit magazines and videotapes. Four magazines and three videotapes in the inventory were found to be obscene. Under a statute that allows the state to seize any property connected to a pattern of criminal behavior, the court ordered Ferris Alexander to forfeit his adult entertainment businesses and their inventories. The government then burned all of the magazines and videotapes.

Alexander maintained that the seizure and destruction of all his magazines and videotapes – which had *not* been found to be obscene and were therefore protected speech – constituted prior restraint. How could a ban on speech be more total than by destroying the speech, he argued? But the Court noted that the term "prior restraint" applied only to orders that forbid certain communications in advance of the communications; this, on the other hand, was only punishment for his obscenity convictions. Prior restraints, by their nature, stop the speech completely and perpetually, Chief Justice William Rehnquist wrote for the Court. Alexander could theoretically open another adult entertainment store the next day, restock with new inventory, and sell videotapes and magazines, all without obtaining prior approval from any court, Rehnquist wrote. The statute that allowed the government to seize property connected with criminal activity did not differentiate between expressive and non-expressive property, he noted, and to do so would encourage criminals to invest their ill-gotten gains in expressive property to protect them from forfeiture. He added:

> By lumping the forfeiture imposed in this case after a full criminal trial with an injunction enjoining future speech, petitioner stretches the term "prior restraint" well beyond the limits established by our cases. To accept [Alexander's] argument would virtually obliterate the distinction, solidly grounded in our cases, between prior restraints and subsequent punishments.

Rehnquist wrote, "[I]t is important for us to delineate with some precision the defining characteristics of prior restraint," but then, oddly, he never did. Several times he noted that prior restraints apply to future speech and subsequent punishments apply to past conduct. But that does not really help, because presumably the punishment for violating a prior restraint would be subsequent to the speech.

In a footnote, Rehnquist traced the history of prior restraint, noting that the doctrine had been expanded from its historical understanding of a licensing system, which would be administered by the executive branch, to include injunctions issued by the judicial branch. But the opinion repeatedly referred to this case as involving statutory forfeiture. In other words, statutes passed by the legislative branch, unless they explicitly set up a licensing scheme or other recognized prior restraint, cannot be prior restraints. A statute that establishes penalties for speech can only be considered subsequent punishment. Otherwise, to characterize any regulation of speech by any of the three branches of government as prior restraint would constitute "the essentially limitless expansion of the term," Rehnquist wrote.

In a dissent that was longer than the majority opinion, Justice Anthony Kennedy vigorously disagreed with Rehnquist's narrow interpretation of prior restraint. His frustration was still evident years later as he wrote the majority opinion in *Citizens United v. Federal Election Commission.*

In *Citizens United,* the Court struck down a federal statute that prohibited corporations and unions from advocating the election or defeat of a candidate shortly before an election. Such advocacy was termed an "electioneering communication."

But because corporations and unions were clever in crafting ads that bordered on express advocacy regarding candidates, the task fell to the FEC to interpret what constituted an "electioneering communication." Justice Kennedy noted that the FEC had adopted 568 pages of regulations, 1,278 pages of explanations for those regulations, and 1,771 advisory opinions. In each case, the FEC applied a two-part, eleven-factor balancing test.

"This regulatory scheme may not be a prior restraint on speech in the strict sense of that term," Kennedy wrote. Speakers technically were not forced to allow the FEC to review their speech beforehand. But as a practical matter, given the complexity of the regulations, speakers who wanted to avoid sanctions "must ask a governmental agency for prior permission to speak." Because the Court was dealing with a statutory restriction that did not explicitly set up a licensing system, Kennedy was constrained by *Alexander* from terming it a prior restraint. But that did not stop him from insisting that it functioned as "the equivalent of prior restraint."

RATIONALES FOR PRIOR RESTRAINT

The doctrine against prior restraint can be considered merely a stepping-stone in the evolution of free speech and press. Having served its purpose, it arguably can be relegated to the dustbin of history. But distinguishing prior restraint from subsequent punishment still makes sense. The extent to which the First Amendment prohibits subsequent punishment is a different question than whether prior restraint should be prohibited. The doctrine against prior restraint accords so wholly with the premises of limited government that disregarding it can be considered antithetical to the very form of government the Constitution prescribes.

Why Distinguish Subsequent Punishment?

Distinguishing prior restraint from subsequent punishment is an important matter. The Supreme Court has said the First Amendment offers protection from subsequent punishment, but the Court has also maintained that prior restraint is the most odious and least tolerable infringement of free speech. It would help to have some justification for the differential treatment beyond the venerable age of the prior restraint doctrine. After all, the point of subsequent punishment is to restrain speech in advance, too. Legislatures enact laws not to fill some prison quota, but to deter conduct beforehand, and laws punishing speech are no different. So how does the fact that the governmental force is applied prior to publication make it worse?

Professor Thomas Emerson attempted to answer that question in an important essay. First, he noted the *breadth* of prior restraint. Because all publications are subject to prior restraint, necessarily more communication is affected than when individual publications are targeted for subsequent punishment.

Second, Emerson emphasized the temporal aspect implicit in the two forms of regulation. With prior restraint, *timing and delay* are in the government's hands. With subsequent punishment, the publication at least reaches the marketplace of ideas, and the timing is at the publisher's discretion. But the requirement of prior review imposes an obvious hitch in the editorial process, and sometimes mere delay can undermine the impact of a story, a factor of which the government is quite aware.

Third, a system of prior restraint has a *propensity toward an adverse decision*. To obtain a judgment after publication, no matter how stacked the trial may be, is still more bother than a system of censorship, which entails, as Emerson wrote, "a simple stroke of the pen." The publisher has practical advantages after publication that are missing beforehand, when the advantages favor government. Thus, Emerson concluded, a system of prior restraint by its very nature makes it easier and more likely that the result will be adverse to the expression.

Similarly, matters of *procedure* favor the government in prior restraint. Prior restraint is an administrative procedure rather than a criminal procedure. In the latter, there are presumptions of innocence, burdens of proof, stricter rules of evidence — all of the trappings that are intended to make courts more deliberative and fairer forums than administrative agencies. Juries are available in criminal proceedings, but in an administrative proceeding the case is heard only by a minor bureaucrat.

Fifth, subsequent punishment provides an opportunity for *public appraisal and criticism.* Administrative proceedings can avoid the glare of publicity, but court hearings have a rich history of openness, which can be said to be more consistent with democracy and the goal of informing public opinion. Furthermore, in a case of subsequent punishment, the speech has already been disseminated and the public can judge for itself the extent of any alleged danger.

Sixth, the *dynamics of prior restraint* are such that absurd and unintelligent administration is foreordained. Emerson noted that the personality of a person willing to be a censor tends toward overzealousness. Not only that, but quite bluntly, "The function of the censor is to censor," Emerson wrote. The job title does not include promotion of expression: When in doubt, excise.

The risk is far greater if the censor approves something that later meets with disapproval than if the censor censors. "The long history of prior restraint reveals over and over again that the personal and institutional forces inherent in the system nearly always end in a stupid, unnecessary, and extreme suppression," Emerson wrote.

Seventh, a system of prior restraint favors *certainty over risk.* Scholars and publishers sometimes note that the advantage of a licensing system is that it gives a seal of approval if a work passes review, and the work is presumably immune from further sanction. But in a system of subsequent punishment, a publisher could be punished even if the publisher intended to remain within the law; the publisher may have made an error in interpretation and face punishment for the error. As Justice Kennedy noted in *Citizens United,* the system of regulation was so complicated that obtaining FEC approval beforehand was the only way to guarantee that the speaker would not be punished afterward, which Kennedy thought was tantamount to prior restraint.

Prior restraint reduces risk, Emerson agreed, but he added that favoring such a system implies a "philosophy of willingness to conform to official opinion and a ... timidity in asserting rights that bodes ill for a spirited and healthy expression of unorthodox and unaccepted opinion."

Finally, prior restraint systems have greater *effectiveness* going for them. When it comes to enforcement, the question is only whether the publication received prior approval. Everybody understands the rules of prior restraint. Indeed, the virtue of the system is its simplicity, at least from government's perspective. Cases are open and shut. Publishers either obey or they don't, and most do. Thus, prior restraint can be distinguished from subsequent punishment, not only definitionally, but rationally.

"These ... considerations which underlie the doctrine of prior restraint ... are the reasons why the doctrine is not simply an arbitrary historical accident, but a rational principle of fundamental weight in the application of the First Amendment," Emerson concluded.

Premises of Prior Restraint

Apart from the definition, differentiation or appropriate treatment of subsequent punishment, prior restraint would be contrary to the First Amendment simply because it is inconsistent with a constitutional system of limited government. Professor Vincent Blasi, with a nod to Milton's *Areopagitica,* identified three premises underlying any system that endorses prior restraint, all of which are inconsistent with limited government and the libertarian theory inherent in the First Amendment:

1. Prior restraint implies trust in the state rather than in the individual and public.
2. Speech is too risky in a democracy.
3. Individuals should have no autonomy from the state.

Blasi believed censorship to be an indignity to both writers and readers because the inherent paternalism of the state associated with censorship implies a general distrust of speakers and audiences. The state is a "suspicious, omnipresent tutor" if it must oversee and approve everything that is disseminated. "No system of political authority premised on the consent of the governed can admit the state to that role, whatever the behavioral consequences," Blasi wrote.

Preoccupation with government power is a trademark of the prior restraint doctrine and libertarian theory generally. Some contemporary free speech theorists are less skeptical of government and more concerned with what they see as the exercise of power by speakers, particularly the media and other corporations engaging in expression. They also are suspicious of the rational capacities of the public and propose a need for a "particularly active and absolute form of intervention by the state" that Blasi noted would be consistent with prior restraint.

Blasi responded that we may distrust the rationality of citizens, but the lesson of the First Amendment is that we distrust the state more. "To trust the censor more than the audience is to alter the relationship between the state and citizen that is central to the philosophy of limited government," Blasi wrote.

The second "troublesome premise" implicit in prior restraint is that speech is no different than other hazardous activities that are licensed or enjoinable, such as driving a vehicle or the practice of medicine. But licensing, Blasi explained, is a method of enforcing social norms. Free speech, by its nature, does not observe such norms; social conformity distorts public discourse. Speech — like democracy — is risky, but that is its virtue. "Only when the public views controversial speakers as normal people, with a legitimate role to play in the social system, can the fragile state-individual balance be maintained," Blasi noted.

The third and perhaps most obvious premise of prior restraint is its subordination of individual autonomy. Blasi contended that prior restraints such as

[L]icensing systems and injunctions coerce or induce speakers to relinquish full control over the details and timing of their communications. These regulatory systems must be premised, therefore, on the notion that either such control is not an essential attribute of the autonomy of speakers, or that such autonomy need not be respected. Either premise is objectionable.

Thus, prior restraints cannot be consistent with the implementation of limited government. Those cases in which the Court has condemned the regulation as a prior restraint aptly illustrate the libertarian principles providing the intellectual foundation for the doctrine against prior restraint: distrust of government, acceptance of the risk inherent in speech and individual autonomy from government.

CASE LAW AND PREMISES

A review of the major cases embracing the prior restraint doctrine yields a treasure trove of commentary and rulings illustrating Blasi's premises.

Distrust of Government

In 1931, the Supreme Court in *Near v. Minnesota* for the first time explicitly adopted the doctrine against prior restraint as constitutional law. In its decision, it referred time and again to the danger of government regulation as a means of deterring criticism of government. The Court expressed concern about governmental abuse of its authority, with regard to both official misconduct and the exercise of the discretion necessary to implement the statute, which was intended to quell seditious libel. In striking the statute, the Court served notice that the prior restraint doctrine had broken free from its historical moorings.

The case involved a ban on speech in advance of publication, based on content; but the ban was in the form of a nuisance statute enforced by judicial injunction. Jay M. Near had published in his *Saturday Press* malicious and scandalous libels adjudged to be nuisances. As partial punishment, he was ordered not to publish any more under threat of contempt of court.

Some Supreme Court justices argued that the law was not a licensing system within the historical meaning of prior restraint but a remedy for past transgressions. The majority disagreed, however, finding that the scheme "must be tested by its operation and effect." Thus understood, the Minnesota law was the "essence of censorship." Writing for the Court, Chief Justice Charles Hughes interpreted the statute as directed, not just at libels of private citizens, but "at the continued publication by newspapers and periodicals of charges against public officers of corruption, malfeasance in office, or serious neglect of duty."

This was a somewhat remarkable conclusion, given that the Court cited no specific language in the statute or in Minnesota

Supreme Court opinions to support its conclusion that the statute concerned primarily libels of public officers. The Minneapolis mayor, a chief of police and a county attorney had been libeled by the defendant, but so had grand jurors, two newspapers and the "Jewish race." The Court, however, emphasized the "operation and effect" of the law when it noted that the newspaper had been targeted because its principal content was criticism of government. Seventeen times in the opinion, the Court expressed concern for protecting expression about official misconduct. Skepticism of government's capacity to oversee publications critical of government was hardly ameliorated by allowing a judge to determine if future issues of the *Saturday Press* were consistent with the "public welfare," the Court noted. If the statute operated to suppress expression critical of official misconduct, the doctrine against prior restraint was designed to thwart its operation as well as its effect.

The majority's expansion of the notion of prior restraint to include judicial injunctions, as well as administrative licensing systems, initiated an academic debate that continues to this day. It is significant, however, that in the Court's first pronouncement on prior restraint, it signaled its intention not to be bound by classical conceptions. Not coincidentally, it is also significant that this first opinion stands as tribute to the checking function, which the framers held dear and which presupposes governmental abuse of its authority.

The Court continued its concern for governmental exercise of discretion in matters relating to speech in a line of prior restraint cases, many of which were closer in kind to the licensing system contemplated by Blackstone. But a prior restraint case five years after *Near* illustrated that the Court considered taxation of the press as well as systems to suppress seditious libel as within the scope of prior restraint. The characteristic that was constant was a concern for government's abuse of its authority.

Grosjean v. American Press Co., Inc. involved a Louisiana tax on selected newspapers that on its face did not even seem to qualify as a subsequent punishment.[2] The tax was imposed, not on content, but on the basis of circulation, with all newspapers that circulated more than 20,000 copies weekly to pay a tax of 2 percent on gross receipts. The tax was imposed by statute, and the penalty for failure to pay the tax was a possible fine of up to $500 as well as imprisonment not exceeding six months.

The Court traced the history of "taxes on knowledge" to the English experience, taking judicial notice of the framers' familiarity with that legacy. Writing for the unanimous Court, Justice George Sutherland observed that stamp taxes and taxes on advertising historically had not been intended to gain revenue, but to control the flow of information regarding government. They

---

[2] Professor Emerson was particularly critical of the Court's application of the prior restraint doctrine in the tax cases. The doctrine could only be relevant to tax cases, he wrote, if it applied to any regulation that inhibited First Amendment freedom. "When employed in this way the concept becomes so broad as to be worthless as a legal rule," Emerson wrote.

shared that characteristic with prior restraint, but of course, the same might have been said of seditious libel laws, which constituted subsequent punishments and which operated concurrently with the English system of taxes on the press. Justice Sutherland concluded his survey of English repression of the press with a quote from eighteenth century scholar and attorney Thomas Erskine, who wrote, "The liberty of opinion keeps governments themselves in due subjection to their duties." The quote, although it is not clear from Sutherland's opinion, dates from the year after the First Amendment was enacted — and was made in defense of freedom from seditious libel.

The *Grosjean* case articulates quite nicely the checking function of the press and the threat that governmental abuse of its authority poses to that essential value of freedom of the press. Using the British government as its example, the Court assailed the "persistent effort" to curtail any criticism, true or false. The "predominant purpose" of the First Amendment was "to preserve an untrammeled press as a vital source of public information." The Court described public opinion as "the most potent of all restraints upon misgovernment." The key to informed public opinion is a free press performing the vital function of the Fourth Estate. "To allow it to be fettered is to fetter ourselves," the Court noted.

From this emphasis on government's sensitivity to criticism and the importance of insulation for critics, the Court concluded that the First Amendment was meant to preclude "any form of previous restraint upon printed publications, or their circulation, including that which had theretofore been effected by these two well-known and odious methods," referring to a stamp tax and a tax on advertising.

A virtue of the prior restraint doctrine as it has come to be construed is that it puts a heavy burden, indeed an insurmountable burden if case outcomes are any indication, on government. While tests and even balancing have been advocated in the same breath as the doctrine against prior restraint, a great strength of the doctrine is that it brings historical weight to bear in asserting outright skepticism of government. Prior restraints are presumed unconstitutional, and it is up to government to bear the heavy burden of attempting to overcome that presumption. The doctrine has a pedigree that no test of compelling or overriding interests can match. The lessons embodied in the doctrine against prior restraint should not be forgotten, but they can easily be lost through mere balancing.

Acceptance of Risk

Worst-case scenarios are integral to the second premise implicit in a system of prior restraint identified by Blasi: risk aversion. In imposing prior restraint, government is attempting to avert the consequences of speech that has yet to be uttered. This necessarily involves the government — including the courts that are passing on the constitutionality of the prior restraint — in

gazing into crystal balls. Rationalizing the need for prior restraint thus lends itself to posing the worst possible consequence of the speech if it were to occur.

The only antidote to threats of worst-case scenarios is straightforward acknowledgment that speech involves risk and that freedom includes freedom for the potent as well as the impotent. "That at any rate is the theory of our Constitution," Justice Oliver Wendell Holmes wrote. We "wager our salvation," he added, "upon imperfect knowledge." He addressed the penchant for concocting worst-case scenarios head-on when he then observed that we must be "eternally vigilant against attempts to check the expression of opinions that we loathe and believe to be fraught with death." Freedom is not for the faint of heart.

Holmes' caveat against caution was tested in the Pentagon Papers case. There, if documents the government had classified as secret were published in the newspapers, then the alleged resultant danger would be "the death of soldiers, the destruction of alliances, the greatly increased difficulty of negotiation with our enemies, the inability of our diplomats to negotiate," as well as prolonging the Vietnam War and extended delay in freeing U.S. prisoners. Possible dangers just do not get any worse.

One might have wondered at this characterization of the danger, however, given that the Pentagon Papers were historical documents relating to U.S. involvement in the Vietnam War. They not only did not give away any planned troop movements or strategic objectives, but they contained nothing the North Vietnamese did not already know. Indeed, the people most ignorant of their content were the constituents of the government that was attempting to conceal them.

The papers, for example, revealed that the U.S. government had engaged in a manipulative public relations campaign aimed at U.S. citizens and foreign allies with little relation to the actual war effort or negotiations, of which the North Vietnamese were, of course, intimately aware. Justice Hugo Black, voting with the majority to allow the *New York Times* and other newspapers to continue publication of a series based on the documents, identified what might have been the real danger that the government perceived: its own embarrassment.

In the last opinion he wrote before he died, Black zeroed in on the government's use of "national security" as a cover for censorship. The phrase demonstrates the government's felicitous choice of words. Advocating "security" is meant to be comforting, and it put the newspapers that would disclose the papers in the role of exposing us to hazards. But Black cautioned that the phrase was "a broad, vague generality." He seemed to suggest that a government whose capacity for deception in conducting war was revealed in the papers would not hesitate to deceive in promising security to its citizens. Free speech involves risks, Black wrote, but the framers of the First Amendment, who fully appreciated what it took to defend a nation, nevertheless understood that free speech provided the only real security.

This paradox of security through risk is only one of many associated with the First Amendment: a freedom to espouse no freedom, freedom for the speech we hate, a right to be wrong. All, however, share an implicit acknowledgment of the risk of free speech. Such paradoxes perhaps explain why Professor Emerson wrote that the theory of freedom of expression "does not come naturally to the ordinary citizen, but needs to be learned." One does not ordinarily choose the more hazardous course, much less associate risk with security. Prior restraint appeals to that impulse favoring the safer path. But the doctrine against prior restraint teaches not only that the government's worst-case scenarios seem not to come true when information is ultimately published, but that attempts to achieve security through suppression pose the greater risk. The risk is not in speech being published, but in it *not* being published. That, as Holmes said, is the theory of our Constitution.

Regard for Individual Autonomy

The final premise of prior restraint that also conflicts with a constitutional system of limited government is a depreciation of individual autonomy. The Court in *Schneider v. State,* for example, recognized that the police had power to promote the public interest in regulating the public streets. But when municipal ordinances sought to license the dissemination of leaflets on those thoroughfares, the Court found that they infringed not only on individual speech but on a system of government:

> This Court has characterized the freedom of speech and that of the press as fundamental personal rights and liberties. The phrase is not an empty one and was not lightly used. It reflects the belief of the framers of the Constitution that exercise of the rights lies at the foundation of free government by free men. It stresses, as do many opinions of this Court, the importance of preventing the restriction of enjoyment of these liberties.... Mere legislative preferences or beliefs respecting matters of public convenience may well support regulation directed at other personal activities, but be insufficient to justify such as diminishes the exercise of rights so vital to the maintenance of democratic institutions.

If speaking in a public forum imposes burdens on the state, such is the price of maintaining individual autonomy. The Court said the ordinance in *Schneider* was particularly odious because it allowed a police officer to act "as a censor," determining what literature could be distributed and who could distribute it, and required pamphleteers to submit to an inquisition, photographing and fingerprinting. Such censorship struck at the heart of free expression because it placed discretion with the officer rather than the speaker. Moreover, the Court made clear that individual autonomy extended not only to the message but to the site of the speech: "[O]ne is not to have the exercise of his liberty of expression in appropriate places abridged on the plea

that it may be exercised in some other place."

The concept of individual autonomy answers the fundamental question in each prior restraint case: "Who is to decide?" The choice of what, when and where to speak is either left to the discretion of the speaker or overruled by the state. Autonomous speech is the condition precedent to the autonomous citizenship contemplated in the democratic model.

First Amendment doctrine, with its focus on individual autonomy, may seem quaint in the eyes of those who advocate that individuals must yield to the public interest, whether the issue involves mandatory motorcycle helmets, zoning or bans on racist speech. But the First Amendment, as exemplified by the prior restraint doctrine in particular, is one of the last areas of constitutional law to uphold the democratic tradition as it was historically understood. If autonomy in speech is rejected, Robert Post observed, the implications go to the core of our belief in self-government, and "beguiling visions of progressive reform" should not obscure the fact that democratic legitimacy, and not just autonomous speech, is at issue.

RECENT CASES

The doctrine against prior restraint shows amazing vitality despite having roots stretching back more than three centuries. Perhaps even more amazing is that cases involving prior restraint persist and questions still emerge. Drawing on those three centuries of history seems to facilitate answering the questions, however.

Origin of a Test

The case in which the Supreme Court most recently employed the prior restraint doctrine shows evidence of distrusting government, embracing risk and prizing individual autonomy; and it contains the Court's most thorough analysis, which ironically was borrowed from some of its earliest First Amendment cases. Those early cases did not even involve prior restraint, and the analysis was taken not from the majority opinions, but from a dissent and a concurring opinion.

The first early case, *Abrams v. United States,* involved a prosecution for publishing two leaflets in 1918 containing objections to U.S. military intervention against the Bolsheviks, who would ultimately form the Soviet Union. In an earlier opinion he had written for the Court, Justice Holmes had framed the issue as "whether the words used are used in such circumstances and are of such a nature as to create a clear and present danger that they will bring about the substantive evils that Congress has a right to prevent." He had endorsed the conviction of speakers in that case, but Harvard Law Professor Zechariah Chafee Jr. prevailed upon Holmes to impart more meaning to the clear and present danger test, which Holmes did in *Abrams.*

When he circulated his dissent to the majority opinion in *Ab-*

rams and defended it at the justices' Saturday conference, Chief Justice Edward White, his long-standing friend and daily companion on the long walk home, asked him not to issue it. When he persisted, three justices took the highly unusual step of calling on him at his home, where his wife joined them in attempting to persuade him not to publish the dissent. Holmes did not relent, and the effect was electric. "A great noise of vilification and praise went up all over the country," wrote biographer Sheldon M. Novick.

In his famous dissent, which has eclipsed the majority opinion and become the law of the land, Holmes stiffened the meaning of a "present danger." "[N]obody can suppose," he wrote, "that the surreptitious publishing of a silly leaflet by an unknown man, without more, would present any immediate danger." Opinions should be allowed "unless they so imminently threaten immediate interference with the lawful and pressing purposes of the law that an immediate check is required to save the country," he wrote. Holmes's stress on the immediacy of the danger before speech should be unprotected presents a nearly impossible hurdle to regulation, but, curiously, it also seems to protect most speech that is unimportant or ineffective. Still, it was a major milestone in the evolution of the First Amendment.

Justices Holmes and Louis Brandeis had a forty-year friendship before Brandeis was appointed to the Court, and they collaborated on some of the great opinions of their era. Brandeis joined in Holmes's dissent in *Abrams*, and Holmes joined Brandeis's concurrence in *Whitney v. California,* a case in which a woman was convicted of criminal syndicalism for joining the Communist Labor Party. Brandeis's opinion concurring in the majority decision seemed to favor her acquittal, but because she did not raise at trial the argument that Brandeis presented, she could not do so on appeal, Brandeis wrote.

This judicial restraint probably left Anita Whitney unimpressed, but Brandeis simply did not have the votes on the Court to overturn her conviction. So whether he labeled his lesson on First Amendment law a concurrence or a dissent seems less important than the fact that it fleshed out the clear and present danger test in a way that lower courts could apply it.

Justice Brandeis pointed out that the Court had not yet determined "when a danger shall be deemed clear; how remote the danger may be and yet be deemed present; and what degree of evil shall be deemed sufficiently substantial to justify resort to abridgement of free speech." First, he turned the question around and suggested that the real danger lay in repression of speech and "that the path of safety lies in the opportunity to discuss freely supposed grievances and proposed remedies."

Justice Brandeis believed that mere fear of serious injury did not justify suppression of speech. "Those who won our independence were not cowards.... They did not exalt order at the cost of liberty," he wrote. In the same libertarian vein, Brandeis indicated that the limited role of the state was to make individuals free to develop their faculties and to avoid "silence coerced by

law — the argument of force in its worst form." He continued:

> To justify suppression of free speech there must be reasonable ground to fear that serious evil will result *if free speech is practiced*. There must be reasonable ground to believe that the danger apprehended is *imminent*. There must be reasonable ground to believe that the evil to be prevented is a *serious* one.

To summarize, the speech must cause the alleged danger, the danger must be immediate, and it must be grave.

Nebraska Press Association

Nearly a half century later, the Court expanded on these themes in its most recent major press prior restraint case, *Nebraska Press Association v. Stuart*. Erwin Simants had been arrested for the murder of six people in a small Nebraska town. Three days later, Judge Hugh Stuart issued an order prohibiting the public dissemination of any testimony or evidence. The Nebraska Press Association appealed the prior restraint.

The Supreme Court granted *certiorari* and used the case to review its decisions involving the "heavy presumption" against the constitutional validity of prior restraint, including *Near v. Minnesota* and the Pentagon Papers case. That heavy presumption translated into a nearly impossible burden on government to justify the exercise of such authority and implicit trust in the state rather than speakers. "The thread running through all these cases is that prior restraints on speech and publication are the most serious and the least tolerable infringement on First Amendment rights," wrote Chief Justice Warren Burger for a unanimous Court.

He distinguished prior restraint from subsequent punishment, noting that penalties for violating a criminal statute or libel judgments do not become effective until after trial and all appeals are ended. "A prior restraint, by contrast and by definition, has an immediate and irreversible sanction," Burger wrote. "If it can be said that a threat of criminal or civil sanctions after publication 'chills' speech, prior restraint 'freezes' it at least for the time."

Chief Justice Burger noted the possible risk that pre-trial publicity posed for a defendant's Sixth Amendment right to a fair trial by unbiased jurors. But he also quoted from an earlier case praising the press as the "handmaiden" of justice, because it "guards against the miscarriage of justice." As Justice Brandeis might have put it, the risk of free speech is real, but the risk of enforced silence is greater. In particular, an effective check on governmental abuse would be missing.

In the Pentagon Papers case, Chief Justice Burger was one of three dissenters voting in favor of prior restraint. He had seemed particularly bothered by the fact that the *New York Times* had three to four months to review and edit the classified documents, but the Court had very few days to digest the case. Why, he asked, after months of deferral, must the right to publish be vindicated so precipitously? He answered his own question five years later in *Nebraska Press Association*, noting it was a matter of the speaker's autonomy:

> Of course, the order at issue ... does not prohibit but only postpones publication. Some news can be delayed and most commentary can even more readily be delayed without serious injury, and there often is a self-imposed delay when responsible editors call for verification of information. But such delays are normally slight and they are self-imposed. Delays imposed by governmental authority are a different matter.

As Justice Brandeis had observed — and Milton before him — thinking and speaking are private, individual matters sensitive to governmental interference. If speakers are to maintain their autonomy, the choice not only of what to say, but when to say it, must be left to individual discretion.

To uphold the prior restraint, Burger wrote:

> [W]e must examine the evidence before the trial judge when the order was entered to determine (a) the nature and extent of pre-trial news coverage; (b) whether other measures would be likely to mitigate the effects of unrestrained pre-trial publicity; and (c) how effectively a restraining order would operate to prevent the threatened danger. The precise terms of the restraining order are also important. We must then consider whether the record supports the entry of a prior restraint on publication, one of the most extraordinary remedies known to our jurisprudence.

First, Chief Justice Burger wrote, the trial judge had reasonably concluded that there would be intensive local and national press coverage. Judge Stuart had found "a clear and present danger that pre-trial publicity *could* impinge upon the defendant's right to a fair trial," the Court observed (emphasis added by the Court). But Stuart was wrong. As Holmes and Brandeis had postulated, a clear and present danger requires immediacy; mere conjecture is insufficient.

Burger wrote that the trial judge's "conclusion as to the impact of such publicity on prospective jurors was of necessity speculative, dealing as he was with factors unknown and unknowable." Nobody could tell what would be disseminated, who would read or view it, what impact it would have, who would be picked as jurors, or whether they would be able to decide the case based solely on the evidence introduced in court. One could not even be certain there would be a trial. Simants could plead guilty — or have a heart attack. When the Court referred to factors unknown and unknowable, the case was over. Once the burden of proof is assigned, that party loses, because it is impossible to prove factors "unknown and unknowable." Because

the government has a heavy burden to overcome the presumption of unconstitutionality, it loses.

Likewise, in the second step of the analysis, Burger noted that the government has the burden of proving no other measures would mitigate the effects of publicity. That, too, is unknown and unknowable, without actually implementing the measures. Multiple options exist: change of venue to a jurisdiction with less publicity, postponement of a trial to allow the effects of publicity to subside, intensive questioning of prospective jurors to determine possible bias, instructions to jurors to avoid publicity and consider only evidence presented in court, sequestration of jurors, restraints on leaks by trial participants, and, of course, a new trial. The obligation to provide a fair trial is on the state, not the press, and if the state holds an unfair trial, it must hold another, fair trial or not try the defendant. The press cannot deny defendants their Sixth Amendment rights.

Third, the Court questioned the effectiveness of the prior restraint. As Brandeis put it, would the danger result if the free speech in question were *not* stopped? Or would the danger only stop if the speech were stopped? In *Nebraska Press Association*, the Court said any danger would exist despite the restraint. The trial court, for example, might have had difficulty implementing its order regarding media outside the court's jurisdiction.

Even more difficult would be stopping a whole community of 850 people from discussing the case and probably generating rumors more damaging to the defendant than publicity would be. Although everybody was restrained from spreading information, the order was hardly enforceable. The townspeople — who constituted the pool of prospective jurors — would gossip no matter what the court decreed. If the restraint would be ineffective, that by itself is a reason for invalidating it.

Finally, the Court noted that the order was defective because it was vague and overbroad. Vague speech regulations inhibit speakers who cannot be sure if they will violate them. A regulation might be constitutional if narrowly crafted, but a regulation that proscribes protected speech as well as unprotected speech is constitutionally suspect. This court order, as modified by the Nebraska appellate court, banned "information strongly implicative of the accused." Would saying Simants had been arrested for six murders be "strongly implicative"? Too vague. If the order covered such an allegation, then it would cover speech that would not prejudice the outcome of a trial because the jury would learn the allegation as soon as the trial began anyway. Therefore, the order was overbroad as well as vague.

Applying the Test

So the case left a blueprint for how the Court would likely approach future prior restraint cases, regardless of whether the restraint involves fair trials. The Court is not willing, apparently, to merely determine if the government regulation qualifies as a prior restraint and declare it unconstitutional on those grounds alone, as it did in *Near v. Minnesota.*

First, the regulation must fit the definition of prior restraint, which has relaxed since the days of King Henry VIII, but is not so elastic to include every restraint on publishing, as the Court illustrated in *Alexander v. United States* (which essentially excluded statutory restrictions from prior restraints). Today, a licensing system would still qualify as prior restraint, unless the government imposed it on its own employees (as with CIA agents), it was a condition of accepting a government subsidy (although this area is still developing and the case law is somewhat inconsistent), or it involved broadcasting or the high school or elementary press. As long as it did not involve a statute, (1) any government prohibition (2) of a specific publication (3) based on its content (4) after the exercise of discretion and (5) in advance of publication would also constitute prior restraint today.

When a regulation is defined as prior restraint, it is presumed unconstitutional, and the government bears a heavy burden to overcome that presumption. This aspect cannot be emphasized too strongly, because the tendency is to give the government the benefit of the doubt and avoid the asserted risk of speech. It is easy to concoct worst-case scenarios and hard to favor an abstract concept such as free speech, but the presumption weights the balance solidly in favor of free speech.

To overcome the presumption of unconstitutionality, the government must prove that the danger is serious *and* imminent, that the speech is the cause of the danger and that stopping the speech will stop the danger, that no alternatives to prior restraint will work, and that the terms of the prior restraint are neither vague nor overbroad. The prior restraint can fail at any of these steps and need fail only one to remain unconstitutional.

A danger can be serious without being imminent, as in the *Nebraska Press Association* case. Likewise, as Brandeis noted, a danger can be imminent without being serious. Advocacy of trespassing could be so persuasive that the speaker's audience immediately sought out backyards to traverse, but even so, it would not rise to the level of a serious danger justifying prior restraint. Seriousness is usually the easiest element of the test to meet, because the government's asserted danger is taken at face value and the government is always able to posit a danger of some magnitude.

Imminence, on the other hand, is generally the element least likely to be demonstrated. Proving something will immediately and inevitably occur is almost impossible. Nobody can know what will happen in the future. The *Nebraska Press Association* Court echoed Brandeis' observation that fear of serious injury alone will not justify suppression when it wrote that the trial judge's conclusions regarding the impact of publicity were necessarily speculative. Conjecture is *always* possible; evidence of imminence rarely so.

But even if the danger is imminent, it need not be caused by the speech. If the danger occurs regardless of whether the speech is practiced, then the rationale for the restraint fails. This element of the test often comes into play when the proscribed speech is already in the public domain, as it was in the Pentagon Papers case where historical data was being suppressed. If the content of the speech is already available elsewhere, even if it poses an imminent danger, then there is no reason to stop the speech in a given case. The question is whether *the speech at issue in the case* causes the danger.

Alternatives to the prior restraint are almost always available to deal with the danger. The question here is not whether an alternative, narrower form of prior restraint would be preferable. That is an overbreadth question. Alternatives to regulating speech altogether are at issue in this context. Even if alternatives would impose substantial costs on government, as in moving the entire trial, regulating speech must be the last resort, not the first.

In any event, to preserve individual autonomy from government, the burden is on government to prove that no means other than infringing on the speaker would adequately address the problem. Publishing something different or at a later time is not an alternative because it shifts the burden to the speaker, when government must do everything possible to defer to the speaker's discretion. The question is not why the speaker wishes to speak, but why the government wants to censor; and the burden is heavy.

Legacy of Nebraska Press Association: CNN

Although the Supreme Court has not considered a prior restraint against the press in recent years, it did have the opportunity in 1990 and declined to do so. The case began when prison officials made tape recordings of conversations between the imprisoned former Panamanian leader Manuel Noriega and his attorney. Cable News Network obtained copies, but Noriega asked a judge to impose a prior restraint on the dissemination of the tapes to preserve his right to a fair trial.

The judge asked CNN to turn over the tapes so he could listen to them and decide whether they imperiled Noriega's fair trial right, but CNN refused. The judge imposed the ban, and CNN appealed. The case is muddied because the refusal to turn over the tapes became the issue that seemed to become more important in the court's mind than the constitutionality of the prior restraint. The case illustrates the legacy of *Nebraska Press Association* in the sense that the judge believed he had to have access to the tapes before he could apply the test. If the *Near v. Minnesota* approach had been in place, it would only have been necessary to define the regulation as a prior restraint and find it unconstitutional, without applying any test. Even though the burden seems impossible to meet after *Nebraska Press Association,* the fact that there is a test suggests that some prior restraints will pass the test; otherwise, why have a test?

As Professors Sigman Splichal and Matthew Bunker have

noted, however, even if the trial judge had assumed the dissemination of the conversations on the tape posed a threat to Noriega's fair trial, without actually obtaining the tapes or hearing them, he could still have applied the test, and the prior restraint would have been unconstitutional. Indeed, the prior restraint would have failed at every step of the test because of the questionable imminence, ineffectiveness of the restraint and availability of alternatives.

In any event, the Supreme Court met and discussed the case on a Sunday morning, which it had not done in forty years, before deciding not to hear it. The denial of *certiorari* provoked a passionate dissent from Justice Thurgood Marshall, joined by Justice Sandra Day O'Connor. He considered the case to be "of extraordinary consequence for freedom of the press." Marshall noted the presumed unconstitutionality of prior restraint and that the proponent of "this drastic remedy" carries a heavy burden to justify it. He continued:

> I do not see how the prior restraint imposed in this case can be reconciled with these teachings. Even more fundamentally, if the lower courts in this case are correct in their remarkable conclusion that publication can be automatically restrained pending application of the demanding test established by *Nebraska Press,* then I think it is imperative that we re-examine the premises and operation of *Nebraska Press* itself. I would grant the stay application and the petition for certiorari.

Justices Marshall and O'Connor are no longer on the Court, of course, and the fact that the Court declined to hear the case means it still has never actually decided in favor of a prior restraint against the press. Perhaps the best that can be said about this case is that it has not served as precedent for any other cases.

Tory v. Cochran

The Supreme Court in 2005 decided a prior restraint case that introduced no new law but raises questions.

In the case, Ulysses Tory had been a client of attorney Johnnie L. Cochran Jr. (O.J. Simpson's lawyer), but he was dissatisfied with Cochran's work. He then engaged in several high-profile criticisms of Cochran, including writing letters to the bar association, picketing Cochran's office and pursuing him in public while chanting threats and insults. As an example of his criticisms, one of the signs he used in the picketing read "Hey Johnnie, How Much Did They Pay $$ You to F*** Me?"

Cochran sued for libel in California, and the court ruled that not only were the libels false and intended to extort money from Cochran, but that damages were an inadequate remedy because Tory said he would continue the campaign of defamation. So the court enjoined Tory and his agents or representatives from uttering, in the form of picketing or otherwise, any statements about Cochran in any public forum.

The decision, the U.S. Supreme Court ruled, was a prior restraint and unanimously found it unconstitutional. It couched its nine-paragraph ruling in terms of causation and overbreadth. Tory's speech no longer represented any threat to Cochran because Cochran had died before the ruling came down. If the speech was not the cause of any danger, then it could not be restrained. Additionally, the terms of the restraint were so broad that the justices noted in oral argument that it prohibited Tory's lawyer from criticizing Cochran — and even prevented Tory and his representatives from saying anything, including praise, regarding Cochran. Thus, the restraint was fatally overbroad.

If the Court had said no more, one might have been satisfied. Indeed, one might even wonder why it had taken the case, because it added nothing to the law, and the California appeals court's opinion upholding the ruling had not even been published. Instead, the Court said the ruling left several questions unanswered, almost inviting further litigation.

Because Cochran had died, the Court said it did not resolve whether a permanent injunction could ever be issued in a defamation case against a public figure (a question First Amendment scholars had assumed had been resolved — in the negative — long ago).[3] Furthermore, the Court said it did not resolve whether the injunction would have been valid before Cochran's death, which was the essential issue in the case. Unless the Court was interested in rewriting decades of prior restraint law, there could only be one outcome to this case. For it to say that unsettled questions remained is, well, unsettling.

Business Week

In 1996, the U.S. Court of Appeals for the Sixth Circuit offered a ringing endorsement of the prior restraint doctrine. Procter & Gamble had sued Bankers Trust, alleging fraud in a business deal. The trial judge authorized the parties before trial to interview each other and collect evidence that would be kept secret, although on file with the court. The secrecy order was intended to protect trade secrets and other confidential information.

The parties later notified the judge that *Business Week* magazine had obtained copies of documents that the parties wanted to keep secret and asked the judge to order *Business Week* not to publish them. He sent a facsimile to McGraw-Hill, publisher of *Business Week,* imposing a prior restraint three hours before the presses would have rolled and without any chance for McGraw-Hill to contest the order.

The next day, McGraw-Hill's lawyers asked the judge to withdraw his order and also filed a request for an expedited appeal with the Sixth Circuit. The Sixth Circuit turned down McGraw-

---

3 *See* ROBERT D. SACK, LIBEL, SLANDER AND RELATED PROBLEMS 361-63 (1980) ("One general rule long adhered to in defamation cases is that courts will not enjoin libels.... The absoluteness of this rule is crucial.").

Hill on procedural grounds, as did Supreme Court Justice John Paul Stevens when McGraw-Hill asked him for an emergency stay of the order. McGraw-Hill was effectively at the mercy of the trial court.

The trial judge conducted hearings off and on for three weeks, during which he was most interested in learning how *Business Week* had obtained the documents in violation of the secrecy order. It turned out that someone in the Procter & Gamble public relations office had notified a *Business Week* reporter that some fascinating documents had been filed in the case, and another *Business Week* reporter had obtained them from an acquaintance at a New York law firm representing Bankers Trust. Apparently neither the reporter who obtained the documents nor the New York lawyer who provided them knew anything about the secrecy order.

Upset that his order had been violated, the trial judge issued a permanent prior restraint ordering *Business Week* not to publish any of the documents it had obtained. But, at the same time, he held that the parties to the case had not given any good reason why the documents should be secret, and he made copies of them public — enabling *Business Week* and everybody else to obtain copies from the courthouse that could be published.

The Sixth Circuit panel concluded that the trial judge was trying to keep his prior restraint order from being appealed when he put the documents on the public record and allowed everybody, including *Business Week,* to publish them. But the Sixth Circuit was not fooled. Chief Judge Gilbert S. Merritt wrote that "appellate courts cannot allow themselves to be done out of their jurisdiction so cleverly.... So long as the permanent injunction remains technically in effect, we will review it as an injunction just as technically."

Merritt then turned to the First Amendment analysis, observing that the order was a "classic prior restraint" and therefore presumed unconstitutional. He applied textbook post-*Nebraska Press Association* analysis, beginning with a heavy burden on the proponent of prior restraint. The interests of Procter & Gamble and Bankers Trust fell vastly short of the "exceptional circumstances" required to justify prior restraint. According to the Sixth Circuit:

Far from falling into that "single, extremely narrow class of cases" where publication would be so dangerous to fundamental government interests as to justify a prior restraint ... the documents in question are standard litigation filings that have now been widely publicized. The private litigants' interest in protecting their vanity or their commercial self-interest simply does not qualify as grounds for imposing a prior restraint. It is not even grounds for keeping the information under seal, as the District Court ultimately and correctly decided.... The permanent injunction, therefore, was patently invalid and should never have been entered.

The court addressed three other bothersome aspects of the case. First, it criticized the trial judge for his extensive investigation into how *Business Week* obtained the documents. Not only did the trial court fail to conduct any First Amendment inquiry before sending the facsimile to *Business Week,* "but it compounded the harm by holding hearings on issues that bore no relation to the right of *Business Week* to disseminate the information in its possession," wrote the appeals court.

Preoccupation with the speaker's motive or knowledge seems to cast the speaker in the role of suspect, when it is government (here, the judge) whose motives are presumed suspect in prior restraint. Inquiring into how *Business Week* obtained the documents shifts the burden from the government to the magazine. In the Pentagon Papers case, the newspaper stories were based on documents that were not only classified, but stolen. Yet the origin of the stories was irrelevant to the outcome.

Second, the appeals court chided the trial court for relying on the Supreme Court opinion in *Seattle Times Co. v. Rhinehart* as authority for its prior restraint. In that case, the Court ruled that if one litigant could be required to disclose confidential information to the opposing litigant, the opposing litigant could be required not to disseminate the information, at least until it was revealed in open court. The Sixth Circuit said *Rhinehart* only applied to the actual parties to a case. *Business Week* was not involved in this case and was not using a court to obtain information from another party — quite the opposite.

Third, the Sixth Circuit disapproved of the temporary prior restraint that stopped the *Business Week* presses and continued while the judge held hearings until the permanent prior restraint was issued. Temporary restraining orders, known in the legal trade as TROs, are common as a means of maintaining the status quo while a court gathers evidence and reaches a decision. Chief Judge Merritt quoted from a First Circuit case involving the *Providence Journal:* "This approach is proper in most instances, and indeed to follow any other course of action would often be irresponsible. But, absent the most compelling circumstances, when that approach results in a prior restraint on pure speech by the press it is not allowed."

A temporary prior restraint is still a prior restraint. As the Sixth Circuit noted in considering if the situation was capable of recurring, there is no three-week exception to the prior restraint rule. Indeed, the court quoted from an opinion by Supreme Court Justice Harry Blackmun that "each passing day may constitute a separate and cognizable infringement of the First Amendment."

The *Providence Journal* case, though, should not be taken too far as authority. The First Circuit held that the newspaper could disobey a prior restraint order that was "transparently invalid" as long as it made a "good faith" effort to appeal it. That was contrary to earlier authority holding that the press should ordinarily abide by an order and work within the judicial system to overturn it, which is what McGraw-Hill did. The Supreme Court soon granted certiorari to hear the *Providence Journal* case.

"I have read the oral argument before the Supreme Court and there is no doubt in my mind that the Supreme Court granted cert to reverse *Providence Journal*," noted Ken Vittor, senior vice president and general counsel for McGraw-Hill at a Practising Law Institute seminar. Perhaps fortunately for the press, media lawyer Floyd Abrams (who also argued the *Nebraska Press Association* case before the Supreme Court) was able to convince the Supreme Court to dismiss the *Providence Journal* case because of a procedural problem with the prosecutor who had been assigned to the case.

Contracts Imposing Prior Restraint

The use of a temporary restraining order to stop publication was also rejected in a more recent case involving John Bolton, former National Security Advisor to former President Donald Trump. Government employees, such as Bolton, with access to classified information are asked to sign Standard Form 312, which requires an employee — even after leaving government employment — to allow the government to review beforehand and approve any publication that might include classified information. And, significantly in the Bolton case, such government approval must be in writing.

Such contracts are generically referred to as "nondisclosure agreements," or NDAs. They are common in industries where employers are trying to protect trade secrets or customer lists. Before becoming president, Trump raised the use of NDAs to an art form, using them regularly to silence women with whom he had affairs, an estranged niece as part of an estate settlement, and even all campaign staffers, including volunteers, in perpetuity. (Other campaigns have used NDAs, just not to the extent that Trump had.)

But when the NDA is imposed by the government, it would seem to implicate the First Amendment and raise the specter of prior restraint. The Supreme Court, however, has decided otherwise.

In a 1980 case, *Snepp v. United States*, the Court ruled that when former CIA agent Frank Snepp III signed the government's form agreeing to prior review and approval, it was simply a contract to which he had voluntarily agreed as a condition of employment. At trial, the government had admitted that nothing in Snepp's book was classified, but contended that Snepp was required to submit his book beforehand anyway, according to the plain terms of the contract.

The *Snepp* Court stoutly disagreed that the government was censoring anything. It was simply asking Snepp to live up to his agreement. Indeed, the Court mused that the CIA might have been able to impose prepublication review even in the absence of an express agreement. The 6-3 decision thus completely avoided any First Amendment questions, including why citizens

can give up their First Amendment rights and agree to prior restraint, even if voluntarily. Should government even be able to ask citizens to waive a right that is supposed to protect them from government?

This total deference to government continued in the *Snepp* Court's discussion of the proper remedy. The government wanted the courts to force Snepp to turn over all profits he obtained from the book. But the lower court had held that, because no classified information was involved, the First Amendment should offer some protection from drastic remedies. The Supreme Court would have none of it, claiming that any other remedy would be too much trouble for the CIA to prove, especially since damages were "unquantifiable." So appropriating all of Snepp's profits resulting from his breach was the only appropriate remedy.

The contract Snepp signed actually had no explicit penalty provision, but the government has since included on every Standard Form 312 a clause forcing government employees to agree to relinquish all profits if they breach the prepublication review agreement.

John Bolton left the government in September 2019 after a year-and-a-half heading the National Security Council. Two months later, he had a contract to write a book, titled *The Room Where It Happened*, about his time in the Trump White House. By December he had submitted a draft manuscript to the agency he formerly oversaw, initiating the prepublication review process. After numerous and extensive edits, he was told in April of 2020 that the manuscript no longer contained classified information and an authorization letter would be forthcoming, possibly that same day.

No letter ever arrived. Instead, after no communication from the government for more than a month, Bolton was informed in June that a new reviewer had been assigned and more edits would be required. By this time, the review process had taken far longer than the time it took to write the book, and Trump had been tweeting since January that the book was "nasty and untrue."

But Bolton, in the meantime and without telling the government, had delivered the manuscript to a publisher, which delayed publication twice before settling on a June 23 release date. As is standard practice in the industry, about two weeks before the release date, the publisher sent out advance review copies and some 200,000 copies to booksellers around the world so that they would be available on June 23.

After the advance copies had already been shipped, the government on June 16 asked a federal court to block publication, the same day late-night talk show host Stephen Colbert showed his audience the copy he had received. (Bolton was scheduled to be a guest the following week). Colbert also played a video clip from the day before in which Attorney General William Barr mistakenly insisted that the book had not yet been released.

The federal court, applying the analysis from *Snepp*, wrote that it is "well-settled that a mandated prepublication review process is not an unconstitutional prior restraint." But in analyzing the requirements for the temporary restraining order that the government was requesting, the court had to consider whether the TRO would prevent "irreparable injury." Because the book was already widely available and its blistering criticisms of Trump were headlining every news outlet, the court said stopping any further publication would not stop further injury.

In other words, even though standard prior restraint analysis did not apply, the court looked at the effectiveness of the restraint, just as with any prior restraint, and the fact that the information was already in the public domain was conclusive. The government claimed a TRO, including restrictions on movie rights and release in audiobook format, could prevent further harm. But the court was unimpressed, noting the "damage was done" and there is "no restoring the status quo."

However, the court said Bolton had taken a risk in publishing without final written authorization. He had "opted out of the review process before its conclusion" to reap publicity and sales. Bolton emphasized his extensive cooperation during the review process and claimed the White House was merely stalling, hoping to delay publication until after the November elections. But none of that was relevant to a *Snepp*-analysis.

No final approval meant Bolton had gambled that the book contained no more information that the government considered classified, but "Bolton was wrong," the court wrote. Now, consistent with *Snepp*, Bolton "stands to lose his profits from the book deal, exposes himself to criminal liability, and imperils the national security," wrote the court.

So it was impractical to stop Bolton's book, but he could still be subject to sanctions.

Requiring Bolton to submit to a review process and citing his failure to obtain the government's final approval sounds more than a little like the licensing system implemented by King Henry VIII. The insistence of courts in such cases to look no further than the language of a contract and their failure to acknowledge any hint of the First Amendment is maddening. Contract law has an age-old refusal to recognize contracts against public policy. The First Amendment would seem to qualify as public policy. Unless public policy means total deference to whatever the Executive Branch says is public policy, courts at least ought to be able to weigh enforcement against a public interest in publication.

The Bolton court noted at one point that if he was upset with the review process, "Bolton could have sued the government and sought relief in court" — as if the court would be willing to tell an Executive Branch intent on delay to speed things up, in an elementary contract case. Several times the court criticized Bolton for not waiting until the review process was complete, so it is mystifying what such a court might do if Bolton had actually sued.

The courts' simplistic reliance on contract law ultimately belies a preference not to get involved — not to second-guess what the Executive Branch has classified, not to determine if the Executive Branch has political motives, not to overhaul a cumbersome review system even though it is weighted toward less speech rather than more.

While such judicial restraint toward the other branches can be laudable in ordinary circumstances, if the First Amendment is at stake, it is fatal to freedom.

Prior Restraint – of Terrorism?

Cryptography, the practice of coding messages so that only the intended receiver can decipher them, dates to at least Julius Caesar. Decrypting, or attempts by unintended receivers to uncover the right "key" to break the code, probably dates back just as far. With the advent of computers, the science has taken a huge leap. The number of possible keys to today's encryption codes is 1 followed by 77 zeroes, a number thought to be approximately equal to the number of atoms in the universe, making the codes virtually unbreakable.

Purchases made over the Internet are encrypted so that credit card data will be secure. Individual or corporate users can have other legitimate uses for encryption. Encryption can even be understood as the digital-age equivalent of the First Amendment right to be anonymous. However, governments are greatly concerned about the use of encryption by terrorists, criminals and spies. For example, Ramzi Yousef, who masterminded the bombing of the World Trade Center in 1993, apparently encrypted files that contained plans to crash eleven airliners; but the National Security Agency was able to crack his password and foil the plot. Al-Qaida operatives have used encryption in their communications, although it is not clear that any encrypted messages were used when they planned the September 11, 2001, attack on the World Trade Center.

In the 1990s, in an effort to keep encryption techniques out of foreign hands, the U.S. government ruled that encryption technology was a "munition." Export of such technology had to be reviewed and licensed — and export included posting on the Internet if foreign nationals might access the technology. Under Department of Commerce regulations, license applications could be held indefinitely, appeals of denials were to be decided "within a reasonable time," and there was no judicial review.

Daniel Bernstein, then a computer science professor at the University of Illinois in Chicago, developed a method of encryption, which he called "Snuffle." When informed he would need a license to distribute his source code within the general academic and scientific communities, he sued, claiming prior restraint.

The Court of Appeals for the Ninth Circuit determined that source code for encryption software was "speech." Computer programmers can read source code, and it expresses ideas little different from equations or graphs used in other fields. This was a controversial finding, to which the dissent objected because source code was "functional" rather than expressive. Computers translate source code into machine language (object code) — ones and zeroes — that then causes computers to work. Because source code controlled a computer without conveying information to humans during this translation, the dissent contended it could not be speech.

But once the majority concluded that source code was, in fact, protected by the First Amendment, the court then found the regulations to be unconstitutional prior restraint. The regulations placed too much discretion in government officials and did not take into account the need for judicial oversight. "To the extent the government's efforts are aimed at interdicting the flow of scientific ideas — these efforts would appear to strike deep into the heartland of the First Amendment," the court wrote.

But what might have happened if this case had occurred after September 11, 2001? A year after the Bernstein case, a professor at Case Western Reserve University wanted to post source code to his Web site, which would constitute exporting the code under the regulations. The Court of Appeals for the Sixth Circuit first overturned the lower court finding that the code was not speech. But, although the expressive elements were protected, the court said the government's interest in regulating the functional elements must also be considered. In language that was prescient of 9/11, the court wrote that the exercise of presidential power on behalf of national security interests could sometimes outweigh free speech interests.

The court returned the case to the lower court because changes in the encryption export regulations had just made it much easier to export source code, but the court's sensitivity to the balance of interests is mindful of a conclusion Professor Fredrick Siebert drew after surveying 300 years of English press law: "The area of freedom contracts and the enforcement of restraints increases as the stresses on the stability of the government and of the structure of society increase."

Prior restraint doctrine does not exist in a vacuum. Judges interpret it, and they are subject to the same anxieties and pressures as anybody else. It follows that judicial opinions are a product of their times. Sensitivity to First Amendment interests might well be waning in this period post-9/11 as people seem willing, even enthusiastic about trading freedom for what they hope to be security. Even the doctrine against prior restraint might not be adequate to protect speech in such a climate.

SUMMARY

Questions remain in this age-old area of the law. If even temporary restraints are so disdained and obviously unconstitutional, should the speaker be able to maintain autonomy and speak at will? Can the judiciary effectively censor the press through TROs in a way that it would not allow the executive branch to do? Are speakers better off to sacrifice principles for pragma-

tism and obey the prior restraint so they can appear before the appellate court with clean hands? It probably helped *Business Week* that it could point out that the only party who had violated the court order was one of the litigants, and it obviously hurt CNN when it refused to turn over the tapes so the judge could review them. And finally what does the future hold for this doctrine?

The prior restraint doctrine will not survive simply because it has a venerable pedigree. The government will continue to attempt to control and manipulate expression, and the doctrine may have to adapt to remain viable. That's what happened in *Near v. Minnesota* when the Court expanded the doctrine to include judicial orders as well as administrative licensing. But the test that the Court used in *Nebraska Press Association* to test the constitutionality of a judicial prior restraint might be considered a step back, because the *Near* Court, and even Blackstone, contemplated a clear rule rather than a balancing test, albeit one heavily weighted in favor of speech. But substituting a test for a clear rule suggests there will be an occasion on which the test will be met and the restraint upheld; otherwise, why not have a clear rule? A test seems to open the door to temporary prior restraints at a minimum, and it may significantly diminish the strength of the doctrine in the long run.

Requiring proof of an imminent danger is the cornerstone of the doctrine against prior restraint, in that it is the component most difficult for the government to prove and thus provides much of the doctrine's force. But there is constant pressure to diminish the imminence requirement in a terrorist-filled world with incessant threats on the Internet against everyone from jurors to presidents.

A recent case is troubling in that regard, although it involves a federal criminal statute and therefore is subsequent punishment and not prior restraint. Harold Turner was upset with an appellate court ruling limiting the right to bear firearms, and he blogged, "These Judges deserve to be killed." He quoted Thomas Jefferson, who wrote that the "tree of liberty must be replenished … with the blood of tyrants," and posted names, pictures, and addresses of the judges, along with pictures of the federal courthouse in which they worked, noting with red arrows the anti-truck bomb barriers.

The Court of Appeals for the Second Circuit affirmed Turner's conviction, rejecting any need for proof that Turner actually intended to carry out an assassination. Notably, the Second Circuit specifically rejected any requirement that the threat posed an immediate danger. It was enough that Turner intended to intimidate the judges and that the judges had a reasonable "apprehension of impending injury." If this inquiry into the fearfulness of people targeted by speech, along with a repudiation of any imminence requirement, were to cross over into prior restraint law, the doctrine might not be dead, but it surely would be crippled.

The Supreme Court has not had a significant prior restraint

case before it for almost forty years, which might be proof by itself of the doctrine's continued vitality. Or it might presage a fresh look at that doctrine when that case eventually does arrive before the Court in a world vastly different from the one confronting John Milton, the framers, or even the newspapers that published the Pentagon Papers. Ultimately, the future of the doctrine depends on those who understand its roots and its rationale and can explain both, whether in editorials, blogs, court papers or coffee shops.

BIBLIOGRAPHY

Articles

Anderson, David A. "The Origins of the Press Clause," 30 *UCLA Law Review* 455 (1983).

Blanchard, Margaret A. "Filling in the Void: Speech and Press in State Courts Prior to Gitlow," *in The First Amendment Reconsidered — New Perspectives on the Meaning of Speech and Press*, Bill Chamberlin, & Charlene Brown, eds. New York: Longman, 1982.

Blasi, Vincent. "Toward a Theory of Prior Restraint: The Central Linkage," 66 *Minnesota Law Review* 69 (1981).

Coyle, Erin K. "Freedom of the Press, 1500-1804," *in The Media in America: A History*, 12th ed., Wm. David Sloan, et al, eds. Northport, Ala.: Vision Press, 2023.

Carter, Edward L., & Brad Clark. "Death of Procedural Safeguards: Prior Restraint, Due Process and the Elusive First Amendment Value of Content Neutrality," 11 *Communication Law and Policy* 225 (2006).

Emerson, Thomas I. "The Doctrine of Prior Restraint," 20 *Law & Contemporary Problems* 648 (1955).

Helle, Steven. "Prior Restraint by the Backdoor," 39 *Villanova Law Review* 817 (1994).

Helle, Steven. "Publicity Does Not Equal Prejudice," 85 *Illinois Bar Journal* 16 (January 1997).

Jeffries, John C. "Rethinking Prior Restraint," 92 *Yale Law Journal* 409 (1983).

Litwack, Thomas R. "The Doctrine of Prior Restraint," 12 *Harvard Civil Rights-Civil Liberties Law Review* 519 (1977).

Post, Robert. "Meiklejohn's Mistake: Individual Autonomy and the Reform of Public Discourse," 64 *University of Colorado Law Review* 1109, 1137 (1993).

Ragan, Fred D. "Justice Oliver Wendell Holmes Jr., Zechariah Chafee Jr., and the Clear and Present Danger Test for Free Speech: The First Year, 1919," 58 *Journal of American History* 42 (1971).

Redish, Martin H. "The Proper Role of the Prior Restraint Doctrine," 70 *Virginia Law Review* 53 (1984).

Scordato, Martin. "Distinction Without a Difference: A Reappraisal of the Doctrine of Prior Restraint," 68 *North Carolina Law Review* 1 (1989).

Splichal, Sigman L., & Matthew D. Bunker. "The Supreme Court and Prior Restraint Doctrine: An Ominous Shift?" 3 *Media Law & Policy* 11 (1994).

Books

Abrams, Floyd. *Speaking Freely: Trials of the First Amendment*. New York: Penguin Books, 2006.

Bickel, Alexander. *The Morality of Consent*. New Haven: Yale University Press, 1975.

Blackstone, William. *Commentaries on the Laws of England*. Philadelphia: J.B. Lippincott Co., 1893 (1769).

Boorstin, Daniel J. *The Mysterious Science of the Law*. Chicago: University of Chicago Press, 1941.

Emerson, Thomas I. *The System of Freedom of Expression*. (1970).

Friendly, Fred W. *Minnesota Rag: The Dramatic Story of the Landmark Supreme Court Case That Gave New Meaning to Freedom of the Press*. New York: Vintage Books, 1981.

Levy, Leonard W. *Emergence of a Free Press*. New York. Oxford University Press, 1985).

Meiklejohn, Alexander. *Free Speech and its Relation to Self-Government*. New York: Harper & Brothers, 1948.

Novick, Sheldon M. *Honorable Justice — The Life of Oliver Wendell Holmes*. New York: Little Brown & Co. 1989.

Rudenstine, David. *The Day the Presses Stopped: A History of the Pentagon Papers Case*. Berkeley: University of California Press, 1996.

Siebert, Fredrick S. *Freedom of the Press in England, 1476-1776*. Cambridge: Harvard University Press, 1965.

Smith, Donald L. *Zechariah Chafee Jr., Defender of Liberty and Law*. New York: Oxford University Press, 1986.

Smith, Jeffrey A. *Printers and Press Freedom — The Ideology of Early American Journalism*. New York: Oxford, 1988.

Ungar, Sanford J. *The Papers & the Papers: An Account of the Legal and Political Battle Over the Pentagon Papers*. New York: Dutton, 1972.

Cases

Abrams v. United States, 250 U.S. 616 (1919).

Alexander v. United States, 509, U.S. 544 (1993).

Bernstein, v. United States, 192 F.3d 1308 (9th Cir. 1999).

Cable News Network, Inc. v. Noriega, 498 U.S. 976 (1990).

Citizens United v. Federal Election Commission, 558 U.S. 310 (2010).

Grosjean v. American Press Co., Inc., 297 U.S. 233 (1936).

In re Providence Journal, 820 F.2d 1354 (1st Cir. 1987).

Junger v. Daley, 209 F.3d 481 (6th Cir. 2000).

McIntyre v. Ohio Elections Communication, 514 U.S. 334 (1995).

Near v. Minnesota, 383 U.S. 697 (1931).

Nebraska Press Association v. Stuart, 427 U.S. 539 (1976).

New York Times Co. v. United States, 403 U.S. 713 (1971).

Procter & Gamble Co. v. Bankers Trust Co., BT Securities Corp., 78 F.3d 219 (6th Cir. 1996).

Schneider v. State, 308 U.S. 147 (1939).

Seattle Times Co. v. Rhinehart, 467 U.S. 20 (1984).

Talley v. California, 362 U.S. 60 (1960).

Tory v. Cochran, 544 U.S. 734 (2005).

United States v. Turner, 720 F.3d 411 (2d Cir. 2013).

Whitney v. California, 274 U.S. 357 (1927).

5

Regulating Pornography

By John C. Watson

☑ **Headnote Questions**

- How are issues of taste and morality tied to the laws regulating pornography, obscenity and indecency?
- How do obscenity, pornography and indecency differ?
- How are federal, state and local governments involved in the legal issue of obscenity?
- How has the Supreme Court defined speech that is obscene and, therefore, not protected by the First Amendment?
- How does the law shield children from inappropriate messages?
- How do old court precedents and new legislation address online pornography?
- How have ratings systems evolved?

Purveyors of sexual messages and speech otherwise deemed socially inappropriate have never lacked audiences or censors. This was true thousands of years ago when cave walls were a primary medium of communication and remains true in the twenty-first century when the Internet had become a top-tier medium for pornography. Societies have been persistent in constraining and punishing speech found to be morally offensive or socially inappropriate. It does not matter whether these messages are carved in stone, written on paper, or measured in bytes.

Even though the U.S. Constitution has given freedom of expression a hallowed place in the First Amendment, restrictions on pornography, indecency and obscenity have grown in fits and starts to become a substantial body of law. These laws, perhaps because they are so closely tied to morality and evolving social mores, are sometimes enforced unevenly and often lack clear, objective rationales and justifications.

Scholars widely agree that all law was originally derived from precepts of morality that condone behavior supporting the peaceful and cooperative survival of society and condemning behaviors inimical to these basic goals. Condemnable behaviors are labeled immoral, evil or bad. Law renders them illegal. Laws regulating sexual expression and offensive messages remain closely tied to morality. This is often reflected in court rulings that espouse rationales grounded in morality and other public policy determinations of what is good or bad for society.

As with other moral judgments, there are greater and lesser evils in this area of law. Legal restrictions and protections vary accordingly. The most morally offensive categories of communication are those that incite violence and those with sexual content. These are "fighting words," "true threats" and "obscenity." They get no First Amendment protection, and legal restrictions and penalties imposed for them can be as rigorous as those imposed on any harmful behavior. Anyone who utters fighting words can be prosecuted. The fighting words concept is loosely defined as speech that is highly likely to provoke an immediate violent response — just as a slap in the face might. True threats are directed communications that reasonably cause a person to fear the infliction of physical injury or death. Obscenity, like fighting words, is also difficult to define beyond the basic requirement that it include sex-themed speech. U.S. Supreme Court Justice Potter Stewart famously wrote in a 1964 obscenity case, *Jacobellis v. Ohio*, that the Court was "trying to define what may be indefinable." But, anyone who creates, sells or conveys obscene messages can be convicted of felonies and sentenced to prison. In a highly publicized 2008 case, for example, Paul F. Little, a pornographer known in the business as "Max Hardcore," was sentenced to nearly four years for distributing obscenity on the Internet and through the mail, according to the *Tampa Tribune* and *Forbes* magazine.

Pornography, which is less sexually offensive than obscenity, gets some First Amendment protection and is in the continuing process of losing some of its moral stigma. This was illustrated to some degree by a federal prosecutor in the Max Hardcore case who, according to *Forbes*, said of the defendant: "What he creates gives mainstream pornography a bad name."

So-called "mainstream pornography" does not include depictions of children. The inclusion of children in sexual communication that would be merely pornographic if adults were depicted, often is transformed into obscenity as a matter of law. The Associated Press reported that a man convicted of trafficking in online child pornography was given a thirty-year federal prison sentence in 2014.

American social mores increasingly label depictions of violence as inappropriate when children are the audience. But the level of public opprobrium as expressed in law remains markedly below the reproach against sexual depictions. In response to public pressure, purveyors of music, movies and video games with violent themes have implemented voluntary rating systems, but efforts to raise the level of legal excoriation to match that of sex-themed speech have failed. In the 2011 case *Brown v. Entertainment Merchants Association*, a seven-justice majority of the Supreme Court found a California law unconstitutional, in part, because it sought to impose the same limitations on violent video games that the First Amendment allows for sex-themed speech directed at children.

Increasing moral condemnation of specific types of violence and invasions of privacy have led to the colloquial linking of the suffix "porn" to some socially and politically unacceptable communication behaviors. For example, the term "revenge porn" refers to depictions of intimate situations that are not necessarily overtly sexual, but usually include nudity in an apparently private circumstance. The term "animal crush porn" has been applied to depictions of the killing of small animals, even when there is no overt sexual content. And "war porn" is the generically applied label for videos of graphic violent military or terrorist attacks. The courts have declined to treat these types of communication as pornography, but legal restrictions have been imposed sometimes on other grounds.

The intensely moral nature of sexual communication law may have contributed to its murkiness and dearth of bright-line definitions. Moral judgments are often gut-level determinations that something is wrong or inappropriate. Such conclusions are not necessarily explicable through a clear path of reasoning.

When legal determinations are tied to morality and issues of taste, they lack some of the long-term predictability common in other areas of law. One of the purposes of written law is to provide the public with behavioral guidelines and notice of what is acceptable and what is not. But morality and taste change in response to a wide variety of cultural, political and religious influences. Victorian influences in the United States in the 1890s, for example, condemned the public display of a woman's naked ankle as indecent and scandalous. During the mid-1960s, television broadcasters would not expose the navel of "Jeannie," the lead female lead character in a situation comedy because they were afraid of viewer backlash or a federal fine for indecency. Not until the 1980s did television commercials dare show women in bras for the first time. By comparison, by the twenty-first century, television commercials for products to treat male erectile dysfunction had become common fare.

PORNOGRAPHY AND THE LAW

Despite its obscurities, the law of morally offensive expression has a traceable path of development and fundamental legal parameters to guide those who convey or receive such messages. An examination of this body of law must necessarily begin with an explanation of the basic terms: obscenity, pornography and indecency.

Indecency is the broadest of the three terms and is applied to perhaps the least morally offensive expression. It refers to messages — sexual and non-sexual — that are considered clearly offensive. Indecency does not necessarily have any of the sexual content of obscenity or pornography but is otherwise considered morally offensive or socially inappropriate. It receives substantial First Amendment protection in the print media and online but is subject to legal restriction in the broadcast media. Indecency is often as much a question of taste, morality and social mores as it is an issue of law. It is nonetheless, a routinely used legal term at the heart of federal legal restrictions in the broadcast media and on the Internet. Broadcast stations, for example, are prohibited from transmitting indecent messages during selected hours of the day.

Indecency was also the term used to refer to the word "fuck" when it was used in a non-sexual, but apparently highly offensive epithet: "Fuck the Draft." Paul Cohen was convicted of disturbing the peace in 1968 because he wore a jacket inscribed with those words. The Supreme Court, in *Cohen v. California*, found no sexual meaning in the words as used and reversed the conviction. Justice John Marshall Harlan observed that the message was distasteful to many people but noted that "it is nevertheless often true that one man's vulgarity is another's lyric." Profanity is often a synonym for indecency in that it also can have no sexual meaning but usually is considered vulgar and offensive expression that can be regulated by law in some contexts. The First Amendment protects indecency in print media, movies and the Internet.

"Pornography" is a term used to label sexually explicit expression. It is indistinguishable from what is euphemistically identified as "erotica." "Pornography" is often used as a term of criticism indicating crass sexual expression. While erotica and pornography may be equally sexual, erotica conveys a somewhat literary nuance. "Pornography" generally indicates a decided lack of delicacy. It is not truly a legal term, but "pornography" often is applied to sexual expression that gets some First Amendment protection. "Hardcore pornography" usually means obscenity.

"Obscenity" is a legal term that refers to material that has been deemed illegal by a court and gets no First Amendment protection. It refers to sexual expression that is disgusting to the senses or abhorrent to morality and to graphic portrayals of sex acts intended to arouse lustful thoughts. The term is often used generically to express disgust or moral outrage in non-sexual contexts; but legally, material must meet a specific court-created test to be deemed obscene.

Supreme Court rulings on sexual expression and morally inappropriate speech fall into two basic areas. First, the Court interprets federal statutes and regulations that control or prohibit the creation and distribution of sexual expression. This body of law includes the Federal Communications Act, rules and regulations of the Federal Communications Commission and U.S. Postal Service, laws controlling imports and exports, and regulations governing interstate commerce. Obscenity laws, like statutes on almost any subject, contain vague provisions that courts must interpret. For example, if U.S. Customs agents in New York City intercept pornographic films shipped from Germany to New Hampshire, the courts must determine whether to apply the laws and standards of New York, Germany or New Hampshire. If statutes are silent, federal appellate courts must articulate rules of law by relying on other legal precedents.

More importantly, the Supreme Court decides how far federal and state governments may go in restricting sexual expression. The Court indicated in 1931 that obscenity was one of a few, narrow classes of expression that is unprotected by the First Amendment. The ruling in *Near v. Minnesota* provided no guidelines about this narrow class. Twenty-six years later, the Court began the difficult task of drawing the line between sexual expression that was obscene (and therefore subject to government bans and criminal prosecution), and sexual expression that was non-obscene (and protected by the First Amendment).

The creation and enforcement of anti-obscenity laws are primarily left to the states. The Supreme Court has determined that the states retain broad police power to prohibit all behavior deemed inimical to the comfort, safety, health and welfare of society. Police power authorizes states to enact laws to protect the peace, good order, morals and health of their communities.

Congress and federal agencies also have created legal restrictions on obscenity, but state supreme courts and legislatures are the sources of the greatest number of obscenity regulations. Local police and prosecutors handle the enforcement of state obscenity law or sometimes choose not to enforce them for political or practical reasons. Neither the First Amendment nor federal statutes require states to enact obscenity laws. Some state judges have effectively exercised their option to decrim-

inalize the sale of obscenity to adults. And in some metropolitan areas, a liberal political environment and a thriving consumer market for sexual material have discouraged the enforcement of anti-obscenity laws. In 2011, during the Democratic administration of President Barack Obama, the U.S. Justice Department's Obscenity Prosecution Task Force was disbanded and had not initiated any such prosecutions since he took office, according to a report in the *Huffington Post*. In 2019, at the end of the Republican administration of President Donald Trump the conservative *Washington Times* complained: "Pornography crackdown vowed by Donald Trump still never materialized." The Republican presidential platform branded pornography a "public health crisis."

PORNOGRAPHY AND SOCIETY

Whether pornography is a threat to public safety, health and morality remains in debate. Some claim the creation and sale of pornography are associated with illicit activities such as gambling, prostitution and illegal drugs. But studies also have concluded that businesses that provide sexually explicit imagery, particularly those online, have thrived largely without the accompanying taint of illegal drugs and prostitution.

Sociologists and political activists are divided on whether adult pornography is harmful. Two presidential commissions have studied the issue. President Lyndon Johnson created the Commission on Obscenity and Pornography in 1968. Two years later, during the Richard Nixon Administration, the commission concluded that neither hard-core nor soft-core pornography leads to antisocial behavior and thus should not be prohibited. Eighteen years later, however, U.S. Attorney General Edwin Meese's Commission on Pornography concluded that pornography was pervasive in society and recommended vigorous enforcement of anti-obscenity laws.

Many people, including some social scientists, oppose obscenity laws. They argue that moderate consumption of pornography — like wine, ice cream or even marijuana — is compatible with physical and mental health. Sallie Tisdale, a journalist and social commentator, defended pornography for women in a 1992 *Harper's* magazine article and in a 1994 book. She wrote: "I want never to forget the bell curve of human desire, or that few of us have much say about where on the curve we land."

Proponents of anti-obscenity laws cite history and research findings to defend their position. They point out that many cultures traditionally have controlled sexual expression. The *Bible* may include bawdy tales of prostitutes and adulterers, but it tells these tales discretely without images of genitals. They point to studies finding that men exposed to explicit videos become more calloused toward women and that there is a strong correlation between consumption of sex-themed magazines for heterosexual men and the incidence of sex crimes against women. Two feminists, Catherine MacKinnon and Andrea Dworkin, were particularly active in fighting pornography, which they define as the graphic, sexually explicit subordination of women. They argue that it presents women "as sexual objects for domination, conquest, violation, exploitation, possession, or use, or through postures or positions of servility or submission or display." An Indianapolis ordinance adopted this argument, but in a 1984 case, *American Booksellers v. Hudnut*, a federal appeals court found it unconstitutional.

Some federal judges, however, have supported attempts by states to restrict pornography and public nudity, even if they addressed actions by wholly consenting adults. Supreme Court Justice Antonin Scalia, for example, observed in a 1991 case, *Barnes v. Glen Theatre*, that Indiana's nudity law would be violated even "if 60,000 fully consenting adults crowded into the Hoosier Dome to display their genitals to one another, even if there were not an offended innocent in the crowd." In 2000, the Court, in *Erie v. Papp*, upheld a Pennsylvania ordinance that banned public nudity and thus prohibited erotic dancers in bars from performing nude. The Court gave state and local government broad latitude for creating and implementing such laws. Two justices said governments need no justification other than public morality to ban nude dancing in public. And four justices insisted on only the slimmest of justifications for such bans, stating that local government could justify the regulations by citing studies from other states and cities that documented secondary effects of nude, barroom dancing. The cited effects often include sex crimes, prostitution and harm to property values.

PORNOGRAPHY AND THE SUPREME COURT

Justice Scalia's colorful observation — part of a lively history of Supreme Court jurisprudence in this area — is from a concurring opinion in a case involving nude dancing. Darlene Miller, a dancer at the Kitty Kat Lounge in South Bend, Indiana, argued that nude dancing was a form of protected expression. Indiana, however, said the state had a right to require all public performers at least to wear pasties and G-strings, and the Supreme Court agreed in a decision that is representative of the Court's history in pornography law.

In his majority opinion in *Barnes*, Chief Justice William Rehnquist conceded that nude dancing was indeed "expressive conduct within the outer perimeters of the First Amendment," but insisted that Indiana had a right to combat public nudity. He observed, however, "It is possible to find a kernel of expression in almost every activity a person undertakes." Byron White, joined by three other justices, dissented and argued that non-obscene, nude dancing performed before consenting adults was protected expression. Justice David Souter joined Scalia in

his attack on the concept that consent should affect the outcome of the case.

This kind of fragmentation dominated Supreme Court jurisprudence for more than thirty years. In *Manual Enterprises v. Day*, the Court clearly indicated for the first time that gay-themed sexual expression was not in and of itself patently offensive or necessarily obscene. The case arrived at the Supreme Court after the U.S. Postal Service seized and refused to deliver copies of magazines that it judged obscene because they displayed pictures of nude men. A fractured majority allowed the magazines to be delivered but reached that result on a variety of rationales. Two justices found the photographs to be no more patently offensive than those in the *Playboy* and *Esquire* magazines of the time. "[T]hese portrayals of the male nude cannot fairly be regarded as more objectionable than many portrayals of the female nude that society tolerates," Justice Harlan wrote. Three other justices indicated that only a court of law and not postal officials could determine whether expression is obscene. Justice William O. Douglas futilely claimed the First Amendment protected the magazines even if they were obscene.

Scattered rationales also were provided in the 1966 case *Memoirs v. Massachusetts*, for which Justice William Brennan presented a three-part test to determine whether a work was obscene. The test would find a work obscene if (1) the dominant theme appealed to a prurient interest in sex; (2) it was patently offensive because it affronted contemporary community standards regarding sexual matters; and (3) the material was utterly without redeeming social value. Two justices joined Brennan's plurality decision finding that the 1749 novel *Memoirs of a Woman of Pleasure* — also known as *Fanny Hill* — was not obscene; two justices concurred and voted to overturn the conviction but for other reasons; another judge wrote a separate concurrence; and three justices filed separate, dissenting opinions.

Justice Douglas, who advocated a strict interpretation of the First Amendment, concurred in the judgment. The First Amendment absolutely protected obscene speech, he wrote: "Publications and utterances were made immune from majoritarian control by the First Amendment, applicable to the States by reason of the Fourteenth. No exceptions were made, not even for obscenity."

The *Memoirs* ruling produced a definition of obscenity that was an expansion of the definition the Court developed in the 1957 case *Roth v. United States*. The newer ruling made it hard to prosecute sex-themed works because it required a finding that works were "utterly without redeeming social value." Most films or books contain a kernel of a story line or smidgen of non-sexual plotting that amount to some social value. Pornographers took pains to make sure this was so to assure First Amendment protections for their work.

The social value test was suggested in *Roth* and formally adopted in *Memoirs*. Under the combined Roth/Memoirs Test, other appellate courts found most sex-themed materials to be non-obscene and thus protected by the Constitution. Adult bookstores and theaters proliferated from the late 1960s through the 1980s, two presidential commissions studied pornography, and the Supreme Court generally ruled in favor of free speech in obscenity cases. Justices, however, were divided on how to define obscenity and whether they should be spending so much time perusing sexual expression. For example:

• In 1964, the Court invalidated a $2,500 fine levied against a Cleveland Heights theater manager who was convicted of obscenity charges for showing *Les Amants*, a French film about an unfaithful wife. It was in this case that Justice Stewart conceded that he could not intelligibly improve on the legal definition of obscenity, "But I know it when I see it, and the motion picture involved in this case is not that."

• In a 1966 case, *Mishkin v. New York*, Justice Hugo Black objected to "saddling this Court with the irksome and inevitably unpopular and unwholesome task of finally deciding by a case-by-case, sight-by-sight personal judgment of the members of this Court what pornography (whatever that means) is too hard core for people to see or read."

• In a 1967 case, *Redrup v. New York*, the Court reversed obscenity convictions from New York, Kentucky and Arkansas for distribution of the publications *High Heels*, *Gent*, *Swank*, *Lust Pool* and *Shame Agent* magazines. Justices disagreed on what rule of law to apply, but deemed the material protected "whichever of these constitutional views is brought to bear."

• In 1968, Justice Harlan noted in *Interstate Circuit v. Dallas* that the Court had published fifty-five separate opinions for 130 obscenity cases since *Roth*, creating a "chaotic state of affairs" that was "unmatched in any other course of constitutional adjudication." He concluded: "[A]nyone who undertakes to examine the Court's decisions since *Roth* which have held particular material obscene or not obscene would find himself in utter bewilderment."

• In 1970, Chief Justice Warren Burger complained in the *Walker v. Ohio* decision about assuming the role of a "supreme and unreviewable board of censorship for the 50 states."

The struggles the Court had in defining and regulating obscenity were mirrored throughout the judicial system. Some scholars, attorneys and judges joined Justices Black and Douglas in opposition to all obscenity laws, but most jurists and observers agreed that the task was unavoidable. Indeed, many so-called absolutists who insist that consenting adults have a right to view whatever they desire, agree that lines must be drawn for material aimed at children or that is obtrusive and unavoidable, such as billboards in public spaces.

If limits must be imposed for materials that are available to children, the central question becomes, "Where are those lines drawn?" In 1973, in *Miller v. California*, the fragmentation on the Supreme Court abated when five justices, for the first time since *Roth*, agreed where some lines should be set. The decision established the basic legal definition of obscenity applied into the twenty-first century.

MILLER V. CALIFORNIA

Marvin Miller sent a mass mailing to California residents promoting four illustrated books (*Intercourse*, *Sex Orgies Illustrated*, *Man-Woman* and *An Illustrated History of Pornography*) and a film (*Marital Intercourse*). A restaurant owner and his mother in Newport Beach who received copies of the brochure complained to police. Miller was eventually charged with violating California's obscenity statute.

The Supreme Court described the brochure as consisting primarily of "pictures and drawings very explicitly depicting men and women in groups of two or more engaged in a variety of sexual activities, with genitals often prominently displayed." Five justices, in an opinion written by Chief Justice Burger, found the brochure obscene under the Court's new definition:

(1) whether the average person, applying contemporary community standards, would find that the work, taken as a whole, appeals to the prurient interest;
(2) whether the work depicts or describes, in a patently offensive way, sexual conduct specifically defined by applicable state law;
(3) whether the work, taken as a whole, lacks serious literary, artistic, political, or scientific value.

The first two parts of the Miller Test were quite similar to the first two parts of the Memoirs Test. In part three, however, the Court rejected the requirement that a work be utterly without redeeming social value and replaced it with the more restrictive requirement that the work lack serious value as determined by the "average person." In addition, the *Memoirs* definition had used the broad adjective "social" to qualify value; the Miller Test specified that the value be literary, artistic, political or scientific, omitting, for example, entertainment value. The Miller Test was a significant alteration of the third part of the Roth/Memoirs by setting aside the implied social or moral expertise of an average person for the actual expertise of a "reasonable person" in areas such as the arts and sciences. The actual expertise requirement was made explicit by the Court's *Pope v. Illinois* ruling in 1987.

On the same day that the Court decided *Miller*, it decided

four other obscenity cases, all by 5-4 votes, clarifying a variety of constitutional provisions in obscenity law. In *Kaplan v. California*, the Court ruled that it is not necessary for a work to use images to be obscene. Words by themselves can be sufficient. In *Paris Adult Theatre I v. Slaton*, the Court confirmed that adult movies could be found obscene, even when they were marketed discreetly. The fact that the theater had a tasteful, non-exploitative exterior and that it restricted its clients to interested adults did not exempt it from obscenity prosecution.

Finally, the Court upheld two federal prosecutions for importing obscene material into the United States for private, personal use and for the transportation of obscene material in common carriers in interstate commerce.

Miller Part 1: The Prurient Interest Test

The first prong of the Miller Test — "Whether the average person, applying contemporary community standards, would find that the work, taken as a whole, appeals to prurient interest" — is the easiest to satisfy. It requires that sexual expression be judged according to average persons — not particularly susceptible and sensitive persons or totally insensitive persons. And the work is judged according to local, contemporary standards, which may vary from community to community. Wrote the *Miller* majority: "It is neither realistic nor constitutionally sound to read the First Amendment as requiring the people of Maine or Mississippi to accept public depiction of conduct found tolerable in Las Vegas or New York City.... People in different states vary in their tastes and attitudes, and this diversity is not to be strangled by the absolutism of imposed uniformity."

The first part of the Miller Test requires that the overall work have a prurient appeal, that is, the work arouses an immoderate or unwholesome interest in sex. The work, however, is judged on its entirety, not on isolated or fleeting passages or scenes that contain sexual descriptions or images. When a Cincinnati art museum was prosecuted for exhibiting photographs by Robert Mapplethorpe, the judge required the 175-photo exhibit to be judged on the basis of seven controversial photos that had been isolated from the others in the exhibit, violating the intent of the Miller Test.

Miller Part 2: The Patent Offensiveness Test

The second prong of the Miller Test is "Whether the work depicts or describes, in a patently offensive way, sexual conduct specifically defined by the applicable state law."

A federal judge who found that *Penthouse* appealed to a prurient interest in sex also found that it satisfied the second part of the Miller Test: The sexual portrayal was sufficiently graphic to be considered patently offensive. Ordinary photographs or drawings of nudes would not satisfy such a requirement, but the 108 photographs in the five photo features went beyond nudity. The judge noted that eighty-seven photos included exposed breasts, buttocks or genitals; nine included actual or simulated lesbian, oral sex; seven alluded to masturbation through the location of fingers in or near genitals; and sixteen photos showed legs spread to expose genitals, with six "close-up photographs showing nothing but women's groins."

The patent offensiveness requirement separates hardcore sexual portrayals from other sexual expression. For a sexual portrayal to be obscene, it must be specifically enumerated in a state obscenity statute. In *Miller*, the Court said such portrayals were of ultimate sexual acts, normal or perverted, actual or simulated, including masturbation, excretory functions and the lewd exhibition of genitals. State statutes that define the behaviors whose portrayals may be obscene read like a catalog of sexual practices for heterosexual and homosexual couples and individuals. A Virginia statute, for example, said obscene material contains content that appeals to "a shameful or morbid interest in nudity, sexual conduct, sexual excitement, excretory functions or products thereof or sadomasochistic abuse."

Thus, communities must restrict prosecutions to works containing explicit portrayals of hard-core sex acts. One year after *Miller*, the city of Albany, Georgia, fined theater manager Billy Jenkins $750 and sentenced him to twelve months of probation for showing the movie *Carnal Knowledge*. Some critics listed the film as among the ten best movies of 1971, and mainstream movie star Ann-Margret received an Academy Award nomination for her performance. The Supreme Court, in *Jenkins v. Georgia*, reversed the conviction and pointed out that juries do not have "unbridled discretion in determining what is 'patently offensive.'" Sexuality may have been the major theme of the movie, the Court said, but it was not obscene: "There is no exhibition whatever of the actors' genitals, lewd or otherwise, during these scenes. There are occasional scenes of nudity, but nudity alone is not enough to make material legally obscene under the Miller standard." The case is a strong reminder to those individuals who mistakenly believe that *Miller* gave communities unlimited power to regulate erotic material.

Subjectivity, imprecision and unpredictability occur in all three parts of the Miller Test. Complicating this subjectivity, tolerance for sexual-themed materials varies from community to community. The concepts of patently offensive and prurient interest vary according to community norms, which the law apparently assumes are reflected in the attitudes of jurors.

Miller Part 3: The Serious Value Test

The third and final determinant of obscenity is "Whether the work, taken as a whole, lacks serious literary, artistic, political or scientific value." Even if a work appeals to the prurient interest and is patently offensive under state law, it must satisfy the third part of the Miller Test to be obscene and to lie outside the protection of the First Amendment. In effect, the third part forces judges into roles of artistic or social critics and evaluate the aesthetic merit of works containing sexual content. Prosecuting and defense attorneys may call expert witnesses to characterize the social value of the work for the jury.

The Transition of the Obscenity Test

The Rationale:

" [I]mplicit in the history of the First Amendment is the rejection of obscenity as utterly without redeeming social importance."

Prurient Interest:

Roth (1957): The average person, applying contemporary community standards must find that the dominant theme of the material, taken as a whole, appeals to the prurient interest.

Roth-Memoirs (1966): The dominant theme of the material, taken as a whole, must appeal to the prurient interest in sex.

Miller (1973): An average person, applying contemporary, local community standards, must find that the work, taken as a whole, appeals to the prurient interest.

Patent Offensiveness:

Roth (1957): The material is patently offensive because it affronts contemporary community standards.

Miller (1973): The work depicts in a patently offensive way sexual conduct specifically defined by applicable state law.

Value of the Work:

Roth (1957): The material is utterly without redeeming social value.

Miller (1973): The work lacks serious literary, artistic, political or scientific value.

The presence of a substantial amount of serious, non-sexual material may salvage a work that contains graphic sex, but the amount of non-sexual material must be substantial. One judge has cautioned: "A quotation from Voltaire in the flyleaf of a book will not constitutionally redeem an otherwise obscene publication." Although some judges have classified *Penthouse* magazine as obscene because of the quantity of explicit, erotic photographs, others have judged it non-obscene because of its

serious articles. The Louisiana Supreme Court in 1980 found that the 228-page, June 1980 issue of *Penthouse* satisfied the first two parts of *Miller*, and that ninety-six pages of photo essays of women satisfied the third part because they constituted hard-core sexual conduct. However, the magazine as a whole was redeemed by sixty-seven pages of articles that had serious value.

Similarly, in 1979, a Boston Municipal Court judge upheld First Amendment protection for the film *Caligula* by a legal thread. A political scientist testified that the film had a serious political theme about absolute power corrupting absolutely, and no witness rebutted the point. The judge ruled that the movie was protected because the government had failed to prove that the film lacked serious political value.

Judges are not free to serve as their own fact finders on the issue of social value. A federal district court judge found the hip-hop lyrics of the 2 Live Crew album *As Nasty As They Wanna Be* obscene; but he ignored the testimony of critics that the music had political significance and literary conventions, and the government presented no evidence on the issue of artistic value. The Eleventh U.S. Court of Appeals reversed the ruling, rejecting the argument that "simply by listening to this musical work, the judge could determine that it had no serious artistic value."

A federal district judge determined in 1991 that a modicum of political or literary value can salvage a work. The judge ruled that a truck driver's bumper sticker, "How's my driving? Call 1-800-EAT-SHIT," had serious literary value because it parodied bumper stickers that encouraged drivers to call truck companies with comments about the driving habits of truck drivers. The judge also said the bumper sticker had serious political value because it protested the "Big Brother" mentality that is promoted by serious versions of the sticker, and it did not satisfy the first two parts of *Miller* because it was not erotic.

Other judges have not been so quick to find redeeming serious value in sexually explicit material. In 1977, the Kentucky Supreme Court upheld an obscenity conviction and accompanying $4,000 fine against the Paducah Fourth Street Cinema for showing the now iconic pornographic movie *Deep Throat*. After viewing the movie, the court held that it lacked serious value: "The story line consists entirely of the sexual activities of Miss Linda Lovelace. We failed to find any serious literary, artistic, political or scientific value in this motion picture." A federal district court, four years later, similarly failed to find serious value in the film *Cinderella-96*, which was described as a translation of the fictional character Cinderella into a bawdy, lusty tale of recurring homosexual and heterosexual encounters. The judge said the "sum and substance of the movie is the almost unbroken string of sexual acts depicted." He concluded that the movie was obscene even though it contained no sexual penetration or ejaculation. And he said it lacked serious literary and artistic value even though it may be entertaining and enjoyable to some viewers.

OBSCENITY AND PUBLIC OPINION

After *Miller v. California* became the binding precedent, obscenity convictions decreased and more sexual materials became available. This may be because the public doesn't want obscenity laws to be strictly enforced. Some prosecutors and judges — those people responsible for enforcing obscenity law — are elected, and members of the public serve on the juries that decide criminal obscenity cases. Studies show that many people use erotica or tolerate its use by others. A 1994 study by University of Chicago Professor Robert T. Michael, for example, reported that 41 percent of men and 16 percent of women questioned said they had purchased auto-erotic materials during the previous twelve months. Twenty-three percent of the men had watched sexually explicit movies, 22 percent had visited clubs with erotic dancers, and 16 percent had purchased sexually explicit books or magazines. Only 34 percent of all subjects said they believed there should be laws prohibiting the sale of pornography to adults.

A 2015 report on a Gallup Poll indicated that 43 percent of Americans had come to believe that pornography is "morally acceptable." This was the highest level of acceptability since polling on the topic began in 2011. The acceptance rate among women, however, was 25 percent.

Other studies report similar results. A 1990 Kinsey Institute survey found that 54 percent of adults questioned had watched adult videos or movies at least once. A 1991 Gallup Poll found that 53 percent of adults either opposed tightening standards in their communities for the sale of sexually explicit material or wanted the standards to be less restrictive. In addition, more than 50 percent of adults said magazines with nudity or that show adults having sexual relations, theaters showing adult movies and sexually explicit video rentals should be available to adults without restrictions or without public displays. Tolerance has increased in the years since the study.

The proliferation of sex-themed magazines, increased explicitness of some major magazines, and growing availability of DVDs and online sex videos are developments that reflect a public that consumes more sex-themed material and is increasingly tolerant of it. This is a public that balks at obscenity prosecutions. Law professor Robert Riggs counted the number of obscenity cases appealed to higher courts before and after *Miller* and found a sharp upward trend from 1969 to 1974, the year after the decision, and an "almost equally sharp down turn" after 1974. Political scientist Harold Leventhal detected similar trends when he surveyed local prosecuting attorneys

about obscenity enforcement before and after *Miller*. Although prosecutors reported an increase in the quantity of obscenity in their communities after 1973, they reported a lower priority for prosecuting obscenity and a drop in the number of obscenity cases. Leventhal concluded that *Miller* failed to spur more obscenity prosecutions. Similarly, former University of Chicago law professor Cass Sunstein observed in 1993 that "realistically speaking, most people involved in the production of sexually explicit work have little to fear from the Miller test."

So, while the three-part Miller Test and the wording of some local obscenity statutes theoretically have made it easier to prosecute obscenity, the public has grown increasingly tolerant of sexual expression and has reduced political pressures on elected officials to enforce obscenity laws. And some members of that public have difficulty when they serve as jurors and are asked to restrict magazines or films that are similar to materials that the jurors may have rented or purchased themselves.

THE SCANT PROTECTION OF OBSCENITY

Miller and its companion cases were aimed at restricting the transportation and sale of explicit sexual expression, but what of the possession of sexually explicit material? Coexisting with the doctrine that obscenity may be regulated is a second doctrine at the core of which is the concept that when people are in the privacy of their homes, the government may not interfere with their personal thought process or their perusal of words or pictures. Under this doctrine, the private possession of objectionable material is legal in nearly every case.

Justice Thurgood Marshall, in *Stanley v. Georgia*, a 1969 case, articulated this concept that the mere possession of obscenity for private use is generally beyond the reach of government. When police searched the home of Robert Eli Stanley for bookmaking equipment, they found no gambling devices but discovered three reels of sexually explicit 8mm film.

In his majority opinion overturning Stanley's conviction, Justice Marshall found that the mere private possession of obscene matter could not be a crime under the Constitution. The state has no right "to control the moral content of a person's thoughts," he wrote, and the right to receive information and ideas is critical. Wrote Marshall: "If the First Amendment means anything, it means that a state has no business telling a man, sitting alone in his own home, what books he may read or what films he may watch. Our whole constitutional heritage rebels at the thought of giving government the power to control men's minds."

Stanley was as much a victory for home sanctity as for free expression. The reach of the *Stanley* ruling, however, was substantially diminished in subsequent cases. Perhaps most notably in 1990 when the Court found the possession of child pornography, even at home, was subject to criminal prosecution. This ruling in *Osborne v. Ohio* reemphasized the Court's finding of a compelling government interest in protecting child victims of pornography as elaborated in *New York v. Ferber*.

State legislatures and supreme courts have minimized obscenity prosecutions. But it is difficult for state legislators to get elected on a platform of decriminalizing obscenity. In 1990, a federal district court judge in Florida told opponents of obscenity laws: "In sum, if persons subscribe to the view that obscenity should be legalized, they should take their petitions to Tallahassee, the Florida capital, not to the steps of the U.S. courthouse." But most state legislatures have been unsympathetic.

Most actions to abolish obscenity laws come from state supreme courts, which are more independent of voters than legislatures are. The most dramatic example is the Oregon case *State v. Henry*. In 1987, the Oregon Supreme Court voted unanimously to decriminalize the sale or ownership of obscenity for adults, though sale of sexually explicit material to minors remained illegal. The court reversed the conviction of Earl Henry, the operator of an adult bookstore in Redmond, ruling that the state constitution's free-expression clause was broader than the First Amendment and protected obscenity. The court reasoned that territorial law existing in 1857, when the constitution was adopted, prohibited only the distribution of obscenity to minors. The court concluded: "In this state any person can write, print, read, say, or sell anything to a consenting adult even though the expression may be generally or universally considered 'obscene.'"

Obscenity protection made other inroads in western states. The Hawaii Supreme Court ruled that the right of privacy, which had been incorporated in its state constitution nine years earlier, protected adult possession of obscenity. The court indicated in a footnote that it was not deciding the issue of child pornography, the sale to minors, the obtrusive public display of pornography, the showing of obscenity to a captive audience, or films that depicted actual killings.

PROTECTING CHILDREN AND JUVENILES

Even when obscenity is decriminalized for consenting adults, courts recognize the need to restrict sexually explicit material from view by juveniles and children. The exception has two manifestations. First, federal and state laws prohibit the sale of sexual materials to minors. Second, federal and state law prohibit the distribution of materials portraying children or juveniles in sexually explicit situations whether in the physical communication media or online.

Variable Obscenity

State and federal laws don't merely ban the sale and virtual transmission of legally obscene materials to minors; they also ban the sale and virtual transmission of sexual materials that would be legal if sold to adults. This approach to regulating material has been called "variable obscenity." The government may be stricter in prohibiting the dissemination of sexual materials to juveniles than to adults.

In a 1968 case, *Ginsberg v. New York*, the Supreme Court upheld a New York statute that made it a crime to sell materials containing nudity to anyone under the age of 16. Sam Ginsberg, the owner of a Bellmore, Long Island, luncheonette, sold two sex-themed magazines to a 16-year-old boy on two occasions. The magazines contained pictures of nude women that were clearly not obscene. The Court upheld the conviction and denied that the statute lacked a rational justification, even though studies neither proved nor disproved a causal link between sex-themed material and the ethical and moral development of youths.

Events decades later demonstrated that the doctrine of variable obscenity remains alive. In 1996, a panel of the U.S. Court of Appeals for the Ninth Circuit upheld a California statute banning the sale of sexually oriented publications from unsupervised news racks. The court held that the California legislature had a compelling interest in shielding juveniles from sexual material that was not obscene for adults. The next year, Phoenix police used a similar Arizona statute to justify seizure of fifteen coin-operated news racks for a local, sexually oriented weekly, *Beat*, which had been published for thirty-three years and had a circulation of 8,500. The publisher, Jerry Evenson, commented: "We're not pornographic. We have no full nudity, there is no profanity. The only thing we have is bare nipples."

The Federal Communications Commission has applied the same logic in prohibiting the use of indecent language on commercial radio. The Supreme Court, in *FCC v. Pacifica*, has said radio may be restricted more than print media because of its intrusiveness and its accessibility to children. The case began when WBAI broadcast a twelve-minute monologue by George Carlin, "Filthy Words," at 2 p.m. His satire was an analysis of the seven words — crude references to sex, excrement, body parts, and so forth — that were banned from broadcasting. Although the station preceded the monologue with an advisory that it contained offensive language, a man who was driving with his young son missed the advisory and tuned in to the middle of the monologue. He complained to the FCC.

The Supreme Court voted 5-4 to uphold possible civil sanctions against the station, but its decision was based on the fact that radio is uniquely available to children. The majority said the decision balanced the significant interests of listeners in their homes against broadcasters' interests. A concurring opinion indicated that the ruling did not apply to the isolated use of an offensive word in a broadcast. Eleven years later, in 1989, the Court underscored the importance of the intrusiveness factor and invalidated a ban on telephone indecency. The FCC was attempting to control the dial-a-porn business that made sexually oriented telephone messages available to people who paid for calls that began with the numbers 900. The Court indicated that the telephone was not nearly as intrusive as the radio: "Placing a telephone call is not the same as tuning in a radio and being taken by surprise by an indecent message."

From 1989 to 1993, while Alfred Sikes was FCC chairman, the commission actively enforced radio's prohibition against indecency and levied fines ranging from $2,000 to $600,000. Most notorious was radio shock-jock Howard Stern, who paid a total of $1.7 million in fines for his off-color morning commentaries. He was cited for his numerous and explicit references to masturbation, fornication, excretory functions and sexual organs. A study of broadcast indecency fines from 1987 to 1997 found that the FCC tended to fine stations "when humor is combined with patently offensive descriptions of sexual or excretory activities or organs, expletives, or sexual innuendo." This was precisely Stern's core product. Stern eventually fled the FCC's jurisdictions and settled into a lucrative career in satellite radio in 2005.

In 2001, the FCC attempted to clarify its indecency ban that is in effect daily from 6 a.m. to 10 p.m. on AM and FM radio and commercial television. The FCC said that it applies three criteria to determine indecency: (1) explicitness or graphic nature of the depiction of sexual or excretory organs or activities; (2) whether the materials dwell on or repeat at length such sexual depictions; (3) the context and whether the depiction appears to pander or titillate or is presented for shock value. The heart of the FCC statement was thirty-two explicit examples from FCC indecency cases, twenty-three of which were ruled indecent. The indecent examples included the *Howard Stern Show* and songs with titles like "Uterus Guy," "You Suck," "Sit on My Face" and "Penis Envy." The nine segments that were found not to be indecent were from the *Geraldo Rivera Show*, the film *Schindler's List* and the National Public Radio show "*All Things Considered.*"

In addition, in 2005, Congress passed and a year later President George W. Bush signed a bill providing for a 10-fold increase in fines the FCC could levy on broadcast stations for airing indecent material. Apparently fed up with sexual references and incidents like the brief exposure of singer Janet Jackson's breast in 2004 Super Bowl half-time performance, Congress set the maximum possible fine for each incident at $325,000. The president signed the Broadcast Decency Enforcement Act of 2005 in June 2006.

Two years later, the Third U.S. Circuit Court of Appeals held that the FCC's fine against CBS was improper because the agency had failed to give adequate notice as to why it was changing its method of determining on-air indecency. The FCC had abandoned its policy of insulating what it called "fleeting expletives" from sanction. The court's ruling was short-lived, however. A year after the CBS ruling, the Supreme Court held in *FCC v. Fox Television Stations* that the FCC did not act improperly when it changed its policy. The Court remanded the CBS case for reconsideration in light of its ruling in the Fox Television case. To further complicate matters, the reversal of *Fox Television Stations* gave the Second Circuit an opportunity to reconsider the case on constitutional grounds. The case was originally considered only on whether the FCC had followed administrative law correctly when it changed the indecency policy. In 2010, the Second Circuit held that the FCC's policy related to indecency violated the First Amendment, and the Supreme Court granted *certiorari*. In 2012, the Court held that the FCC did not give adequate notice to Fox Television Stations and ABC for the broadcast of an episode of *NYPD Blue* and, therefore, the standards as applied to the broadcasts were vague. The Court set aside the FCC's orders.

The Supreme Court indicated in a 1975 case, *Erznoznik v. Jacksonville*, that there were limits to how far it would go to shelter children and disinterested adults from offensive speech that was not legally obscene. It ruled that a city ordinance prohibiting the showing of films with nudity in drive-in theaters with screens visible from streets or public places was unconstitutional. The theater was prosecuted for the R-rated film *Class of '74*. The screen was visible from two city streets and a church parking lot. The Court said the censorship was not justified by the limited privacy interests of persons on public streets who could simply look away when confronted by offensive material. It said that "all nudity cannot be deemed obscene even as to minors." Such a rule would bar films with pictures of baby's buttocks, nude bodies of war victims, cultures in which nudity is indigenous, the opening of art exhibits and bathers on a nude beach.

The Supreme Court applied similar logic when it invalidated the Communications Decency Act of 1996. The act made it a crime to communicate indecent material on the Internet to anyone 17 or younger. It defined "indecency" as patently offensive descriptions of sexual or excretory activities or organs. The Supreme Court said in *Reno v. American Civil Liberties Union* that the act would violate the First Amendment because it would allow Internet users to be punished for disseminating such things as the seven "dirty words" of the George Carlin monologue, discussions of prison rape or safe sexual practices, nude artistic images or, arguably, the card catalog of the Carnegie Library. The Court concluded that the Internet was not as available to children as radio and television and that it was unconstitutional to deprive adults of sexual matter that was indecent but not obscene. The Court said banning such material "threatens to torch a large segment of the Internet community" and was like "burning the house to roast the pig."

In a 2000 ruling, *United States v. Playboy Entertainment Group, Inc.*, the Supreme Court again invalidated a provision of the Telecommunications Act of 1996 that had restricted the dissemination of indecent and erotic material. Two sections of the act had restricted the broadcasting by cable television of sexually oriented programming such as *Playboy Television* and *Spice*. The act required cable systems to fully scramble such programs so that the occasional and accidental bleeding of sexual images would not be available to children, or to delay the broadcasts to the safe harbor time period of 10 p.m. to 6 a.m., when children were less likely to be watching. Most cable systems opted for the delayed broadcasting because the technology for effective scrambling of signals was too expensive. Five justices agreed that the regulation unconstitutionally burdened the disseminators of programs that were indecent and sexual but not obscene. The majority favored the less restrictive and less intrusive alternative of requiring cable systems to inform their subscribers of a blocking option that would entirely block such sexual channels from their home televisions.

The *Reno v. ACLU* ruling provided First Amendment protection for indecency on the Internet but not for obscenity. Distributors of obscenity on the Internet have been successfully prosecuted. In addition, in 2006, the Supreme Court let stand a ruling by a federal three-judge panel for the Southern District of New York holding the obscenity provision of the Communications Decency Act was not overbroad. The federal court held that the plaintiff failed to meet its burden proving that the community standards prong of the Miller Test was not applicable to the widespread scope of the Internet.

Congress has not given up in its attempt to protect children from sexual materials on the Internet. In 1998, following the *Reno* decision, it passed a statute that was narrower than the former Communications Decency Act. The new act, the Child Online Protection Act, prohibited easily accessible, commercial sexual materials on the World Wide Web that were harmful to minors. The law provided a three-part test, similar to the Miller Test, to determine what content was harmful. Two of the three prongs were based on the application of community standards, which could mean local standards.

A U.S. court of appeals ruled that this use of community standards rendered the law substantially overbroad. The Supreme Court's 2002 ruling *Ashcroft v. American Civil Liberties Union* reversed the holding and ruled that it was just as valid to apply local standards to the Internet as to films, magazines and dial-a-porn telephone conversations, as the Court had in previous cases.

In 2004, in its second opinion in the case — *Ashcroft v. ACLU* — the Supreme Court found unconstitutional the COPA provision that required Internet providers of porn to verify the age of customers. A five-justice majority found the age verification was not the least restrictive means of shielding minors from Internet pornography. The Court concluded that filters and blocking software on home computers were more effective methods.

Congress's third attempt to shield children from Internet sexual expression met with success. In 2000, Congress passed the Children's Internet Protection Act, which required libraries that received federal subsidies to place filters on all their computers connected to the Internet. The purpose of the filters was to block child pornography and overtly sexual material that was inappropriate for children.

In a plurality opinion by Chief Justice Rehnquist, the Court upheld CIPA in its 2003 ruling, *United States v. American Library Association*. It held: "Because public libraries have traditionally excluded pornographic material from their other collections, Congress could reasonably impose a parallel limitation on its Internet assistance program." It noted that the statute allowed libraries to disconnect the filters for adults.

The availability of sexual material on the Internet continues to trouble many people, especially parents and lawmakers.

Child Pornography

The Constitution protects many portrayals of adults in sexual situations. But material that portrays minors is another matter. The Supreme Court, Congress, state supreme courts and legislatures have been unequivocal in authorizing criminalization of child pornography. In 1982, the Supreme Court upheld a state statute that prohibited the dissemination of material with sexual performances by children under the age of 16. *New York v. Ferber* involved a Manhattan store that sold films of young boys masturbating. The Court conceded that material depicting children in sexual situations could be prosecuted even if it would not be obscene had it depicted adults in the same situation. But, in reversing the state's highest appellate court, the Court said the paramount concern in such cases was protecting children who were portrayed in such materials from psychological, emotional and mental harm. This was clearly a compelling state interest that justified some limits on expression.

Eight years later in *Osborne v. Ohio* the Supreme Court upheld an Ohio law that prohibited the possession of materials depicting nude children unless they served a bona fide artistic, scientific or educational purpose. Clyde Osborne was sentenced to six months in prison for possession of four photographs of nude juvenile males in sexually explicit positions. The Court said the gravity of the state interest in protecting victims of child pornography justified the limits on free expression. The Ohio Supreme Court specifically limited its ruling to the lewd exhibition or graphic focus on genitals to prevent punishment for possession of innocuous photographs of naked children. The legal proscription of child pornography has become so unequivocal that children have been prosecuted for victimizing themselves by sexting. In an illustrative case from 2019, *In re: S.K. No. 41*, the Maryland Court of Appeals upheld penalties imposed on a 16-year old girl who shared with her friends a text-message video of herself engaged in a sex act. Half of the fifty states however, through statutes or common law, have since exempted from prosecution any minors engaged in this behavior. Adult participants in sexting with minors remain liable to prosecution. Former U.S. Rep Anthony Weiner of New York's 9th District pleaded guilty in 2017 when charged with sending explicit sexual texts to a 15-year-old girl.

Child pornography, then, is one of the few categories of legally taboo speech in American society. However, during its 2001-02 term the Supreme Court found unconstitutional a federal law that criminalized images that did not involve real children but were computer images of fictitious children engaged in imaginary sexual conduct. The statute made illegal a visual depiction that appeared to be or "convey[ed] the impression" of a minor engaged in explicit sex. In a 6-3 opinion, the Court concluded in *Ashcroft v. Free Speech Coalition* that "The Government has shown no more than a remote connection between speech that might encourage thoughts or impulses and any resulting child abuse."

In 2008, however, the Court upheld the constitutionality of a federal law that makes it a crime to advertise material as child pornography, regardless of whether actual children are involved. Under the law, a crime occurs when an advertiser believes or intends for the customer to believe that the advertised material depicts real children.

PANDERING AND ZONING

Most of this chapter has analyzed the definitional approach for restricting inappropriate or sex-themed expression. Zoning laws and the concept of pandering are other approaches for controlling such material. The more obscure of the two is pandering.

Pandering

The classic pandering case is *Ginzburg v. United States*. Ralph Ginzburg was sentenced to five years in federal prison and fined $42,000 because of the method he used to promote his sex-themed but non-obscene books and periodicals. What was thought to be a liberal Supreme Court upheld the conviction by a 5-4 vote. Earl Warren and William Brennan voted to uphold the conviction because of Ginzburg's blatant pandering: "The business of purveying textual or graphic matter openly advertised to appeal to the erotic interest of their customers."

Ginzburg — a former articles editor for *Esquire* and staff writer for NBC and *Reader's Digest* — mailed nine million copies of a brochure to promote the book *The Housewife's Handbook on Selective Promiscuity*, the newsletter *Liaison*; and *Eros*, the hardcover quarterly devoted to love and sex. The mailings generated 150,000, $25 subscriptions to *Eros*.

The Supreme Court said Ginzburg's method of promotion could be used to judge the content of the works: "Where the purveyor's sole emphasis is on the sexually provocative aspects of his publications, that fact may be decisive in the determination of obscenity." Ginzburg had highlighted the erotic nature of his publications by mailing the promotions from cities whose names had sexual connotations: Intercourse and Blue Ball, Pennsylvania, and Middlesex, New Jersey.

Civil libertarians denounced the decision. They pointed out that none of Ginzburg's publications were even close to satisfying the court's own definition of obscenity. *Eros* had received a number of national graphics awards, including one from the National Society of Art Directors. In order to secure a conviction, federal prosecutors had moved the trial from New York City to more conservative Philadelphia, where the mayor had narrowly won election on a promise to rid the city of smut, and the police department's obscenity control squad recently had arrested twenty-two magazine dealers and confiscated seventeen van loads of magazines. Ginzburg's appeal to the Supreme Court was supported by briefs of the American Civil Liberties Union, the Authors League of America and a group of writers that included literary icons Joseph Heller, James Jones, Norman Mailer and Arthur Miller.

Zoning

A decade after *Ginzburg*, the Supreme Court approved another non-content approach for the control of obscenity. In *Young v. American Mini Theatres, Inc.*, it allowed cities to use zoning laws to limit the location and concentration of businesses that specialize in sex-themed media. The Pussy Cat, an adult theater in what had been a corner gas station, challenged a Detroit ordinance. The law said an adult business could not be located within 1,000 feet of two other adult businesses, or within 500 feet of a residential neighborhood. Adult businesses included pool halls, pawnshops and adult bookstores and theaters. The intent of the ordinance was to prevent the concentration of such businesses on one street.

In an opinion by Justice John Paul Stevens, the Court upheld the Detroit ordinance. Stevens wrote that the ordinance did not impose content limitations on the creators of adult movies or significantly restrict the viewing of such movies. He concluded that the impact of the ordinance on free expression was at most incidental and minimal. Justice Stevens attempted to create a doctrine granting sexual speech less protection than political speech, noting that "it is manifest that society's interest in protecting this type of expression is of a wholly different, and lesser, magnitude, than the interest in untrammeled political debate." But only a minority of justices joined him on that point.

In 2002, the Supreme Court again found it was constitutional for cities to limit the geographic concentration of sex-themed businesses. In *City of Los Angeles v. Alameda Books, Inc.*, it upheld a Los Angeles ordinance that prohibited the presence of more than one adult business in a building. The Court said that such uses of zoning laws must be backed up by studies that document a relationship between a concentration of adult business and undesirable secondary effects such as increases in crimes such as prostitution, robbery and assault.

Rudolph Giuliani, who was then the mayor of New York City, used a Detroit-type ordinance to banish topless bars and X-rated peep shows from the Times Square area. And the highest court in the state, the New York Court of Appeals, upheld the law. The unanimous decision noted that the number of adult establishments in New York City had grown from nine in 1965 to 177 in 1993; 107 of these were in Manhattan.

DVDs, the Internet and the growth of cable television with adult networks have diminished the significance of the *Young* decision. Across the United States, adult theaters have virtually disappeared.

RATINGS AND LABELING

Young helped to shield disinterested adults from unwanted sexual expression. It empowered cities to isolate adult businesses from homes, schools and churches and made it easier for disinterested adults to avoid such businesses. Offensive businesses that are unobtrusive and easily avoided are easier to tolerate. The voluntary labeling of movies, recordings and video games has had the same effect. It gives adults fair warning about the explicit content of media and assists them in avoiding material they find offensive for themselves or their children.

The Motion Picture Association of America initiated the most successful of the rating systems after Jack Valenti took over as president in 1966. That year a new kind of frankness emerged in movies. *Who's Afraid of Virginia Woolf* included the word "screw" and the phrase "hump the hostess." More movies contained nudity. Because of the fear of government censorship, the movie industry decided to create its own system for rating films. The system has changed over the years. As it exists today, the system has five categories:

• G General Audiences. All ages are admitted. The film contains nothing in language, nudity and sex, or violence that would offend parents whose children view the film. Snippets of language may go beyond polite conversation, but they are common, everyday expressions.

• PG Parental Guidance Suggested. Some material may not be suitable for children. There may be some profanity, violence or brief nudity, but these elements are not intense. There is no drug use content.

• PG-13 Parents Strongly Cautioned. Some material may be inappropriate for children under 13. The rating is required for drug use content or use of harsher, sexually derived words.

• R Restricted. The admission of people under age 17 requires accompanying parent or adult guardian. The movie contains some adult material: hard language, tough violence, nudity within sensual scenes or drug abuse.

• NC-17 No Children Under 17 Admitted. The content of the movie is patently inappropriate for youngsters. The rating does not necessarily mean the content is obscene or pornographic. It can mean the presence of violence or sex or aberrational behavior or drug use that is too strong and therefore off-limits for viewing by children.

Leaders in the motion picture industry consider the movie rating system a success. The National Association of Theater Owners and the Video Software Dealers Association have embraced it. Polls conducted by the Opinion Research Corporation of Princeton, New Jersey, show that three-quarters of parents with children found the system very useful or fairly useful in selecting movies for their children.

The recording and video games industries have also adopted ratings, but in a more limited way. In 1985, the Recording Industry Association of America agreed to encourage its members to place the warning "Explicit Lyrics — Parental Advisory" on recordings containing references to explicit sex, violence or substance abuse. Instead of the warning, song lyrics may be printed on the back of the album cover. In 1994, the Software Publishers Association, following threats from Congress, agreed to encourage its members to label computer and video games. Games are labeled for age appropriateness and for the explicitness of violence, nudity or sex, and language.

The major advantage of such ratings is that, because they alert consumers to content, they tend to discourage the involvement of government in controlling that content. Congress has not been fully satisfied with the actions of the software industry, however, and several bills aimed at the industry were introduced but did not pass the 107th Congress.

And in 1996, with pressure from Congress, most TV networks agreed to a voluntary rating system. The six classifications are:

• TV-Y. Children's programs acceptable for kids of all ages.

• TV-Y7. Children's programs for ages seven and older that

might have material upsetting to younger kids.

• TV-G. Appropriate for audiences of all ages.

• TV-PG. Parental guidance suggested, may contain violence, sexual material or offensive language.

• TV-14. Inappropriate for kids under 14 because of more intense violence and sexual content.

• TV-MA. Not for children under 17, may contain sex, profane language or graphic violence.

Additional rating subcategories were the following: V — violence, S — sexual situations, L — coarse language, D — suggestive dialogue and FV — fantasy violence. Television sets with "V-chips" may be programmed to restrict access to different categories of programs.

SUMMARY

The landmark Supreme Court ruling in *Miller v. California* was not greatly heralded by either side of the sexual expression divide. In its aftermath, sexual-themed materials have become more available. Some of this may be attributed to technological developments that have provided easy access to the materials in private dwellings instead of public places. Increased access has occurred despite the ongoing efforts of virtually every state legislature to draft restrictive statutes. Sex-themed materials also have become quite commonplace in Canada. Under Canadian supreme court rules, portrayals of explicit sex are legal if they do not include degradation or violence.

Social mores are also arguably responsible because they clearly have grown quite tolerant of unobtrusive erotica. This often translates into less pressure on prosecutors and police to enforce obscenity laws and jurors who are less easily offended.

Nonetheless, the divide over sexual expression remains. It is part of what are referred to as the culture wars.

BIBLIOGRAPHY

Articles

Breslin, Susannah. "Adult Director Max Hardcore Released From Prison," *Forbes*, http://www.forbes.Com/sites/susannah breslin/2011/07/21/adult-director-max-hardcore-released-from -prison-2/.

Dugan, Andrew. "Women Differ on Morals of Sex, Relationships," *Gallup.com*, June 19, 2015, https://news.gallup.com/poll/183719/men-women-differ-morals-sex-relationships.aspx.

Gerstein, Josh. "Holder Accused of Neglecting Porn," *Politico*, May 16, 2011, https://www.politico.com/story/2011/04/holder-accused-of-neglecting-porn-053314.

Harris, Ron. "Grand Theft Auto' Publishers Settle with FTC," NBC, http://www.nbcnews.com/id/13227126/ns/technology_an d_science-games/t/grand-theft-auto-publishers-settle-ftc/ (updated June 9, 2006).

Hughes, Kyonzte. "Rating & Labeling Entertainment," Freedom Forum Institute, https://www.freedomforuminstitute.org/first -amendment-center/topics/freedom-of-speech-2/arts-first-ame ndment-overview/rating-labeling-entertainment/ (updated May 2006).

Leber, Rebecca. "Is Revenge Porn Legal in Your State? Based on This Map, it Probably Is, " *New Republic*, Sept. 3, 2014, https://newrepublic.com/article/119295/revenge-porn-laws-sta te-map-shows-theyre-rare-us.

Leventhal, Harold. "An Empirical Inquiry into the Effects of Miller v. California on the Control of Obscenity," 52 *New York University Law Review* 810 (1977).

Linz, Daniel. "Estimating Community Standards: The Use of Social Science Evidence in an Obscenity Prosecution," 55 *Public Opinion Quarterly* 80 (Spring 1991).

Mordock, Jeff. "Pornography Crackdown Vowed by Donald Trump Still Never Materialized, *Washington Times*, Dec. 25, 2019, https://www.washingtontimes.com/news/2019/dec/25/pornography-crackdown-vowed-trump-still-never-mate/.

Porter, David. "Major Child Porn Distributor Sentenced to 30 Years," https//www.nydailynews.com/sdut-founder-of-child-po rn-site gets 30-years-in-prison-2014jun17-story.html.

Riggs, Robert. "Miller v. California: An Empirical Note," 1981 *Brigham Young University Law Review* 247.

Ross, Philip. "More Americans Say Pornography is Morally Acceptable," *International Business Times*, June 5, 2018, https://www.ibtimes.com/porn-morally-acceptable-almost-half-men-say-yes-women-less-accepting-sex-relationship-1976503.

Silvestri, Elaine. "Filmmaker Receives 46-month Sentence," *Tampa Tribune*, Oct. 4, 2008, at Metro 1.

Weiser, Benjamin and Rashbaum, William K. "Anthony Weiner Pleads Guilty to Federal Obscenity Charge," May 20, 2017, https://www.nytimes.com/2017/05/19/nyregion/anthony-weiner-guilty-plea-sexting.html

Wright, Paul, Robert Tokunaga, & Ashely Kraus. "A Meta-Analysis of Pornography Consumption and Actual Acts of Sexual Aggression in General Population Studies," 66 *Journal of Communication* 183 (2016).

Books

Dworkin, Andrea, & Catherine MacKinnon. *Pornography and Civil Rights: A New Day for Women's Equality*. Minneapolis, Minn.: Organizing Against Pornography, 1988.

Hester, Helen. *Beyond Explicit: Pornography and the Displacement of Sex*. New York: State University of New York, 2014.

Lasky, Melvin J. *Profanity, Obscenity and the Media*. Somerset, N.J.: Transaction, 2004.

Michael, Robert T. *Sex in America: A Definitive Survey*. New York, N.Y.: Little, Brown, 1994.

Semonche, John. *Censoring Sex*. Lanham, Md.: Rowman & Littlefield, 2007.

Strossen, Nadine. *Defending Pornography: Free Speech, Sex, and the Fight for Women's Rights*. New York: Scribner, 1995.

Sunstein, Cass. *Democracy and the Problem of Free Speech*. New York, N.Y.: The Free Press, 1995.

Cases

American Booksellers Association v. Hudnut, 771 F.2d 323 (7th Cir. 1984).

Ashcroft v. ACLU, 542 U.S. 656 (2004).

Ashcroft v. American Civil Liberties Union, 535 U.S. 564 (2002).

Ashcroft v. Free Speech Coalition, 535 U.S. 234 (2002).

Barnes v. Glen Theatre, 501 U.S. 560 (1991).

Brown v. Entertainment Merchants Association, 564 U.S. 786 (2011).

City of Los Angeles v. Alameda Books, Inc., 535 U.S. 425 (2002).

Cohen v. California, 403 U.S. 15 (1971).

Erie v. Pap's A.M., 529 U.S. 277 (2000).

Erznoznik v. Jacksonville, 422 U.S. 205 (1975).

FCC v. CBS, 556 U.S. 1218 (2009).

FCC v. Fox Television Stations, 556 U.S. 502 (2009).

FCC v. Fox Television Stations, 567 U.S. 239 (2012).

FCC v. Pacifica Foundation, 438 U.S. 726 (1978).

Ginsberg v. New York, 390 U.S. 629 (1968).

Ginzburg v. United States, 383 U.S. 463 (1966).

In re: S.K. No. 41, 215 A.3d 300 (Md. 2019).

Interstate Circuit v. Dallas, 390 U.S. 676 (1968).

Jacobellis v. Ohio, 378 U.S. 184 (1964).

Jenkins v. Georgia, 418 U.S. 153 (1974).

Kaplan v. California, 413 U.S. 114 (1973).

Manual Enterprises v. Day, 370 U.S. 478 (1962).

Memoirs v. Massachusetts, 383 U.S. 413 (1966).

Miller v. California, 413 U.S. 15 (1973).

Mishkin v. New York, 383 U.S. 502 (1966).

Near v. Minnesota 283 U.S. 697 (1931).

New York v. Ferber, 458 U.S. 747 (1982).

Osborne v. Ohio, 495 U.S. 103 (1990).

Paris Adult Theatre I v. Slaton, 413 U.S. 49 (1973).

Pope v. Illinois, 481 U.S. 497 (1987).

Redrup v. New York, 386 U.S. 767 (1967).

Reno v. ACLU, 521 U.S. 844 (1977).

Roth v. United States, 354 U.S. 476 (1957).

Stanley v. Georgia, 394 U.S. 557 (1969).

State v. Henry, 732 P.2d 9 (Or. 1987).

United States v. Am. Library Ass'n, 539 U.S. 194 (2003).

United States v. Playboy Entm't, 529 U.S. 803 (2000).

Walker v. Ohio, 398 U.S. 434 (1970).

Young v. American Mini Theatres, Inc., Young v. American Mini Theatres, Inc., 427 U.S. 50 (1976).

Web Site

Enforcement Policies Regarding Broadcast Indecency, http://www.fcc.gov.

Defamation

By Kyu Ho Youm

Freedom of speech is not absolute. It must be balanced against other competing social interests. One area in which such balancing must occur is that of defamation. As the U.S. Supreme Court noted in *Gertz v. Robert Welch, Inc.*, "[A]bsolute protection for the communications media requires a total sacrifice of the competing value served by the law of defamation."

The libel law of a society indicates to a large extent how the society balances the importance of reputational interests with freedom of speech. Harm to reputation has been a criminal offense or a civil wrong since civilization's earliest days, but the social and cultural approach to reputation as a value varies from society to society. Professor Robert C. Post elaborates in a 1986 law review article:

Defamation law would operate differently in a deference society than in a market society. In the latter, reputation is a quintessentially private possession; it is created by individual effort and is of importance primarily to those who have created it. Reputation's claim to legal protection is neither greater nor less than the claim to public protection of similar private goods. The preservation of honor in a deference society, on the other hand, entails more than the protection of merely individual interests. Since honor is not created by individual labor, but instead by shared social perceptions that transcend the behavior of particular persons, honor is "public good, not merely a private possession."

In the United States, defamation was one of the earliest legal actions available against the press, and it is still the most common legal danger. Libel remains an occupational hazard for professional and non-professional communicators. Indeed, as libel law expert W. Wat Hopkins noted in 2021, "In the last half-dozen years or so, the number of defamation suits by and against public figures has grown considerably."

In June 2022, for example, actor Johnny Depp won a jury verdict against his former wife, Amber Heard, for defamation over her *Washington Post* op-ed of 2018. He was awarded $10.35 million in damages. More recently, Fox News was liable for more than $787 million to Dominion Voting Systems in the largest ever settlement in a defamation lawsuit.

Libel has the very real possibility of chilling speech, particularly when one considers the ramifications of a libel suit. As attorney Barbara Dill writes:

Libel law in the United States is at a critical juncture. The old broken formula of sue-and-be-sued is not working well for anyone but lawyers. It costs too much, takes too long, and clogs the courts with fencing matches that end most often in technical decisions that bypass the fundamental issues and satisfy neither side.

The chill caused by libel law is clearly an irony, since press freedom is protected as a constitutional right but reputation is not. In many ways, First Amendment scholar Frederick Schauer writes, "[T]he American approach ... reflects a society in which the press is considered to occupy a much more important role in the resolution of public issues. The press occupies a special position in the American system, a position that accounts for its strong protection against inhibiting defamation laws."

Libel suits are common, and they are not limited to traditional mainstream media and professional communicators. So-called "citizen journalists" or bloggers on social media are often the targets of libel litigation. In an important Internet libel case, *Obsidian Finance Group v. Cox*, the Ninth U.S. Circuit Court of Appeals held in 2014 that under the First Amendment, bloggers with no institutional media connections are no different from professional journalists formally affiliated with the traditional press. "In defamation cases," the court stated, "the public-figure status of a plaintiff and the public importance of the statement at issue not the identity of the speaker — provide the First Amendment touchstone."

Attorney Bruce Sanford identifies these key cyberlibel issues:

- Should courts treat the Internet like print media or television?
- Does the new forum impact the public official/public figure inquiry?
- When online "journalists" are not backed by editors and lawyers, should they be held to the same standards of care as traditional journalists?
- Can liability for defamation arise out of "linking" to a site with libelous content?

In any case, instead of being passive, traditional and new media practitioners can be proactive in an attempt to stay out of trouble and to provide themselves with more protection should they be sued.

This chapter first reviews defamation law from the plaintiff's perspective and then provides an overview of libel defense strategies. It focuses on the elements of a cause of action for libel and related areas, including the technological impact of cyberspace and the emerging legal issues confronting news media and individuals around the world. It also explores various libel defenses the media use in accomplishing a great social good by publishing allegedly defamatory material.

DEFAMATION DEFINED

Defamation — the publication of material that would tend to hold one up to hatred, ridicule, contempt or scorn — consists of twin torts: libel and slander. In general, libel is the publication of defamatory matter by written or printed words or by some other physical form. Slander is defamatory communication by spoken words, gestures or other transitory means.

The distinction between libel and slander originated when relatively few people could read, and the spoken word was more credible. Since then, the written word has gained more credibility, and defamation by writing is perceived to cause greater harm. More recently, however, new modes of communication have developed that often make the distinction between libel and slander obsolete. Defamation by means of television or radio, for example, might have more impact and greater reach than that by a small newspaper. Modern legal guides such as *Restatement (Second) of Torts* suggest that, instead of the form of medium, courts should consider the area of dissemination, the deliberate and premeditated character of a publication and the persistence of the defamation when classifying a defamatory statement as libel or slander.

Jurisdictions disagree on whether defamation by electronic means should be defined as libel or slander. Most states do not distinguish libel from slander with regard to broadcasting; but four, including California, treat defamatory radio and television broadcasts as slander; and thirteen states, including New York, treat it as libel. In *Shor v. Billingsley,* a New York court explained its rationale:

When account is taken of the vast and far-flung audience reached by radio today, often far greater in number than the readers of the largest metropolitan newspaper, it is evident that the broadcast of scandalous utterances is in general as potentially harmful ... as a publication by writing. That defamation by radio, in the absence of a script or transcription, lacks the measure of durability possessed by written libel, in nowise lessens its capacity for harm.

Some states — Connecticut and Tennessee are two — make a distinction between a statement broadcast from a script — libel — and that which is ad-libbed — slander. An appellate court in Georgia, noting that television broadcasting contains both libel and slander, coined the word "defamacast" to describe broadcast defamation. The court said, "Perhaps the most perplexing problem is whether defamatory material shown on television should be classified as a libel, a slander or in some third category." The court decided to classify this type of material:

Believing as we do that the common law must adapt, and classically has adapted, to meet new situations, we now make that "frank recognition..." that defamation by radio and television falls into a new category, thus completing the triptych.

In this category, defamation by broadcast or "defamacast" is actionable *per se,* according to the Georgia Court of Appeals in *American Broadcasting Paramount-Theaters v. Simpson.*

While debate on the issue continues, an increasing number of jurisdictions are accepting the position that, because of the wide dissemination and the increased power of the broadcast media, defamation by electronic means is closer to libel than slander.

THE RATIONALE AND REACH OF LIBEL LAW

Libel law protects the reputational interests of individuals because it involves statements about them made by others. Legal scholar David Anderson has identified four types of reputational harm in the context of relational interest. The defamation may (1) interfere with the plaintiff's existing relationships with other people; (2) interfere with future relationships; (3) destroy a favorable public image; or (4) create a negative public image for a person who previously had no public image at all.

Libel law also serves other important societal interests. It attempts to compensate for economic and emotional injury and promotes human dignity by providing a civilized forum in which a dispute is settled.

More importantly, libel law acts as a deterrent on the publication of false and injurious speech through the award of damages. In *Keeton v. Hustler,* the U.S. Supreme Court has noted, for example, that a state "may rightly employ its libel laws to discourage the deception of its citizens." In addition, libel law serves a vital social interest by providing a check on media power. As showcased by the case of *Dominion Voting Systems v. Fox News Network,* libel law opens the newsgathering and decision-making process of the media to public scrutiny and accountability. A federal judge in a libel action by former Israeli Defense Minister Ariel Sharon against *Time* magazine explained:

Time has refused to issue any correction or to print plaintiff's denial. Only through the litigation process has plaintiff been able to uncover and publish the evidence from which *Time* claimed to have learned the contents of [a secret document relating to the Beirut massacre in 1982]. And only through this avenue has he been able to bring to light the process by which the allegedly offending statement came to be written, including evidence of the possible motivations and truthfulness of its author. That this process has proved enormously expensive, and painfully contentious, is as much the product of

Time's all-out litigation strategy as of any plan by plaintiff to intimidate the press.

Meanwhile, libel law is subject to jurisdictional issues. Indeed, this is strikingly relevant, albeit not frequently, when the ecclesiastical abstention doctrine is invoked. In 2021, for example, the Texas Supreme Court held in the case *In re Diocese of Lubbock* that it had no jurisdiction over a deacon's libel claim relating to the diocese's publication of a list of sexually abusive clergy. The court reasoned that the publication of the list was intertwined with the diocese's internal investigation of the sexual abuse of minors by clergy.

Constitutional and State Law

Although the Constitution does not explicitly recognize reputational rights, courts have often noted the value of a good name. In an oft-quoted opinion, Justice Potter Stewart, in *Rosenblatt v. Baer,* characterized an individual's right to protection of reputation as "a concept at the root of any decent system of ordered liberty." He explained: "The protection of private personality, like the protection of life itself, is left primarily to the individual States under the Ninth and Tenth Amendments. But this does not mean that the right is entitled to any less recognition by this Court as a basic of our constitutional system." The Supreme Court, therefore, in *Milkovivh v. Lorain Journal,* has recognized that "society has a pervasive and strong interest in preventing and redressing attacks upon reputation."

The Constitution, of course, is not the only source of law to be used in balancing free speech and reputational rights. State constitutions and common law play a significant role in protecting press rights and in allowing individuals to protect their reputations. State statutes can also affect libel conflicts. Statutes of limitations — laws that prevent stale lawsuits from being adjudicated — and retraction statutes — which can mitigate or eliminate some damages — are examples of state laws that directly affect libel.

In addition, the First Amendment principle that prior restraint is presumptively unconstitutional applies to attempts to restrain material because it may be defamatory. In 2005, the Supreme Court refused to rule on the question of whether the First Amendment ever may allow a permanent injunction against defamation relating to prior restraint. In *Tory v. Cochran,* the Court sidestepped the substantive First Amendment issues over the injunction attorney Johnnie L. Cochran Jr. had obtained to prevent his former client Ulysses Tory from his continuing defamation.[1] When Cochran died while the Supreme Court reviewed the California court's injunction, the Court

---

[1] For a detailed discussion of *Tory v. Cochran, see* Chapter 4.

ruled that the injunction was an overbroad prior restraint upon speech because it lacked "plausible justification."

Regardless, several state supreme courts have addressed injunction as a possible option in libel law. They recognized a possibility of defamatory statements being subject to prior restraint in limited circumstances.

In 2007, for example, the California Supreme Court ruled that an injunction can be issued to prohibit repetition of defamatory statements. In *Balvoa Island Village Inn, Inc. v. Lemen*, the California high court reasoned:

> [P]reventing a person from speaking or publishing something that, allegedly, would constitute a libel if spoken or published is far different from issuing a post-trial injunction *after* a statement that already has been uttered has been found to constitute defamation. Prohibiting a person from making a statement or publishing a writing *before* that statement is spoken or the writing is published is far different from prohibiting a defendant from *repeating* a statement or *republishing* a writing that has been determined at trial to be defamatory and, thus, unlawful. This distinction is hardly novel.

In 2010, the Kentucky Supreme Court followed suit in adopting the so-called "modern rule" permitting injunctions against defamation. In *Hill v. Petrotech Resources Corp.*, it wrote:

> [D]efamatory speech may be enjoined only after the trial court's final determination by a preponderance of the evidence that the speech at issue is, in fact, false, and only then upon the condition that the injunction be narrowly tailored to limit the prohibited speech to that which has been judicially determined to be false.

But the First U.S. Circuit Court of Appeals rejected the modern rule in 2018. The court held in *Sindi v. El-Moslimany* that anti-libel injunctions against repetition of adjudicated defamatory statements violate the First Amendment because such injunctions do not pay attention to the protected or unprotected context of the statements. "The cardinal vice of the injunction" at issue, the federal appellate court stated, "is its failure to make any allowance for contextual variation." The court continued that "[r]efined to bare essence," the injunction bans "repeating certain words, regardless of their purpose in employing them," so it likely prohibits protected speech more extensively than necessary under the First Amendment.

Criminal Libel

As the Media Law Resource Center noted, "[I]t is hard to square modern First Amendment principles with laws that purport to criminalize statements that allegedly harm reputation." Colorado repealed its criminal libel law in 2012. But at least eleven states have statutes that allow the government to prosecute people for libel, and criminal libel prosecutions continue. In his in-depth study of criminal libel, journalism scholar David Pritchard stated that criminal libel is more frequently used than media law texts acknowledge. He wrote that the Internet is an increasingly important factor that precipitates criminal libel prosecutions. A New Hampshire man, for example, was arrested in 2018 under New Hampshire criminal libel law for his online comment on Exeter Police Chief William Shupe. But his criminal libel charges were dropped because there was no evidence of his knowledge of the comment's falsity

The Supreme Court has *not* repudiated criminal libel. Indeed, in *Garrison v. Louisiana*, it extended the actual malice rule — knowledge of falsity or reckless disregard of the truth — to criminal libel.

Criminal libel had its genesis in *De Libellis Famosis*, an English case in which Lord Coke delineated the principal points of the action:

> Every libel is made either against a private man, or against a magistrate or public person. If it be against a private man it deserves a severe punishment, for although the libel be made against one, yet it incites all those of the same family, kindred or society to revenge, and so tends *per consequens* to quarrels and breach of the peace, and may be the cause of the shedding of blood and greater inconvenience; if it be against a magistrate, or other public person, it is a greater offense; for it concerns not only the breach of the peace, but also the scandal of Government; for what greater scandal of Government can there be than to have corrupt and wicked magistrates to be appointed by the King to govern his subjects?

Courts have approached criminal libel in various ways, usually based on the actual malice requirement. In *Fitts v. Kolb* of 1991, for example, a U.S. district court struck down South Carolina's criminal libel statute, finding it unconstitutional because it based liability on common law malice — ill will, spite or hatred — rather than actual malice. Four years later, however, the Tenth U.S. Circuit Court of Appeals in *Phelps v. Hamilton* upheld Kansas's criminal libel statute. The court held that the law is not unconstitutional on its face because it requires actual malice to be proved in libel cases involving matters of public concern. The First Circuit in *Frese v. Formella* was no different in holding in 2022 that New Hampshire's criminal libel law is constitutional under the Supreme Court's decision in *Garrison*.

The First Circuit, in *Mangual v. Rotger-Sabat*, struck down Puerto Rico's criminal libel law on the ground that it lacked the actual malice requirement and truth as a defense. Likewise, in

2007, the Washington Court of Appeals in *Parmelee v. O'Neel* held the Washington criminal libel statute unconstitutional because it punished a false defamatory statement made without actual malice or a true defamatory statement made with no good motives or intent. Further, the Washington appellate court found that the criminal libel law was fatally overbroad and vague. The court reasoned that the law allowed punishment of permitted speech and that it did not define "malice," so creating a possible confusion between the common law malice and actual malice. Similarly, a California appeals court in *Summit Bank v. Rogers* struck down a 1917 state law that criminalized making false statements or disseminating false rumors about a bank's financial condition. The court found that the pre-actual malice statute did not clearly require that the prosecutor prove the defendant's knowledge of falsity or reckless disregard for the truth.

Regardless, criminal libel is not necessarily an exercise in futility. Professor Pritchard's empirical research concludes:

> Criminal libel is a legitimate legal tool to use when the reputations of private figures have been harmed by defamatory comments that have nothing to do with public issues. Criminal libel can be especially useful for people of limited means, those who would have difficulty finding lawyers to pursue civil lawsuits for libel. Criminal libel may also be useful in curbing defamatory gossip on the Internet.

THE PLAINTIFF'S CASE

Before the Supreme Court constitutionalized libel law in 1964 with *New York Times Co. v. Sullivan*, the basic requirement for a plaintiff in making a case for defamation was proof that the defendant published a statement about the plaintiff that had a tendency to harm the plaintiff's reputation in the community or to discourage other people from associating or dealing with the plaintiff. The burden was on the plaintiff to prove three essential elements: identification of the plaintiff in the allegedly defamatory material, publication of the material by the defendant, and the defamatory nature of the material.

But the requirements in a modern libel action are not that simple. To win damages, especially in libel actions against the media, a plaintiff must establish that: (1) a false *and* defamatory statement of fact concerning the plaintiff was published to a third party, (2) the publication was not privileged and was made with fault on the part of the publisher, and (3) the publication caused actual injury.

For cyberlibel, a plaintiff has to identify the originator(s) of libel who posted anonymously on the Internet. The plaintiff asks a court to order ISPs to identify the defamer. For several years, many courts have followed a test established by a New Jersey appellate court in the case *Dendrite International, Inc. v.*

Doe. Applying the so-called "Dendrite Test," for example, a Tennessee circuit court in *Swartz v. Doe* held that to determine whether a plaintiff is entitled to discover the identity of an anonymous defendant, the plaintiff must:

1. Attempt to notify an anonymous online defendant that he or she is the subject of a subpoena or application for order of disclosure;
2. give the defendant a reasonable time to file opposition to the application;
3. identify the exact statements purportedly made by each anonymous online defendant that give rise to each claim;
4. make a prima facie or substantial showing of proof for each element of each cause of action.

If a plaintiff has successfully complied with the first four requirements and the court concludes that a substantial showing of proof has been made, the fifth and final step is for the court to balance the First Amendment interests of the anonymous defendant against the strength of the plaintiff's prima facie case and the need for disclosure to allow the claims to proceed.

Falsity

Under the common law, when a libel action was filed, statements upon which the action was based were presumed to be false. As a matter of constitutional law, however, that presumption of falsity has been rejected. Libel plaintiffs now must prove the statements are false, even if they were made with ill will.

Judge Robert Sack of the Second U.S. Circuit Court of Appeals, in the highly acclaimed treatise *Sack on Defamation*, wrote that under the constitutional rule, "Truth is usually now not a *defense*. Proof of falsity is instead part of the plaintiff's case, at least in defamation suits brought by public officials, or involving communications about public issues, or both."

Meanwhile, the falsity requirement should not concern the trivial inaccuracies of the challenged statement. As the Tenth Circuit observed in 2011, the plaintiff must establish that the defamatory statement is not only false but material as well. "To qualify as *material* the alleged misstatement must be likely to cause reasonable people to think 'significantly less favorably' about the plaintiff than they would if they knew the truth," the federal appeals court explained in *Bustos v. A&E Television Networks*. "[A] misstatement is not actionable if the comparative harm to the plaintiff's reputation is real but only modest."

Defamation

In addition to being false, offending material must be defamatory. Identifying defamatory language is the first order of business in libel law. As libel law scholar Philip Wittenberg wrote, however, "[W]ords are not single faced. They have many facets and may have many interpretations. Their values change with time, with place, and with association. Whether a word has a libelous connotation will therefore require analysis and perception in terms of its milieu and period." Earlier, Supreme Court Justice Oliver Wendell Holmes observed in *Towne v. Eisner*: "A word is not a crystal, transparent and unchanged; it is the skin of a living thought and may vary greatly in color and content according to the circumstances and the time in which it is used." Thus, the same words may communicate different meanings in different contexts.

Words can be ambiguous. Love, democracy, communism and other words are capable of many connotations and interpretations. One cannot say with assurance that a word is or is not defamatory without placing it in time, in location, and in association so that its meaning can be determined. As the Hawaii Supreme Court held in *Beamer v. Nishiki*, whether a statement is defamatory "depends, among other factors, upon the temper of times, the current of contemporary public opinion, with the result that a word, harmless in one age, in one community, may be highly damaging to reputation at another time or in a different place." In *Yonaty v. Mincolla*, for example, a New York appellate court held in 2012 that falsely calling someone lesbian, gay or bisexual is not defamatory *per se*. It reasoned: "[P]rior cases categorizing statements that falsely impute homosexuality as defamatory *per se* are based on the flawed premise that it is shameful and disgraceful to be described as lesbian, gay or bisexual."

Compendiums of words cannot be considered a foolproof formula to divining how courts will rule on similar language, but they can often be warning signs for possible trouble. In addition, there are categories of words that are especially sensitive. According to media lawyer Neil Rosini, words are defamatory, for example, if they

- impute to another a loathsome disease;
- accuse another of serious sexual misconduct;
- impugn another's honesty or integrity;
- accuse another of committing a crime or of being arrested or indicted;
- allege racial, ethnic or religious bigotry;
- impugn another's financial health or credit-worthiness;
- accuse another of associating with criminals or others of unsavory character;
- assert incompetence or lack of ability in one's trade, business, profession or office.

Interpreting Defamation. Defamation is recipient-oriented. That is, it hinges on how the language is interpreted by its recipients.

"Red-Flag Words"

Attorney and libel expert Bruce Sanford has listed a number of so-called "red-flag words" that courts often consider defamatory. They are:

addict, adulteration of products, adultery, AIDS, alcoholic, altered records, atheist, bad moral character, bankrupt, bigamist, blacklisted, blackmail, booze-hound, bribery, brothel, buys votes, cheats, child abuse, collusion, con artist, confidence man, corruption, coward, crook, deadbeat, defaulter, divorced, double crosser, drug abuser, drunkard, ex-convict, fawning sycophant, fraud, gambling den, gangster, gay, graft, groveling office seeker, herpes, hit-man, hypocrite, illegitimate, illicit relation, incompetent, infidelity, informer, insider trading, intemperate, intimate, intolerance, Jekyll-Hyde personality, kept woman, Ku Klux Klan, Mafia, manipulate, mental illness, mobster, moral delinquency, mouthpiece, Nazi, neo-Nazi, paramour, peeping Tom, perjurer, plagiarist, pockets public funds, profiteering, prostitute, rape/rapist, scam, scandalmonger, scoundrel, seducer, sham, sharp dealing, shyster, slacker, smooth and tricky, smuggler, sneaky, solid influence, sold out, spy, stool pigeon, stuffed the ballot box, suicide, swindle, taken, thief, unethical, unmarried mother, unprofessional, unsound mind, unworthy of credit, vice den, villain.

From Bruce W. Sanford, *Libel and Privacy* § 4.13 (2d ed. 2022).

Thus, the first step in analyzing the defamatory nature of a statement is determining whether the readers could interpret the words to be defamatory and whether they did so. The value judgments, knowledge and background of recipients will affect their interpretations of statements. For example, people who support abortion as a constitutional right of privacy would not consider it defamatory for a person to be depicted as being "pro-choice," while those who view abortion as morally reprehensible might lose their reputations among a certain group by being so depicted. So, whose understanding of a defamatory statement is used in establishing the defamatory nature of the statement?

The *Restatement (Second) of Torts*, a tract designed to explain the law, states:

It is enough that the communication would tend to prejudice [the plaintiff] in the eyes of *a substantial and respectable minority* of [the community but] it is not enough that the communication would be derogatory in the view of a single individual or a very small group of persons, if the group is not large enough to constitute a substantial minority [emphasis added].

As an example, a prison inmate was unsuccessful in maintaining a libel action when he was identified as an FBI informant because, the Delaware Superior Court found *in Saunders v. WHYY*, he was not accused of unlawful or improper conduct. Noting that the defamatory statement must expose the plaintiff to public ridicule "in the minds of 'right thinking persons' or among 'a considerable and respectable class of people,'" the court stated:

> It is true that a charge of informing may bring opprobrium from one's fellow inmates in the prison community. However, it is not one's reputation in a limited community in which attitudes and social values may depart substantially from those prevailing generally which an action for defamation is designed to protect.

Rules of Construction. Most states use the reasonable construction rule to determine the defamatory nature of a statement. The meaning of a communication, according to the *Restatement,* "is that which the recipient correctly, or mistakenly but reasonably, understands it was intended to express." The rule does not allow a strained interpretation. In *Kelly v. Arrington,* the Alabama Supreme Court provided a good explication of the rule:

> [T]he printed words are to be taken in their natural meaning, and according to the sense in which they appear to have been used and the idea they are adapted to convey to those who read them. A forced construction is not to be put upon them in order to relieve the defendant from liability, nor are they to be subjected to the critical analysis of a trained legal mind, but must be construed and determined by the natural and probable effect on the mind of the average lay reader.

The innocent-construction rule in Illinois, as set forth by the Illinois Supreme Court in *Chapski v. Copley Press,* requires a statement "to be considered in context, with the words and the implications there from given their natural and obvious meaning; if, as so construed, the statement may reasonably be innocently interpreted or reasonably be interpreted as referring to someone other than the plaintiff it cannot be actionable *per se.*" The rule has been under considerable attack over the years, but in 2006 the Illinois Supreme Court upheld it because, the court said, it advances free speech interests and promotes the robust discussion of daily affairs.

In Ohio, the innocent construction rule was first recognized by the Ohio Supreme Court in 1983. And the common law libel defense has never been questioned. In recent years, it has more regularly applied. In 2023, for example, while refusing to find the word "prey" innocent, the Ohio Court of Appeals in Hartman v. Kerch restated the rule: "If allegedly defamatory words are susceptible to two meanings, one defamatory and one innocent, the defamatory meaning should be rejected, and the innocent meaning adopted.

The *Restatement* declares that a report of a single act of mis-

conduct in the course of a person's business, trade, profession or office may be sufficient to support a libel action, even though the charge does not imply a habitual course of conduct. A number of states, however, have adopted the single-instance rule, which provides that a charge of ignorance or a mistake on a single occasion is not actionable unless special damages can be shown. The rule is based on the common-sense premise that people make mistakes, and to state that a professional has made a mistake in a specific instance should not cause damage because the statement only implies that the person is human.

Implication. Defamation by implication occurs when false impressions arise from truthful statements. It demonstrates the larger problem of determining the meaning of an allegedly defamatory communication by examining the words in context. The Texas Supreme Court, whose analysis of defamation by implication in *Dallas Morning News v. Tatum* is refreshingly informative, held in *Turner v. KTRK Television*: "A publication can convey a false and defamatory meaning by omitting or juxtaposing facts, even though all the story's individual statements considered in isolation were literally true or non-defamatory." One example of such defamation by omission is a story the *Memphis Press-Scimitar* published. It reported that Mrs. Ruth A. Nichols was treated for a bullet wound she received when another woman found her with the woman's husband in the Nichols home. According to witnesses, the woman fired at her husband and then at Mrs. Nichols. The story was true. The Tennessee Supreme Court held in *Memphis Publishing Co. v. Nichols,* however, that the story was defamatory because it omitted crucial facts. What the paper did not report was that Mrs. Nichols and the suspect's husband were not alone in the home. Mrs. Nichols' husband and two neighbors were also there, and Mr. Nichols had attempted to prevent the shooting.

Defamation through implication often arises in one of three contexts: (1) when a writer tries to guide a reader to a conclusion without stating the conclusion; (2) when a writer is ambiguous, offering multiple meanings, at least one of which is defamatory; (3) when a writer juxtaposes one message with another, creating an implication that is not necessarily intended.

One media law text finds that proof of defamation by implication requires a combination of elements, defined by the terms "inducement," "innuendo" and "colloquium," explained here:

> If the plaintiffs themselves are not directly named they must show by "colloquium" that the statements were "of and concerning" them. If it is still not clear how the plaintiffs have been defamed, they must plead extrinsic facts that would permit a defamatory meaning to be applied to defendants' words. This allegation of extrinsic facts is called the "inducement...." Where a statement is not clearly defamatory on its

face it is the function of the innuendo to assert the meaning that plaintiff attaches to the passage and any additions by colloquium and inducement. The innuendo is not a fact but is the plaintiff's assertion of how the passage would be understood by those who heard the defendant's words and knew the additional unstated facts.

To state, for example, that John Doe ran his car into a utility pole is not defamatory since he has every right to do so. But when it is specifically pleaded as "inducement" that Doe insured the car and, as "innuendo," that the statement is construed to mean that he was defrauding the insurance company, a charge of property damage is clearly implied, which is defamatory.

The Supreme Court has not addressed the issue of whether those who defame through implication are liable for damages. Several lower courts, however — including courts in Connecticut, the District of Columbia, Louisiana and Michigan — have declined to recognize liability for defamatory implications. The basis for the rulings appears to be this premise, according to Judge Sack:

> If unrestrained ... the theory of libel by implication would allow a jury to draw whatever inferences it wished, truthful or otherwise, from statements of fact. It would thereby permit liability for the mere tone of a publication, for statements that are in substance opinion or true, or for statements about public persons that do not pass the "actual malice" test because they do not constitute knowing falsity or "reckless disregard" for the truth.

In *Forsher v. Bugliosi*, the California Supreme Court, for example, noted that a false and defamatory meaning cannot be based on "the fact that some person might, with extra sensitive perception, understand such a meaning.... Rather, the test ... is whether by reasonable implication a defamatory meaning may be found in the communication." On the other hand, an increasing number of jurisdictions have accepted libel by implication. In 2007, the Iowa Supreme Court in *Stevens v. Iowa Newspapers*, expressly adopted the principle of defamation by implication. "Otherwise," it stated, "by a careful choice of words in juxtaposition of statements in a publication, a potential defendant may make statements that are true yet just as damaging as if they were actually false." More recently, in recognizing defamation by implication in 2019, the Idaho Supreme Court in *Verity v. USA Today* followed the Iowa Supreme Court in *Stevens*.

Libel *Per Se* and Libel *Per Quod*. A statement that is libelous *per se* is defamatory on its face. That is, the defamation is apparent in the statement. If additional information is required before a statement is defamatory, the statement is libelous *per quod*, and

a plaintiff must prove special damages — that there was, in fact, a loss of money — before the plaintiff can recover.

The distinction between libel *per se* and libel *per quod* was weakened in 1974 when, in *Gertz v. Robert Welch, Inc.*, the Supreme Court required plaintiffs to prove damages before recovering. For example, the Missouri Supreme Court no longer recognizes a distinction between libel *per se* and libel *per quod*. That court stated in *Nazeri v. Missouri Valley College* that the rule created unjustifiable inequities by requiring a higher standard of proof for certain defamations:

> [I]n defamation cases the old rules of *per se* and *per quod* do not apply and plaintiff need only to plead and prove the unified defamation elements. In short, plaintiffs need not concern themselves with whether the defamation was *per se* or *per quod*, or with whether special damages exist, but must prove actual damages in all cases.

In twenty-six jurisdictions, however, the *per se/per quod* distinction remains as a rule of law. Iowa is one of them. In *Bierman v. Weier*, the Iowa Supreme Court refused to abrogate libel *per se*. Beth Weier and her father, Gail Bierman, sued Scott Weier and Author Solutions, Inc., a vanity press. In his memoir, Scott Weier said his former wife, Beth, as a child had been molested by Bierman. In granting summary judgment for the plaintiffs, the trial court ruled that the allegations by the non-media defendants were defamatory *per se*. Iowa defamation law distinguishes media from non-media defendants: "[L]ibel *per se* is available only when a private figure plaintiff sues a non-media defendant for certain kinds of defamatory statements that do not concern a matter of public importance."

Noting that neither the First Amendment nor the Iowa Constitution compelled abolition of the libel *per se/per quod* distinction, the Iowa Supreme Court in *Bierman* found that the libel *per se* doctrine was useful when actual damages are difficult to prove. The court further stated that "[w]e are not persuaded ... that the Internet's ability to restore reputations matches its ability to destroy them."

Statements of Fact

For an allegedly defamatory statement to be actionable — that is, for a lawsuit to be based upon the statement — the statement must be one of fact rather than of opinion. In *Gertz*, the Supreme Court held:

> Under the First Amendment there is no such thing as a false idea. However pernicious an opinion may seem, we depend for its correction not on the conscience of judges and juries but on the competition of other ideas. But there is no constitu-

tional value in false statements of fact.

And in *Milkovich v. Lorain Journal* the Court held that for a statement to be actionable, it must be provably false.

The threshold question facing the opinion defense is how to distinguish fact from opinion. The judge decides whether a statement is a statement of fact or opinion. If the judge cannot determine whether a particular statement constitutes fact or opinion, the jury makes the determination.

Identification

In order to win a libel action, a plaintiff must prove that he or she was identified, that is, that the defamation was "of and concerning" the plaintiff. Identification has nothing to do with the intent of the publisher of the defamation. As Paul Ashley, author of *Say It Safely,* put it, "The test is not whom the story intends to name but who a part of the audience may reasonably think is named — 'not who is meant but who is hit.'"

Identification does not always mean that the plaintiff must be named. The plaintiff can be identified by other information within the published material or by extrinsic facts not included in the published material. And the plaintiff need not show every viewer or reader of the material identified the plaintiff, but that some significant number did.

A landmark Illinois case, *John v. Tribune Co.*, provides a good example of how identification can cause unique problems. The case began when the *Chicago Tribune* reported about a police raid on a prostitution operation in an apartment house. Two articles identified the arrested owner as Dorothy Clark, also known as "Dolores Reising, 57, alias Eve Spiro and Eve John." By sheer coincidence, a woman whose maiden name was Eve Spiro and whose name at the time of the raid was Eve John was living in the basement of the raided building. She was a practicing psychologist and was not involved with the prostitution operation. She sued for libel. The Illinois Supreme Court in *John* held that the alias names could not be read as identifying Eve Spiro John as the target of the publication. Thus, there was no identification of the plaintiff in the *Tribune* story.

Pictures of persons identified by fictitious names can also create headaches for the media. In 1982, *TV Guide* published an ad for an upcoming television documentary series on teenage pregnancy. The ad's heading asked in large, bold letters: "GUESS WHAT LORI FOUND OUT TODAY." In the middle of the advertisement was a photograph of a diary that contained the handwritten entry: "Dear Diary: I found out today that I'm pregnant. What will I do now?" Directly below the diary was a photograph of a teenager embracing a young man.

Libby Sue Chumley sued *TV Guide* for a false implication that she was pregnant. She claimed she was the girl in the pic-

ture and that she was not and had never been pregnant. She further asserted that she never engaged in sexual relations with the young man in the photograph or with anyone else.

In 1984, the Georgia Supreme Court in *Triangle Publications v. Chumley* ruled that the ad was "of and concerning" Chumley. It rejected the argument that the ad did not identify Chumley because "Lori" was the name used in the ad even though the photograph was of Chumley. The court reasoned that the bold print of the advertisement and the strategic placement of the photo made it possible for people to interpret Chumley to be "Lori," a pregnant teenager.

In a "libel in fiction" claim, the U.S. Court of Appeals for the Second Circuit found that the producers of *Wolf of Wall Street* had no actual malice in making false and defamatory statements about Andrew Greene, a former executive at the real-life brokerage firm, Stratton Oakmont, that was featured in the 2013 film. In *Greene v. Paramount Pictures*, the federal appeals court reasoned that the film makers "took appropriate steps to ensure that no one would be defamed by the film" and that no reasonable viewer would believe that Paramount Pictures intended the character in the movie, Nicky "Rugrat" Koskoff, to depict Green. The Second Circuit also noted that the defendants were aware that the Koskoff character was a fictitious character comprised of three different people. And the court paid additional attention to a disclaimer in the fictional film.

In addition, the Supreme Court has said that races or other large groups of people cannot win libel actions because individual members of the groups must be identified. The *Restatement* delineates the "small group libel doctrine" this way:

> One who publishes defamatory matter concerning a group or class of persons is subject to liability to an individual member of it if, but only if: (a) the group or class is so small that the matter can reasonably be understood to refer to the member; or (b) the circumstances of publication reasonably give rise to the conclusion that there is a particular reference to the member.

The rationale for the rule, according to media attorney Rex Heinke, is that, "First, defamatory statements do little damage to the reputation of any member of a group larger than twenty-five if the defamation refers to all members of the group.... Second, the price to be paid by making such statements actionable is simply too high" for freedom of expression.

The cut-off point for identification probably ranges from about twenty-five to about one hundred. For example, the Second Circuit applied the small group libel doctrine in 2017 in finding that the three members of the fifty-three-member Phi Kappa Psi fraternity at the University of Virginia had a plausible libel claim against *Rolling Stone* over its 2014 article on the alleged fraternity's gang rape. The Second Circuit in *Elias v. Rolling Stone* reasoned: "Taking the allegations in the Article together, a reader could plausibly conclude that many or all fraternity members participated in alleged gang rape as an initiation ritual and all members knowingly turned a blind eye to the brutal crimes."

More recently, the South Carolina Court of Appeals in *Garrard v. Charleston County School District* held that a high school football team, which the defendant newspaper called "racist douchebags," was not "a small group," so the newspaper article challenged did not concern any of the team members. The court explained: "The article did not reference any names nor did it include any pictures of the members of the football team." Plus, the court found, the newspaper published no fact or commentary "specific to any particular member" of the team.

While members of groups can be defamed if the groups are small enough, it is almost impossible for family members to be defamed based on the activities of other members of the family. A father cannot be defamed, for example, because of a report that his son was charged with some crime.

Publication

Publication is essential to a libel plaintiff's case. It is probably the easiest element to prove when the lawsuit involves the media. Legally, publication occurs when defamatory material is intentionally or negligently disseminated to someone other than the person defamed. As the New York Court of Appeals in *Ostrowe v. Lee* put it, "A defamatory writing is not published if it is read by no one but the one defamed. Published it is, however, as soon as read by anyone else."

The form of publication is irrelevant. Defamatory material can be published in written or spoken form or on computer bulletin boards. Especially noteworthy, however, is the congressional attempt to immunize online publication of defamatory statements from liability. In 1996, Congress passed the Communications Decency Act. Sec. 230 provides, "No provider or user of an interactive computer service shall be treated as the publisher or speaker of any information provided by another information content provider." Thus, federal law protects online service providers from state law causes of action for defamation.

And, while repetition of a defamation generally consists of a new and separate libel, repetition by the defamed person does not. Similarly, while each person involved in the publication of defamatory material may be sued, unless the involvement is direct, there is not likely to be liability. News vendors, book sellers and libraries, for example, are not subject to liability for publishing defamatory material if they had no reason to suspect that the material was defamatory.

The accurate republication of defamatory statements within quotation marks is automatically a republication. And, since accuracy is not necessarily the equivalent of truth, simply reporting what another person has said is no defense except where the neutral-reportage doctrine or the "third-party allegation" defense or the fair report privilege is recognized.

At one time, each separate publication of a defamatory statement could prompt a cause of action. For example, if a newspaper sold 500,000 copies of an edition containing a libelous statement, a plaintiff could bring 500,000 lawsuits. But courts have recognized the inherent unfairness of such a rule, and many have adopted the single-publication rule. The rule requires a plaintiff to recover all damages suffered from a libel published in any one edition of a magazine or newspaper in one action. This, of course, does not necessarily foreclose multiple causes of action against several defendants for a defamatory statement. Each person who is responsible for publication of the defamatory statement may be held liable for the publication.

The date of publication of an alleged libel is important because courts do not like to hear old lawsuits. Therefore, each jurisdiction has a statute of limitations, which bars legal actions after certain periods of time. The statute of limitations for libel actions in most states is one or two years. The key, therefore, is determining the actual date of publication of the libel. If each republication constitutes a new publication, therefore, a new statute of limitations applies to each republication.

Courts that have applied the single-publication rule, however, have held that the statute of limitations begins to run with the first publication. This single-publication rule applies to Internet postings. That is, "[D]espite the continued public availability," Judge Sack wrote extra-judicially, "there is a single publication at the time the posting is made, and the statute of limitations begins to run then." Will making changes to a Web page restart the statute of limitations? The New Jersey Supreme Court held in *Petro-Lubricant Testing Laboratories, Inc. v. Adelman* (emphasis added): "[A] republication occurs to an online publication if an author makes a *material and substantive* change to the original defamatory article." In addition, courts have distinguished between a "republication" and a "repetition" of the libel, the latter not being a publication for purposes of a lawsuit. An example of a repetition would be the distribution of a syndicated column. The publication occurred, a federal district court held in *Givens v. Quinn*, with the distribution of the column, and each printing of the column thereafter was a repetition, not a republication. The statute of limitations of the state where the column first appeared should apply, the court held.

Fault: Actual Malice

U.S. libel law is exceedingly complex, and one of the best examples of that complexity might be the various degrees of fault.

Public figures and public officials are required to prove actual malice — knowledge of falsity or reckless disregard for the truth — before they can win libel actions. Private persons, on the other hand, must only prove negligence in most states in order to win, but must prove actual malice if they want to win punitive or presumed damages.

The actual malice rule, which originated for constitutional purposes in *New York Times Co. v. Sullivan,* is derived from the constitutional right to express oneself about matters of public concern. Against the background of "a profound national commitment to the principle that debate on public issues should be uninhibited, robust, and wide-open," the Supreme Court declared, "erroneous statement is inevitable in free debate, and ... it must be protected if the freedoms of expression are to have the 'breathing space' that they 'need to survive.'"

Times v. Sullivan arose from an advertisement published in the March 29, 1960, issue of the *New York Times.* The full-page ad, "Heed Their Rising Voices," was placed by the Committee to Defend Martin Luther King and the Struggle for Freedom in the South and, among other things, solicited funds for the legal defense of Dr. King. It started thus:

As the whole world knows by now, thousands of Southern Negro students are engaged in widespread non-violent demonstrations in positive affirmation of the right to live in human dignity as guaranteed by the U.S. Constitution. In their efforts to uphold these guarantees, they are being met by an unprecedented wave of terror by those who would deny and negate that document which the whole world looks upon as setting the pattern for modern freedom.

The advertisement alleged repressive actions taken by local authorities against civil rights demonstrations in the South:

In Montgomery, Alabama, after students sang "My Country, 'Tis of Thee" on the State Capitol steps, their leaders were expelled from school, and truckloads of police armed with shotguns and tear-gas ringed the Alabama State College Campus. When the entire student body protested to state authorities by refusing to re-register, their dining hall was padlocked in an attempt to starve them into submission.

The advertisement, without naming any individuals or organizations, asserted that "the Southern violators of the Constitution" were "determined to destroy the one man who, more than any other, symbolizes the new spirit now sweeping the South — the Rev. Dr. Martin Luther King Jr., world-famous leader of the Montgomery Bus Protest." It continued:

Again and again the Southern violators have answered Dr.

King's peaceful protests with intimidation and violence. They have bombed his home almost killing his wife and child. They have assaulted his person. They have arrested him seven times — for "speeding," "loitering" and similar "offenses." And now they have charged him with "perjury" — a felony under which they could imprison him for ten years.

L.B. Sullivan, a commissioner of public affairs for Montgomery, sued the New York Times Co. for libel. He claimed that because he was the commissioner responsible for supervision of the Montgomery police, the advertisement's allegations of police wrongdoing libeled him. He sought $500,000 in damages, and a jury awarded him the entire amount. The Alabama Supreme Court affirmed the judgment, holding that the *Times* was irresponsible in publishing the false advertisement because the paper could have verified the allegations in the advertisement by checking its own files prior to publication. The Alabama court curtly rejected the *New York Times'* argument that the U.S. Constitution protected the advertisement in a single sentence: "The First Amendment of the U.S. Constitution does not protect libelous publications."

The New York Times Co. appealed the decision to the U.S. Supreme Court. In 1964, the Court reversed the Alabama court decision unanimously. It was a stunning victory for free press and free speech. Professor Harry Kalven of the University of Chicago Law School quoted Alexander Meiklejohn, who had argued for years that political expression relating to the government should be immune from punishment, as characterizing the *Times* decision as "an occasion for dancing in the streets."

Justice William Brennan, who wrote the opinion for the Court, began with the "general proposition that freedom of expression upon public questions is secured by the First Amendment." Noting the First Amendment's guarantee of freedom of expression as a right of American citizens, Justice Brennan wrote that the *Times* case should be examined "against the background of a profound national commitment to the principle that debate on public issues should be uninhibited, robust, and wide-open, and that it may well include vehement, caustic, and sometimes unpleasantly sharp attacks on government and public officials." Justice Brennan wrote that the advertisement in question was "an expression of grievance and protest on one of the major public issues of our time" and thus entitled to the constitutional protection. However, "The question is whether it forfeits that protection by the falsity of some of its factual statements and by its alleged defamation of respondent."

Justice Brennan answered by stating that "the First Amendment guarantees have consistently refused to recognize an exception for any test of truth." He recognized the flexibility of the concept of truth and warned against the chilling effect of penalizing honest mistakes: "A rule compelling the critic of official conduct to guarantee the truth of all his factual assertions — and to do so on pain of libel judgment virtually unlimited in amount — leads to a comparable 'self-censorship.'"

Therefore, the Court established that a public official could win a libel action based upon criticism of official conduct only if the official could prove actual malice, defined as knowledge of falsity or reckless disregard for truth or falsity. "Actual malice" does not mean hatred, ill will or spite, which is the definition of common law malice.

The Supreme Court has specifically said that actual malice is a subjective rather than objective standard. That means that the standard reflects an attempt by a publisher to, as Justice Brennan wrote in *Times v. Sullivan*, injure through knowing or reckless falsehood. Thus, the conduct of a libel defendant is often examined to determine whether there is objective evidence of the subjective standard.

Knowledge of Falsity. Actual malice is proved much more often by showing reckless disregard on the part of the defendant than by showing knowing falsity. One reason — perhaps the foremost reason — is that professional communicators rarely publish anything knowing it is false. But there are exceptions. One was when Ralph Ginzburg published in *Fact* magazine that some psychiatrists he surveyed found Republican presidential candidate Barry Goldwater to be mentally unstable. Goldwater sued for libel, and his attorneys were able to show in *Goldwater v. Ginzburg* that the survey results were actually very favorable toward Goldwater, but Ginzburg ignored the positive comments and focused only on the negative. In addition, there was evidence that the publisher of the article knew before the survey was distributed what the tenor of the article would be. Goldwater was able to meet the actual malice standard by showing that, although the statements Ginzburg made were true individually, collectively they misrepresented the truth; that is, they were false and that the author knew this but published them anyway.

While knowledge of falsity can be easily applied, it's not easily proved. Because "[t]he knowledge of falsity prong of Times Rule Actual Malice is based on a determination of what the publisher knew or did not know at the time of publication," libel law expert Wat Hopkins wrote in 1989; the defendant's state of mind at the time of publication is key. Proving state of mind with convincing clarity can be challenging at the least. Rarely will a libel defendant admit knowledge of falsity, so, most often, plaintiffs must use objective evidence. That's difficult, but it can be done. When editorial writers at a newspaper asserted that a public official was a liar, for example, but articles in the same newspaper demonstrated that the official had not lied, the Illinois Court of Appeals in *Costello v. Capital Citizens Commissions* found the editorial writers to have acted with actual malice, for they *knew* their statements were false.

A plaintiff's claim that a publication is false, while signaling that a publisher should investigate further, is not sufficient, standing alone, to show knowledge of falsity, particularly in the face of evidence from reliable, objective sources. If the evidence from those sources raised questions about the truth of the material to be published, it's a different story. As Hopkins wrote in his book on *Sullivan*, "To publish in the face of such evidence would be to publish with knowledge of falsity. Similarly, to publish charges with little or no support for those charges has also been determined to be publishing with knowledge of falsity, as has the selective use of information to the detriment of the plaintiff."

Thus, the determination of knowledge of falsity rests on what the libel defendant knew at the time of publication. And what the publisher knew often rests on the extent of the investigation before publication, along with the interpretation, editing and presentation of the material. In *Herbert v. Lando,* for example, the Supreme Court concluded that a plaintiff could inquire as to a defendant's state of mind while preparing a report. Questions about why the defendant believed and disbelieved certain sources, why the defendant used some material over other material and like issues were permissible, Justice Byron White wrote for the majority.

Former Army Col. Anthony Herbert contended that he was defamed in a *60 Minutes* segment. Producer Barry Lando and correspondent Mike Wallace argued that the First Amendment protected them from testifying as to their thought processes or state of mind in editing and producing the program. The Supreme Court disagreed, finding that state of mind was central to actual malice. In a 1968 case, *St. Amant v. Thompson*, which is detailed in *Reckless Disregard* by media law professor Eric Robinson, the Court had held, "There must be sufficient evidence to permit the conclusion that the defendant in fact entertained serious doubts as to the truth of his publication." The assertion by a defendant that he or she believed the publication to be true is inadequate standing alone, but may be sufficient when not refuted by the plaintiff.

What a libel defendant knew at the time of publication was also central to the 1984 case *Bose Corporation v. Consumers Union of United States.* Bose filed suit against the publisher of *Consumer Reports* magazine for statements critical of stereo speakers developed by the company. Bose convinced a jury that the magazine had published false statements with actual malice. The First Circuit reversed, however, and the Supreme Court upheld the reversal. Bose had succeeded in showing that the author of the critical report might not have expressed himself well and might have attempted at trial to cover up for that poor expression. That proof, the Court said, however, was irrelevant. What was important was the author's "state of mind when he wrote his initial report, or when he checked the article against that report."

In short, it becomes essential to explore the libel defendant's state of mind at the time of the preparation and publication of the defamation in order to learn whether actual malice existed. The libel defendant should recognize that these are likely to be probed and should be prepared to justify both the actions and the state of mind that led to the choices made.

The publisher's state of mind toward the investigation and the material that is eventually published is also key to the question of knowledge of falsity. Indeed, the publisher's state of mind toward the *subject* of the report may be irrelevant because ill will toward the plaintiff is not sufficient to demonstrate actual malice. Ill will, however, may be introduced to demonstrate a defendant's motive for lying or publishing with reckless disregard for the truth. As the New York appellate court noted in *DiLorenzo v. New York News,* while "the concepts underlying malice and actual malice are not the same ... this does not preclude a relationship between them." When courts permit evidence of ill will, hatred or spite to be introduced, they usually admonish juries that those elements, standing alone, can never establish actual malice.

Courts have also indicated that knowledge of falsity can be demonstrated by the way material is written, edited or presented. This may be particularly true with headlines, as Hopkins wrote:

When large headlines are not literally defamatory, for example, but raise the implication of wrongdoing not supported by the texts of the articles over which they appear, a libel verdict for a public official can stand because of sufficient evidence that the headlines were published with actual malice. When the headlines are merely ambiguous, however, there is no knowledge of falsity. Similarly, ambiguous language or internal inconsistencies in news stories, standing alone, are insufficient evidence of actual malice.

In the Internet era, headlines emerge as a new issue in defamation law. As Judge Sack of noted in *Sack on Defamation,* "Indeed ... print media may be risking a legal challenge to a headline as the print analog of 'clickbait' by using inflammatory language in a headline and physically isolating the headline from the article to which it refers." Indeed, "clickbait defamation" is far from a whimsical notion. In 2020, the prominent Harvard Law Professor Lawrence Lessig sued the *New York Times,* although he later withdrew his clickbait defamation lawsuit. According to Lessig, the *Times* defamed him by resorting to the "use of a shocking headline and/or lede to entice readers to click on a particular article," although the paper was "fully aware" that clickbaiting could defame its targets.

In addition to a media defendant's state of mind, the editorial policies that govern or guide actions can play a role in the determination of predisposition. The idea that a media defendant preconceived a story line, and then proceeded to skew reporting to fit that preconception, is evidence of knowledge of falsity. In *Burnett v. National Enquirer,* for example, the trial court suggested that the *Enquirer's* editorial predisposition may have contributed to its judgment. Entertainer Carol Burnett argued that the *National Enquirer* had falsely portrayed her as being "drunk, rude, uncaring, and abusive" in a Washington restaurant. At trial, a reporter for the *Enquirer* testified that the article about Burnett was published even though he was unable to verify its accuracy.

Similarly, *Tavoulares v. Washington Post Co.* resulted in an opinion that troubles journalists but that courts may believe they need to follow. A *Washington Post* article implied that William Tavoulares, the president of Mobil Oil Co., misused his position by setting up his son to head an international tanker fleet. A federal jury awarded Tavoulares $2 million in damages. Before the full Court of Appeals for the District of Columbia overturned the verdict, a panel of that court had held that the *Post's* predisposition toward "hard-hitting investigative journalism" could be considered as evidence relevant to actual malice. The suggestion that a practice generally revered in journalism could be used against a libel defendant sent shock waves through the field. Those feelings were eased, however, when a full-panel rehearing by the District of Columbia Circuit reversed, throwing out the verdict and ruling that actual malice had not been proven. Adding to the relief was the court's assertion that a media organization's reputation for aggressive reporting was not to be taken as evidence of actual malice.

Pressure exerted by newsroom supervisors to produce high-impact stories may also be construed as a predisposition toward certain kinds of stories with specific plot lines. Such pressure may contribute to reporters skewing facts to fit such predilections. Libel expert Rodney Smolla places this phenomenon within the context of freedom of expression:

At the very core of our first amendment jurisprudence lies the elemental wisdom that government has no business prescribing what is orthodox, genteel, or polite in politics and culture. A publication or broadcast outlet is not to be penalized because of its unique boldness, style, or flair. Indeed, in an era in which one of the great *economic* tendencies in the media is toward consolidation and centralization, often resulting in "play it safe" editorial styles that make all news sound the same, the first amendment's protection for those media outlets with special courage or uniqueness is more vital than ever. To actually preconceive a story is one thing — such an act is quite properly probative of actual malice — but merely to have an editorial image or slant is quite another.

Thus, when circumstances permit, proving falsity can be easier than exploring a defendant's state of mind. It simply stands to reason that it is much more difficult to prove a particular state of mind compared to presenting evidence that suggests reckless oversights. But what happens when a defendant admits to altering an interviewee's quotations? Arguably, that is an example of knowing falsity. That is, if quotations were knowingly altered to the extent that their meaning was materially transformed, then the journalist must have been aware of the fact that they were false. Traditionally, journalistic practice suggests that words bracketed by quotation marks are the exact words of the person to whom they are attributed. When a journalist knowingly changes this material, the quoted information arguably has been knowingly falsified.

While that might be the case, publishing knowing falsehoods is only one element of a public figure's burden of proof. In *Masson v. New Yorker Magazine, Inc.,* the Supreme Court ruled that even the deliberate misquotation of a public figure cannot be libelous unless the wording materially changes the meaning of what was really said. It stated that in *Masson* the meaning had not been transformed. On remand, a federal district court jury ruled in favor of the journalist, even though she had admitted to condensing certain statements by the plaintiff.

In a non-media libel case in 2014, *Air Wisconsin Airlines Corp. v. Hoeper,* the Supreme Court applied the "material falsity" standard of actual malice. In determining that Air Wisconsin was not liable under a federal law for reporting to the Transportation Security Administration with no actual malice that one of its pilots was possibly armed and "mentally unstable." The Court said statements will not be considered materially false unless they would have affected the intended recipient of them in a different way than the truth.

Reckless Disregard. Reckless disregard for whether material is true or false, like knowledge of falsity, is a subjective test. But it can often be determined by the publisher's actions rather than by thought processes, state of mind or predisposition at the time of publication. Knowledge of falsity focuses on what the publisher knew; reckless disregard focuses on what the publisher reasonably *should have known.* The focus of the actual malice inquiry, as Hopkins observed in his 1993 study of actual malice, "is on a defendant's attitude toward the truth or falsity of the publication," on "subjective awareness of its probable falsity" and on "actual doubts as to its accuracy." And Smolla agrees: The "inquiry in 'actual malice' focuses largely on the defendant's belief regarding truthfulness."

For recklessness to rise to the level of actual malice, it must be significant — it must be tantamount to lying; it must be obvious that the publisher did not care about the truth of the information. When publishers have demonstrated adequate inves-

tigation of potentially libelous charges, courts have typically ruled that there was no reckless disregard. Thus, a plaintiff cannot prove reckless disregard if the defendant can show the statements were adequately investigated prior to publication.

The seriousness of the charges being made is also weighed. The more serious the material in question, the more detailed an investigation into its truth should be. In this connection, the "recklessness" of the actual malice rule is a concept of relativity in American tort law on reckless behavior. Judge Richard Posner of the Seventh Circuit stated in *United States v. Boyd* that if a person publishes a defamatory false statement recklessly, "the potential harm that it creates [to reputation] … is wildly disproportionate to any benefits that the activity might be expected to confer." In addition, reckless disregard is more likely to be found when sources for published material are anonymous, biased or of questionable reputation. Courts look to the number of reputable sources when determining whether a sufficient investigation was conducted.

The Supreme Court in *Garrison v. Louisiana* has provided guidance as to the meaning of reckless disregard. It has, for example, called reckless disregard publishing with a "high degree of awareness of their probable falsity." And it held in *St. Amant v. Thompson,* for reckless disregard to exist, "there must be sufficient evidence to permit the conclusion that the defendant in fact entertained serious doubts as to the truth of his publication." Whether a defendant had such serious doubts can be established by circumstantial evidence including determining what the defendant's thoughts were leading up to publication of the challenged statements.

The mere failure to investigate charges is not sufficient, standing alone, to prove reckless disregard. Publishers often rely on the work of reputable writers. If there is no reason to doubt the truth of material those writers submitted, publishers don't have to conduct independent investigations. If plaintiffs can show that publishers had doubts about the truth of such material or reasonably should have had doubts, however, that's a different story. In such cases, the question of reckless disregard may be open. In short, a publisher must be able to demonstrate a reasonable belief in the truth of the published material. That may sometimes require an investigation into the facts, but the belief may also be based on the reputation of the original author. To establish actual malice, plaintiffs must go beyond proving that "a reporter failed to show significant initiative in corroborating, verifying, or further investigating the defamatory story at issue." Rodney Smolla wrote:

[T]he mere failure to investigate, even when that failure to investigate is less than reasonable or responsible journalism, does not in and of itself meet the actual malice test. There must be some evidence of subjective suspicion that further investigation is needed. That evidence, of course, can be met by circumstantial data, including such things as the reliability or unreliability of the source or the inherent implausibility of the allegation, but something other than the stark failure to pursue investigation must be established.

Regardless, the actual malice rule has been criticized over the years for being overly media-protective at the expense of reputational interests. Most recently, Supreme Court Justices Clarence Thomas and Neil Gorsuch have argued, albeit in concurring in or dissenting from the Court's denials of certiorari, that actual malice should be reconsidered. Professor Hopkins predicts that the Court will "very likely" review actual malice in the near future. He doubts that the Court will abolish or modify the rule substantially. Instead, the Court may opt for "some fine tuning" of actual malice.

Indeed, the most recent federal court of appeals case, *Coral Ridge Ministries Media v. Amazon.Com* might provide the Supreme Court an opportunity to revisit actual malice. The Florida evangelical Christian ministry sued the Alabama-based Southern Poverty Law Center for defamation when the SPLC designated it an LGBTQ-hate group on its "hate map." In 2021, the Eleventh Circuit held that the ministry did not prove actual malice on the part of SPLC when it was placed on the hate map. The court found little evidence for a reasonable conclusion that SPLC "'actually entertained serious doubts as to the veracity' of its hate group definition and that definition's application to Coral Ridge, or that SPLC was 'highly aware' that the definition and its application was 'probably false.'"

Fault: Negligence

At a minimum, the Supreme Court said in *Gertz v. Welch*, private persons seeking damages for the publication of false defamations related to matters of public interest must at least prove negligence. As a result, most states have ruled that negligence is the standard of fault for private-person libel plaintiffs.

Negligence has been defined in a variety of ways, but it is generally defined as failure to act as a reasonably or ordinarily careful person would under similar circumstances. A second definition — known as "journalistic malpractice" — is failure to adhere to standards of reporting and writing that are common to the news industry.

The reasonable care standard requires a libel plaintiff to establish that a libel defendant did not operate in a reasonable way, that is, that a reasonable person would have operated in a way significantly different from that of the defendant. The Arizona Supreme Court in *Peagler v. Phoenix Newspapers* defined negligence this way:

[C]onduct which creates an unreasonable risk of harm. It is the failure to use that amount of care which a reasonably prudent person would use under like circumstances. The question which the jury must determine from the preponderance of the evidence ... is whether the defendants acted reasonably in attempting to discover the truth or falsity or the defamatory character of the publication.

Most states have adopted the reasonable person definition of negligence, but some — including Iowa, Kansas and Oklahoma — define negligence as journalistic malpractice. The *Restatement* defines journalistic malpractice this way:

The defendant, if a professional disseminator of news, such as a newspaper, a magazine or a broadcasting station, or an employee, such as a reporter, is held to the skill and experience normally possessed by members of that profession.... Customs and practices within the profession are relevant in applying the negligence standard, which is, to a substantial degree, set by the profession itself, though a custom is not controlling.... If the defendant is an ordinary citizen, customs of the community as a whole may be relevant.

Regardless of the definition of negligence, some factors seem common when courts have ruled that defendants published material negligently. In his 1985 study of negligence as an actionable standard in post-*Gertz* cases, Hopkins identified three general negligence rules:

(1) [I]f there is a discrepancy between what a reporter says he was told by a source and what the source said he told the reporter, the court is more likely to believe the source and find that negligence is likely; (2) courts are likely to rule that negligence could be established if media representatives make little or no effort to contact a person against whom accusations are made or if a medium bases a story later found to be false upon a single source; (3) courts are likely to rule that negligence could be established if media fail to get all the information they should.

Actual Injury

Even if libel plaintiffs can prove they were identified in false, defamatory publications, and even if they can prove the requisite degree of fault, they must still prove actual injury to reputation in order to recover damages, especially when the challenged statement relates to a matter of public concern. The New Mexico Supreme Court held in *Smith v. Durden*: "Injury to reputation is the very essence of the tort of defamation. Evidence of humiliation and mental anguish, without evidence of actual injury to reputation, is insufficient to establish a cause of action for defamation."

Warning against the "danger of media self-censorship" resulting from jury discretion in assessing punitive damages, the Supreme Court said in *Gertz* that "punitive damages are wholly irrelevant to the state interest that justifies a negligence standard for private defamation actions. They are not compensation for injury. Instead, they are private fines levied by civil juries to punish reprehensible conduct and to deter its future occurrence." The Court noted, however, that the private libel plaintiff who establishes liability under a less demanding standard than actual malice may be limited to recovery of "only such damages as are sufficient to compensate him for actual injury."

In a libel action, five types of damages are recognized.

Nominal damages are awarded to plaintiffs who have not suffered from provable injury to their reputations. They are granted in very small amounts, usually $1, and are awarded where a plaintiff does not seek compensation for loss, but a vindication of reputation in the form of a declaration that a published statement is false.

Compensatory damages are awarded for actual injury. They compensate, not for out-of-pocket loss, but for harm to a reputation, humiliation, suffering and mental anguish. Awards must be based upon the evidence, but if the damages are not outrageous, a jury can award damages in its own discretion. Corporate defamation plaintiffs, unlike natural person plaintiffs, cannot recover damages for internal emotional distress. Compensatory damages are sometimes called "general damages."

Presumed damages are a form of compensatory damages. The Supreme Court in *Dun & Bradstreet, Inc. v. Greenmoss Builders* stated that their purpose is to "further ... the state interest in providing remedies for defamation by ensuring that those remedies are effective." They may be awarded without any actual proof of reputational injury. The New Jersey Supreme Court in *W.J.A. v. D.A.* has noted the heightened value of presumed damages to a private victim of non-public-concern online defamation who cannot prove actual damages. The court held that "private persons face the real risk of harm through the modern ease of defamatory publications now possible through use of the Internet." Presumed damages vindicate the dignitary and peace-of-mind interest in one's reputation that may be impaired through the misuse of the Internet. Permitting reputational damages to be presumed in a defamation action arising in that setting serves a legitimate interest, one that ought not be jettisoned from our common law.

Special damages are designed to compensate for actual pecuniary loss. Evidence must demonstrate an actual amount of money the plaintiff lost as a result of the defamation.

Punitive or exemplary damages are designed to punish the defendant for outrageous and willful defamation. They are de-signed to deter the defendant and others from repeating similar actions. Actual malice must be proved for recovery of punitive damages. Four states — Massachusetts, Michigan, Oregon and Washington — do not recognize punitive damages, and others have capped the amount of punitive damages a plaintiff can win. Some states require that both actual malice and common law malice be established in seeking punitive damages for libel.

PUBLIC PERSONS

The Supreme Court has established that two categories of libel plaintiffs — public officials and public figures — must prove actual malice in order to win libel actions. In addition, the Court has defined three types of public figure: all-purposes, limited-purposes and involuntary.

Public Officials

Public officials for purposes of the actual malice rule are persons in government who are in or appear to be in policy-making roles. The Supreme Court in *Rosenblatt v. Baer* indicated that "the 'public official' designation applies at the very least to those among the hierarchy of government employees who have or appear to the public to have, substantial responsibility for or control over the conduct of governmental affairs." The trial judge determines whether a plaintiff is a public official.

Determining just who qualifies as a public official is reasonably, but not entirely, clear-cut. In a 1979 case, *Hutchinson v. Proxmire*, the Supreme Court made it clear that "public official" is not synonymous with "public employee." Whether a public employee is in or appears to be in a position to make policy and whether the employee has ready access to the media are key factors in determining his or her status.

A public official must establish that a defamatory statement was directed at the official rather than at his or her government unit. This is at the heart of First Amendment philosophy — that under the Constitution there is no such thing as seditious libel: that is, libel of the government. As the Texas Court of Appeals stated in *Cox Texas Newspapers L.P. v. Penick*, "An impersonal attack criticizing the actions of a governmental agency without referring specifically to its agents, without more, will not support a claim of libel by the head of that agency."

A person remains a public official for the purposes of the actual malice rule even after leaving office, at least with regard to stories that refer to conduct while in office. The passing of time, however, eventually may erode public interest in the office-holder's conduct so that the *New York Times* rule would no longer apply. According to the *Rosenblatt* Court, there may be cases "where a person is so far removed from a former position of authority that comment on the manner in which he performed his responsibilities no longer has the interest necessary to justify the *New York Times* rule." But this exception is rare.

Any statement that touches on an official's fitness for office — even if the statement is about the official's private life — is considered protected. Said the Supreme Court in *Garrison*:

> The *New York Times* rule is not rendered inapplicable merely because an official's private reputation, as well as his public reputation, is harmed. The public-official rule protects the paramount public interest in a free flow of information to the people concerning public officials.... To this end, anything which might touch on an official's fitness for office is relevant.

Public Figures

In 1967, the actual malice rule was expanded to include public figures. In *Curtis Publishing Co. v. Butts,* the Supreme Court ruled that there was little legal difference between persons who have widespread fame and notoriety — public figures — and public officials. "Many who do not hold public office at the moment," wrote Chief Justice Earl Warren, "are nevertheless intimately involved in the resolution of important public questions or, by reason of their fame, shape events in areas of concern to society at large."

The rule was established in a roundabout way. Justice John Marshall Harlan had written a plurality opinion differentiating between public officials and public figures, but he also differentiated between the rules that should apply to the two categories. Chief Justice Warren wrote that the actual malice rule should apply to both categories of libel plaintiffs, and a sufficient number of justices joined his opinion so as to establish that rule.

The actual malice rule was extended in 1971 to any defamatory story involving matters of public or general interest, but the expansion was short-lived. In *Rosenbloom v. Metromedia, Inc.,* a plurality of the Court had favored a rule that required private people involved in matters of public interest to prove actual malice when suing for libel based upon discussion of those matters. But the "Rosenbloom Rule" lasted only three years. In 1974, a 5-4 Court majority definitively rejected the rule by overruling *Rosenbloom* in *Gertz v. Robert Welch.*

The *Gertz* case started in 1969 when *American Opinion,* a monthly periodical published by the John Birch Society, a far-right organization founded by Robert Welch, published an article critical of a Chicago civil liberties lawyer, Elmer Gertz. Gertz had been retained by the family of an African-American man who had been shot and killed by Chicago policeman Richard Nuccio. The article charged that Gertz, who was hired to initiate a wrongful death suit against Chicago and Nuccio, was the architect of the "frame-up" in the earlier prosecution of Nuccio for second-degree murder. It claimed that the prose-

cution was part of a Communist effort to discredit the Chicago police. The article declared, in part:

> The file on Elmer Gertz in Chicago Police Intelligence takes a big Irish cop to lift.... He has been an official of the Marxist League for Industrial Democracy, originally known as the Intercollegiate Socialist Society, which has advocated the violent seizure of our government.... In fact, the only thing Chicagoans need to know about Gertz is that he is one of the original officers, and has been Vice President, of the Communist National Lawyers Guild ... which probably did more than any other outfit to plan the Communist attack on the Chicago police during the 1968 Democratic Convention.

Gertz sued Robert Welch, Inc., publisher of *American Opinion,* for libel. He said the statements about him were false. He had no criminal record, contrary to the implications of the article. He was not a member of the Marxist League for Industrial Democracy. Further, although he had been a member of the National Lawyers Guild fifteen years earlier, the Guild was not a Communist organization. Neither had he anything to do with the prosecution of Nuccio for murder.

Gertz claimed he was injured both as an individual and as an attorney. He sought $100,000 in actual damages and $500,000 in punitive damages. In 1970, a jury awarded him $50,000 in damages, but the trial judge set aside the verdict because, he said, since the article discussed Gertz's public activity, the actual malice rule should apply. Gertz appealed, but the U.S. Court of Appeals for the Seventh Circuit applied *Rosenbloom* and affirmed the trial judge's ruling, stating that there was no clear and convincing evidence of actual malice.

In his appeal to the Supreme Court, Gertz argued in part:

> Is every attorney, representing a client, to be exposed to the most scurrilous attacks, with absolutely no recourse? May a defamer concoct wholly fictitious stories about such an attorney which have no legitimate connections with the matter at hand? Are the members of the legal profession such public figures that they imperil their very livelihood to all unfounded attacks with absolutely no recourse? These issues must be considered very carefully and fully, not in an offhand manner.

The Supreme Court agreed, holding that the actual malice rule applies to private-person libel plaintiffs only when they seek presumed or punitive damages. Other than that, the Court said, states could determine the fault standard for private-person libel plaintiffs, so long as states did not allow liability without some degree of fault. The Court explained the distinction between public and private persons:

Public officials and public figures usually enjoy significantly greater access to the channels of effective communication and hence have a more realistic opportunity to counteract false statements than private individuals normally enjoy. Private individuals are therefore more vulnerable to injury, and the state interest in protecting them is correspondingly greater. More important than the likelihood that private individuals will lack effective opportunities for rebuttal, there is a compelling normative consideration underlying the distinction between public and private defamation plaintiffs. An individual who decides to seek governmental office must accept certain necessary consequences of that involvement in public affairs. He runs the risk of closer public scrutiny than might otherwise be the case.

In *Gertz,* the Court also differentiated between three types of public figures, whether natural or corporate. General or all-purpose public figures are persons who have achieved pervasive fame or notoriety in their communities or are pervasively involved in the affairs of society. It is not easy to become an all-purpose public figure. The category is generally reserved for those people who have become so-called "household names" — that is, celebrities.

Far more common than the all-purpose public figure is the limited-purpose public figure. Limited-purpose public figures have "thrust themselves to the forefront of particular controversies in order to influence the resolution of issues involved." This means, first, a public controversy must exist and, second, the nature and extent of the plaintiff's participation in that controversy must be determined. While it is clear that newsworthiness and public figure status are not synonymous, some courts have held that a person who creates a public controversy in order to affect the outcome of some public issue has met the limited-purposes criteria.

The Court also acknowledged that involuntary public figures may exist — at least in theory — but that such cases would be rare. Yet, an individual could be thrust into a matter of public controversy not merely through voluntary actions but also through bad luck. It is possible to become a public figure through no purposeful action. Recently, however, two law journal authors have questioned the notion of "involuntary public figures" in the Internet law era. Derigan Silver and Loryn Rumsey wrote in *Communication Law and Policy* in 2022: "Most importantly, the involuntary public figure is no longer a viable concept in the age of viral media content, and courts should abandon it. Already fraught with problems throughout its history, the involuntary public figure concept is especially damaging when applied to viral content."

The *Gertz* Court saw a relationship between public figures and public officials, in part, because individuals in both groups tend to have access to the media and, therefore, have the ability to set the record straight when inaccuracies occur. Private figures, on the other hand, usually have limited access to the media and are, therefore, more vulnerable to irreparable injury. In addition, there is a certain degree of risk that accompanies those in the public eye. While public officials "must accept certain necessary consequences [regarding their] involvement in public affairs," they also "run the risk of closer public scrutiny than might otherwise be the case.... Those classified as public figures stand in a similar position.... [T]he communications media are entitled to act on the assumption that public officials and public figures have voluntarily exposed themselves to increased risk of injury from defamatory falsehoods concerning them." The Court noted that society's stake in news about private figures is not as great as when public people are involved. Society places a high value in protecting private figures against libel, so the level of fault they are required to meet is less demanding than it is for public people.

Distinguishing between public and private figures, however, is not easy. As one federal district court pointed out, it "is much like trying to nail a jelly fish to the wall." Being in the public eye and being a public figure are not the same. The case of Mary Alice Firestone is an example. She was married to the heir to the Firestone Rubber Co. fortune, was a prominent member of Palm Beach society and even subscribed to a clipping service so she could keep track of news published about her. In addition, when she and her husband became involved in a notorious divorce proceeding, she held daily press conferences. When she sued *Time* for incorrectly reporting that her husband was granted a divorce because of her adultery and extreme cruelty — rather than because "neither party is domesticated" — it seemed certain that she would be categorized as a public figure for libel purposes. But the Supreme Court in *Time Inc. v. Firestone* said no. The Court said that a large number of people might be interested in the problems of the extremely wealthy, but those were not the kinds of matters the Court had in mind when it referred to a public controversy.

A plaintiff cannot be made public merely by the actions of the media. This bootstrapping occurs when media defendants attach themselves to the protection of the actual malice standard by pointing to their own allegedly libelous media coverage of the plaintiff as evidence that the plaintiff is a public figure. The Supreme Court in *Hutchinson* said, "Clearly, those charged with defamation cannot, by their own conduct, create their own defense by making the claimant a public figure." As a result, courts have noted that the public controversy at issue must have existed prior to the publication upon which the defamation claim is based. However, a court that rigidly applies the pre-existing controversy requirement may punish legitimate reporting that uncovers specific acts of wrongdoing. Courts, therefore, attempt to strike a delicate balance between which came first — the controversy or the story about the controversy.

Just as a media organization is not permitted to bootstrap itself into creating its own defense, a plaintiff may not avoid the actual malice standard by claiming that the attention was unwanted. The proper question is not whether the plaintiff volunteered for the publicity but whether the plaintiff volunteered for an activity from which publicity would foreseeably arise.

In 2020, the Third Circuit held in *McCafferty v. Newsweek Media Group* that C.M., a 12-year-old "politically vocal" boy in Philadelphia, was a limited-purpose public figure, since he voluntarily injected himself into the political controversies enveloping President Donald Trump and his critics. In 2016, before turning 12, his public endorsement of then-candidate Trump attracted media attention at home and abroad as "Philly's Biggest Trump Supporter." Thus, voluntary entry into a sphere of activity, especially controversial, is sufficient to satisfy this element of the public figure inquiry.

Because the Supreme Court has said that someone with widespread fame or notoriety is a public figure, the individual's prominence is important in determining public-figure status. Moreover, that prominence may apply to a narrowly drawn context. Merely being an executive within a prominent and influential company does not by itself make a person a public figure. Professionals are typically not public figures, but under certain circumstances they can be. For example, voluntary use of controversial or unorthodox techniques may be enough to confer public-figure status. Publicly defending such methods or adopting other controversial stands also tends to bring about public status. Thus, according to a federal district court in *Renner v. Donsbach*, a doctor who had written extensively on health issues as a newspaper columnist, who was also the author of various journal articles, and who had appeared on at least one nationally broadcast television program discussing health and nutrition issues was held to be a public figure for a limited range of issues — those pertaining to health and nutrition.

An individual may assume public-figure status within small publics but may revert to being a private figure in larger spheres. For example, a professor may be a public figure on campus and in the adjacent academic community but a private person beyond those boundaries. The professor, therefore, may be a public figure for purposes of an article in the university newspaper but not for purposes of a regional newspaper or a national magazine. Thus, the professor's public-figure status is restricted. Similarly, an individual can attain the status of an all-purpose public figure within a particular geographical area, according to the Montana Supreme Court in *Williams v. Pasma*.

The passage of time may theoretically permit some people who were once public figures to regain private-figure status. To revert to private-figure status, it is likely that a plaintiff would need to demonstrate that the original status as a public figure was not connected to events or controversies that have become part of the permanent historical consciousness of the country.

The Lasting Impact of Gertz v. Welch

Gertz, the most important libel case since *New York Times Co. v. Sullivan,* established a new set of guidelines for balancing the constitutional right of free speech against concerns for reputational interests.

First, the Court reaffirmed that public figures, along with public officials, must prove actual malice in libel cases involving matters of public concern.

Second, the Court held that "so long as they do not impose liability without fault, the states may define for themselves the appropriate standard of liability for a publisher or broadcaster of a defamatory falsehood injurious to a private individual," at least where a defamatory statement "makes substantial danger to reputation apparent."

Third, the Court stated that presumed or punitive damages may not be awarded absent a showing of actual malice. Those who cannot prove actual malice, the Court said, may be compensated only for actual injury. In a later case, *Dun & Bradstreet, Inc. v. Greenmoss Builders, Inc.* the Court held that the actual malice requirement for punitive damages does not apply to material "of purely private concern."

As a result of *Gertz,* more than forty jurisdictions, including the District of Columbia, Puerto Rico and Virgin Islands, have established negligence as the private-person fault standard; five states — Alaska, Colorado, Indiana, Kansas and New Jersey — have apparently adopted a variation of the Rosenbloom Rule; and one state, New York, requires "gross irresponsibility" when matters of public concern are involved. The New York Court of Appeals held in *Chapadeau v. Utica Observer-Dispatch* that when the content of the article is arguably within the sphere of legitimate public concern, which is reasonably related to matters warranting public exposition, the party defamed may recover if he or she can establish "by a preponderance of the evidence, that the publisher acted in a grossly irresponsible manner without due consideration for the standards of information gathering and dissemination ordinarily followed by responsible parties." The "gross irresponsibility" standard in New York for private-figure libel plaintiffs is considered closer to "actual malice" than to negligence when it comes to difficulty of proof. Indeed, Judge Sack of the Second Circuit noted: "It is almost as difficult as 'actual malice' for plaintiffs to meet in most cases and more difficult in some."

Significantly, New York expanded its anti-SLAPP (Strategic Lawsuit Against Public Participation) statute in 2020. The statute provides:

THE LIBEL PLAINTIFF'S
BURDEN OF PROOF

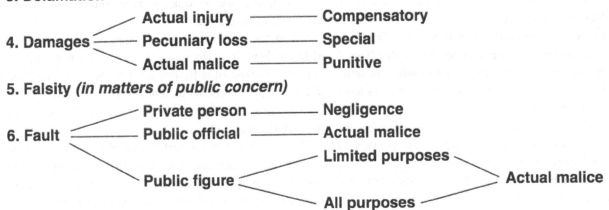

1. **Publication**
2. **Identification**
3. **Defamation**

4. **Damages**
   - Actual injury ———— Compensatory
   - Pecuniary loss ———— Special
   - Actual malice ———— Punitive

5. **Falsity** *(in matters of public concern)*

6. **Fault**
   - Private person ———— Negligence
   - Public official ———— Actual malice
   - Public figure
     - Limited purposes ⟶ Actual malice
     - All purposes

In an action involving public petition and participation, damages may only be recovered if the plaintiff, in addition to all other necessary elements, shall have established *by clear and convincing evidence* that any communication which gives rise to the action was made with knowledge of its falsity or with reckless disregard of whether it was false, where the truth or falsity of such communication is material to the cause of action at issue (emphasis added).

As First Amendment scholar Jeff Kosseff commented in 2022, the codification of the *Sullivan* actual malice, as the state legislature of New York did, will "proactively" counter the potential harm to freedom of speech and the press from the rising anti-*Sullivan* momentum.

DEFENSE STRATEGIES

The libel defendant is by no means defenseless. Any of a number of defenses or defense strategies is available to help prevent liability, depending on the circumstances of a case.

In libel law, the rights of individuals to be secure in their reputations are weighed against the rights of publishers to be heard on issues important to self-government. Broadly speaking, libel defenses assert that important issues of public concern should be debated in a free, open and uninhibited manner. A li-

bel suit today, thanks to the precedent that *Times v. Sullivan* established, can be defended on constitutional grounds as well as through the common law.

Libel defenses begin by attempting to defeat the plaintiff's case. By refuting any of the plaintiff's claims, a defense may be successful. For example, the Tenth Circuit, in *Lamb v. Rizzo,* upheld a federal district court's dismissal of a libel suit because the plaintiff had suffered no reputational harm from two news stories. The federal appeals court reasoned that he had too tarnished a reputation as a convicted murderer to be further damaged when the stories were published.

If defeating an element of the plaintiff's case doesn't work, defendants then may try to assert affirmative defenses.

THE CONSTITUTIONAL DEFENSE

The First Amendment protects the freedoms of speech and press. Therein lies the heart of the so-called "constitutional defense" in libel law. The Supreme Court in *Citizen Publishing Co. v. United States* has recognized that free speech is vital because it ensures individual self-fulfillment and that it is a social good because it contributes to the search for truth. The First Amendment "rests on the assumption that the widest possible dissemination of information from diverse and antagonistic sources is essential to the welfare of the public." Moreover, as Justice Louis Brandeis wrote in *Whitney v. California* during the era in which the Court truly began to interpret the meaning and scope of the First Amendment, "[F]reedom to think as you will and speak as you think are means indispensable to the discovery and spread of political truth."

Thus, a libel defense, of sorts, has developed out of the notion that contributing significantly to public knowledge and information is important, and freedom of expression is a key element in the process.

The question becomes, does the speech contribute to what the *Sullivan* Court has termed the "profound national commitment to the principle that debate on public issues should be uninhibited, robust, and wide-open?" At a base level, a media organization's defense on constitutional grounds is a claim that limiting its ability to convey information is an abridgment of First Amendment guarantees of free speech and press. Carrying this argument to its logical conclusion, then, finding a media defendant responsible for libel abridges constitutionally protected freedoms. Moreover, knowing that a guilty verdict is possible in the wake of critical or less-than-positive statements about an individual may also limit freedom by producing a chilling effect. That is, the media may be less inclined to publish critical statements if they know that dangers may lie ahead in a libel trial.

The ability to criticize the government and government officials was central to *Times v. Sullivan*. At the root of Justice Brennan's opinion was the notion that statements about public officials — people who hold government positions — are most deserving of constitutional protection. The freedom to be critical of government and government officials, after all, was the basis and justification for the First Amendment's protection of speech and the press from interference by the state. Some scholars, in fact, have taken an unconditional approach to the issue. Alexander Meiklejohn, for example, has written that speech relevant to self-government is absolutely protected under the First Amendment. Harry Kalven wrote that the central meaning of the First Amendment is uninhibited discussion of governmental affairs: "Political freedom ends when government can use its powers and its courts to silence its critics."

It was the critical nature of the ability of citizens to criticize government and government officials that prompted Justice Brennan to appropriate the actual malice standard from state libel law and establish it as a constitutional rule. Unless a defendant's statement about a public plaintiff was made knowing it was false, or with reckless disregard for its truth, the defense will be successful. The scope of the standard was soon thereafter expanded to apply to more than public official plaintiffs.

As previously indicated, the Supreme Court, in *Curtis Publishing Co.*, applied the actual malice standard to public figures, that is, individuals who either possess widespread fame or notoriety or who have thrust themselves into a public controversy in order to influence its outcome.

Chief Justice Warren justified the extension, writing that the "differentiation between public figures and public officials and adoption of separate standards of proof for each have no basis in law, logic, or First Amendment policy." The case established the principle that many people who do not hold governmental office are nevertheless intimately enough involved in the resolution of public issues that, like public officials, they should be required to prove the defendant acted with actual malice.

Because of the dramatic difference in the level of fault required of public and private libel plaintiffs, defendants often try hard to demonstrate that a plaintiff is a public person. This effort, of course, while not purely a defense, is considered part of the so-called "constitutional defense" given that it stems from the actual malice concept. It is certainly an issue that libel defendants should consider as they formulate their strategies. How a libel suit unfolds hinges on this determination.

The Nature of the Statement

Not only is the categorization of the plaintiff important, but the nature of the statement at issue is as well. In *Dun & Bradstreet v. Greenmoss Builders* a private-person plaintiff contended that material the Supreme Court said was a matter of private concern defamed him. A Dun & Bradstreet credit report sent to five subscribers inaccurately reported that Greenmoss Builders had declared bankruptcy. Justice Lewis Powell, for the majority, wrote that the purpose of the speaker and the nature and size of the audience are among the criteria for determining when speech involves matters of public concern. Thus, the Court sought to establish minimal standards of fault not only depending on the status of the plaintiff but also according to the nature of the subject matter.

Opinion

The opinion defense has both constitutional and common law roots, causing discussion of this complex area of the law to become muddled. Traditionally, opinion as a defense stemmed from the common law. But the ability to voice opinions, particularly about issues of public concern, is now recognized as also being at the heart of the First Amendment's protection of expression. Constitutional derivations of the opinion defense are analyzed here; the common law components of opinion follow.

To attempt to separate statements of fact from statements of opinion is to venture onto one of the law's most slippery of slopes, yet to do so is vital in establishing the boundaries of the protection. In addition, state-to-state variations make the distinction all the more difficult.

In *Gertz*, the Supreme Court stated: "Under the First Amendment there is no such thing as a false idea. However pernicious an opinion may seem, we depend for its correction not on the conscience of judges and juries but on the competition of other ideas." The question remained, however, just what is an opinion, and how is it different from a statement of fact?

The defining case in this area is *Ollman v. Evans,* a 1984 ruling by the D.C. Circuit Court of Appeals. A college professor sued newspaper columnists Rowland Evans and Robert Novak, who wrote that he had no status within the profession and that he used his classroom as an instrument to prepare for a Marxist revolution. The court split in its decision. Judge Antonin Scalia decided that the columnists wrote a "classic and coolly crafted libel," but the majority, led by Judge Kenneth Starr, found the column to be opinion protected by the First Amendment and the principles enunciated in *Gertz.* Judge Robert Bork concurred. Moreover, Judge Starr noted the difficulty in distinguishing opinion from fact and attempted to simplify the task by establishing a four-part test, now known as the Ollman Test:

1. The inquiry must analyze the common usage or meaning of the words.

2. Is the statement verifiable — "objectively capable of proof or disproof"? In other words, can the statement be proven either true or false?

3. What is the linguistic or journalistic context in which the statement occurs? The article or column must be considered as a whole: "The language of the entire column may signal that a specific statement that, standing alone, would appear to be factual, is in fact a statement of opinion."

4. What is the "broader social context into which the statement fits?"

Opinion was initially granted a wide berth of protection. Then — six years after *Ollman* and sixteen years after *Gertz* — came *Milkovich v. Lorain Journal.* It reframed the opinion defense. It also forced recognition of the idea that where pure opinion may not exist, mixed opinion may. In *Milkovich,* a high school wrestling coach sued when a local newspaper columnist indicated that the coach lied under oath about his role in a brawl during a match. For the first time, the Supreme Court addressed the "false idea" statement from *Gertz.* "[W]e do not think this passage from *Gertz* was intended to create a wholesale defamation exemption for anything that might be labeled 'opinion,'" Chief Justice William Rehnquist wrote. "Not only would such an interpretation be contrary to the tenor and context of the passage, but it would also ignore the fact that expressions of 'opinion' may often imply an assertion of objective fact." He wrote that facts can disguise themselves as opinions and that, when they do, they imply a knowledge of hidden facts that led to the opinion. While *Milkovich* holds that opinion is not protected as a category of speech, it provides a framework in which opinion *is* protected. That is, since an opinion cannot be proved false, it cannot be the basis for a successful libel action.

As noted above, opinion defenses are not limited to the constitutional category. "Fair comment and criticism" and "letters to the editor" are common law defenses.

Neutral Reportage

Neutral reportage is another defense with a constitutional foundation. It was first enunciated in 1977 in *Edwards v. National Audubon Society.* Neutral reportage protects accurate, unbiased reporting of accusations by prominent, responsible persons about public figures. Courts that have adopted the neutral reporting rule have done so because news value attaches when public persons make such statements. The Second U.S. Circuit Court of Appeals, in *Edwards,* overturned a jury verdict against the *New York Times,* saying it was constitutionally impermissible to hold the newspaper liable:

[W]hen a responsible, prominent organization ... makes serious charges against a public figure, the First Amendment protects the accurate and disinterested reporting of those charges, regardless of the reporter's private views of their validity.... We do not believe that the press may be required under the First Amendment to suppress newsworthy statements merely because it has serious doubts regarding their truth.

Since the Supreme Court had said that serious doubts about a statement's truth constitutes actual malice, *Edwards* seemed to carve out an exception within the definition of actual malice. Neutral reportage, it seemed, would create even greater breathing space for a media industry already provided latitude *via* the actual malice standard.

In the three decades since its inception, several states — Alabama, Florida, Georgia, Illinois, Louisiana, Oklahoma, Vermont and Washington — and the District of Columbia have accepted neutral reportage in some form. In addition, on the federal appeals level, the Fourth, Seventh and Tenth Circuit Courts have joined the Second in recognizing the privilege. Yet the judiciary has hardly embraced it. Indeed, a significant number of courts have rejected the libel defense, reasoning that it is neither First-Amendment-mandated nor justifiable on policy grounds. The rejection by the Pennsylvania Supreme Court of neutral reportage is illustrative. In *Norton v. Glenn,* the Pennsylvania high court held that the First Amendment creates no special rights for the news media in libel law over and above those enjoyed by ordinary citizens. The court also stated that unless the Supreme Court changes the actual malice standard further in favor of the media, there is no public policy justification for adoption of the neutral reportage privilege.[2]

The Supreme Court has had virtually nothing to say about neutral reportage. While it remains an option in the libel defendant's strategy, the inconsistent manner in which courts have accepted neutral reportage makes it an increasingly unreliable defense. Indeed, neutral reportage has rarely been asserted by media libel defendants for nearly twenty years.

One recent exception was the unsuccessful invocation by Fox News Network of the libel defense when sued by US Dominion for libel. In March 2023, the Delaware Superior Court rejected FNN's neutral reportage argument. The court found that FNN was "not disinterested" in reporting election-fraud allegations.

(For a discussion of neutral reportage as a libel defense in foreign law, see the "Globalization of U.S. Libel Law" section later in this chapter.)

COMMON LAW DEFENSES

Libel defendants may also utilize defenses that originate with the common law. Traditional state rules governing libel law largely stem from laws and principles handed down through generations of legal precedent, mainly from English law. Early in the sixteenth century, the common law courts began to recognize a claim for defamation and, with it, various defenses. These grew out of the recognition that there is sometimes an interest in the free flow of information that is so important that some allowance for error must be made.

Fair Comment and Criticism

Imagine a situation in which a newspaper publishes a highly critical review of a local theater production. Should the subjects of the review be able to file a libel claim? At the turn of the century, the *Des Moines Leader* republished a review of an act by "The Cherry Sisters." Among other statements, the reviewer described one sister as "an old jade," a second as "a capering monstrosity," and the three of them as "strange creatures." When the sisters sued for libel, the Iowa Supreme Court in *Cherry v. Des Moines Leader* accepted the *Leader's* defense:

One who goes upon the stage to exhibit himself to the public, or who gives any kind of a performance to which the public is invited, may be freely criticised [sic].... [E]ntire freedom of expression is guaranteed [sic] to dramatic critics, provided they are not actuated by malice or evil purpose in what they write.

Thus began the development of the fair comment and criti-

cism doctrine. Originally the privilege provided only modest coverage, protecting commentary only when it was based on true facts, but over time it has expanded. Still, to qualify for the privilege, commentary must be fair, it must be made without common law malice (that is, ill will), and it must accurately reflect the opinion of the commentator.

Fair comment and criticism is a common-law privilege that protects critics from lawsuits by individuals in the public eye. A "critic" can be anyone who comments on an individual. A person in the public eye is anyone who enters a public sphere: artist, entertainer, dramatist, writer, teacher, member of the clergy — anyone who moves in and out of the public eye, either professionally or as an amateur. The privilege also protects commentary on institutions whose activities are of interest to the public or where matters of public interest are concerned.

Fair comment and criticism protects criticism based on facts that are stated, privileged or otherwise known to be available to the public. If the challenged statement conveys or implies a defamatory message, this defense may be lost and the implication may be the basis of a libel suit.

The statement-of-fact requirement for the plaintiff raises challenges to Twitter users given that "tweets" are limited to 280 characters. As FindLaw columnist Julie Hilden noted: "[T]he limit may … have a serious — and probably unanticipated — downside: It may make Twitter a trap for the unwary when it comes to libel suits." Given that the word limit offers not enough space to allow supporting facts for an opinion, Twitter users should be wary of potentially defamatory comments.

Truth

As the Tenth Circuit cogently observed, American defamation law protects "a good reputation honestly earned," not an undeserved reputation that has been damaged by the disclosure of hidden facts. Thus, truth is a complete defense in a libel case. If a statement must be false for liability to attach, it cannot be the basis of a successful libel suit if, in fact, it is true. Truth can be asserted as a libel defense even where a person's criminal conviction was expunged but that conviction was subsequently publicized. "Although our expungement statute generally permits a person whose record has been expunged to misrepresent his past," the New Jersey Supreme Court stated in *G.D. v. Kenny*, "it does not alter the metaphysical truth of his past, nor does it impose a regime of silence on those who know the truth." In 2009, however, the First Circuit, applying Massachusetts libel law, held in *Noonan v. Staples* that true but defamatory statements about a private person relating to a matter of private concern can be actionable if published maliciously.

Meanwhile, a number of misconceptions exist about the truth defense, and it is not easy to prove. For years, truth was consid-

---

[2] For the most recent judicial rejection of neutral reportage as a libel defense under the First Amendment, *see* U.S. Dominion, Inc. v. Fox News Network (Del. Super. Ct. 2023), https://perma.cc/6Y9F-KWMN.

ered a noble defense. After all, the media are supposed to be in the business of rooting out and publishing the truth. Modern libel law, however, has turned the truth-falsity distinction on its ear. As the Supreme Court held in *Philadelphia Newspapers v. Hepps,* the burden of proving falsity lies with the plaintiff, especially when the news media are sued for defamation relating to a matter of public interest.

Just because the burden of proof lies with the plaintiff, however, a libel defendant does not stand idly by. The defendant's attorneys may attempt to demonstrate that the disputed material is true. The attorneys will do this by cross-examining the plaintiff's witnesses and, possibly, by producing evidence of truth. In such circumstances — and even when a defendant advances a defense of truth — the defendant need not demonstrate that a defamatory statement is completely true in order to maintain the defense. Substantial truth is all that is required. As the D.C. Circuit held in *Liberty Lobby v. Dow Jones,* "Slight inaccuracies of expression are immaterial provided that the defamatory charge is true in substance." The Supreme Court in *Masson* has agreed, holding that substantial truth would absolve a defendant even if the defendant cannot justify every word of the alleged defamatory matter; it is sufficient if the substance of the charge be proved true, irrespective of the slight inaccuracy in the details. Minor inaccuracies do not amount to falsity so long as the substance, the gist, the sting of the libelous charge can be justified.

Substantial truth means, for example, that if a newspaper reported that an individual was in police custody when, in fact, the individual had been released on bail, the story would be substantially true, because the individual had been in custody and it was only a quirk in time that had caused the mistake. If, however, a newspaper published that an individual had been charged with a crime when the individual had only been questioned and released, the story would not be substantially true. In short, the substantial truth defense can protect a libel defendant when *minor* inaccuracies appear in a report.

A phenomenon unique to the broadcast media may play a role in libel cases and, in turn, may have a bearing on the truth defense. Broadcasters have the ability to alter a message — and its believability, that is, its perceived "truth" — with voice inflections. A libel suit was filed against a Chicago television station claiming that one of its reporters gave a false impression of what had actually occurred, and thereby defamed the plaintiffs, with his skeptical tone of voice. That is, while his words themselves were innocent enough, the tone with which they were delivered was at the root of the libel claim. The federal judge in *Hanash and Yousef v. WFLD,* however, agreed with the defendant's position that the tone alone could not support the defamation suit, and he dismissed it.

It is worthwhile to note a growing trend in lawsuits against media defendants. Plaintiffs are circumventing the issue of truth in the defendant's stories by filing suit for transgressions other than libel. A good example is *Food Lion v. Capital Cities/ABC,* in which a supermarket chain that was unhappy with a television news magazine segment on its food preparation practices sued, not for libel, but because of the techniques used in gathering the information. This strategy enabled Food Lion to entirely bypass any obligation of proving that the broadcast was false. Thus, whereas libel may have been the preferred sword for plaintiffs in cases like this, lawyers are more frequently advising clients to avoid the realm in which the media have the shield of both constitutional and common law protection at their disposal. (The *Food Lion* case also is discussed in Chapter 18.)

Fair Report Privilege

Within some spheres of society, it is so vitally important that people be allowed to speak without fear of being sued for libel that they are granted immunity from liability. This privilege — called "absolute privilege" — typically occurs within the context of carrying out the business of government. Nothing a government official says that is relevant to the official's duties can be the subject of a successful libel suit. A corporation is no different in its absolute privilege when it provides an allegedly defamatory investigatory report to a government agency. As the Texas Supreme Court held in *Shell Oil Co. v. Writt,* compelled cooperation by companies with the federal Department of Justice will not expose them to liability for defamation. Moreover, an open society demands that members of the public have access to information relating to government proceedings. It logically follows, then, that people reporting on these proceedings or other absolutely privileged information also have the protection of privilege. This privilege, however, is often conditioned or qualified on the fair and accurate reporting of the proceeding and is generally known as "qualified privilege."

The privilege may be lost if the allegedly defamatory material is published with common law malice, if it is not fair, if the gist of the article is not substantially correct, or if the author draws conclusions or adds comments to the official report. According to the Illinois Supreme Court in *Solaia Technology v. Specialty Publishing Co.* and the Tennessee Supreme Court in *Funk v. Scripps Media,* however, it is not defeated by either common law malice or actual malice. Sometimes referred to as the "fair report" or "official report" privilege, it is recognized by common law or statute in at least forty-seven states and the District of Columbia, and it proves to be an exception to the rule of republication, discussed later in this chapter.

The fair report privilege protects media reports of official government actions, regardless of possible defamatory elements in those reports. The rationale is that citizens in a participatory democracy are entitled to such information. According to the Fourth Circuit in *Lee v. Dong-A Ilbo*, however, that entitlement rarely extends to official reports issued by governments other than those in the United States.

Hyperlinking to a defamatory source is protected by the fair report privilege. In *Adelson v. Harrison*, a federal district court in New York applied the fair report privilege under Nevada libel law in holding hyperlinking nonactionable. This hyperlink libel case arose from allegations made in a separate wrongful termination suit by an ex-employee against Sheldon Adelson, a Las Vegas businessman. Adelson was alleged to have approved "prostitution strategy" for his casino business. The National Jewish Democratic Council posted an article on its Web site claiming that Adelson "personally approved" of prostitution in his Macau casinos and hyperlinked to an Associated Press story.

In connection with the source attribution as a requirement for the fair report privilege, the federal court found: "The hyperlink is the twenty-first century equivalent of the footnote for purposes of attribution in defamation law, because it has become a well-recognized means for an author or the Internet to attribute source." The court added that shielding libel defendants from liability for hyperlinking to their sources is "good public policy," since it helps facilitate access to information of public interest.

More recently, a federal district court in Florida followed *Adelson*. In *Gubarev v. BuzzFeed, Inc.*, the court ruled in late 2018 that BuzzFeed's article on the so-called "Trump Dossier" was protected by the fair report privilege when it was hyperlinked to the CNN report on the "official actions" on the dossier.

The privilege covers officials and proceedings in the executive, judicial and legislative branches of local, state and federal governments and, often, private individuals communicating with the government.

Executive Branch. Reports on the official statements and proceedings of people in the administrative — or executive — branch of government are typically privileged. The reports and hearings administrators are required by law to prepare and conduct are covered, particularly when the information contained therein has been made available to the public.

In 2020, the Minnesota Supreme Court in *Larson v. Gannett Co.* applied to an official news conference and press release. The court held that the balance of the public's right to know against an individual's reputational interest "weighs in favor of applying the fair and accurate reporting privilege to news reports of information disseminated by law enforcement officers about a matter of public concern at an official press conference or in an official press release,"

Similarly, the Third Circuit in *Lee v. TMZ Productions* ruled in 2017 that New Jersey's fair report privilege covered the "full,

fair, and accurate" news articles on a New York attorney general's press conference and press release describing a drug and prostitution ring.

Meanwhile, the fair report privilege is not always confined to reports of official statements or of official actions. It may apply to news reports based on information provided by *nonofficial* sources, if the reports are fair and accurate. In 2010, the Massachusetts Supreme Judicial Court stated in *Howell v. Enterprise Publishing Co.*:

> The privilege to report official actions would mean very little, … if to qualify for its protection, the media were limited to reporting such [official] actions solely on the basis of on-the-record statements by high-ranking (authorized to speak) officials or published official documents. Consequently, the privilege extends to reports of official actions based on information provided by nonofficial third-party sources. It should be of no moment that a reporter's source is, in fact, a high official, a low official, or a mere witness who overheard the proceedings, so long as it is official action that is reported.

Law enforcement agencies are included as part of the executive branch of government, so reports of police activity are conditionally privileged. Official reports and statements by police officials and officers qualify. A 2009 Arkansas case illustrates how the privilege can work. A man who was mentioned in a police report about an alleged rape sued the *Courier News* for libel after the newspaper published a story based on the inaccurate report. He argued that the newspaper's story was not fair and not privileged. The Arkansas Supreme Court, in *Whiteside v. Russellville Newspapers*, disagreed, holding that the news story about the rape allegations comprised the information from the report as recounted to the police by the victim's cousin. The court found that if the gist of the publication is in essence accurate, "some minor conflicts in what was alleged will not eliminate the privilege."

Not every statement by a public official is privileged, however. In 2019, for example, the Tennessee Supreme Court in *Burke v. Sparta Newspapers, Inc.*, refused to apply the fair report privilege to a nonpublic, one-on-one interview between a newspaper reporter and a detective of a county sheriff's department. The privilege, the Tennessee court held, "encompasses only *public* proceedings or official actions of government that have been made *public.*"

Legislative Branch. Reports about the proceedings of Congress, state legislatures and local governing bodies are privileged. In addition, reports on documents — petitions and complaints, for example — that are filed with or submitted to these bodies are also privileged. It is important to remember, however, that documents coming from legislative meetings are not privileged until officials take possession of them.

Judicial Branch. Reports about judicial activities — the courts — are conditionally privileged unless otherwise codified. So media accounts of testimony, depositions, arguments, trials, verdicts, opinions and orders — those aspects that are typically open or available to the public — are among the proceedings covered. Also, documents that relate to the judicial branch are also typically privileged. Conversely, those parts of the judicial process that are closed are not privileged.

As a Massachusetts judge, Oliver Wendell Holmes was among those who reasoned in *Cowley v. Pulsifer* that the public should be provided with information about judicial proceedings because "those who administer justice should act under a sense of public responsibility." Nearly a century later, another Massachusetts court in *Liquori v. Republican Co.* echoed Holmes and held that the value of granting privilege to media reports about the courts is "the security which publicity gives for the proper administration of justice."

Non-Publication and Republication

Since a plaintiff in a libel case must prove that a defamatory statement was published, a defendant may prevail by showing he or she did not publish the statement, that the statement was not understood by a third party, or that it was published so long ago (one year or more, depending on the state) that the statute of limitations expired.

Since republication, a narrow exception to the single publication rule, is considered tantamount to publication, there is virtually no defense in arguing that the defendant merely repeated a defamatory statement. As the D.C. Circuit Court of Appeals ruled in *Liberty Lobby v. Dow Jones & Co.*, "[O]ne who republishes a defamatory statement 'adopts' it as his own and is liable in equal measure to the original defamer." Moreover, media are especially prone to libel suits for repeating defamatory statements because plaintiffs tend to sue defendants who are best able to pay damages. The original publisher is not as likely to be as financially capable as a media organization.

Meanwhile, does the posting of new articles referencing or hyperlinking to a previously published defamatory story constitute republication? In *Salyer v. Southern Poverty Law Center*, a federal district court in Kentucky answered no. The court held that a mere reference to a defamatory article "does not present the *defamatory contents* of the article to [a] new audience," while it may bring the article's "existence" to the attention of the audience. Further, the court found that the hyperlink, a new method of access to the referenced article, did not republish the article. For the hyperlink neither restated the defamatory

article nor changed the contents of that article. From a policy perspective, the court reasoned, finding republication by hyperlink would undercut the single publication rule:

Websites are frequently, if not constantly, updated. Methods of access to portions of the website can change on a regular basis and links to previous posts on a website are constantly added and taken away from sites. Therefore, to find that a new link to an unchanged article posted long ago on a website republishes that article would result in a continual retriggering of the limitations period.

More recently, a New York appeals court held in *Biro v. Condé Nast* that an email from Conde Nast to *New Yorker* magazine subscribers containing a hyperlink to a *New Yorker* article does not constitute republication.

Letters to the Editor

While the publication of letters to the editor represents a form of republication, letters are typically viewed as expressions of opinions rather than statements of fact. For that reason, newspapers and magazines have won most cases based on the publication of letters. Courts have sought to provide protection for their publication, often viewing them as part of an open forum for the general public.

The placement of a letter can have a bearing in determining whether it qualifies as opinion. That is, by appearing in a section of a newspaper or magazine that is clearly set aside for letters expressing opinions, a letter is much more likely to be viewed by a court as an expression of opinion.

Courts have held that some letters to the editor have combined opinion and facts. Often cases based on such expressions end in favor of libel plaintiffs. For example, a Florida appellate court ruled in *Madsen v. Buie* that a letter questioning a child psychologist's qualifications was defamatory because it was this sort of mixed expression and, therefore, not privileged. On the other hand, the Ohio Supreme Court, in *Wampler v. Higgins*, supported the notion that writers of letters to the editor enjoy the same constitutional protection for opinions as journalists do: "The robust exchange of ideas that occurs each day on the editorial pages of our state's newspapers could indeed suffer if the non-media authors of letters to the editor published in these forums were denied the same constitutional protections enjoyed by the editors themselves." Thus, the authors of letters that the news media publish are as shielded as the media themselves.

The Wire Service Defense

Another exception to the republication rule is the publication of information from a business that expressly provides information to news organizations. This "wire service defense" is available to libel defendants if four factors are met:

(1) the defendant received the copy in which the defamatory statements are contained from a reputable news gathering agency;

(2) the defendant did not know the story was false;

(3) nothing on the face of the story could have reasonably alerted the defendant that it may have been incorrect; and

(4) the original wire service story was republished without substantial change.

In short, the wire service defense holds that the accurate republication of a story that a reputable news agency provided does not constitute fault as a matter of law.

The wire service defense originated with the 1933 case *Layne v. Tribune Co.* The Florida Supreme Court held that republication of wire service reports could not be libelous unless the publisher acted in a negligent, reckless or careless manner. "No newspaper could ... assume in advance the burden of specially verifying every item of news reported to it by established news gathering agencies," the court held.

In *McKinney v. Avery Journal,* a North Carolina Court of Appeals case, and in *Auvril v. CBS,* a federal district court case in Washington state, the wire service defense has succeeded even when a newspaper published a story that relied on past wire-service articles and when a CBS affiliate broadcast network news reports. Though by no means universally accepted, at least thirteen jurisdictions have adopted the wire service defense: Alaska, the District of Columbia, Florida, Georgia, Hawaii, Kentucky, Louisiana, Massachusetts, Missouri, New York, North Carolina, Wisconsin and Puerto Rico.

But what happens if the Associated Press republishes defamatory articles from reputable newspapers? The "reverse wire service defense" protects the AP from liability. The Massachusetts Court of Appeals in *Reilly v. Associated Press,* calling the relationship between the AP and its member newspapers and other media outlet members "symbiotic," noted that the AP employs its own staff to report original news stories but also often relies upon member newspapers as additional wire sources.

Online Republication

Publication of online material by Internet service providers is related to publication and republication. The issue in libel law is whether an online service can be held liable for defamatory statements that are published through that service.

The defining case in this area is *Zeran v. America Online.* The case dealt with the issue of an ISP as publisher, but did so in light of the passage of the Communications Decency Act in 1996. Kenneth Zeran sued America Online when the company

included his name and telephone number in a series of bulletin board notices that advertised t-shirts and other items glorifying the 1995 bombing of a federal building in Oklahoma City. The inclusion of his name was part of a hoax by an unknown individual. A relevant section of the CDA stipulates that no provider of an interactive computer service may be treated as the publisher of information provided by some entity other than the provider. A U.S. district court ruled that while the CDA does not preempt all state law actions of this nature, it did preempt Zeran's claim of negligence by AOL because it conflicts with both the language and purposes of the CDA. On appeal, the Fourth U.S. Circuit Court of Appeals ruled that this section of the CDA "plainly immunizes computer service providers like AOL for liability for information that originates with third parties." Thus, an online libel defendant may be able to utilize the CDA when similar circumstances present themselves.

Barrett v. Rosenthal, the California Supreme Court's application of the CDA on the basis of the *Zeran* precedent, is illustrative. Adopting *Zeran's* ruling that the CDA protects both "publishers" and subsequent "distributors" against defamation liability for online republication, the California court, stated that there is no practical distinction between active and passive use of interactive computer services. Hence, the court concluded that Internet users cannot be held liable for posting defamatory statements prepared by someone else.

On the other hand, the Ninth Circuit, in *Fair Housing Council of San Fernando Valley v. Roommates.com,* a 2008 *en banc* decision, held that Roommates.com was ineligible for immunity as a "developer" under the CDA when it "materially" contributed to creating the allegedly illegal content relating to housing discrimination under the federal Fair Housing Act. In a recent Internet libel case, however, the New York Court of Appeals did not find the kind of "material" change that had deprived Roommates.com of CDA immunity in the Ninth Circuit's ruling. New York's highest court held in *Shiamili v. Real Estate Group of New York, Inc.* that the defendant blog operators did not materially alter a defamatory comment by a user when they moved it to a stand-alone post and gave it a heading. The court said: "Reposting content created and initially posted by a third party is well-within 'a publisher's traditional editorial functions.'"

The Libel-Proof Plaintiff

A libel defendant may be able to invoke the concept of the "libel-proof plaintiff." When an individual's reputation is so bad that even a false accusation could not further harm it, the individual is considered to be libel-proof and cannot win a defamation suit. The libel-proof doctrine was first articulated as a libel defense in *Cardillo v. Doubleday Co., Inc.,* a 1975 case. Since then, two separate prongs of the libel-proof doctrine have developed: in-

THE DEFENDANT'S CASE

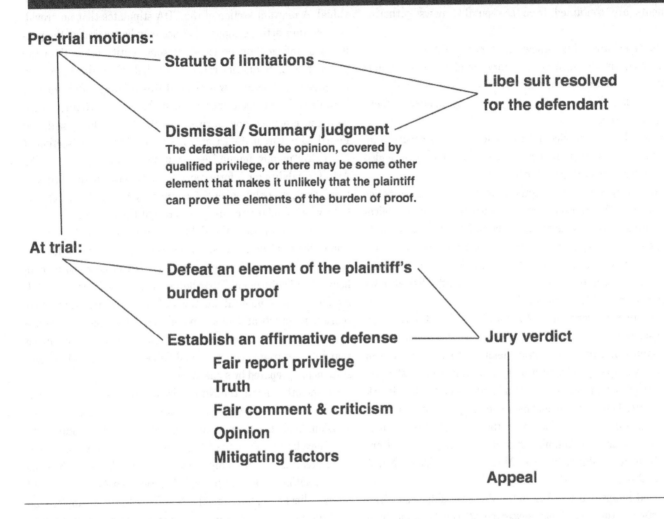

Pre-trial motions:

Statute of limitations ────────────▶ **Libel suit resolved for the defendant**

Dismissal / Summary judgment
The defamation may be opinion, covered by qualified privilege, or there may be some other element that makes it unlikely that the plaintiff can prove the elements of the burden of proof.

At trial:

Defeat an element of the plaintiff's burden of proof

Establish an affirmative defense ────────────▶ **Jury verdict**
    Fair report privilege
    Truth
    Fair comment & criticism
    Opinion
    Mitigating factors

Appeal

---

cremental harm and issue-specific publication.

Incremental Harm. If an individual is identified in an article as thief, child molester and tax evader, and if all the charges are true, does it make any difference if the individual is also identified falsely as a kidnapper? The doctrine of incremental harm says no. In such a case, the publisher could probably win, arguing that the single false statement causes harm that is merely incremental beyond what already exists and, therefore, is not grounds for a libel suit. In short, the false statement causes no significant harm to the reputation beyond that caused by the true statements, which are protected.

One of the leading incremental harm cases is *Herbert v. Lando*. Anthony Herbert, a retired Army officer, sued CBS over statements made about him in a segment of *60 Minutes*. The segment questioned the validity of his claim that the U.S. Army had punished him for trying to disclose information about massacres by American forces in South Vietnam. The Second Cir-

cuit ruled that if the charge that Herbert lied about reporting war crimes was not actionable, "other statements, even those that might be found to have been published with actual malice should not be actionable if they merely imply the same view, and are simply an outgrowth of and subsidiary to those claims upon which it has been held there can be no recovery."

In several cases, however, the incremental harm doctrine has failed as a defense. A noteworthy example was the rejection of the doctrine in *Liberty Lobby, Inc. v. Anderson*. Journalist Jack Anderson described the founder of Liberty Lobby as a racist, fascist, anti-Semitic and neo-Nazi. Anderson argued that previous publications had already so irreparably tarnished the plaintiff's reputation that the libel-proof doctrine should apply. In an opinion written by Judge Antonin Scalia, the D.C. Circuit rejected the claim, ruling that "we cannot envision how a court would go about determining that someone's reputation had already been 'irreparably' damaged — i.e., that no new reader could be reached by the freshest libel."

Nevertheless, the doctrine, which the First Amendment does not mandate, remains a valuable defense weapon, particularly against frivolous libel suits, and especially given the Supreme Court's opinion in *Masson* that states are free to adopt the doctrine as they see fit.

Issue-Specific Publication. Courts recognizing the issue-specific doctrine have found that libel plaintiffs with tarnished reputations with regard to a particular issue are libel-proof *only with respect to that topic area.* Libel claims pursued in the issue-specific context, the New Hampshire Supreme Court held in *Thomas v. Telegraph Publishing Co.*, require proof not only

that the plaintiff engaged in criminal or anti-social behavior in the past, but also that his activities were widely reported to the public. The evidence on the nature of the conduct, the number of offenses, and the degree and range of publicity received must make it clear, as a matter of law, that the plaintiff's reputation could not have suffered from the publication of the false and libelous statement.

In one case, for example, the defendant had published an article that said the plaintiff had used his relationship with actress Elizabeth Taylor for financial gain. A federal district court in California held in *Wynberg v. National Enquirer* that the plaintiff had a "reputation for taking advantage of women generally, and of Miss Taylor specifically." It ruled that "[a]n individual who engages in certain anti-social or criminal behavior and suffers a diminished reputation may be 'libel-proof' as a matter of law, as it *relates to that specific behavior.*"

More recently, however, Howard K. Stern, a former attorney and companion of Anna Nicole Smith, was found not to be libel-proof. A federal district court held that Stern's bad reputation as Smith's "principal enabler" could still be further damaged by the false "promiscuous homosexual sex" or "pimping" assertions in defendant Rita Cosby's book *Blonde Ambition: The Untold Story Behind Anna Nicole Smith's Death.* U.S. District Judge Denny Chinn in *Stern v. Cosby* stated: "That someone has been falsely called a thief in the past does not mean that he is immune from further injury if he is falsely called a thief again."

Thus, the doctrine of the libel-proof plaintiff may serve a defendant who has published otherwise defamatory statements about an individual whose reputation is already so sullied as to render additional accusations moot, regardless of their falsity. The doctrine may apply to accusations of any nature or to those that relate only to a specific issue.

OTHER DEFENSE ISSUES

While not defenses *per se*, several other issues can have a bear-

ing on — and even strengthen — a libel defense.

Responsible Reporting

As part of a defense strategy, a libel defendant may attempt to demonstrate that it conducted itself in a responsible way. Within the context of a media organization, responsible reporting may be demonstrated through attempts to show that journalists acted without negligence or reckless disregard of the truth.

In attempting to prove that a libel defendant acted with reckless disregard, a plaintiff is likely to attempt to build a case bit by bit, demonstrating irresponsibility or carelessness in publishing. Courts have said that no single element is sufficient to prove clearly and convincingly that a defendant acted with actual malice, but each can be used as evidence. A libel defendant who is aware of certain claims of irresponsibility or carelessness, therefore, can be prepared to refute them. Some of the claims might be the following:

- failure to investigate sufficiently;
- failure to interview parties who have knowledge of facts related to the story, including the subject of the report;
- reliance on previously published material;
- reliance on biased stories or sources;
- inaccurate reporting;
- reporting from a specific point of view in an investigative story;
- refusal to retract or correct if facts warrant;
- absence of a fixed deadline;
- ill will or hatred toward the plaintiff, that is, common law malice.

Even if media defendants are unable to escape liability altogether, by refuting these points, and demonstrating responsible reporting, they are likely to mitigate damages.

A case in Ohio illustrates how a court may consider one or more of these elements. Within the context of a libel suit, a state appellate court concluded that a reporter's failure to interview one of the police officers accused of brutality in a series of reports could be regarded as negligent behavior. The Ohio Court of Appeals in *Early v. Toledo Blade* ruled, however, that the irresponsibility alone did not support the officer's claim that the reporter had acted with actual malice. Conversely, a television journalist argued that his reporting methods were responsible by maintaining that he spent four days interviewing thirty people and reviewing 500 pages of court records in preparing the story. That contributed to the Texas Court of Appeals in *Dolcefino and KTRK Television v. Turner* overturning a libel judgment against him.

Retractions, apologies and corrections for reputation-damaging reports can also be considered examples of "responsible reporting." In the eyes of the law, their impact varies greatly from state to state. In some states, a prompt and complete apology, correction and retraction will protect a defendant from punitive damages. In other states, jurors merely consider retractions in determining the amount of damages.

While a retraction or apology is not a defense, a potential defendant is often advised to correct possibly libelous errors due to the correction's ability to alleviate the statement's defamatory sting in the eyes of a court. Admitting errors may be regarded as an aspect of responsible reporting.[3] Moreover, many states have retraction laws that provide varying degrees of protection. Typically, they require a plaintiff to give a publisher an opportunity to retract a statement prior to initiating a libel suit. If the publisher honors the request in a timely manner, the retraction may reduce the damages that the plaintiff may seek should a lawsuit be filed. It should be noted, however, that the plaintiff may use a retraction, apology or correction as a defendant's admission of liability.

Summary Judgment

A judge may summarily decide certain points of a case and issue a judgment dismissing the case. Summary judgment can occur at any of several junctures in litigation.

A judge may issue a summary judgment on grounds that there is no genuine issue as to material fact. Generally, this is a result of a plaintiff being unable to meet at least one element in the plaintiff's burden of proof. The Supreme Court held in *Mourning v. Family Publications Service* that when considering motions for summary judgment, courts "must view the facts and inferences to be drawn from them in the light most favorable to the opposing party." The rationale is that, if the summary judgment is granted, the plaintiff's opportunity to prove a case is ended, but if the defendant's motion for summary judgment is denied, the defendant still has an opportunity to prove its case.

Summary judgments are seen as important tools for protecting free expression, particularly in an environment in which plaintiffs have harassed the media by filing frivolous lawsuits. Allowing judges to dismiss claims without merit tackles the chilling effect on media coverage that these lawsuits can have. As the D.C. Circuit in *Washington Post Co. v. Keogh* explained:

In the First Amendment area, summary procedures are even more essential. For the stake here, if harassment succeeds, is free debate. One of the purposes of the [*New York*] *Times* [ac-

tual malice] principle, in addition to protecting persons from being cast in damages in libel suits filed by public officials, is to prevent persons from being discouraged in the full and free exercise of First Amendment rights with respect to the conduct of their government. The threat of being put to the defense of a lawsuit brought by a popular public official may be as chilling to the exercise of First Amendment freedoms as fear of the outcome of the lawsuit itself, especially to advocates of unpopular causes.

Until 1979, summary judgment was a preferred method of dealing with libel cases involving actual malice. When the defense submitted a motion for summary judgment — based on the contention that the plaintiff could not prove actual malice — the judge would either grant or deny it. If granted, the case was over; if denied, the case went to trial. In 1979, Chief Justice Warren Burger in *Hutchinson* cast doubt on the appropriateness of summary judgment because any examination of actual malice "calls a defendant's state of mind into question." Such a circumstance, he argued, "does not readily lend itself to summary disposition." While some lower courts took Burger's admonition to heart — using it as a basis for denying summary judgment — motions for summary judgment continued to be granted more often than not. Then, in 1986, Justice Byron White in *Anderson v. Liberty Lobby* wrote that in deciding whether to grant motions for summary judgment, trial judges should decide if public plaintiffs can meet the actual malice standard by "clear and convincing evidence." If not, summary judgment should be granted. In short, White's opinion suggests that summary judgment remains a viable option.

Today, in an effort to curtail the increasing cost of defending libel suits, judges may be more apt to grant motions for summary. About 80 percent of libel insurance costs are incurred, not through the compensation of injured plaintiffs, but merely in defense costs. Estimates regarding the average defense cost vary but typically range from $100,000 to $200,000. In major cases, defendants have spent millions of dollars. Moreover, they have discovered that juries are increasingly unsympathetic toward them. The median jury award increased from $200,000 in the early 1980s to an average of $1.5 million over the decade. The Media Law Resource Center found in the early 2000s that libel judgments against the media averaged $1.8 million in 2001. In fact, juries seem to be punishing some defendants — those whose content or newsgathering techniques they find distasteful — particularly hard with punitive damages. Verdicts can reach into the millions, making it appear that juries base their decisions at least in part on a defendant's perceived unsavory nature. In the wake of these awards, legal scholar Nicole B. Casarez wrote, such awards "[fly] in the face of the First Amendment which protects unorthodox as well as mainstream speech."

---

[3] It should be acknowledged that retractions and/or apologies are sometimes discouraged by those who advise potential media defendants. To retract or apologize, they say, is tantamount to an admission of guilt, thus increasing the challenge of mounting a successful defense.

While approximately two-thirds of jury verdicts in media libel cases are rendered against media defendants, about 75 percent are reversed or reduced on appeal. The bottom line — and not necessarily a reassuring one — for those facing a libel suit may be that media defendants tend to win on the law rather than having to rely on the often emotion-based conclusions of jurors.

GLOBALIZATION OF U.S. LIBEL LAW: JURISDICTION AND CHOICE OF LAW ISSUES

Now broadcasters and publications transcend the boundaries of one country, causing complicated problems for potential libel plaintiffs and defendants. Such is increasingly the case with Internet communicators, both institutional and individual. The site where a lawsuit is adjudicated is, in legal parlance, the "place of wrong," that is, the place where the alleged injury occurred. In past years, the place of wrong for libel actions was the jurisdiction where the defamatory publication was made, regardless of where it originated. More recently, however, libel actions have been adjudicated in the place with the most significant relationship to the case. Generally, the *Restatement* states, the place with the most significant relationship to the case is the jurisdiction in which the plaintiff lives or works.

The determination of which law should govern in multi-state or multi-nation lawsuits is called the "choice of law" issue. Transnational media litigation, which often involves libel cases in foreign countries against media defendants in the United States, is growing. This is especially true of libel involving the Internet. A good illustration is the High Court of Australia's 2002 decision in *Dow Jones & Co. v. Gutnick*. Australian businessman Joseph Gutnick sued the U.S. company Dow Jones & Co. in the Supreme Court of Victoria for defamation in connection with online material published in *Barron's Online* magazine. Noting that Victoria residents downloaded the material at issue, the Australian court held that when a defamatory statement is accessible to and read by ISP subscribers in an Australian state, a court of that state has jurisdiction to hear an action for defamation relating to the statements.

In a 2005 Internet libel case, however, a Canadian appellate court refused to exercise jurisdiction over an American newspaper. In *Bangoura v. Washington Post,* the Ontario Court of Appeal held that there was "simply no real and substantial connection" between the libel action and Ontario. Cheickh Bangoura, a native of Guinea, who moved to Ontario in 2000, sued the *Washington Post* and three reporters for defamation. In 1997, the *Washington Post* had published two articles claiming that Bangoura, then a U.N. official in Kenya, engaged in sexual harassment, financial improprieties and nepotism.

Generally, American courts hold that the First Amendment protects U.S. libel defendants from foreign judgments if they are brought to the United States for enforcement. In *Bachchan v. India Abroad Publications, Inc.,* for example, an Indian national living in London asked a New York state court to enforce a libel verdict the plaintiff won in England against the publisher of a newspaper and news service in the United States. Judge Shirley Fingerhood found that England's lack of an equivalent to the First Amendment to be significant and ruled that enforcing a foreign libel judgment would seriously jeopardize the First Amendment protections of speech and the press.

The Maryland Court of Appeals, in *Telnikoff v. Matusevitch,* reached a similar conclusion five years later. A U.S. citizen was successfully sued in England for a letter he had written to the editor of the London *Daily Telegraph*. When the writer returned to Maryland, the plaintiff asked American courts to enforce the libel judgment. The Maryland Court of Appeals, however, noting England's adherence to strict liability in libel actions, the presumptive falsity of alleged defamations, the lack of distinction between private and public figures and differences in defenses, concluded that defamation law was totally different in England "in virtually every significant respect." The principles of libel law applied to the suit in England, the court held, were "so contrary to Maryland defamation law, and to the policy of freedom of the press" that the judgment should not be recognized.

In 2001, a federal district judge in California held the French court's order against Yahoo! unenforceable in the United States. U.S. District Judge Jeremy Fogel stated in *Yahoo! Inc. v. La Ligue Contre le Racisme et l'Antisemitisme,* "Although France has the sovereign right to regulate what speech is permissible in France, this Court may not enforce a foreign order that violates the protections of the U.S. Constitution by chilling protected speech that occurs simultaneously within our borders."

In an effort to preempt various free speech issues arising from libel tourism abroad,[4] state and federal lawmakers have taken legislative initiatives. In 2008, the New York legislature passed the Libel Terrorism Protection Act, which requires New York courts to dismiss foreign libel judgment as unenforceable if the foreign laws underlying the judgments are less protective of speech and the press than the First Amendment or the state constitution. California, Florida, Illinois, Maryland and Utah have also enacted similar laws.

In 2010, President Barack Obama signed federal legislation that bars domestic enforcement of foreign libel judgments against Americans if the judgments are inconsistent with the First Amendment. The act, modeled on the New York libel tourism law, was designed to protect American news media, journalists, ISPs, and others from libel litigation overseas. The SPEECH (Securing the Protection of Our Enduring and Estab-

---

4 "Libel tourism" refers to "the use of libel judgments ... in jurisdictions with claimant-friendly libel laws — and little or no connection to the author or purported libelous material....." Ehrenfeld v. Bin Mahfouz, 881 N.E.2d 830, 834 (N.Y. 2007).

lished Constitutional Heritage) Act enables a U.S. publisher or author sued abroad to collect attorneys' fees if the foreign judgment is successfully opposed. Libel tourism is not necessarily limited to the traditional media. Postings on Facebook, Twitter and other social media can be subject to libel tourism abroad.

In 2013, the Fifth Circuit held in *Trout Point Lodge, Ltd. v. Handshoe* that the SPEECH Act barred enforcement of a Canadian defamation judgment. Canadian residents sued a Mississippi-based blogger in a Nova Scotia court for defamation. They won a default judgment against the blogger, which included injunctive relief, in addition to $252,000 in damages and costs. When they sought to enforce their Canadian judgment, the federal district court in Mississippi refused, citing the SPEECH Act. The Fifth Circuit, affirming the district court ruling, reasoned that Canadian law, an offshoot of U.K. law, was less protective of free speech than American law and that a Mississippi court would not have found defamation on the facts and circumstances involved. The blogger, as the prevailing party under the SPEECH Act, was awarded an attorney's fee of $48,000.

The gap between the United States and the rest of the world remains considerable. American libel law is decidedly more media-friendly than the laws of other laws countries. As media law scholar Kyu Ho Youm noted in the early 2010s, however, free speech defenses, including the *Sullivan* actual malice standard, for the news media against liability for libel are increasingly accepted in other countries. In *Jameel v. Wall Street Journal Europe*, the United Kingdom House of Lords, a body that functions as the highest appellate court in England, held that responsible news reporting on a matter of public interest should preclude liability although it resulted in false defamatory stories. More importantly, the Law Lords in *Jameel* recognized neutral reportage as a libel defense in a way similar to that of the Second Circuit in *Edwards v. National Audubon Society*. Especially Lord Leonard H. Hoffmann's comment on reportage in *Jameel* is provocative. "[T]here are cases ('reportage') in which the public interest lies simply in the fact that the statement was made, when it may be clear that the publisher does not subscribe to any belief in its truth," Lord Hoffmann stated. "[Here] the defense is not affected by the newspaper's inability to prove the truth of the statement at the trial." The U.K. common law reportage defense was incorporated into the Defamation Act of 2013. In 2009, the Canadian Supreme Court embraced "reportage" as part of its new "responsible communication" defense in libel law. The Court in *Grant v. Torstar* held:

If a dispute is itself a matter of public interest and the allegations are fairly reported, the publisher should incur no liability even if some of the statements made may be defamatory and untrue, provided: (1) the report attributes the statement to a person, preferably identified, thereby avoiding total un-

accountability; (2) the report indicates, expressly or implicitly, that its truth has not been verified; (3) the report sets out both sides of the dispute fairly; and (4) the report provides the context in which the statements were made.

Further, Argentina and Spain are other countries that incorporate neutral reportage, although the libel defense is increasingly questionable in U.S. law.

SUMMARY

Defamation law is designed to protect reputations so that individual interests are not harmed, while the guarantees of free expression are designed to promote the gathering and dissemination of information. Reputational rights are recognized in every society as a significant interest, but the degree of protection by law or custom varies greatly from country to country.

In the United States, though free expression is vigorously protected, libel law is one of the most visible legal restraints on expression. In recent years, the chill on expression caused by libel law has been a growing concern for the media. On the other hand, those critical of the excesses of the press welcome some degree of press chill. Notwithstanding the debate, there is no denying that libel law serves as a necessary mechanism for the balance between reputational rights and press freedom.

There are two types of defamation: libel – written defamation – and slander – spoken defamation. The traditional distinction between libel and slander is not as clear-cut as it once was because of new modes of communication. Broadcast defamation, for example, is more often than not treated as libel.

Nearly all libel cases are civil actions, in which plaintiffs claim monetary damages for reputational harm from defamatory statements. Libel is still recognized as a crime in some jurisdictions, but criminal libel statutes are rarely invoked.

To establish a cause of action against a non-media libel defendant, a plaintiff must prove that he or she was identified in a statement that was published to a third person, and that the statement was defamatory. When a media organization is the defendant, the plaintiff must establish two additional elements: (1) that the publication resulted from fault on the part of the defendant and (2) that the plaintiff suffered actual injury from publication of the defamatory statement. But the Ninth Circuit ruling of 2013 on the First Amendment right of bloggers questions the media and non-media distinctions.

Libel as a tort — a civil wrong — is premised on the requirement that a statement be false and defamatory. Thus, falsity is essential to a libel claim. Therefore, a libel claim for a statement of opinion — which cannot be proved to be true or false — cannot stand.

"Truth" in libel law is not synonymous with "accuracy." Verbatim quotations in a news story may be accurate but may not necessarily be true. "Truth" means that the substance of the quoted statement is factually verifiable.

It is difficult to determine when some language is defamatory; other language is clearly defamatory. The meanings of words change with the time, place and manner in which they are used. In the majority of jurisdictions, the libel *per se* and libel *per quod* rules are still followed. Libel *per se* refers to words and phrases that are defamatory on their face and need no additional information. Libel *per quod* refers to a statement that is not defamatory in and of itself but that can be made defamatory if additional facts are known.

Family members or relatives of libel plaintiffs can rarely claim damages for libels unless they can individually establish that they suffered from damage to their reputations because of the publication of defamatory statements about them. Identification is not necessarily the specific reference to a plaintiff by name. If a plaintiff is identifiable to those who were exposed to the publication, the identification requirement is met. Individuals who are members of groups have increasing difficulty proving they were identified as the size of the group grows.

Publication has little to do with the ordinary meaning of printing or broadcasting a defamatory statement. Instead, it means that material is disseminated to someone other than the defamed person. Publication is rarely an issue in media libel actions because defamatory statements are usually disseminated to a wide audience when media publish them. Republication of a libelous statement can constitute a cause of action separate from the original publication. Whoever is substantially and directly involved in publishing a defamatory statement is liable and thus can be sued.

Libel plaintiffs must prove fault, but the degree of fault depends upon the status of the plaintiff. In most states, private persons are required to prove negligence in order to win compensatory damages for defamatory statements involving a matter of public concern. Public figures and public officials must prove actual malice in order to win compensatory damages. In addition, every libel plaintiff must prove actual malice in order to win punitive or presumed damages. As the Supreme Court of Minnesota held in *Maethner v. Someplace Safe, Inc.*, in 2019, recovery of presumed damages for a private plaintiff is contingent upon proof of actual malice.

Does actual malice as a private figure's proof element in winning presumed damages hinge on the status of the libel defendant — that is, media or non-media defamer? Indeed, the Oregon Supreme Court is currently reviewing the challenge to *Wheeler v. Green* (1979), in which the court held that actual malice was required as proof in claiming presumed damages in libel actions by private plaintiffs against *media* defendants.

Libel defendants have at their disposal a variety of tools to use to defend themselves. Typically, their first option is to seek summary judgment. If there is reason to believe that the plaintiff is unable to prove all the elements of the burden of proof — whether on constitutional or common law grounds — a defense attorney may be able to prevail with a summary judgment.

When a case goes to trial, defendants can use both constitutional and common law defenses. Among the defenses in the latter category, truth is regarded as the most definitive, given that it refutes any claim that a statement is false. Other common law defenses for media defendants include the privilege of reporting the proceedings of all government branches. The privilege is qualified on the reporting being fair and accurate.

At the heart of the constitutional defense is the notion that there is a First Amendment value embedded in the media's freedom to express themselves. The creation of actual malice was designed to provide an additional layer of protection for media defendants in reporting about public officials. The doctrine was later extended to public figures. Thus, establishing the nature of the plaintiff is key. Libel defendants seek to have plaintiffs categorized as public because they then have to prove the defendant acted with actual malice — knowledge of falsity or reckless disregard for the truth.

Media organizations and their employees have the right to express opinions, and that right has its roots in the First Amendment freedom of the press. However, defining what qualifies as opinion has been a challenge, and largely rests with the four-part Ollman Test. The protection of opinion is also derived from the common law. Those who are in the public eye subject themselves to fair comment and criticism by the media.

To some extent, defending against a libel accusation involves refuting the elements of the plaintiff's case — that is, contesting the plaintiff's attempts to prove that the definition of libel was met. Given that one of those elements is that the statement at issue is false, if the defendant can prove that it is true, the defense is successful. Similarly, because publication is an element of the plaintiff's case, a defendant may attempt to prove that its publication qualifies as one of the exceptions to the republication rule — neutral reportage, the wire service defense, or online republication. With regard to the latter, the Communication Decency Act of 1996 offers protection to computer service providers.

Finally, media defendants want to portray themselves as reliable and trustworthy organizations that conduct themselves responsibly. While not a defense, *per se*, this representation can only help the defendant's image in the eyes of the court and jury. Moreover, journalistic integrity is simply the proper way to conduct business and often tends to be the best way to avoid libel suits in the first place — and that is often the best defense.

Libel actions resulting from multi-state publications of defamatory statements create various choices of law questions for plaintiffs. The law of the state with "the most significant relationship" to the libel action is generally applied. Foreign libel judgments against transnational U.S. media cannot be enforced in the United States when they are found to violate First Amendment standards on freedom of speech and the press. New York and other states have passed "libel terrorism" laws intended to protect American journalists, writers and publishers from foreign defamation judgments.

BIBLIOGRAPHY

Articles

Anderson, David A. "Reputation, Compensation, and Proof," 25 *William and Mary Law Review* 747 (1984).

Ardia, David S. "Freedom of Speech, Defamation, and Injunctions," 55 *William and Mary Law Review* 1 (2013).

Bunker, Matthew D. "Famous in a Small Town: Indeterminacy and Doctrinal Confusion in Micro Public Figure Doctrine," 70 *Mercer Law Review* 381 (2018-2019).

Casarez, Nicole B. "Punitive Damages in Defamation Actions: An Area of Libel Law Worth Reforming," 32 *Duquesne Law Review* 667 (1994).

Elder, David. "Truth, Accuracy and Neutral Reportage: Beheading the Media Jabberwock's Attempts to Circumvent New York Times v. Sullivan," 9 *Vanderbilt Journal of Entertainment and Technology Law* 551 (2007).

Fu, Angela. "What Does the *Depp v. Heard* Verdict Mean for the Media? It's Hard to Say." *Poynter*, June 13, 2022, https://bit.ly/3HGd2x1.

Hilden, Julie. "Libel by Twitter?: The Suit Against Kim Kardashian Over the "Cookie Diet," *FindLaw*, Jan. 4, 2010, https://perma.cc/S8PA-PXJS.

Hopkins, W. Wat. "Good News or Bad for the Press? Actual Malice as Purposeful Avoidance of the Truth," 14 *Newspaper Research Journal* 99 (Summer/Fall 1993).

Kalven, Harry, Jr. "The New York Times Case: A Note on 'The Central Meaning of the First Amendment,'" 1964 *Supreme Court Review* 199.

LaCasse, Alex. "Exeter Man Charged with Defaming Police Chief," *EDGE Radio*, May 31, 2018, seacoastonline.com, https://perma.cc/H7VZ-EP4F.

Lisby, Gregory C. "No Place in the Law: The Ignominy of Criminal Libel in American Jurisprudence," 9 *Communication Law and Policy* 433 (2004).

McAdoo, Paul R. & Leita Walker, "Minnesota and Tennessee Tackle the Fair Report Privilege," 32 *Communications Lawyer* 6 (Winter 2020).

Post, Robert C. "The Social Foundations of Defamation Law: Reputation and the Constitution," 74 *California Law Review* 691 (1986).

"Preface, Criminalizing Speech About Reputation: The Legacy of Criminal Libel in the U.S. After Sullivan & Garrison," *Media Law Resource Center Bulletin*, March 2003.

Pritchard, David. "Rethinking Criminal Libel: An Empirical Study," 14 *Communication Law and Policy* 3 (2009).

Schauer, Frederick. "Social Foundations of the Law of Defamation: A Comparative Analysis," 1 *Journal of Media Law and Practice* 1 (1980).

Silver, Derigan & Loryn Rumsey, "Going Viral: Limited-Purpose Public Figures, Involuntary Public Figures, and Viral Media Content," 27 *Communication Law and Policy* 49 (2022).

Volokh, Eugene. "Anti-Libel Injunctions," 168 *University of Pennsylvania Law Review* 73 (2019).

Wimmer, Kurt. "Toward a World Rule of Law: Freedom of Expression," 603 *The Annals of the American Academy of Political and Social Sciences* 202 (2006).

Youm, Kyu Ho. "'Actual Malice' in U.S. Defamation Law: The Minority of One Doctrine in the World?" 4 *Journal of International Media and Entertainment Law* 1 (2011-12).

_____. "The 'Actual Malice' of *New York Times Co. v. Sullivan*: A Free Speech Touchstone in a Global Century," 19 *Communication Law and Policy* 185 (2014).

_____. "The Interface Between American and Foreign Libel Law: U.S. Courts Refuse to Enforce Libel Judgments," 49 *International and Comparative Law Quarterly* 131 (2000).

Books

Barbas, Samantha. *Actual Malice: Civil Rights and Freedom of the Press in* New York Times v. Sullivan. Oakland, Calif.: University of California Press, 2023.

Elder, David A. *Defamation: A Lawyer's Guide*. Deerfield, Ill.: Clark Boardman Callaghan, 2023.

Glasser, Charles J., Jr., ed. *International Libel & Privacy Handbook: A Global Reference for Journalists, Publishers, Webmasters, and Lawyers*, 2022-2023 ed. New York: LexisNexis, 2022.

Hopkins, W. Wat. *Actual Malice Twenty-Five Years After Times v. Sullivan*. New York: Prager, 1989.

Melkonian, Harry. *Defamation, Libel Tourism, and the SPEECH Act of 2010: The First Amendment Colliding with the Common Law*. Amherst, N.Y.: Cambria Press, 2011.

Restatement (Second) of Torts. Philadelphia, Pa.: American Law Institute, 1977.

Robinson, Eric P. *Reckless Disregard: St. Amant v. Thompson and the Transformation of Libel Law*. Baton Rouge, La.: Louisiana State University Press, 2018.

Sack, Robert D. *Sack on Defamation: Libel, Slander, and Related Problems*, 4th ed. New York: Practising Law Institute, 2023.

Sanford, Bruce W. *Libel and Privacy,* 2d ed. New York: Wolters Kluwer, 2022.

Smolla, Rodney A. *Law of Defamation,* 3d ed. St. Paul, Minn.: Thomson Reuters, 2023.

Cases

Adelson v. Harris, 973 F. Supp. 2d 467 (S.D.N.Y. 2013), *aff'd,* 876 F.3D 413 (2d Cir. 2017).

Air Wisconsin Airlines Corp. v. Hoeper, 134 S. Ct. 852 (2014).

American Broadcasting-Paramount Theatres, Inc. v. Simpson, 126 S.E.2d 873 (Ga. Ct. App. 1962).

Anderson v. Liberty Lobby, 477 U.S. 242 (1986).

Auvril v. CBS, 140 F.R.D. 450 (E.D. Wash. 1991).

Bachchan v. India Abroad Publications, Inc., 585 N.Y.S.2d 266 (Sup. Ct. N.Y. Co. 1992).

Balvoa Island Village Inn, Inc. v. Lemen, 156 P.3d 339 (Cal. 2007).

Bangoura v. Washington Post, 258 D.L.R.4th 341 (Ont. Ct. App. 2005).

Barrett v. Rosenthal, 146 F.3d 510 (Cal. 2006).

Beamer v. Nishiki, 670 P.2d 1264 (Haw. 1983).

Bierman v. Weier, 826 N.W.2d 436 (Iowa 2013).

Biro v. Condé Nast, 171 A.D.3d 463 (N.Y. App. Div. 2019).

Bose Corp. v. Consumers Union of United States, 446 U.S. 485 (1984).

Burke v. Sparta Newspapers, Inc., 592 S.W.3d 116 (Tenn. 2019).

Burnett v. National Enquirer, 193 Cal. Rptr. 206 (Cal. Ct. App. 1983).

Bustos v. A&E Television Networks, 646 F.3d 762 (10th Cir. 2011).

Cardillo v. Doubleday Co., Inc., 518 F.2d 638 (2d Cir. 1975).

Chapadeau v. Utica Observer-Dispatch, 341 N.E.2d 569 (N.Y. 1975).

Chapski v. Copley Press, 442 N.E.2d 195 (Ill. 1982).

Cherry v. Des Moines Leader, 86 N.W. 323 (Iowa 1901).

Citizen Publishing Co. v. United States, 394 U.S. 131 (1969).

Coral Ridge Ministries Media v. Amazon.Com, No. 1914125 (11th Cir. July 28, 2021), petition for cert. pending (Aug. 15, 2021).

Costello v. Capital Cities Commissions, 505 N.E.2d 701 (Ill. Ct. App. 1987).

Cowley v. Pulsifer, 137 Mass. 392 (1884).

Cox Texas Newspapers L.P. v. Penick, 219 S.W.3d 425 (Tex. App. 2007).

Curtis Publishing Co. v. Butts, 388 U.S. 130 (1967).

Dallas Morning News, Inc. v. Tatum, 554 S.W.3d 614 (Tex. 2018).

Dendrite International, Inc. v. Doe, 775 A.2d 756 (N.J. Super. Ct. App. Div. 2001).

DiLorenzo v. New York News, 432 N.Y.S. 2d 483 (App. Div. 1981).

Dolcefino and KTRK Television, Inc. v. Turner, 987 S.W. 2d 100 (Tex. 1998).

Dow Jones & Co. v. Gutnick, 194 A.L.R. 433 (2003).

Dun & Bradstreet, Inc. v. Greenmoss Builders, Inc., 472 U.S. 749 (1985).

Early v. Toledo Blade, 720 N.E.2d 107 (Ohio Ct. App. 1998).

Edwards v. National Audubon Society, Inc., 556 F.2d 113 (2d Cir. 1977).

Elias v. Rolling Stone, LLC, 872 F.3d 97 (2d Cir. 2017).

Fair Housing Council of San Fernando Valley v. Roommates.com LLC, 52 F.3d 1157 (9th Cir. 2008) (en banc).

Fitts v. Kolb., 779 F. Supp. 1502 (D.S.C. 1991).

Food Lion v. Capital Cities/ ABC, 964 F. Supp. 956 (M.D.N.C. 1997).

Food Lion, Inc. v. Capital Cities/ABC, 194 F.3d 505 (4th Cir. 1999).

Forsher v. Bugliosi, 608 P.2d 716 (Cal. 1980).

Frese v. Formella, 53 F.4th 1 (1st Cir. 2022).

Funk v. Scripps Media, Inc., 570 S.W.3d 205 (Tenn. 2019).

G.D. v. Kenny, 15 A.3d 300 (N.J. 2011).

Garrard v. Charleston County School District, 429 S.Ct. 170 (2019).

Garrison v. Louisiana, 379 U.S. 64 (1964).

Gertz v. Robert Welch, Inc., 418 U.S. 341 (1974).

Givens v. Quinn, 877 F. Supp. 485 (W.D. Mo. 1994).

Goldwater v. Ginzburg, 414 F.2d 324 (2d Cir. 1969).

Grant v. Torstar, 2009 S.C.C. 61.

Greene v. Paramount Pictures Corp., 813 Fed. Appx. 728 (2d Cir. 2020).

Gubarev v. BuzzFeed, Inc, 340 F. Supp. 3d 1303 (S.D. Fla. 2018).

Hanash and Yousef v. WFLD, 1998 U.S. Dist. Lexis 17738 (N.D. Ill. 1998).

Hartman v. Kerch, No. CV-21-946506, 2023 WL 4006566 (Ohio Ct. App. June 15, 2023).

Herbert v. Lando, 441 U.S. 153 (1979).

Hill v. Petrotech Resources Corp., 325 S.W.3d 302 (Ky. 2010).

Howell v. Enterprise Publishing Co., 920 N.E.2d 1 (Mass. 2010).

Hutchinson v. Proxmire, 443 U.S. 111 (1979).

Jameel v. Wall Street Journal Europe, [2006] U.K.H.L. 44.

John v. Tribune Co., 181 N.E.2d 105 (Ill. 1962).

Keeton v. Hustler, 465 U.S. 770 (1984).

Kelly v. Arrington, 624 So. 2d 546 (Ala. 1993).

Lamb v. Rizzo, 391 F.3d 1133 (10th Cir. 2004).

Larson v. Gannett Co., 940 N.W.2d 120 (Minn. 2020).

Layne v. Tribune Co., 146 So. 234 (Fla. 1933) (en banc).

Lee v. Dong-A Ilbo, 849 F.2d 876 (4th Cir. 1988).

Lee v. TMZ Prods. Inc., 45 Media L. Rep. (BNA) 2545 (3d Cir. 2017) (non-precedential).

Lessig v. New York Times Co., No. 1:20-cv-10060 (D. Mass.

Filed Jan. 13, 2020; filed April 13, 2020): https://perma.cc/5HSA-HXS8.

Liberty Lobby v. Dow Jones, 838 F.2d 1287 (D.C. Cir. 1988).

Liberty Lobby, Inc. v. Anderson, 746 F.2d 1563 (D.C. Cir. 1984), *rev'd*, 477 U.S. 242 (1986).

Liquori v. Republican Co., 396 N.E.2d 726 (Mass. App. 1979).

Lubbock, In re, No. 20-0127, 2021 WL 2386 (Tex. June 11, 2021).

Madsen v. Buie, 454 So. 2d 727 (Fla. Dist. Ct. App. 1984).

Maethner v. Someplace Safe, Inc., 929 N.W.2d 868 (Minn. 2019).

Mangual v. Rotger-Sabat, 317 F.3d 45 (1st Cir. 2003).

Masson v. New Yorker Magazine, Inc., 501 U.S. 496 (1991).

McCafferty v. Newsweek Media Group, 955 F.3d 352 (3d Cir. 2020).

McKinney v. Avery Journal, 393 S.E.2d 295 (N.C. Ct. App. 1990).

Memphis Publishing Co. v. Nichols, 569 S.W.2d 412 (Tenn. 1978).

Milkovich v. Lorain Journal Co., 497 U.S. 1 (1990).

Mourning v. Family Publications Serv., 411 U.S. 356 (1973).

Nazeri v. Missouri Valley College, 860 S.W.2d 303 (Mo. 1993) (en banc).

New York Times Co. v. Sullivan, 376 U.S. 254 (1964).

Noonan v. Staples, Inc., 556 F.3d 20 (1st Cir. 2009), *rehearing en banc denied*, 561 F.3d 4 (1st Cir. 2009).

Norton v. Glenn, 860 A.2d 48, 53 (Pa. 2004).

Obsidian Finance Group, LLC v. Cox, 740 F.3d 1284 (9th Cir. 2014), *cert denied*, 134 S. Ct. 2680 (2014).

Ollman v. Evans, 750 F.2d 970 (D.C. Cir. 1984).

Ostrowe v. Lee, 175 N.E. 505 (N.Y. 1931).

Parmelee v. O'Neel, 186 P.3d 1094 (Wash. Ct. App. 2008), *rev'd in part*, 229 P.3d 723 (Wash. 2010).

Peagler v. Phoenix Newspapers, Inc., 560 P.2d 1216 (Ariz. 1977).

Petro-Lubricant Testing Laboratories, Inc. v. Adelman, 184 A.3d 457 (N.J., 2018).

Philadelphia Newspapers, Inc. v. Hepps, 475 U.S. 767 (1986).

Reilly v. Associated Press, 797 N.E.2d 1204 (Mass. Ct. App. 2003).

Renner v. Donsbach, 749 F. Supp. 987 (W.D. Mo. 1990).

Rosenblatt v. Baer, 383 U.S. 75 (1966).

Rosenbloom v. Metromedia, Inc., 403 U.S. 29 (1971).

Salyer v. Southern Poverty Law Ctr., Inc., 701 F. Supp. 2d 912 (W.D. Ky. 2009).

Saunders v. WHYY, 382 A.2d 257 (Del. Super. Ct. 1978).

Sharon v. Time, 599 F. Supp. 538 (S.D.N.Y. 1985).

Shell Oil Co. v. Writt, 464 S.W.3d 650 (Tex. 2015).

Shiamili v. Real Estate Group of New York, Inc., 952 N.E.2d 1011 (N.Y. 2011).

Shor v. Billingsley, 158 N.Y.S.2d 476 (N.Y. Sup. Ct. 1956).

Sindi v. El-Mosliman, 896 F.3d 1 (5th Cir. 2018).

Smith v. Durden, 276 P.3d 943 (N.M. 2012).

Solaia Technology, LLC v. Specialty Publishing Co., 852 N.E.2d 825 (Ill. 2006).

St. Amant v. Thompson, 390 U.S. 727, 731 (1968).

Stern v. Cosby, 645 F. Supp. 2d 258 (S.D.N.Y. 2009).

Stevens v. Iowa Newspapers, Inc., 728 N.E.2d 823 (Iowa 2007).

Summit Bank v. Rogers, 142 Cal. Rptr. 3d 40 (Ct. App. 2012).

Swartz v. Doe, 37 Med. L. Rep (BNA) 2485 (Tenn. Cir. Ct. 2009).

Tavoulares v. Washington Post Co., 759 F.2d 90, 121 (D.C. Cir. 1985), *rev'd* 817 F.2d 762 (D.C. Cir. 1987) (en banc).

Telnikoff v. Matusevitch, 702 A.2d 230 (Md. 1997).

Thomas v. Telegraph Publishing Co., 929 A.2d 993 (N.H. 2007).

Time, Inc. v. Firestone, 424 U.S. 488 (1976).

Tory v. Cochran, 544 U.S. 734 (2005).

Towne v. Eisner, 245 U.S. 418 (1918).

Triangle Publications v. Chumley, 317 S.E.2d 534 (Ga. 1984).

Trout Point Lodge, Ltd. v. Handshoe, 729 F.3d 481 (5th Cir. 2013).

Turner v. KTRK Television, Inc., 38 S.W.3d 103 (Tex. 2000).

United States v. Boyd, 475 F.3d 875 (7th Cir. 2007).

US Dominion, Inc. v. Fox News Network (Del. Super. Ct. 2023), https://perma.cc/6Y9F-KWMN

Verity v. USA TODAY, LLC, 436 P.3d 653 (Idaho 2019).

W.J.A. v. D.A., 43 A.3d 1248 (N.J. 2012).

Wampler v. Higgins, 752 N.E.2d 962 (Ohio 2001).

Washington Post Co. v. Keogh, 365 F.2d 965 (D.C. Cir. 1966).

Whiteside v. Russellville Newspapers, Inc., 295 S.W.3d 798 (Ark. 2009).

Whitney v. California, 274 U.S. 354 (1927).

Williams v. Pasma, 656 P.2d 212 (Mont. 1982).

Wynberg v. National Enquirer, 564 F. Supp. 924 (C.D. Cal. 1982).

Yahoo! Inc. v. La Ligue Contre le Racisme et l'Anti semitisme, 145 F. Supp. 2d 1168 (N.D. Cal. 2001), *rev'd en banc*, 433 F.3d 1199 (9th Cir.), *cert. denied*, 547 U.S. 1163 (2006).

Yonaty v. Mincolla, 945 N.Y.S.2d 774 (N.Y. App. Div. 2012).

Zeran v. America Online, 129 F.3d 327 (4th Cir. 1997).

Other Sources

Communications Decency Act, 47 U.S.C. § 230(c) (Supp. 1996).

New York Civil Rights Law § 74 (2014).

New York Civil Rights Law § 76-1a(2) (2020).

Libel Terrorism Protection Act, N.Y.C.P.L.R. § 302 (2008).

Securing the Protection of Our Enduring and Established Constitutional Heritage Act, 28 U.S.C. §§ 4101-4105 (2010).

7

Regulating Student Expression

By Mark Goodman and Erica Salkin

 Headnote Questions

- How do the free expression rights of students in public schools differ from those of other citizens?
- How are the free expression rights of high school and college students different?
- Why is it important that student publications be identified as designated public forums?
- What legal avenues do private school students have for protecting their free expression?
- Under what circumstances can public school or college officials restrict the free expression rights of students?

North Paulding High School sophomore Hannah Watters was worried. It was August 2020, and on the second day of classes, her school's hallways were packed with students, shoulder to shoulder with few masks in sight despite the ongoing COVID pandemic. She did what many high school students would do: she pulled out her phone, took a photo, and posted it to social media. Shortly afterward, she was suspended for five days for violating the student code of conduct at the Paulding County high school.

Many cried foul, especially after the principal of the school announced that any student found criticizing the school via social media could be disciplined. News outlets across the country picked up the story, and Georgia School Superintendent Richard Woods released a statement encouraging schools to ensure that students and staff were not penalized for expressing their concerns. Hannah's suspension was ultimately lifted (and removed from her record), and the student later told CNN that she would do it all again, stating "I'd like to say that this is some good and necessary trouble, so I don't regret posting this because it needed to be said."

Hannah's story highlights the tension inherent in questions of student expressive freedom. As careful readers of the Constitution will note, nothing in the text of the First Amendment limits its application by age or ability. We do, though, commonly see location of the speech as a key factor in determining the level of First Amendment protection rather than the individual who is speaking. Certain environments have essential needs that require a special consideration of the role of free expres-

sion. For example, prisoners have First Amendment protection, but it is applied in light of the particular needs of the prison setting.

Students in school are not prisoners. But the challenges to their free speech and the confusion over the legal protections to which they are entitled are frequently disturbingly similar. What is settled law is that student speech at public schools enjoys a degree of First Amendment protection. That has been the unmistakable holding of the U.S. Supreme Court for almost 100 years. Yet, those First Amendment rights must be applied "in light of the special characteristics of the school environment," the Court held in the landmark case *Tinker v. Des Moines Independent Community School District*.

Because the courts have defined student rights based in the school setting, this chapter will do so as well. It will discuss the differences between expressive rights of students in high schools and colleges, focusing on relevant Supreme Court decisions and lower court rulings that apply. It will also explore the more limited legal protections for private school students and discuss the increasingly important role state law is playing in defining students' free expression and free press rights.

PUBLIC HIGH SCHOOLS

Defining First Amendment protections afforded to students at public high schools is a complex task. The Supreme Court has waded into the murky waters of student free expression rights a handful of times over the decades, and each ruling seems to make the law more confusing.

The earliest student free expression cases in the United States reach back to the late 1800s and early 1900s. These decisions generally supported the decisions of schools to penalize students for speech that would disrupt schooling or subvert the authority of teachers or principals.[1] In 1915, a high school senior named Earl Wooster was expelled from his Fresno city high school for speaking out about his school's lack of adequate fire exits and safety materials. His expulsion was upheld by a California appeals court, which noted that the speech was intended to belittle the school board and was thus punishable. Wooster, who might be considered an "early-20th-century Hannah Watters" also refused to apologize for his remarks, which "accentuated his misconduct" in the court's eyes.

In 1923, the Court in *Meyer v. Nebraska* and *Bartels v. Iowa*, recognized that students have some First Amendment protection. But the Court's 1943 decision in *West Virginia Board of Education v. Barnette* was the first clear indication of where the Court would end up in protecting students expressing unpopular views. *Barnette* focused on whether public school officials could compel students to salute the American flag and recite the Pledge of Allegiance. Some Jehovah's Witnesses, whose faith demands allegiance only to God and who consider saluting the flag worship of a graven image, brought suit after their children were expelled for refusing to do so. The Supreme Court upheld their claim of First Amendment infringement by a 6-3 vote. Independent of the fact that the parents' objection was based on their religious faith, the Court said the government could not compel even children to express views with which they disagreed absent a compelling justification. The Court rejected the West Virginia requirement as in conflict with the First Amendment protections for free speech afforded all Americans.

The seminal Supreme Court decision recognizing First Amendment protection for public school students is the 1969 case *Tinker v. Des Moines Independent Community School District*. In *Tinker*, Iowa public school students John and Mary Beth Tinker and their friend Chris Eckhardt wore black armbands to school to express their concern about U.S. involvement in the Vietnam War and were suspended as a result. The three students contested the punishment as a violation of their First Amendment rights. The Supreme Court, by a 7-2 vote, ultimately agreed, ruling that neither students nor teachers "shed their constitutional rights to freedom of speech or expression at the schoolhouse gate."

The Court held:

In order for the State in the person of school officials to justify prohibition of a particular expression of opinion, it must be able to show that its action was caused by something more than a mere desire to avoid the discomfort and unpleasantness that always accompany an unpopular viewpoint.

But the Court added: "[C]onduct by the student, in class or out of it, which for any reason ... materially disrupts classwork or involves substantial disorder or invasion of the rights of others is, of course, not immunized by the constitutional guarantee of freedom of speech." The Court concluded that the school had provided no evidence of material and substantial disruption or invasion of the rights of others and thus rejected the school's punishment.

This *Tinker* standard — requiring school officials to show or reasonably predict material and substantial disruption or invasion of the rights of others — has become the key legal test for when school officials will be allowed to censor or punish student expression. It remains the most important precedent on student speech protections.

For almost twenty years, *Tinker* was the only Supreme Court legal standard for when student speech could be censored at public secondary schools. But in 1986, the Court carved out an additional exception to student speech protections. In *Bethel School District v. Fraser*, a 7-2 majority upheld a school's punishment of Renton, Washington, high school senior Matthew Fraser for delivering a speech at a school assembly that contained what the Court described as an "elaborate, graphic, and explicit sexual metaphor." In nominating his friend for a student government office, Fraser said:

I know a man who is firm — he's firm in his pants, he's firm in his shirt, his character is firm — but most ... of all, his belief in you, the students of Bethel, is firm. Jeff Kuhlman is a man who takes his point and pounds it in. If necessary, he'll take an issue and nail it to the wall. He doesn't attack things in spurts — he drives hard, pushing and pushing until finally — he succeeds. Jeff is a man who will go to the very end — even the climax, for each and every one of you.

So vote for Jeff for A. S. B. vice-president — he'll never come between you and the best our high school can be.

Fraser was suspended from school and, unsurprisingly, removed from the list of students eligible for selection as a graduation speaker. He contested the punishment, and ultimately, the Supreme Court upheld the school's discipline. The rights of students to speak freely when at school "are not automatically coextensive with the rights of adults in other settings," the Court held.

Bethel has come to stand for the proposition that the First Amendment does not prohibit school officials from silencing or punishing student expression at school that is vulgar, lewd, in-

---

[1] *See* Lander v. Seaver, 32 Vt. 114 (1859); State ex rel Dresser v. District Board of School District 1, 116 N.W. 232 (Wisc 1908).

decent or "plainly offensive." Most courts regard the holding as a narrow one that has little relevance to most mainstream student expression.

Two years later, in *Hazelwood School District v. Kuhlmeier*, a 5-3 majority of the Supreme Court allowed a school's censorship of stories about teen pregnancy and divorce in a Missouri high school student newspaper that was tied to a journalism class. The majority concluded that when student expression occurs in a school-sponsored context, school officials can censor if they can demonstrate that their actions have a "valid educational purpose" or are "reasonably related to legitimate pedagogical concerns," a significantly lesser level of protection than given to independent student speech at issue in the *Tinker* case. However, the Court also said that this limitation only applied when the school had not, by policy or practice, designated the student publication as a public forum for student expression. Therefore, student press freedom advocates recommend student media staffs take steps to establish their publications as "designated public forums" where student editors make the content decisions.

In applying the *Hazelwood* ruling, lower courts have disagreed about whether it also requires school officials to act in a way that is viewpoint neutral, meaning the government restriction cannot be based upon the viewpoint of the speaker. The requirement applies to government censorship even in nonpublic forums. The Supreme Court has not yet clarified whether the requirement extends to the school context under *Hazelwood*.

Hazelwood prompted a significant increase in the censorship of school-sponsored student media. In addition to student newspapers and yearbooks, *Hazelwood* has been used to suppress books and films from school curricula as well as student theatrical performances. But it is important to remember that despite the deference the *Hazelwood* standard gives to acts of censorship by school officials, it is not an absolute license to censor. One court case illustrates this point.

Student journalists at Utica High School in Michigan wrote a news story and editorial about a lawsuit filed against the school district. A family living near the district's bus parking lot claimed members became ill from breathing the fumes of vehicles left idling. The parking lot was near the high school athletic field and an elementary school playground, so the potential health risks had special relevance to the newspaper's readers. School officials refused to comment for the students' story and ultimately ordered the newspaper adviser not to allow students to cover the topic.

Student editor Katy Dean sued her school for violating students' First Amendment rights after she was unable to persuade officials to reconsider their decision. In *Dean v. Utica Community Schools*, a federal district court ruled in her favor.

The court offered several justifications for its conclusion.

First, it noted the newspaper had been operating as a limited public forum for student expression. As the newspaper adviser testified in court, for more than twenty years no school official had censored or reviewed the newspaper before publication, and the paper's policies gave content control to student editors. Thus, the court concluded, limitations of the *Hazelwood* standard did not apply, even though the publication was school-sponsored. Second, the court said even if the publication were subject to the *Hazelwood* censorship standard, the school could not meet it. It was not educationally reasonable for school officials to censor an accurate story about a lawsuit filed against the district.

Furthermore, the court held that even if the publication was subject to *Hazelwood* limitations and even if the censorship was considered educationally reasonable, the school's actions were not "viewpoint neutral." Because the school's motivation for censoring was clearly to silence a viewpoint with which it disagreed — that of the family who filed the lawsuit — the school's actions could not stand. A school official testified that the school would have allowed the story to be published if the students had taken the school's side in reporting the lawsuit. The *Dean* case points out how, even under the constraints of the *Hazelwood* ruling, high school students may have a legitimate basis for legally contesting their school's acts of censorship.

The next major Supreme Court decisions involving high school students' free speech rights is *Morse v. Frederick* in 2007. In *Morse*, the Court upheld the right of Juneau, Alaska, school officials to punish a high school student for conveying what the Court found to be a drug-related message at a school event. Joseph Frederick was suspended after he and friends held up a fourteen-foot banner that said, "Bong Hits 4 Jesus" as the Olympic Torch Relay passed en route to the Salt Lake City Winter Olympics. School officials said the banner promoted illegal drug use. Frederick said he believed the message was nonsense but hoped it would get him on television.

In rejecting Frederick's First Amendment claim, the Court held that the special characteristics of the school environment and the governmental interest in stopping student drug abuse allow schools to restrict student expression that they reasonably regard as promoting illegal drug use. The Court rejected the school's argument that it be allowed to censor speech simply because school officials find it offensive or in conflict with the school's educational mission. "[M]uch political and religious speech might be perceived as offensive to some," the Court held.

Justice Samuel Alito wrote a concurring opinion encouraging a narrow reading of the Court's holding in *Morse*. He wrote that the case

goes no further than to hold that a public school may restrict speech that a reasonable observer would interpret as advocating illegal drug use. ... [I]t provides no support for any restriction of speech that can plausibly be interpreted as commenting on any political or social issue, including speech on issues such as "the wisdom of the war on drugs or of legalizing marijuana for medicinal use."

These four Supreme Court decisions represent the currently recognized legal justifications for censorship of student expression at public high schools and show how convoluted student First Amendment protections have become. From 1969 until 1986, there was one legal standard for censorship of student speech: material and substantial disruption or invasion of the rights of others as described in the *Tinker* ruling. Thanks to the subsequent decisions, there are now four justifications public school officials can use to justify their acts of censorship:

1. When the expression will create a material and substantial disruption of school activities or an invasion of the rights of others (*Tinker*).
2. When the expression is pervasively vulgar, lewd or indecent (*Bethel*).
3. When the expression advocates illegal drug use (*Morse*).
4. When the student expression is school-sponsored and not in a designated public forum, but only as long as the school's censorship is viewpoint neutral (at least in some jurisdictions) *and* is based on a reasonable educational justification (*Hazelwood*).

In 2021, the Supreme Court for the first time handed down a decision exploring the ability of public secondary school officials to censor or punish off-campus speech. The case, *Mahanoy Area School District v. B.L.*, involved a Pennsylvania high school student who was suspended from the cheerleading squad after she posted a message from home to her personal Snapchat account that contained vulgarity (middle fingers raised and use of the f-word). The Supreme Court majority concluded 8-1 that her off-campus speech was protected by the First Amendment. The Court rejected the view that school officials could never punish off-campus speech by students, but left to future cases the defining of the precise contexts where such speech will be protected. Lower courts have struggled to consistently apply *Mahanoy* to situations involving student expression, with many citing the conflict between the long-held *in loco parentis* doctrine applied to K-12 schools and the question of realistic boundaries. If schools can regulate online speech, what stops them from regulating *all* student expression at *all* times? In other words, when is a student *not* a student for purposes of the First Amendment? *Mahanoy* did not answer this question, and absent Supreme Court guidance, this remains unclear.

PUBLIC COLLEGES

Historically, public college and university students have been afforded strong First Amendment protection — much stronger than that of high school students. In contrast to the focus on order and discipline reflected in the high school cases, the Supreme Court has stated that its own decisions "leave no room for the view that, because of the acknowledged need for order, First Amendment protections should apply with less force on college campuses than in the community at large." The college classroom and its surrounding environs, the Court said in *Healy v. James*, are "peculiarly the 'marketplace of ideas.'"

The Supreme Court's decision in *Papish v. Board of Curators of the University of Missouri* provides a clear illustration of the stark contrast between the way the Court regards high school students' First Amendment rights and those of public college and university students. You will recall that in the *Bethel* case the Court allowed high school officials to punish the use of sexually suggestive or vulgar language. In *Papish,* a case involving a college student, the Court took a very different position.

Barbara Papish was a graduate journalism student at the University of Missouri-Columbia who was involved in distributing on campus a controversial publication called the *Free Press Underground*. There were two things in the publication to which university officials objected:

First, on the front cover the publishers had reproduced a political cartoon previously printed in another newspaper depicting policemen raping the Statue of Liberty and the Goddess of Justice. The caption under the cartoon read: "...With Liberty and Justice for All." Secondly, the issue contained an article entitled "M____f____ Acquitted," which discussed the trial and acquittal on an assault charge of a New York City youth who was a member of an organization known as "Up Against the Wall, M____f____."

Papish was expelled for her role in the publication's distribution and contested the punishment as a violation of her First Amendment rights. The Supreme Court agreed. "[T]he mere dissemination of ideas — no matter how offensive to good taste — on a state university campus may not be shut off in the name alone of 'conventions of decency,'" the Court held.

In *Healy* and *Papish*, the Court kept the *Tinker* standard as a legitimate justification for censorship of student expression in the college environment. However, because the college environment differs in significant ways from K-12, courts generally have been less likely to find material and substantial disruption resulting from speech at a college than at a high school.

Courts have also been quick to reject other more indirect forms of censorship, especially of the college student press, when there is no evidence of substantial disruption. Public university officials (including student government leaders) have been told they may not withdraw or deny funding or discipline publication staff members based on the content they publish or require prior approval of articles.[2]

After the Court allowed certain kinds of limitations on the First Amendment rights of students in its *Hazelwood* decision, some college and university officials began pushing for an application of the *Hazelwood* analysis to college students. In a footnote to the *Hazelwood* opinion, the Court said, "We need not now decide whether the same degree of deference [to school officials' acts of censorship] is appropriate with respect to school-sponsored expressive activities at the college and university level." Lower courts have found use for Hazelwood in university student expression situations, however, using it to protect a university administrator who censored a student newspaper and uphold disciplinary actions taken against students whose speech violated curricular policies. Although the Supreme Court has yet to revisit and definitively decide the issue, lower courts have disagreed, and the question remains in dispute.

PRIVATE SCHOOLS

Because public schools are government agencies, censorship by school officials constitutes state action and is limited by the First Amendment, as are the actions of other government officials. Private school officials in high schools and colleges are not government agents, thus, the First Amendment protections for free speech and free press don't apply to their efforts to censor or punish student speech. Some have attempted to create state actor status for private schools based on their similarity to their public counterparts, especially for schools that receive public funding through other means. This approach was rejected by the Supreme Court in 1982, which noted that the country's long history of private education showed schooling was never an exclusive role of the state.

Legal protection for private school students must come from somewhere other than the Constitution. California and Rhode Island have enacted statutory protections for private school students. Some courts have found protections for free speech at private schools in free expression provisions in state constitutions.[3] But the most likely source of free expression protection

for private school students is school policy. If a private school includes protection for rights in a student handbook or other policy document, some courts have concluded those policies can be legally enforced as the terms of a contract if school officials ignore them.[4] There is also opportunity, albeit limited, to support free expression in private schools through exploration of mission statements, which courts have used to establish purpose, context and meaning of an organization and the reasonable expectations a participant might have of it. Without the protections of the First Amendment, private school students unquestionably have a greater challenge in defending their free speech and free press rights. But they are not without options.

STATE LAW PROTECTIONS

As indicated previously, the Supreme Court's *Hazelwood* decision is unpopular among educators who believe in the importance of a free student press.[5] Within hours of the decision, student free press advocates began discussing ways to work around the more limited protections afforded school-sponsored speech established in that ruling. It soon became clear that state laws could be one way to limit the impact of *Hazelwood*.

On the day of the ruling, a student newspaper at Homestead High School in Cupertino, California, was experiencing its own censorship conflict. After learning of the Supreme Court's decision, the school principal ordered the publication staff not to publish a story about AIDS that the students had been working on for months. The staff and its adviser sought outside help and learned that in the 1970s the California legislature had enacted a state statute protecting student press rights. By the 1980s, the statute received little attention because of the belief that it duplicated rights students were afforded under the *Tinker* standard. But after *Hazelwood* limited the application of *Tinker* to school-sponsored speech, something the California statute did not do, the law took on new importance. It effectively provided

[2] *See* Rosenberger v. Rector and Visitors of the Univ. of Virginia, 515 U.S. 819 (1995); The Koala v. Khosla, 931 F.3d 887 (9th Cir. 2019); Stanley v. Magrath, 719 F.2d 279 (8th Cir. 1983); Schiff v. Williams, 519 F.2d 257 (5th Cir. 1975); Joyner v. Whiting, 477 F.2d 456, 460 (4th Cir. 1973); Antonelli v. Hammond, 308 F. Supp. 1329 (D. Mass. 1970); Milliner v. Turner, 436 So.2d 1300 (La. Ct. App. 1983); Mazart v. State, 441 N.Y.S.2d 600 (N.Y.Ct.Cl. 1981); Trujillo v. Love, 322 F. Supp. 1266 (D. Colo. 1971).

[3] *See* State v. Schmid, 423 A.2d 615 (N.J. 1980), *appeal dismissed*, 455 U.S. 100 (1980) (holding that Princeton University violated the New Jersey Constitution when it had an individual arrested for distributing political literature on campus); Common-

wealth v. Tate, 432 A.2d 1382 (Pa. 1981) (holding that the Pennsylvania Constitution does not allow Muhlenberg College administrators to have protesters distributing leaflets arrested and charged with trespassing); Abramowitz v. Boston Univ., CIV No. 82680 (Mass. Sup. Ct. Suffolk Div., Dec. 2, 1986) (holding that the Massachusetts Constitution prohibited Boston University from removing political posters students placed in their dorm room windows).

[4] *See, e.g.,* Ross v. Creighton Univ., 957 F.2d 410, 416 (7th Cir. 1992) ("It is held generally in the United States that the 'basic legal relation between a student and a private university or college is contractual in nature. The catalogues, bulletins, circulars, and regulations of the institution made available to the matriculant become a part of the contract'" (citations omitted)). *See also Guide for the Private School Press*, STUDENT PRESS L. CTR ONLINE, June 28, 2021, http://www.splc.org/article/2012/12/legal-guide-for-the-private-school-press_1201 (providing practical and legal suggestions for private school students fighting censorship).

[5] *See* Hank Reichman, *Hazelwood Day of Action: Thirty Years is Too Many*, ACADEME BLOG, June 28, 2021, https://academeblog.org/2018/01/17/hazelwood-day-of-action-thirty-years-is-too-many/; Journalism Education Association Statement on Student Free Expression, June 28, 2021, http://jea.org/wp/home/about-jea/statements/#free.

under state law the rights students were previously thought to have under the First Amendment. "California public school students still enjoy substantial 'freedom of the press' despite the recent U.S. Supreme Court decision to the controversy," stated the California State Superintendent of Public Instruction.

California provided the example that, as of May 2023, has resulted in seventeen states enacting legal protections for high school students' free press and free speech rights.[6] No two state laws are worded exactly the same, but they all attempt to codify *Tinker*'s material and substantial disruption standard as the key requirement before school officials can censor. Twelve of the state laws also provide explicit protection for journalism teachers or media advisers, protecting them from punishment based on what their students publish.[7] Two states, California and Rhode Island, have enacted statutory protections for private school students, and thirteen states have statutes that provide state law protections to public college and university students as well.[8] It is fair to say that in each of these states, students have greater protection than they would in a state without a statute. But now, more than ever, the rights secondary school students have depend on where they live.

Concern among political conservatives about efforts to silence their voices on campuses has prompted a growing effort to legislatively prohibit public colleges and universities from disallowing controversial speakers on campus or limiting protests on campus to student "free speech zones." As of May 2023, twenty-two states had enacted laws banning free speech zones and opening up public spaces on campus to student expression, with more under consideration by their state legislatures.

SUMMARY

It is not a surprise that students and educators frequently express frustration when attempting to define the extent of First Amendment protections in schools. The same Supreme Court that says, "America's public schools are the nurseries of democracy. Our representative democracy only works if we protect the marketplace of ideas." (in *Mahanoy Area School District v. B.L.*) creates a standard that allows school officials to censor student speech when the censorship is "reasonably related to legitimate pedagogical concerns" (in *Hazelwood v. Kuhlmeier*). The lack of clarity by the courts has opened the door to the states defining student free expression rights and creating a patchwork of laws across the nation.

---

[6] Arkansas, California, Colorado, Illinois, Iowa, Hawaii, Kansas, Maryland, Massachusetts, Nevada, New Jersey, North Dakota, Oregon, Rhode Island, Vermont, Washington, West Virginia.

[7] Arkansas (college level only), California, Colorado, Hawaii, Kansas, Maryland, New Jersey, North Dakota, Rhode Island, Vermont, Washington, West Virginia.

[8] Arkansas, California, Hawaii, Illinois, Maryland, Nevada, New Jersey, North Dakota, Oregon, Rhode Island, Vermont, Washington, West Virginia.

BIBLIOGRAPHY

Articles

Carter, Edward L. & Kevin R. Kemper. "Applying Hazelwood to College Speech: Forum Doctrine and Government Speech in the U.S. Courts of Appeals," 48 *South Texas Law Review* 157 (2006).

"Guide for the Private School Press," *Student Press Law Center Online*, May 23, 2022, http://www.splc.org/article/2012/12/legal-guide-for-the-private-school-press_1201.

Hurley, Michael. "Georgia Improves Upon Free Speech Law by Enacting FORUM Act," May 3, 2022, https://www.thefire.org/georgia-improves-upon-free-speech-law-by-enacting-forum-act

"Legal Guide to Hazelwood and Viewpoint Suppression," *Student Press Law Center Online*, May 23, 2022, https://splc.org/2015/11/differing-opinions_0501/.

LoMonte, Frank. "What Public Forum Status Means for Your Student Publication," *Student Press Law Center Online*, May 23, 2022, http://www.splc.org/article/2014/07/what-public-forum-doctrine-means-for-your-student-publication.

Reichman, Hank. "Hazelwood Day of Action: Thirty Years is Too Many," *Academe Blog*, May 23, 2022, https://academeblog.org/2018/01/17/hazelwood-day-of-action-thirty-years-is-too-many/.

Strapagiel, Lauren. "Two Students Say They Were Suspended From Their Georgia High School For Posting Photos Of Crowded Hallways," Buzzfeed News, Aug. 6, 2020, https://www.buzzfeednews.com/article/laurenstrapagiel/north-paulding-high-school-suspensions-for-hallway-photos

Sullivan, Cheryl. "California Law on Student Free Speech Left Intact by High Court Ruling," *Christian Science Monitor*, Jan. 29, 1988, https://www.csmonitor.com/1988/0119/anews.html.

Tagami, Ty. "Paulding Lifts Suspensions of Two Students after Viral Photos," The Atlanta Journal-Constitution, Aug. 7, 2020, https://www.ajc.com/education/paulding-family-pushes-back-on-school-suspension-over-crowded-hall-photo/2XTUNBDA2NDF7I2RHFLXR2MR4M/

Book

Law of the Student Press, Arlington, Va.: Student Press Law Center, 4th Ed. 2013.

Cases

Abramowitz v. Boston University, CIV No. 82680 (Mass. Sup. Ct. Suffolk Div., Dec. 2, 1986).

Antonelli v. Hammond, 308 F. Supp. 1329 (D. Mass. 1970).

(1969).

Bartels v. Iowa, 262 U. S. 404 (1923).

Bethel School District v. Fraser, 478 U.S. 675 (1986).

Boring v. Buncombe County Board of Education, 98 F.3d 1474 (4th Cir. 1996).

Commonwealth v. Tate, 432 A.2d 1382 (Pa. 1981).

Dean v. Utica Community Schools, 345 F. Supp. 2d 799 (E.D. Mich. 2004).

Hazelwood School District v. Kuhlmeier, 484 U.S. 260 (1988).

Healy v. James, 408 U.S. 169 (1972).

Hosty v. Carter, 412 F.3d 731 (7th Cir. 2005).

Joyner v. Whiting, 477 F.2d 456 (4th Cir. 1973).

Keeton v. Anderson-Wiley, 664 F.3d 865 (11th Cir. 2011).

The Koala v. Khosla, 931 F.3d 887 (9th Cir. 2019).

Krizek v. Board of Education, 713 F. Supp. 1131 (N.D. Ill. 1989).

Mahanoy Area School District v. B.L., 141 S. Ct. 2038 (2021).

Mazart v. State, 441 N.Y.S.2d 600 (N.Y.Ct.Cl. 1981).

Meyer v. Nebraska, 262 U.S. 390 (1923).

Milliner v. Turner, 436 So.2d 1300 (La. Ct. App. 1983).

Morse v. Frederick, 551 U.S. 393 (2007).

Papish v. Board of Curators of the University of Missouri, 410 U.S. 667 (1973).

Rendell-Baker v. Kohn, 457 U.S. 830 (1982).

Rosenberger v. Rector and Visitors of the University of Virginia, 515 U.S. 819 (1995).

Ross v. Creighton University, 957 F.2d 410 (7th Cir. 1992).

Schiff v. Williams, 519 F.2d 257 (5th Cir. 1975).

Stanley v. Magrath, 719 F.2d 279 (8th Cir. 1983).

State v. Schmid, 423 A.2d 615 (N.J. 1980).

Tinker v. Des Moines Independent Community School District, 393 U.S. 503 (1969).

Trujillo v. Love, 322 F. Supp. 1266 (D. Colo. 1971).

Turner v. Safley, 482 U.S. 78 (1987).

Virgil v. School Board of Columbia County, 677 F. Supp. 1547 (M.D. Fla. 1988).

West Virginia Board of Education v. Barnette, 319 U.S. 624 (1943).

Wooster v. Sunderland, 27 Cal. App. 51 (Court of Appeals of California, 1st Appellate Dist. 1915).

Other Sources

Exec. Order No. 13864, 84 FR 11401 (March 21, 2019).

Press Release, California State Department of Education, Honig Clarifies Status of Students' "Freedom of the Press," Mar. 18, 1988.

State Statutes Protecting Private School Students' Free Speech and Press Rights

Cal. Ed. Code §§ 48950 & 94367 (1972).

R.I. Gen. Laws § 16-109-1 — 16-109-3 (2017).

State Statutes Protecting Public College and University Students' Free Speech and Press Rights

Ark. Code §§ 6-60-1001 — 6-60-1003 (2019).

Cal. Ed. Code §§ 76120, 66301 & 94367 (1972).

Hawaii Rev. Stat. §304A-951 (2022).

110 Ill. Comp. Stat. § 13 (2007).

Md. Code Ann., Ed. § 15-119 (2016).

Nev. Rev. Stat. Ann. § 396.5475 (2017).

N.J. Rev. Stat. § 18A:62-67 (2021).

N.D. Cent. Code § 15-10-55 (2015).

Or. Rev. Stat. § 351.649 (2007).

R.I. Gen. Laws §§ 16-109-1—16-109-3 (2017).

Vt. Stat. Ann. tit. 16 §§ 180 & 1623 (2017).

Wash. Rev. Code § 28B.10.037 (2018).

W. Va. Code §§18B-21-1—18B-21-4 (2023) (citation pending).

State Statutes Protecting Public High School Students' Free Speech and Press Rights

Ark. Code §§ 6-18-1201—6-18-1204 (1994).

Cal. Ed. Code §§ 48957 (1972).

Colo. Rev. Stat. § 22-1-120 (1990).

105 Ill. Comp. Stat. § 80 (2016).

Hawaii Rev. Stat. §302A-451 (2022).

Iowa Code § 280.22 (1989).

Kan. Stat. Ann. §§ 72.1504-72.1506 (1992).

Md. Code, Ed. § 7-121 (2016).

Mass. Gen. Laws ch. 71, § 82 (1988).

Nev. Rev. Stat. Ann. § 388.077 (2017).

N.J. Rev. Stat. §§ 18A:36-44—18A:36-45 (2021).

N.D. Cent. Code § 15.1-19-25 (2015).

Or. Rev. Stat. § 336.477 (2007).

R.I. Gen. Laws §§ 16-109-1—16-109-3 (2017).

Vt. Stat. Ann. tit. 16 §§ 180 & 1623 (2017).

Wash. Rev. Code § 28A.600.027 (2018).

W. Va. Code §§18B-21-1—18B-21-4 (2023) (citation pending).

8

Regulating Advertising

By Robert L. Kerr

☑ **Headnote Questions**

- What is commercial speech?
- How has constitutional protection for commercial speech changed over the years?
- Why doesn't commercial speech get the same First Amendment protection as other forms of speech?
- What is the four-part test courts use to determine the constitutionality of government restrictions on commercial speech?
- What recent Supreme Court ruling has raised questions in the lower courts about application of that four-part test?
- What is the Federal Trade Commission's role in regulating advertising?
- How does the Federal Trade Commission define deceptive advertising?
- What remedies can the Federal Trade Commission use to stop deceptive ads from being disseminated?
- What other remedies are available to prevent the dissemination of deceptive ads?
- How does the advertising industry regulate itself?

In announcing some four decades ago the beginning of the age of First Amendment protection for advertising, Justice Harry Blackmun observed, "So long as we preserve a predominantly free enterprise economy, the allocation of our resources in large measure will be made through numerous private economic decisions. It is a matter of public interest that those decisions, in the aggregate, be intelligent and well informed." Writing in 1976 in *Virginia State Board of Pharmacy v. Virginia Citizens Consumer Council*, Justice Blackmun could not have imagined the dizzying degree to which technology would soon make it possible for rapidly escalating advertising techniques to enter every nook and cranny of the private lives in which those economic decisions would be made.

When Blackmun died in 1994, he would have been familiar with a world in which advertising was widely present in consumers' lives *via* television and radio, in newspapers and magazines, on billboards and buses, selling everything from the latest movie to the next president. But he could have known nothing about the way Facebook and countless other digital, cyber-networked entities would soon be able to collect and market infinitely more data than ever before on virtually every aspect of consumers' activities, making their economic decisions less private than ever, if indeed truly private at all.

He could not have known of the imminent arrival of algo-rithmic, peer-to-peer, and viral marketing in which individuals would be paid to surveil and influence, often surreptitiously, the economic decisions of friends and neighbors in cyberspace, or of a blogosphere in which apparent social commentary would actually be commercially purposed. He probably could not have imagined an age in which the story lines of so many tales told *via* film, television, Webcast, graphic novel, video game and even textbook would be shaped to one degree or another by product placements, or one when technology giants like Google would consider ways to advertise inside individuals' automobiles, on their wristwatches and eyeglasses, and in their homes *via* wired devices such as their thermostats. Justice Blackmun would be like almost everyone else online today in having difficulty grasping the breathtaking extent to which the newest algorithmic "relevance" methods utilize social media and other digital profiling efforts to "microtarget" ever smaller target audiences and create information cocoons, bubbles, and silos. As Ronald Collins and David Skover have characterized it, advertising today often has "less to do with facts than image" and advances "more a total cultural system" in which "truth is that which sells."

The unprecedented degree of digitally networked advertising intrusion into private lives reached, in 2018, what increasingly is shaping up as a watershed tipping point in related regulatory activity. Revelations of more than 87 million Facebook users' private data being misused by a consulting firm involved in advertising to influence the 2016 presidential campaign signaled greatly increased attention from the Federal Trade Commission, as reported in *CQ* and many other sources, which has extensive powers to regulate deceptive communications made to users by Internet firms. The scandal brought revived attention to a consent agreement with Facebook, announced by the FTC in 2012, in which it pledged to protect user data and not share it with advertisers. In 2019, Facebook was fined $5 billion by the FTC for the 2018 revelations.

Both members of Congress and Facebook founder and Chief Executive Officer Mark Zuckerberg spoke of the need and inevitability of greater regulation of social media at high-profile hearings at the Capitol in early 2018, reported by *The Economist* and other sources. Development of such regulation now looms as the most active area of commercial-speech law in coming years, driven by growing awareness of how automated, personalized digital advertising can be grounded in a model based on deceptively mining and manipulating private personal data without consent or knowledge. Regulation aimed at addressing such concerns went into effect in 2018 in the European Union, as reported in *The New York Times* and elsewhere, with the impact of the General Data Protection Regulation promising to extend beyond Europe due to the Internet's borderless nature. In 2020, the California Consumer Privacy Act, with many provisions similar to the European legislation, went into effect. By 2021, a *Times* account observed, "Around the world, governments are moving simultaneously to limit the power of tech companies with an urgency and breadth that no single industry had experienced before."

In an age when so much traditional advertising has morphed into forms more difficult to test for truth, advertising nevertheless remains a highly regulated field. Despite so many technological changes, the legal basis continues for commercial messages to be regulated at the federal level most directly by the Federal Trade Commission, but also by agencies such as the Food and Drug Administration and the Securities and Exchange Commission. Similar agencies at the state level also regulate advertising. At the same time, advertising is protected from such regulation in more ways than ever by a First Amendment doctrine that has evolved dramatically over the years since the landmark ruling in which Justice Blackmun framed the matter in terms of the public interest.

That dramatic evolution of First Amendment doctrine on commercial speech since the 1970s and the parade of cases that have shaped it have generated extensive scholarly debate over whether the broadened protections have gone too far or not far enough. And the most recent ruling on the subject by the U.S. Supreme Court suggests it may be prepared to push the evolution of the doctrine considerably further.

Cases continue to test the Court's definition of commercial speech, in *Pittsburgh Press Co. v. Pittsburgh Commission on Human Relations*, as expression that does "no more than propose a commercial transaction" or is "solely motivated by the desire for profit." Scholars continue to debate whether it is paternalistic to provide consumers with some protection from unscrupulous advertisers or whether advertising techniques have largely surpassed consumers' abilities to detect deception. The tension in the debate is inherent in the reality of commercial speech's dual nature. It is speech that both conveys information and establishes transactional promises between buyer and seller. In the political-social context, informational speech receives almost absolute First Amendment protection from government restriction. But in the well-established context of preserving the fair-bargaining process, as Daniel A. Farber has emphasized, expression involved in contractual arrangements "is not the sort of 'speech' to which the First Amendment Applies." Thus, arguments that commercial speech should be treated identically to political speech face the enduring question, as expressed by Reza R. Dibadj, of "why a government that can regulate an underlying commercial transaction should not be able to regulate speech promoting the same commercial transaction."

CONSTITUTIONAL PROTECTION FOR COMMERCIAL SPEECH

While the debate continues, it is clear that the commercial speech doctrine today is a far different one from that of the mid-twentieth century era when the Supreme Court dispatched the question of First Amendment protection for advertising almost dismissively. In *Valentine v. Chrestensen*, in 1942, the Court deemed that its answer required only a four-page opinion and declared unanimously that no such protection was justified because the "Constitution imposes no ... restraint on government as respects purely commercial advertising."

That challenge reached the Court through the creative efforts of F.J. Chrestensen to promote tours of a Navy submarine he had moored at a pier in New York City. Upon learning that passing out fliers advertising his tours to pedestrians violated a city anti-litter code — which did not apply to political handbills — Chrestensen had his fliers reprinted with a message on the flip side criticizing the city law. Despite his assertion that his speech thus had been rendered political and protected, police officials said he was still violating the ordinance, and he sued to enjoin the government from interfering with his distribution of advertising that he argued was constitutionally protected. The Court rejected his challenge, declaring that the "affixing of the protest against official conduct to the advertising circular" was clearly only "for the purpose of evading the prohibition of the ordinance," but noting that future cases could well involve more complicated questions in this area of First Amendment law.

And how they have. Over the course of a long series of cases moving far beyond some key elements of *Valentine*, the Court has focused on shaping a doctrine that continues to sharply distinguish commercial from political expression, but emphasizes protection for truthful advertising on the reasoning that it advances a public good for consumers to receive accurate commercial information. At the same time, the Court's holdings in those cases have not wavered on the government's power to regulate false or deceptive advertising.

The Court first signaled the potential for a shift away from *Valentine*'s rejection of First Amendment protection for advertising in 1964's *New York Times Co. v. Sullivan*, in the course of constitutionalizing libel law in that landmark ruling. The case involved a full-page advertisement for a civil rights organization published in the *New York Times* that criticized officials in Montgomery, Alabama, for their handling of civil rights protests and sought financial support for the civil rights movement. L.B. Sullivan, the Montgomery police commissioner, brought the libel action, contending that false assertions in the ad regarding police activity had defamed him. His attorneys maintained that *Valentine*'s holding meant the *Times* could argue no First Amendment defense in the case, because the alleged libel appeared in an advertisement. But the Court found that argument "wholly misplaced" in that the speech in question in *Valentine* had amounted to an effort to evade a city ordinance in order to promote a commercial venture while the speech in *Sullivan* concerned "matters of the highest public interest and concern." It held that in the context of the facts of that case, the advertising format alone could not bar the speech involved from First Amendment protection, which eventually offered the opening for other cases to make their way toward the Court on other commercial-speech questions.

Nine years later, the *Pittsburgh Press* challenged a city regulation barring help-wanted advertisements segregated according to male or female interest, asking the Court to "abrogate the distinction between commercial and other speech." The Court suggested that it might be willing to give constitutional protection to "an ordinary commercial proposal" but found that the facts of the *Pittsburgh Press* case did not warrant it because "discrimination in employment is not only commercial activity, it is illegal commercial activity."

In rejecting the newspaper's argument, the Court said the ads resembled the speech in *Valentine* more than that of *Sullivan* in that they did not express a position on "whether, as a matter of social policy, certain positions ought to be filed by members of one or the other sex, nor ... criticize the ordinance." Because a help-wanted ad "is no more than a proposal of possible employment," it represented "classic examples of commercial speech." The Court noted, however, that it might well consider some degree of First Amendment protection for advertising for an ordi-

nary commercial proposal not tainted by illegality.

The next year provided evidence of how difficult the Court found it was to sort out the questions involved in First Amendment protection for commercial speech, in a case in which it was unable to form a majority for an opinion concerning a challenge to a ban on political advertising on city buses. In *Lehman v. City of Shaker Heights*, a majority upheld the ban, but only three justices joined the plurality opinion by Justice Harry Blackmun that declared the buses did not constitute a public forum for First Amendment purposes, so the city was free to allow commercial advertising on cards posted inside the buses while not accepting political advertising, because the city was only "engaged in commerce" in providing bus service.

A year after that, seven justices found greater agreement in declaring unconstitutional a Virginia statute that banned publication of any advertisement for abortion services. In *Bigelow v. Virginia*, the Court distinguished the ad in question, noting that it contained truthful information for a service that was legal in the state where the abortion services were offered (New York) and of public interest in the state where it was published (Virginia), even though abortions were illegal there. While once again holding that commercial speech was not without constitutional protection, the Court still declined to decide "the precise extent to which the First Amendment permits regulation of advertising that is related to activities the State may legitimately regulate or even prohibit." *Bigelow* came just two years after the 1973 *Roe v. Wade* ruling that declared individuals' decisions on abortion within the constitutionally protected right of privacy.

Expanding Protection for Purely Commercial Speech

After that series of cases, in which the Court established its willingness to protect political ads as well as ads promoting legal activities in the public interest, it squarely addressed the issue of First Amendment protection for purely commercial advertisements in 1976 in *Virginia State Board of Pharmacy v. Virginia Citizens Consumer Council*. In striking down a state prohibition on pharmacists advertising the price of prescription drugs, the Court focused on preventing government from blocking the dissemination of truthful information to citizens: "Virginia is free to require whatever professional standards it wishes of its pharmacists.... But it may not do so by keeping the public in ignorance of the entirely lawful terms that competing pharmacists are offering." The pharmacy board had argued that the restriction was necessary to avoid pressure on pharmacists to participate in aggressive price competition rather than developing relationships with customers, possibly endangering consumers' health and harming the pharmacists' status as professionals, and potentially pushing some conscientious pharmacists out of business while raising advertising costs that would be passed on to consumers in the form of higher drug prices.

It was not pharmacists who challenged the regulation, but the non-profit Virginia Citizens Consumer Council, which was not actually barred from advertising pharmaceutical prices, as Justice William Rehnquist noted in a dissenting opinion. The group argued, however, that consumers had a First Amendment right to *receive* information from pharmacists, which would allow them to find the drugs they needed at the best prices.

In agreeing, the Supreme Court recognized for the first time that the First Amendment protects purely commercial advertising by focusing on "the free flow of commercial information," noting that a consumer's interest in commercial information "may be as keen, if not keener by far, than his interest in the day's most urgent political debate." That free flow of information, the Court reasoned, is also crucial to the development of intelligent opinions about how to reform or regulate the economic system.

It emphasized, however, that the government was still free to regulate ads that were false, misleading, deceptive or that promote illegal products or services, making clear that the First Amendment "does not prohibit the State from insuring that the stream of commercial information flow cleanly as well as freely." The Court also detailed why "commonsense differences" between commercial speech and other, protected types of speech made government regulation of untruthful commercial speech more tolerable. First, advertisers may easily verify their commercial speech because they disseminate information about their own product or service and, therefore, know more about it than anyone else. In contrast, reporters and political commentators must rely on other sources as the basis for the information they distribute. Second, commercial speech is hardier than other types of speech because it is so necessary for generating profits that regulation would not chill an advertiser's speech.

A year later, in *Linmark Associates v. Willingboro*, the Court emphasized its focus on preventing government from denying citizens truthful information in declaring unconstitutional a city ban on the posting of signs advertising homes for sale. The purpose of the ordinance was argued to be promoting racial integration by preventing "panic selling ... by whites who feared that the township was becoming all black, and that property values would decline." The Court declared, however, that if "dissemination of this information can be restricted, then every locality in the country can suppress any facts that reflect poorly on the locality," and that restricting government from denying citizens "information that is neither false nor misleading" was precisely the point of *Virginia Pharmacy*.

The same year, the Court, in *Bates v. State Bar of Arizona*, relied on *Virginia Pharmacy* to invalidate an Arizona state bar regulation that prohibited lawyers from advertising prices for legal services in the mass media. The state bar had argued that

advertising would make lawyers less dignified and professional, stir up unnecessary lawsuits, and result in higher costs for legal services. The Supreme Court rejected all of those arguments, asserting that *Virginia Pharmacy* made it clear that the "choice between the dangers of suppressing information and the dangers arising from its free flow was seen as precisely the choice 'that the First Amendment makes for us.'" Because people who have a legitimate need for legal services may not know where to turn for advice or may be afraid that legal services will cost too much, advertising could help them in such situations, the Court noted. It also emphasized its view that there was nothing inherently misleading about lawyers advertising the cost of routine legal services as important to its decision, because "the leeway for untruthful or misleading expression that has been allowed in other contexts has little force in the commercial arena."

A year later, the Court found cause to qualify its holding on advertising by attorneys in *Ohralik v. Ohio State Bar Association*. The case involved a First Amendment challenge to sanctions against an attorney who had utilized undue influence and misrepresentation in ways Justice Thurgood Marshall called "classic examples of 'ambulance chasing'" to induce two 18-year-old women to hire him to represent them in relation to an automobile accident in which they were injured. In a unanimous ruling, the Court declared that in-person solicitation by attorneys "does not stand on a par with truthful advertising about the availability and terms of routine legal services, let alone with forms of speech more traditionally within the concern of the First Amendment." More broadly, the *Ohralik* opinion, authored by Justice Lewis Powell, reasserted why distinctions between advertising and more protected expression were justified. It emphasized that the Court's decisions had "afforded commercial speech a limited measure of protection, commensurate with its subordinate position in the scale of First Amendment values" and that requiring equal protection for commercial and noncommercial speech "could invite dilution, simply by a leveling process, of the force of the Amendment's guarantee with respect to the latter kind of speech."

The Central Hudson Test

Two years later, Justice Powell went much further to formally establish the commercial-speech doctrine for maintaining the distinction between advertising and more protected expression. In *Central Hudson Gas & Electric Co. v. Public Service Commission of New York*, he enunciated a formal test for determining the extent of First Amendment protection for commercial speech. In striking down a New York state law that sought to conserve energy by banning all advertising that promoted the use of electricity, the Court put forth a standardized four-part test of intermediate scrutiny to determine whether a government regulation on advertising is constitutional.

The test, as articulated in *Central Hudson* and applied to the facts of that case, unfolded in this manner:

(1) The test first asks *whether the advertising that is regulated is misleading and whether it concerns a legal product or service.* Neither a misleading ad nor one for an illegal product or service receives any First Amendment protection. In *Central Hudson*, the New York Public Service Commission did not claim that the advertising at issue was misleading, deceptive or for any illegal activity, so that meant the Court's analysis continued to the second question.

(2) The second part of the Central Hudson Test asks *whether the asserted governmental interest is substantial.* This part of the test requires government to show that it has a substantial interest in protecting the health, safety, morals and aesthetics of the public — rather than a compelling interest, a much more rigorous standard which the Court considers very few government interests to meet. In *Central Hudson*, the government's asserted interest in energy conservation was certainly a substantial one, the Court concluded.

(3) Third, the Central Hudson Test asks *whether the regulation directly advances the asserted governmental interest.* In *Central Hudson*, the Court found there must be an immediate connection between advertising and electrical consumption, because otherwise the company would not have been advertising. Therefore, a restriction on advertising would reduce electrical consumption, directly advancing the government's interest.

(4) Finally, the test asks *whether the regulation is "no more extensive than necessary"* to serve the governmental interest. The Court concluded that the regulation at issue in *Central Hudson* failed the test, finding it to be more extensive than necessary because it banned ads even for electric services or devices that were energy efficient.

Thus, the Court ruled that because the challenged regulation reached "all promotional advertising, regardless of the impact ... on overall energy use ... the energy conservation rationale, as important as it is, cannot justify suppressing information" that could reduce total energy consumption.

Three years later, the Court provided its most substantial guidance for distinguishing between commercial and noncommercial speech in 1983's *Bolger v. Youngs Drug Products Corp.* To determine if a condom manufacturer's flyers and pamphlets promoting its products — but also discussing venereal disease and family planning — could be considered commercial messages subject to federal regulation, the Court developed a three-part test that considered the combination of the advertising format of the messages, reference to a specific product, and the economic motivation for disseminating the messages. It stressed that one of those three factors by itself would not necessarily prove dispositive, but, when considered together, the messages

in question were "properly characterized as commercial speech ... notwithstanding the fact that they contain discussions of important public issues." Further, the Court emphasized advertisers' ability to separate commercial messages from noncommercial messages: "A company has the full panoply of protections available to its direct comments on public issues, so there is no reason for providing similar constitutional protection when such statements are made in the context of commercial transactions."

In 1986, the Court applied the test in *Posadas de Puerto Rico Associates v. Tourism Company of Puerto Rico* and upheld a ban on casino ads in Puerto Rico. The island had legalized gambling to promote tourism but banned casino ads because it did not want to encourage Puerto Ricans to gamble. The majority applied the Central Hudson Test and found the ban to be constitutional in that its restriction on a form of commercial speech advanced a substantial government interest (promoting the public welfare by reducing demand for gambling) in a manner that was no more extensive than necessary. Justice Rehnquist's majority opinion asserted that even though casino gambling was legal in Puerto Rico, "the Puerto Rico Legislature surely could have prohibited casino gambling by the residents of Puerto Rico altogether. In our view, the greater power to completely ban casino gambling necessarily includes the lesser power to ban advertising of casino gambling."

Writing in dissent, however, Justice William J. Brennan argued that *Posadas* had gone too far beyond the Court's prior commercial-speech cases that had accepted regulation of "dissemination of information that is false, deceptive, or misleading ... or that proposes an illegal transaction," but not restrictions "designed to deprive consumers of accurate information about products and services legally offered for sale."

Three years later, a regulation by the State University of New York prohibiting private commercial activities in university facilities was upheld in *Board of Trustees, State University of New York v. Fox.* The university said the regulation sought to prevent commercial exploitation of students, maintain an educational atmosphere on campus, promote student safety, and protect residential tranquility. In applying the Central Hudson Test for the majority, Justice Antonin Scalia articulated at some length the basis in the Court's precedents for interpreting the meaning of the fourth part of the test as asking only whether a "reasonable fit" existed between the asserted governmental interest and the challenged regulation. That interpretation allowed more leeway for regulation of commercial speech than would the "least restrictive means" standard that the challengers of the university's regulation had argued should be used.

Recent Cases and Trends

The potential narrowing of protection for advertising in *Posadas* and *Board of Trustees* was counterbalanced by rulings in the 1990s that stiffened the government's burden in the Central Hudson Test, particularly the third and fourth prongs. In 1993's *Cincinnati v. Discovery Network*, the Court ruled unconstitutional a city ban on use of newsracks on city streets to distribute commercial handbills. It found a lack of reasonable fit between the city's purpose of promoting the safety and aesthetics of public streets and the banning of commercial, but not noncommercial, newsracks. The Court emphasized that the ban's distinction between commercial and noncommercial speech bore "no relationship whatsoever to the particular interests that the city has asserted" because "commercial newsracks are no greater an eyesore than the [noncommercial] newsracks permitted."

The same year, in *Edenfield v. Fane*, the Court ruled unconstitutional a state ban on certified public accountants' personal solicitation of prospective clients, declaring the state had not demonstrated that the regulation advanced the interests asserted. To the contrary, the Court found the rule threatened citizens' access to complete and accurate commercial information, because the speech in question sought "to communicate no more than truthful, non-deceptive information proposing a lawful commercial transaction." The Court, also in 1993, in *United States v. Edge Broadcasting*, upheld a federal law prohibiting lottery advertising by radio stations located in states where lotteries are not legal, applying the Central Hudson Test to conclude that the regulation advanced North Carolina's anti-gambling policy without unduly interfering with lotteries sponsored by nearby states.

In the 1990s, the Court began moving even more aggressively to strengthen the Central Hudson Test and to emphasize its determination to protect the dissemination of truthful, factual information from government regulation that seeks to discourage activities that are otherwise legal. In 1995, the Court held a federal law prohibiting beer labels from advertising alcohol content to be unconstitutional because it failed both the third and fourth prongs of the Central Hudson Test. In *Rubin v. Coors Brewing Co.*, the government had asserted that allowing alcohol content on beer labels would lead to strength wars among brewers, which would in turn lead to an increase in alcoholism. The Court held that although preventing strength wars did represent a substantial interest, the government had failed to show that the regulation advanced its interest in a "direct and material way." The federal government allowed the labels of distilled spirits to disclose alcohol content, required the labels of some wine bottles to do so and did not prohibit brewers from indicating alcohol content in advertisements. Additionally, the regulation failed the Court's application of the fourth prong, the Court concluded, because there were less restrictive alternatives that would have advanced the government's interest, such as directly limiting the alcohol content of beer or prohibiting marketing

that emphasized strong alcohol content.

The next year, in *44 Liquormart v. Rhode Island*, the Court unanimously struck down two Rhode Island statutes that prohibited the advertisement of alcohol prices anywhere in the state except at the point of purchase. The state maintained that the ban served the substantial government interest of reducing alcohol consumption among its residents, because if alcohol retailers could advertise their prices, prices would fall and consumption would rise.

The Court was splintered in its reasoning, however, demonstrating again how challenging it often finds First Amendment questions involving advertising. No more than four justices could agree on what test should be applied to the commercial-speech regulations involved, and a majority agreement could only be reached on the judgment and the application of the Twenty-First Amendment to the issue. Justice John Paul Stevens delivered the Court's opinion concerning the Twenty-First Amendment issue and the facts and procedure of the case, but no more than three justices joined him in any other parts of his opinion. On the question of the constitutional grant to states of broad regulatory power over the commerce of alcohol, the Court held that power granted by the "Twenty-First Amendment does not qualify the constitutional prohibition against laws abridging the freedom of speech embodied in the First Amendment." Because the state presented no evidentiary support, the Court said it could not agree that the ban would significantly advance the state's interest in promoting temperance.

Only two justices joined Stevens's argument that more rigorous scrutiny than *Central Hudson* intermediate scrutiny should be applied to regulations that prohibit "the dissemination of truthful, nonmisleading commercial messages for reasons unrelated to the preservation of a fair bargaining process." In contrast, four justices specifically rejected any such departure from the Central Hudson Test for considering First Amendment protection of commercial speech, declaring that the challenged regulation would fail the fourth prong of the test because it was more extensive than necessary to serve its stated interest.

In a part of Justice Stevens's opinion joined by three other justices, that plurality declared that its earlier decision in *Posadas* was incorrect. "*Posadas* erroneously performed the First Amendment analysis," the plurality held, declaring that the government "does not have the broad discretion to suppress truthful, non-misleading information." A plurality declared that, henceforth, the Court would apply a more stringent constitutional review when the government completely suppresses truthful expression.

In *Lorillard Tobacco v. Reilly*, five years later, the Court sought to provide some clarification of its commercial-speech doctrine. It noted that the petitioners challenging state regulations on outdoor tobacco advertising had urged the Court to "reject the *Central Hudson* analysis and apply strict scrutiny" on the grounds that some justices in the earlier cases had "expressed doubts about the *Central Hudson* analysis and whether it should apply in certain cases." Pointing out that the same argument had been raised in *Greater New Orleans Broadcasting v. United States* two years earlier, the *Lorillard* Court found, as in that case, "no need to break new ground. *Central Hudson*, as applied in our more recent commercial speech cases, provides an adequate basis for decision." So in *Lorillard*, the Court applied the Central Hudson Test and concluded that the regulations involving advertising of cigars and smokeless tobacco failed the test as more extensive than necessary to advance the government's substantial interest in preventing underage tobacco use. It declared that while the government's interest in preventing minors' tobacco use was

> substantial, and even compelling ... it is no less true that the sale and use of tobacco products by adults is a legal activity. We must consider that tobacco retailers and manufacturers have an interest in conveying truthful information about their products to adults, and adults have a corresponding interest in receiving truthful information about tobacco products.

In 2009, Congress enacted the Family Smoking Prevention and Tobacco Control Act, giving the Food and Drug Administration extensive regulatory control over tobacco. Tobacco companies then challenged FDA guidelines that required a significant portion of tobacco packaging be reserved for health warnings, restricted commercial marketing of "modified risk tobacco products" (those promoted as representing relatively less risk of disease or harm than others), banned statements that convey the impression FDA regulation means that tobacco products are safer, limited the use of colorful tobacco displays and ads, barred the distribution of free samples of tobacco products in most locations as well as brand-name tobacco sponsorship of athletic and social events, and banned "continuity programs" (distribution of free items as rewards for tobacco purchase). A district court judge upheld most of the regulations in *Commonwealth Brands v. United States*, though not the limitations on use of colorful displays and ads and the ban on statements of relative safety. A federal appeals court, in *Discount Tobacco City & Lottery v. United States* in 2012, affirmed most of the lower court ruling, but reversed its striking down of the ban on statements of relative safety and its upholding of the ban on continuity programs. The Supreme Court declined to hear the appeal. Application of the Central Hudson Test was central to both rulings. In a second challenge, brought against FDA guidelines issued under the act in *R.J. Reynolds, et al. v. F.D.A.*, which called for graphic warnings on cigarette packs and in ad-

vertising about the health consequences of tobacco use, another district court judge applied strict scrutiny rather than the Central Hudson Test in striking down the regulation. A federal appeals court held that the Central Hudson Test was the appropriate standard, but that the government had failed to satisfy the test's burden of showing that the regulation directly advanced the government's interest in reducing smoking rates.

In *Thompson v. Western States Medical Center*, the Supreme Court struck down provisions of the federal Food and Drug Administration Modernization Act of 1997 that precluded pharmacists from advertising compounded drugs. Under the act, compounded drugs — those custom-made for patients by pharmacists — did not have to comply with the FDA's drug approval process if providers refrained from advertising or promoting them. This restriction sought to balance the government's interests in protecting public health through the FDA approval process for manufactured drugs and continuing to permit pharmacists to compound drugs that had not been tested for safety or efficacy. After a group of licensed pharmacies challenged the limitation as a violation of their free-speech rights, the Supreme Court ruled 5-4 that the restriction was too broad. While acknowledging that protecting the integrity of the FDA's drug approval process was a substantial interest, the Court held that the interest could have been advanced by other means that did not include restrictions on speech: "We have made clear that if the Government could achieve its interests in a manner that does not restrict speech, or that restricts less speech, the Government must do so."

Thus, over the years since it first enunciated a test for commercial speech cases, the Court has expanded protection for such speech, but no majority has found a need to depart from the Central Hudson Test. Although some justices have argued for equal protection for noncommercial speech and truthful, non-misleading commercial speech, the Court's holdings have focused on preventing government from denying citizens truthful information while maintaining *Central Hudson* as an effective means for achieving that. Thus, the Court's commercial-speech doctrine has placed a priority on protecting truth in advertising. Scholarship such as Robert Kerr's article "A Justice's Surprise That Has Stood Its Ground" has asserted that the *Hudson*-centric doctrine has endured so long, despite repeated challenges, because of the way the Court's four-part test successfully institutionalized a difficult balancing between protecting the informational component of advertising and maintaining preservation of the fair-bargaining process in its contractual component.

Questions About the Future of the Doctrine

In its most recent major commercial-speech case, the Supreme

Court raised considerable questions as to where its doctrine may be headed. In *Sorrell v. IMS Health Inc.*, decided in 2011, the Court ruled unconstitutional a Vermont statute that restricted the sale, disclosure and use of prescriber histories for marketing purposes without a physician's consent. The act targeted the practice of collecting data on the prescriptions individual physicians write and selling that data to pharmaceutical companies who, in turn, use the information to better market their drugs to doctors. According to the majority, Vermont was essentially trying to curb the effective promotion of brand-name prescription drugs in favor of generic alternatives. Thus, it held that the statute restricted speech based on its content and on the identity of the speaker and, therefore, warranted heightened constitutional scrutiny under the First Amendment. Vermont argued that the speech involved was commercial speech and deserving of less protection. But the Court noted that the statute's restrictions on speech would not survive regardless of the scrutiny level used. Citing its *Bates* decision, the Court reaffirmed the strong interest consumers have in receiving free-flowing commercial information and said that interest is especially important "in the fields of medicine and public health, where information can save lives."

The full impact of the *Sorrell* case on the commercial-speech doctrine remains to be seen. The Court did not abandon its *Central Hudson* analysis as the constitutional test for restrictions, but it indicated it would scrutinize regulations more stringently if they disfavored particular speakers and messages. For the *Sorrell* Court, the Vermont law's placing of restrictions on marketing in that manner disfavored "speech with a particular content" and "specific speakers, namely pharmaceutical manufacturers" and, thus, imposed "burdens that are based on the content of speech and that are aimed at a particular viewpoint." The implications of *Sorrell* — that commercial speech potentially can be considered nothing more than a protected viewpoint, rather than part of a contractual offering between seller and buyer — along with the holding that government may not burden the expression of such viewpoints when non-commercial speakers are not similarly burdened, appear to be potentially expansive. The ruling raises questions about further ramifications for a commercial-speech doctrine that long has permitted many regulations on commercial speakers that would not be permissible on noncommercial speakers. Justice Stephen Breyer argued in dissent that the *Sorrell* majority had at the least applied "an unforgiving brand of 'intermediate' scrutiny" that if extended in future cases "would work at cross-purposes" with the Court's established commercial-speech doctrine.

The Court has not addressed *Sorrell* substantially in any of its commercial-speech rulings since then, but in concurring with the judgment in *Reed v. Town of Gilbert* in 2015, Justice Breyer pressed the argument that *Reed* and *Sorrell* both represent a dangerous trend of relying excessively on strict scrutiny when a lesser standard of review could resolve an issue. In *Reed*, the Court struck down an Arizona municipal sign code as unconstitutional content regulation because even though it did not discriminate against any viewpoint, it singled out subject matter for differential treatment by imposing shorter time limits on temporary directional signs than on political signs. Both Breyer's separate concurrence and Justice Elena Kagan's concurrence joined by Breyer and Justice Ruth Bader Ginsburg, contended the same ruling could have been reached through a lesser level of scrutiny, with Kagan insisting there was "no reason why such an easy case calls for us to cast a constitutional pall on reasonable regulations quite unlike the law before us." She warned that by potentially declaring that "strict scrutiny applies to every sign ordinance in every town across this country containing a subject-matter exemption, ... courts will discover that thousands of towns have such ordinances," and this "Court may soon find itself a veritable Supreme Board of Sign Review." In 2022's *City of Austin v. Reagan National Advertising*, a 6-3 majority at the Court held that a city restriction on digital billboards that distinguished between on-premise and off-premise signs was content-neutral and should not be subject to strict scrutiny, remanding it to the lower courts for facial review under intermediate scrutiny. The ruling suggests that a sign regulation that provides different treatment for on-premise and off-premise signs will not automatically render such a regulation in violation of the First Amendment.

If Justice Kagan's "Supreme Board of Sign Review" forecast has not yet literally come to pass, plaintiffs in the years since *Sorrell* have seized upon it to argue challenges against a stunning plethora of regulated activity, as detailed in the law-review article by Robert Kerr, "Desperately Seeking Coherence," an extensive recent review of lower-court activity. The arguments as to why an ever more diverse range of activities should be understood in the post-*Sorrell* era as worthy of First Amendment protection against regulation helps to illustrate the challenges facing lower courts. The myriad efforts of lower courts to address that rapidly growing body of *Sorrell*-grounded claims have only begun to bring the nature of the ruling's impact on the doctrine into focus, but that process is far from coalescing into a consistent understanding.

Some lower courts have declared that *Sorrell* did not replace the intermediate-scrutiny analysis of the Central Hudson Test, while others have distinguished *Sorrell* by emphasizing various essential facts that differ from key elements of *Sorrell*. Some lower courts have held that *Sorrell* "adjusted" or "refined" the commercial-speech doctrine so as to require heightened judicial scrutiny on any content-based regulation of commercial expression. Those courts have specifically applied the fourth prong of the Central Hudson Test in a manner that combines the second through fourth prongs in a new configuration — thus implementing the heightened level of scrutiny that the *Sorrell* Court actually left unspecified.

Other lower courts have applied *Sorrell* in a manner that stresses a heightened level of scrutiny, but less clearly focused on a *Sorrell*-adjusted fourth prong of the Central Hudson Test. Some courts have focused on a new step of determining first whether a challenged regulation on commercial speech is content-based, but then still proceeding with the Central Hudson Test in a relatively traditional manner — quite possibly *because Sorrell* did not actually define the heightened scrutiny that should be applied. Other courts seem to be applying a more aggressive Central Hudson Test that focuses primarily on targeting "paternalism" in regulating commercial speech, and some courts have applied other particulars from *Sorrell* less systematically to strike down challenged regulations.

A potential opportunity for the Supreme Court to address more clearly how *Sorrell* should be applied, and whether it altered the nature of *Central Hudson* analysis in the commercial-speech doctrine, could develop out of the stark disagreement between two recent panels of appellate judges in the Ninth Circuit that directly contradicted each other.

In a *Sorrell*-grounded First Amendment challenge to state regulations on in-store liquid-crystal-display alcohol advertising, a three-judge panel for the Ninth Circuit in 2016 reversed the district court's ruling in concluding that *Sorrell* required "heightened judicial scrutiny of content-based restrictions on non-misleading commercial speech regarding lawful products," rather than *Central Hudson*'s intermediate scrutiny. In *Retail Digital Network, LLC v. Appelsmith*, that court found that even though *Sorrell* did not apply heightened scrutiny, it modified the Central Hudson Test by holding heightened scrutiny could be applied through focusing on an adjusted fourth prong of the test. It cited decisions in the Second, Third, and Eighth circuits in support of that holding.

However, shortly after that decision, the Ninth Circuit voted to rehear the case en banc, and an eleven-judge panel in 2017 declared that "*Sorrell* did not modify the *Central Hudson* standard." It found that the *Sorrell* Court "referred to 'heightened scrutiny' within the context of deciding whether [the challenged law] regulated speech whatsoever," and only in response to the state's argument that the law should be subject to rational-basis review as a non-speech regulation of commerce – not in relation to *Central Hudson* intermediate scrutiny. It further emphasized that the fact that the *Sorrell* Court "entertained the potential application of a 'stricter form of judicial scrutiny' but ultimately still applied *Central Hudson*, while clearly acknowledging that "the government's legitimate interest in protecting consumers from 'commercial harms,' explains 'why commercial speech can be subject to greater governmental regulation than

noncommercial speech.'" The eleven-judge panel declared such key points from *Sorrell* make clear that "one of the core principles that animates the Court's approach to commercial speech" remains intact after *Sorrell*. In support of its conclusion that the established Central Hudson Test had not been altered, that panel cited decisions in the Second, Fourth, Sixth, and Eighth circuits. To date, the Ninth Circuit's en banc holding has been cited positively by the federal district courts for the Eastern District of Pennsylvania and the D.C. Circuit, as well as by the Ninth Circuit in a separate case, and negatively by none.

One additional element of potential instability regarding the future of the commercial-speech doctrine may have been introduced *via* the Court's 2010 ruling in *Citizens United v. Federal Election Commission*. In that case, a 5-4 majority, more sweepingly than ever, protected corporate political media spending from regulation aimed at preventing corruption of candidate campaigns, ruling for the first time that corporations may make unlimited political expenditures directly from their treasuries and declaring unconstitutional virtually any limits on spending of that type. That extended First Amendment protection of such unlimited political expenditures (already in place for human beings) to corporate beings on the reasoning that "the First Amendment does not allow political speech restrictions based on a speaker's corporate identity." Although *Citizens United* was not itself a commercial-speech case, the sweeping ruling freed a vast array of political advertising from government regulation and has raised questions of its potential impact on regulation of commercial speech by corporations. For example, if future challenges of such regulation should successfully advance arguments that "any speech by a commercial entity must be, to some degree, commercial" and thus establish that "corporate speech is also commercial speech," Robert Sprague and Mary Ellen Wells have proposed, will the First Amendment then permit corporate commercial speech to be regulated as extensively as it has been to date?

REGULATION OF DECEPTIVE ADVERTISING

Commercial speech can be regulated at both the federal and state levels, but the primary regulatory body is the century-old Federal Trade Commission. It has long been such an established fact of life for the advertising industry that, for example, an early episode of the acclaimed television drama *Mad Men* featured a discussion about dealing with the FTC in the 1950s at the fictional ad agency on which the show focused. In the episode, the agency's executives respond to the concerns of a client, frustrated at being unable to fight the FTC, by helping creatively craft a campaign strategy that will carefully walk as close as possible to the line of deceptive advertising without actually crossing it. Having a sense of where the FTC draws that line is crucial to advertising practitioners — and to consumers concerned about deceptive or misleading advertising.

The FTC in the Twenty-First Century

The FTC's regulation of deceptive advertising must be considered in the context of what it has described on its Web site as its broader mission to prevent "anticompetitive, deceptive, and unfair business practices" and enhance "informed consumer choice ... without unduly burdening legitimate business activity." Established by Congress in 1914, the FTC is declared by the *United States Code* as "the only federal agency with both consumer protection and competition jurisdiction in broad sectors of the economy." An agency that was born when technologies like motion pictures and radio were transforming the nation's economy now operates in an age shaped by the transformative forces of wireless communications, the Internet, and Big Data. As the FTC enters its second century, it is actively interfacing its mission with rapidly evolving digital technological developments to advance a cyber-age understanding of Justice Blackmun's vision in which intelligent, well-informed consumer decision-making is prioritized as a matter of public interest.

In a world in which the "Internet of Things" means more and more aspects of consumer activity are constantly tracked by an ever increasing array of Internet-connected sensors, "Today's currency is data," declared Edith Ramirez, recent chairwoman of the FTC, in 2014. She outlined a broad approach for the agency in which its activities are targeted at "areas where we can have the greatest impact for consumers" and "address the problems that affect them in their day-to-day lives," as reported in *The New York Times*. To that end, the FTC in recent years has advanced its mandate to maintain competition and protect consumers with a creative and expansive cyber sensibility grounded in "tried-and-true tools of law enforcement, sound public policy, and consumer education," as it characterized it on its Web site. Among recent manifestations of that approach:

• The agency has increasingly focused on the way that the media through which advertising is utilized can be intertwined with digital intrusions upon consumer privacy. In 2015, for example, Ramirez publicly pressed the makers of tech gadgets to make data security a priority and to give consumers more control over the data that is gathered on them digitally for advertising and other purposes in a growing market worth billions. The FTC has also recently increased its investigations and enforcement actions related to the collecting and selling of consumer data. "Your smart TV and Tablet may track whether you watch the History Channel or reality television, but ... will this information be used to paint a picture of you that you won't see but that others will," Ramirez said in remarks at an interna-

tional electronics trade show. "People who might make decisions about whether you are shown ads for organic food or junk food, ... and what offers of credit and other products you receive?"

• In a 2014 example of FTC action concerning data collection that involved deceptive advertising, the mobile-messaging app Snapchat agreed in a consent order to settle charges by the agency that user messages did not "disappear" in the way the company had represented the service — in fact, others could save the messages without being detected. "If a company markets privacy and security as key selling points in pitching its service to consumers, it is critical that it keep that promise," Ramirez said in an FTC press release on the case, in which the private data of millions of Snapchat users were accessed illegally. "Any company that makes misrepresentations to consumers about its privacy and security practices risks FTC action." In settling, the Associated Press reported, Snapchat agreed to be monitored by an outside privacy expert for twenty years in an arrangement similar to settlements Google, Facebook and Myspace agreed to in recent years.

• In the FTC's first case involving crowdfunding, it reached a settlement in 2015 with a project creator who deceptively raised money from consumers online through representations in a Kickstarter campaign that he planned to produce a board game — when in fact he spent most of the money on unrelated personal expenses such as rent payments and moving expenses and never produced a game. According to an FTC press release, the settlement order with Erik Chevalier imposed a $111,793 judgment, suspended on the basis of his inability to pay it unless he were to be found to have misrepresented his financial condition.

• In another 2015 settlement that demonstrated the agency's increased focus on so-called "revenge" Web sites, the FTC shut down the activities of a man who was deceptively advertising a legal service that would get nude photos of women posted online without their permission. The photos were actually from a revenge porn site that the man operated by obtaining photos from the women's former boyfriends. The settlement barred Craig Brittain, who had promoted his purported legal service as "Takedown Lawyer," from engaging in any further "revenge porn" activity and required that he destroy all the images and personal contact information he had collected, according to an FTC press release.

• In 2022, the maker of TurboTax software for filing online tax returns was accused of misleadingly advertising free services that actually steered consumers into paid services. The company agreed to pay back $141 million to four million consumers, in action also involving the attorney general of New York State, after the FTC alleged it had employed multiple deceptive and unfair trade practices, including buying search-engine advertisements that guided people into services that incurred fees and blocking the landing page for its free service from appearing in search-engine results.

• In a 2023 settlement, the FTC alleged the popular drug-discount app GoodRx deceptively shared details on users' illnesses and medicines with advertising firms. The FTC accused the app's developer, GoodRx Holdings, of wrongful disclosing sensitive personal data on millions of users' intimate health information, such as prescription medications and illnesses, with companies like Facebook and Google without authorization. It marked the first time the agency brought an enforcement action using its Health Breach Notification Rule, which requires health apps and connected devices to notify users of the unauthorized sharing of their health data, as well as the first time the FTC sought to prohibit a company from sharing users' health data for advertising purposes. The company agreed to pay a $1.5 million civil penalty for violating the rule.

When Ramirez began her tenure at the agency in 2010, the *New York Times* reported her observation that "most everyday Americans really don't know much about what the FTC does." As part of the agency's efforts to raise awareness of its activities, it began reaching out to the public *via* Twitter and Facebook, an online subscription service for its press releases and the so-called "complaint assistant" to aid in the reporting of fraud and abuse, and a toll-free help line. Despite its heightened cyber-profile and its intensified focus on maintaining competition and protecting consumers in the digital world, its fundamental tools for regulating deceptive advertising are well established and remain at the core of its activity. The continuing vigor of the agency's role was most recently highlighted by the 2021 appointment as FTC chair Lina Khan, who has published extensively on the deceptive practices, antitrust issues and other dangers of Big Tech. Her appointment signals what a former FTC chair described in the *New York Times* as "the boldest vision for the agency in its history."

That vision has aggressively extended the FTC's crackdown on data and privacy protection. That has included, for example, seeking a ban on the collection of young people's personal data by Meta, Facebook's parent company, and fining Twitter $150 million over alleged violations of a previous data-privacy settlement, plus expanding the agreement's terms to prohibit Twitter from using certain data to target ads, while blocking Twitter owner Elon Musk's personal efforts to intervene.

Such efforts by the FTC are now imperative, Khan has set forth in the *New York Times*, in light of the way many tech companies' business models have become based on "the widespread hoarding and sale of our personal data" through the development of "endlessly invasive ways to track" consumers "at extraordinary cost to our privacy and security." All that is being compounded, Kahn detailed, by the "race to deploy and monetize" artificial intelligence, already "turbocharging fraud" by

employing chatbots to "scam people, fake websites and fake consumer reviews." In response, she promised the FTC will be vigorously cracking down on unfair or deceptive practices grounded in A.I.-enhanced "business models or practices involving the mass exploitation of their users."

The FTC and Deceptive Advertising

The FTC's five commissioners are nominated by the president and confirmed by the Senate for terms of seven years. No more than three may be of the same political party. The FTC administers a variety of federal statutes that, according to the FTC Policy on Deception, "promote competition and protect the public from unfair and deceptive acts and practices in the advertising and marketing of goods and services." Regional offices are responsible for enforcing regulations, investigating complaints and educating the public. The FTC focuses on national advertising, referring purely local concerns to state and local government agencies. While the staff monitors national ad campaigns for potentially deceptive claims, letters from consumers or businesses, congressional inquiries, or news stories on consumer or economic topics may also trigger FTC investigations.

The FTC is responsible for protecting consumers from both unfair and deceptive advertising, according to its Truth in Advertising statement: "When consumers see or hear an advertisement, whether it's on the Internet, radio or television, or anywhere else, federal law says that ad must be truthful, not misleading, and when appropriate, backed by scientific evidence." In enforcing truth-in-advertising laws, the FTC "applies the same standards no matter where an ad appears in newspapers and magazines, online, in the mail, or on billboards or buses."

The agency gives especially close attention to advertising claims that can affect consumers in terms of health or finances, such as claims about food, over-the-counter drugs, dietary supplements, alcohol, tobacco and technology. It also monitors and creates reports about advertising-industry practices regarding the marketing of food and violent media to children.

The Commission defines "unfairness" as an act or practice that "causes or is likely to cause substantial injury to consumers, which is not reasonably avoidable by consumers themselves and not outweighed by countervailing benefits to consumers or to competition," according to 1994 amendments to the FTC Act. Unfairness arises more often in a business's relationship with a consumer than in advertising; for example, a company may be found to have acted unfairly if it coerces a customer to buy expensive unnecessary parts or services.

The FTC is more concerned with deception than with unfairness. The Commission defines a deceptive ad as one that contains a material representation, omission or practice that is likely to mislead a consumer acting reasonably under the circumstances. The definition, then, has three key parts:

• *The representation, omission or practice must be material.* "Material" means the representation, omission or practice "is likely to affect the consumer's conduct or decision with regard to a product or service," according to the FTC Policy Statement on Deception. Types of material statements include those about the health, safety, cost, quality, durability, performance or efficacy of a product or service. A claim such as "You will save 50 percent with our long distance service" would be material because it is a statement about price that is likely to influence a consumer's purchasing decision.

Express claims as to the attributes of a product are always considered material. Ads involving health and safety are usually presumed to be material, as are those containing information that pertains to a product's central characteristic. A Colgate-Palmolive claim that its Rapid Shave shaving cream was so good it could be used to shave sandpaper is an example of a material representation. In the TV commercial, Rapid Shave was apparently spread on sandpaper and then a few seconds later shaved off. The FTC complained that the ad was deceptive and a material misrepresentation because it used not sandpaper but sand sprinkled on glass. Colgate-Palmolive argued that the product really could shave sandpaper if left on long enough, but that on TV the sand and the paper were the same color. Glass had to be used to get the proper visual impression. The Supreme Court agreed in *FTC v. Colgate-Palmolive Co.* with the FTC that this was a material misrepresentation.

Not all fake demonstrations will result in an allegation of material misrepresentation. Only those that are used to suggest a product attribute will be. For example, a fake television could be used in an ad for satellite TV service because no claim about the quality of the television is being made. A fake television could not be used to advertise the television itself, especially if the ad were extolling the virtues of the sharp, clear quality of the screen image.

• *The representation, omission or practice must be likely to mislead.* An ad does not have to actually mislead or cause deception so long as it appears likely to do so. A deceptive statement may mislead expressly ("Using Listerine prevents colds," for example) or by implication, in which the ad suggests that the product contains certain elements or does certain things, as held in *Warner-Lambert Co. v. FTC.* Omission of important or material information can make an ad deceptive. For example, if a company advertised that people could save 50 percent with its long distance service but failed to say that it required customers to spend at least $100 to get the savings, the omission would make the claim misleading.

• *The representation, omission or practice must be likely to mislead a reasonable consumer.* The FTC has said in its Policy on Deception that the key question is "whether the consumer's interpretation or reaction is reasonable." The FTC said in *Heinz W. Kirchner* that it does not seek to protect people who are "foolish or feeble-minded." In addition, the FTC will consider the intended audience for the ad in deciding whether an ad is deceptive. For example, for a claim in an advertisement targeting children, the agency would evaluate the ad from the perspective of how reasonable children of the age group targeted would be likely to respond. Similarly, the agency would evaluate a claim in a prescription drug ad directed to doctors taking into account the knowledge and sophistication of the highly educated target audience. Also, the FTC will evaluate the impact of the advertisement *as a whole* on reasonable consumers, rather than focusing on isolated, out-of-context words or imagery.

In addition to standards for deceptive advertising, since 1971 the FTC has required prior substantiation of advertising claims. Advertisers must be able to substantiate the explicit and implied statements in ads that make objective claims about products and services before the claims are made. That is, they must have "a reasonable basis" for their claims before they make them. Without such a basis, companies are deemed to have violated Section 5 of the FTC Act, according to the FTC Policy Statement Regarding Advertising Substantiation. An advertiser must have at least the level of evidence the ad says exists.

In 2010's *Dannon Co., Inc.,* the FTC settled a lawsuit in which it alleged the Dannon Company exaggerated the health benefits of its Activia yogurt and DanActive dairy drink. In its Activia ads, Dannon claimed the yogurt relieved temporary irregularity because it contained probiotics. It did not, however, tell consumers that three servings a day of Activia were required to produce the benefit. As part of the settlement, Dannon agreed to stop making the irregularity claim unless it conveyed that three servings per day were required or it obtained scientific evidence to substantiate that the benefit can be achieved from a smaller amount. With respect to DanActive, Dannon agreed to stop claiming the drink would help people avoid catching colds and the flu unless the FDA approves the claim.

Exaggerations or hyperbole in ads are considered *puffery* and are not generally deemed deceptive by the FTC. Puffery claims are considered to be ones that reasonable people do not believe are true qualities and are incapable of being proven true or false. They usually involve subjective matters such as taste or appearance. Examples of puffery would be describing a soft drink as the "World's Best" or "the perfect summer drink."

Testimonials and endorsements by experts, celebrities or even ordinary people, on the other hand, are regulated because they are considered to carry special weight with consumers. Under guidelines adopted by the FTC in 2009, ads featuring a customer who lost 100 pounds on a weight-loss program, for example, can no longer hide behind a disclaimer that "Results Are Not Typical." The ads must now show the results that consumers most likely can expect. The 2009 Guides Concerning the Use of Endorsements and Testimonials in Advertising also reveal the FTC's concern about the use of fictitious consumer reviews online. Now "material connections" between a reviewer and a company must be disclosed. One of the first complaints under the new guidelines was against Reverb Communications, a communications company that had its interns pose as ordinary customers posting game reviews on the iTunes store Web site. In 2011, Legacy Learning Systems, a company that sells guitar-lesson DVDs, was ordered to pay $250,000 to settle charges that it used "Review Ad" affiliates to promote its courses through endorsements in articles, blogs and other online outlets. According to the FTC, the endorsements generated more than $5 million in sales for the company.

The FTC engages in a number of activities to help prevent deceptive ads from appearing in the marketplace including:

• *Advisory opinions.* An advertiser may seek an advisory opinion from FTC commissioners or FTC staff on a proposed advertisement or specific issue of concern. An advisory opinion is a statement giving an informed judgment about a legal question or issue. The Commission may provide an advisory opinion if the request "involves a substantial or novel question of fact or law and there is no clear Commission or court precedent" and the request is a matter of significant public interest, according to the *Code of Federal Regulations.* Because advisory opinions are only opinions and are not legally binding, the Commission may later reconsider the question and rescind or revoke its opinion. Advisory opinions become part of the public record after they are issued.

• *Industry guides.* The FTC publishes detailed guides that tell advertisers how to avoid creating advertising that is deceptive. Some of the guides, for example, describe how advertisers may avoid deception in the use of the word "free." The Commission has also created industry guides specific to advertising for particular types of products, such as jewelry, dietary supplements and food. The FTC may take action against an advertiser who fails to comply with industry guides.

• *Policy statements.* The FTC may publicize its regulatory philosophy in a policy statement, also according to the *Code of Federal Regulations.* For example, the FTC issued a policy statement about comparative advertising after examining the ad industry's codes and standards. Finding that its codes and standards seemed to discourage the use of comparative advertising, the FTC wanted to clearly state its position that "industry self-regulation should not restrain the use by advertisers of truthful comparative advertising." The FTC's policy on comparative advertising "encourages the naming of, or reference to, competi-

tors, but requires clarity, and, if necessary, disclosure to avoid deception of the consumer.... Comparative advertising, when truthful and non-deceptive, is a source of important information to consumers and assists them in making rational purchase decisions." An example of what the FTC considers deceptive in comparative advertising involved a Kentucky Fried Chicken ad, in which the company implied that eating two Original Recipe fried chicken breasts was better for an individual's health than eating a Burger King Whopper. In fact, while two KFC Original Recipe fried chicken breasts were found in *KFC Corp.* to have slightly less total fat and saturated fat than the Whopper, they had more trans-fat, cholesterol, sodium and calories.

• *Rulemaking.* The FTC may establish Trade Regulation Rules, which have the force of federal law, to address widespread deceptive practices. The commission holds informal hearings at which interested parties and the public may participate and give their opinions about the proposed rule.

If the FTC decides that an ad is deceptive, it has a number of remedies at its disposal. One problem the FTC has is that ad campaigns can be over long before the FTC catches up with the company and brings a complaint. On the other hand, the FTC does have publicity working in its favor. Companies do not like the negative publicity that comes with a charge of false advertising; so publicity can be a powerful sanction.

The FTC also has a series of remedies it invokes when it finds that an advertisement may be deceptive, including:

• *Consent agreements.* If the FTC believes an ad is deceptive, it may issue a complaint to the advertiser detailing its charges. The advertiser may then choose to settle the charges with the FTC by signing a consent agreement. Generally, the advertiser does not admit liability but agrees to start or stop doing something, such as running a particular ad or making specific claims in an ad. The agreement also provides that the advertiser waives the right to judicial review. The FTC places proposed consent agreements on the record for sixty days to allow public comment before they become final.

• *Cease-and-desist orders.* If a consent agreement cannot be reached and the advertiser chooses to fight the charges, the FTC's complaint will be adjudicated before an FTC administrative law judge in a proceeding similar to a trial. At the end of this quasi-judicial proceeding, the judge will issue a decision stating findings of fact and conclusions of law and recommending either a cease-and-desist order or dismissal of the complaint. A cease-and-desist order is an order to start or stop doing something. The decision of the judge may be appealed to the full commission. The advertiser may appeal the commission's decision to a federal court of appeals, and either party may appeal that decision to the Supreme Court.

• *Corrective advertising.* In some cases the FTC will require a company to correct its advertising message in future ads to clear up any misleading impressions that were left from the deceptive ads. This remedy is usually reserved for long-running and successful ad campaigns where the FTC fears the public will be left with false information. For example, Novartis was ordered in 1999 to state in its future advertising for Doan's Pills that "there is no evidence that Doan's is more effective than other pain relievers for back pain."

• *Court injunctions.* Rather than taking an administrative route first, federal law allows the FTC to go directly to federal court to seek a preliminary or permanent injunction in cases of ongoing consumer fraud in an attempt to stop it before too many consumers are harmed. In 2011, it sought such an injunction to stop the use of fake news sites to sell weight loss products. The FTC stated in a press release that headlines such as "Acai Berry Diet Exposed: Miracle Diet or Scam?" on a Web site like "News 6 News Alert" were actually being used to promote the product by deceptively representing the article as an objective news report.

• *Civil and criminal penalties.* The FTC can ask a federal district court to impose civil penalties for a number of reasons, including to reimburse all consumers who bought an advertiser's product, because an advertiser violated a federal statute that imposes fines on violators, or because an advertiser has violated an FTC order. To get consumer redress, according to federal law, the FTC must show that an advertiser demonstrated conduct that a "reasonable man would have known under the circumstances was dishonest or fraudulent." The FTC can also refer cases to the Justice Department for criminal prosecution.

The FTC is active in regulating advertising and marketing practices on the Internet. Advertising on the Internet must conform to the same rules as advertising in other media.

Legal Liability

The basic defense against any false advertising complaint is truth, that is, providing evidence that proves the product does what the ad says it does or has the attributes the ad claims it does. Advertising agencies may be held legally liable, along with their clients, for deceptive claims, because they have a responsibility to independently check claims made in ads. Public-relations agencies have the same obligation, a Public Relations Society of America forum emphasized recently, even though many PR practitioners believe they are beyond FTC concerns because of the differences in what they and advertising practitioners do. However, Ann Willets has written on the "Voice of Public Relations" Web page, that it is advisable for PR firms to have a reasonable basis to support all claims made in content they disseminate for clients; include clear and conspicuous disclosures to ensure content is not false, deceptive or misleading; design content so it will specifically not mislead the audience for whom it is targeted; inform their clients of the need to comply with FTC guides and include disclosures when endorsers are paid to provide opinions in content.

Lanham Act

At the federal level, the Lanham Act also provides redress for individuals and businesses harmed by false or deceptive advertising. The Lanham Act is the federal trademark protection law, but it contains a section dealing with advertising. Section 43(a) reads, in part:

> Any person who ... in commercial advertising or promotion, misrepresents the nature, characteristics, qualities, or geographic origin of his or her or another person's goods, services, or commercial activities, shall be liable in a civil action by any person who believes that he or she is or is likely to be damaged by such act.

The section creates what a federal district court in *Estate of Presley v. Russen* called a "distinct federal statutory tort designed to afford broad protection against various forms of unfair competition and false advertising."

Because of the Lanham Act's focus on protection of commercial interests, as opposed to consumers, courts have not generally given consumers standing to bring an action under Section 43(a). The act allows businesses or people to sue others for competitive harm arising from false advertising. For a claim, the plaintiff must establish that the advertiser made a false representation about a product or service; that the representation deceives, or has a tendency to deceive, a substantial segment of the target audience; that the representation is material; and that it resulted or is likely to result in injury to the plaintiff. Although the elements are similar to the FTC's standards for deceptive advertising, the biggest difference is the requirement of injury. In Lanham Act cases, the plaintiff must show that it has or is likely to have suffered commercial harm by the defendant's deceptive advertising claims. The plaintiff also must show that the claim was in fact false and not just that the advertiser lacked prior substantiation.

State Laws

All fifty states have enacted legislation similar to the Federal Trade Commission Act, prohibiting deceptive advertising. Unlike the federal law, however, most of the state statutes permit private lawsuits to be brought by consumers and competitors against advertisers and allow plaintiffs to sue for damages in addition to an injunction stopping the ads. Some national advertisers, such as tobacco companies and airlines, have sought to avoid state penalties by claiming the state law is pre-empted by federal law. Commercial speech is an area of law that is shared by the state and federal governments. When a conflict between the two arises, the federal law takes precedence.

When it was sued by smokers of its light cigarettes, Altria Group, the parent company of Philip Morris, argued that the Maine Unfair Trade Practices Act was pre-empted by the Federal Cigarette Labeling and Advertising Act. But the Supreme Court, in a 5-4 decision in *Altria Group, Inc. v. Good* in 2008, held that the Labeling Act did not pre-empt a state-law fraud claim. The respondents claimed that light cigarettes were advertised as delivering less tar and nicotine than regular cigarettes, which the company knew was not true.

A year earlier, Philip Morris had been foiled in a similar case in its attempt to remove to federal district court a state-court case brought against it in Arkansas. The suit claimed that the company violated Arkansas' unfair business practice laws by advertising some of its cigarettes as "light" when in fact the tests had been manipulated to register lower levels of tar and nicotine than were actually present in the cigarettes. The company, in turn, argued that the plaintiffs were challenging the use of the test, which was an approved FTC method, and therefore were suing the company for acting under the FTC. The Supreme Court unanimously held in *Watson v. Philip Morris Cos.* In 2007 that Philip Morris was not "acting under" the FTC, but was simply regulated by it. Therefore, the case was to stay in the Arkansas court.

Industry Self-Regulation

The advertising industry has developed a variety of methods for self-regulation. The Advertising Self-Regulatory Council establishes the policies and procedures of the National Advertising Division, the National Advertising Review Board and the Children's Advertising Review Unit. The Council of Better Business Bureaus administers this self-regulatory system.

The National Advertising Division. The NAD, which was created in 1971, "uses a unique, hybrid form of alternative dispute resolution, working with in-house counsel, marketing executives, research and development departments and outside consultants to decide whether [disputed advertising] claims have been substantiated," according to the Advertising Self-Regulatory Council. Self-regulation allows advertisers to resolve disputes quickly and inexpensively, without government involvement and assessment of penalties. The NAD reviews national advertising and investigates complaints about the truth or accuracy of claims. It

focuses on product performance, superiority, and scientific and technical claims, and maintains, "National advertisers who use the NAD process find it to be significantly less expensive than litigation. By utilizing the NAD process, cost-conscious companies save hundreds of thousands of dollars typically spent seeking reparation through the courts."

While the NAD cannot force an advertiser to comply with a recommendation or accept its findings, it exerts pressure on advertisers by publishing its conclusions in the *NAD Case Reports* and by issuing news releases announcing decisions. For example, in 2012 NAD released a "Seller Beware" statement recommending that Discover Financial Services more clearly disclose limitations on its cash-back promotions. It also recommended that Sonic disclose that its "Free Coffee with any Breakfast Burrito" promotional offer did not apply to the Junior Breakfast Burrito, but only to premium burritos. The NAD will also refer cases to the FTC if a company does not comply with NAD recommendations.

The National Advertising Review Board. Either an advertiser whose claim is in question or a challenger of a claim may appeal a finding of the NAD to the National Advertising Review Board. The NARB is a group of advertising professionals who work in ad agencies, companies that advertise, academia and government, and who work in panels to decide NAD appeals. If an advertiser does not accept the NARB panel's decisions and recommendations, which the Advertising Self-Regulatory Council characterizes as "extremely rare," the NARB refers the case to an appropriate law-enforcement agency.

The Children's Advertising Review Unit. To combat misleading and socially irresponsible advertising aimed at children, the advertising industry created the Children's Advertising Review Unit in 1974. CARU "evaluates child-directed advertising and promotional material in all media to advance truthfulness, accuracy and consistency." When such advertising is found to be "misleading, inaccurate, or inconsistent with CARU's guidelines, according to the Advertising Self-Regulatory Council, CARU seeks change through the voluntary cooperation of advertisers." In 2016, for example, a CARU review recommended that the maker of Aquabeads (a child crafting product) revise an ad representation — "Spray with water, and the beads magically stick together" — to more accurately disclose that users must allow time for the beads to dry before they stick together after being sprayed with water.

A section of CARU's guidelines highlights issues "including children's privacy, that are unique to the Internet and online sites directed at children age 12 and under," which formed the basis of the federal Children's Online Privacy Protection Act of 1998.

SUMMARY

Commercial speech can be defined as expression that proposes a commercial transaction or is related solely to the economic interests of a speaker and the speaker's audience. The saga of the development of constitutional protection for commercial speech began in 1942 with a Supreme Court pronouncement that commercial advertising received no First Amendment protection. The Court modified that initial view, saying in 1977 that the First Amendment protects even purely commercial expression, though government remains free to constitutionally restrict advertising that is false, misleading or deceptive, or promoted illegal products or services. The Court has ruled that commercial speech receives a lower level of protection than other types of expression because the truth of its content is more easily verified and because it is an economic necessity for companies; thus, commercial advertising can better tolerate government regulation.

In 1980, the Court articulated a four-part test, commonly referred to as the "Central Hudson Test," to determine whether a regulation on commercial speech is constitutional:

(1) Is the commercial speech true and not misleading, and does it advertise a legal product or service?

(2) Is the asserted governmental interest substantial?

(3) Does the regulation directly advance the governmental interest?

(4) Is the regulation no more extensive than necessary to serve the governmental interest?

The Court later clarified the fourth part of that test as requiring a reasonable fit between the regulation and the governmental interest. But a few years after that, the Court further revised its application of the Central Hudson Test so as to make it a more substantial burden for government to meet, in particular requiring greater proof to support government assertions that regulations pass the Central Hudson Test. In its most recent commercial-speech ruling, the Court's application of *Central Hudson* suggested support for an even more stringent level of assessment of government regulation related to advertising. Although some justices have argued for the same broad protection accorded noncommercial speech to be extended to truthful, non-misleading commercial speech, the Court's holdings on balance have focused more sharply on preventing government from denying citizens truthful information while maintaining the Central Hudson Test as an effective means for achieving that. Thus, the Court's commercial-speech doctrine has placed a high priority on protecting and maintaining truth in advertising and preserving the fair-bargaining process. Most recently, lower courts have contended over whether the Court's 2011 *Sorrell* ruling may have altered *Central Hudson* analysis, a debate that remains in progress.

The FTC is the federal governmental agency that regulates deceptive advertising in the United States. Its definition of a deceptive ad is one that contains a representation, omission or practice that is material and likely to mislead a consumer acting reasonably in the circumstances.

The commission uses various tools — offering advisory opinions to advertisers, issuing policy statements, publishing industry guides, making rules and requiring substantiation — to try to prevent deceptive advertising from appearing in the marketplace. Once advertisers disseminate deceptive claims to consumers, the FTC seeks remedies — through a consent agreement, cease-and-desist order, injunction, or civil or criminal penalties — to stop such claims from continuing to deceive consumers and to seek redress for harms advertisers have inflicted on consumers.

Competitors and others harmed by false and deceptive advertising can seek redress through the Lanham Act. In Lanham Act cases, the plaintiff must show that it has suffered or is likely to suffer commercial harm by the defendant's false and deceptive claims. State laws also regulate advertising, and many allow consumers and competitors to sue for damages in addition to injunctive relief.

Self-regulation by the advertising industry can be an effective and quick way of addressing concerns about deceptive or unsupported claims in national advertising and about various issues relating to children's exposure to advertising. The National Advertising Division, Children's Advertising Review Unit, and National Advertising Review Board, which all operate as part of the Better Business Bureau, are the main industry groups involved in the self-regulatory process.

BIBLIOGRAPHY

Articles

An, Soontae. "From a Business Pursuit to a Means of Expression: The Supreme Court's Disputes Over Commercial Speech," 8 *Communication Law and Policy* 201 (2003).

Associated Press, "FTC Says Snapchat Deceived Customers," *Yahoo News*, May 8, 2014, https://www.yahoo.com/news/ftc-says-snapchat-deceived-customers-175603664--finance.html.

Browne, M. Neil, Lauren Frances Biksacky & Alex Frondorf. "Advertising to Children and the Commercial Speech Doctrine: Political and Constitutional Limitations," 58 *Drake Law Review* 67 (2009).

Collins, Ronald K.L. & David M. Skover. "Commerce and Communication," 71 *Texas Law Review* 697 (1993).

Croxall, Daniel J. "Cheers to Central Hudson: How Traditional Intermediate Scrutiny Helps Keep Independent Craft Beer Viable," 113 *Northwestern University Law Review* 1 (2018).

Dibadj, Reza R. "The Political Economy of Commercial Speech," 58 *South Carolina Law Review* 913 (2007).

Farber, Daniel A. "Commercial Speech and First Amendment Theory," 74 *Northwest Law Review* 372 (1979).

"For Facebook, the FTC Looms," *CQ Magazine*, Apr. 16, 2018, http://library.cqpress.com/cqweekly/weeklyreport115-0000052 97873.

Hamm, Richard. "Off the Streets: The Origins of the Doctrine of Commercial Speech," 57 *American Journal of Legal History* 495 (2017).

Hoefges, Michael. "Protecting Tobacco Advertising Under the Commercial Speech Doctrine: The Constitutional Impact of Lorillard Tobacco Co.," 8 *Communication Law and Policy* 267 (2003).

Kahn, Lina, "We Must Regulate A.I. Here's How," *N.Y. Times*, May 3, 2023, https://www.nytimes.com/2023/04/03/opinion/ai-lina-khan-ftc-technology.html.

Kerr, Robert L. "A Justice's Surprise That Has Stood Its Ground: The Enduring Value of the Commercial Speech Doctrine's Powellian Balance," 13 *Journalism & Communication Monographs* 215 (2012).

—. "Desperately Seeking Coherence: The Lower Courts Struggle to Determine the Meaning of Sorrell for the Commercial Speech Doctrine," 7 *Journal of Media Law & Ethics* 1 (2019).

—. "From *Sullivan* to *Nike*: Will the Noble Purpose of the Landmark Free Speech Case be Subverted to Immunize False Advertising?" 9 *Communication Law & Policy* 525 (2004).

McGeveran, William. "Disclosure, Endorsement, and Identity in Social Marketing," 2009 *University of Illinois Law Review* 1105 (2009).

"New Privacy Law Makes Europe World's Leading Tech Watchdog," *N.Y. Times*, May 25, 2018, at A1.

Piety, Tamara. "'A Necessary Cost of Freedom?' The Incoherence of *Sorrell v. IMS*," 64 *Alabama Law Review* 1 (2012).

Post, Robert. "The Constitutional Status of Commercial Speech," 48 *UCLA Law Review* 1 (2000).

Schwartz, Victor E., Cary Silverman, Michael J. Hulka & Christopher E. Appel. "Marketing Pharmaceutical Products in the Twenty-First Century: An Analysis of the Continued Viability of Traditional Principles of Laws in the Age of Direct-to-Consumer Advertising," 32 *Harvard Journal of Law & Public Policy* 333 (2009).

Sprague, Robert & Mary Ellen Wells. "The Supreme Court as Prometheus: Breathing Life into the Corporate Supercitizen," 49 *American Business Law Journal* 507 (2012).

Stern, Nat. "In Defense of the Imprecise Definition of Commercial Speech," 52 *Maryland Law Review* 55 (1999).

Tushnet, Rebecca. "It Depends on What the Meaning of 'False' Is: Falsity and Misleadingness in Commercial Speech Doctrine," 41 *Loyola Los Angeles Law Review* 227 (2007).

Vladeck, David C. "Lessons from a Story Untold: *Nike v. Kasky* Reconsidered," 54 *Case Western Reserve Law Review* 1049 (2004).

Wu, Felix T. "The Commercial Difference," 58 *William & Mary Law Review* 2005 (2017).

Wyatt, Edward. "Edith Ramirez is Raising the F.T.C.'s Voice," *N.Y. Times*, Dec. 21, 2014, at B1.

Book

Piety, Tamara. *Brandishing the First Amendment: Commercial Expression in America*. Ann Arbor: University of Michigan Press, 2012.

Cases

44 Liquormart v. Rhode Island, 517 U.S. 484 (1996).

Altria Group, Inc. v. Good, et al., 555 U.S. 70 (2008).

Bates v. State Bar of Arizona, 433 U.S. 350 (1977).

Bigelow v. Virginia, 421 U.S. 809 (1975).

Bolger v. Youngs Drug Products Corp, 463 U.S. 60 (1983).

Central Hudson Gas & Electric Company v. Public Service Commission of New York, 447 U.S. 557 (1980).

Chamber of Commerce for Greater Philadelphia v. City of Philadelphia, 319 F. Supp. 3d 773 (E.D. Pa. 2018).

Cincinnati v. Discovery Network, 492 U.S. 469 (1989).

City of Austin v. Reagan National Advertising, 2022 U.S. LEXIS 2098.

Commonwealth Brands Inc. et al. v. United States, 678 F. Supp. 2d 512 (W.D. Ky. 2010).

Dannon Co., Inc., 2010 WL 5199606 (No. 082-3158) (F.T.C. Dec. 15, 2010) (consent order).

Discount Tobacco City & Lottery et al. v. United States, 674 F.3d 509 (6th Cir. 2012), *cert. denied*, American Snuff Company v. United States, 569 U.S. 946 (2013).

Edenfield v. Fane, 507 U.S. 761 (1993).

Estate of Presley v. Russen, 513 F. Supp. 1339, 1376 (D.N.J. 1981).

FTC v. Colgate-Palmolive Co., 380 U.S. 374 (1963).

Greater New Orleans Broadcasting v. United States, 527 U.S. 173 (1999).

Heinz W. Kirchner, 63 F.T.C. 1282, 1290 (1963).

KFC Corp., 138 F.T.C. 422 (2004) (consent order).

Legacy Learning Systems, Inc., 2011 WL 2415390 (No. C-4323) (F.T.C. June 1, 2011) (consent order).

Lehman v. City of Shaker Heights, 418 U.S. 298 (1974).

Linmark Associates v. Willingboro, 431 U.S. 86 (1977).

Lorillard Tobacco v. Reilly, 533 U.S. 525 (2001).

Nicopure Labs, LLC v. FDA, 266 F. Supp. 3d 360 (D.C. Cir. 2017).

Novartis Consumer Health, Inc., 127 F.T.C. 580 (F.T.C. May 27, 1999).

Ohralik v. Ohio State Bar Association, 436 U.S. 447 (1978).

Posadas de Puerto Rico Associates v. Tourism Company of Puerto Rico, 478 U.S. 328 (1986).

Reed v. Town of Gilbert, 135 S. Ct. 2218 (2015).

Retail Digital Network, LLC v. Appelsmith, 945 F. Supp. 2d 1119 (C.D. Cal. 2013).

Retail Digital Network, LLC v. Appelsmith, 810 F.3d 638 (9th Cir. 2016).

Retail Digital Network, LLC v. Prieto, 861 F.3d 839 (9th Cir. 2017).

Reverb Communications, Inc., 2010 WL 4897037 (No. C-4310) (F.T.C. Nov. 22, 2010) (consent order).

R.J. Reynolds, et al. v. F.D.A., 696 F.3d 1205 (D.C. Cir. 2012).

R.J. Reynolds, et al. v. F.D.A., 845 F. Supp. 2d 266 (D.D.C. 2012).

Roe v. Wade, 410 U.S. 113 (1973).

Rubin v. Coors Brewing Co., 514 U.S. 476 (1995).

Snapchat, Inc., 2010 (No. C-4501) (F.T.C. Dec. 23, 2014) (consent order).

Sorrell v. IMS Health Inc., 564 U.S. 552 (2011).

Thompson v. Western States Medical Center, 535 U.S. 357 (2002).

United States v. Edge Broadcasting, 514 U.S. 418 (1993).

Valentine v. Chrestensen, 316 U.S. 52 (1942).

Virginia State Bd. of Pharmacy v. Virginia Citizens Consumer Council, 425 U.S. 748 (1976).

Warner-Lambert Co. v. FTC, 562 F.2d 749 (D.C. Cir. 1977).

Watson v. Philip Morris Cos., Inc., 551 U.S. 142 (2007).

Other Sources

"About CARU," Advertising Self-Regulatory Council, http://www.asrcreviews.org/about-caru/ (accessed May 21, 2019).

"About NAD," Advertising Self-Regulatory Council, http://www.asrcreviews.org/how-nad-works/.

Better Business Bureau Advertising Review Programs Web site, http://www.bbb.org/advertising.

"CARU Recommends International Playthings Better Disclose Drying Time for 'Aquabeads' Product; Company Says it Will Do So," Advertising Self-Regulatory Council, http://www.asrc reviews.org/caru-recommends-international-playthings-better-disclose-drying-time-for-aquabeads-product-company-says-it-will-do-so/.

Federal Trade Commission Web site, http://www.ftc.gov.

FTC Act Amendments of 1994, 15 U.S.C.A. § 45(n) (West Supp. 1995).

FTC Approves Final Settlement with Facebook (Aug. 10, 2012), https://www.ftc.gov/news-events/press-releases/2012/08/ftc-ap proves-final-settlement-facebook.

"FTC Policy on Deception," 16 C.F.R. § 0.1 (1999).

"FTC Policy Statement on Deception," Oct. 14, 1983, https://www.ftc.gov/system/files/documents/public_statements/4105 31/831014deceptionstmt.pdf.

"FTC Policy Statement Regarding Advertising Substantiation," https://www.ftc.gov/public-statements/1983/03/ftc-policy-state ment-regarding-advertising-substantiation.

"Guides Concerning the Use of Endorsements and Testimonials in Advertising" 16 C.F.R. § 255 (2009), https://www.ftc.gov/sites/default/files/attachments/press-releases/ftc-publishes-fi nal-guides-governing-endorsements-testimonials/091005revis edendorsementguides.pdf.

"NARB Process," Advertising Self-Regulatory Council, http://www.asrcreviews.org/how-the-narb-process-works/.

"Opening Remarks of FTC Chairwoman Edith Ramirez Privacy and the IoT: Navigating Policy Issues International Consum er Electronics Show Las Vegas, Nevada." Jan. 6, 2015, *available at* https://www.ftc.gov/system/files/documents/pub lic_st atements/617191/150106cessspeech.pdf.

Press Release, FTC, "Crowdfunding Project Creator Settles FTC Charges of Deception" (June 11, 2015), https://www.ftc.gov/news-events/press-releases/2015/06/crowdfunding-project-cre ator-settles-ftc-charges-deception.

Press Release, FTC, "FTC Seeks to Halt 10 Operators of Fake News Sites from Making Deceptive Claims about Acai Berry Weight Loss Products" (Apr. 19, 2011), https:// www.ftc.gov/news-events/press-releases/2011/04/ftc-seeks-halt-10-operator s-fake-news-sites-making-deceptive.

Press Release, FTC, "FTC Enforcement Action to Bar GoodRx from Sharing Consumers' Sensitive Health Info for Advertis ing" (Feb. 1, 2023), https://www.ftc.gov/news-events/news/pre ss-releases/2023/02/ftc-enforcement-action-bar-goodrx-sharin g-consumers-sensitive-health-info-advertising.

Press Release, FTC, "Snapchat Settles FTC Charges That Prom ises of Disappearing Messages Were False" (May 8, 2014), https://www.ftc.gov/news-events/press-releases/ 2014/05/snap chat-settles-ftc-charges-promises-disappearing-messages-were

Ramirez, Edith. "After 100 Years, Looking Ahead to Our Next Century," Sept. 26, 2014, https://www.ftc.gov/news-events/blogs/competition-matters/2014/09/after-100-years-looking-ah ead-our-next-century.

Seller Beware, "NAD Deals a Double Whammy on Two Con sumer Promotions," June 26, 2012, https://www.consumeradv ertisinglawblog.com/2012/week26/index.html.

"Truth in Advertising" (2015), https://www.ftc.gov/news-events/media-resources/truth-advertising.

Willets, Ann. "PR & Advertising: The Lines Continue to Blur, PRSAY," Sept. 17, 2014, http://prsay.prsa.org/index.php/2014 //09/17/pr-advertising-the-lines-continue-to-blur.

Regulating Public Relations

By Karla K. Gower

☑ Headnote Questions

- To what extent do corporations have constitutional protection for their speech?
- Why do public relations practitioners need to understand securities law?
- What is the role of the Food and Drug Administration, and how does the agency impact public relations?
- What is required for a negligence action?
- What is required for a "non-compete" clause in a public relations practitioner's employment contract to be enforceable?

Public relations requires knowledge of laws affecting both communication and management. PR practitioners "speak" for their clients on a broad range of political, economic, technological, social and cultural issues. Like journalists, they inform, and like advertisers, they persuade. They seek to provide publics with knowledge about their clients, and to persuade them to think favorably about those clients, ultimately moving publics to action, whether voting in a particular way or buying a particular product or service. Thus, public relations crosses many legal categories, from the traditional media law areas of defamation, privacy and access to information, to the more business-oriented ones of commercial speech, contracts and regulation.

While nonprofits, religious organizations, political candidates, celebrities and activists — among others — all engage in PR activities, this chapter will focus on legal issues affecting the public relations endeavors of business entities. Specifically, it will discuss the law as it affects corporate speech, as opposed to commercial speech, which was described in Chapter 8. The U.S. Supreme Court has defined commercial speech two ways. In *Dun & Bradstreet v. Greenmoss Builders*, it was described as speech that does "no more than propose a commercial transaction." More than a decade earlier, the Court in *Pittsburgh Press v. Pittsburgh Commission on Human Relations,* defined it as speech "solely motivated by the desire for profit." Corporate speech, on the other hand, is speech by a corporation on issues of importance to society and that is not tied directly to the promotion of the corporation's products or services.

CONSTITUTIONAL PROTECTION FOR CORPORATE SPEECH

Corporations have long had certain recognized rights under the Constitution. For example, they are considered "persons" for purposes of the equal protection and due process clauses of the Fourteenth Amendment. And the Fifth Amendment protects them against double jeopardy. But, as seen in Chapter 8, the First Amendment historically did not protect what might be termed economic or commercial expression. The assumption was that only expression contributing to informed self-government, or political speech, was worthy of protection. Economic or commercial speech was considered a business activity, not an act of expression. There was no fear, it was believed, that government regulation would chill companies' speech. Businesses would always find a way to communicate to consumers about their products or services.

In the 1978 case *First National Bank of Boston v. Bellotti,* the Supreme Court ruled for the first time that the First Amendment protects corporate speech. First National had sought to inform Massachusetts citizens of the bank's position regarding an upcoming state constitutional amendment referendum that would decide whether the state could impose a flat income tax rate. Massachusetts prohibited corporations from spending money on political referenda unless the issue directly impacted their businesses. In this case, it clearly did not. The sharply divided Court declared that the bank's "speech" was "indispensable to decision-making in a democracy" regardless of whether that speech came from a corporation or an individual. In other words, the Court held that it was the speech that determined protection, not the nature of the speaker.

The *Belotti* decision was subsequently expanded to include ideological groups and entities — those formed to disseminate political ideas, rather than amass economic capital.

Although *Bellotti* is considered the Magna Carta of corporate speech doctrine, it by no means settled all questions regarding the role of corporations in public life, their influence on the democratic process, and their involvement in the political sphere through monetary contributions to campaigns and parties.

Two years prior to *Bellotti*, the Supreme Court, in *Buckley v. Valeo*, had upheld limits on contributions to candidates and political parties on the grounds that large contributions create fears of improper influence on the political process and undermine citizens' faith in government honesty and integrity. Thus, limits were valid as long as a regulation was "closely drawn" and matched a "sufficiently important [governmental] interest," the Court held, writing that "a limitation upon the amount that any one person or group may contribute to a candidate or political committee entails only a marginal restriction upon the contributor's ability to engage in free communication." At the same time, the Court rejected limits on independent expenditures in support of candidates. Such expenditures did not represent a corrupting influence the way that contributions did. More importantly, restrictions on "the amount of money a person or group can spend on political communication during a campaign necessarily reduces the quantity of expression by restricting the number of issues discussed, the depth of their exploration, and the size of the audience reached."

In 2002, Congress again tackled the issue of money and politics, enacting the Bipartisan Campaign Reform Act, what the *New York Times* called at the time, "[T]he most ambitious effort since Watergate to reduce the influence of big donations on the political process." The statute was immediately challenged in eleven separate lawsuits, which were consolidated into a single action: *McConnell v. Federal Election Commission*. A special three-judge panel upheld much of the statute but found that its two most important provisions were unconstitutional infringements of free expression: its restrictions on large political donations from corporations and labor unions to political parties for "party-building activities," known as "soft money" contributions; and its prohibitions against those same entities using their general treasuries to pay for electioneering communications (communication that mentions a candidate) within a month or so of an election. Concluding that the soft money restrictions only minimally affected free speech, the Supreme Court reversed the lower court's ruling, while upholding its decision regarding electioneering communications. Yet, the Court overturned this provision, too, in 2007, when it concluded that such election advertising by groups is "core political speech," which could not be

censored — effectively, though not explicitly, gutting its four-year-old *McConnell* ruling.

This evisceration of *McConnell* continued in 2010 with the Court's ruling in *Citizens United v. Federal Elections Commission*, which also overturned its twenty-year-old ruling in *Austin v. Michigan Chamber of Commerce*. In *Austin*, the Court upheld a ban on the use of corporate general treasury funds for expenditures in state elections. Such expenditures could only come from a segregated account set up specifically for political purposes and to which employees and stockholders could voluntarily contribute. In *Citizens United*, involving a 2008 film documentary critique of presidential hopeful Hillary Clinton, the Court allowed corporations and unions to spend monies directly from their treasuries to advocate political positions and outcomes, as long as the messages were produced independently and not associated with any candidate's campaign. The First Amendment, the Court said, "does not permit laws that force speakers to retain a campaign finance attorney, conduct demographic marketing research, or seek declaratory rulings before discussing the most salient political issues of our day."

Most recently, in *McCutcheon v. Federal Election Commission*, the Supreme Court held that the BCRA's aggregate limits on the amount of money a donor may contribute in total to all candidates are an unconstitutional restriction under the First Amendment because they have nothing to do with the prevention of quid pro quo corruption.

Moreover, the lines separating corporate action from corporate expression, and corporate commercial speech from corporate political speech, are still uncertain and — some would say — artificial, in that giving money and spending money are essentially the same to a corporation. As corporations can only express themselves by disbursing money, they would prefer that all expressive activity be deemed corporate speech, which the First Amendment protects, rather than action, which may be regulated. And, too, they would prefer that all corporate speech be deemed political speech, which requires a higher level of judicial scrutiny to justify regulation than does commercial speech. But the question of what is and is not corporate political or corporate commercial speech is not easily answered.

In an attempt to provide more predictability, the Court, in *Central Hudson Gas & Electric Corp. v. Public Service Commission*, differentiated between commercial and political advertising and established a four-part test for determining when commercial speech may be regulated. As a result, the First Amendment protects commercial expression as long as it promotes lawful products and services and unless the regulation comes within certain narrow circumstances. But even the *Central Hudson* case has come under fire from legal scholars who argue that it provides no real clarification on how to distinguish between corporate and commercial speech and that in any event such a distinction is unworkable.[1]

The issue was presented to the California Supreme Court in a direct way in 2002. In *Nike v. Kasky*, the court concluded that Nike's defense of its corporate reputation and controversial business and labor practices in Southeast Asia *via* traditional PR strategies and tactics constituted commercial expression because (1) Nike was a corporate speaker, (2) the expression was motivated primarily by pecuniary interests, and (3) the targets were consumers and potential consumers. The court also held that Nike's speech was not political speech because the debate was over Nike's own operations and not corporate America's labor practices in general. Having found the expression to be commercial and not political, the California court then held that the state's false advertising statute could regulate Nike's speech and penalize Nike for its falsity.

The decision is troubling because the test the court used to determine that the speech was commercial (nature of speaker, motivation and intended audience) makes most corporate speech, even on political and social issues, commercial and, therefore, subject to less First Amendment protection. It also ignores the reality of the public debate. Nike was responding to activists who had full First Amendment rights and who had intentionally targeted the company. Nike could not respond in general as the California court had suggested because the debate was not framed in general terms. The Supreme Court, however, refused to hear the case on the basis that the appeal was premature and sent it back for trial. The case was later settled out of court, leaving the important question of whether Nike's speech was political or commercial unanswered.

REGULATING THE SPEECH OF CORPORATIONS

While corporations' speech has First Amendment protection, it still is highly regulated. Some of the federal agencies that directly impact the practice of public relations are the Securities and Exchange Commission, the Food and Drug Administration, and the Federal Trade Commission, which is discussed in the previous chapter. While, arguably, it is impossible for a PR practitioner to have a complete knowledge of every federal and state law and regulation that impacts a particular corporate or public communication, the practitioner should be aware of certain important concepts and definitions regularly used by each administrative agency with which his or her client deals.

Lobbying

Federal and state laws impact the way businesses do business. For example, acts to protect the environment can force corpora-

tions to engage in greener technologies and practices, potentially increasing production costs. Legislation can also protect businesses from the unscrupulous activities of competitors. Thus, corporations have an interest in what laws are passed and what regulations those laws impose.

To protect their interests, corporations, as well as associations and nonprofit organizations, lobby legislators. The goal is either to avoid legislation altogether or to help shape it in ways favorable to the organization. Lobbying politicians is not a new phenomenon. It dates from at least the early days of the British parliamentary system. In the United States, the First Amendment protects lobbying because it encompasses both freedom of speech and the right to petition government for grievances. However, the government is permitted to regulate lobbying activities to prevent corruption of the democratic process.

Lobbying is controlled by the Lobbying Disclosure Act of 1995, which defines lobbyists as individuals who made more than one contact with a legislator on behalf of a client and who spent at least 20 percent of their time during a three-month period providing that service to the client. A contact is defined as "any oral, written, or electronic communication to a covered official that is made on behalf of a client" with a purpose of influencing that official.

Grassroots lobbying, which attempts to influence public opinion to pressure the government to act on an issue, is generally not considered lobbying for the purposes of the act.

Lobbyists who make more than $3,000 in a quarterly period for their services and in-house lobbyists who expect to spend more than $14,000 on lobbying activities in a three-month period must register with the government. They are also required to file statements identifying their clients and detailing the general areas and specific issues on which they have lobbied.

Lobbyists who work for foreign clients also must disclose their activities. Prior to World War II, Congress became concerned with the distribution of pro-German and Communist literature in the United States. To control this "un-American propaganda," Congress passed the Foreign Agents Registration Act of 1938. A foreign agent acts "as a public relations counsel, publicity agent, information-service employee or political consultant" or engages in "political activities" for a foreign client. A foreign client can be foreign government entities, political organizations, businesses, nonprofits, or even individuals.

Securities and Exchange Commission

The Securities and Exchange Commission oversees financial markets and grew out of the stock market crash of 1929. Congress passed the Securities Act of 1933 and the Securities Exchange Act of 1934 in response to concerns that speculators partly caused the Great Depression. The 1934 Act created the

---

[1] The four-part "Central Hudson test" is discussed in Chapter 8.

SEC to "administer federal securities laws and issue rules and regulations to provide protection for investors and ensure that the securities markets are fair and honest." President Franklin Roosevelt, in a 1933 message to the House of Representatives, stated the SEC's guiding principle: "No essentially important element [may] be concealed from the buying public." The purpose of the agency and the myriad of securities laws enacted in the early 1930s, the Supreme Court said in *SEC v. Capital Gaines Research Bureau*, is "to substitute a philosophy of full disclosure for the philosophy of *caveat emptor* and thus to achieve a high standard of business ethics in the ... industry."

The SEC operates on the assumption that transparency leads to greater levels of trust. Thus, it seeks to level the playing field for all investors by requiring truthful, complete and timely disclosure to the public of information about publicly traded companies that could be important to an investor's decision to buy, sell or hold stocks or other securities.

The 1933 Act, also called the "Truth in Securities Act," deals with new issues of stock. It requires that, before any security may be offered for sale to the public, a registration statement disclosing financial and other information about the issuing company be filed with the SEC. While the SEC reviews the material, no press releases, news conferences or other mass media publicity encouraging the sale of the new securities on behalf of the corporation are permitted, although the company may still publish regular information through its normal channels, such as its Web site. The only advertisements allowed during this waiting period are "tombstone" ads, text-based ads with no graphics or persuasive techniques that simply identify the company and the number of securities to be issued.

After the SEC deems the registration effective, the stock is sold in an initial public offering. No earnings forecasts or research reports may be issued on behalf of the company, however, for forty days, the "quiet period," after the IPO.

The Securities Exchange Act of 1934, on the other hand, applies to stock already publicly traded. Its purposes are to ensure full disclosure of timely and pertinent information and to prevent deception or manipulation of prices. As a result, the SEC requires reports to be filed periodically detailing a company's financial state, its future plans and other information that could affect an investor's decision regarding that company's securities.

The best-known report is Form 10-K, which companies must file with the SEC annually. In it, a company discloses specific information about its financial status and direction. Form 10-K is the basis of the annual report that companies must give shareholders no less than fifteen days prior to the company's annual meeting. PR professionals are often involved in writing the narrative portion of annual reports, including the letter to the shareholders from the president/CEO, and thus need to be aware of the SEC rules to avoid liability.

In addition to the annual report, the SEC requires timely and accurate disclosure of material facts or claims impacting the company. A fact is material if it would influence an individual's decision to buy, sell or hold a particular stock. The claim need not actually influence an investor's decision to buy, nor must the investor actually lose money for the claim to be considered deceptive. The material fact must only have the capacity to affect an investor's choices. Such an omission — however inadvertent — makes the information false and misleading, according to the SEC. As the Supreme Court said in *TSC Industries v. Northway*, there must be a substantial likelihood that the disclosure of the omitted fact would have been viewed by the reasonable investor as having significantly altered the "total mix" of information available.

Corporations traditionally considered material facts requiring disclosure as those that would affect a company's earnings by 5 percent or more. But for the SEC, the question is whether a reasonable investor would consider the information important or material in the context of the company's overall financial situation. Such extensive disclosure requirements reinforce Congress' belief that "honest markets" depend on "honest publicity."

Failure or delay in disclosing material information can be evidence of a company's deceptive or misleading actions or even proof of intention to defraud. On the other hand, the information must be "available and ripe for publication" before a duty to disclose commences. To be ripe under this requirement, according to the court in *Financial Industrial Fund v. McDonnell Douglas*, the content must be verified sufficiently to permit the officers and directors to have full confidence in its accuracy.

As with advertising, corporate release of knowingly false and misleading information may be equated with fraudulent misrepresentation and may even give rise to private enforcement actions, as long as the misrepresentation actually caused a loss. As the Supreme Court stated in *Virginia Bankshares v. Sandberg*, information may be fraudulently misrepresentative when a corporation uses "indefinite and unverifiable" terms — such as "high value" or "fair" — in public communication. In fact, "such conclusory terms in an economic context are reasonably understood to rest on a factual basis that justifies them as accurate, the absence of which renders them misleading." Corporate expression "should be to inform, not to challenge, the reader's critical wits."

Disclosure that is made with honesty of purpose and freedom from fraudulent intent, without the knowledge of any circumstances that would cause a reasonable individual to inquire further, is good faith disclosure.

The courts and the SEC have made it clear that PR agencies cannot escape liability for misleading investors by saying they relied on the company's representations. A PR agency must undertake a reasonable investigation to satisfy itself that the representations are accurate.

Regulation FD (fair disclosure), an SEC rule that went into effect in 2000, is designed to make important corporate information available to individual investors by prohibiting unfair selective disclosure. The rule extended the duty to disclose information to include the practice of giving corporate news first to stock analysts and mutual fund managers before announcing it publicly, as well as to disclose corporate executives' cancellations of stock purchases. Under Regulation FD, if the nonpublic, material information is disclosed intentionally, distribution of the same information to the public must be made simultaneously. If the disclosure is unintentional, the information must then be released to the public promptly, usually within twenty-four hours, *via* recognized channels of distribution.

In 2012, the SEC investigated whether Reed Hastings, the CEO of Netflix, violated Regulation FD when he posted on his personal Facebook page that Netflix had streamed one billion hours of content in June of that year. That was a record for the company, but Netflix had not disclosed it publicly. The SEC decided not to take action against Hastings, opting instead to clarify that companies must inform the public about which channels of communication, including social media platforms, they will use to disseminate nonpublic, material information. As the SEC noted in its news release, "Without such notice, the investing public would be forced to keep pace with a changing and expanding universe of potential disclosure channels, a virtually impossible task."

The SEC also prohibits insider trading. In modern corporate law, the term "insider" is generally defined as anyone who has company information that is not available to the general public. Corporate officers and directors obviously fall into this category. PR professionals, at times, also may be so classified. An insider must act on the nonpublic information for personal gain in order to be in violation of the law. Individuals can still be guilty of insider trading, however, even if they did not act on the information but tipped off others, such as family members and friends, who in turn acted on the information. For example, in 2022, the SEC, in its first cryptocurrency case, charged a Coinbase manager and his brother with insider trading. The manager helped coordinate Coinbase's public listing announcements that included what crypto assets would be made available for trading. From June 2021 to April 2022, the manager tipped off his brother about the timing and content of the upcoming announcements. His brother then purchased the assets and, after the announcements, sold them for a profit. The two were sentenced to prison for wire fraud and ordered to forfeit $892,500.

At the heart of the ban on insider trading and tipping is the concept of fiduciary duty. Those who manage a corporation and their advisors owe a duty to the corporation's shareholders to act at all times in the best interests of the corporation. That fi-

duciary duty is breached when insiders use nonpublic material information to trade a corporation's shares and may well subject the corporation and its directors and officers to lawsuits by the SEC and individual investors.

The best known of the SEC insider cases in the last 20 years involved Martha Stewart. She was accused of selling her shares in the biopharmaceutical firm ImClone Systems, Inc., in 2001. The SEC alleged that she did so after her broker told her that ImClone's CEO had sold his. ImClone at the time was seeking approval from the Food and Drug Administration for a new cancer drug. The actions of ImClone's CEO suggested that the FDA was going to deny the company's application, prompting Stewart to sell her shares, according to the SEC. It settled its civil lawsuit with Stewart when she agreed to a five-year ban on serving as a director of a public company and a five-year limitation on her services as an officer, and to pay a $195,081 fine.

Food and Drug Administration

According to the FDA's Web site, Congress initially enacted the Pure Food and Drug Act of 1906 after Upton Sinclair and other muckraking journalists exposed the hazardous conditions of the food and drugs being sold to the public. The act prohibited the interstate transport of unlawful food and drugs. To be "unlawful," food could not include any ingredients "that would substitute for the food, conceal damage, pose a health hazard, or constitute a filthy or decomposed substance." Drugs had to indicate the presence of certain dangerous ingredients on their labels. But according to the Supreme Court, the 1906 law did not apply to false therapeutic claims. No testing of drugs for safety was required. Thus, products such as Radithor, a tonic that contained radium and subjected users to a slow and painful death, were protected. It took a drug called "Elixir Sulfanilamide," marketed by a Tennessee company as a new wonder drug in the treatment of streptococcal infections, to prompt changes. Elixir Sulfanilamide contained the highly toxic compound antifreeze and killed 100 people, many of them children, in fifteen states over a two-month period in 1937. The incident led to the enactment of the 1938 Food, Drug and Cosmetic Act, the basis of the current law. Today, the FDA regulates food, drugs, medical devices, vaccines, cosmetics, and radiation-emitting, veterinary and tobacco products.

Specifically, the FDA is concerned about claims on a product's packaging, which includes "all labels and other written, printed, or graphic matter upon any article or any of its containers or wrappers, or accompanying such article," though it also regulates the advertising of all prescription drugs. A product is deemed to be misbranded "unless its labeling bears adequate directions for use." The regulation covers pharmaceutical trade and generic names, pesticides and similar products, and promotional materials. The Federal Trade Commission, not the FDA, controls the contents of book, magazine, or non-label advertising of food and non-prescription drug products, and evaluates them under a "truthful and not misleading" standard.

In general, the FDA bars all health claims on labels without prior approval. The Food and Drug Administration Modernization Act of 1994 allowed health claims on food labels if supported by authoritative statements from certain health research and protection agencies, such as the National Academy of Sciences, provided that the FDA was given pre-marketing notice.

Concerned about too-strict regulations on dietary supplements, Congress enacted the Dietary Supplement Health and Education Act of 1994, which allows certain health claims on the labels of dietary supplements without petitioning the FDA for approval. The claims may include statements that dietary supplements restore nutrient deficiency, claims regarding how the human body uses the nutrient and proclamations that dietary supplements contribute to one's general well-being. Yet these may only be made if the manufacturer has substantiated the claim as "truthful and not misleading," if the label expressly states that the FDA has not evaluated the claim, and if the FDA is notified thirty days before the claim is made.

In response to congressional passage of the Nutrition Labeling and Education Act of 1990, the FDA enacted regulations allowing health claims to be made only when there is significant scientific agreement among experts that the claim is supported by evidence. A lawsuit claiming that the requirements were an unlawful prior restraint of truthful commercial speech by the FDA was determined in 1998 to be without merit.

In 2002, the FDA reviewed its rules about what corporations may say about products (specifically, food, drugs, cosmetics or supplements). The review came after the Supreme Court overturned a ban on pharmacies from advertising the availability of "compounded" pharmaceuticals (drugs pharmacists mix themselves for the specific needs of certain patients) in *Thompson v. Western States Medical Center*. Scolding the government for its failure to consider alternatives to a complete advertising ban, the Court offered a ringing defense of free expression: "If the First Amendment means anything, it means that regulating speech must be a last — not first — resort." In response, the FDA said it would continue pursuing the regulation of products to protect the public but would attempt to ensure that any such regulations comply with the First Amendment.

Seven years later, the 2009 Family Smoking Prevention and Tobacco Control Act (TCA) gave the FDA extensive regulatory control over tobacco for the first time since the U.S. surgeon general declared smoking a health hazard in 1966. In response, the FDA adopted regulations that restricted the advertising, sale and distribution of cigarettes and smokeless tobacco to minors. Even before those restrictions took effect in 2010, tobacco companies challenged the provision that prohibited the use of color on labels and in advertisements, claiming it was more extensive than necessary to reduce minors' tobacco use. A U.S. district court agreed, finding in *Commonwealth Brands, Inc. v. United States*, that the ban on all uses of color demonstrated a lack of tailoring.

Undeterred, the FDA decided to require color warnings that graphically depict the negative health consequences of smoking. The warnings were to occupy the top half of the front and back of all cigarette packages. The Sixth Circuit ruled that regulations requiring the warnings, which were to take effect in 2012, were constitutional. The D.C. Circuit Court of Appeals, however, in *R.J. Reynolds Tobacco v. FDA*, held that the same requirements were unconstitutional. The D.C. court applied the *Central Hudson* standard to the regulation because the case involved compelled commercial disclosure. In concluding that the graphic warnings did not pass the Central Hudson Test, the court noted that the FDA did not present any evidence showing that the graphic warnings would accomplish the agency's objective of reducing the number of smokers.

In 2013, the FDA decided not to appeal the decision to the Supreme Court. Instead, in 2020, it issued a second graphics-warning regulation. R.J. Reynolds sued again on the same grounds. In 2022, the U.S. District Court for the Eastern District of Texas granted partial summary judgment to the tobacco company, ruling that the FDA's graphic warning requirement violated the First Amendment. The court declined, however, to hold that the provision requiring such labels in general was unconstitutional. In 2023, the FDA appealed the district court's decision to the Fifth Circuit.

In 2016, the FDA finalized a rule extending its reach to all tobacco products, including "hookah, e-cigarettes, dissolvables, smokeless tobacco, cigarettes, all cigars, roll-your-own tobacco, pipe tobacco, and future tobacco products." The rule prevents the sale of such products to anyone under the age of 18 and requires FDA approval for the sale of all tobacco products that have come on the market since 2007. Despite legal challenges from e-cigarette manufacturers, the FDA's pre-sale approval requirement was ruled constitutional in 2019. In 2021, the FDA, for the first time, approved the marketing of three tobacco-flavored e-cigarette products. The R. J. Reynolds Vapor Company was able to satisfy the FDA that the products could benefit addicted adults who switch to e-cigarettes by reducing their tobacco consumption.

National Labor Relations Board

In 1935, Congress passed the National Labor Relations Act to protect the rights of both employees and employers and to encourage collective bargaining. The act was a formal recognition of the inequality of bargaining power between employees and employers and an attempt to balance that power. While labor law is a relatively settled legal area, social media have taken the National Labor Relations Board into uncharted waters. At issue for the NLRB is the extent to which a company can control employees' use of social media.

In 2014, an administrative law judge ruled that four provisions of the social media policy of the Kroger grocery chain were unlawfully broad and violated the employees' speech rights. One of the provisions required workers to include a disclaimer that they did not represent the company if they identified themselves as Kroger employees and published "any work-related information online." The judge wrote that "the requirement that a disclaimer be posted by the employee every time he or she speaks on work-related issues and is identifiable as an employee of the employer, is unduly burdensome ... and will have a tendency to chill legitimate" speech about labor issues.

The other provisions barred the use of Kroger's logo or insignia without permission; the discussion of confidential or proprietary information including "rumors, speculation or personnel matters;" and the engagement in "behavior that would be inappropriate at work." In each case, the judge found the restrictions to be overly broad. PR practitioners, who typically help develop such policies, should ensure their clients' policies are in compliance with NLRB rules.

TORT LAW

A tort is a legal wrong that results in damages to a person or property caused by the actions or omissions of another individual. Tort law has three purposes: compensation, justice and deterrence. It deals with fairly compensating individuals for losses that the actions of others caused. The harms, at a minimum, may be physical (such as battery, trespass to land, or intrusion upon physical solitude), mental (such as infliction of emotional distress) or reputational (such as defamation or misappropriation). There are three types of torts:

- negligent (the defendant did not intend to cause harm);
- intentional (the defendant caused harm intentionally); and
- strict liability (the defendant is liable regardless of intention or negligence).

A negligent tort has four elements, all of which must be present for a plaintiff to be successful:

(1) the defendant must owe the plaintiff a duty of care;
(2) the defendant must have breached that duty;
(3) the plaintiff must have been injured or harmed; and
(4) the breach of duty must have caused the harm.

Everyone has a duty to protect others from harms that his or her actions or omissions cause. The degree of required care varies, but it is always based on what a reasonable person would have done under the circumstances. Doctors, for example, are held to the standard of care expected of a reasonable member of the medical profession. Defendants breach their duty of care by falling short of what a reasonable person would have done.

The most important element of negligence is causation. Did the defendant's actions cause the harm? The actions must be the actual cause (the plaintiff would not have been injured but for the defendant's actions) and the proximate cause. Proximate cause operates as a policy limit to actual causation liability. The question the courts ask is, was the injury or harm foreseeable? For example, in a two-car collision, a passenger was ejected and thrown thirty feet. His leg was impaled on the remains of a municipal drainpipe. The passenger sued the village for negligence. The court held that the accident was not foreseeable, describing the circumstances as "tragically bizarre" and possibly even a unique outcome. The opposite result came in *Weirum v. RKO General*. In that case, a radio station held a promotion in which a disc jockey, popular with teens, drove to unspecified locations around the city. The first person to physically locate the DJ would receive a prize. Two teens in separate cars decided to follow the DJ. As they raced each other on the highway to get to the DJ first, one forced another car into the center divider, killing its driver. The deceased's family sued the radio station for negligence, arguing that it should have known teens would drive recklessly to win the contest. The court agreed that it was foreseeable that "defender's youthful listeners ... would race to arrive first at the next site and in their haste would disregard the demands of highway safety."

Product Liability

Product liability is the liability of manufacturers and sellers for damages their defective products cause. A PR practitioner has a duty to warn consumers of dangerous conditions associated with a product.

The general rule is that for a duty to warn to exist, a product must be dangerous beyond the extent to which a reasonable consumer, with common knowledge about the product's characteristics, would use it. To mitigate a product's inherent danger, a seller could be required to provide directions for use of the product. If a product contains a dangerous ingredient — or one whose danger is not widely known or that an average consumer would not reasonably expect to find contained in the product — a seller could be required to provide a warning with each sale of the product. For example, warnings as to appropriate use are generally required for poisonous drugs.

To determine the adequacy of directions or warnings, judges must balance the likelihood the product would cause the harm with the burden on the manufacturer of providing an adequate warning. An adequate warning will provide a fair indication of the nature and degree of intensity of the dangers involved. According to the court in *Seley v. G.D. Searle Co.*, a warning that is "unduly delayed, reluctant in tone, or lacking in a sense of urgency" may be found to be unreasonable. Adequacy also requires resolving other questions: How explicit must the warning be? In whose language must the warning be made? At what point is a warning sufficient?

When a product's label meets a federal statute's labeling requirements, the manufacturer is usually protected from tort lawsuits brought in state courts, although the Supreme Court has ruled that neither federal regulatory approval nor advertising control completely shields drug companies and cigarette manufacturers from claims of fraudulent deception.

The same rule applies to manufacturers' product warranties and marketing promises. In *Hauter v. Zogarts*, a company that promoted its "Golfing Gizmo" as "completely safe" was held liable when a 13-year-old boy hit the ball in an unusual manner and was struck in the head when the ball bounced back. The device consisted of a golf ball attached to an elastic cord. It was supposed to allow users to improve their swings without having to retrieve balls. The company's promotional literature urged users to "drive the ball with full power" since the "ball will not hit player." The court upheld an award based on claims of breach of warranty and misrepresentation.

Strict liability is often applied in cases involving dangerous or defective products. With strict liability, the manufacturers or sellers of a product are liable for damages that result from the use of the product even if they were not negligent in producing or selling it. The application of strict liability is a matter of public policy and is an attempt to protect consumers.

Misrepresentation

The core of the intentional tort of misrepresentation is a person's reliance on a false statement. Thus, fraudulent misrepresentation requires:

(1) a false statement that is material — substantially central to a person's decision,

(2) knowledge of the falsity on the part of the communicator,

(3) an intention to induce others to make economic decisions based upon the statement, and

(4) damages caused by reliance on the statement.

Negligent misrepresentation occurs when a PR practitioner makes a false representation of a material fact in his or her professional capacity, when the practitioner fails to use reasonable care to determine the statement's truth, and when the practitioner owes a duty to the person who justifiably relied on it, causing damages. However, the general rule is that nondisclo-

sure, when two parties are dealing independently and knowingly, "at arm's length," is not grounds for a misrepresentation claim. Third parties, such as PR agencies, are not generally liable for negligent misrepresentation unless they:

(1) know their statements will be used for a particular purpose,

(2) know another specific party will rely on their statements, and

(3) are somehow linked to that party and understand the consequences of that party's reliance on their statements.

Interference in a Business Relationship

Tortious interference in a business relationship is an example of an intentional tort. There are two types of tortious interference. The first occurs when an individual convinces another to breach a contract with a third entity. The second occurs when an individual acts to prevent another from successfully establishing or maintaining a business relationship. Such a claim requires that:

(1) there was some sort of a contractual or beneficial business relationship between two parties,

(2) the defendant was aware of the relationship,

(3) the defendant intentionally caused a breach in that relationship, and

(4) damage resulted.

For example, if a PR practitioner at Agency A learns that a competitor, Agency B, is pitching its services to a new company in town and the Agency A practitioner calls the company and says that Agency B does lousy work, causing the company not to hire Agency B, that action is unethical according to PRSA's Code of Conduct. In addition, the Agency A practitioner could be sued for tortious interference in a business relationship.

In the early twentieth century, corporations used the tort as a weapon to keep employees from joining labor unions. More recently, in what ended up a PR fiasco for Texaco, Pennzoil filed a tortious interference claim when Texaco topped Pennzoil's offer for Getty Oil — interfering with the two companies' agreement. The result was a verdict of $7.53 billion in actual damages and $2.5 billion in punitive damages for Pennzoil, a final appeal to the Supreme Court, and an ultimate settlement of $3 billion.

CONTRACT LAW

Because public relations involves the marketing of corporate ideas and ideals, as well as the defense of economic actions and transactions (such as contracts), a close, symbiotic relationship exists between business law and public relations law.

At its simplest, a contract consists of an offer, acceptance of the offer, and consideration. The offer must be specific, such as "I am offering my car for sale for $1,000." If someone agrees to the price, there is acceptance. If the person responds instead with "I'll pay you $900 for the car," that is a new offer and requires the seller's acceptance. For a valid contract, there must be consideration, an exchange of something of value by each party. In the car example, the car and the purchase price serve as consideration. If your friend says he will give you his car when he graduates, there is no consideration and his "promise" is not enforceable. He can do whatever he wants with the car after graduation, and you are out of luck.

Contracts do not need to be in writing to be valid although some are required by law to be so, and others should be written because of their complexity, the length of the contractual duration or their importance.

Contracts such as release forms and consent agreements are often used in public relations to secure the right to use the name or likeness of someone in public relations materials. Although releases may not be necessary in every situation, the basic rule of thumb is that if the use is commercial — if it is for purposes of trade — releases are necessary. An ideal consent release should be in writing and contain these elements:

(1) consideration or exchange of value,

(2) identification of parties' names and ages,

(3) a statement as to the agreement's scope and duration,

(4) words binding one's legal successors and representatives, and

(5) a statement that the agreement is the full agreement, that no promises were made not plainly stated in the release.

It is also wise to keep the agreement broader than the specific purpose at hand to protect future uses of the material.

Under contract law, minors, usually under the age of 18, are considered too young to understand the significance of a contract. Therefore, they may disaffirm any contract they sign. Typically, PR practitioners have the parents or guardians sign on the behalf of the minor, but care must be taken whenever minors are being used in promotional materials.

Contracts with Clients

PR practitioners and their clients typically sign contracts stipulating:

• the terms of work to be produced, timeliness, deadlines, billing routines, the use of free-lancers through sub-contracting and other pertinent data;
• the terms of supplying information, timetables for review of work and payment schedules.

Once contracts are signed, both parties must satisfy their parts of the bargain. In other words, they must deliver the consideration provided for in the contract. In the case of the PR

practitioner, that might mean a campaign plan, for example. But what if the client does not like the plan or considers it of inferior quality? As long as the client provides an honest evaluation of the work, the client can cancel the contract on the basis that the practitioner did not fulfill the terms of the contract to its satisfaction.

Employment Contracts

Most new practitioners for organizations or PR agencies are required to sign employment contracts. Such contracts set out the expectations of the employer and employee. They allow termination only for cause. Two other provisions typically found in employment contracts governing PR positions are non-compete covenants and confidentiality agreements.

Non-Compete Covenants. A covenant not to compete restricts the employment of a PR practitioner by a company's competitors in order to protect a company's trade secrets, customer contacts and other intellectual property. The common law prohibition against contracts in restraint of trade is one of the oldest and most firmly established in the law. Public policy concerns still generally disfavor such restraints and favor an individual's freedom of contract and right to work. Essentially, non-compete clauses must not deny the practitioner the right to earn a living.

Thus, such clauses in employment agreements must be reasonable in both duration (time) and space (geography). Is the time or geographic limitation greater than required to protect the employer's interests? Do the limitations impose an undue hardship on the employee's ability to profit from his or her skills? Is either limitation injurious to the public's interest, which favors free competition in the market?

Because such agreements typically favor the employer, courts place the initial burden on the employer to prove that the non-compete clause is reasonable, is fairly related to and is necessary to protect the employer's business interests or activities. The employer is not entitled to protection against ordinary competition in the market. For example, even if a business were national in scope, an agreement not to compete anywhere in the nation would be unreasonable.

In January 2023, the FTC proposed a new rule that would ban employers from imposing noncompete agreements on their employees on the grounds that such agreements hurt workers and harm competition. After receiving significant public comments on the proposed rule, the FTC has delayed its vote on the ban until April 2024.

Confidentiality Agreements. Most employment contracts for PR positions require a confidentiality or nondisclosure agreement because PR practitioners are often privy to their clients' confidential and proprietary information. Clients want to know that information is protected from disclosure to competitors and the public. PR professionals are not like doctors, ministers and attorneys who have a legally privileged relationship with patients and clients. Thus, the nondisclosure agreement is used to create a confidential relationship to protect nonpublic business information. It should be noted that the confidentiality agreement will not necessarily protect you from being required to disclose what you know before a judge.

Ownership of Work and Proposals

In most situations, the materials PR professionals prepare for an employer are "works for hire." The case may be different, however, if a PR professional is a freelancer or independent contractor and not an employee. The Supreme Court ruled in the 1989 case of *Community for Creative Non-Violence v. Reid*, that, unless an express contractual agreement exists to the contrary, independent contractors own the copyright to works they create. Historically, corporate clients assumed they owned such works-made-for-hire because they had contracted with PR practitioners to create particular campaigns, programs, projects or plans. A close look at the works-made-for-hire provisions of the Copyright Act of 1976, however, reveals that the corporation owns the finished work only if the creator is an employee acting "within the scope of his or her employment." Other works, "specifically ordered or commissioned," require an express agreement "that the work is to be considered a work-made-for-hire." Even then, the corporation may not own all rights to the work, because the Copyright Act defines a "work-made-for-hire" in a limited way, as "a contribution to a collective work, as a part of a motion picture or other audio-visual work, as a translation, as a supplementary work, as a compilation, as an instructional text, as a test, as answer material for a test, or as an atlas."

Generally, PR campaigns, projects, programs or plans created by independent practitioners do not fit into any of these categories and, thus, continue to be owned by their creators even if the copyright is assigned to the corporation. So corporations and PR practitioners should carefully agree to the origin and ownership of PR plans in very specific contractual terms. Because prospective clients can easily use part or all of a proposal after having seen it during a presentation, a statement of ownership should be included on the proposal's title page.

SUMMARY

Public relations, which generally may be defined as the explanation of business or institutional concerns to the public, involves the communication of corporate ideas and ideals and the defense of economic actions and transactions. Public relations law

has been described as plain, old business law polished with a veneer of First Amendment protections. In fact, it is not really an area of law — such as defamation or copyright — but a study of the application of other areas of law to the practice of public relations. Thus, a close, symbiotic relationship exists between public relations law and the general laws of business.

While corporations today have First Amendment speech rights, the level of protection for that speech depends on how the speech is classified. Corporate speech on issues of political and social importance tends to have greater protection than does commercial speech. But deciding what is political and what is commercial is not easy when it comes to corporate speech. Courts continue to struggle with the extent of the influence and power of corporate speech in the political process and how best to treat blended corporate and commercial speech.

In addition to the constitutional questions, however, PR professionals need an understanding of federal regulations impacting their clients' industries such as the SEC, the FDA and NLRB to ensure they and their clients do not run afoul of the law. Similarly, they must be careful not to misrepresent a company's products or services to the public or they open the company and themselves up to litigation.

In the area of employment law, PR practitioners must understand who owns the plans they create and the extent of their non-compete clauses. Finally, PR practitioners should be aware of the potential legal consequences of their promises and agreements, whether written or oral.

BIBLIOGRAPHY

Articles

Huang, Jidong, Frank Chaloupka & Geoffrey T. Fong. "Cigarette Graphic Warning Labels and Smoking Prevalence in Canada: A Critical Examination and Reformulation of the FDA Regulatory Impact Analysis," 23 *Tobacco Control* 7 (2014).

Lewis, Neil A. & Richard A. Oppel Jr. "U.S. Court Issues Discordant Ruling on Campaign Law," *New York Times*, May 3, 2003, at A14.

Silver, Derigan & Dan V. Kozlowski. "Preserving the Law's Coherence: *Citizens United v. FEC* and Stare Decisis," 21 *Communication Law and Policy* 39 (2016).

Books

Gower, Karla K. *Legal and Ethical Considerations for Public Relations*. 3d ed. Long Grove, Ill.: Waveland Press, 2018.

Moore, Roy L., Carmen Maye & Erik L. Collins. *Advertising & Public Relations Law*. 2d ed. New York: Routledge, 2010.

Cases

Austin v. Michigan Chamber of Commerce, 494 U.S. 652 (1990).

Buckley v. Valeo, 424 U.S. 1 (1976).

Central Hudson Gas & Electric Corp. v. Public Service Commission, 447 U.S. 577 (1980).

Citizens United v. Federal Elections Commission, 558 U.S. 310 (2010).

Commonwealth Brands, Inc. v. United States, 678 F. Supp. 2d 512 (W.D. Ky. 2010).

Community for Creative Non-Violence v. Reid, 490 U.S. 730 (1989).

Dun & Bradstreet v. Greenmoss Builders, Inc., 472 U.S. 749 (1985).

Financial Industrial Fund v. McDonnell Douglas Corp., 474 F. 2d 514 (10th Cir. 1973).

First National Bank of Boston v. Bellotti, 435 U.S. 765 (1978).

Hauter v. Zogarts, 534 P.2d 377 (Cal. 1975).

Kroger Co. of Michigan v. Granger, NLRB, No. 07-CA-098566 (Apr. 22, 2014).

McConnell v. Federal Election Commission, 251 F. Supp. 2d 176 (D. D.C. 2002).

McCutcheon v. Federal Election Commission, 572 U.S. 185 (2014).

Nicopure Labs, LLC v. FDA, et al., 266 F. Supp. 3d (D.D.C. 2017), *affirmed*, 944 F. 3d 267 (D.C. Cir. Dec. 10, 2019).

Nike v. Kasky, 45 P.3d 243 (Cal. 2002), *cert dismissed as improvidently granted*, 539 U.S. 654 (2003).

Pittsburgh Press Co. v. Pittsburgh Commission on Human Relations, 413 U.S. 376 (1973).

R.J. Reynolds Tobacco Co. v. FDA, 696 F.3d. 1205 (D.C. Cir. 2012).

R.J. Reynolds Tobacco Co., et al. v. FDA, No. 6:20-cv-00176 (E.D. Tex. May 21, 2021).

R.J. Reynolds Tobacco Co., et al. v. FDA, No. 23-60128 (5th Cir. 2023).

SEC v. Capital Gaines Research Bureau, 375 U.S. 180 (1963).

Seley v. G.D. Searle Co., 423 N.E. 2d 831 (Ohio 1981).

Texaco v. Pennzoil, 485 U.S. 994 (1988); 729 S.W.2d 768 (Tex. App. 1987).

Thompson v. Western States Medical Center, 535 U.S. 357 (2002).

TSC Industries v. Northway, 426 U.S. 438 (1976).

Virginia Bankshares v. Sandberg, 501 U.S. 1083 (1991).

Weirum v. RKO General, 539 P. 2d 36 (Cal. 1975).

Broadcast Regulation

By Stuart N. Brotman

☑ **Headnote Questions**

- Why are broadcasting media regulated differently than print media?
- What role does Congress and the courts play in broadcast regulation?
- What are the powers of the Federal Communications Commission?
- What are the main structural regulations of the broadcast media?
- What are the main content regulations of the broadcast media?

Broadcast regulation is one of the most complex and dynamic areas of communication law. To better understand how broadcasting came to be regulated as it is today, it is necessary to review some of its history. But, first, it is crucial to understand exactly what a "broadcasting" service is and what it is not. A broadcast service is one that is distributed over the air and is intended for and free to the general public. Thus, broadcasting refers to local radio and television stations serving specific communities across the country. "Broadcast" should not be used when referring to transmission systems or program networks distributed by cable or satellite services (ESPN or Comedy Central, for example) or to the Internet and programming services distributed online (Netflix or Pandora, for example).

THE DEVELOPMENT OF BROADCAST REGULATION

Few people involved in radio's development, which began more than 100 years ago, foresaw its becoming a form of mass communication. "Wireless," as it was called, initially was considered an extension of the telegraph and the telephone. Only much later did it become a mass medium.

Broadcasting's Early History

Guglielmo Marconi, considered the first person to send radio signals without wires, believed his "wireless radio," used for ship-to-shore and ship-to-ship radio transmissions, would be commercially successful. He competed fiercely with rival companies to retain rights to his invention. Employees of Marconi Wireless Company of America, for example, refused to recognize signals sent to shore from ships using equipment that other firms manufactured. Concern that distress signals might be ignored led Congress to adopt the Wireless Ship Act of 1910, which required large ships to have wireless equipment and radio operators on board. The law also made it illegal not to retransmit or answer wireless transmissions from ships. The 1910 law was the first American regulation of devices using the electromagnetic spectrum, a natural resource through which radio signals are transmitted.

When ships began using wireless equipment, many radio signals filled the spectrum. They would interfere with each other, so only static was heard, causing problems for ships throughout the world. In an effort to deal with the problem, representatives from a number of countries met to establish certain standards for radio use. They also insisted that individual nations adopt laws requiring that the standards be followed. This agreement and one tragic event led to the United States replacing the 1910 law with the Radio Act of 1912.

The Radio Act of 1912

The tragedy was the sinking of the *Titanic*. The supposedly unsinkable ship hit an iceberg in the Atlantic Ocean, and more than 1,500 people died. The irony that tied the *Titanic* tragedy to broadcast regulation was the fact that a ship only a few miles away could have saved many lives. No one on the nearby ship knew of the *Titanic's* desperate radio transmissions, however, because even though the ship met the provisions of the 1910 Act and possessed the required radio equipment, the radio operator had gone off duty. While the 1910 Act required radio equipment, it did not require a radio operator to be on duty.

The *Titanic* tragedy focused public and congressional attention on radio legislation. Congress adopted the 1912 Act, which, in addition to closing some of the loopholes of the earlier act, became the first law directly affecting commercial radio. Among other provisions, it allowed the U.S. Secretary of Commerce to award licenses for radio stations and to assign the spectrum frequencies those stations would use. In an era when wireless was considered a point-to-point medium, the 1912 Act worked well enough. Dramatic changes in the use of wireless, however, soon demonstrated the act's limitations.

Following World War I, rather than simply communicate with each other, wireless hobbyists began using their stations to deliver information and entertainment to broader audiences. This form of mass communication, which became known as "broadcasting," quickly became popular with listeners and caught the attention of major electronics manufacturers. General Electric, Westinghouse, the Radio Corporation of America and other companies, anticipating the revenue potential of broadcasting, began acquiring radio licenses around the country. The problems with the 1912 Act became apparent. Although the act gave the secretary of commerce the power to grant licenses, it did not allow him to reject license applications. All he could do was award a license to anyone who applied. The secretary faced other limitations as well. Station operators would unhesitatingly change frequencies and the heights of transmission towers. An operator might even move a station from one city to another. Under the 1912 statute, federal courts ruled, Secretary of Commerce Herbert Hoover had no power to control these actions. The U.S. Attorney General agreed.

So, as commercial radio began to develop, the government granted and registered licenses, but could neither refuse a license to an applicant nor limit the purposes for which radio stations were used. This inability to control the use of the spectrum led to serious interference problems. By 1920, many commercial broadcasters and hobbyists believed radio was doomed as a public medium unless the government could control both the number of radio stations on the air and the broadcast frequencies. In an attempt to deal with the chaos on the airwaves, Hoover convened several radio conferences between 1922 and 1926 but could not convince radio station owners to cooperate with one another. At first, Congress ignored calls to adopt legislation controlling radio broadcasting. In most major cities, interference constantly interrupted radio stations' signals. Eventually, the problem became so serious that Congress cooperated.

The Radio Act of 1927

Recognizing radio's importance to the public and the country's commerce, and realizing the need to control spectrum use, Congress enacted the Radio Act of 1927. The act established a five-member Federal Radio Commission, each commissioner representing a different region of the country. The FRC was given the power to grant and deny radio station licenses, assign frequencies and prevent spectrum interference, but it did not have the power to censor content.

The 1927 Act was important because it was the first law giving the U.S. government, through Congress and the FRC, control over radio broadcasting to the public. The act required the FRC to act in the "public interest, convenience or necessity," the standard the Federal Communications Commission still uses in broadcast regulation. The act also established that broadcast stations were not to be regulated as common carriers, that is, the licensee was responsible for the content of the station's transmissions. The 1927 law did not explicitly give the federal government exclusive jurisdiction over broadcast regulation, but the U.S. Supreme Court later interpreted it as doing so and as forbidding the states from interfering. Each of these points continues to be an important element in broadcast regulation.

The Communications Act of 1934

In adopting the 1927 Act, Congress expected that the FRC could be disbanded after completing its task of allocating licenses to radio stations, but it soon became apparent that the federal government would need to oversee broadcasting on a continuing basis. Another problem was that the 1927 Act had added yet another federal agency, the FRC, to others with control over spectrum use and telephony, including the Interstate Commerce Commission, the Department of Commerce and the Postmaster General's Office. To continue jurisdiction over broadcasting, but also to simplify the regulatory process, Congress adopted the Communications Act of 1934, establishing the Federal Communications Commission. FCC jurisdiction extends to "radio and wire communication service," that is, broadcasting and various aspects of telephone service. The 1934 Act replaced the 1927 law, and the FCC became the successor to the FRC.

More than eighty years since the adoption of the 1934 Act, the FCC has had to decide how to deal with satellites, mobile telephony, and other new technologies that use the spectrum but which, of course, were not mentioned in the act and were not imagined by any member of Congress in 1934. To address these new technologies, Congress has amended the act many times. The most recent major amendment came when Congress adopted the Telecommunications Act of 1996. That act significantly altered many rules regarding market entry and operational aspects of various communications media.

RATIONALES FOR BROADCAST REGULATION

The First Amendment to the Constitution states that the government "shall make no law ... abridging the freedom of speech, or of the press." Does that mean broadcasters have the same First Amendment rights as publishers of the print media? The Supreme Court has said "No," holding that various mass media may be treated differently under the First Amendment, and, indeed, broadcasters' First Amendment rights are not equal to those of the print media.

Print vs. Broadcasting

When the Supreme Court began deciding cases involving broadcasting, it had judicial precedent for not treating the industry the same as the print media. From 1915 until 1952, the Court held that motion pictures were entertainment and, therefore, not entitled to First Amendment protection. As radio developed into a major mass medium, it primarily offered entertainment. By the mid-1930s, First Amendment rights essentially had been applied only to the print media, and federal courts found no reason to extend the same type of protection to broadcasting. Just one year after the Supreme Court ruled in *Near v. Minnesota* that a state could not stop a newspaper from printing "malicious, scandalous, and defamatory" attacks on public officials, a federal appellate court upheld the FRC in denying a radio license renewal to a church whose minister, Dr. Robert Shuler, used the station to attack government officials, labor unions and religions other than his own.

The Supreme Court took a similar approach in 1964, when a small Pennsylvania radio station carried a fifteen-minute program in which the Rev. Billy James Hargis attacked Fred J. Cook, the author of *Goldwater — Extremist on the Right*. Hargis said Cook was fired as a newspaper reporter because he made false charges against city officials and that he had worked for a Communist publication, denounced then FBI chief J. Edgar Hoover and the CIA, and set out to "destroy Barry Goldwater," Republican presidential candidate in 1964. When Cook learned of the broadcast, he asked the station for free time to reply under the FCC's personal attack rule. It refused. Cook complained to the FCC, which ordered the station to offer him on-air response time. The station appealed to the courts.

In 1969, the Supreme Court found in *Red Lion Broadcasting Co. v. FCC* that "those who are licensed stand no better than those to whom licenses are refused. A license permits broadcasting, but the licensee has no constitutional right ... to monopolize a radio frequency to the exclusion of his fellow citizens." Therefore, the Court held, the First Amendment does not prohibit "re-quir[ing] a broadcaster to permit answers to personal attacks occurring in the course of discussing controversial issues."

Five years later, the Supreme Court heard a case in which a newspaper refused to abide by a state statute requiring papers to provide free space for candidates they criticized. The *Miami Herald* had published an editorial critical of a candidate for the Florida House of Representatives. When he demanded space for a response under Florida law and the newspaper refused, he sued. The Supreme Court, in *Miami Herald Publishing Co. v. Tornillo,* held that it is unconstitutional for the government to force a newspaper to publish material it chooses not to. The Court said that a "responsible press is an undoubtedly desirable goal, but press responsibility is not mandated by the Constitution and like many other virtues it cannot be legislated."

The Court thought of "press" as "print media," not broadcasting. *Red Lion* required a radio station to provide a right of reply, while the Court held in *Tornillo* that the same requirement could not be applied to newspapers. This does not mean broadcasters have no First Amendment rights. The Court has found that they do. But it has said that "of all forms of communication, it is broadcasting that has received the most limited First Amendment protection." Courts have used several rationales for the proposition that print media have greater First Amendment rights than broadcasters. The rationales are spectrum scarcity, the concept of public trusteeship, pervasiveness and the special impact broadcast media can have, especially on children.

Spectrum Scarcity

The electromagnetic spectrum is the array of energy that includes radio waves. Broadcast radio and television stations use transmitters to send radio waves to receiving antennas. Transmitters radiate thousands to millions of radio waves per second, depending on the frequency at which stations broadcast. The FCC assigns frequencies to stations and requires them to transmit only on those frequencies.

Groups of frequencies can be used only for certain types of broadcasting. Television, AM radio and FM radio are assigned frequencies within a certain portion of the spectrum. Because of the way the federal government has allocated the spectrum for broadcasters' use, only a limited number of radio and TV stations can be on the air. Adding more would cause harmful interference. Therefore, only a relatively few companies may use the spectrum for broadcasting. So there is a notion of spectrum scarcity; there are not enough frequencies to allow all who want to broadcast to do so. Courts have decided that Congress may impose certain obligations to serve the public on those granted broadcast licenses.

However, most cities have more radio and TV stations than print newspapers. Where, then, is the scarcity? As the courts see it, this is not simply a matter of numbers. There are so few print newspapers because a newspaper is very costly to begin and operate, and advertisers and subscribers for competing newspapers are limited. This is an economic limitation, the courts say, while spectrum scarcity is a physical and technical limitation, that is, a limitation of nature. No matter how much money might be available to begin a new broadcast station, if there is no room on the broadcast spectrum — if a station cannot be added without causing signal interference with other stations — the new station may not go on the air.

Therefore, the award of a broadcast license is considered to be a grant of a privilege. Another person or company who wants to communicate by owning a broadcast station simply may not do so if no frequencies are available in the area.

The Supreme Court adopted the spectrum scarcity rationale in 1943. The Court was straightforward, stating that radio's "facilities are limited; they are not available to all who may wish to use them; the radio spectrum simply is not large enough to accommodate everybody. There is a fixed natural limitation upon the number of stations that can operate without interfering with one another." *Red Lion* echoed the point later: "[I]t is idle to posit an unabridgeable First Amendment right to broadcast comparable to the right of every individual to speak, write, or publish."

The Concept of Public Trusteeship

Unlike some countries where the government owns and controls all or most broadcasting outlets, in the United States nearly all commercial stations are privately owned. But because the spectrum allocation and licensing process remains in the government's hands, those who are given licenses hold portions of the spectrum in trust for the public, that is, they are public trustees. The courts have said that Congress and the FCC may require them to operate in the public interest as part of the privilege of holding broadcast licenses. The Supreme Court has accepted this approach, stating in *Red Lion*:

There is nothing in the First Amendment which prevents the Government from ... requiring a licensee to ... conduct himself as a proxy or fiduciary with obligations to present those views and voices which are representative of his community.... [T]he people as a whole retain their interest in free speech by radio and their collective right to have the medium function consistently with the ends and purposes of the First Amendment. It is the right of the viewers and listeners, not the right of the broadcasters, which is paramount.... Licenses to broadcast do not confer ownership of designated frequencies, but only the temporary privilege of using them.

In 1973, four years after deciding *Red Lion*, the Court refined this point. The CBS network refused to accept advertisements from the Business Executives' Move for a Vietnam Peace, which, together with the Democratic National Committee, asked the FCC to rule that broadcasters could not "refuse to sell time to responsible entities ... for comment on public issues." The FCC rejected the request. The Supreme Court ruled that broadcasters did not have to take any and all advertisements.

Red Lion, which held that a radio station must give time for an individual to reply to a personal attack, and the CBS case, which held that broadcasters need not sell time for commercials about public issues, may not be as contradictory as they appear. The two decisions suggest that there is no general right for the public to have access to broadcast stations. But Congress may require access under certain circumstances, such as when a political candidate running for federal office wants to purchase airtime to reach the public. This still leaves broadcasters less protected than the print media under the First Amendment.

The spectrum scarcity and public trustee rationales have been criticized often as unsupportable. By the mid-1980s, even the Supreme Court suggested that it would consider a "signal from Congress or the FCC that technological developments have advanced so far that some revision of the system of broadcast regulation may be required." That is, the Court recognized that, since audiences may receive video signals from cable TV, satellites, microwave transmissions and other technologies, spectrum scarcity may not limit communication through the electronic media. Moreover, new technologies exist to put more signals on the broadcast bands without causing interference. For example, in the year 2000, the FCC authorized a new, low-power FM radio service, which when fully implemented could add thousands of additional stations across the country. Also, the move from analog to digital transmission (discussed later in this chapter) allows existing broadcast stations to deliver multiple programming channels simultaneously over their facilities.

It has been argued that even if there is a spectrum scarcity, all goods are scarce to some degree. for example, newsprint is scarce and expensive. Does that justify government control of newspapers or limits on publishers' First Amendment rights?

Pervasiveness

Another rationale courts use to justify differential First Amendment treatment of broadcasters is that radio and television are ubiquitous — they are heard and seen in homes, stores and in many other places, and are constantly intrusive, especially on the lives of children. Further, a listener or viewer has no idea what is being broadcast until a receiver is turned on.

Exactly that kind of confrontation was at the center of a case in which the Supreme Court noted that broadcasting is different from other media. In *FCC v. Pacifica*, a child inadvertently was exposed to indecent language when his father turned on the car radio. The Court said that with many forms of speech — like movies or words on jackets — people have a responsibility to avoid the communication; they can turn their heads or avert their eyes, for example. But, the Court said, radio and television are omnipresent; they are intruders rather than forms of communication people invite into their lives. The Court was particularly concerned that when broadcast radio or television comes into the home, children may be exposed to material their parents do not want them to see or hear. Broadcasting's intrusiveness and omnipresence make it unique among mass media. These characteristics justify treating broadcast radio and television differently than print media under the First Amendment.

Special Impact

Congress and a few federal courts have articulated an additional rationale for broadcast regulation: that radio and television have a greater impact on audiences than do print media. For example, when considering a law forbidding cigarette and small cigar advertising on television, a federal appellate court in the 1960s, without clearly explaining the grounds for its assertion, stated:

> [A]n ordinary habitual television watcher can avoid these commercials only by frequently leaving the room, changing the channel, or doing some other such affirmative act. It is difficult to calculate the subliminal impact of this pervasive propaganda, which may be heard even if not listened to, but it may reasonably be thought greater than the impact of the written word.

In 1996, as part of the enactment of the Telecommunications Act, Congress decided that televised violence presented enough of a threat to the well-being of children that it required a voluntary system that rated television violence, profanity and sexual content that could be used with a required piece of technology, called the v-chip, for all U.S. television sets. This will be discussed later in the chapter.

In addition, the Supreme Court has said that sexually indecent broadcast programming can have a powerful impact on children. In *Pacifica*, it said that while parents may be able to shield their children from offensive books or motion pictures, broadcasting is "uniquely accessible to children, even those too young to read." As a result, an indecent broadcast could instantly enlarge the vocabulary of very young children. The Court found that, in order to protect children, the FCC could constitutionally channel indecent broadcasts to times when children were less likely to be in the audience.

THE FEDERAL COMMUNICATIONS COMMISSION

The FCC is responsible for regulating broadcasting, other spectrum uses such as satellite communications and amateur radio, and various aspects of wired and wireless telephony and broadband service.

Structure of the FCC

The FCC is one of the federal government's independent agencies, similar in that respect to the Securities and Exchange Commission and the Federal Trade Commission. But like them, the FCC is not truly independent. Congress allocates the FCC's budget in a bill that the president must approve. Its five members are selected by the president and confirmed by the Senate. They serve five-year terms and can be reappointed. The president decides which of the five commissioners will be designated as chairman. While the FCC is not intended to be political — only three of the five commissioners can be from the same political party — political considerations play a part in the appointment process and in some of its decisions.

The FCC employs more than 2,000 staff members across seven bureaus. Of these seven bureaus, two are particularly relevant to broadcasters:

- The Media Bureau administers the policy and licensing programs related to electronic mass media, including broadcast radio, television and cable TV. It also handles post-licensing matters related to direct-to-home satellite services, for example, the Dish television network and Sirius/XM radio.
- The Enforcement Bureau resolves complaints involving radio frequency interference, indecent communications, and false distress signals, among others.

Powers of the FCC

As an independent regulatory agency, the FCC has judicial, legislative and executive powers.

Judicial Power. When the FCC makes decisions that affect individual licensees — taking action to revoke a license, for example — it acts much as a court does. Administrative law judges within the FCC initially decide cases that deal with individual parties. An ALJ will hold a hearing that might look much like a trial. Counsel represent the parties to the hearing. They present evidence and witnesses, and witnesses may be cross-examined. After all the evidence is presented, the ALJ weighs it and writes an opinion, referred to as the "Initial Decision." This decision is restricted to the record evidence that is presented in the case. A losing party may appeal the decision to the five commissioners.

Legislative Power. The FCC also acts much as a legislative body, adopting regulations affecting an entire industry. The FCC or an interested outside party may initiate the legislative process. When a decision is made to begin the process, FCC staff members prepare a Notice of Proposed Rule Making, stating what regulations the FCC is considering adopting, changing or rescinding, and explaining the reasons behind the proposed changes. When the commissioners agree on the NPRM's language, they make it public. Members of the public — including companies and lobbying groups representing companies that may be affected by the rules — submit comments to the FCC. The Commission makes them public and then accepts reply comments. The staff and commissioners review the comments and replies, discuss the proposed rules and finally adopt a Report and Order. The regulations in the order may be the same as those originally proposed in the NPRM, or they may be different, based on the public comment or changes made by commissioners for other reasons. After an order is released, members of the public may ask the FCC to reconsider the decision, which it may or may not do.

Executive Power. The FCC may impose an array of penalties to enforce its decisions, rules, regulations and policies — from a letter of reprimand inserted into a licensee's file, to a fine, to renewing a license for less than a full term, to non-renewal or revocation of a license. Short-term license renewals and non-renewals are harsh penalties, and the FCC normally prefers to impose no more than a fine, called a "forfeiture," when it finds a licensee has violated the rules.

Final Commission decisions, whether adjudicative, legislative or enforcement in nature, may be appealed to a federal court. That court's decision may then be appealed to the U.S. Supreme Court. An appellate court typically gives deference to the FCC's interpretation of the Communications Act. Under a separate law, the Administrative Procedures Act of 1946, a reviewing court may overturn an FCC policy decision if it is found to be "arbitrary, capricious [or] an abuse of discretion."

The Public Interest Standard

In both the 1927 and the 1934 acts, Congress required the FCC to regulate broadcast licensees so that they function in the "public interest, convenience and necessity." Adopted from the 1887 Interstate Commerce Act, the public interest standard is supposed to govern FCC decisions. The Communications Act does not define the term, leaving it to the FCC and the courts to give it substance — thus allowing flexibility in establishing policies and deciding cases. There are several problems with this continuing ambiguity. The FCC may give the words different meanings at different times, for example, depending upon its make-

up. It has used the standard both to adopt and later reject the same regulation, and the Commission and the courts cannot always agree on what the term means.

The FCC's predecessor, the FRC, issued several statements providing technical and content guidelines for radio that it believed were required to meet the public interest. These suggestions included ways to limit spectrum interference, provide radio signals to much of the country, limit the private use of commercial radio frequencies and provide well-rounded programming. The FRC also recommended that it would be in the public interest for stations to limit the "use of phonograph records" as program material.

In addition, the FRC applied the public interest standard when evaluating broadcast content. For example, in the 1920s, Dr. John R. Brinkley aired a program called the

> Medical Question Box, devoted to diagnosing and prescribing treatment of cases from symptoms given in letters.... Patients are not known to the doctor except by means of their letters.... The doctor usually advises that the writer of the letter is suffering from a certain ailment, and recommends the procurement from one of the members of the Brinkley Pharmaceutical Association, of one or more of Dr. Brinkley's prescriptions.... [For instance,] "Sunflower State, from Dresden Kans[as]. Probably he has gall stones. No, I don't mean that, I mean kidney stones. My advice to you is to put him on Prescription No. 80 and 50 for men, also 64. I think that he will be a whole lot better. Also drink a lot of water."

The FRC refused to renew the station's license, stating that Brinkley's programs did not serve the public interest. On appeal, the court agreed that Brinkley operated the station only to earn revenue for himself and that public health was being endangered. Brinkley argued that his First Amendment rights were being abridged, but the court found that the FCC "has merely exercised its undoubted right to take note of appellant's past conduct, which is not censorship."

A few years later, the FRC refused to renew a station licensed to a church. It found that the Rev. Robert Shuler used the airwaves to attack public officials and various religious groups. On appeal, the court upheld the FRC's decision, finding that:

> The evidence abundantly sustains the conclusion of the Commission that the continuance of the broadcasting programs is not in the public interest.... [I]t is manifest, we think, that it is not narrowing the ordinary conception of "public interest" in declaring his broadcasts — without facts to sustain or to justify them — not within that term.

The interplay between the FCC and the courts often has

helped define the public interest. For example, the Supreme Court agreed with the FCC that it could not take into consideration any possible impact on an existing radio station's revenues when it granted a license for a new station in the same city. The public interest meant being concerned with the public, not the licensee, the Court said. Three years later, it reinforced this interpretation in *National Broadcasting Co. v. FCC*: "The 'public interest' to be served under the Communications Act is ... the interest of the listening public." The Court has held that judges have limited powers to overturn a public interest determination. If the FCC balances the various interests at stake, it is up to the Commission to define the public interest.

In 1946, the FCC attempted to give station licensees better guidance about how to operate in the public interest. A set of informal programming guidelines — known as the "Blue Book" after the color of its cover — suggested that stations broadcast non-sponsored programs, live programs originated locally, and programs "devoted to public discussions." The Blue Book also urged stations to limit the number of commercials and to be careful of their content. Although broadcasters feared the Blue Book was an attempt by the FCC to scrutinize programming practices, in fact, the Commission never denied the renewal of a station's license for violation of Blue Book guidelines.

In 1960, the FCC replaced the Blue Book with a formal statement that specified fourteen program categories as "the major elements usually necessary to meet the public interest." The categories included children's, religious, educational, public affairs, agricultural, news, sports, entertainment and weather programs, and "opportunit[ies] for self-expression, ... the development and use of local talent" and "service to minority groups."

After decades of protecting the public interest by imposing specific regulations on broadcast stations, the FCC in the 1980s moved toward an economic marketplace approach. It said that competition among stations and from other forms of electronic media would be sufficient to ensure that licensees operate in the public interest and that extensive regulation was unnecessary.

The FCC took significant steps to deregulate broadcast radio in 1981 and television in 1984. It eliminated a number of programming guidelines; requirements for surveying community leaders, interest groups and individuals to ascertain programming needs and preferences; most limits on how much time could be used for commercials; complex license renewal processes; certain technical rules; and a number of other minor regulations. But it left many other rules in place.

Whether adding new regulations or deregulating, the FCC consistently tries to grapple with how to interpret the concept of public interest. In attempting to understand the meaning, it may be safe to say that "the public interest" means what the FCC says it means at any given time, subject to congressional oversight and judicial review.

STATION LICENSING

In large part, the Federal Radio Commission was created to ensure that stations broadcast without interfering with other stations' signals. That responsibility continues, but today the FCC's duties extend much further. The Communications Act of 1934 gave the FCC the authority to allocate frequencies to individual communities around the country and then license those frequencies to companies that the Commission has decided may operate radio and TV stations. The act requires that the FCC do this in a "fair, efficient and equitable" manner.

The Commission first must decide which portions of the spectrum will be used for what purposes — satellite transmissions, AM or FM radio, cellular communications, or for public safety uses. The FCC shares spectrum allocation responsibilities with the National Telecommunications and Information Administration of the U.S. Department of Commerce. NTIA allocates all spectrum used by the federal government, and the FCC allocates everything else. As technology evolves and demand for the spectrum continues to grow, the FCC's job of allocating this valuable resource becomes more complex and demanding. For this reason, in 2010 a new spectrum task force was created to ensure that burgeoning mobile services will have sufficient spectrum for continued development and growth. One implemented proposal regarding the allocation of spectrum allowed television broadcasters to give up part of their spectrum for use by mobile service operators through a complex spectrum auction process. As an incentive to relinquish a chunk of their spectrum, television broadcasters will receive a portion of the proceeds generated through these spectrum auctions. In 2012, Congress gave the FCC the authority to conduct these "incentive auctions." In 2014, the Commission adopted a Report and Order implementing the auctions, which began in 2016. With the process completed in 2017, companies eager to boost their wireless broadband offerings agreed to pay $19.77 billion for 70 MHz of broadcast spectrum for repurposing. Television stations agreed to relinquish some of the airwaves they use for a little more than $10 billion.

The Commission released a public notice formally beginning the thirty-nine-month period, known as the repacking process, during which time some TV stations will need to transition to new channel assignments. The FCC will reauthorize and relicense the facilities of the remaining broadcast television stations that receive new channel assignments in the repacking, or because they have won their auction bid to move to a different frequency band or to channel share. New channel assignments were designed to minimize costs by maximizing the number of channel "stays," or stations assigned to their pre-auction channels instead of being assigned to new channels; minimizing the maximum aggregate new interference experienced by any station; avoiding reassignment of stations with high anticipated relocation costs; and prioritizing assignments to channel 5 in the Low-VHF band and off of channel 14 in the UHF band.

Those stations that must move to new channels will have to modify their existing facilities (for example, antennas and transmission lines) to transmit on different frequencies. Then they must test their equipment. Unless a station's new channel is "available" (that is, free from interference caused by other stations), it will need to coordinate carefully with one or more other stations to prevent the testing from causing interference. With hundreds of stations needing to move to new channels, there is the potential for a traffic jam in which a station can't move to its new channel until a second station moves, and that station, in turn, must wait for a third station to move, and so on. Stations whose moves are dependent on another's move are called "linked stations," and these links can span dozens of stations across a large geographic area. Linked stations can switch to their new channels simultaneously to break up the congestion points, but doing so requires careful coordination.

Congress allocated $1 billion for a TV Broadcaster Relocation Fund ($600 million in fiscal year 2018 and $400 million in fiscal year 2019) to be used to reimburse relocation costs of eligible broadcasters and multichannel video programming distributors, TV translator stations and low-power TV stations, and FM broadcast radio stations. The FCC may use up to $50 million from this appropriation for consumer education.

License Requirements

The Communications Act of 1934 makes it illegal to operate a broadcast radio or television station in the United States without an FCC license. Stations operating without licenses — sometimes referred to as "pirate stations" — can be subject to civil fines, court injunctions, seizures of equipment, and even criminal penalties including jail time. According to the Communications Act, all applicants for broadcast licenses must be technically, financially and legally qualified.

To be technically qualified, an applicant must have access to technical expertise sufficient to operate the station. That means having sufficiently planned for the equipment and engineering personnel needed. To be financially qualified, an applicant must demonstrate sufficient financial backing, through funds on hand or loan commitments, to run the station for the first three months without advertising or other income.

There are several aspects to being legally qualified. The first criterion is U.S. citizenship. The Communications Act forbids granting a broadcast license to foreign governments or alien individuals, or their representatives, or to foreign corporations. In addition, foreign interests may own no more than 20 percent of the stock of a corporation holding a broadcast license. For a cor-

poration that is controlled by another corporation, the controlling entity may not have more than 25 percent of its stock owned or voted by foreign interests.

A second licensing criterion is that the applicant be of good character. The FCC will not award licenses to companies run or controlled by individuals who have engaged in fraudulent conduct or have been convicted of felonies or of violating antitrust laws involving the media. It is particularly concerned with applicants who have lied or made misrepresentations to the Commission. For example, it revoked the licenses of Contemporary Media, whose sole shareholder, Michael Rice, was convicted of sexually abusing children. Contemporary Media informed the FCC of Rice's arrest and told the Commission that he was removed from his managerial role of the company as a result of the arrest. However, the FCC later learned that Rice was actually involved in the business affairs of his company after his conviction, and it revoked the company's licenses and construction permits. Contemporary Media appealed the FCC's decision, but the U.S. Court of Appeals for the District of Columbia Circuit upheld it as reasonable. While the fact that Contemporary Media lied to the FCC probably tipped the balance against the licensee, this case generally ratified the Commission's authority to base its licensing decisions on the issue of character.

The final aspect of being legally qualified to be a licensee relates to the FCC's media ownership rules. In certain instances, regulations forbid one company from owning more than a specified number of stations in a market. If an applicant for a license is not eligible to own the station for which it is applying due to the ownership rules, it may not be awarded the license. These specific ownership regulations will be discussed below under the heading "Structural Regulation of Broadcasting."

Applying for a license

Before filing a broadcast application with the FCC, would-be broadcasters must ascertain whether a frequency is available for the area they wish to serve. To do that, they usually hire an engineering consulting firm. Assuming an appropriate frequency is available, applicants must wait for the FCC to announce that frequency's availability before submitting their applications. The Commission makes these announcements periodically, on no apparent systematic schedule. The announcements are made several months before applications are due so that applicants have notice and time to prepare their applications.

Mutually Exclusive Applications

If two or more entities apply for the same frequency, the FCC must choose one. Prior to 1993, it held full-blown evidentiary hearings to determine which applicant would best serve the public interest. To make such a determination, it applied a set of comparative standards that it developed in 1965. These criteria included diversification of ownership (the FCC preferred applicants who did not already own broadcast stations), integration of ownership and management (whether station owners were involved in the station's day-to-day management), prior broadcast experience and the likely reach of a station's signal.

For many years, the FCC's comparative hearing process was heavily criticized. Even the FCC characterized its own method as one that "can be described most charitably as laborious, exceedingly time consuming, expensive and often resulting in choices based on, at most, marginal differences."

Then, in the 1993 case of *Bechtel v. FCC*, a federal appellate court rejected one of the comparative factors the FCC had been using. The court held that the FCC had offered no proof that the criterion favoring integration of ownership and management had led to better broadcast service than absentee ownership did. Consequently, there was no evidence that using the integration factor was in the public interest. Because of the *Bechtel* decision, the agency stopped using comparative hearings in these kinds of licensing cases.

As early as 1982, the FCC experimented with lotteries to grant certain kinds of licenses, including low-power television. But it moved away from lotteries shortly thereafter. It continued to search for ways to deal with mutually exclusive applications but took no final action. Congress finally resolved the matter in the Balanced Budget Act of 1997, which required the FCC to use auctions to award licenses when there are mutually exclusive applications. In order to assure that licenses do not always go to the applicant with the deepest pockets, and to help diversify the ownership of broadcast media, the FCC provides what it calls "bidding credits" to applicants who own three or fewer existing media outlets. The credits allow applicants to bid more money for the license than they have. Since the auction process took effect in 1998, more than 1,160 broadcast frequencies have been licensed to applicants who could bid the most, adding nearly $345 million to the U.S. Treasury.

License Renewals

Both radio and TV station licenses are awarded for eight-year periods, after which the licenses must be renewed. The renewal application is much smaller and simpler than the application for the original license. Licensees who have engaged in serious misconduct during the license term may not have their licenses renewed, but the vast majority of license renewal applications are routinely granted.

The Telecommunications Act of 1996 requires the FCC to take a two-step approach to license renewal. First, it must decide whether to renew the current license holder, without con-

sidering whether the public interest would be better served by a different licensee. It must renew the license unless it finds that the incumbent broadcaster has not operated in the public interest, has committed serious violations of the Communications Act or FCC rules, or in any other way has shown a pattern of abusing the law or FCC regulations. The Commission also is to consider any comments submitted by the public to the station or the FCC about a licensee's performance. If it decides under these standards that a license should not be renewed, it then will move to the second step and put the license up for auction. While the Telecommunications Act of 1996 seems to ensure that most broadcast licenses will be renewed, the FCC still may refuse to renew a license on grounds that the station owner has not operated in the public interest.

Transferring Broadcast Licenses

A broadcast station's facilities — such as its transmitter, compact disc players, desks and trucks — belong to the station owner and can be sold to anyone at any time. But the facilities are useless without a license to broadcast. The license belongs to the federal government and is granted to a licensee for a specified period of time. If the licensee — the station owner — wants to sell the station, it is unlikely anyone would purchase it without also being able to use the station's license, and that requires asking the FCC to transfer the license. Generally, the FCC will transfer a license upon request if the new licensee meets the basic criteria.

Public Involvement in Licensing

It may seem obvious that, since the FCC's standard is the public interest, the public should have a voice in the decision-making process. It took a federal court decision, however, to require that the FCC allow public involvement.

In 1964, a nonprofit group accused TV station WLBT in Jackson, Mississippi, of selecting its programming based on racial bias. The FCC, presuming that it represented the public and, therefore, that the public need not be involved, would not allow the group to participate in the license renewal proceeding. But a federal appellate court held that members of the public had a right to be part of the process. On remand, the FCC renewed WLBT's license, but the Fourth U.S. Circuit Court of Appeals overturned that decision. The court said that when the public participates in FCC proceedings, it only has to draw the Commission's attention to pertinent issues; the public is not required to prove the charges are true. The Commission must investigate the claims, if it decides they have credence.

Since 1966, then, members of the public have been able to participate in licensing proceedings. The FCC may set certain limits, such as allowing participation only by groups representing listeners or viewers who actually will be affected by the FCC's action. The usual method of public participation is the filing of what is called a "petition to deny" the granting of a construction permit, license renewal, or transfer application. The Commission may reject the petition or attempt to gather additional information needed to make a decision on the complaint.

Another station may intervene in the process also, either because it believes its signal will be degraded if the FCC grants or renews a license, or because it claims it will suffer financially. But a claim that it will lose revenue is not sufficient grounds for denying or not renewing a license. The FCC is not required to protect other broadcasters' economic interests from competition.

Regulatory Fees

For seven decades, broadcasters paid essentially nothing to the federal government, which did not charge fees for licenses. The costs of obtaining a license were substantial, but they were for engineering studies and attorneys' fees to assist with the application process. Beginning in 1989, Congress authorized the FCC to impose and collect application processing fees. These fees, which range from around $5,000 for a new commercial TV station construction permit to $200 for a renewal application, go directly to the U.S. Treasury and are not available to the FCC. Beginning in 1993, in an effort to recover the FCC's costs, Congress required the Commission to collect additional regulatory fees. These fees range from several hundred dollars to more than $60,000 per year, depending on the type of service — AM, FM, TV — and the size of the market in which the station operates. These regulatory fees, which are set by Congress each fiscal year, cover nearly all of the agency's total costs.

Broadcast Networks

Many programs that broadcast television stations carry are, or once were, network shows. The same was true of radio from 1930 to 1952. A "network" distributes programs to stations, and the stations broadcast the programs. For example, NBC sends *The Tonight Show* to more than 200 stations throughout the country, all of which receive the program the same evening, although networks send programs at several different times to accommodate the country's different time zones. That makes NBC a commercial broadcast network, as are ABC, CBS, Fox, CW, and Univision, the nation's largest Spanish language network. Most of the stations receiving network programs are known as affiliates because they have contractual obligations to carry the programming the networks distribute. Some stations, however, are licensed to the networks and are known as "O & O's" — owned and operated by the networks.

The FCC licenses only broadcast stations. "Broadcasting" means sending a signal intended for general reception. The signals a network sends — *via* satellite today, formerly by a nationwide network of terrestrial microwave links — are meant only for the stations affiliated with the network, not for the general public. Therefore, networks do not broadcast and are not licensed by the FCC. Each of the major networks has licenses for several TV stations it owns and operates. So the FCC, which licenses the stations, has indirect control over the networks. Also, courts have allowed the FCC to set rules for the networks because of their contractual relations with the stations, over which the FCC does have jurisdiction.

STRUCTURAL REGULATION OF BROADCASTING

In order to fulfill its public interest goals without intruding on a licensee's programming discretion, the FCC often adopts rules regulating the structure of the broadcast industry. The rules, for example, set limits on the number of stations a company may own in a single market or restrict the kinds of businesses in which a licensee may engage.

The FCC long has acted on the assumption that the public interest is best served when many different licensees operate stations. Diverse ownership, it asserted, would lead to diverse viewpoints in programming and increased economic competition. For decades, the FCC has limited the number of stations, as well as other media outlets, a single owner can control.

The ownership restrictions were designed to prevent undue concentration of ownership at both the national and the local levels. The national rules first limited the number of stations that a company could own to seven AM, seven FM and seven TV (no more than five of which could be VHF stations). In the 1980s and 1990s, the FCC modified the national ownership limits several times, finally setting the limits at twenty AM, twenty FM and twelve TV stations. It also added a requirement for television group ownership: The stations could collectively cover no more than 25 percent of the nation's TV households. Another rule prohibited one company from controlling two television broadcast networks. Networks were also not allowed to own cable television systems.

At the local level, the anti-duopoly rule limited a licensee to one station of the same service in a market. (AM radio, FM radio and television each is a "service.") The rule barred an entity from owning both a commercial television station and a radio station in the same market (although this rule was often waived to permit such combinations). There were also cross-ownership restrictions: A company could not, for example, own a cable system and a broadcast station in the same local market.

Over the years, the FCC significantly amended these rules. Moreover, Congress sharply modified some ownership limits in the Telecommunications Act of 1996. The act further directed the FCC periodically to review whether the remaining ownership restrictions continued to serve the public interest.

Radio

Congress, in the 1996 Act, rescinded the national ownership limits for radio stations. Thus, one company may own as many stations throughout the country as it wants. Rules continue to restrict ownership within each local market. The limit depends on the number of stations in the market:

- In communities with up to fourteen radio stations, a licensee may have no more than five radio operations, no more than three of which may be AM or FM stations; and no single licensee may control more than half of the total radio stations in a market.
- In markets with fifteen to twenty-nine radio stations, one owner may control up to six radio stations, but no more than four AM or four FM stations.
- In communities with thirty to forty-four radio stations, one owner may control up to seven radio stations, but no more than four AM or four FM stations.
- In markets with forty-five or more radio stations, one owner may control up to eight radio stations, but no more than five AM or five FM stations.

The FCC's 2007 Order did not change these limitations, but the Commission amended its definition of "local radio markets" in an effort to make the rules more predictable and understandable.

Television

The 1996 Act removed all limits on the number of TV stations one company may own, but owners could not control stations collectively capable of reaching more than 35 percent of the country's households with television sets. The FCC was forced to review the 35 percent rule after the D.C. Circuit Court ordered it to justify whether keeping the rule continued to serve the public interest. The FCC then raised the coverage cap to 45 percent, finding that there was a need to retain some ownership limits but that increasing the limits would benefit the public by allowing large group owners, such as the broadcast networks, to expand their holdings and funnel increased revenues into expensive, high-quality programming. Congress subsequently amended this provision so that group-owned stations could cover no more than 39 percent of U.S. television households.

At the local level, an entity formerly was permitted to own two TV stations in the same market if (1) the "digital noise limited service contours" of the stations do not overlap or (2) at least one of the stations is not ranked among the top-four stations in the market and at least eight independently owned stations would remain in the market following the combination.

In 2017, however, the FCC eliminated the requirement that at least eight independently owned TV stations must remain in the market following the combination of two TV stations in a market. According to the Commission, eliminating the requirement will allow broadcasters, particularly in small and mid-sized markets, to realize the benefits of common ownership and to better serve their local communities.

The FCC also modified the prohibition against common ownership of two top-four rated stations in a local market. While retaining the underlying prohibition, it adopted an option for applicants to seek case-by-case review of a transaction in order to account for circumstances in which strict application of the Top-Four Prohibition may be unwarranted.

TV stations in the same market also now are permitted to enter into Joint Sales Agreements that involve the sale of more than 15 percent of the weekly advertising time of a station (brokered station) by another in-market station (brokering station), without having this be attributable under the Commission's ownership rules.

Media Cross Ownership

The FCC historically maintained two separate cross-ownership restrictions — one regulating the common ownership of radio and TV stations in the same market and the other regulating the common ownership of broadcast stations and newspapers in the same market: two TV stations and four radio stations in markets with ten additional voices. In 2017, the FCC eliminated as antiquated both the rules restricting radio-television cross-ownership and prohibiting newspaper-broadcast cross-ownership. The rules, according to the Commission, are outdated considering the explosive growth of the number and variety of sources of local news and information.

In 2021, the U.S. Supreme Court unanimously reversed a decision of the U.S. Court of Appeals for the Third Circuit that had vacated these deregulatory changes to the ownership rules. In *FCC v. Prometheus Radio Project*, the Court held that the FCC reasonably determined to eliminate the newspaper/broadcast cross-ownership rule and the radio/television cross-ownership rule and to relax the local television ownership rule.

This decision is the latest in an extensive litigation history concerning the FCC's media ownership rules. The Court recognized that these rules were "adopted ... in an early-cable and pre-Internet age when media sources were more limited," and remain subject to review by the FCC every four years under Section 202(h) of the Communications Act of 1934, as amended.

As the Court explained, in order "[t]o ensure that the FCC's ownership rules do not remain in place simply through inertia, Section 202(h) ... directs the FCC to review its ownership rules every four years to determine whether those rules remain 'necessary in the public interest as the result of competition.'" The FCC "'shall repeal or modify' any rules that it determines are 'no longer in the public interest.'" Section 202(h) "establishes an iterative process that requires the FCC to keep pace with industry developments and to regularly reassess how its rules function in the marketplace."

Despite "technological advances [that] challenged the traditional dominance of daily print newspapers, local radio stations, and local television stations," the FCC's media ownership rules remained largely intact due to successive decisions of the Third Circuit. Beginning in 2003, the same divided panel of the Third Circuit repeatedly struck down FCC attempts to provide regulatory relief to broadcasters and newspaper publishers, with the most recent decisions based on a view that the FCC needed to do more to establish that deregulatory rule changes would not harm minority and female ownership diversity.

The matter returned to the Third Circuit after the FCC decided to eliminate the newspaper/broadcast cross-ownership rule and the radio/television cross-ownership rule and to relax the local television ownership rule. The Commission determined that the rules at issue no longer serve the FCC's public interest goals of competition, localism and viewpoint diversity. It also found that altering these rules was not likely to harm minority and female ownership diversity based on available data and a lack of countervailing evidence. The Third Circuit , however, directed the agency to "ascertain on record evidence" the impact that any rule changes would have on minority and female ownership, "whether through new empirical research or an in-depth theoretical analysis."

The Supreme Court ruled that "[i]n analyzing whether to repeal or modify its existing ownership rules, the FCC considered the record evidence and reasonably concluded that the three ownership rules at issue were no longer necessary to serve the agency's public interest goals of competition, localism, and viewpoint diversity, and that the rule changes were not likely to harm minority and female ownership." Consequently, the Court strongly rejected arguments that the FCC needed to go to greater lengths to support its determination regarding minority and female ownership diversity, confirming that there is nothing Section 202(h) or any other statute that "requires the FCC to conduct its own empirical or statistical studies before exercising its discretion under Section 202(h)" to repeal or modify rules found to be no longer in the public interest.

In light of the Court's decision, the FCC's 2017 decision to eliminate the cross-ownership rules and the local television ownership rule's "eight voices" test and to replace a flat ban on

owning two top-four TV stations with a case-by-case review was reinstated. In addition, the television joint sales agreement attribution rule was eliminated under the same Court reasoning. The Court's decision, however, did not directly impact the 39 percent national television ownership cap or the local radio subcaps for AM and FM ownership. The subcaps limit the combination of AM or FM stations that a company can own in a radio market, based on a formula reflecting the number of competing stations in a particular market.

Broadcast Networks

At one time, broadcast networks could not own cable television systems, but Congress ordered the rescission of the rule in the Telecommunications Act of 1996. The dual network rule, which prohibits a company from owning two national television broadcast networks, still exists, but the FCC has interpreted the rule to prohibit only the merger of the four major commercial television networks: ABC, CBS, NBC and Fox.

REGULATION OF BROADCAST PROGRAMMING

The Communications Act forbids the FCC from censoring broadcast programming, but that has not prevented the FCC and Congress from adopting a number of regulations and laws affecting broadcast content. Some broadcasters argue that these limitations amount to censorship, but courts generally have allowed content requirements and restrictions.

Formats

While most TV stations offer a broad selection of programming, radio stations adopt formats with a relatively limited range of content. A radio station's format may be country-western music, adult-oriented albums, oldies or another sub-genre of rock, sports or news and talk. Listeners tune to a station because of its particular programming and may be upset if the station changes formats. This is particularly true if the format is unusual — jazz, classical music or children's programming, for example. Indeed, at one time courts told the FCC that the public interest requires the Commission to give approval, and to allow citizens' groups to have an opportunity to express their views, before a station could change a unique format.

Several years later, however, the Commission decided that stations should be able to choose their formats without FCC approval, based upon the rationale that market forces should determine the formats of the large number of stations on the air. The Supreme Court upheld that decision. Stations now may change formats at will, no longer needing FCC permission, the rationale being that if a sufficient number of listeners will support a station offering a particular format, a station in the market will respond to that consumer demand.

Fairness Doctrine

Broadcasters have argued that many rules and laws affecting programming conflict with their First Amendment rights, but the fairness doctrine particularly nettled them. The FCC developed the doctrine in a number of decisions beginning in 1949. It required broadcasters to inform audiences about controversial issues of public importance in the stations' license areas and to present contrasting viewpoints. This was to be done in overall programming, not necessarily through any individual program. The Supreme Court, in *Red Lion Broadcasting v. FCC*, effectively upheld the FCC's right (but not duty) to impose fairness requirements.

By the mid-1980s, however, the FCC began to question whether it needed the doctrine, since the number of broadcast and other outlets had grown significantly. The Commission also concluded that the doctrine in fact had a chilling effect on speech because broadcasters often avoided controversial issues altogether rather than open themselves to complaints about presenting contrasting viewpoints. For these reasons, the FCC rescinded the doctrine in 1987, a decision the courts upheld.

Indecent Programming

No electronic media may carry obscene material. The First Amendment protects obscenity on radio or television no more than in any other mass medium. In addition to possibly violating criminal laws, broadcasters who air obscene material are subject to stiff fines for not complying with FCC rules. Broadcasters, however, are also forbidden from airing "indecent or profane" programs, a restriction not placed on other media.

During broadcasting's first fifty years, no station was punished solely for airing indecent material. But in the 1970s, the face of radio was changing, and some stations allowed — indeed, encouraged — on-air personalities to discuss sexual topics in a joking way, often at times when children could be listening. Reacting to complaints from the public, the FCC fined some stations and stated that it expected such programming to stop, a decision the D.C. Circuit Court of Appeals upheld.

Then, in 1973, the FCC was faced with what it considered an egregious example of indecent material. During a weekday mid-afternoon, a father and son driving through New York City turned on the radio and heard on WBAI, an FM station licensed to the Pacifica Foundation, a portion of an album by comedian George Carlin. Recorded live, the twelve-minute routine was based on Carlin's list of seven words "you can't say on the public ... airwaves." The father complained to the FCC, and, after a

hearing, the Commission warned Pacifica that if it broadcast indecent programming again, the FCC could impose sanctions. Pacifica appealed, and the Supreme Court upheld the FCC.

In *FCC v. Pacifica*, the Court adopted the FCC's definition of indecent language as words that "describe, in terms patently offensive as measured by contemporary community standards for the broadcast medium, sexual or excretory activities and organs, at times of the day where there is reasonable risk that children may be in the audience." The Court recognized that the restriction on indecent programming limited broadcasters' speech rights but found it acceptable because (1) broadcasting is pervasive, and (2) the Carlin monologue was aired at a time children likely could be listening. Both points were important.

First, the Court assumed that people could be exposed to radio or television at any time, in any place, with little control over what they would hear or see. Because broadcasting differs in this regard from print media, which normally require a decision to purchase and a conscious effort to read, broadcasters' First Amendment rights could be narrowed. Second, since the primary concern was preventing children from being exposed to indecent programming, the FCC and Supreme Court did not hold that stations never could carry such material. Rather, they could not air indecent material when children were likely to hear or see it. Accordingly, the FCC has chosen 10 p.m. to 6 a.m. as a so-called "safe harbor" during which broadcasters are permitted to carry indecent programming.

Until a few years ago, most indecency fines were levied against radio stations, usually for broadcasts involving live shows that featured sexually graphic or suggestive discussions, expletives or lewd songs. In an effort to help the broadcast industry avoid violating the indecency rules, the FCC issued a Policy Statement in 2001 that listed the various factors the Commission uses to determine whether material is indecent.

Several notable events in 2003 and 2004 led both the FCC and Congress to reconsider the ways indecent and profane broadcasts are regulated. First came a string of high-profile violations involving radio shock jocks. One instance involved the "Opie and Anthony Show," during which descriptions of couples having sex in St. Patrick's Cathedral in New York City were aired live. Another involved a call-in show in which callers described in detail explicit sexual and excretory experiences. The incident most credited with provoking Congress, however, was the famous "costume malfunction" during the 2004 Super Bowl halftime show in which Janet Jackson's breast briefly was revealed, which the FCC subsequently ruled was indecent. In response to these and other violations and the resulting complaints from thousands of citizens, in 2006, Congress amended the Communications Act to raise the permissible penalty for airing indecent language from $32,500 to $325,000 per incident.

In another development, the FCC, in a departure from long-established practice, announced that it would begin to act against stations airing what the FCC called "fleeting expletives." The issue arose when Bono, while accepting a Golden Globe award on live television, said the award was "f***ing brilliant." After review, the FCC's Enforcement Bureau, citing precedent, declared that the one-time, fleeting use of the word — even though it was broadcast outside the safe harbor — was not indecent. The word was used as an adjective, not as a reference to sexual activity. Congress responded with resolutions condemning the decision. Several months later, the full Commission reversed the bureau's decision, finding the use of the word to be actionable and indicating that future use of such language outside the safe harbor will result in forfeitures.

Based on this decision, many television licensees declined to carry the award-winning World War II movie *Saving Private Ryan* due to the its strong language. Several stations did carry the program, and many complaints about the language were filed at the Commission. The FCC ruled that the program was not indecent because the language was integral to the film's objective of presenting the horror of war. However, when musicians used the same language in a critically acclaimed documentary on the blues, the FCC ruled the language was indecent. In 2006, the FCC declared that use of the word "shit" outside the safe harbor also was actionable and could lead to sanctions. However, it decided that use of the word "bullshitter" during *The Early Show* was not actionable because the word was said in the context of a *bona fide* news interview. Further complicating the matter, the FCC stated in the same proceeding that there is "no outright news exemption from our indecency rules."

The broadcast networks challenged several of the FCC actions in court, citing both procedural errors and First Amendment concerns. In 2010, the U.S. Court of Appeals for the Second Circuit ruled that the FCC's policy was unconstitutionally vague and created a chilling effect on protected speech. However, when the Supreme Court considered the case in 2012, it vacated the Second Circuit's First Amendment decision. In a very narrow ruling, the Court concluded that the FCC's specific sanctions in the cases being appealed violated the broadcasters' Fifth Amendment due process rights because the broadcasts occurred before the FCC's announced change in its indecency policy; the broadcasters accordingly had no notice that the broadcasts would be actionable. The Supreme Court declined to address the First Amendment issue, however.

The Court decision essentially leaves the FCC's indecency policies intact. However, in 2013, the FCC opened a proceeding seeking comment on whether to continue its current enforcement policies (the ones that led to all the recent litigation) or go back to its pre-fleeting expletive policy by focusing only on egregious cases. No decision had been made in the proceeding.

Children's Programming

For decades, Congress and the FCC have sparred with networks over children's programming. Early on, the battle involved excessive violence in shows children watched. Later, advocates for better children's programming convinced Congress that there simply were not enough shows that helped children learn about themselves and their world. Congress held a number of hearings and tried to convince network executives to pay more attention to the quality of children's programs.

Finally, in 1990, Congress adopted a law requiring stations to provide certain types of children's programs, which essentially meant that networks and syndicators would need to supply the shows. The statute also limited the amount of commercial time that could be inserted before, during and after children's programming on broadcast stations and cable networks.

The Children's Television Act requires stations to provide programming intended for children 16 years old or younger that will serve their "educational and information needs." The law also encourages stations to offer educational and information programming that is meant for families — adults, as well as children. Nature programming is an example. Additionally, the act suggests that broadcast television stations could show their concern about children's programming in other ways. They could air announcements for children's shows on public television, for example, or help pay for study guides for educational and information programs. The law did not specify how much programming aimed at children would be required for a station to be in compliance, but the voluntary activities could help convince the FCC that a station has met the requirements.

By the mid-1990s, several FCC commissioners and some members of Congress asserted that broadcasters were not fulfilling their responsibilities under the Children's Television Act. To give the law more teeth, in 1996, the FCC adopted rules making it clear what TV stations must do. They are to broadcast three hours per week of programs designed to serve children's intellectual/cognitive and social/emotional needs. Programs are required to be at least thirty minutes long, regularly scheduled on a weekly basis and broadcast between 7 a.m. and 10 p.m. The rules establish what is termed "core programming," and stations' compliance with the rules is considered at license renewal. For broadcasters that multicast (provide more than one simultaneous program stream), three additional hours of programming are required for every full-time free program stream. Program streams broadcast less than full time are required to provide children's programming on a pro rata basis.

A TV station that does not broadcast quite three hours of core programming can still have its license renewed by airing public service announcements, programs fewer than thirty minutes in length and programs not scheduled weekly — all of which are designed to meet children's intellectual and emotional needs and which the station persuades the FCC are equivalent to meeting the three-hour requirement. Stations not coming within either of these categories will have to convince the FCC that they deserve to have their licenses renewed.

While the programming requirements apply to commercial broadcast stations and not to cable television networks, the Children's Television Act has commercial limits that apply to both. It restricts advertising time before, during and after programming directed at children 12 years old and younger. Commercials are limited to twelve minutes per hour during the week and ten and one-half minutes per hour on Saturdays and Sundays. These limits are prorated; a half-hour program may carry only six minutes of commercials on Thursday afternoon, for example. The FCC also has ruled that characters in children's programs may not appear in commercials before, during or after the programs. In 2004, it added rules to deal with special considerations relating to children's Web sites. Television programs that target children 12 and younger may not display Web addresses that lead children to commercial sites that include e-commerce or advertising. Only sites that contain primarily program related and other noncommercial content may be listed in children's programs.

V-Chip and Television Program Ratings

In the 1990s, rumblings from the public and politicians about the perceived amount of violence and sex on television rose to a roar. Congress addressed the complaints in the Telecommunications Act of 1996, which required that, beginning in 1998, all television sets sold in the United States include a means for viewers to prevent certain programs from being seen on the sets. A microprocessor chip — called a "v-chip" — within the set picks up an electronic signal embedded within certain television programs. The signal indicates the program's rating. The v-chip in a set may be instructed to prevent programs rated for mature audiences, for example, from being seen on that set.

In conjunction with the v-chip, Congress mandated the development of a voluntary rating system for TV programs. There are two sets of parental guidelines, as the ratings are known. One category applies to programs designed solely for children: TV-Y means a program is appropriate for all children; TV-Y7 means a program is designed for children aged seven and above. The second rating category applies to programs designed for the entire audience: TV-G means that most parents would find the program suitable for all ages; TV-PG means the program contains material that parents may find unsuitable for younger children; TV-14 means it contains some material that parents may find unsuitable for children younger than 14; TV-MA means a program is specifically designed for an adult audience

and is, therefore, unsuitable for children younger than 17. Additionally, the ratings include letters that identify various types of content: "V" stands for violence, "FV" for fantasy violence, "S" for sexual material, "L" for strong language, and "D" for suggestive dialogue. Sports and news programs are not rated.

While the law does not require a rating to be applied to any individual program, once a program is rated, the rating must be embedded in the signal carrying the show. In 2000, the FCC released a survey indicating that all the broadcast television networks and most of the basic cable television networks were encoding their programming.

Responding to public concern about the coarsening of TV content, several members of Congress asked the FCC to study television violence and its impact on children. The Commission began its inquiry in 2004 and issued its report to Congress in 2007. The report agreed with many commenters that there is strong evidence that exposure to violence in the media can increase aggressive behavior in children, but that existing devices for shielding children from such programming, such as the v-chip, are not effective. Consequently, the FCC recommended that Congress pass legislation requiring broadcasters to channel violent programming to time periods when children are less likely to be in the audience, much like the regulations that currently apply to indecent and profane programming. Congress has not formally reacted to the FCC's proposal.

Political Broadcasting

Under Section 315 of the Communications Act, once a legally qualified candidate for an elective office has used a broadcast station — has been given or sold time — all other legally qualified candidates for the same office must be given equal opportunities. That is, candidates for the same office have the right to approximately the same amount of time during a period of the day when they are likely to be seen or heard by the same size and type of audience. Section 315 applies to candidates running for all types of elective office — local, state or federal.

While the FCC has held, essentially, that the public interest requires candidates to be given access to broadcast stations, Congress made certain of that for those running for federal offices. Section 312(a)(7) of the Communications Act requires broadcast stations to give federal candidates "reasonable access" to radio and television audiences. The term "reasonable access" is interpreted liberally. In 1980, the Carter-Mondale Committee asked ABC, CBS and NBC to sell it thirty minutes of time. The networks refused, and the Supreme Court upheld the FCC's decision that the refusal violated section 312(a)(7). The Commission also has stated that "reasonable access" does not mean free time for federal candidates; stations may charge candidates for air time, a ruling also upheld in federal court.

Section 312(a)(7) guarantees that a candidate for federal office cannot be denied time on broadcast stations. Otherwise, federal candidates are subject to the provisions of Section 315, just as are candidates for non-federal offices.

A point of contention between broadcasters and candidates for federal office has been the length of political ads. Broadcasters usually sell time to commercial advertisers in thirty- and sixty-second slots. But some candidates have sought to buy five-minute time slots in order to present a more detailed message. Consequently, the FCC issued an order stating that candidates may not be barred from purchasing advertising time in lengths most useful for their purposes simply because broadcasters traditionally sell time in thirty- and sixty-second slots.

Legally Qualified Candidate. A legally qualified candidate is one who has announced publicly that he or she is running for an elective office. This means more than telling a few friends. The person must have made a widely disseminated statement. Second, the person must meet qualifications for the office — age or residency, for example. Third, the person must either (a) have qualified for a place on the ballot, usually by having a sufficient number of registered voters sign a nominating petition or being nominated by a political party, or (b) be a publicly committed write-in candidate. Independent candidates can be legally qualified, and even candidates with no reasonable chance of winning the election can insist upon equal opportunities.

A candidate claiming equal opportunity in reaction to another's appearance must be running for the same office. Clearly, two candidates seeking the mayor's seat or two seeking a Senate seat are running for the same office. But other scenarios are not so clear. Assume two Republicans are running in a primary election for mayor, as are two Democrats. A Republican buys a minute of time on a radio station, and one of the Democrats insists on a similar purchase. Under Section 315, the station need not sell time to the Democrat. The FCC has ruled that the Democrat and Republican are not running for the same office: The Democrat is running for the Democratic nomination, and the Republican for the Republican nomination. If both candidates were to win their primary races and face each other in the general election, they would be running for the same office, and so would any third-party or independent candidates for that office.

A station could avoid all these problems by not selling advertising time to any candidates for state and local offices under Section 315, although the FCC has indicated it would frown on such action. But the requirement under Section 312(a)(7) that broadcast stations offer reasonable access for federal candidates essentially means that a station must sell time to even the first candidate for a federal office asking to run an advertisement.

Use. "Using" a station, which triggers Section 315 for competing candidates, happens when a candidate or the candidate's picture or identifiable voice appears on the air. This can be a campaign commercial, or it can be an appearance on a station's cooking show with no mention of the election. There is no use if the appearance is disparaging, which would occur, for example, if an opponent used the candidate's picture in a belittling way.

In 1959, Congress amended Section 315 by specifying four news exemptions to the use rule. In these instances, even if a candidate's voice or picture is used on the air, Section 315 does not apply because there has been no use under the law. Congress' intent was to be certain that Section 315 did not artificially limit news coverage of political campaigns and candidates. The exemptions are:

(1) On-the-spot coverage of a news event will not trigger Section 315. The FCC and courts have ruled that press conferences and speeches by candidates generally will be considered news events, and coverage of them will not constitute a use. Similarly, debates among candidates are news events and, therefore, exempted from Section 315 regardless of who sponsors them – the candidates, broadcasters or a nonpartisan group. The FCC and the courts have said that it is not required that all candidates for an office be included in a debate, and those who are excluded cannot claim time under Section 315. In 1998, the Supreme Court said that even state-owned public television stations may exclude minor political candidates from on-air debates. The 6-3 opinion held that public stations could exercise their journalistic discretion as long as the exclusion of minority candidates was not based on the candidate's views. In 1996, the FCC allowed ABC, Fox and the Public Broadcasting Service to provide free debate time for the major party presidential candidates. It held that the candidates' appearances would be exempt from the equal opportunities requirement of Section 315 as coverage of a bona fide news event.

(2) An appearance on a regularly scheduled newscast is not considered a use. The appearance could be an interview with a candidate, coverage of a candidate's campaign or other such activities. Courts have interpreted this exception broadly. Candidates appearing on *Face the Nation*, for example, a television program featuring discussions among panelists as well as presentations of news events, are considered to be involved in news coverage, even though the appearance was not in a typical newscast. The FCC does not interpret the broadcast exemption broadly in relation to on-air personalities who are running for office. While it may seem, for example, that a news program anchor who is a political candidate would come under the newscast exemption, the FCC has held otherwise. Congress recognized that the broadcasting of news about candidates for public office is important to viewers, so it amended Section 315 to exclude appearances by candidates in newscasts. Appearing in a news story, however, and appearing on a news program as a re-

porter or anchor are not the same. A person presenting the news does not help the public learn more about the campaign; it simply gives the candidate an unfair opportunity to become known. Therefore, an anchor on a Sacramento station who was a candidate for town council in a nearby community had to choose between being on the air or being a candidate during the campaign period. Had he been both, the station would have been required to offer more than thirty hours of free time to other candidates for the same office to comply with the requirements of Section 315.

(3) A candidate's appearance on a regularly scheduled news interview program is not a use and does not trigger Section 315. Interview programs such as *Meet the Press* and *Face the Nation* are exempt. The FCC has extended the definition of a "news interview program" to include *The Today Show*, *Entertainment Tonight* and similar programs. Even interview segments of call-in talk shows can be exempt. To fall under the exemption, the program must have been regularly scheduled beginning well before the election period, and the station must control the content, format and guests.

(4) A candidate's appearance on a news documentary program is not a use if the appearance is incidental to the campaign. For example, a water engineer running for governor could be in a documentary about water conservation in the state. But a documentary about the political views of a mayoral candidate would not qualify under the exemption.

Application of Section 315. Section 315 applies whenever there are two or more legally qualified candidates for the same elective office. That may be only a short time before an election, or months prior to an election.

Requesting Time and Public File Requirements. Under Section 315, a candidate whose opponent has used a broadcast station must ask for equal opportunity. Candidates must make requests for time within seven days of the appearance that triggered Section 315. The station has no obligation to notify candidates of prior uses. Stations, though, must keep public files with information about candidates who have appeared and those who have requested time.

Lowest Unit Rate. Section 315 provides that candidates purchasing time for political commercials must be charged no more than the station's most favored advertiser would pay. That is, whatever the rate would be for the advertiser who purchases the most minutes during the year on a station is the rate a candidate would be charged. This is true even if that minute is the only time the candidate will purchase during the entire campaign. But if the appearance triggering Section 315 was free to the first candidate — for example, a candidate appears on a lo-

cal children's program only to read a story aloud — opponents may demand equivalent free time.

The lowest-unit-rate provision takes effect forty-five days before a primary election and sixty days before a general or special election. Outside those periods, stations may charge candidates what any other advertiser would be charged (not just their best advertiser) for comparable advertising time.

Content of Political Commercials. Broadcast stations cannot edit political advertisements, nor can they refuse to run a candidate's commercial because they believe the message will offend an audience. At the same time, stations are not liable for anything said or shown in political commercials. Broadcasters cannot be sued for libel, invasion of privacy or any other tort based on material in a candidate's presentation under Section 315.

The general rule that political ads may not be censored was severely tested in the 1990s when some candidates chose to show aborted fetuses as part of their commercials. A Georgia candidate for the U.S. House of Representatives included in a commercial depictions of "the actual surgical procedure for abortion ... [including] graphic depictions and descriptions of female genitalia, the uterus, excreted uterine fluid, dismembered fetal body parts, and aborted fetuses." The FCC held that while such commercials are not indecent, TV stations may decide to carry such advertisements only in the safe harbor hours used for indecent programming if they find that the commercials could be harmful to children. But a federal appellate court found that this would permit "broadcasters to take the content of a political advertisement into account" in determining whether to confine the commercial to the safe harbor period, allowing broadcasters "standardless discretion." The court said that, on balance, candidates' rights as specified in sections 315 and 312(a)(7) of the Communications Act took precedence over concerns about children being exposed to possibly offensive material.

Ballot Issues. Section 315 applies only to candidates for public offices and not to ballot issues. Supporters and opponents of such issues may purchase broadcast time if they wish, but there is no requirement that such time be sold or that equal opportunities be provided.

Other Programming Requirements

The FCC has imposed on broadcasters several other rules affecting program content. When those rules have been challenged as violating broadcasters' First Amendment rights, courts have generally upheld them.

Lotteries. A lottery is a contest that has a prize of more than token value, uses chance rather than skill to determine winners, and requires some form of consideration — like the purchase of a ticket — to enter. FCC rules and federal criminal laws have long restricted the information broadcasters may carry about lotteries. The exception has been state-run lotteries in states where the stations are located.

Congress changed all that in 1988. Broadcasters may carry information about certain lotteries. As before, they can provide facts about state lotteries if the station is located in a state that has a lottery. They may also carry news or advertisements for gaming conducted by Native American tribes. And they may provide information about a lottery legal in the state where it is conducted and that a governmental or nonprofit organization offers or is sponsored by a person or company not primarily in the business of sponsoring lotteries. Thus, reports or advertisements for bingo games at churches or a cereal company giving away an automobile are acceptable if state law permits. But until recently, stations could not carry information or advertisements for private (non-Native American) gambling casinos or sports betting. In 1999, the Supreme Court unanimously struck down the ban on television and radio advertising of private casino gambling in states where such gambling is legal, finding that the ban was "so pierced by exemptions and inconsistencies that the government cannot hope to exonerate it."

Sponsorship Identification. Broadcasters must identify clearly any individual or group providing money, or anything else of value, in return for the dissemination of a message. The purpose of the rule is to ensure that viewers and listeners will not confuse paid advertising with entertainment or news programs. If the sponsor is obvious — a cereal, a laundry detergent, a fast food restaurant — the requirement is met. Other messages are not so clearly identifiable. If, for example, a local company provides funds for a "Clean Up The Parks" ad campaign, the ads must carry the company's name as a sponsor.

Hoaxes and News Distortion. The FCC prohibits the broadcasting of hoaxes. Under the regulation, a hoax occurs when a station knowingly broadcasts false reports of crimes or catastrophes that "directly cause foreseeable — immediate, substantial and actual public harm."

WALE-AM radio in Providence, Rhode Island, perpetuated a hoax in 1991 when the news director announced over the air that a WALE talk show host had been shot in the head while outside the station's studio. About ten minutes later, the station stated that the shooting had been a dramatization. Before the second announcement, several police officers and several members of the media rushed to the scene. WALE apologized and offered to repay the Providence Police Department for any costs resulting from the hoax. The FCC admonished the station's owner, citing the Commission's policy "requiring licensees to

program their stations in the public interest."

The FCC also has a policy against news distortion. One example of distortion occurred when a Chicago TV station had a group of people stage a gathering at which marijuana was smoked in order to film a "pot party." The FCC expressed its concern about manufacturing news but did not threaten action against the station. In another instance, the CBS documentary *Hunger in America* showed a child said to be suffering from malnutrition but who was afflicted with a different illness. The FCC took no action against CBS but used the case to establish a policy forbidding intentional news distortion. The Commission, however, distinguishes deliberate distortion from a mistake or negligent reporting.

Cigarette and Alcohol Advertising. Concerned with the costs to public health that cigarette smoking causes, Congress made it "unlawful to advertise cigarettes on any medium of electronic communication" starting in 1971. The law was upheld despite a challenge based on broadcasters' First Amendment rights. Contrary to popular belief, the advertising of alcoholic beverages on broadcast stations has never been illegal (at least since the end of Prohibition), though the distilled spirits industry voluntarily declined to purchase broadcast ads for many years. This voluntary ad ban was abandoned in the 1990s.

Disclosure of Advertising by Foreign Governments. The FCC requires broadcasters to disclose when foreign governments or their representatives lease time on their airwaves.

Although U.S. law restricts foreign governments and their representatives from holding a broadcast license directly, foreign governmental entities can and do purchase time on domestic broadcast stations. These rules require on-air disclosure for broadcast programming aired through a leased airtime agreement sponsored by any entity or individual that is a foreign government, a foreign political party, an agent acting on behalf of such entities, or a U.S.-based foreign media outlet based on definitions drawn from the Foreign Agents Registration Act of 1938 and the Communications Act of 1934, as amended.

In addition, if a station is airing foreign government-provided programming pursuant to a lease agreement, it is required to include such disclosures in its Online Public Inspection File.

NONCOMMERCIAL BROADCASTING

Certain parts of the broadcast spectrum are set aside for use by noncommercial stations. Radio broadcasters were using the AM band before any government agency could consider whether to reserve frequency assignments for noncommercial uses. The FCC, however, was able to set aside portions of the FM band and reserve certain television frequencies for nonprofit organizations, usually educational institutions and state governments, but also religious groups. It recognized that some educational institutions might be tempted to sell their stations to commercial broadcasters, in part because of the high costs of keeping a station on the air, unless certain frequencies were reserved only for nonprofit, educational use.

In 1967, Congress aided noncommercial broadcasting by adopting the Public Broadcasting Act, which established the Corporation for Public Broadcasting, an agency through which government and other funding is used to produce programming for noncommercial stations. The FCC has no jurisdiction to enforce any provisions of the Public Broadcasting Act, such as that requiring "strict adherence to objectivity and balance in all programs or series of programs of a controversial nature."

One section of the act insisting on objectivity and another forbidding noncommercial stations from supporting political candidates raise questions of First Amendment protection for public stations. The Supreme Court rejected the provision forbidding public stations from supporting political candidates and the Public Broadcasting Act's ban on noncommercial stations editorializing. It said that First Amendment protection of journalistic freedom also should apply to public stations.

Most public broadcast stations receive federal and possibly state funds, and government agencies own many of them. The tension between the public nature of noncommercial stations and First Amendment freedoms was reflected in the *Death of a Princess* case. The docudrama, intended for showing on public TV, portrayed the execution in Saudi Arabia of a woman and her lover accused of adultery. The government of Saudi Arabia objected strongly to it, and several public television stations decided not to carry it. Viewers took government-owned stations in Alabama and Houston, Texas, to court, hoping to force them to broadcast the program. In part, the suits claimed that the public stations were arms of the government and were engaging in censorship, as well as violating viewers' First Amendment rights. A federal appellate court found that, as licensees under the Communications Act, the stations were permitted to use their editorial judgment in selecting what programs to carry.

Most of the regulations that apply to commercial broadcast stations also apply to noncommercial stations, but there are several differences. In comparative licensing situations, for example, Congress has forbidden the use of auctions in awarding noncommercial licenses. Accordingly, the FCC has developed a point system that compares criteria such as local diversity and technical superiority. Another regulatory difference relates to multiple- and cross-ownership limitations, which do not apply to noncommercial licensees. Finally, as the name implies, noncommercial stations are not permitted to carry advertisements. However, they are permitted to acknowledge entities that contribute money to the station or underwrite programming. These underwriting announcements differ from commercial advertising in that they contain no qualitative statements about the underwriter's products or services, they cannot make comparisons among products, they cannot provide price information, and there can be no calls to action or inducements to purchase.

THE MOVE TO DIGITAL

Following almost ten years of study and testing, the FCC, in consultation with various industry groups, adopted a new digital television transmission standard in 1996. The new standard, which allows for transmission of multiple program streams as well as high-definition television, replaced the analog transmission standard that broadcasters used since the 1940s. The Commission initially proposed a ten-year transition period during which broadcasters and consumers would replace their incompatible analog transmission and receiving equipment with new digital equipment. Every full-power television broadcaster was given a second six-megahertz channel on which to broadcast its digital signal. During the transition, all broadcasters sent out two signals, the old analog signal and the new digital signal. At the end of the transition period, which Congress extended to 2009, all full-power television broadcasters ended their analog transmissions and broadcast solely using their digital signals. The spectrum no longer being used for analog broadcasting was auctioned for other uses. The auction, which was held in 2008, netted the government nearly $20 billion.

The transition to digital broadcasting for terrestrial radio has been much simpler than the television transition. For radio, the FCC has approved a digital transmission system that allows stations to provide both analog and digital signals on the same frequency simultaneously. Accordingly, this system, known as "In-Band On-Channel," does not require the allocation of additional frequencies. Digital radio, currently marketed as "HD Radio," provides much higher quality signals plus the ability to broadcast more than one program stream at the same time.

In 2017, the FCC adopted new rules to let television broadcasters use the Next Generation broadcast television transmission standard, also called ATSC 3.0, on a voluntary, market-driven basis.

The Next Generation TV standard will let broadcasters provide consumers with more vivid pictures and sound, including Ultra High Definition television and superior reception, mobile viewing capabilities, advanced emergency alerts, better accessibility features, localized content, and interactive educational children's content.

The upgraded technology will merge the capabilities of over-the-air broadcasting with the broadband viewing and information delivery methods of the Internet using the same 6 MHz channels presently allocated for digital television.

Broadcasters electing to use Next Generation TV are required to partner with another local station in the same market to simulcast programming in the current DTV standard so that viewers can continue to receive their existing broadcast service without having to purchase new equipment. Next Gen TV signals also are subject to the public interest obligations that currently apply to television broadcasters.

EQUAL EMPLOYMENT OPPORTUNITIES

The FCC, in conjunction with the Equal Employment Opportunity Commission, a federal agency established in 1964, requires that broadcasters not discriminate in hiring, promoting or firing on the basis of race, gender, religion, color or national origin. While the EEOC is expected to notify the FCC of any discrimination complaints filed against broadcast licensees, the FCC also enforces its own equal employment rules.

These regulations require licensees to widely disseminate information concerning full-time job vacancies, provide notice of full-time job vacancies to recruitment organizations, and complete a series of longer-term recruitment initiatives — such as job fairs, internships and mentoring programs — over a two-year period.

SUMMARY

The broadcast media play an integral role in the dissemination of news and information, but the Supreme Court has said that of all forms of mass media, broadcasting has the least protection under the First Amendment. In other words, as long as the FCC issues licenses, broadcasters are required to serve the public interest, which subjects them to more regulation than other mass media. That is, of course, unless the Supreme Court reverses itself and rules that all media are entitled to the same rights under the First Amendment.

As new technologies emerge, will the FCC or the courts eventually change the definition of "scarcity"? Forecasting the answers to these questions is not easy, but at some point — given the continuing expansion of available information and entertainment choices for the public — the regulatory scheme under which broadcasting operates may well change.

Until then, however, it will continue issuing licenses, reviewing the transfer of licenses, making spectrum allocations, settling controversies among competing parties, issuing fines, and developing policies that will affect the broadcast media as well as other communication technologies. But the FCC will not be doing all of this on its own. Regardless of whether its powers are changed or limited in any way, the FCC will always operate under the watchful eye of Congress and the courts.

BIBLIOGRAPHY

Articles

Fowler, Mark & Daniel Brenner. "A Marketplace Approach to Broadcast Regulation," 60 *Texas Law Review* 207 (January 1982).

Hopkins, W. Wat. "When Does F*** Not Mean F***? FCC v. Fox Television Stations and a Call for Protecting Emotive Speech," 64 *Federal Communications Law Journal* 1 (December 2011).

Books

Brotman, Stuart N. *The First Amendment Lives On: Conversations Commemorating Hugh M. Hefner's Legacy of Enduring Free Speech and Free Press Values.* Columbia, Mo.: University of Missouri Press, 2022.

Einstein, Mara. *Media Diversity: Economics, Ownership, and the FCC.* Mahwah, N.J.: Lawrence Erlbaum Associates, 2004.

Kahn, Frank J. *Documents of American Broadcasting*, 4th ed. New York: Pearson, 1984.

Lipschultz, Jeremy H. *Broadcast Indecency: F.C.C., Regulation and the First Amendment.* Boston: Focal Press, 1996.

McCall, Jeffrey. *Viewer Discretion Advised: Taking Control of Mass Media Influences.* New York: Rowman & Littlefield Publishers, 2007.

Minow, Newton N. & Craig L. LaMay. *Abandoned in the Wasteland: Children, Television, and the First Amendment.* New York: Hill and Wang, 1995.

Powe, Lucas A., Jr. *American Broadcasting and the First Amendment.* Berkeley, Calif.: University of California Press, 1987.

Tillinghast, Charles H. *American Broadcast Regulation and the First Amendment: Another Look.* Ames: Iowa State University Press, 2000.

Cases

Accuracy in Media, Inc. v. FCC, 521 F.2d 288 (D.C. Cir. 1975).

American Family Association v. FCC, 365 F.3d 1156 (D.C. Cir. 2004).

Arkansas AFL-CIO v. FCC, 11 F.3d 1430 (8th Cir. 1993).

Arkansas Educational Television Commission v. Forbes, 523 U.S. 666 (1998).

Banzhaf v. FCC, 405 F.2d 1082 (D.C. Cir. 1968).

Barnstone v. University of Houston, KUHT-TV, 487 F. Supp. 1347 (S.D. Tex. 1980).

Bechtel v. FCC, 10 F.3d 875 (D.C. Cir. 1993).

Becker v. FCC, 95 F.3d 75 (D.C. Cir. 1996).

Branch v. FCC, 824 F.2d 37 (D.C. Cir. 1987).

Capital Broadcasting Co. v. Mitchell, 333 F. Supp. 582 (D.C. 1971).

CBS Corp. v. FCC, 535 F.3d 167 (3d Cir. 2008).

CBS Corp. v. FCC, 663 F.3d 122 (3d Cir. 2011).

CBS, Inc. v. FCC, 453 U.S. 367 (1981).

Citizens Committee to Preserve the Voice of the Arts in Atlanta v. FCC, 436 F.2d 263 (D.C. Cir. 1970).

Citizens Committee to Save WEFM v. FCC, 506 F.2d 246 (D.C. Cir. 1973).

Columbia Broadcasting System v. Democratic National Committee, 412 U.S. 94 (1973).

Contemporary Media, Inc. v. FCC, 214 F.3d 187 (D.C. Cir. 2000).

Farmers Educational & Cooperative Union of America v. WDAY, 360 U.S. 525 (1959).

FCC v. CBS Corp., 556 U.S. 1213 (2009).

FCC v. Fox Television Stations, Inc., 556 U.S. 502 (2009).

FCC v. Fox Television Stations, Inc., 567 U.S. 239 (2012)

FCC v. League of Women Voters, 468 U.S. 364 (1984).

FCC v. Pacifica Foundation, 438 U.S. 726, 748 (1978).

FCC v. Prometheus Radio Project, 141 S. Ct. 1150 (2021).

Federal Radio Commission v. Nelson Brothers, 289 U.S. 266 (1933).

Fox Television Stations v. FCC, 280 F.3d. 1027 (D.C. Cir. 2002).

Gillette Communications of Atlanta v. Becker, 807 F. Supp. 757, 763 (N.D. Ga. 1992).

Great Lakes Broadcasting Co. v. F.R.C. 37 F.2d 993 (D.C. Cir. 1930).

Greater New Orleans Broadcasting Association v. United States, 527 U.S. 173 (1999).

Henry v. FCC, 302 F.2d 191 (D.C. Cir. 1962).

Hoover v. Intercity Radio Co., 286 F. 1002 (D.C. Cir. 1923).

Illinois Citizens Committee for Broadcasting v. FCC, 515 F.2d 397 (D.C. Cir. 1974).

Johnson v. FCC, 829 F.2d 157 (D.C. Cir. 1987).

Joseph Burstyn, Inc. v. Wilson, 343 U.S. 495 (1952).

Kennedy for President Committee v. FCC, 636 F.2d 417 (D.C. Cir. 1980).

KFKB Broad. Association v. Federal Radio Commission, 47 F.2d 670 (D.C. Cir. 1931).

Miami Herald Publishing Co. v. Tornillo, 418 U.S. 241 (1974).

Muir v. Alabama Educational Television Commission, 688 F.2d 1033 (5th Cir. 1982) (*en banc*).

Mutual Film Corp. v. Industrial Commission of Ohio, 236 U.S. 230 (1915).

National Broadcasting Co. v. FCC, 319 U.S. 190, 213 (1943).

Near v. Minnesota, 283 U.S. 697 (1931).

Office of Communication of the United Church of Christ v. FCC, 707 F.2d 1413 (D.C. Cir. 1983).

Office of Communication of the United Church of Christ v. FCC, 359 F.2d 994 (D.C. Cir. 1966).

FCC, 824 F.3d 33 (3d Cir. 2016).

Red Lion Broadcasting Co. v. FCC, 395 U.S. 367 (1969).

Robinson v. American Broadcasting Co., 441 F.2d 1396 (6th Cir. 1971).

Robinson v. FCC, 334 F.2d 534 (D.C. Cir. 1964).

Sanders Brothers v. FCC, 309 U.S. 470 (1940).

Syracuse Peace Council v. FCC, 867 F.2d 654 (D.C. Cir. 1989).

Trinity Methodist Church, South v. Federal Radio Commission, 62 F.2d 850 (D.C. Cir. 1932).

United States v. Zenith Radio Corp., 12 F.2d 614 (N.D. Ill. 1926).

WNCN Listener's Guild, 450 U.S. 582 (1981).

11

Regulating Cable Communication

By Matt Jackson

☑ **Headnote Questions**

- What is the legal history of cable television?
- What are the rationales for the government's regulation of the cable industry?
- What level of First Amendment protection does cable enjoy?
- Why do courts allow more stringent governmental structural regulations on cable than on the print media?
- What kinds of regulations are designed to protect each of the various cable-related interest groups — broadcasters, programmers, Internet content providers, competitors, consumers?

Cable is one of the primary communication pathways into the home, providing most Americans with their television programming, broadband (high speed) Internet access, and sometimes their telephone service as well. Cable operators dominated the television industry in the late twentieth century and early part of the twenty-first century but providing high speed internet service has become their primary business since 2014. As broadband (high speed) Internet access becomes ubiquitous, millions of households have canceled their cable service in favor of myriad streaming options. According to the Internet and Television Association, thirty-nine million households subscribed to cable pay television service in the United States in 2022. Cable companies also provided high speed broadband Internet service to eighty-two million households, landline telephone service to twenty-one million households and mobile telephone service to ten million customers.

While cable is still the dominant wired distribution technology for high speed Internet service and subscription television, its pay-TV dominance is steadily eroding. Over the last twenty-five years, cable has lost a significant number of pay-TV subscribers; first to direct broadcast satellite competitors, then to telephone companies, and most recently to streaming services. Cable subscriptions peaked in 2000 at sixty-eight million households, compared to thirty-nine million households in 2022. The "cord-cutting" trend continues to accelerate. Almost six million households canceled their cable television service in 2022, a 6 percent drop in subscribers. Comcast, the country's largest cable company, lost almost two million subscribers in 2022. As dis-

cussed later, this decline in cable subscriptions has led to a loss of revenue for local and state franchise authorities, which typically collect a five percent tax on cable service.

Broadband (high-speed) Internet access has become the primary product sold by cable companies. With eighty-two million broadband customers, the industry now has more than twice as many broadband subscribers as pay-TV subscribers. Almost 75 percent of American households rely on a cable company for their residential Internet access. It should be noted that most consumers also get Internet access through their mobile telephone provider. Cable companies have begun to compete with these incumbent wireless providers, with ten million Americans now getting their mobile phone service through their cable company.

Given its size and central role in our culture since the 1970s, it is no surprise that the cable industry has drawn the attention of regulators, politicians and consumer advocates. Cable originally was regulated because it posed a threat to over-the-air broadcasting. Regulators were concerned that cable would siphon away the audience for local TV stations. Cable regulations then evolved in response to concerns about monopoly power, since initially just one cable operator served each local market. Today, regulators are trying to foster competition between the cable, satellite, telephone, broadcast and Internet industries to make sure consumers have adequate choices for television, telephone and Internet service and a wide range of diverse viewpoints.

Government regulators try to protect consumers and preserve

competition in all large industries, but cable, broadcasting and other forms of telecommunications receive special attention because of their central role in transmitting speech. Policymakers recognize that these media are important to the proper functioning of democracy. Comcast, Charter Communications and a handful of similar large corporations control the communications infrastructure that citizens rely on for information and political participation. So, in addition to normal concerns regarding competition, cable regulation also is based on free speech principles and a desire to foster a marketplace of ideas. But regulators must avoid violating the First Amendment rights of cable operators in their attempt to promote the First Amendment rights of others.

The Constitution was written long before the invention of the electronic communication technologies that dominate our world today, so it is not always clear how the First Amendment should be applied to a new technology. The U.S. Supreme Court has recognized that the unique traits of each mass medium permit different constitutional standards. However, the most important characteristics of a new technology often are not apparent until after the public has adopted it.

Convergence of the media industries also creates problems for policymakers. Originally, cable merely provided video programming. Today, cable operators offer Internet access, telephone service, interactive TV and other new services. As the distinctions between cable companies, telephone companies and broadcasters blur, their different regulatory schemes come into conflict. For example, phone companies have to share their wires with competing phone companies. Now that cable companies offer telephone and Internet service, should they have to share their cable wires as well? As another example, your telephone provider is not allowed to alter or interrupt the information transmitted during a phone call. Should Internet access providers also be prohibited from interfering with the content that consumers try to view online?

For First Amendment purposes, cable regulations can be classified broadly as either structural or content-based. Most content-based cable regulation is similar to content-based regulation of broadcasting and print. For example, the standards for defamation and invasion of privacy apply to cable the same way they apply to other media. Content-based cable regulations usually must pass strict scrutiny in order to be constitutional.

The structural regulation of cable is grounded in modern economic theory. As a general rule, economists believe companies behave best when faced with competition. Competition leads to efficient use of resources, a wide range of choices for consumers, and continual product innovation. When there is little or no competition, companies with market power can take advantage of consumers, suppliers and would-be competitors. Antitrust law, which is applied to all industries, is designed to preserve competition in the marketplace.

Some industries have unique characteristics that make competition more difficult to achieve or sustain. The large infrastructure costs and economies of scale involved in operating a cable system led many regulators to believe that cable, like the telephone industry, was a natural monopoly. In other words, it would be more efficient for one company to run a single cable down the street and serve every house than for two separate companies to run separate cables down the street with each company serving half the houses. Theoretically, one company could offer the service more cheaply than two competing companies. Therefore, most cities initially granted one cable company a monopoly franchise. But without a competitor, a company might raise prices since consumers would have no alternative. Similarly, a monopoly cable provider can take advantage of program suppliers (cable networks like Comedy Central and ESPN) because the program supplier has few other potential customers for its programming in that geographic location.

Because of this history of monopoly franchises, most homes are served by only one cable operator, typically a huge company known as a multiple system operator, or MSO, that operates hundreds of local cable systems and serves millions of subscribers nationwide. Thus, regulators impose special structural regulations on operators so that they cannot abuse their monopoly position. Today regulators are trying to promote competition between cable, telephone, direct broadcast systems and wireless companies in the hope that it will reduce the need for regulation. Often the regulations created to encourage competition are just as complex as the regulations that apply when there is no competition. As discussed later in this chapter, cable structural regulations are usually evaluated under the First Amendment standard of intermediate scrutiny.

Sometimes the law contains elements of both content and structural regulation — for example, the access and must-carry requirements discussed later in this chapter. This creates special problems for First Amendment analysis. On the one hand, the purpose of these laws is to assure citizens have access to a robust marketplace of ideas. Lawmakers are concerned when one company has the ability to control much of what consumers see or hear. At the same time, the Supreme Court has said that these companies have First Amendment rights as well.

To make matters even more complex, cable operators must negotiate franchise agreements with local communities for the right to run cables over (or under) city streets. Broadcasters, who don't need wires to distribute their signals, don't need permission to use the public rights-of-way. Thus, cable companies must deal with both federal and local regulations. As we shall see, many times this results in conflicting rules.

HISTORY OF CABLE TELEVISION REGULATION

When cable TV was introduced in the late 1940s, broadcasters welcomed it because it expanded the audience for local stations by physically extending the reach of broadcast signals. Cable providers erected tall antennas to pick up TV signals and strung coaxial cables to transmit them to homes unable to receive the broadcast signal clearly.

Beginning in the mid-1950s, these community antenna television systems, as they were known, began using microwave technology to import signals from distant TV stations. Cable subscribers now had more channels to choose from. Local broadcasters quickly realized that the new channels would siphon away parts of their audiences, ultimately reducing advertising revenues, so broadcasters asked the Federal Communications Commission to control the cable industry.

The FCC was caught in a bind. On the one hand, increased viewing choices clearly promoted its mandate to serve the public interest and foster diversity. But broadcasters argued that if cable viewers stopped watching local TV stations, the stations would go bankrupt, leaving those homes that did not subscribe to cable without any television at all. Broadcasters reminded the FCC that part of its mandate was to promote broadcasting.

One unanswered question was whether the FCC had the authority to regulate cable at all. When Congress adopted the Communications Act of 1934, it created a framework for regulating broadcasting and wire communications like telegraph and telephone. The act gave the FCC power over common carriers — companies that allow anyone to use their facilities and do not limit or control the content that can be transmitted — and over broadcasting. At that time, Congress could not have envisioned cable TV. Consequently, the FCC initially said the act did not grant it power to regulate cable, for its jurisdiction was limited to radio, broadcast television, other technologies using the electromagnetic spectrum and common carriers. Through the 1950s, the FCC refused to assume control over cable, even at the request of broadcasters.

Early Federal Regulation of Cable Television

As cable grew, broadcasters continued to call for regulation. In the 1960s, the FCC decided it could regulate cable because of the effect cable had on broadcast TV. In *Carter Mountain Transmission Corp. v. FCC* in 1962, the FCC said the general language of the Communications Act gave it jurisdiction over cable because cable involves interstate communication by wire and because cable might harm efficient TV service. The FCC was concerned that TV stations, particularly UHF stations (which had weaker signals than VHF stations) and stations in smaller markets, could be harmed financially, even driven off

the air, if viewers switched from local stations to stations imported by cable from other cities.

In 1968, the U.S. Supreme Court supported the FCC's interpretation, ruling in *United States v. Southwestern Cable Co.* that because the Communications Act of 1934 gave the FCC responsibility to foster the growth of broadcast television, the FCC could regulate cable as long as the regulation was "reasonably ancillary" to the Commission's jurisdiction over broadcast television. Therefore, the FCC could regulate cable in order to protect broadcasting even though the Communications Act never mentions cable.[1] The Court's opinion did not mention the First Amendment at all.

As technology improved, national cable networks emerged, providing programming that was not available on broadcast stations. These new networks transmitted their signals to a satellite that retransmitted the signals to cable operators all over the country, which then distributed the signals to cable customers. At first, the FCC tried to restrict the growth of cable networks by creating complex rules that prevented cable companies from taking advantage of the new satellite technology. The rules prevented premium channels — channels for which a subscription is required, such as HBO — from carrying movies between three and ten years old or most major sporting events. The rules were designed to prevent premium channels from siphoning away popular programming from free, over-the-air broadcast stations. After the Court of Appeals for the District of Columbia struck down the Commission's pay cable rules in *Home Box Office v. FCC*, subscription-based premium channels began to prosper.

Early Local Regulation of Cable Television

The number of cable subscribers skyrocketed between 1975 and 1985, and cable operators, local authorities, broadcasters and program producers disagreed about who should regulate cable and how it should be regulated. Each group lobbied the FCC and Congress for rules favoring its own interests. The FCC prevented city and state authorities from regulating pay TV. Yet states, counties and local governments imposed extensive requirements on cable systems through an elaborate franchising process. Local governments had authority over cable systems because cable systems must run their wires from the head end to subscribers' homes over streets and other public land. Local authorities control public rights-of-way and, therefore, can impose conditions, in the form of franchise agreements, on cable.

A franchise is essentially a contract between the two parties.

---

[1] The FCC's ancillary power to regulate new technologies would be called into question by an appellate court in 2010. That court ruled in *Comcast v. FCC*, 600 F.3d 642 (D.C. Cir. 2010) that the FCC did not have unlimited authority to regulate cable Internet service.

Many franchising authorities wanted to control programming, the rates cable systems charged, the customer services they provided, and other aspects of cable business. Franchising authorities also required cable systems to pay a portion of their revenues in return for permission to use public rights-of-way. Many of the early agreements imposed such a heavy burden on new cable operators that the systems failed. In *Capital Cities Cable, Inc. v. Crisp*, the Supreme Court helped reduce this problem when it held that the FCC, not local authorities, had broad power regarding cable and that certain regulatory powers belonged to the commission alone.

The Cable Acts and the Telecommunications Act

In 1984, thirty-five years after the introduction of CATV and fifty years after the adoption of the Communications Act, Congress decided the law needed to be amended to include cable regulation. It adopted the Cable Communications Policy Act of 1984 to distinguish the areas of responsibility of local and federal authorities. The 1984 Cable Act freed cable operators to determine the prices they would charge subscribers and forced cable systems to provide service to their entire franchise areas instead of ignoring low-income neighborhoods. The law also limited the fees local franchising authorities could charge cable operators and prevented franchisers from arbitrarily refusing to renew a cable operator's franchise. By deregulating cable television, the act permitted increased growth of cable.

But soon complaints arose that the cable industry was interested more in profits than service. Customers complained about rapidly rising prices. Localities complained about unfulfilled franchise obligations. So Congress, believing the 1984 Act had eliminated too much regulation, again amended the 1934 Communications Act with the Cable Television Consumer Protection and Competition Act of 1992. Among other provisions, it gave local TV broadcast stations the choice of requiring cable systems to carry their signals (must-carry) or to insist on payment or other compensation for being carried (retransmission consent). The act also regulated rates for many cable services and required the FCC to adopt rules to allow cable television's competitors to have access to much of the programming cable TV carries. While the 1984 Act was designed to *deregulate* the cable industry, the 1992 Act was passed to *re-regulate* the industry.

Four years later, again changing its mind, Congress passed the Telecommunications Act of 1996. The law reduced some regulations affecting cable and eliminated others. It focused on increasing competition — rather than regulation — to assure communications serve in the public interest. It reflected a belief among lawmakers and many economists that regulations were stifling, rather than protecting, competition. At the same time, rapid changes in technology (particularly wireless technology) made policymakers question the assumption that cable and telephone industries were natural monopolies. Instead, they reasoned that phone companies, terrestrial and satellite wireless companies, and even electric companies (which have wires into every home) could offer the same services as cable companies.

The Telecommunications Act sought to encourage competition by allowing local telephone companies, long distance phone companies and cable companies to enter each other's businesses. Instead of fostering competition, though, the law initially prompted mergers and buyouts among the companies, leading to more consolidation. The act maintained preexisting cable system content requirements but prohibited the FCC from imposing new content obligations on cable operators. It also required the FCC to review its ownership rules every two years with a mandate to repeal or modify any rule that is no longer in the public interest.

As noted at the beginning of this chapter, cable operators now face more competition than ever before. The number of households subscribing to cable peaked in 2001 at 66.9 million homes. By 2018 that number had declined to fifty-one million homes, a decrease of 24 percent.

CABLE AND THE FIRST AMENDMENT

In 1986, the Supreme Court held for the first time that cable operators clearly had First Amendment interests and enjoyed some level of constitutional protection. In *Los Angeles v. Preferred Communications, Inc.*, it held that cable TV operators engage in "some of the aspects of speech and the communication of ideas as do the traditional enterprises of newspapers and book publishers." A franchising authority could not use its franchising process to grant a cable monopoly, it ruled. Instead, it held that Los Angeles was required to show that its interests in refusing to issue a competing franchise outweighed the cable applicant's First Amendment interests.

In 1991, the Court held in *Leathers v. Medlock* that cable is "engaged in 'speech' under the First Amendment." Nevertheless, it found that a state could tax cable system revenues, even if other mass media aren't taxed, so long as the tax is unrelated to speech and is a non-discriminatory, property and service tax applied to a large number of other businesses. In neither of these two cases did the Court specify what standards courts should use to determine whether a cable operator's First Amendment rights had been abridged.

The Court finally did so in *Turner Broadcasting System, Inc. v. FCC*. In response to a First Amendment challenge to the must-carry provisions of the 1992 Cable Act, the Court drew a distinction between content-based and content-neutral regulations and upheld the constitutionality of the must-carry rules, which require cable systems to carry local broadcast programming. It held that the First Amendment must be applied to cable TV in two ways. First, regulations directed at programming content must pass the strict scrutiny test. That is, the government must show that the law directly advances the least restrictive means to protect a compelling governmental interest of the highest order. This is the same standard applied to content regulations of newspapers.[2]

If a cable regulation is not directed at content, however, and imposes only an incidental burden on a cable operator's speech, the Court held that the regulation need be tested only under the intermediate First Amendment standard established in *United States v. O'Brien* and *Ward v. Rock Against Racism.* Intermediate scrutiny of content-neutral regulations requires the government to show that the regulation is a reasonable way to achieve an important or substantial government interest. Here again, the Court applied the same level of protection it would afford to core First Amendment speakers such as newspapers. In general, structural regulations of cable are treated as content-neutral and thus face only intermediate scrutiny.

CABLE STRUCTURAL REGULATIONS

Cable operators face many structural regulations. This stems, in part, from the government's early view of cable as a video delivery business that was not engaged in speech in the same way as a newspaper or broadcast station. Instead, cable was viewed as a threat to free speech since it threatened the viability of free, over-the-air broadcast stations, especially marginal TV stations. In addition, cable was assumed to be a natural monopoly. Congress and the FCC imposed ownership and rate regulations to protect consumers and program producers from unfair business practices on the part of large cable operators. However, many regulations are being rescinded as cable operators face more competition from DBS providers, telephone companies, and online video streaming services.

Cable Competition

Cable is the dominant multichannel television distribution technology in the United States. Of the more than 5,000 individual cable systems, most are owned by a handful of large multiple system operators. According to the National Cable and Telecommunications Association (renamed the Internet and Television Association but still using the acronym NCTA), the four largest MSOs (Comcast, Charter, Cox and Altice) reached almost 90 percent of all U.S. cable subscribers. Comcast, the largest, with sixteen million cable subscribers, controls television for almost one out of every eight homes with television.

Cable faces stiff competition from satellite TV (DirecTV — owned by AT&T — and Dish network) and telephone companies like Verizon and AT&T. However, the greatest competition is now coming from so-called "over the top" services like Netflix, Hulu and Amazon Prime, and more recently Disney Plus, Peacock and Max. Many individual television networks like Showtime and ESPN also offer stand-alone subscription services delivered *via* the Internet. However, approximately thirty percent of households still pay a traditional cable operator for television service. Cable became popular in the 1970s and 80s. At its peak in 2000, almost 70 percent of households subscribed to cable television service. This led Congress and the FCC to impose rate regulation, ownership size limits, and various access requirements on cable operators to promote competition.

Rate Regulation

For decades, cable TV operators, the FCC and franchising authorities have received complaints about cable rates. Attempts to limit rates have competed with concerns that cable's growth as a business would be stunted if government interfered by setting prices. In 1971, the FCC prohibited franchising authorities from regulating rates for pay-per-channel services but did not address rate regulation for other cable services.

The 1984 Cable Act restricted the ability of local franchising authorities to regulate cable rates. Cable prices rose rapidly, and Congress reimposed rate regulation in the 1992 Cable Act. Under it, each local franchising authority regulated the basic tier of local broadcast and public access channels, and the FCC regulated the cable tier (including the common package of cable networks such as CNN, MTV, ESPN and TBS). Premium channels such as HBO and Showtime, digital cable services and pay-per-view channels remained unregulated. The FCC's regulation of the cable tier expired in 1999. Currently, only the basic tier faces rate regulation by the franchise authority and only if the cable company has no effective competition.

In 2015, the FCC issued a new order creating a presumption that all cable systems face effective competition because most households have access to DBS and Internet based subscription services. Thus, any local franchising authority that wants to regulate the basic tier price must first demonstrate that the cable provider does not face effective competition. In other words, the burden now is on the local government to prove it should be allowed to regulate basic cable rates rather than on the cable operator to demonstrate that it should not be subject to rate regulation. In 2019, the FCC ruled that Charter Communications faced effective competition in thirty-two Massachusetts counties, thereby prohibiting the state from regulating Charter's basic tier rates. Massachusetts has sued to overturn the FCC's decision (*Massachusetts Department of Telecommunications and*

---

[2] *See, e.g.,* Miami Herald Publ'g Co. v. Tornillo, 418 U.S. 241 (1974) (applying strict scrutiny to content-based regulation of newspapers).

Cable v. FCC).

According to the FCC's most recent Communications Marketplace Report, from 2012 to 2017, cable expanded basic tier rates rose an average of 4.1 percent per year. This compares to a Consumer Price Index annual increase of about 1.3 percent during the same period. Cable rates thus rose more than three times as fast as the general rate of inflation. However, cable operators also expanded the number of channels included in the expanded basic tier. When examining the price per channel for cable service, the average price per channel decreased by 0.8 percent per year over the same five-year period.

Many states have passed consumer protection laws requiring cable companies to give subscribers a pro-rated refund if they cancel their cable service in the middle of a billing period. Altice, one of the largest cable MSOs in the United States, challenged a New Jersey law that required pro-rated refunds, arguing that the requirement was preempted by the federal law that governs rate regulation. The New Jersey Supreme Court rejected that argument, holding that the law does not regulate the rate that Altice can charge customers, but rather regulates whether customers can be charged for a service that has been cancelled.

Another aspect of competition relevant to college students and the one-third of Americans who live in an apartment building is cable and Internet competition in privately owned buildings. For many years cable and Internet companies would negotiate exclusive contracts with the owners of large apartment buildings. The provider would share revenue with the building owner, and the building owner would block competing providers from the building in return. Tenants would have no choice of cable or Internet provider. In 2022, the FCC adopted a new rule prohibiting some types of exclusive agreements and requiring disclosure of other exclusive marketing deals.

Ownership Restrictions

In addition to rate regulation, cable operators face various ownership and conduct restrictions. This is because the government historically has been concerned with cable's position as a monopoly bottleneck that controls consumers' access to video programming. At one time, federal law and FCC rules designed to prevent concentration of media ownership prohibited the owner of a broadcast TV station from owning a cable system in the same area. The purpose of the so-called "cross-ownership rule," adopted by the FCC in 1970 and made part of the 1984 Cable Act, was to protect diversity of ownership and content. The ban on broadcast-cable cross-ownership was intended to prevent a broadcast owner from favoring the owner's station and refusing to carry competing broadcasters on the cable system.

In 1992, the FCC recommended that Congress repeal the cross-ownership ban, in part because the must-carry rules (discussed later in this chapter) would prevent discrimination against other local stations. Congress took that action in the Telecommunications Act of 1996, but the FCC never repealed its version of the rule. In *Fox Television Stations v. FCC,* the U.S. Court of Appeals for the D.C. Circuit struck down the FCC cross-ownership ban. It said the FCC had failed to justify why the rule should be kept, but it did not evaluate whether the rule violated the First Amendment. Cable systems now may own local TV stations.

Another cross-ownership rule imposed by the 1992 Cable Act generally prohibited a cable operator from owning a wireless cable or a satellite master antenna television system (both of which will be discussed in the next chapter) in the same area served by the cable system. The 1996 Act removed that joint ownership ban if the cable system faces competition from another company providing multi-channel video service. There are no legal restrictions on ownership of cable systems by citizens of other countries or owners of newspapers or other print media in the areas the cable system serves.

Horizontal and Vertical Ownership Limits

Some of the most contested ownership rules deal with horizontal and vertical integration. The 1992 Cable Act directed the FCC to impose ownership limits to make sure cable operators won't have so much power as gatekeepers that they are able to prevent competing or unpopular views from being heard. The primary purpose of the rules is to prevent large cable companies — MSOs like Comcast and Charter that own hundreds of local cable systems — from discriminating against independent cable networks.

One contributing issue was increased ownership of cable networks by cable system operators (vertical integration). Congress expressed concern that companies that own their own networks might exclude competing networks from reaching viewers. For example, Time Warner might refuse to carry MSNBC or Fox News because both of those networks compete with CNN, which Time Warner owned at the time. In response to this potential for unfair competition, a provision of the 1992 Act ordered the FCC to adopt rules to limit the number of cable networks owned or partially owned by the MSO that the owner could carry on its cable systems.

The FCC vertical ownership rules (Development of Competition and Diversity in Video Programming Distribution and Carriage, 1993) stated that no more than 40 percent of a cable system's first seventy-five channels may be used for programming affiliated with the system's owner. The remaining 60 percent had to be made available for broadcast TV stations and cable programming in which the system's owner has no more than a 5 percent interest. Slightly more of a system's channels may be used for programming in which the system owner has an interest if minority individuals or businesses control the services. (This rule is to help promote minority-owned networks to increase diversity in the marketplace of ideas.) If a system has more than seventy-five channels, the regulation does not affect those additional channels.

For example, Comcast owns all of the NBC Universal cable networks (USA, MSNBC, Bravo, Golf Channel, SyFy, NBC Sports Network and others). In communities where Comcast operates the local cable franchise, only 40 percent of the first seventy-five channels can be Comcast-owned networks. Regulators feared that, otherwise, an MSO might refuse to carry cable networks that competed with its own cable networks. For example, Comcast might refuse to carry ESPN or Fox News since they compete with NBC Sports and MSNBC respectively. The vertical ownership rule was designed to promote competition among program suppliers and ensure diversity of programming.

Congress also directed the FCC to establish horizontal ownership limits. The horizontal limits prevent one MSO from owning cable systems in too many cities. Policymakers wanted to prevent one MSO from becoming so large that it could take advantage of program suppliers. For example, assume that a new independent cable network is being launched. If one MSO controlled 60 percent of the nation's cable subscribers and refused to carry that network, the network would likely fail because it cannot reach that 60 percent of the population.

The FCC initially imposed a 30 percent national limit on the number of subscribers one MSO may control. It assumed that a new cable channel would need to reach at least 40 percent of the nation's homes to be viable. If each MSO was limited to a 30 percent reach, a new channel would have a chance to succeed even if the two largest MSOs refused to carry it since their combined reach would only control 60 percent of the population. The FCC believed this would encourage diversity of programming and prevent the largest MSOs from refusing to pay a fair price to carry new cable networks.

In 2000, Time Warner and AT&T, the two largest MSOs at the time, challenged the horizontal and vertical ownership rules. In *Time Warner Entertainment Co. v. United States*, the D.C. Circuit Court of Appeals ruled that the regulations were content-neutral and should be reviewed under intermediate scrutiny. It said Congress and the FCC could impose some ownership limits without infringing on the First Amendment rights of cable operators. In 2001, however, the same court ruled that the FCC had not provided adequate justification for the specific 30 percent horizontal limit or the 40 percent vertical limit that it had chosen.

In 2007, the FCC issued an order using new calculations to justify maintaining the 30 percent horizontal ownership limit.

Comcast and other cable operators immediately challenged the justification for the rule. In *Comcast Corp. v. FCC*, the D.C. Circuit vacated the 30 percent limit again. It said the FCC's new formula for determining the horizontal ownership limit was arbitrary and capricious, in large part because it did not take into account increasing competition from DBS companies like Dish network and DirecTV. The FCC likely will have to raise the ownership limit above 30 percent in order to pass judicial scrutiny. It has now been more than ten years since the courts threw out the FCC's horizontal ownership rules and almost twenty years since the vertical ownership limits were rejected. There is no indication that the FCC intends to reinstate either of these ownership rules soon.

To further ensure that independent networks have access to cable subscribers, the 1992 Cable Act also gave the FCC the authority to review complaints about anticompetitive behavior when cable operators negotiate with cable networks. The FCC can intervene when an operator (1) demands a financial interest in the network, (2) requires exclusive rights or penalizes the network for not granting exclusive rights, or (3) discriminates against nonaffiliated networks in terms or conditions of carriage. In 2011, for example, the FCC ruled in *Tennis Channel v. Comcast Cable Communications* that Comcast had unfairly discriminated against the Tennis Channel by placing it on a premium tier that subscribers had to pay extra to receive, resulting in a very small potential audience, while Comcast's own sports networks were available on a more popular programming tier with a much larger potential audience. However, in *Comcast Cable v. FCC*, the D.C. Circuit Court of Appeals reversed the FCC and held that there was insufficient evidence to prove that Comcast had discriminated against the Tennis Channel.

In another sports-related case, the Justice Department sued DirecTV for colluding with other Los Angeles area multichannel providers to drive down the per subscriber carriage fee being asked for by SportsNet LA, which carries Los Angeles Dodgers baseball games. According to the *New York Times*, DirecTV was accused of working with the other providers to all reject SportsNet's asking price. Since the providers were all working together, they didn't have to fear that a competing provider would add SportsNet to its lineup.

In 2020, the Supreme Court issued a ruling in a racial discrimination lawsuit involving carriage of cable networks. Entertainment Studios Network had sought carriage placement for some of its channels on Comcast cable systems. When Comcast refused, ESN sued, claiming racial discrimination under the 1866 Civil Rights Act. In *National Association of African American-Owned Media v. Comcast Corp.* a unanimous Supreme Court held that the lawsuit could only go forward if the plaintiffs could prove that race was *the* reason for the decision rather than a contributing factor. Comcast had offered legitimate business reasons for why it did not reach a deal with ESN. The court decision has wide ranging implications beyond the media industry, requiring a higher standard of proof for any lawsuit under the 1866 Civil Rights Act.

Access to Cable Networks

The preceding horizontal and vertical ownership rules were designed to make sure independent networks have a fair chance at getting distributed by large cable MSOs. Congress was also concerned that MSOs would try to harm competing distributors by not allowing other distributors to carry popular cable networks that are owned by the MSOs. The 1992 Cable Act required companies that supply affiliated cable systems with programming *via* satellite to offer such programming to the company's competitors as well. The act prevents cable systems and programmers from entering into exclusive agreements or in other ways limiting access to programming by other multi-channel video distributors such as direct broadcast satellite systems or telephone companies. In other words, Comcast, which owns USA network, must allow DBS provider DirecTV, telephone company Verizon, and other competitors to offer USA network to their customers as well.

The purpose of this rule was to create more competition and reduce the power of large MSOs. If one company had the exclusive right to distribute the most popular cable networks, few consumers would be willing to switch to a competing distributor. Notice that like the vertical and horizontal ownership rules discussed previously, the concern is potential anticompetitive behavior by large, vertically integrated cable operators. Whereas the vertical and horizontal ownership rules are primarily aimed at protecting independent content *producers* (cable networks) by making sure that cable operators carry networks they *don't own*, the access rules are primarily aimed at protecting competing *distributors* by making sure cable operators share the networks they *do own*.

The ban on exclusive agreements between cable programmers and cable operators expired in 2012. While cable operators like Comcast and Charter are no longer preemptively banned from refusing to offer their affiliated networks to competing distributors, the FCC retains the right to approve or deny exclusive arrangements on a case-by-case basis.

The ban on exclusive contracts between cable-affiliated networks and cable operators never covered networks that rely on terrestrial distribution. Many MSOs have regional sports or news channels that are not distributed *via* satellite. The MSOs do not normally have to share these networks with competitors. However, in 2010, the FCC passed a rule granting the agency the power to prohibit exclusive contracts for terrestrial delivered networks on a case-by-case basis. The FCC was concerned

that, if cable operators such as Comcast withhold their popular regional sports networks, the practice will put telephone and satellite competitors at a disadvantage.

CABLE ACCESS REGULATIONS

As mentioned earlier, cable was initially regulated because local broadcasters felt threatened by its ability to import distant signals and add original, cable-only programming. Another aspect of this concern was that attaching a coaxial cable to the back of a television set effectively meant unplugging the antenna. If viewers wanted to watch a local station that the cable system didn't carry, they would have to switch back and forth between cable reception and antenna reception. Broadcasters and the FCC believed most viewers would not be willing to make the extra effort (this was before remote controls were popular), meaning that local stations not carried by the cable system would lose that portion of their audience who subscribed to cable. The broadcasters wanted to make sure they had access to cable subscribers. The FCC and Congress were concerned that a local station could lose so many viewers that it might go out of business, leaving those viewers who *don't* subscribe to cable with fewer stations to choose from. This led to a long evolution of must-carry rules.

The basic premise is that the local cable operator is a gatekeeper with the ability to determine which channels viewers can receive. Many critics believe this power threatens the marketplace of ideas. Regulators also feared that cable operators would have an incentive not to carry local broadcast stations because they compete for advertising revenues. If 60 percent of homes in a community subscribe to cable and station A is not available on the local cable system, then station A is effectively cut off from 60 percent of the local audience. Advertisers then might stop advertising on station A and purchase commercial time directly from the local cable operator instead.

Must-Carry Rules

Although the FCC began in 1965 to adopt rules forcing cable to carry broadcast stations, in *Century Communications v. FCC* and *Quincy Cable v. FCC* federal appellate courts ruled that the so-called "must-carry rules" infringed on cable operators' First Amendment rights. The courts did not say the rules could never be applied but that the FCC had not adequately demonstrated why it favored broadcasters' concerns over cable operators' rights. In the 1992 Cable Act, Congress tried to resolve the problem by allowing a TV station either to choose must-carry status with the local cable system or to negotiate with it on the terms for retransmitting the station's signal. The latter option is called "retransmission consent." The rules implicate the First

Amendment rights of cable system operators and cable networks. Operators are forced to carry local stations regardless of whether they want to. The rules also affect the free speech rights of cable networks because they reduce the number of cable networks that a local system may carry. If a system has 100 channels and fifteen have to be set aside for local broadcast stations, the system won't be able to carry as many cable networks. Turner Broadcasting, owner of TBS, TNT and CNN, sued to have the rules declared unconstitutional.

In 1994, in *Turner Broadcasting System, Inc. v. FCC,* called *"Turner I"* to differentiate it from a later iteration of the case, the Supreme Court considered whether the must-carry rules were content-neutral. The Court found that the rules did not impermissibly favor broadcast programming but were a content-neutral means to protect the broadcast industry and enhance competition. The majority said the rules were content-neutral because they merely favored one mode of delivery (free, over the air broadcasting) over another mode of delivery (pay cable) without regard to the specific content being delivered:

It is true that the must-carry provisions distinguish between speakers in the television programming market. But they do so based only upon the manner in which speakers transmit their messages to viewers, and not upon the messages they carry: Broadcasters, which transmit over the airwaves, are favored, while cable programmers, which do not, are disfavored. Cable operators, too, are burdened by the carriage obligations, but only because they control access to the cable conduit. So long as they are not a subtle means of exercising a content preference, speaker distinctions of this nature are not presumed invalid under the First Amendment.

The Court held:

Our review of the Act and its various findings persuades us that Congress' overriding objective in enacting must-carry was not to favor programming of a particular subject matter, viewpoint, or format, but rather to preserve access to free TV programming for the 40 percent of Americans without cable.

In contrasting the case to *Miami Herald v. Tornillo,* in which the Supreme Court struck down a state right-of-reply law applying to newspapers, the majority noted that the Florida law punished newspapers based on their editorial content, while the must-carry law was not based on a cable operator's programming decisions. Cable systems had to adhere to the must-carry requirements regardless of which cable networks they picked, while the right-of-reply law in *Tornillo* was only enforced when a newspaper criticized a candidate for public office. Unlike the Florida papers, cable operators were not being punished for

choosing specific programming to include on their systems.

The Supreme Court remanded the case to the district court to determine if the rules were necessary and narrowly tailored. The lower court found them constitutional, and, in 1997, the Supreme Court agreed. By a 5-4 vote, it said in the second *Turner Broadcasting System v. FCC* case — called *"Turner II"* — that the must-carry rules were a proper, content-neutral means to protect the broadcast industry from extinction, an appropriate way the government could assure that cable operators would not force broadcasters out of business and deprive consumers of programming.

In a sharp dissent, Justice Sandra Day O'Connor wrote that the majority opinion in *Turner II* actually supported the argument that the must-carry rules were an unconstitutional content-based means to promote the speech of broadcasters over cable operators. She wrote that Congress stated that it specifically wanted to protect local and educational programming. Therefore, the law was based at least in part on the content of the broadcasters' speech. Justice O'Connor — joined by Justices Antonin Scalia, Clarence Thomas and Ruth Bader Ginsburg — would have applied strict scrutiny to the must-carry rules and struck them down as favoring local (broadcast) speech over national (cable) speech.

Generally, the must-carry rules apply to all except the smallest cable operations. All full-power commercial stations in a community served by a cable system may demand to be carried. Every three years, commercial TV stations must decide whether to negotiate terms for carriage or to demand carriage under the must-carry standards. Rules also require non-commercial stations to be carried, but they cannot choose to negotiate for carriage under the retransmission consent rules.

Retransmission agreements continue to foster controversy as companies that own broadcast stations demand cash or prime channel space for their cable networks in return for giving the cable operator permission to carry their local broadcast stations. Over the past few years, cable operators have started paying cash to local stations, providing an important source of revenue as local advertising revenues decline.

Digital Must-Carry

In 2009, all full-power TV stations in the United States switched from analog to digital transmission. With a digital signal, it is possible for a broadcast station to transmit more than one program at a time (multicasting) and to transmit other information as well (electronic program guides and Internet services, for example). Broadcasters wanted the FCC to require cable systems to carry all their digital content, including programs sent on secondary channels. Should a cable operator be forced to carry all of a station's digital signal or just the primary program on its main channel? The FCC has ruled that, for now, the cable operator only has to carry the primary video program and program-related content such as closed captioning or v-chip data. In addition, if a broadcast station provides a high definition signal to the cable provider, the cable provider must deliver the signal to homes in the HD format (rather than reducing the quality to save bandwidth).

Leased-Access Channels

The must-carry rules grew out of a concern that a local cable system is usually a monopoly provider that controls the programming options for subscribers. As discussed earlier, this concern is alleviated in part by the vertical ownership restrictions that force cable operators to carry cable networks in which they don't have a financial interest. To foster competition and a marketplace of ideas, additional access requirements have been imposed on cable operators as well.

The 1984 Cable Act requires large cable systems to provide channels for purchase or lease by commercial users and allows franchising authorities to negotiate with cable systems to offer channel capacity for use by the public and by educational and governmental organizations (called PEG channels). Requirements for commercial leased-access channels and PEG channels do not violate cable operators' First Amendment rights, according to a federal appellate court.

Under the 1984 Act, cable systems with thirty-six to fifty-four channels must designate 10 percent of the channels for this purpose. Systems with fifty-five or more channels must set aside 15 percent for leased access. Anyone who wants to put programming on the cable system may lease these channels for a fee. The FCC has jurisdiction over the rates, terms and conditions of commercial leased-access contracts. Cable systems often use these channels for purposes other than leased access, such as carrying cable network programming, until they are requested for leased-access purposes. Under the 1992 Cable Act, a cable system may use up to one-third of its leased-access channels for certain educational or minority cable programming services and still count the channels as being used for leased access.

While the purpose of the leased-access provisions was to make sure alternative viewpoints could be heard on cable systems, as a practical matter few programmers can afford to lease a channel full-time. This severely limits the potential audience for any program transmitted on a leased-access channel. Under the Barack Obama Administration in 2008, the FCC adopted a new formula for determining the maximum rate a cable operator may charge for leased access and required cable operators to offer part-time leased access in the hope that this would make leased access more affordable for programmers who want to start a commercial network. However that rule was replaced by

the FCC in 2019 under the Trump Administration. The new leased access rules eliminate the requirement for part-time leased access and generally favor cable operators.

Leased-Access Content Restrictions

Cable operators generally act as common carriers of commercial, leased-access channels; they do not control the content they deliver. But the 1992 Cable Act gave cable systems the right to reject leased-access programming that the operator "reasonably believes describes or depicts sexual or excretory activities or organs in a patently offensive manner as measured by contemporary community standards." The 1996 Telecommunications Act permits a cable system operator to refuse to carry a program or portion of a program "which contains obscenity, indecency or nudity" on a commercial, leased-access channel.

Congress also developed a complex method of segregating indecent leased-access material that operators carried. The Communications Decency Act of 1996 required cable operators to put all such programming on separate channels scrambled or blocked in some way. A subscriber was required to ask in writing for such a channel to be unblocked and, later, could also ask for it to be re-blocked. The cable operator has thirty days to comply with a written request for unblocking or re-blocking.

In 1996, a divided Supreme Court reviewed a First Amendment challenge to the law's indecency and obscenity restrictions and in *Denver Area Educational Telecommunications Consortium v. FCC* upheld the provision permitting cable operators to reject obscene programming. But the Court rejected the parts of the law that required operators to segregate indecent material and force subscribers to request it. Several justices noted that, unlike obscenity, indecency is protected by the First Amendment. They said alternative means that would interfere less with viewers' First Amendment rights could still protect children and sensitive viewers from the material. They also expressed concern that cable customers who wanted access to some or all of the segregated programming might hesitate to request access in writing for fear their names would be released.

The U.S. Court of Appeals for the Second Circuit in *Life Without Shame v. Time Warner* dismissed a First Amendment challenge against Time Warner Communications for its refusal to transmit sexually explicit and violent sexual programming over its leased-access channels. However, the court also ruled that Time Warner had infringed the free expression rights of programmers through its blanket refusal to consider future programming submissions from any programmer who had submitted programs Time Warner deemed indecent. The court enjoined Time Warner from applying its blanket refusal policy.

PEG Access Channels

The 1984 Cable Act permits, but does not require, franchising authorities (local communities) to negotiate with cable operators to provide access channels for educational institutions, the public and governmental bodies. The agreements need not require all three types of programming, and a system may devote one channel to multiple purposes. For example, it could use one channel for educational access during daytime hours and for governmental access during the evening.

Access channels grew out of competitive offerings from cable operators attempting to obtain franchises in large cities. Beginning decades ago, cable operators promised PEG access and other features as a means to win franchises. Then, in 1969, the FCC encouraged cable operators to offer PEG channels and in 1972 required them to do so. In 1979, in *FCC v. Midwest Video Corp.*, the Supreme Court ruled that the FCC did not have the authority to require PEG channels, but it did not prevent cable systems and franchising authorities from voluntarily agreeing to have them. Finally, the 1984 Cable Act gave franchising authorities the specific right to negotiate with cable operators to have PEG channels. As more states adopt statewide franchising agreements, those laws are less likely to require PEG channels than the older, local franchising agreements.

In 2019, Maine enacted a law requiring cable operators to place PEG channels near local broadcast channels on the cable lineup, transmit PEG signals at the same signal quality as local broadcast stations, and include PEG program information in the electronic programming guide. Maine passed the law because many cable operators were moving PEG channels to very high channel numbers, making them hard to find, and reducing the signal quality from HD to SD, resulting in poor picture quality. The NCTA sued on behalf of cable operators, asserting that Maine's law was preempted by federal law and violated the First Amendment. In *NCTA-Internet & TV Association v. Frey*, a federal district court ruled against the NCTA. The court held that the rules are not preempted because they fall under the category of state consumer protection laws permitted by federal cable law. In addition, the court rejected the NCTA's First Amendment claims, noting that cable operators have no editorial control or discretion over PEG channels; it is the franchise authority that ultimately controls PEG channel content (see PEG Channel Content Restrictions below for a discussion of First Amendment application to PEG channels).

PEG Channel Content Restrictions

Cable operators have limited control over the content of PEG channels and are not liable for material they cannot prohibit. This means a cable system cannot eliminate specific program-

ming or public-access provisions to exclude ideas it dislikes or disfavors. For example, when the Ku Klux Klan attempted to offer a program on the Kansas City, Missouri, cable system's public-access channel, the city council removed the public-access channel requirement from the city's cable franchise. With the requirement gone, the operator stopped providing the channel, and the Klan had no way to offer its program. It sued the cable system. In *Missouri Knights of the Ku Klux Klan v. Kansas City*, a federal district court ruled in favor of the Klan because the city could not show that it had not eliminated the channel requirement as a way to limit the Klan's First Amendment rights to free speech. The city re-established the public-access provision, and the Klan presented its program.

The 1984 Cable Act says franchising authorities and cable systems may agree that cable services — including PEG channels — will not present material that is "obscene or otherwise unprotected by the United States Constitution." The 1992 Act went further. It allowed cable operators to prohibit "obscene material or sexually explicit content or material soliciting or promoting unlawful conduct" on PEG channels and withdrew operators' protection against lawsuits based on the presentation of such material. In the *Denver Area* case, the Supreme Court found this provision violated the First Amendment. It said both public and private groups provided sufficient oversight of public-access channels to exclude the type of material to which Congress objected. Moreover, the government had not provided sufficient evidence to demonstrate that further control by the cable operator was required to protect children from indecent material. The Court also said cable operators permitted to exclude programming from public-access channels might restrict borderline material that otherwise might be protected under the First Amendment.

In *McClellan v. Cablevision of Connecticut, Inc.*, the U.S. Court of Appeals for the Second Circuit upheld the right of an independent program producer to broadcast a sexually explicit show on public-access channels. It said that although the 1984 Cable Act permits local authorities to enforce franchise agreements and control the operation of public-access channels, the law also prohibits cable operators from exercising editorial control over public-access programming and assures that cable systems provide the widest possible diversity of information services and sources to the public.

In *Nationalist Television v. Access Houston Cable*, the Fifth Circuit found that a Houston franchise rule giving preference to locally produced programming on PEG access channels permissibly advanced the government interest in programming diversity. The court said the city's practice of charging a fee for all non-locally produced programming was a constitutional, content-neutral rule that did not distinguish between favored and disfavored speech. Instead, the court said, the rule advanced the city's substantial interest in promoting localism. The court of appeals then remanded the case to the lower court to determine whether the general fee schedule was narrowly tailored to advance this interest.

In 2019, in a 5-4 decision, the Supreme Court held in *Manhattan Community Access Corp. v. DeeDee Halleck* that when the government authorizes a private entity to operate PEG channels, that entity is not considered a state actor for First Amendment purposes. Therefore, the entity that operates the PEG channels has editorial discretion and is not constrained by the First Amendment. However, if the government operates the PEG channels itself, then the First Amendment would apply in evaluating a refusal to carry a specific program. This case overturns dicta in the *Denver Area* case from 1996 that a public access channel is a type of public forum where speakers have First Amendment rights.

Access Rules and the First Amendment

Notwithstanding the restrictions on obscene and indecent content discussed previously, the motivation behind the access rules is that, for the 50 percent of homes that subscribe to cable, the cable operator controls which programs and channels are available. Newspapers and other print publishers do not have the burden of must-carry, leased access or other access requirements. All of these structural access rules imposed on cable operators very likely would be struck down as unconstitutional if applied to newspapers. Why the different treatment between the two industries? The Supreme Court provided some insight in its *Turner I* decision:

> Although a daily newspaper and a cable operator both may enjoy monopoly status in a given locale, the cable operator exercises far greater control over access to the relevant medium. A daily newspaper ... does not possess the power to obstruct readers' access to other competing publications.... The same is not true of cable. When an individual subscribes to cable, the physical connection between the TV set and the cable network gives the cable operator bottleneck, or gatekeeper, control.... A cable operator, unlike speakers in other media, can thus silence the voice of competing speakers with a mere flick of the switch.

So while a local newspaper may have a larger monopoly than the local cable provider, you can have multiple newspapers delivered to your door whereas you could only have one cable system connected to your television. In a certain sense, the Court is justifying cable regulation based on the scarcity of inputs on the back of a TV set just as it justified broadcast regulation based on the scarcity of frequencies. Newer digital TV sets often have multiple inputs that viewers can easily select using a remote control device. If viewers can now easily switch between multiple content providers that are all plugged into the back of the television, should that change the First Amendment analysis of these regulations? Does the availability of Internet streaming (Netflix and Hulu, for example) reduce the power of cable operators to control access to information?

LOCAL CABLE REGULATION

As previously indicated, cable operators must adhere to local as well as federal regulations because their cables are placed on public property. Congress has periodically given and then taken away the power of local authorities to regulate cable franchises. Local laws, also, cannot violate the First Amendment or other constitutional restrictions.

Cable System Franchises

The 1984 Cable Act made it clear that local and state authorities have a right to grant cable franchises and that a cable system must have a franchise in order to offer service. Traditionally, local municipalities awarded franchises, with a few states offering statewide franchises. As telephone companies attempt to get into the video distribution business, they have lobbied for statewide franchises, arguing that negotiating with hundreds of individual municipalities creates a barrier to entry that makes it harder to compete with incumbent cable operators. Twenty-seven states have passed statewide franchising laws. In 2006, Congress considered but ultimately rejected a proposal to allow companies to obtain a national franchise to offer cable service.

The 1992 Cable Act forbids authorities from awarding exclusive franchises. That is, they cannot agree to grant one, and only one, franchise. At first, communities liked awarding exclusive franchises because they could then ask for more in return from the cable operator. The prohibition on exclusive franchises is supposed to encourage competition. A city can also own a cable system, even in competition with a cable company offering service in the municipality.

Most communities have franchised only one company to offer cable service because other companies have not sought franchises. These companies do not want to invest the large amount of money necessary to build competing cable systems (known as "overbuilds"). This is in large part because of the economies of scale that led observers to refer to cable as a natural monopoly.

Courts have also ruled that technologies competing with cable generally are not required to obtain franchises from local government. The U.S. Courts of Appeals for the Seventh and Fifth circuits ruled in 1999 that neither satellite master antenna television systems nor telephone video systems are required to obtain franchises to offer video to consumers.

In 2006, the FCC passed new rules to make it easier for cable companies to obtain local franchises. Local authorities now have to adhere to strict FCC-specified deadlines in making franchising decisions. The rules limit the ability of local franchise authorities to impose build-out requirements or to impose conditions that would exceed the 5 percent cap on franchise fees.

Cable Franchise Provisions

Franchises can be short or hundreds of pages long, depending on the complexity of the agreement between the franchising authority and cable system. Certain provisions, however, will be found in most franchises.

Franchise fees. For decades, authorities have required cable systems to pay franchise fees as part of the agreement to use public rights-of-way. At one time, fees were set as high as 36 percent of a system's revenues. In 1972, the FCC limited the fees, and the 1984 Cable Act set a fee ceiling of 5 percent of gross annual revenues. The act does not define "gross annual revenues," allowing cable operators and authorities to negotiate definitions. Some cable operators have argued that having to pay any franchise fees violates their First Amendment rights, but most courts hearing such cases have decided that cable's use of public rights-of-way justifies imposing fees (see *Group W Cable v. Santa Cruz*). In *City of Minneapolis v. Time Warner Cable, Inc.*, a federal district court ruled that under federal law, the 5 percent fee could only be applied to revenues from cable services. Minneapolis wanted to include revenues from cable modem service as well. The court noted that the FCC had already declared that cable modem Internet access did not constitute a cable service.

In 2019, the FCC imposed sweeping new rules regarding franchise fees in its Third Report and Order. The rules prohibit any broadband or telecommunications regulation of mixed use facilities as part of a cable franchise agreement, stated that in-kind cable contributions such as free or discounted cable service to governments and schools and costs associated with PEG channels would count toward the 5 percent franchise fee, and established that FCC franchising rules would also apply to state franchising authorities. These rules will likely result in significant revenue losses for local and state franchise authorities and reduced funding for PEG channels. Multiple localities across the country sued the FCC to have the new rules vacated. In a per curiam opinion in *City of Eugene, Oregon v. FCC*, the Sixth Circuit Court of Appeals refused to issue a preliminary injunction before a trial. The court ruled that the FCC's new interpretation allowing in-kind contributions to count toward franchise fee requirements likely was reasonable.

The latest battle over franchise fees involves streaming ser-

vices. As noted above, a federal court held that local communities may impose a 5 percent franchise fee only on revenue from cable television service — not revenue from Internet or telephone service. As more consumers cancel their pay television cable service and shift to Internet streaming services, the amount of money paid to local communities as a franchise fee declines. To make up for that loss, some communities want to apply the franchise fee to streaming services like Netflix and Disney Plus. Municipalities and state legislatures in at least thirteen states have attempted to require streaming services to sign a franchise agreement and pay a percentage of revenues as a fee. Courts in California, Arkansas, Texas Nevada, Georgia and Ohio have already dismissed lawsuits by municipalities in those states. In *City of Maple Heights, Ohio v. Netflix, Inc.* the Ohio Supreme Court held that streaming services are not video service providers under Ohio law and cannot be forced to pay a franchise fee. Most recently, in *Gwinnett County v. Netflix, Inc.* the Georgia Court of Appeals reached the same conclusion.

Programming. The 1984 Cable Act allows franchising authorities to specify broad categories of video programming that the cable operator must carry, such as movies, children's programming, sports and public affairs. They, however, are not permitted to specify which programming services a cable system must provide (those such as CNN or ESPN) or to forbid a cable operator from offering specific services.

Duration. Franchises also specify the agreement's duration, which typically is from eight to fifteen years. Most franchises specify that the cable operator must ask the franchising authority's permission to transfer or sell to a new owner. Most cable owners invest heavily in the equipment needed to operate their systems and hope to renew franchises and continue providing service beyond the initial franchise period. The 1984 Cable Act established a franchise renewal process that creates renewal expectancy so that cable operators would be willing to invest in upgrading their systems. As we shall see in the next section, local governments have attempted to use the franchising process as a means to regulate new services offered by cable companies.

CABLE AND THE INTERNET

Perhaps no change within the cable industry has created as many problems for regulators as broadband (high speed) access to the Internet. As the Internet and the World Wide Web rapidly increased in popularity in the 1990s, consumers became interested in broadband access. Broadband access allows users to surf the Web and download Web pages, software, audio and video literally hundreds of times faster than a standard telephone modem. For example, a ten-megabyte file that would take twenty-four minutes to download using a 56k modem can be downloaded via a cable modem in less than twenty seconds. Broadband speeds also are necessary to stream video from services such as Netflix, Amazon Prime Video, Disney Plus, HBO Max and Hulu.

There are many ways to achieve a broadband connection, including cable modems, digital subscriber line telephone service, known as DSL, wireless and satellite. The two most popular methods for high speed Internet service to the home are cable modems offered by cable operators and DSL offered by telephone companies. In 2022, more than 89 percent of American households had high speed Internet access at home, with 75 percent relying on a cable operator for their broadband connection. It should be noted that most individuals can also connect to the Internet through their wireless telephone provider (AT&T, Verizon, T-Mobile, for example). Note that for the ten million users that obtain wireless service through a cable operator, the fixed line and wireless Internet access are both controlled by the same company.

In the days of dial-up Internet connections, you would use a phone landline to call your ISP every time you wanted to connect to the Internet. You could choose which ISP you wanted to use since each had its own set of phone numbers with which to call to connect. The phone company owned the telephone wire that went to your house, but it was not allowed to restrict what phone numbers you chose to dial.

With a cable modem, users connect to the Internet using a coaxial cable connection rather than a telephone wire. The cable company was not regulated as a common carrier, so it did not have to give you a choice of ISPs. Most cable companies own their own ISP service. So if you are a Comcast cable customer you are forced to use Comcast's Internet service. In 2005, the FCC ruled that telephone companies would not have to share their broadband DSL lines either, putting them on equal regulatory footing with cable operators. This meant whether you subscribed to broadband Internet access through your cable company or your telephone company, you might not get any choice regarding the company that provides the Internet access.

Open Access Requirements

As more Internet users switched to cable modems and DSL, competitors and consumer groups became afraid that cable-affiliated ISPs would favor cable-affiliated content providers. For example, if you get your broadband access through Comcast, maybe Comcast-owned Web sites like MSNBC.com will download faster than competing Web sites like Fox.com or Google news. This is similar to the previous discussion that cable operators would favor affiliated cable networks over competing networks. The horizontal and vertical ownership limits, leased access rules, and access to cable networks were all designed to prevent these types of anti-competitive practices in the provi-

sion of cable TV service. Independent ISPs and consumer groups wanted laws that require cable operators to provide open Internet access so that competing ISPs can lease the cable wires to reach customers as well.

Cable operators referred to such demands as "forced access." They argued that the cable wire is their private property and that they would have no incentive to spend the money to build broadband networks if they then have to share the networks with competitors. In addition, they argue that the current lack of regulation encourages investment in competing broadband technologies such as DSL and wireless access.

In 1999, the FCC released a report stating that it did not intend to require open access. At that time, telephone companies had to lease their DSL lines to competitors. In other words, an independent ISP like Earthlink could lease wires from a telephone company to offer broadband DSL service, but it could not lease wires from a cable company to offer broadband cable service. (As discussed above, the FCC stopped requiring telephone companies to share their DSL wires in 2005.)

Meanwhile, AT&T was completing its mergers with TCI and MediaOne, two large MSOs, and the new company was beginning to offer @Home broadband access through its cable lines. A number of ISPs, including AOL, lobbied the government to force AT&T to provide open access to its cable customers. The FCC refused to require open access, but consumers and competitors convinced some local franchise authorities to require open access as a condition of the franchise transfer or renewal. This resulted in court cases in three different cities where the local franchise was being transferred to AT&T. In all three cases, the courts held that cities could not require open access as a condition of the cable franchise agreement.

AT&T v. City of Portland began when AT&T sued the franchising authority for refusing to grant a franchise transfer. The authority required that the franchise could be transferred only if AT&T agreed to provide open access for competing ISPs. The district court rejected AT&T's argument that Portland did not have authority to impose such a requirement, but the Court of Appeals for the Ninth Circuit reversed the decision. It stated that cable Internet access is a telecommunications service, not a cable service, and that the Communications Act bars local franchising authorities from regulating telecommunications services. In a Virginia case involving Media One and Henrico County, the Fourth U.S. Circuit Court of Appeals reached a similar conclusion.

In both cases, the courts distinguished between (1) the provision of Internet content and services (such as email access and Web storage space on the ISP's server) and (2) the provision of transmission services between the ISP and the subscriber. Both courts concluded that the connection between the subscriber and the ISP, whether *via* a copper telephone line operated by the local telephone company or a coaxial cable operated by the cable company, should be classified as a telecommunications service. While such a classification precluded local franchise authorities from demanding open access as a condition of franchise approval, it left the door open for the FCC to begin regulating cable Internet access as a telecommunications service. This could result in the imposition of common carrier requirements and force cable companies to contribute to the universal service fund to support affordable telephone service unless the FCC chose to forebear from imposing those requirements.

In the Florida case of *Comcast Cablevision of Broward County v. Broward County,* a district judge held that the franchise authority's attempt to impose open access requirements violated the First Amendment. The court reasoned that the open access requirement was a content-based regulation similar to that in *Miami Herald v. Tornillo* because the cable operator is essentially punished if it chooses to offer Internet access. The court also said that even if the regulation were content-neutral it would fail intermediate scrutiny because the county did not conduct adequate fact-finding to establish that a substantial governmental interest was at risk.

After initially lobbying for regulations requiring open access to cable modems, AOL abruptly changed its position upon acquiring Time Warner cable systems. Time Warner's holdings included Time Warner Cable, the second largest MSO in the nation with 12.7 million subscribers. After the merger was complete, AOL owned its own cable wires, and it began to oppose government regulation in this area. Ironically, the Federal Trade Commission and the FCC required AOL Time Warner to provide open access for competing ISPs as a condition of allowing the two companies to merge, even though there is no general requirement that other MSOs have to offer open access. Thus, after AOL bought its own cable company and stopped lobbying for open access, it became the only cable company required to provide open access.[3]

In 2002, in its *Internet Over Cable* declaratory ruling, the FCC issued a ruling that cable modem service would be classified as an information service rather than as a telecommunications service or cable service. This important decision prevented local governments from requiring open access to cable modems or regulating cable Internet service in any way. The ruling also meant that cable companies could avoid any of the common carrier regulations that telephone companies face. The FCC eliminated most of the open access regulations imposed on telephone DSL lines as well.

In declaring cable modem service to be an information service, the commission ignored the *Portland* court analysis that cable modem service has two components: information service (such as Web pages and email) and telecommunications (the transmission of data between the cable head end and the home subscriber). Instead, the FCC said cable modem service is a "single, integrated service." It also ruled that cable service is interstate because most Internet data cross state borders. This means that state regulators don't have jurisdiction to regulate cable modems. The FCC also issued a Notice of Proposed Rulemaking to decide what regulations (if any) should be imposed on cable modem service. Independent ISPs and consumer groups appealed the ruling to the Court of Appeals for the Ninth Circuit, the same court that ruled cable Internet access is a telecommunications service in the *Portland* case. In 2003, the court ruled in *Brand X Internet Service v. FCC* that its *Portland* decision was binding precedent that controlled its review of the FCC's ruling. Therefore, it stated that it was compelled to vacate the FCC's determination that cable modem service did not include a telecommunications service. In 2005, the Supreme Court resolved this conflict between the *Portland* decision and the FCC's ruling regarding the proper classification of cable modem Internet service. The Court held in *National Cable and Telecommunication Association v. Brand X Internet Services* that the FCC's classification of cable modem service as an information service (rather than a telecommunications service) was reasonable. Furthermore, it said that when a court precedent conflicts with an agency's interpretation, the court must accept the agency's interpretation *unless* the statute is unambiguous and contrary to the agency's interpretation.

Network Neutrality

Network neutrality is a recent policy issue that has replaced calls for open access. Whereas open access would require a cable company or other broadband provider to share its wires with competing ISPs, network neutrality requires commercial ISPs to treat all content and applications equally. In other words, it focuses on how an ISP manages the data that flows through its wires. Some policymakers are concerned that the companies that control the physical infrastructure of the Internet (mostly large cable and telephone companies) will discriminate against certain types of content by charging more, slowing the connection speed, or blocking access to that content entirely. Why would an ISP discriminate? It might want to promote its own content, harm a potential competitor, favor a content partner, manage bandwidth, charge more money, or even block content with which it disagrees. Network neutrality advocates favor regulations requiring ISPs to treat all Internet content equally.

The issue gained prominence in 2008 when it was revealed

---

[3] In 2010, AOL Time Warner split, creating three separate companies: AOL, Time Warner Entertainment and Time Warner Cable. Since the merger has been dissolved, the FCC has proposed eliminating the special open access requirements that were put in place in 2001. Commission Seeks Comment on Time Warner Cable's Request to Terminate Remaining AOL Time Warner Merger Condition, DA-12-921, June 12, 2012.

that Comcast, the largest broadband ISP, was blocking its subscribers from connecting to BitTorrent, a popular P2P file sharing service. Comcast was using fake packets repeatedly to close the P2P connection. It claimed the move was necessary to prevent users from causing an online traffic jam. Critics argued that Comcast was really concerned that as P2P file sharing grew in popularity, it would threaten Comcast's cable revenues. In addition to its interference with P2P applications, Comcast began reducing the bandwidth available for customers who did the most downloading. In Florida, Comcast settled with the attorney general after complaints that it never notified customers what the bandwidth limit would be.

In 2005, the FCC ruled in its Appropriate Framework for Broadband Access to the Internet over Wireline Facilities report that Comcast was discriminating against some of its customers. This decision was significant, in part, because the FCC asserted its authority to enforce its Internet Policy Statement and regulate how companies manage their Internet networks. It stated:

> Although Comcast asserts that its conduct is necessary to ease network congestion, we conclude that the company's discriminatory and arbitrary practice unduly squelches the dynamic benefits of an open and accessible Internet and does not constitute reasonable network management. Moreover, Comcast's failure to disclose the company's practice to its customers has compounded the harm.

The FCC ordered Comcast to stop blocking BitTorrent and to publicly disclose all of its future network management policies. Comcast appealed the ruling. In a very important decision, the appellate court ruled in *Comcast v. FCC* in 2010 that the FCC did not have jurisdiction to regulate Comcast's Internet management practices. The Communications Act gives the FCC explicit authority to regulate telecommunications services (Title II), broadcast services (Title III) and cable services (Title VI). At times, the FCC can also use its ancillary authority under Title I to regulate information services. However, in this case the court held that the FCC can exercise its ancillary authority only in conjunction with its "statutorily mandated responsibilities." Regulating Comcast's network management practices was not tied to any of the specific provisions in the Communications Act. Therefore, the appeals court held, the FCC does not have jurisdiction over this aspect of Comcast's Internet access service.

Notwithstanding the court ruling against it, the FCC issued the *Preserving the Open Internet* order in 2010, new network neutrality rules for fixed broadband providers (wireline cable and telephone companies) and mobile broadband providers (cellular phone companies). The rules had three key components: (1) transparency — broadband providers (fixed and mobile) must be transparent about their network management practices; (2) no blocking — fixed broadband providers may not block any lawful content or applications, while mobile broadband providers can block some devices and applications (but not competing voice applications); and (3) no unreasonable discrimination — fixed broadband providers cannot discriminate in transmitting lawful traffic.

The impetus for the rules was the concern that most homes get their broadband Internet access from either their cable company or their telephone company. The FCC was concerned that cable and telephone companies would discriminate against Internet services, applications and content that compete with their traditional video and telephone services. After all, Comcast does not want subscribers to sign up for Internet service and cancel their cable service, and Verizon does not want subscribers to cancel their telephone service.

As Netflix, Hulu, Amazon and other companies offer online video streaming services, many consumers are "cordcutting," that is, canceling their cable or DBS video service and relying on streaming Internet services for television viewing. Internet providers like Comcast wanted to charge streaming companies like Netflix an additional fee to guarantee the broadband speed necessary for smooth viewing. Consumer groups complain that while Netflix and Hulu can afford to pay additional fees, a new company that wants to compete with them would be unable to afford the fee, resulting in less competition, which would harm consumers. In addition, if cable operators begin charging Netflix a higher fee for access to a fast lane, Netflix will ultimately pass the cost to consumers in the form of higher subscription fees. The FCC and consumer groups feared that cable companies would either slow or block access to content that competes with their own offerings, or extort higher fees from those companies.

After the FCC issued its new network neutrality rules in 2010, Verizon sued, arguing the FCC did not have the authority to impose the rules. In *Verizon v. FCC*, a federal appeals court again struck down the rules. It held that the FCC could not impose common carrier style regulations on Internet access unless it first classifies Internet access as a telecommunications service. Remember that in a series of decisions going back to the FCC's *Broadband Over Cable* ruling in 2002, the agency had explicitly rejected classifying Internet access as a telecommunications service subject to common carrier regulation. In response to the court decision, the FCC opened a new inquiry to develop network neutrality rules that would pass judicial scrutiny.

The FCC's 2015 Open Internet Order

In 2015, the FCC issued a landmark network neutrality ruling known as the "Open Internet Order." The Commission expanded the rules it had tried to implement in 2010 but which had been overturned by the appeals court. Recall that the court stated that some of the rules would only be valid if Internet access were classified as a telecommunications service. So in its new order, the FCC discarded its 2002 classification of Internet access as an "information service" and declared that Internet access would now be considered a "telecommunications service" and, therefore, subject to tighter regulation.

The new open Internet rules expanded upon the principles from the FCC's 2010 order that had been vacated by the courts. In the 2010 order, the FCC applied one set of rules to wireline broadband providers like Comcast, and a different set of rules to wireless broadband providers that use cellular networks like AT&T, Sprint and Verizon. The new 2015 rules applied equally to wireline and wireless broadband providers.

The new rules imposed three restrictions on broadband providers: (1) no blocking of lawful content, applications or services; (2) no throttling — reducing the speed or quality on the basis of content, service or application; and (3) no paid prioritization — accepting or charging additional money for better or faster service for certain content, service, or applications. In addition, the FCC maintained the transparency rule from the 2010 order that requires broadband providers to disclose their network management and pricing practices. To prevent broadband providers from using loopholes to get around the new rules, the FCC also added a catch-all rule that prohibits unreasonable interference or disadvantage imposed on consumers or edge providers (the companies like Netflix, Facebook, Google and Twitter that provide the content, services and applications that consumers use).

While the FCC reclassified broadband access as a telecommunications service to justify its jurisdiction to impose these new rules, the agency also chose to forbear from enforcing other aspects of Title II telecommunications common-carrier regulation. For example, broadband providers were not required to provide open access to competing ISPs, and they are not subject to rate regulation.

Cable and telecommunications providers immediately challenged the new FCC rules in court. In *U.S. Telecommunications Association v. FCC*, the D.C. Circuit Court of Appeals ruled in favor of the FCC, holding that the FCC has the authority to reclassify broadband Internet access as a telecommunications service. Referring to the Supreme Court's decision in *Brand X Internet Services v. FCC*, the appeals court stated that it is proper for the FCC to consider the end user's perspective when classifying a service and that the FCC was reasonable to assert that end users consider Internet access as a standalone service that "transmits messages unadulterated by computer processing." In its earlier 2002 order classifying Internet access as an information service, the FCC had noted that the service combines information processing such as email with a transmis-

sion service to create one integrated service. In its 2015 Open Internet Order, the FCC noted that many consumers consider access to third-party content and services as separate from the email and other add-on services offered by their Internet service provider.

The new network neutrality rules went into effect in 2015. When Donald Trump was elected president in 2016, the FCC switched to a Republican majority with Republican Ajit Pai as chairman. He had voted against the Open Internet Order when he was a commissioner. As chairman, he proposed rescinding the order and reclassifying Internet service as an information service once again. In 2017, the FCC voted to repeal its network neutrality rules in its Restoring Internet Freedom order. After the FCC decision, large ISPs like Comcast and AT&T stated that they will not block or throttle content, and the Republican majority on the FCC argued that the repeal of the rules will lead to more investment and better service for consumers. Public interest groups still fear that ISPs will institute discriminatory practices that will harm innovation and consumers.

The new rules changed the classification of Internet access back to an "information service" subject to Title I regulation, rather than a "telecommunications service" subject to Title II (common carrier) regulation. The rules also repeal three of the four network neutrality rules (no blocking, no throttling, and no paid prioritization). The only rule still in effect is a transparency requirement: Broadband providers must disclose their network management and pricing rules. Thus, if a provider chooses to block or throttle certain content or engage in paid prioritization, it must make that information publicly available. The new FCC order also prohibits states or cities from passing their own network neutrality rules — arguing that since Internet traffic flows easily over state lines, it would be too difficult for ISPs to deal with different rules in each state.

The repeal of the network neutrality rules took effect in 2018. While the FCC has the power to enforce its transparency rules, the primary regulation of ISPs shifts from the FCC to the Federal Trade Commission. Multiple groups filed lawsuits to overturn the FCC's 2017 decision and restore the rules that were passed in 2015.

In *Mozilla Corp. v. FCC*, an appellate court upheld the FCC's reclassification of Internet access as an information service subject to Title I regulation. However, the court remanded the rules back to the FCC because the agency had not adequately considered how the change would impact some of its other regulations. More importantly, the court vacated the FCC broad prohibition on states or cities from passing their own network neutrality rules. Instead the FCC must evaluate each current or future state or local regulation individually to determine if it should be preempted by federal law.

California passed its own statewide network neutrality rules after the FCC repealed the federal rules. A group of Internet trade associations sued California, arguing that only the federal government has the authority to impose network neutrality rules. The first court decision to consider this argument was the Ninth Circuit in *ACA Connects American Communications Association v. Bonta* in 2022. The appeals court refused to apply a preliminary injunction against the California law, noting that once the FCC reclassified broadband Internet as an information service (rather than a telecommunications service), the agency gave up its authority to regulate broadband providers as telecommunications common carriers. In other words, by reclassifying Internet access as an information service, the FCC opened the door to allow states to regulate network neutrality at the local level.

A similar case is currently being considered by the Second Circuit in *New York State Telecommunications Association v. James.* New York passed a law requiring broadband providers to offer discounted Internet plans to low-income households. Broadband providers sued, arguing that this is a form of common carrier rate regulation preempted by the FCC's 2018 Restoring Internet Freedom order that rescinded most of the network neutrality rules. The district court issued an injunction barring enforcement of the law. The state of New York appealed, arguing, like California, that once the FCC's Restoring Internet Freedom order classified broadband as an information service, the agency relinquished jurisdiction over broadband, giving states freedom to impose their own regulations.

Another area of controversy is broadband providers' desire to offer usage-based pricing. Comcast, the nation's largest broadband provider, announced plans in 2014 to charge extra to customers who use more than 300 gigabytes per month. Public interest groups are concerned that Comcast will put Internet video providers like Netflix at a disadvantage by metering customers' usage of Netflix while offering unlimited usage of Comcast's own video-on-demand offerings. The Department of Justice in 2012 began investigating whether such a policy is a violation of antitrust law, but the DOJ does not appear to be actively pursuing the issue.

Pole Attachment Agreements

Cable operators need permission to attach cables to poles or run them through underground conduits that are owned by telephone or electric companies. To prevent the companies from charging unreasonably high rental prices or refusing cable use entirely, Congress adopted the Pole Attachment Act in 1978. Its purpose was to make sure new companies were able to compete. It gave the FCC authority to regulate the rates, terms and conditions of agreements between most pole owners and cable systems. In addition, the Telecommunications Act of 1996 *requires*

pole owners to allow cable companies to rent pole or conduit space. It also extended the pole attachment provisions to cable operators' use of poles or conduits for non-video services — such as data or voice transmissions — that compete with telephone offerings. The law permits a state, rather than the FCC, to oversee pole rental contracts within the state. Nearly twenty states have decided to do so.

The FCC is struggling to determine the fees cable Internet service providers should be charged for pole use and the status of wireless carriers that attach their equipment to poles. In 1998, the FCC established a formula for fees for pole attachments by cable and wireless telephone services unable to negotiate terms in states that do not regulate pole attachments. Internet services carried by cable have been charged at the rate applied to cable services, which is less than half the rate applied to telephone services. Utility companies challenged these rules.

The Eleventh U.S. Circuit Court of Appeals ruled the FCC did not have authority to require pole attachments for wireless providers or to set the rates for Internet service providers. In 2002, the Supreme Court overturned the ruling in *Gulf Power v. United States* and held that the FCC *does* have authority to set rates for any cable company pole attachment even if the attachment is used for purposes beyond providing cable services.

In 2011, the FCC adopted an order that established new rules for setting pole attachment rates to reduce some of the disparity between the pole attachment rates paid by cable providers and telecommunications providers. However, cable and small telephone providers complained that the new rules still allowed pole owners to charge higher rates for telecommunications services. They petitioned the FCC at the time to reconsider its pole attachment rules. The 2015 Open Internet Order that reclassified Internet access as a telecommunications service created the possibility that utility pole owners can raise the rate they charge broadband providers (including cable companies) by as much as 70 percent. The NCTA has requested that the FCC reconsider its 2011 petition in order to prevent the potential rate increase for pole attachments. In *Mozilla,* the appellate court ordered the FCC to reconsider the impact of its network neutrality repeal on pole attachment regulation. Existing pole attachment regulations are focused on cable and telecommunications services — not information services. Under the Open Internet Order, a standalone ISP would not get any rate protection if its equipment doesn't also transmit telecommunications or cable signals.

CONTENT AND PROGRAMMING REGULATIONS

Despite court decisions establishing that the First Amendment protects cable from content-based regulations, Congress has placed a variety of content-related and access regulations on cable TV. Courts have allowed many of the laws to stand.

Sexually Explicit Programming on Commercial Channels

Congress has also tried to regulate sexually explicit programming on cable. The 1996 Telecommunications Act required the FCC to establish rules regarding such programming on channels used primarily for such material (Playboy and other adult channels, for example). The FCC issued a regulation that the channels must be fully scrambled or blocked, unless a subscriber chooses to receive them. The purpose was to address the problem of signal bleed whereby the audio or portions of the video are still viewable even though a channel has been scrambled. The rule required cable operators who do not completely scramble such channels to provide a safe harbor free of sexually oriented programming from 6 a.m. until 10 p.m.

In *United States v. Playboy Entertainment Group*, the Supreme Court applied strict scrutiny to strike down the rule as a content-based restriction that violated the First Amendment. The 5-4 decision found that the law improperly singled out particular programmers. Since blocking methods were either very expensive or not completely effective, most cable operators had to limit the transmission of sexually oriented channels to between 10 p.m. and 6 a.m. Thus, many adult viewers, including those who do not have children, were being denied access. Another provision of the law already required cable operators to block access to channels for individual households on request — clearly a less restrictive alternative solution. The Court held the government had not demonstrated that the harm was real or that a less restrictive alternative was unavailable.

Other Content Laws and Rules

Cable systems also must comply with certain federal laws and FCC rules that apply to broadcasters regarding political advertising, bans on carrying obscene material, limitations on information about lotteries and sponsorship identification rules. Cable systems must comply with the limits on commercial time during children's programs, but unlike broadcast stations, they do not have to provide three hours of children's educational programming per week.

OTHER CABLE REGULATION ISSUES

Cable operators face numerous other regulations, some of which are briefly covered here.

Interactive Television

Digital technology has created countless opportunities for in-teractive TV. Services include program guides, personal video recorders like TiVo and Replay, video on demand and other enhanced services like immediate product purchases while viewing TV. Many of the new interactive services are available through the Internet or sophisticated set-top boxes. In 2001, the FCC opened an inquiry to determine if large, vertically integrated cable operators might discriminate in favor of affiliated ITV providers. This is similar to the concern that cable operators would favor affiliated networks that eventually led to the vertical ownership limits.

Another issue related to interactive TV is the provision of set-top boxes. Digital cable and video-on-demand are areas of huge growth for cable systems. Subscribers typically rent set-top boxes from the cable provider to access these services. The boxes integrate digital video recorders and navigation features for changing channels with security features to prevent cable theft.

To stimulate competition and give consumers more choices, in 2007, the FCC ordered cable companies to separate out the boxes' security function from the other features. Consumers could then buy a third-party box or digital TV from a local store and insert the cable company's security card (known as a Cable-CARD) into the box or TV to receive programming rather than being forced to rent boxes from the cable company. One problem with the rules is that the CableCARD standard only works with one-way cable signals. Video on demand and switched digital video both incorporate two-way signals between the customer and the cable company. Therefore, third-party boxes can't access these functions, forcing consumers to rely on the cable company's own set-top box. In 2009, the FCC held that cable companies may migrate channels to SDV technology even though it is incompatible with CableCARD technology and reduces the functionality of third party set-top boxes.

In 2010, the FCC issued a Notice of Inquiry to develop a new policy regarding set-top boxes. The CableCARD initiative had not achieved its intended effect of creating competition for set-top boxes. Since 2007, when the new rules took effect, more than 97 percent of consumers continued to rent their set-top boxes directly from their cable companies. Cable and satellite providers currently earn almost $20 billion per year renting set-top boxes to consumers.

The FCC began to consider new software-based set-top box rules in 2016. The rules would create open technical standards for any third-party equipment manufacturer or software developer to access pay TV content. Cable providers vigorously oppose the new rules, which they claim would give large tech companies like Google and Apple an unfair advantage, by allowing them to collect consumer data, sell advertising, and integrate streaming services with traditional pay television. Cable companies and cable networks also assert the new rules would increase the problem of video piracy and threaten consumer privacy. As Brian Fung wrote in the *Washington Post*, the cable industry recently proposed a compromise whereby the industry would develop an app that would replace the set-top box entirely. With the cable industry strongly opposed to the FCC's proposal and consumer groups strongly opposed to the industry's alternative solution, it is unclear if any decision will be made in the near future.

Exclusivity and Non-Duplication Rules

The FCC has adopted two rules in addition to must-carry designed to protect broadcast stations from cable competition: syndicated exclusivity and network non-duplication. Syndicated programming is sold by exclusive contract to individual stations in different cities. When cable systems import distant stations' signals, the signals may include the same syndicated programming being shown by a local station under an exclusive contract. To address this duplication and protect local stations, the FCC adopted syndicated exclusivity rules in its Cable Television Report and Order in 1972. The rules permit a local station to require a cable system to black out any syndicated program on an imported signal that the station also was carrying. The commission rescinded the rules in 1980 but reinstated them in 1988. They remain in force and have been upheld as content-neutral by the Court of Appeals for the D.C. Circuit in *United Video v. FCC*. Similar rules for network programs allow stations affiliated with a broadcast network to demand that a cable system black out network programming being carried on an imported station affiliated with the same network.

Another FCC rule prohibited a cable or satellite operator from televising a local sporting event if the telecast has been blacked out on local broadcast stations. The FCC repealed the rule in 2014, though a professional sports league can still require blackouts through its private contracts with broadcast stations and cable providers. In 2012, the NFL relaxed its rule to allow the local team to decide if a game will be blacked out as long as 85 percent of the tickets have been sold.

Cable and Copyright

Broadcast programming is protected under copyright law, which, as discussed in Chapter 13, requires that permission be granted for use of the material. Broadcast TV stations, or the networks with which the stations are affiliated, pay the producers of television programming for the right to broadcast their shows. Similarly, when cable systems began to retransmit local broadcast signals, program producers argued that cable TV was required to obtain permission as well. Producers said that they had sold their shows to broadcast television, not to cable. Broadcast stations also argued that cable should be required to obtain permission to carry local programming — like evening news shows — for which local stations held the copyrights.

In 1968 *(Fortnightly Corp. v. United Artists Television)* and again in 1974 *(Teleprompter Corp. v. Columbia Broadcasting System)*, the Supreme Court held that a cable system's retransmission of a broadcast station's signal did not violate the copyright law in effect at the time. Instead, the Court said the cable was simply an extension of the viewer's antenna. Program producers and broadcasters reached a compromise with cable operators that Congress adopted as part of the Copyright Act of 1976. The law's compulsory copyright license for broadcast TV and radio programs permits cable operators to carry such programming for a fee without asking permission. A complex formula determines the amount each cable system must pay, but the fee is less than what the system would pay if it negotiated separately with the copyright holder of each individual program. Cable payments are made to a fund administered through the U.S. Copyright Office, which distributes the money to the copyright holders. The broadcast stations and networks do not receive any of the money unless they are the copyright owners. In 2008, the Copyright Office issued a report recommending that the compulsory license be phased out, after which cable systems would have to negotiate directly with the copyright owners for the right to retransmit the programs carried on distant broadcast stations. In 2010, Congress passed a law amending the compulsory license to cover payments when a cable system retransmits multiple video streams (multicasting) from a broadcast station. The law also directs the Copyright Office to conduct a new inquiry into whether the compulsory licenses should be phased out.

A company called Aereo thought it found a loophole in the compulsory licensing law and began offering low-cost subscriptions to local TV programming. It invented a tiny antenna less than an inch long that could receive local TV signals. Aereo installed thousands of the antennas at its office. A consumer could rent an antenna, and Aereo would send the TV programming to the consumer *via* the Internet. Program producers and local TV stations sued Aereo for copyright infringement for publicly performing their copyrighted content. Like the cable industry in the late 1960s and early 1970s, Aereo argued it should not have to pay local TV stations for programming because subscribers were still using their own remote antennas, which the Supreme Court had said was permissible. In *ABC v. Aereo*, the Court rejected Aereo's argument, noting that Congress had closed that loophole when it passed the Copyright Act of 1976.

As consumers and the various industries switched from analog to digital television, program producers were concerned that viewers would begin to trade movies and TV programs on the Internet the same way they trade MP3 music files. HBO would find it difficult to rent or sell DVD copies of *Game of Thrones* if consumers were trading the episodes for free. In addition, fewer viewers might subscribe to HBO if they could get the programs for free on the Internet. To prevent the illegal trading of copyrighted programs, cable companies, broadcast outlets, copyright owners and consumer electronics manufacturers began developing special encryption software and digital watermarks to prevent consumers from copying and/or distributing TV programs.

In order to speed the transition from analog to digital broadcasting, the FCC passed a rule in 2003 that would have required all digital TV receivers manufactured after July 1, 2005, to recognize a "broadcast flag" — a digital code inserted in the broadcast to prevent redistribution of the content. Thus, the FCC was requiring copyright protection measures be built into TV sets. In *American Library Association v. FCC*, the Court of Appeals for the D.C. Circuit struck down the requirement and ruled that the FCC had exceeded its statutory authority. The court reasoned that the FCC can impose requirements related to the reception of TV signals, but that it could not impose requirements controlling TV sets *after* the transmission is complete.

In yet another copyright battle, a group of cable networks sued Cablevision when it announced it would offer customers a remote digital video recorder feature. Many households use Tivo or another type of DVR to record shows for later viewing. The Supreme Court has ruled that this form of time shifting is not a copyright infringement. Cablevision wanted to offer a service where the programs are recorded and stored at the company's head end rather than in the subscriber's set-top box. Copyright owners sued, claiming that if Cablevision stores the recordings at its offices, it is no longer considered a fair use and should instead be considered copyright infringement. An appeals court ruled in favor of Cablevision, holding that the new service does not constitute infringement in *Cartoon Network v. CSC Holdings*.

Cable Companies as Telephone Providers

The Telecommunications Act of 1996 opened local telephone service to competition. For nearly 100 years, a residential telephone user could obtain service from only one local company. But the 1996 Act permits any firm to offer local phone service and requires phone companies to make their facilities available, on a nondiscriminatory basis, to others who want to compete in the local telephone market. In return, local phone companies are allowed to offer long distance service.

Congress incorrectly expected cable to seize the opportunity provided by the 1996 Act to rush into and provide competition in the lucrative local telephone market. After all, local telephone service providers earned more than $66 billion a year, nearly three times the $23 billion in revenues earned from cable TV service at the time. Moreover, cable lines — already in near-

ly two-thirds of American homes and passing more than 95 percent of homes — were permitted to carry a full range of communications services: local telephone, Internet access, cable video, online banking and other services. But such communications packages require fiber optic cable, and many operators hesitated to make the major investment necessary to upgrade their coaxial lines. Other cable operators entered the telephone market carefully and selectively because they lacked experience or expertise in interactive services billed by usage.

In its 2009 annual report on competition, the FCC noted that most cable companies were waiting for improved Internet protocol telephony technology before trying to offer telephone service on a large scale. At that time, about 8.5 million customers got some form of telephone service through their cable company. This number began to grow as cable companies marketed the "triple play" of cable, Internet access and telephone service more aggressively. Today, twenty-five million households subscribe to landline telephone service through cable companies and eight million customers get their wireless telephone service from a cable company.

Cable Customer Privacy

In the 1984 Cable Act, Congress reacted to a concern that cable companies could collect private information about their customers and share that information with others without subscribers' permission. Congress particularly focused on cable company access to customer information through cable's two-way capabilities, such as banking-from-home. Most of these two-way services have not fully developed yet, but cable systems are limited in the information they may gather and release.

Such private information includes the customer's name, address, telephone number, cable services taken and other information that identifies a particular subscriber. Cable systems annually must inform customers in writing what private information the system collects, what use it makes of the information, to whom the information is disclosed and why, how long the information will be kept by the system, when and where the customer may see the information, the limits placed by law on the system's right to collect and disclose private information, and what steps the customer may take if the cable system violates those limitations.

Without a customer's permission, a cable operator may collect only the private information needed to offer cable or other services ordered by the customer and to be certain customers are not stealing services. Similarly, a cable operator may not release the information to others without permission except as needed to provide services to the customer or for the system's legitimate business needs, such as giving information to a company that sends the cable system's monthly bills.

The foregoing rules, however, apply only to cable service, not to high speed Internet service. In 2006, a cable modem customer sued Comcast for collecting IP addresses and URLs from the Web sites that its customers visited. The U.S. Court of Appeals for the Sixth Circuit ruled in *Klimas v. Comcast Communications* that the privacy rules that restrict collecting personal data only apply to cable service and not to other services offered by the provider.

In 2016, the FCC passed new privacy rules for broadband providers. The new rules require providers to obtain opt-in consent from consumers before using customer information for certain purposes. The FCC developed three categories of information: (1) ISPs would have implied customer consent to use information necessary to provide service and billing; (2) ISPs would be allowed to use customer data to market affiliated services unless consumers opt-out of sharing such data, and (3) consumers would have to opt-in before ISPs could use customer information for other purposes. The rules applied to broadband providers such as telephone and cable companies, but not edge providers such as Facebook, Twitter or Google. These rules followed from the FCC's recent classification of broadband providers as common carriers subject to Title II regulations discussed earlier in this chapter. After the 2016 election of Donald Trump, the Republican-controlled Congress passed a law repealing the new FCC privacy rules.

Another privacy issue is government wiretapping. In 1994, Congress passed the Communications Assistance for Law Enforcement Act, requiring telecommunications carriers to ensure that law enforcement can engage in electronic surveillance using their telecommunications networks. In 2005, the FCC ruled that facilities-based ISPs and Voice over Internet Protocol (VoIP or "Internet telephony") providers also had to comply with CALEA, calling them telecommunications carriers even though they are generally classified as information service providers by the FCC.

Equal Employment Opportunity Requirements

The FCC has had equal employment opportunity rules for broadcasters and cable systems in place for twenty-five years, but the 1984 and 1992 cable acts codify these rules for cable systems and other multi-channel video programming providers. Generally, the law forbids cable systems and their corporate owners from discriminating on the basis of national origin, race, color, age, religion or gender in employment.

The rules also require that employees in certain job categories, such as managers and technicians, reasonably reflect the makeup of the pool of possible employees in the cable system's area. Further, cable systems and their owners had to establish programs to ensure that no discrimination occurred in any phase of employment, including hiring, training, promotions and firing. However the validity of the rules was put into doubt when the D.C. Circuit Court of Appeals in 2001 rejected similar rules which the FCC had put into place for broadcasters in *Md/DC/DE Broadcasters Association v. FCC*.

The FCC created new rules in 2002 for broadcasters and cable companies that require them to conduct broad outreach when filling job vacancies and file an annual report concerning their EEO efforts. Under these new rules cable companies do not have to show that the racial makeup of their employees reflected that of the community.

Theft of Cable Service

Cable companies lose millions of dollars each year because of theft of cable services. Individuals tap into cable wires to obtain service without being subscribers, or they may use illegal set-top boxes to receive premium channels. The 1984 Cable Act forbids intercepting or receiving any cable service, or assisting anyone in doing so. Violators face up to two years in jail, $50,000 in fines or both. The law also forbids the manufacture and distribution of equipment intended to be used to steal cable service. Another section of the Communications Act makes it illegal to intercept signals not intended for the general public and to manufacture or sell equipment used to intercept such signals. Additionally, more than forty states enacted laws that may be used to prosecute theft of cable service.

A la Carte Pricing

In recent years, consumer interest groups have called on Congress to require cable companies to offer all their channels *a la carte*, as opposed to the bundled tiers that consumers must now purchase. Advocates for *a la carte* argue that consumers should not have to pay for channels they don't watch. The FCC has supported this approach as one way to help deal with the issue of violent content, since consumers would have the option to purchase only family friendly networks.[4] The cable industry opposes a mandatory *a la carte* option, arguing that consumers won't save any money because each channel will be more expensive on an *a la carte* basis. Opponents of *a la carte* also argue that it will reduce diversity since many less popular and minority-oriented networks will go out of business.

In *Brantley v. NBC Universal*, the Ninth Circuit dismissed a lawsuit by consumers that programming deals between companies that own multiple networks and cable operators harmed competition and violated the Sherman Act. Companies like Dis-

---

[4] *See* Violent Television Programming and Its Impact on Children (FCC 07-50), 22 F.C.C.R. 2979 (Apr. 25, 2007), 47.

ney operate multiple cable networks, some more popular than others. Disney sometimes requires a cable operator to carry all of its networks even though the operator might only want ESPN. The appeals court held that there was no evidence that bundling networks instead of offering each channel *a la carte* harmed competition.

In an interesting twist, Cablevision, a large cable operator, sued Viacom for forcing Cablevision to carry Viacom's less popular channels in order to gain access to Viacom's popular channels, including Nickelodeon, MTV, BET and Comedy Central. Cablevision argued that this policy violated antitrust law by creating a tying arrangement. A classic example of tying occurred in the movie industry in the 1940s when film distributors forced theater chains into block-booking arrangements. The distributors required movie theaters to book less popular "B" movies in order to gain access to the most popular films. In *United States v. Paramount Pictures,* the Supreme Court ruled in 1948 that this practice violated antitrust law. Cablevision argued that Viacom was engaging in a similar anticompetitive practice. In 2014, a federal district court ruled that Cablevision's lawsuit against Viacom could proceed, but as Meg James wrote in the *Los Angeles Times*, the companies settled the suit a year later without disclosing the terms. It was ironic that Cablevision sued for the right to purchase cable channels from suppliers on an *a la carte* basis while simultaneously refusing to offer the same type of choice to its own customers.

The debate over *a la carte* pricing has receded somewhat as individual networks like HBO, NBC and CBS and third-party providers like Hulu and Sling TV offer alternatives to standard cable bundles. However, in 2019, Maine passed a law requiring cable companies to offer *a la carte* pricing in addition to their traditional programming tiers. Comcast sued, arguing that the Maine rules were preempted by federal law and a violation of the First Amendment. In *Comcast of Maine/New Hampshire v. Mills* the district court rejected the preemption claim but issued a preliminary injunction on the grounds that the Maine law likely violated cable operators' First Amendment rights. The court rejected the cable companies' argument that bundling channels in programming tiers was a form of editorial discretion protected by the First Amendment. But the court agreed that the law burdened cable operators and then applied intermediate scrutiny. The court said the state does have an important interest in ensuring its citizens have access to cable programming at affordable rates but the state had failed to provide any evidence that the *a la carte* law would actually lead to lower costs or greater consumer choice.

Expanding Internet Access

In the twentieth century, policymakers recognized that access to telephones was crucial for participation in modern life, much like electricity. The government instituted many policies and subsidies to expand telephone networks to rural areas and low income households. The goal was "universal service," to ensure that everyone had access to a telephone. Today, access to the Internet is essential for participating in society, and the primary concern is the "digital divide" and the "broadband divide"— the gap between those who have high speed Internet access and those who don't.

The emergence of the COVID-19 pandemic in 2020 increased the necessity of broadband Internet access for remote work, school, and daily life. This created a new urgency for expanding broadband networks. In 2022, the federal government allocated $65 billion to expand broadband networks, including $14 billion in subsidies to Internet providers to lower the cost for low income consumers to thirty dollars per month. The fund is expected to lower costs for up to forty-eight million households until 2026.

Mergers and Competition

As discussed earlier, many structural regulations have been put in place to protect cable's competitors and consumers from unfair competition. When two large media companies merge, policymakers must weigh the costs and benefits of increased consolidation. The FCC and other government agencies often impose special conditions on the new company before allowing the merger to take place. For example, when Time Warner Cable acquired some of Adelphia's cable systems, the FCC ordered Time Warner to negotiate with unaffiliated regional sports networks. The FCC was concerned Time Warner would refuse to carry those networks to drive them out of business and then acquire their popular sports programming. The FCC determined that Time Warner treated one of those networks unfairly when it placed the network on a digital tier rather than the analog tier that had significantly more subscribers.

In 2009, Comcast, America's largest cable company, announced plans to merge with NBC Universal, owner of two national broadcast networks, twenty-six TV stations, a production studio and multiple cable networks. Both companies were already vertically integrated, with each owning film and television production companies, national TV networks and local outlets. Comcast is also the nation's largest broadband provider.

Public interest groups opposed the merger, concerned that it would continue the trend of very large media conglomerates becoming even larger, making it harder for new independent voices to succeed. In addition, NBC was part owner of Hulu, an online TV service. Hulu, along with services like Netflix, competes with Comcast. Opponents of the merger feared that once Comcast acquired NBC, it would shut down Hulu and restrict other competitors from distributing NBC's popular content.

The FCC and the Department of Justice approved the merger in 2011. Both imposed conditions on the new company. Comcast must make its online video content available to other distributors at nondiscriminatory rates, and Comcast cannot restrict online video content through its broadband Internet service. These conditions are to ensure that Comcast does not try to put Hulu or other online video services out of business.

In addition, Comcast agreed to offer stand-alone broadband service for customers who do not want to subscribe to cable TV. Comcast was also required to offer discounted Internet access to low income households and extend its high speed networks to more rural communities, schools and libraries. The NBC and Telemundo local TV stations owned by the newly merged company agreed to produce more local news and television programming. Comcast also agreed to add additional minority oriented cable networks to its lineup.

New mega-mergers are proposed almost every year. In 2014, Comcast sought to acquire Time Warner Cable, the country's second largest cable provider for $45 billion. The merger would have given Comcast more than 30 million subscribers and merged the largest and third-largest ISPs in the country. The companies abandoned the proposed merger in the face of opposition by regulators in 2015.

In 2015, the FCC approved AT&T's acquisition of DirecTV, the nation's largest DBS provider with more than twenty million subscribers (second only to Comcast with twenty-two million). AT&T is the country's second largest wireless phone company and also the second largest Internet access company (behind Comcast). Even before acquiring DirecTV, AT&T provided pay TV service to more than 5.9 million households, making it the third largest wireline television provider behind Comcast and Time Warner. AT&T was competing with DirecTV for video subscribers in the markets where AT&T operates. The merger gave AT&T control of DirecTV's twenty million DBS subscribers.

Much as Comcast argued in its failed attempt to merge with Time Warner, AT&T had argued that its proposed merger with DirecTV should be approved because the pay TV industry faces increasing competition from Netflix, Hulu, Amazon, and other Internet video providers. Furthermore, more people now access the Internet through smart phones and other wireless devices than through fixed broadband access provided by cable and telephone companies.

In 2016, Charter Communications, the nation's third largest MSO, acquired both Time Warner (the second largest MSO) and Bright House Networks. The $65 billion merger gave Charter close to twenty-four million customers, making it the second largest cable company behind Comcast. The deal was approved by the Department of Justice and the FCC under the condition that Charter not impose data caps on broadband customers and not to prohibit content providers from distributing programming online. Altice, a European cable and telephone company also completed its acquisition of Cablevision, a large MSO in the New York metropolitan region. Charter, the second largest MSO is now interested in merging with Cox, the third largest MSO.

The merger trend shows no sign of slowing. AT&T completed an $85 billion merger with Time Warner in 2018. Time Warner is one of the largest content producers in the world. It owns HBO, TBS, TNT, CNN, Headline News, and Warner Brothers, one of the largest movie producers in the world. In *United States v. AT&T* the Department of Justice sued to block the merger arguing that it would harm consumers and competitors. Specifically, the DOJ argued that once AT&T acquired Time Warner, it would raise the rates that other MVPDs have to pay for Time Warner television networks and that AT&T would also try to harm "virtual" pay TV providers like Sling TV. But the U.S. District Court for the District of Columbia ruled against the DOJ, and the merger was allowed to proceed. Note that the AT&T-Time Warner merger was a vertical merger: a content distributor (AT&T) acquiring a content producer (Time Warner).

The next year, two of the largest content producers struck a deal in what was primarily a horizontal merger between Disney and 21st Century Fox. Disney, one of the largest content producers in the world and owner of Star Wars, Marvel, Pixar, ABC and ESPN, completed its purchase of 21st Century Fox for $73 billion in 2019. Disney acquired the Fox film and TV studios, FX, National Geographic, and Fox's stake in Hulu, giving Disney majority control of the streaming service. News Corporation, the corporate owner of Fox, kept Fox News, the Fox broadcast network and Fox Sports.

The most recent mega merger, between WarnerMedia and Discovery Media was completed in 2022. AT&T purchased WarnerMedia in 2018 for $85 billion to try to compete with the other major vertically integrated companies like Comcast. After just a few years, AT&T spun off Warner Media in a $43 billion merger with Discovery Networks. The new horizontally integrated company, Warner Bros. Discovery, combines the Warner Brothers movie and television studios, HBO, Cinemax, TNT, TBS, Cartoon Network and the HBO Max streaming service with Discovery's Food Network, HGTV, other reality networks and Discovery streaming service. AT&T retreats from owning content producers to focus on its distribution networks and emerging 5G high speed networks.

SUMMARY

Since cable television's commercial development in the 1950s, Congress, the FCC and the courts have vacillated about how it should be regulated. In general, Congress and the FCC have imposed regulation on cable operators when cable's growth and market dominance appeared to jeopardize over-the-air broadcasting or the public's interest in diverse content, quality service and fair pricing. Cable also has been regulated to protect the public, especially children, from indecent or obscene programming. Although the courts view cable systems as part of the media protected by the First Amendment, some regulations treat cable more like a common carrier or public utility and require that the public, government and educational institutions, and even competitors, have access to a cable system's delivery network. Cable operators face such a complex array of regulations in part because of their size and economic power and in part because of their central role in disseminating news and other content and connecting consumers to the Internet.

In the 1960s, the FCC asserted its authority to regulate cable TV as "reasonably ancillary" to its obligation to protect an efficient broadcast system. The Supreme Court agreed and generally has deferred to the power of Congress to regulate cable. In fact, the Court has affirmed the authority of the FCC, rather than local or state governments, to regulate many aspects of cable systems. However, local governments maintain some power through their franchising authority. Congress finally gave the FCC explicit authority to regulate cable in 1984.

While the Supreme Court and lower courts have generally deferred to the FCC's policy decisions with regard to cable, in a few instances they have blocked FCC regulations. The FCC still has not adequately justified its cable ownership rules. But in a major FCC win, in 2016, the D.C. Circuit said the agency had the authority to reclassify broadband Internet access as a telecommunications service subject to strict regulation — and in 2019 the same court said the FCC could change its mind (again) and reclassify Internet access as an information service once again.

In 1986, the Supreme Court said in *Los Angeles v. Preferred Communications* that cable operators enjoy some First Amendment protection. The Court has reviewed most structural regulation of the cable industry under intermediate scrutiny and generally has upheld content-neutral laws that advance the government's dedication to providing broad access, encouraging a diversity of programming, or controlling excessive market power. In 2000, however, the Court, in *United States v. Playboy Entertainment*, afforded cable full First Amendment protection and also applied strict scrutiny to strike down a federal law requiring cable operators to fully scramble indecent programming.

As consumers spend more time using the Internet and watching video entertainment through providers such as Netflix, Amazon and Hulu, cable companies are becoming more important as broadband Internet providers than as pay TV providers. As Ian Morris wrote in 2017 in *Forbes*, Netflix now has more U.S.

subscribers (fifty million) than all of the major cable MSOs combined (not including DBS or telephone video subscribers). In fact, cable operators now have twice as many broadband customers than cable customers.

Cable regulation is strongly influenced by the party in control of the White House, since the president controls the majority of the FCC and can veto legislation passed by Congress. During the eight years of the Democratic Obama administration, the FCC strove to enact network neutrality rules popular with consumers and edge providers. Donald Trump's Republican administration overturned many of those rules. President Biden's Democratic administration is prioritizing consumer protections once again. But even under a Democratic administration, the FCC tried to be business- and innovation-friendly.

Policymakers continue to be driven by the belief that competition serves the public interest and protects both competitors and consumers better than regulation. Most regulatory efforts are designed to be short-term measures to protect small competitors until they are strong enough to compete with large established ones. These regulatory efforts are complicated by the convergence of cable, telephone and Internet services; each with its own history of regulation. More than two decades after the passage of the Telecommunications Act of 1996, increases in competition have been modest at best. Cable operators now control only fifty percent of the subscription TV market, down from 95 percent just twenty years ago. As high speed Internet access becomes ubiquitous, traditional broadcast and cable TV providers will face increasing competition from Internet streaming services. Internet service will increase in importance as more consumers cancel their cable TV and watch video online. The debate over network neutrality will occupy policymakers for the foreseeable future.

Cable companies now offer three major products: subscription video programming, broadband Internet access and wired and wireless telephone service. Competition continues to increase for all these products. Online video services like Netflix, Hulu, and Amazon Prime Video offer competing bundles of programming while individual content companies like HBO, Showtime, Viacom, Disney and NBCUniversal begin to offer their own stand-alone content services. In addition, "virtual" cable companies like YouTubeTV, SlingTV, and Hulu LiveTV compete with cable companies by offering the same television network bundles, but without the physical infrastructure that traditional companies like Comcast use.

The long term projection is that cable (and satellite) TV providers will continue to lose video customers. At the same time, more Americans now connect to the Internet through their wireless carrier such as AT&T or Verizon or T-Mobile, than through a wired service. Cable broadband still has an advantage in speed while the wireless carriers have the advantage of mobility. As 5G mobile WIFI is implemented, wireless Internet will begin to catch up in terms of speed. Both wired and wireless Internet providers and their relationship with edge providers like Netflix, Google, Facebook and Amazon will be the key focus for regulators going forward. Time will tell if the changing regulatory landscape serves to enhance competition and the marketplace of ideas.

BIBLIOGRAPHY

Articles

Barnes, Brooks. "Buying Fox, Disney Shapes Media's Future," *New York Times,* Dec. 17, 2017, at A1.

Bogage, Jacob. "Low-wage Earners to get high-speed Internet for $30 in Biden program." *Washington Post*, May 9, 2022, https://www.washingtonpost.com/business/2022/05/09/biden-internet-discount/.

Bologna, Michael. "Netflix, Hulu in Growing Fight with Cities over Streaming Money," *Bloomberg News*, Oct. 12, 2021, https://news.bloombergtax.com/daily-tax-report-state/netflix-hulu-in-growing-fight-with-cities-over-streaming-money.

Chen, Kathy. "AOL Changes Tune in Debate on Cable Access," *Wall Street Journal*, Feb. 14, 2000, at B5.

Collins, Keith. "How the Repeal of Net Neutrality Could Affect You," *New York Times*, Jun. 12, 2018, at B3.

Farrell, Mike. "Cable, Telcos Will Fight for Broadband Market Share as Growth Opportunities Wane, Kagan Says," *NextTV*, May 10, 2022, https://www.nexttv.com/news/cable-telcos-will-fight-for-broadband-market-share-as-growth-opportunities-wane-kagan-says.

Fung, Brian. "Cable Firms Offer Plan to Ditch Boxes and Compromise to Regulations," *Washington Post,* June 18, 2016, at A13.

Internet and Television Association. "Industry Data," https://www.ncta.com/industry-data.

James, Meg. "Viacom and Cablevision Settle Lawsuit Over Bundles," *Los Angeles Times*, Oct. 17, 2015, http:// www.latimes.com/entertainment/envelope/cotown/la-et-ct-viacom-cablevision-settle-lawsuit-over-channel-bundles-20141016-story.html.

Kang, Cecilia. "Flurry of Lawsuits Filed in Net Neutrality Fight," *New York Times*, Jan. 17, 2017, at B2.

Labaton, Stephen. "FCC Approves AOL-Time Warner Deal, With Conditions," *New York Times*, Jan. 12, 2001, at C1.

Lewontin, Max. "Charter Finalizes Time Warner Purchase: Is Era of 'Mega Cable' Here?" *Christian Science Monitor*, May 18, 2016, http://csmonitor.com/Technology/2016/0518/Charter-finalizes-Time-Warner-purchase-is=era-of-mega-cable-here.

Littleton, Cynthia. "Comcast Scrambles as Disney Gains New Momentum on 21st Century Fox Deal," *Variety*, June 27, 2018, https://variety.com/2018/biz/news/comcast-21st-century-fox-disney-bid-regional-sports-networks-1202859661/.

McGinley, Devin. "Cable Providers in the US," *IBISWorld Industry Report 51711a*, December 2018, https://www.ibisworld.com/united-states/market-research-reports/cable-providers-industry/.

Morris, Ian. "Netflix is Now Bigger Than Cable TV," *Forbes*, June 13, 2017, https://www.forbes.com/sites/ianmorris/2017/06/13/netflix-is-now-bigger-than-cable-tv/#53681 640158b.

Sandomir, Richard. *"Justice Dept. Alleges Collusion in Dodgers TV Standoff," New York Times*, Nov. 3, 2016, at B12.

Books

Aufderheide, Patricia. *Communications Policy and the Public Interest: The Telecommunications Act of 1996*. New York: Guilford Press, 1999.

Brock, Gerald W. *Telecommunication Policy for the Information Age: From Monopoly to Competition*. Cambridge: Harvard University Press, 1994.

Crandall, Robert W. *Cable Television: Regulation or Competition*. Washington, D.C.: Brookings Institution, 1996.

Crawford, Susan. *Captive Audience: The Telecom Industry and Monopoly in the New Gilded Age*. New Haven: Yale University Press, 2013.

Ferris, Charles D., Frank Lloyd, & Thomas J. Casey. *Cable Television Law*. New York: Mathew Bender, 1984-1998.

Huber, Peter W., et al. *The Telecommunications Act of 1996: Special Report*. Boston: Little, Brown, 1996.

Parsons, Patrick. R. *Cable Television and the First Amendment*. New York: Free Press, 1987.

Pool, Ithiel de Sola. *Technologies of Freedom*. Cambridge, Mass.: Belknap Press, 1983.

Cases

ABC, Inc. v. Aereo, Inc., 573 U.S. 431 (2014).

ACA Connects American Communications Association v. Bonta, 24 F.4th 1233 (9th Cir. 2022).

Alliance for Community. Media v. FCC, 529 F.3d 763 (6th Cir. 2008).

American Council on Education v. FCC, 451 F.3d 226 (D.C. Cir. 2006).

American Library Association v. FCC, 406 F.3d 689 (D.C. Cir. 2005).

AT&T Corp. v. City of Portland, 216 F.3d 871 (9th Cir. 2000).

Brand X Internet Servvice v. FCC, 345 F.3d 1120 (9th Cir. 2003), *rev'd sub nom*, National Cable and Telecommunications Association v. Brand X Internet Services, 545 U.S. 967 (2005).

Brantley v. NBC Universal, Inc., 675 F.3d 1192 (9th Cir. 2012).

Cablevision Systems Corp. v. FCC, 597 F.3d 1306 (D.C. Cir. 2010).

Cablevision Systems Corp. v. Viacom International Inc., 2014 U.S. Dist. Lexis 84498 (S.D.N.Y. June 20, 2014).

Capital Cities Cable, Inc. v. Crisp, 467 U.S. 691 (1984).

Cartoon Network LP v. CSC Holdings, Inc., 536 F.3d 121 (2d Cir. 2008).

Carter Mountain Transmission Corp. v. FCC, 321 F.2d 359 (D.C. Cir. 1963), *affirming* Carter Mountain Transmission Corp., 32 F.C.C. 459 (1962).

Century Communications Corp. v. FCC, 835 F.2d 292 (D.C. Cir. 1987).

City of Austin v. Southwestern Bell Video Services, 193 F.3d 309 (5th Cir. 1999).

City of Chicago v. FCC, 199 F.3d 424 (7th Cir. 1999).

City of Eugene, Oregon v. FCC, Case No. 19-4161 (6th Cir. Mar. 19, 2020).

City of Maple Heights, Ohio v. Netflix, Inc., 2022-Ohio-4174 Supreme Court of Ohio, Nov. 30, 2022).

City of Minneapolis v. Time Warner Cable, Inc., 2005 U.S. Dist. Lexis 27743 (D. Minn. Nov. 10, 2005) (unpublished opinion).

Comcast Cable Communications v. FCC, 717 F.3d 982 (D.C. Cir. 2013).

Comcast Cablevision of Broward County v. Broward County, 124 F. Supp. 2d 685 (S.D. Fla. 2000).

Comcast Corp. v. FCC, 579 F.3d 1 (D.C. Cir. 2009).

Comcast Corp. v. FCC, 600 F.3d 642 (D.C. Cir. 2010).

Comcast of Maine/New Hampshire, Inc. v. Mills, 2019 U.S. Dist. LEXIS 219159 (D. Maine, Dec. 20, 2019).

Denver Area Educational Telecommunications Consortium, Inc. v. FCC, 518 U.S. 727 (1996).

FCC v. Midwest Video Corp., 440 U.S. 689 (1979).

Fortnightly Corp. v. United Artists Television, Inc., 392 U.S. 390 (1968).

Fox Television Stations, Inc. v. FCC, 280 F.3d 1027 (D.C. Cir. 2002).

Group W Cable, Inc. v. City of Santa Cruz, 679 F. Supp. 977 (N.D. Cal. 1988).

Gulf Power Co. v. United States, 208 F.3d 1263 (11th Cir. 2000), *rev'd sub nom.* National Cable & Telecommunications Association v. Gulf Power Co., 534 U.S. 327 (2002).

Gwinnett County v. Netflix, Inc., 885 S.E.2d 177 (Mar. 8, 2023).

Home Box Office v. FCC, 567 F.2d 9 (D.C. Cir. 1977).

In re Alleged Failure of Altice USA, Inc., 291 A.3d 790 (Supreme Court of N.J. April 3, 2023).

Klimas v. Comcast Comm'ns Inc., 465 F.3d 271 (6th Cir. 2006).

Leathers v. Medlock, 499 U.S. 439 (1991).

Life Without Shame v. Time Warner Entertainment Co., 191 F.3d 256 (2nd Cir. 1999).

Los Angeles v. Preferred Communications, Inc., 476 U.S. 488 (1986).

Manhattan Community Access Corp. v. Halleck, 139 S. Ct. 1921 (2019).

Massachusetts Department of Telecommunications and Cable v. FCC, Docket 19-2282 (1st Cir. Dec. 23, 2019).

McClellan v. Cablevision of Connecticut, Inc., 149 F.3d 161 (2nd Cir. 1998).

Md/DC/DE Broadcasters Association v. FCC, 236 F.3d 13 (D.C. Cir. 2001).

Media One Group, Inc. v. County of Henrico, 257 F.3d 356 (4th Cir. 2001).

Miami Herald v. Tornillo, 418 U.S. 241 (1974).

Mid-Atlantic Sports Network v. Time Warner Cable Inc., DA 08-2441 (Media Bureau), 23 F.C.C.R. 15783 (Oct. 30, 2008).

Missouri Knights of the Ku Klux Klan v. Kansas City, 723 F. Supp. 1347 (W.D. Mo. 1989).

National Association of African American-Owned Media v. Comcast Corp., 2020 U.S. App LEXIS 14575 (No. 18-1171, Mar. 23, 2020).

National Cable and Telecommunication Association v. Brand X Internet Services, 545 U.S. 967 (2005).

Nationalist Television v. Access Houston Cable, 179 F.3d 188 (5th Cir. 1999).

NCTA-Internet & Television Association v. Frey, 2020 U.S. Dist. LEXIS 41682 (D. Maine, Mar. 11, 2020).

New York State Telecommunications Association v. James, 544 F. Supp. 3d 269 (E.D.N.Y. 2021).

Quincy Cable TV, Inc. v. FCC, 768 F.2d 1434 (D.C. Cir. 1985).

Teleprompter Corp. v. Columbia Broadcasting System, 415 U.S. 394 (1974).

Tennis Channel v. Comcast Cable Communications, 27 F.C.C.R. 8508 (2012), *rev'd sub nom* 30 F.C.C.R. 849 (2015).

Time Warner Cable Inc. v. Hudson, 667 F.3d 630 (5th Cir. 2012).

Time Warner Entertainment Co. v. FCC, 93 F.3d 957 (D.C. Cir. 1996).

Time Warner Entertainment Co. v. United States, 211 F.3d 1313 (D.C. Cir. 2000).

Time Warner Entertainment Co. v. United States, 240 F.3d 1126 (D.C. Cir. 2001).

Turner Broadcasting System v. FCC, 512 U.S. 622 (1994) (*Turner I*).

Turner Broadcasting System v. FCC, 520 U.S. 180 (1997) (*Turner II*).

United States v. AT&T Inc., 310 F. Supp. 3d 161 (D. D.C. 2018).

United States v. O'Brien, 391 U.S. 367 (1968).

United States v. Paramount Pictures, 334 U.S. 131 (1948).

United States v. Playboy Entertainment Group, 529 U.S. 803

(2000).

United States v. Southwestern Cable Co., 392 U.S. 157 (1968).

United Video, Inc. v. FCC, 890 F.2d 1173 (D.C. Cir. 1989).

U.S. Telecommunications Association v. FCC, 825 F.3d 674 (D.C. Cir. 2016).

Verizon v. FCC, 740 F.3d 623 (D.C. Cir. 2014).

Ward v. Rock Against Racism, 491 U.S. 781 (1989).

Statutes and Agency Documents

Cable Communications Policy Act of 1984, Pub. L. No. 98-549, 98 Stat. 2779 (1984).

Cable Television Consumer Protection and Competition Act of 1992, Pub. L. No. 102-385, 106 Stat. 1460 (1992).

Communications Assistance for Law Enforcement Act Pub. L. No. 103-414, 108 Stat. 4279 (1994).

FCC. Appropriate Framework for Broadband Access to the Internet over Wireline Facilities, FCC 05-151, 20 F.C.C.R. 14986 (Sept. 23, 2005).

FCC. Cable Television Report and Order, 36 F.C.C. 2d 143 (1972).

FCC. Communications Assistance for Law Enforcement Act (CALEA) and Broadband Access and Services (FCC 05-153), 70 Fed. Reg. 59704 (Oct. 13, 2005).

FCC. Communications Marketplace Report (FCC 18-181), 33 F.C.C.R. 12558 (Dec. 26, 2018).

FCC. Community Antenna Television System, 20 F.C.C. 2d 201 (1969).

FCC. Development of Competition and Diversity in Video Programming Distribution and Carriage, 8 F.C.C.R. 8565 (1993); 47 U.S.C. § 536 (2000).

FCC. *In re* Commission's Cable Horizontal and Vertical Ownership Limits, Fourth Report and Order (FCC 07-219), 23 F.C.C.R. 2134 (Feb. 11, 2008).

FCC. *In re* Inquiry Concerning High-Speed Access to the Internet Over Cable and Other Facilities, Internet Over Cable Declaratory Ruling: Appropriate Regulatory Treatment for Broadband Access to the Internet Over Cable Facilities (FCC 02-77), 17 F.C.C.R. 4798 (2002).

FCC. *In re* Formal Complaint of Free Press and Public Knowledge Against Comcast Corporation for Secretly Degrading Peer-to-Peer Applications, FCC 08-183, 23 F.C.C.R. 13028 (Aug. 20, 2008).

FCC. *In re* Improving Competitive Broadband Access to Multiple Tenant Environments (FCC 22-12), Feb. 15, 2022, 87 Fed. Reg. 17181 (Mar. 28, 2022).

FCC. *In re* Nondiscrimination in the Distribution of Interactive Television Services Over Cable (FCC 01-15), 66 Fed. Reg. 7913 (Jan. 26, 2001).

FCC. *In re* Protecting the Privacy of Customers of Broadband and Other Telecommunications Services (FCC 16-148), Nov. 2, 2016, 81 Fed. Reg. 87274 (Jan. 3, 2017).

FCC. Leased Commercial Access (FCC 07-208), 23 F.C.C.R. 2909 (Feb. 1, 2008).

FCC. Preserving the Open Internet Order, FCC 10-201, 25 F.C.C.R. 17905 (Dec. 23, 2010).

FCC. Protecting and Promoting the Open Internet, FCC 14-61, 29 F.C.C.R. 5561 (May 15, 2014).

FCC. Protecting and Promoting the Open Internet, FCC 15-24, adopted Mar. 12, 2015, 80 Fed. Reg. 19737 (Apr. 13, 2015).

FCC. Revision of the Commission's Program Access Rules (FCC 12-123), 56 C.R. 1271 (Oct. 5, 2012).

FCC, Restoring Internet Freedom, FCC 17-166, Jan. 4, 2018.

FCC. Sports Blackout Rules, FCC 14-141, 29 F.C.C.R. 12053 (Sept. 30, 2014).

FCC. Syndicated Exclusivity Rules, 79 F.C.C. 2d 663 (1980); *In re* Rules Relating to Program Exclusivity in the Cable and Broadcast Industries, 3 F.C.C.R. 5299 (1988).

FCC. Third Report and Order (FCC 19-80), 84 F.R. 44725 (Aug. 27, 2019), *In re* Implementation of Section 621(a)(1) of the Cable Communications Policy Act of 1984.

FCC. Video Device Competition; Implementation of Section 304 of the Telecommunications Act of 1996: Commercial Availability of Navigation Devices; Compatibility Between Cable Systems and Consumer Electronics Equipment (FCC 10-60), 25 F.C.C.R. 4275 (Apr. 21, 2010).

Telecommunications Act of 1996, Pub. L. No. 104-104, 110 Stat. 56 (1996).

12

New Communication Technologies

By Jeremy Harris Lipschultz

☑ **Headnote Questions**

- How have the Internet and social media redefined communication law, regulation and policy?
- How have recent U.S. Supreme Court and appellate decisions set digital law precedent?
- How has emerging data privacy law created new rights and responsibilities?
- How will artifical intelligence (AI) disrupt the media law and policy landscape?

A Pennsylvania high school freshman, angry about not making the varsity cheerleading squad, posted two Snapchat photos from a local convenience store. Public school officials suspended the girl for flipping her middle finger and using the word "fuck." The U.S. Supeme Court, in *Mahanoy v. B.L.*, quoted her as saying. "F*** school f*** softball f*** cheer f*** everything." One of Brandi Levy's Snapchat friends took a screenshot that was shared with cheerleaders and later the coach. The Supreme Court voted 8-1 that off-campus, First Amendment speech in this case was protected. However, it followed the Court's earlier language in the landmark case *Tinker v. Des Moines Independent School District* that public school administrators may punish students for inappropriate social media use, if they could show "it would create a substantial interference in, or disruption of, the school's efforts."

Ubiquitous smartphone use by students, as well as government employees and others, has created a fluid First Amendment law and emerging technology regulation. In the Mahanoy case, dissenting Justice Clarence Thomas unsuccessfully argued that "speech location is a much trickier question than the majority acknowledges." Mobile phones are one important technology among many that have created emerging federal court cases and conflicts. Newer communication technologies, such as voice commands, facial recognition and artificial intelligence natural language chatbots, continue to evolve on the Internet, social media and mobile apps. Rapid technological change typically leads to new laws and regulation, social conflicts and case law, as traditional issues must be reconsidered.

There are an *estimated* 1.98 billion active Web sites, but fewer than 400 million are active at any given time. Search engine optimization business is worth more than $46 billion, and may reach $235 billion by 2030. Every second, Google estimates it receives more than 99,000 searches — or more than 3.6 trillion per year. About 2.85 billion global Facebook users represent a slice of social media communication that also happens on Instagram, Snapchat, YouTube, TikTok, Linkedin and millions of daily blogs. There are billions of YouTube views each month, and Google data suggest that about 80 percent are from outside the United States in hundreds of languages. As digital media allow individuals to take on roles as publishers (through blogs, podcasts, Twitter, Facebook, Instagram, IGTV, TikTok, Reddit, Snapchat and other social postings), there are new freedoms *and* responsibilities.

The Federal Trade Commission used commercial speech law in warning bloggers to disclose financial interests when endorsing products or services, and it also reminded Instagram celebrities about disclosure rules. The FTC found that the hashtags #ad, #sp and #sponsored are not clear paid promotional disclosure of financial interests to followers and fans. In one letter, it wrote that

[If] you are endorsing a brand and have a "material connection" with the marketer (that is, a connection or relationship that might affect the weight or credibility that your followers give the endorsement), then your connection should be clearly and conspicuously disclosed, unless the connection is already clear from the context of the endorsement. Material connections could consist of a business or family relationship, or your receipt of payment, free products or services, or other incentives to promote the brand.

The FTC has the power to fine violators. While social media users have a lot of freedom, errors in judgment may spark litigation. At the same time, the U.S. Supreme Court has begun to articulate how First Amendment rights are important because political and legal commercial speech happens online.

From Wikileaks to the National Security Agency PRISM case, technologies may alter traditional norms of privacy, journalism and law. The desire for open access to information clashes with the need for counter-terrorism national security programs. The Aministrative Office of the United States Courts in 2020 reported that the Foreign Intelligence Surveillance Court denied twenty applications in full, thirty-eight in part, modified 264, and granted 688. The data were required to be reported under the USA Freedom Act of 2015. Digital technologies make it easier for the government to snoop, but courts provide some protection.

The broader backdrop of rapid diffusion, adoption and convergence of mobile devices, Internet and social communication technologies, and mobile apps make it easier for smartphone users to communicate from almost anywhere. Smartphones also made it (1) easier for the government to monitor and spy on citizens, including journalists; (2) possible for retail apps to track consumer or employee location and movement (as well as location and spread of the COVID-19 Coronavirus during a global pandemic); and (3) more likely for there to be patent, copyright and intellectual property disputes.

A ubiquitous mobile media environment is giving rise to new interest in so-called "big data" privacy protection. For example, cloud-based computing — such as DropBox, Google Drive, Amazon's AWS and Apple's Cloud (which store files at remote servers) — make it difficult to establish clear property rights over shared content. The federal government has been slow to respond, but state laws also are important. In Illinois, for example, a biometerics data privacy law allowed for a settlement with Facebook over collection and use of facial recognition data. In 2022, users received about $400 payments. Other states — California is one — led the way in constructing stronger data privacy frameworks. The California Consumer Privacy Act of 2018 offers consumers some control over data that businesses collect by making explicit a right to know, right to delete, right to opt-out and right to non-discrimination. The state attorney general and California Department of Justice interpret and enforce business disclosure of personal information and data rights.

Popular social media sites ask users to guard their privacy but then collect and use personal data based upon terms of service end-user agreements, with few legal restrictions in the United States. At the same time, site rules allowed Twitter to flag former President Donald Trump's @realDonaldTrump tweets that promoted false information or hate: "This Tweet violated Twitter Rules about [specific topic]. However, Twitter has determined that it may be in the public's interest for the Tweet to remain accessible." Twitter ultimately banned Trump's account, even though it had more than 80 million followers, on grounds that his tweets promoted the attack on the U.S. Capitol on January 6, 2021. A district court judge in San Francisco a year later rejected Trump's lawsuit based that claimed Twitter was a state actor. Trump eventually was reinstated by Twitter, Facebook and YouTube.

CALIFORNIA CONSUMER PRIVACY ACT OF 2018 (UPDATED 2023)

The California constitution was amended in 1972 to add privacy as an "inalienable" right of state residents. In 2018, the lawmakers added language to give consumers a right to opt-out (but not opt-in) of personal data collection under CCPA. Consumers have a right to know and right to delete business data. Other states followed the lead and also included biometric data, such as facial recognition.

TITLE 1.81.5. California Consumer Privacy Act of 2018 [1798.100 - 1798.199]
(Title 1.81.5 added by Stats. 2018, Ch. 55, Sec. 3.) 1798.100

(a) A consumer shall have the right to request that a business that collects a consumer's personal information disclose to that consumer the categories and specific pieces of personal information the business has collected.

(b) A business that collects a consumer's personal information shall, at or before the point of collection, inform consumers as to the categories of personal information to be collected and the purposes for which the categories of personal information shall be used. A business shall not collect additional categories of personal information or use personal information collected for additional purposes without providing the consumer with notice consistent with this section.

(c) A business shall provide the information specified in subdivision (a) to a consumer only upon receipt of a verifiable consumer request.

(d) A business that receives a verifiable consumer request from a consumer to access personal information shall promptly take steps to disclose and deliver, free of charge to the consumer, the personal information required by this section....

(e) This section shall not require a business to retain any personal information collected for a single, one-time transaction, if such information is not sold or retained by the business or to reidentify or otherwise link information that is not maintained in a manner that would be considered personal information.

(Amended by Stats. 2019, Ch. 757, Sec. 1. (AB 1355) Effective January 1, 2020.

Source: California Attorney General. https://oag.ca.gov/privacy/ccpa

A Florida law sought to stop sites from deplatforming political candidates, but a federal judge found that government had no legitimate interest within a First Amendment context. The Fifth U.S. Circuit Court of Appeals, however, in 2022 overturned a lower court and upheld a social media law in Texas that allowed citizens to sue sites.

Meanwhile, entrepreneur Elon Musk headed a group that purchased Twitter, took it private, reinstated banned acocunts and loosened content limits. Trump operative Roger Stone earlier had returned to Twitter ("Well bitches I'm back…") with a new account — only to be banned within minutes. Meanwhile, conservative app Parler failed in its initial antitrust case against Amazon Web Services, after it suspended it. The app deplatforming raised concerns about Amazon and other growing corporate power over the Internet. Parler reopened, and Trump's Truth Social app, at the same time, struggled to attract broad adoption and use.

Privacy law also is developing within a context of concern over the contractual power of Twitter and Facebook to filter and manage content. While the California Consumer Privacy Act of 2018 is considered the most sweeping in the nation, the opt-out provisions are not as tough as Europe's General Data Protection Regulation that treats privacy as a fundamental right based upon the international law concept of human dignity.

A 2020 Executive Order by then President Trump responded to Twitter's editing: "In a country that has long cherished the freedom of expression, we cannot allow a limited number of online platforms to hand pick the speech that Americans may access and convey on the Internet." Civil liability site protection designed to allow for removal of obscene, violent or harmful content, the order claimed, was not made law and extended to protected political speech:

It is the policy of the United States to ensure that … this provision is not distorted to provide liability protection for online platforms that — far from acting in 'good faith' to remove objectionable content — instead engage in deceptive or pretextual actions (often contrary to their stated terms of service) to stifle viewpoints with which they disagree.

Congress held hearings on the law that protects online sites from being sued by content creators, and Florida passed a law that prohibits sites from "knowingly deplatforming" political candidates. The Electronic Frontier Foundation is among those organizations that call potential fines of up to $250,000 per day an unconstitutional violation of social media company rights.

In *Biden v. Knight First Amendment Institute* in 2021, the Court vacated as moot an earlier decision that Donald Trump's tweets were a public forum, and the admininstration could not block accounts that criticized the former president. The Court's reasoning was that Trump was no longer president. Justice Thomas wrote that "it seems rather odd to say that something is a government forum when a private company has unrestricted authority to do away with it."

The global distribution of unfiltered media across a mosaic of legal systems and structures means technological freedom as a trend is colliding with governmental, corporate and individual desires to control messages. At the dawn of the digital age, Irving Fang observed that while Internet headquarters was based in Reston, Virginia, the decision was made to "not have a single central command and control point." Instead, computer nodes distributed communication through packet switching that created, in effect, a new public utilty. Rapid global growth of social network sites created an inevitable clash between various national laws and regulatory systems.

Social media have spawned litigation. As journalism professor Chip Stewart observed, "Centuries of jurisprudence about media law provides a foundation for understanding the particular challenges we face when using social media. However, courts, lawmakers and regulators have done little to keep up with these challenges, particularly for media professionals." In 2020, the Trump administration attempted to ban the social media app TikTok over its Chinese ownership, but lost in court. At the same time, TikTok left Hong Kong over an ongoing political crisis. Facebook, Twitter, Google and other U.S. companies stopped processing user data requests from Beijing in an application of new state security laws in China.

Online communication requires an identifiable Internet protocol address, but a user may try to hide behind an app. Yik Yak went out of business amid federal harassment complaints by students at the University of Mary Washington in Virginia. Some Internet service providers, under pressure, removed controversial Web pages. The General Data Protection Regulation took effect in Europe in 2018, and many U.S. sites fell under compliance. The regulation defined "personal data" as, "any information relating to an identified or identifiable natural person … who can be identified, directly or indirectly, in particular by reference to an identifier." Following the Cambridge Analytica 2016 election data scandal, Facebook's Mark Zuckerberg told Congress: "But it's clear now that we didn't do enough to prevent these tools from being used for harm, as well. And that goes for fake news, for foreign interference in elections, and hate speech, as well as developers and data privacy."

The lack of data transparency is considered a problem. Senator Ted Cruz of Texas chaired a key committee and has been a vocal critic of Facebook, Google and Twitter for failing to answer basic questions about the nature of content filtering and possible political bias. The use of secret and ever-changing algorithms serves to make it difficult to judge decision-making, but also attempts to respond to social marketers gaming the system to capture free attention for commercial sites.

Further, the explosion of user-created Internet video is one important challenge to traditional norms about copyright and content property law. YouTube and similar sites must police users in order to respond to media company complaints about copyright infringement in use of music and video. Changes in policy have made it more difficult for niche content creators to monetize and be paid for their work. Earlier, there were attempts to limit the power of Internet Service Providers.

FACEBOOK COMMUNITY STANDARDS AND HATE SPEECH DELETION

Hate speech laws around the world, with their myriad definitions, present a challenge to Facebook to manage its more than two billion user accounts. Its Community Standards attempt to promote "responsible communications" and a feeling of safety. Facebook reported that its growing teams of more than 4,500 employees "deal with reported content," and delete about 288,000 posts each month. Facebook has a difficult challenge of operating as "an open platform for all ideas, a place where we want to encourage self-expression, connection and sharing." Its rules focus on "bullying, harassing and threatening someone."" For example:

- "Our current definition of hate speech is anything that directly attacks people based on what are known as their 'protected characteristics' — race, ethnicity, national origin, religious affiliation, sexual orientation, sex, gender, gender identity, or serious disability or disease."
- U.S. Constitutional protection is distinguished from German laws forbidding "incitement to hatred" and others restricting "blasphemy."
- "Often the most difficult edge cases involve language that seems designed to provoke strong feelings, making the discussion even more heated — and a dispassionate look at the context (like country of speaker or audience) more important."
- Immigration debate posts, for example, cross a Facebook line if they are "calls for violence against migrants" or are "duhumanizing references to them — such as comparisons to animals, to filth or to trash."
- "There are times someone might share something that would otherwise be considered hate speech but for non-hateful reasons, such as making a self-deprecating joke or quoting lyrics from a song."
- "If we fail to remove content that you report because you think it is hate speech, it feels like we're not living up to the values in our Community Standards. When we remove something you posted and believe is a reasonable political view, it can feel like censorship."

Facebook claims a First Amendment right to manage communities by curating content. Artificial intelligence tools are expected in the future to be used to filter hate speech, as well as "spam," "nudity" and "bullying." Facebook also has tightened restrictions of political and other advertising. It also faced a 2020 boycott by major brands using Facebook and Instagram advertising.

Source: Richard Allen, Facebook, Hard Questions: Hate Speech, June 27, 2017, http://news room.fb.com/news/2017/06/hard-questions-hate-speech/.

The D.C. Circuit Court of Appeals backed a Federal Communications Commission Open Internet Order to treat ISPs as common carriers that were required to offer neutral and nondiscriminatory access.

Data suggest that Internet freedom is spreading across the globe at the same time as governments, corporations and others use political, economic, technological and social power to push back. New technologies spread adoption of new ideas. Web use exploded after its introduction to the public around 1994. Now, the number of users worldwide is estimated at about 5.2 billion, and 4.8 billion (59.9 percent) are on social media sites. Data, however, do not explain what social media theorist Jeremy Hunsinger describes as *how* technological changes transform "the legal system of torts from a punitive one to a profitable one."

Data painted enormous growth on every continent, and it was most dramatic in Asia. China has more broadband connections than the United States. China took the lead in the number of Internet users in 2009, and now about 73 percent of its 1.4 billion people use the Internet. Developing nations were experiencing the fastest growth in online use. However, freedom continued to be a concern, as China pressured computer manufacturers to preinstall filtering software and resist outside nudging to be more open. Digital media have been disruptive of traditional social norms and values, and some elected politicians question why huge social media companies should have the power to decide what we read, see and watch.

LARGEST NATIONAL INTERNET USERS (2020-23)

Country 2023	Users	2022 Rank	%Penetration 2023 (2020)
1. China	1,051,140,000	1	73.7 (62.8)%
2. India	836,860,000	2	59.5 (40.9)
3. United States	307,200,000	3	91.2 (88.5)
4. Indonesia	196,000,000	5	71.6 (64.1)
5. Brazil	165,300,000	4	77.1 (70.8)
6. Nigeria	136,203,231	7	63.8 (55.5)
7. Pakistan	130,000,000.	NA	60.8 (54.0)
8. Russia	129,800,000	8	89.5 (76.1)
9. Bangladesh	126,210,000	9	75.9 (54.8)
10. Japan	117,400,000	7	94.2(93.5)
World Total Est	**5,385,798,406**		**67.9 (59.7)**

Source: Internet World Stats (June 13, 2023).
https://www.internetworldstats.com/stats.htm

Note: It took a decade to reach one billion Internet users, but the second billion was reached just five years later in 2010. Seven years later, by the end of 2017, there were more than 4 billion global users. Mexico, Iran, Germany, the Phillipines, Turkey, Vietnam, the United Kingdom, France, Egypt, South Korea, Spain, Thailand, Italy, Poland, and Canada are among the top twenty-five nations. China officially blocks Facebook and many other Western siites.

Beyond blocking in top Internet countries, many have their own popular social networks. No U.S. city is among the top 10 for Facebook users: 1. Bangkok, 2. Jakarta, 3. Dhaka, 4. Mexico City, 5. Istanbul, 6. New Delhi, 7. Lima, 8. Cairo, 9. Sao Paulo, and 10. Ho Chi Minh. Simon Kemp, India Overtakes the USA to Become Facebook's #1 Country (July 13, 2017). https://thenextweb.com/contributors/2017/07/13/india-over-takes-usa-become-facebooks-top-country/.

A majority Internet world users are in Asia (54.2%), followed by Europe (13.9.3%), Africa (11.2%), Latin America (9.9%), North America (6.5%), the Middle East (3.8%), and Oceania/Australia (0.6%). *See* Internet Usage Statistics (June 12, 2023). https://www.internetworldstats.com/stats.htm.

From re-licensing of Google in China to so-called "right to be forgotten" European online rules, law-based management requires online platforms and their users to accept government filtering in various countries, including France and Germany. Meanwhile, rapid Internet growth is happening in Bangladesh, India, Indonesia, Iran, Thailand, Turkey, the Phillipines, Vietnam and other developing nations. The global digital transformation is driving political movements toward more individual and social freedom, at the same time as economic growth sparks entrepreneurial opportunities for change.

Frequently, countries seek to limit the spread of online speech that challenges state power, promotes terrorism, damages individual or national reputation, incites ethnic division, or is considered pornographic. Typically, most nations have laws that allow for criminal libel cases, pornography and blasphemy prosecution, and prior restraints. The optimistic view is that new communication technologies promote U.S.-style online freedom of expression, but change always smashes into a desire to retain the status quo. India, for example, seemed to be following the Chinese model by blocking TikTok and many other apps in 2020. Other countries, Turkey is one, forced social media companies to register and respond to national concerns about provocative content. A United Kingdom Digital Markets Unit empowered consumers and threatened fines. In the United States, former President Barack Obama called for new regulation to fight political disinformation campaigns waged by Russia and other countries: "The very design of these platforms seems to be tilting us in the wrong direction."

Futurist David Mathison was early to observe: "Because of today's technology, almost anyone can be an author, musician, filmmaker, journalist, politician, blogger, cartoonist, podcaster, speaker, radio or TV host, or licensor." New technologies allow interactive collaboration, and the author of this chapter has used Twitter (@JeremyHL) for ongoing discussions with thousands of sources and subjects and even plan formal presentations. The Internet and social media remain paradoxical because they offer users wide communication freedom at the same time as they also bring new data surveillance tools to those in power. While U.S. usage is very high, the country represents a very small slice of global Internet activity. At the same time, artifical intelligence (AI) apps Chat GPT4 and OpenAI E DALL·E startled the world with a potential to influence and alter human communication.

Ubiquitous U.S. Internet access and use may be contrasted with the emerging world and its rapid growth and development. More than half of the countries with the largest number of online users are relative newcomers to the list. It is clear that mobile and social media use will drive continued growth in interest, as social messaging and video are valuable to marketers. Awareness that we are being watched more than any time in human history increases the probability that there is a chilling effect on free speech. At the heart of the technological revolution is the empowerment of individuals to exercise free speech, but there are limits through subsequent punishment. For example, Egypt in 2020 arrested doctors speaking out about COVID-19 during the global pandemic, as nurses and doctors took to TikTok and other social media sites. In the United States, disputes lead to more frequent case law and interpretation, such as the following:

• In *Keefe v. Adams* the Supreme Court denied review of an Eighth Circuit decision against a nursing student removed from a community college professional program because his Facebook posts violated a nursing ethics code. Legal scholars raised concerns over courts deferring to university use of professional standards that limit First Amendment freedom of expression.

• In *Minnesota v. Tatro,* the state supreme court upheld discipline against a mortuary science student for Facebook wall posts she claimed were "satire" about a body in the university lab. Case law inconsistencies in the Eighth Circuit and elsewhere have not been clarified by the U.S. Supreme Court.

High school, community college and university students may be punished, if they have agreed to student ethical conduct rules that have the power of contract law. This area of law and policy truly includes virtually every First Amendment topic you read in the other chapters of this textbook.

Web3 non-fungible tokens burst onto the blockchain online spaces with a promise of using crypto currencies to protect and sell authenticated copies of intellectual property (IP), but AI syntheized online content without attribution or payments to creators.

CONVERGING VOICE, DATA AND VIDEO

The convergence of text, photographs, audio and video presents challenges — from libel and privacy to obscenity and copyright issues. The First Amendment on the one hand is seen as differing in the video area in which fewer restrictions exist, but, as one scholar wrote, "subject to restrictions from any country, regardless of whether that country is part of the video providers' intended audience."

Digital technology unleashed stiff competition among video services. Some regulatory battles were about which companies and technologies would survive and prosper. Telecommunication deregulation, for example, allowed phone companies to provide video and cable companies to offer phone services. Such cross-media competition came at a time of mergers and corporate consolidation. Some critics worried that telecommunication cartels threatened to monopolize mass media and the Internet. Lawmakers and the FCC debated such issues as net neutrality, pricing, connection speeds and bandwidth concerns. Net neutrality issues included the desire of cable companies to offer premium download speeds that could favor some content providers over others. Web and smartphone speeds also vary, and regulators and courts must decide what constitutes fair competition.

Network Neutrality

The U.S. Court of Appeals for the D.C. Circuit rejected portions of the FCC Open Internet Order developed in 2010 addressing network neutrality and other issues. In 2014, in *Verizon v. FCC*, a three-judge panel relied upon a previous FCC definition of broadband cable as information service providers rather than telecommunications common carriers. While the court upheld FCC authority to encourage broadband infrastructure deployment under the Telecommunication Act of 1996, the Open Internet Order went further in requiring disclosure of traffic speeds, anti-blocking and anti-discrimination requirements: "Even though the Commission has general authority to regulate in this arena, it may not impose requirements that contravene express statutory mandates." The court distinguished legal issues of Internet backbone networks, broadband providers, edge providers (Amazon and Google, for example) and end users. Users of Facebook, however, "may often act as edge providers by creating and sharing content that is consumed by other end users."

In *National Cable & Telecommunications Association v. Brand X Internet Services*, the Supreme Court upheld FCC classification of cable through its reasonable interpretation of vague language in the 1996 Act. When Comcast subscribers later complained about slowed peer-to-peer services, the FCC ordered disclosure in 2008. The D.C. Circuit, however, vacated the order, ruling in *Comcast Corp. v. FCC* that the FCC failed to demonstrate regulatory authority over network management.

The FCC went forward with Open Internet proceedings. Faced with a contrary *Comcast* decision, it sought to reclassify broadband. The successful *Verizon* appeal was based on (1) lack of FCC regulatory authority, (2) arbitrary and capricious rules, and (3) actions contrary to the 1996 Act. By attempting to reclassify broadband as a common carrier, the FCC did so without identifying its statutory authority.]

The Ninth U.S. Circuit Court of Appeals, however, upheld California's Open Internet Net Neutrality law, and technology companies in 2022 dropped their legal challenges. The law bars ISPs from throttling Internet speeds for economic advantage to some over other streaming services.

The FCC's ISP common carrier re-classification in 2015 was first decided a year later by a three-judge panel. Six months after the D.C. Circuit Court of Appeals heard *United States Telecommunications Association v. FCC*, the court voted 2-1 to deny a petition for review of the FCC Order. The government rules blocked ISPs from purposely slowing speeds from specific sites. In its motion to dismiss, the FCC told the court that the rules were carefully tailored to favor Internet openness.

Importantly, the panel that decided *United States Telecommunications Association*, addressed application of the rules to emerging mobile technologies: The FCC found that mobile broadband — like all broadband — is a telecommunication service subject to common carrier regulation under Title II of the

Communications Act. The majority also recognized the mobile marketplace and a projection that more than 90 percent of broadband may be mobile and smart by the time the book you are reading now was published. The FCC "permissibly found that mobile broadband now qualifies as interconnected because it gives subscribers the ability to communicate to all users of the newly defined public switched network." The majority quoted the FCC Order: "Broadband users should be able to expect that they will be entitled to the same Internet openness protections no matter what technology they use to access the Internet." The Trump Administration under FCC Chair Ajit Pai, however, repealed net neutrality. Pai argued that the policies were based upon "hypothetical harms and hysterical prophesies of doom," and that the decision restores FTC authority.

The common carrier telecommunications service classification had explicitly rejected First Amendment issues: "The absence of any First Amendment concern in the context of common carriers rests on the understanding that such entities, insofar as they are subject to equal access mandates, merely facilitate the transmission of speech of others rather than engage in speech in their own right." The majority observed that broadband providers offered no messages and little editorial control over content. Instead, the FCC views broadband as "mere conduits for the messages of others." The majority distinguished any case where a broadband provider also operates a news or weather channel, exercises content decisions and qualifies for First Amendment protection. However, most broadband providers do not exercise editorial judgment similar to a newspaper or cable TV operation. "In that regard," the court held, "the role of broadband providers is analogous to that of telephone companies: They act as neutral, indiscriminant platforms for transmission of speech of any and all users." Broadband providers make an argument similar to the huge social and digital platforms.

While broadband providers may face network capacity issues, the majority concluded that the issues are temporary. The FCC defined broadband in data marketing terms — allowing end users to send and receive data across "all or substantially all Internet endpoints."

In *Verizon v. FCC*, the D.C. Circuit struck down an FCC attempt to address net neutrality. In 2015, however, the FCC voted to treat ISPs as common carriers similar to telephone companies, and a panel of the same court upheld the order. In *United States Telecommunictions Association v. FCC*, the D.C. Circuit denied en banc review of the 2015 decision, but also acknowledged that the FCC appeared ready to replace the rule. A majority had found that the FCC has authority to create Internet rules, and ISPs have no First Amendment shield against net neutrality obligations. The court cited the *Brand X* case as Supreme Court precedent for FCC authority. It noted that the rules applied only to those "broadband providers that hold themselves out as neutral, indiscriminate conduits" and raise "reasonable expectations of a customer" that desired content will not be blocked or access speeds throttled.

FCC AND FTC ISSUE AGENDAS

Administrative law agencies, such as the FCC and FTC, derive delegated regulatory authority from Congress to create rules based upon complexity and specialized knowledge.

FCC Key Issues
- Measuring fixed broadband
- Communications marketplace
- Rural Internet connection
- Mobile digital divide
- Library universal service

FTC Key Issues
- Children's Online Privacy Protection Act (COPPA)
- Online frauds, refunds and cease and desist letters
- Identity theft
- Antitrust complaints and merger reviews
- Robocalls
- Cloud computing
- Social media financial transparency

Sources: FCC.gov and FTC.gov (2023).

The First Amendment and Online Communication

A review of new media begins with free expression theory and practice, but it must go beyond the law to view social change in an increasingly technological world. Defamation, as we saw in Chapter 6, is one example of how law may be defined within unique cultural contexts around the world. Social media sites, such as Twitter, spark new cases and issues. In 2019, Twitter used its contract rights with users to blur some tweets that might be viewed as harmful.

At the same time, there is the potential for social media interaction to be subpoenaed in a case. Lawyers representing employers and employees have been among those warning about the legal dangers of social media posts. The tech Web site Mashable.com identified five potential lawsuit areas: company secrets, invasion of privacy, defamation, trademark violations and wrongful employee termination claims. In 2009, for example, Horizon Group Management, which managed rental property in Chicago, sued tenant Amanda Bonnen for $50,000 after she tweeted: "You should just come anyway. Who said sleeping in a moldy apartment was bad for you? Horizon realty thinks it's okay." Bonnen had just twenty followers on Twitter. The libel lawsuit claimed the tweet damaged Horizon's reputation. A Cook County judge dismissed the case, finding the tweet was too vague.

Twitter changed its Terms of Service in a number of important ways. Silha Center for the Study of Media Ethics & Law Research Assistant Scott Memmel reported in 2016 that Twitter sought to stop violent, harrassing and terroristic tweets. Twitter labels "hateful conduct" as threatening speech based on "race, ethnicity, national origin, sexual orientation, gender, gender identity, religious affiliation, age, disability, or disease." The future of First Amendment freedoms rests, in part, on speakers' ability to use social media platforms. Twitter and other sites, however, exercise editorial judgment and filtering. By flagging some of President Trump's tweets and closing other controversial accounts, sites risk the possibility that they could lose lawsuit immunity or even face new regulation.

The First Amendment does not mention new technologies, but lawmakers, regulators and the courts have attempted a variety of strategies to apply it. For example, the Supreme Court recognized that the unique traits of each mass medium may permit different constitutional standards. Yet new technology characteristics often are not apparent until long after an introduction. Congress, the FCC, the FTC, other regulators applying administrative law, and the courts must choose to (1) regulate an emerging technology before it is well understood or widely used; (2) regulate during the uncertain developmental and evolutionary period; (3) attempt to formulate logical and consistent regulatory models after the new technology is in general use; or (4) avoid regulation altogether.

Legislation frequently is challenged in the courts on First Amendment grounds. State privacy law, for example, remains an unsystematic set of measures related to arrest, banking, medical and school records, computer crime and justice, government data, employment and other issues, according to the Electronic Privacy Information Center and others. Adding to confusion is the FTC's implementation of the Children's Online Privacy Protection Act, known as COPPA, originally part of congressional attempts to protect children in cyberspace. Sites had to require operators to post privacy policies, provide notice and obtain parental consent prior to collecting certain personal information from children. The rule allowed Internet operators to submit individual regulatory plans for dealing with children younger than 13, and many Web sites responded by restricting access. Legal scholars raised constitutional concerns about, among other aspects, the chat room restrictions of COPPA, which require parental consent and may not be narrowly tailored.

Often, it is unclear whether, or how much, the technology of a medium should affect the legal protection of the message conveyed. History of a technology appears to affect the courts' willingness to apply the First Amendment. The result is a highly detailed, often inconsistent and confusing array of regulations and rulings.

While state legislation may be designed to solve the nagging concern of, for example, email spam, this problem goes beyond the full reach of law and regulation. Even technological solutions, such as filtering software, fail to stop all unwanted email. The FTC continues to prosecute those who send spam — in one case winning a $2.5 million judgment for CAN-SPAM violations. The FTC rule was aimed at protecting identifiable information such as names, addresses, email addresses and phone numbers. In response, about 147 individuals and corporations filed comments with the FTC. Retailer Amazon.com, for example, complained that the rule was "likely to interfere with the overall customer experience and inherent benefits of the Internet." The FTC sought more authority over Internet consumer privacy because fewer than half of the Web sites in the study had implemented adequate privacy protections. In the end, Internet e-commerce and shopping continued to grow under the new rules.

Video Services and Telephone Company History

The Communications Act of 1934 identified telephone companies as common carriers that had to provide non-discriminatory services at similar rates to anyone wishing to send and receive messages over their systems. Different portions of the act govern phone companies, broadcast stations and cable systems, making the law cumbersome. As fiber optic technologies developed, many government regulators believed phone companies would use their large size, universal penetration and economic power to drive other multi-channel video providers out of business. Of course, cable and broadcast lobbyists helped fuel these fears within the political, policy-making system. Concerns about phone company behavior pre-date the break-up initiated in the 1970s and later settled.

The problem of ownership concentration was known from the dawn of the telephone age. The dominance was so great that the federal government filed lawsuits against the original AT&T in 1914 and again in 1956. The government charged that AT&T violated antitrust laws by attempting to monopolize local and national telecommunications markets for service and equipment. Each time, AT&T would sign a consent decree, promising that it would no longer engage in the impermissible actions, but change was rarely seen.

Similar concerns arose during the early years of the cable industry, when many phone companies owned cable systems. They often needed to string above-ground lines, but local governments sometimes refused to allow cable operators to erect their own poles, which was inefficient. So, cable operators rented or leased space on existing poles that telephone or power companies owned. From cable's earliest days and through the 1960s, though, the FCC heard many complaints that affiliated cable operators were not being allowed to rent space on telephone poles. Likewise, the market concentration of Facebook (and Instagram), Google (and YouTube), Twitter and Amazon reflect similar concerns about too few players with control over too much. Facebook's control of Instagram, WhatsApp and Messenger reflect market dominance that may require the federal government to respond. In one example, Google+ was ended because even they could not compete.

New technologies historically begin with entrepreneurial innovation that eventually leads to a relatively small group of survivors. For example, In 1960, the FCC responded by adopting the telephone-cable cross-ownership ban to eliminate the incentive for phone companies to discriminate against cable competitors. In 1974, the U.S. Department of Justice filed a third antitrust suit against AT&T, claiming that the 1956 consent decree had failed to prevent monopoly. Originally, there were twenty-two Bell Operating Companies, which were reorganized into seven Regional Bell Operating Companies. The new agreement, settled in 1982, became known as the "Modification of the Final Judgment." It forced AT&T to sell off its local telephone service divisions, and AT&T then became only a long-distance provider. The newly formed regional and local phone companies were limited to local phone services.

Congress adopted the FCC's cross-ownership ban as part of the 1984 Cable Act. It prevented all telephone companies — including approximately 2,500 independent phone companies not formerly affiliated with AT&T — from owning or operating cable systems. Regulation typically comes in conflict with large businesses seeking synergies with others.

The original seven RBOCs (now merged to three — AT&T, Lumen Technologies and Verizon) became the nation's largest providers of local phone service: Ameritech, Bell Atlantic, Bell South, Nynex, Pacifio Telesis, Southwestern Bell and USWest. They chafed at many restrictions in the MFJ, including the ban on information services. In 1991, federal district judge Harold Greene oversaw the consent decree and essentially removed the information services ban. However, that left in place the 1984 Cable Act ban on telephone-cable cross-ownership. Several RBOCs sued and argued that the ban abridged their First Amendment rights to free speech. Beginning in 1993, every court that heard such a case agreed.

While the RBOCs were challenging the Cable Act ban, the FCC also gave phone companies a way to be involved in video. In 1992, it allowed the RBOCs to offer a common carrier video service called "video dialtone." With it, a phone company used its wires and support services to provide video similar to television signal quality. Telephone companies had to provide the service on a non-discriminatory, first-come-first-served basis. The companies, historically viewed as common carriers, provided households access to shared long distance lines. In this environment, the phone companies were not involved in content or editing. Video services, however, redefined the phone companies.

The Telecommunications Act of 1996 eliminated the telephone-cable cross-ownership ban and allowed local phone companies to provide video programming in one of three ways:

• A firm offering local telephone service could also own a cable system as a subsidiary company. Telephone-owned systems would need to comply with all of the laws and local and state cable franchise requirements.

• A telephone company could operate a common carrier video service similar to VDT (although that term is no longer used) on a first-come-first-served basis. Under this approach, its video service would be regulated much as its common carrier telephone service.

• The Open Video System providers served both as common carriers of others' programming and as program providers. If outside demand for video carriage exceeds system capacity, then the OVS provider may program no more than one-third of its channels, with the remainder offered to other providers on a first-come-first-served basis. The systems were not required to obtain franchises, but local governments could require OVS fees equivalent to the franchise fees of a cable operator. By acting as video common carriers, OVS providers are absolved of some regulatory obligations. A phone company could offer video services through what is called "wireless cable." Wireless technology is further discussed later in the chapter and is perhaps the most important development in the new media technology area.

The RBOCs challenged other provisions of the 1996 law. They argued that it unfairly punishes them by requiring delays until competition exists before they may provide advanced services. In 1998, a federal circuit court upheld the FCC's effective-competition standard before allowing a RBOC to offer long-distance

services. The court later rejected another RBOC's constitutional challenge to the Telecommunications Act's mandate that Bell companies provide electronic publishing only through separate affiliates. It said the rule was a well-justified, content-neutral mechanism to prevent monopolies and unfair competition. The Supreme Court refused to review.

Rates, Services and Access

Rates for service and competitor access to new marketplaces continue to be important issues. The D.C. Circuit Court of Appeals, after two previous interventions, refused to overturn the FCC method for determining fair charges for coinless pay telephone calls. The same court vacated one FCC order that would have transferred licenses from Ameritech to SBC Communications as part of a merger and forced regulators to revisit the scope of services allowed to be included. Companies and the FCC also have bickered over the release of required audit data that the FCC uses to determine fairness of rates.

Merger mania abounded among the so-called "Baby Bells" and others, and, in 2000, the FCC reviewed a proposed merger between the nation's second and third largest long-distance providers. The merger would have placed 80 percent of the residential long-distance market in the hands, once again, of two companies, AT&T and MCI (WorldCom). However, they called off the $129 billion deal following regulatory challenges in the United States and Europe. This turned out to be a pause, as mergers again later accelerated more than a decade later.

By 2002, a national economic downturn and questionable business practices led to a dramatic shakeout of the more than 600 competing telecommunications companies. Global Crossing and McLeodUSA filed for bankruptcy. WorldCom collapsed, admitted to $11 billion in fraud, agreed to pay shareholders $500 million, and signed on to a settlement that included a $1.5-billion Securities and Exchange Commission fine. The deal allowed MCI to continue to operate the business.

From a regulatory perspective, two questions involving the mergers and telecommunication companies (known as "telcos") are (1) Is there a settling point between free-wheeling marketplace economics and regulatory limits on monopolization of the market? and (2) What role will the courts play in managing the telecommunication marketplace in such an environment?

The Supreme Court, in two important cases in 2002, addressed key issues raised by expanding phone services and wireless delivery methods. In *National Cable & Telecommunications Association v. Gulf Power*, it held that the FCC had authority under the Pole Attachments Act to set reasonable rates and conditions for high-speed Internet, traditional cable and wireless services. It found that "the subject matter here is technical, complex, and dynamic; and as a general rule, agencies have authority to fill the gaps where the statutes are silent."

Moreover, in *Verizon Communications v. FCC,* the Court upheld rules requiring large local phone companies to allow new competitors reasonably priced access to existing networks. The decision was hailed as a victory for smaller competitors but was by no means the end of telephone powerhouses' attempts to retain a competitive advantage. In *AT&T v. FCC,* the D.C. Circuit Court of Appeals said regulators may allow Bell operating companies to have expanded access to new long-distance customers, if the competitors have access to local networks that meet the public interest. In *SBC v. FCC,* circuit judges denied review of $6 million in FCC fines for merger agreement violations.

The three proposed remaining "Baby Bell" RBOC phone companies — the new AT&T, Qwest and Verizon — earlier had faced millions of dollars in fines because they withheld or delayed competitors' access to lines and equipment, a small price to pay to gain a competitive edge in a business worth billions of dollars. By 2004, the FCC drafted new rules promoting competition, including the so-called "Pulver Order" that unregulated free voice over the Internet and sparked a flurry of online innovation. The inability to settle the issues at first threatened AT&T and MCI, long-distance companies. However, mergers pushed MCI to Verizon, and the SBC deals assumed the AT&T brand. The U.S. House of Representatives voted in 2007 to deregulate the business further and allow Baby Bells to offer DSL Internet service without being required to provide competitors with access to equipment and networks, but the issues remained unresolved. Nevertheless, the business deals continued.

Huge mergers were back in the news in 2019, as the U.S. Department of Justice signed-off on a deal worth at least $26 billion. T-Mobile and Sprint were on track to combine as the nation's second largest wireless group. Sprint's agreement to sell Boost Mobile was a regulatory requirement. This positioned the merged brand among the three consumer options that included AT&T and Verizon.

A D.C. Circuit panel earlier had approved AT&T's purchase of Time Warner, which owns CNN and other media properties. The new WarnerMedia brand antitrust dispute with the U.S. Department of Justice had begun in 2016 in an $85 billion deal that led to HBO rate increases and an end to unlimited data pricing. Concern also has been expressed about the willingness of the wireless companies to share private data with other businesses and the government.

There are core First Amendment issues. In 2008, the FBI director apologized to the *New York Times* and *Washington Post* for not following DOJ rules in 2004, and obtained reporters' telephone records in violation of federal law. These were among "hundreds of cases" that utilized an "exigent circumstance" exception. We now know that the practice continued during the Trump Administration and at the start of the Biden presidency.

NSA SURVEILLANCE PROS AND CONS

The political debate over NSA surveillance programs raises important issues in the balance between freedom and the desire to be safe from terrorist attacks. Despite some changes offered by President Barack Obama following the Edward Snowden disclosures, some say more reform is needed to protect U.S. citizens from electronic data collection.

David Cole, legal affairs correspondent for *The Nation,* writes: "Americans from the right and left have voiced concerns.... But privacy advocates will have to keep pressing their cause if they want real reform.... True reform would replace that mass surveillance with a more targeted approach, one that authorizes intrusive surveillance when the agency has reason to suspect a person of wrongdoing or of being a foreign agent, but not otherwise" (*Real NSA Reform Still Needed,* THE NATION, Feb. 10, 2014, at 3-4).

Arthur Herman and John Yoo, writing in the *National Review,* defended NSA "bulk collection" of telephone and email data: "President Obama could continue a program that takes advantage of America's technological superiority, meets the requirements of constitutional law, and has proven effective in stopping terrorist attack.... With an eleven-judge panel overseeing every step, NSA handles data with a lot more care than Facebook or Google" (*A Defense of Bulk Surveillance,* NAT'L REV., Apr. 7, 2014, at 31-33).

In *Smith v. Maryland,* 442 U.S. 735 (1979), the Supreme Court found no constitutional right to hide telephone numbers already available to telephone companies. They are considered third parties that weaken a case for individual privacy protection. The Court may need to revisit the issue based upon the new technologies for using computer algorithms to dissect big data in search of behavioral patterns across social networks.

The 2013 disclosure by Edward Snowden of widespread NSA surveillance of telephone and computer records sparked media coverage and public debate. Former President Barack Obama maintained the post 9/11 programs were developed in the George W. Bush Administration. The spying aimed at protecting the nation from future enemy attacks has been funded by Congress and reviewed in the federal courts. There remains room, though, to debate boundaries within a free society.

Glenn Greenwald first reported the government snooping in *The Guardian* in 2013, and journalists James Risen and Laura Poitras followed a year later in *The New York Times.* Among the revelations from Snowden data was that the NSA was developing facial recognition systems from digital photographs. The Electronic Frontier Foundation fought the data collection system. The passage of the USA Freedom Law in 2015 followed expiration of Section 215 of the USA PATRIOT Act provisions. The new instructions revert some provisions to the law in 2001. One commentator wrote: "[T]he government is seemingly back to only being able to request a court order to obtain business records from common carriers, public accommodation facilities, physical storage facilities, and vehicle rental facilities, per the pre-PATRIOT Act and current version of Section 1862(a)."

The EFF challenged several laws, including Section 702 of the FISA Amendments Act, which the NSA has used to collect without warrants telephone and email big data from company computers through fiber optic cables. Other EFF cases of interest included issues ranging from fair use in copyright law, Fourth Amendment privacy related to cellphone tracking, and the Allow States and Victims to Fight Online Sex Trafficking Act of 2017. Beyond government issues, consumers must deal with corporate providers of service. Early DSL high-speed Internet competition was one issue.

Robocalls and the First Amendment

In *Barr v. American Association of Political Consultants* in 2020 the Supreme Court rejected amendments from 2015 to the Telephone Consumer Protection Act of 1991. These would have allowed for government-backed student loan and mortgage collection robocalls. Generally, automated telephone calls to landlines and mobile phones are prohibited under the Telephone Consumer Protection Act of 1991.

The Supreme Court affirmed the Fourth Circuit ruling that, by singling out two industries, TCPA changes amounted to content-based restrictions that could not survive strict scrutiny. The 6-3 decision relied on Americans' "disdain for robocalls," laws passed to restrict them as well as the fact that the act "generally prohibits robocalls to cell phones and home phones." A group of political consultants and pollsters had sought to use the new exceptions as a way to strike down the general law. Their argument worked in the Eastern District of North Carolina but was vacated on appeal. "The Court of Appeals therefore invalidated the government-debt exception and severed it from the robocall restriction," the Supreme Court held. It cited *Police Department of Chicago v. Mosley, Hudgens v. NLRB,* and *Reed v. Town of Gilbert* when it concluded that while the First Amendment allows for time, place and manner restrictions, these cannot discriminate based upon expressive content.

Consumers and Corporations

Consumers sometimes find their interests at odds with those of the large corporations. Two days after FCC rules cracking down on slamming were to go into effect in 1999, for example, the D.C. Circuit halted enforcement, but its order did not address the validity of the rules. The FCC defined slamming as unauthorized changes in the preferred telephone carrier of a consumer, such as switching a consumer without an explicit request. While courts have upheld the FCC's regulation of slamming, fines have been vacated when imposed simply because a telephone company could not prove the actual line subscriber had agreed to the service charge.

Similarly, there has been concern about telemarketing. When the public complained about the prevalence of unsolicited telephone sales calls, the FTC responded with a national "Do Not Call" list in 2003. In the first day alone, 735,000 numbers were registered. Still, consumers continue to complain.

The 1984 AT&T divestiture left regional monopolies called Incumbent Local Exchange Carriers, but ILECs were left out of the long-distance market until deregulation in 1996. Upstart Competitive Local Exchange Carriers, however, went to court to challenge what they insisted were antitrust and unfair trade practices. The 1996 Act requires that ILEC's share network resources with competitors, but it is not a simple matter to guarantee access to fair pricing, open markets and reasonable compensation. The Supreme Court, in 2007, reviewed common carrier provisions of the Communications Act and mandated *just and reasonable* charges to customers *and* suppliers.

The telephone market continues to evolve, as regulators address new competition of voice over Internet protocol services, including requiring help in subsidizing rural, educational, library and low income access. Meaningful competition has produced cases between communication giants.

THE FCC AND SLAMMING

Slamming has been the single largest source of complaints to the Commission for several years. The number rose from 12,795 in 1996 to 23,484 in 1999. FCC rules were at the core of the agency's efforts to eliminate slamming by giving consumers meaningful recourse against deceptive switching of carriers. Thereafter, there was a decline in slamming complaints the FCC received (with local phone companies also reporting similar declines) after April 1999.

The FCC has levied fines of more than $15 million for slamming violations. However, in 2006-07 there was only one $85,000 consent decree with Long Distance Consolidated Billing Co., and this followed a $4 million consent decree with Sprint Communications Company. In that case, it was alleged that consumers shopping at Sprint PC retail stores had their exchange services changed without authorization. Sprint could not provide the FCC with records showing that it had followed verification procedures before making changes. The FCC continues to encourage consumers to file complaints against companies that change service without their approval. In 2008 the FCC proposed a $5,084,000 fine against one carrier. *See* http://www.fcc.gov/eb/tcd/slam.html.

More than two-thirds of states administer anti-slamming rules, but the FCC early in the Trump Administration removed pages and reduced federal focus on regulation, but consumer protection reremerged in the Biden Administration. https://www.fcc.gov/general/consumer-policy-issues

OTHER MEDIA

A variety of emerging consumer technologies has raised numerous legal issues. Systems for delivering video into the home have been particularly problematic for regulators. As Internet video compression improved, however, consumers had amazing new options for watching news, entertainment and sports across a variety of mobile and fixed devices.

Direct-to-Home Services

Cable systems provide service to a majority of multichannel

video consumers, but the industry is rapidly losing customers to Internet video. Netflix, Hulu, HBO, MLB, CBSN and others are attracting growing audiences.

In 1934, when Congress passed the Communications Act, it did not envision satellites. Science fiction writer Arthur C. Clarke first advanced this concept — known as "geosynchronous orbit" — in 1945. It is not surprising, then, that the Communications Act did not mention broadcast satellites that use modern technologies such as digital band compression to beam down hundreds of channels of video programming. For about thirty years, before the rapid rise of Internet streaming video, satellite TV was a very important delivery system.

The FCC has jurisdiction over direct broadcast satellites because they use the electromagnetic spectrum to send signals to receiving dishes. The FCC licenses all DBS operations. In 1982, when it faced the issue of how to regulate DBS, it realized that DBS could be seen as (1) a broadcasting service, distributing signals to terrestrial antennas, just as broadcast stations do, or (2) a service much like local phone companies, renting space on the satellite to send signals. The FCC chose to adopt simplified, flexible regulations to allow DBS to develop. Broadcasters challenged the fairness of the rules, and a federal appellate court disagreed, in part, with the FCC's strategy. It found that DBS met many legal characteristics of a broadcast medium and could be regulated only to the extent that the FCC could justify distinctions. The court said DBS could be regulated as a non-local broadcast service without local programming obligations. A later court decision held that DBS was more like subscription services than broadcasting because it does not use the spectrum to transmit to the public. The FCC used the term "direct-to-home" for services sending video signals to receivers in the United States, and required technical standard agreements with Mexico and other Latin American nations. Operators such as DirecTV and Dish Network formerly offered this service using high-power signals. Another company, Prime-Star, offered DBS service using medium power.

Under international agreements, the United States had eight positions for DTH satellites in the geosynchronous orbit. Each position used up to thirty-two transmission channels. Digital signal compression allowed for several signals to transmit in the portion of the spectrum previously needed for a single signal; hundreds of channels may fit on a single satellite. The FCC shifted from awarding these orbital positions through competitive hearings or by lottery to auctions for the slots.

Satellite operators must comply with federal laws and FCC regulations, but they also must operate under standards set by the International Telecommunications Union, the worldwide body overseeing spectrum use. U.S. satellite operators also need not strictly comply with ITU rules, but ultimately the ITU must approve the deviations from its standards, or the operators must come into compliance.

The 1992 Cable Act required the FCC to establish certain public interest obligations of satellite operators, such as rules regarding political communication, retransmission consent (but not the must-carry rules) and equal employment opportunities. Broadcasters and cable operators argued that DBS had an unfair competitive edge and should have been subjected to government mandated must-carry rules. In 1998, the FCC adopted rules requiring DBS providers to set aside 4 percent of their channel capacity for noncommercial educational or informational programming, as required by the public interest section of the law. The FCC has interpreted the 1992 Act to apply these requirements to DBS operators.

A federal appellate court held that satellite operators, like cable operators, may use the compulsory copyright license. Echo-Star, a leading DBS provider, brought a federal lawsuit against the television networks to obtain legal permission for a retransmission of programming to residents where over-the-air reception of local signals is marginal.

The broadcast regulation system was originally designed to aid local broadcasters because it was believed they had an ability to serve the unique "public interest, convenience or necessity" of a particular community. Under the 1992 Cable Act, the FCC was instructed to determine whether DBS operators also should be subject to such "localism" rules. Under the Communications Act of 1934, the FCC employed its licensing power to promote local ownership and programming. The FCC, though, was unable to determine how a service that sends a signal nationally and offers a wide variety of programming options could be concerned with localism in the same way as a local broadcast station. Regardless, the general trend toward deregulation has led to declining emphasis on the concept of localism in the licensing process. The 1996 Act limited the ability of cities, homeowners' associations and others to restrict satellite dishes; Congress' intent was to ensure that DBS growth would not be stymied. By consolidating and streamlining DBS regulation, the FCC promoted more competition with cable, whose rates continued to climb.

Satellite Master Antenna Television Systems

A satellite master antenna television system, also called "private cable," is essentially a cable system contained within an apartment building or several buildings. Similar to cable, a SMATV system collects local TV signals through an antenna and satellite signals through receiving dishes, all placed on top of a building. It sends the signals through wires that run through the building, into individual apartments. The SMATV system may serve other commonly owned buildings on the same plot of private land, and the system's wires will run to and through each building. If the wires go across public rights-of-way, such as public streets, the operation becomes a cable, not a SMATV, system. The FCC has chosen to impose few regulatory burdens on SMATV systems, thus allowing them to develop into competition for cable. Further, it has held that there can be no local or state regulation of SMATV.

Wireless Cable

In 1970, the FCC dedicated a portion of the spectrum to a service for business communications. By 1974, it realized that part of the spectrum could be used to send video signals to subscribers and established the "Multipoint Distribution Service." The FCC permitted two video channels to be provided in the country's fifty largest markets and one video channel in other markets.

The business soon became known as "Multichannel Multipoint Distribution Service." Wireless cable sent as many as thirty-three channels by microwave signals to antennas on subscribers' homes. Since it used microwaves, part of the electromagnetic spectrum, the FCC licensed and regulated it. Because it did not cross public rights-of-way, it was not considered a cable system and didn't require a local franchise.

The FCC did not permit cities or states to regulate wireless cable, and, as with satellite operators, the Commission allowed wireless operators to act as conduits for other video programmers or to themselves provide programming. In either case, the Commission imposed very few regulatory requirements on wireless cable, but it must approve any non-subscription service supplied by MDS or MMDS. As with DBS, wireless cable services must comply with the retransmission consent rules requiring operators to obtain permission from any broadcast stations that the wireless cable service carries.

In 1997, the FCC issued its first rulings preempting restrictions on the installation and use of satellite dishes imposed by local governments and homeowners associations in four states. It also began a proceeding to adopt more flexible regulation of wireless cable and to encourage its use for interactive services. In a 1998 decision intended to strengthen the foundering wireless cable industry, the Commission adopted rules that allowed MDS operators to offer two-way digital services.

The FCC used auctions to award hundreds of wireless cable licenses. As technological advances enabled wireless cable operators to offer a number of video signals on each of their thirty-three channels through digital signal compression, licenses became more valuable. Several phone companies expressed an interest in purchasing wireless cable operations because the 1996 Telecommunications Act permits telephone companies to provide video services through wireless cable.

In 1998, the FCC auctioned portions of the local MDS spectrum, which uses transmitters to send voice, data or video to within a six-mile radius. The FCC awarded more than 859 local MDS, or LMDS, licenses and raised approximately $580 million. The FCC did not permit local telephone or cable companies to bid for most licenses, hoping that other smaller companies would develop competitive LMDS services. In recent years, digital and Internet video access replaced many of the older technologies that tend to persist in smaller, rural communities that still lack high-speed Internet access.

Digital Television

"Digital television" is a term applied to technological standards for advanced television, affecting both the transmission and widescreen display of signals. The first high-definition TV sets were introduced in 1998. Traditional analog sets can display HDTV only if they are used with an external ATSC tuner converter. The conversion to digital from analog was slowed by the historic investment in traditional analog television systems. The transmission standard in use in the United States since 1941 is called NTSC (for the National Television System Committee, which suggested its adoption to the FCC).

DTV development, initially called HDTV, began in Japan in the 1960s. Later work was undertaken in Europe on a different DTV standard incompatible with the Japanese technology. The United States began work on DTV late, but the delay gave American companies a digital rather than an analog transmission scheme. In 1987, the FCC established the Advisory Committee on Advanced Television Systems to coordinate American research. After years of work, the so-called "Grand Alliance," comprised of the companies that had been competing to develop DTV, agreed upon a technical standard different from Japanese and European electronic engineering.

In 1996, the FCC approved an ATSC standard, which differed from that used in Europe and much of the rest of the world. ATSC addressed signal transmission protocols, giving TV manufacturers the confidence to build and sell sets able to receive DTV signals. Televisions compatible with both the Grand Alliance and the FCC standards reached the market, and broadcasters and cable companies began to provide digital programming while simulcasting existing analog programs. Most desktop and laptop computers today feature video cards and DVD drives capable of handling theater-quality digital video.

In 1997, the Commission gave current full-power television broadcasters a second channel to use for DTV. A decade later, DTV broadcasts became a reality in the United States. It was a challenging transition for broadcasters and the public. In 1998, the FCC affirmed its commitment that conversion to DTV be completed by 2006, when analog channels were first scheduled to go dark. However, in early 2006, a provision of the Deficit Reduction Act delayed the death of analog television until 2009. Some analog signals went dark then, and the remainder finally made the transition in June 2009. Consumers wanting to watch broadcast television needed sets capable of receiving digital signals, or set-top converter boxes to make reception possible. The government offered coupons to help pay for the cost of converters and, additionally, some computer users purchased HDTV tuner cards.

Digital channels may be used for high definition television, or "multiplexing" — up to four TV signals, but not HDTV. Using compression, several signals, plus data and other services, such as paging, may be provided on the spectrum space previously devoted to one channel. The 1996 Act states that if broadcasters are given second channels, and they use them to provide services for which they charge a fee, they must compensate the federal government for using those channels.

Beyond the technologies themselves, regulators are concerned about fraudulent marketing practices to consumers, such as pressuring customers to change providers.

Interactive Video and Data Services

Interactive Video and Data Services combine data transmission and interactivity to permit home shopping, banking and other services. Some IVDS providers entered the business by buying available portions of the spectrum through FCC auctions that offered preferences for women and minorities. In 1997, a federal circuit court ruled that a constitutional challenge to these preferences must be reviewed on its merits by the FCC. An IVDS provider argued that the preferences unconstitutionally favored select groups and inflated auction prices.

These developments were less important than the low-cost access available with the World Wide Web. Anyone may launch a multimedia site and attempt to compete with major media players without approval from government regulators.

THE INTERNET

The ubiquitous Internet offers global email, information and entertainment. It has grown from a handful of sites in 1994, to the primary global online advertising method. These numbers grow dramatically each year, and the trend is toward global access. The number of Web pages has surpassed one trillion, and everyone seems to agree that the Internet will continue to expand and be a dominant force for years to come — particularly in Asia and in underdeveloped nations. To assure the continued strength and growth of this network, some Internet service providers are lobbying Congress for laws requiring local cable TV companies to provide access to their lines for Internet use. This policy is known as "unbundling" or "open access."

The Internet presents legal problems, some of which are familiar and others that are new. For example, communication through the Internet can be undertaken anonymously, copyrighted material can be distributed without the copyright holder's permission, and information stored on computers can be obtained by people with no right to it. As time passed, it became clearer that the Web was less revolutionary than first predicted and more an extension of traditional media in terms of American communication law. One of the toughest challenges is how to define offensive material. YouTube (Google) in 2019 removed and de-monitized hate speech videos without full transparency in its decision-making process.

The Internet and Indecency

A portion of the Telecommunications Act of 1996, called the Communications Decency Act, made it illegal to knowingly send or make available to minors any indecent or obscene material. The CDA was one of four unsuccessful U.S. government attempts (under two presidents and three sessions of Congress) to restrict or filter access by children to pornography, particularly on the Internet. The CDA of 1996, the Child Pornography Prevention Act of 1996, and the Child Online Protection Act of 1998 all have failed a number of various legal challenges. In 2003, however, the Supreme Court reversed a lower court and upheld the Children's Internet Protection Act of 2000. (See the box "Five Key Court Cases.")

The Supreme Court found part of the CDA's indecency provisions unconstitutional. In *Reno v. ACLU* it acknowledged Congress's concern with preventing children from being the targets of, or having access to, sexually explicit communications, but it said the CDA's ban on indecency was vague and overbroad. The law did not define indecency in a way that conformed to previous Court decisions.

In a ruling against the law that would have defined as criminal making such content accessible to children, the Court distinguished the Internet from broadcasting. The Internet does not use the limited public spectrum, and people are not as likely to be exposed inadvertently to sexually explicit material on the Internet as on broadcast stations. Accordingly, adult Internet users should not suffer the reduced First Amendment protections that apply to radio and television station operators, the Court reasoned. However, the *Reno* Court concluded that obscene material may be banned from the Internet because the First Amendment does not protect any obscene messages, regardless of medium. Most importantly, the Court treated Web site operators as publishers: "Publishers may either make their material available to the entire pool of Internet users, or confine access to a selected group, such as those willing to pay for the privilege."

FIVE KEY COURT CASES: NARROWLY TAILORING LAWS THAT RESTRICT INTERNET FREE SPEECH

Between 1997 and 2004 the Supreme Court addressed issues related to Internet pornography, obscenity and indecency in five important opinions:

• In *Reno v. ACLU* (1997), the Court found unconstitutional portions of the Communications Decency Act, which was part of the Telecommunications Act of 1996. It found the language too vague and rejected Justice Sandra Day O'Connor's call for zoning the Internet.

• In *Ashcroft v. ACLU* (2002), the Court voted 8-1 to remand the Child Online Protection Act of 1998 to lower courts to reconsider application of the obscenity test from *Miller v. California* (1973). The case appeared to apply the traditional obscenity test to Internet content. It was remanded again in 2004 on a 5-4 decision to seek fresh evidence comparing site age verification blocking to user-based filtering software. In 2007, District Judge Lowell Reed found that software filters "are far more effective than COPA would be at protecting children from sexually explicit material," and he struck down the law as "not narrowly tailored to Congress' compelling interest." He issued an injunction against enforcement. The law would have made it federally criminal to offer any commercial "harmful" communication to minors on the Web, punishable with fines and imprisonment. The ruling means that Congress is free to draft a narrower law that addresses constitutional concerns.

• In *Ashcroft v. Free Speech Coalition* (2002), the Court, by a 6-3 vote, rejected a ban on "virtual" child pornography, as defined in the Child Pornography Prevention Act of 1996, as violating the First Amendment.

• In *United States v. American Library Association* (2003), a lower court decision was reversed in a 6-3 vote. The Children's Internet Protection Act of 2000, which requires libraries supported by federal funds to install filtering software on computers, was found to be a constitutional and effective measure to block pornographic images that are deemed harmful to children. The Supreme Court rejected First Amendment arguments that public libraries are a public forum subject to the strict scrutiny standard. Instead, libraries make content-based decisions.

• In *Ashcroft v. ACLU* (2004) (*Ashcroft II*), the Supreme Court, by a 5-4 vote, blocked the latest iteration of COPA. The Court remanded the case to a lower court and sought fresh evidence on filtering software effectiveness.

The Court has consistently called for narrowly tailored restrictions on Internet speech and application of traditional obscenity law. The Internet has been viewed as similar to print media with respect to the First Amendment.

The *Reno* decision reflected the Court's position in *Sable Communications v. FCC*, when it held that Congress may prohibit obscene telephone communications but may not ban indecent "dial-a-porn" messages available *via* telephone for a fee. Although the Court had ruled in *FCC v. Pacifica Foundation* that the FCC could restrict indecency on broadcast stations, it found in *Sable Communications* that telephones are markedly different from broadcasting. Radio is ubiquitous, uniquely powerful and accessible to children, the Court held.

On the other hand, a person must consciously choose to access a dial-a-porn service. Likewise, people pay to gain access to the Internet, and filtering software is available to assist parents in protecting their children from offensive messages. In addition, pornography sites often are supported by additional user subscription fees. Congress later adopted a law requiring dial-a-

porn businesses to make their services available only through a pre-subscription arrangement, credit card payment or other method that would make it difficult for children to gain access. Attempts to enact similar restrictions for the Internet have been more problematic.

While courts use the *Miller v. California* definition of obscenity for print and visual media, questions existed about applying it to the Internet. For example, the Sixth U.S. Circuit Court of Appeals upheld the conviction on federal obscenity charges of two people who operated a computer bulletin board from their California home, offering sexually explicit materials. The couple was charged in Memphis with transmitting obscene material. A postal official had obtained computer files and ordered six videotapes. A jury found that the material violated local community standards and convicted the couple of transporting obscene images across state lines *via* the Internet. In *United States v. Thomas*, the court rejected the argument that the ruling effectively established a national standard for obscenity, contrary to the Supreme Court's Miller Test, or that upholding the conviction would mandate that all material sent over the Internet be no more explicit than permitted by the most restrictive community.

Concerned by the high Court's elimination of the CDA's online indecency ban, Congress enacted and President Bill Clinton signed the Child Online Protection Act in 1998 to help prevent children from accessing harmful material. Six months later, the U.S. Department of Justice was in the U.S. Court of Appeals for the Third Circuit to challenge a district court order that enjoined enforcement of the new law.

In 1999, a federal judge in Pennsylvania stopped application of Congress's second attempt to shield children from Internet pornography. COPA would have required commercial Web sites to collect credit card numbers or some other proof of age before allowing users to access targeted materials. The law called for a $50,000 fine and up to six months in prison for any commercial provider who knowingly made harmful material available to minors under the age of 17. In 2000, an appeals court struck another blow to COPA by upholding the district court ruling. The Third U.S. Circuit held that the ACLU's attack on the constitutionality of the act would likely succeed.

In 2002, the Supreme Court held in *Ashcroft v. ACLU* that community standards may be used to identify material that is harmful to minors. Ruling on COPA, the Court found the use of *Miller v. California* language distinguishable because all three prongs of the test must be used. While the earlier *Reno* decision failed because only the patently offensive standard was utilized, the COPA statute also employed *Miller's* prurient interest and serious value tests. Justice Clarence Thomas, writing for the 8-1 majority, reiterated that, unlike the first two prongs, the third allows a court to set aside community standards in favor of "whether a reasonable person would find ... value in the material, taken as a whole." The decision then remanded the case for further review by lower courts.

Only Justice John Paul Stevens dissented: "In the context of the Internet ... community standards become a sword rather than a shield. If a prurient appeal is offensive in a puritan village, it may be a crime to post it on the World Wide Web."

In 2004, the Supreme Court sided 5-4 with a lower court decision to block COPA, but it remanded the case to update evidence on the effectiveness of Internet filters, as well as other existing laws and technologies. In an opinion written by Justice Anthony Kennedy, the Court held, "Content-based prohibitions, enforced by severe criminal penalties, have the constant potential to be a repressive force in the lives and thoughts of free people." The Court noted that Congress passed two other laws, one prohibiting misleading domain names and another creating a "Dot Kids" domain. The idea to create separate Internet domain space for children, however, has not become popular. A for-profit company owns .kids, and the second-level kids.us project has been inactive since 2012.

The decision to return the case to the district court relied on the *Reno* decision and the idea that filtering software satisfies the least restrictive means test better than forcing commercial Web sites to verify user age. The Court, however, refused to accept the appellate court conclusion that use of community standards was overbroad. It distinguished the differences between the district court opinion, which held that the statute must be narrowly tailored to serve a compelling government interest, and the appellate court's unconstitutional finding, which the majority refused to accept without fresh evidence.

The majority placed the burden on government to find less restrictive alternatives: "The purpose of the test is to ensure that speech is restricted no further than necessary to achieve the goal, for it is important to assure that legitimate speech is not chilled or punished." Minors may be able to obtain credit cards and access pornographic Web sites, and filters are not entirely effective. However, they go beyond Web sites and may also be used to block email. The majority concluded that parents and libraries may be encouraged to use filters.

The Court was severely divided, however, on whether filters solve the problem, as well as how best to fit restrictions within the requirements of the First Amendment. Justices Stevens and Ruth Bader Ginsburg would have taken it further. Their concurrence supported the appellate court reasoning that use of community standards warranted striking down the law as unconstitutional. However, Justice Antonin Scalia dissented, arguing that restricting commercial pornography is consistent with existing law. Justice Stephen Breyer's dissent, meantime, argued that COPA advanced a compelling interest and followed the Miller Test.

In 2007, District Court Judge Lowell Reed appeared to settle the question by ruling that software filters were more effective than COPA in protecting children from harmful material and that the legislation was "impermissibly vague and overbroad" when applying the strict scrutiny test. In *ACLU v. Gonzalez,* he wrote:

Because COPA suppresses a large amount of speech that adults have a constitutional right to receive, under the strict scrutiny standard, COPA may only be upheld as constitutional if defendant meets the burden of proving that COPA is narrowly tailored to the compelling interest that COPA was enacted to serve and there are no less restrictive alternatives.

The Supreme Court had let stand a lower court ruling upholding another part of the Communications Decency Act. The Court issued a one-sentence order that allowed the government to enforce a CDA ban on obscene and indecent email intended to harass or annoy a recipient. In *ApolloMedia Corp. v. Reno,* a San Francisco company challenged a provision that made it a felony to initiate "the transmission of, any comment, request, suggestion, proposal, image, or other communication which is obscene, lewd, lascivious, filthy, or indecent, with intent to annoy, abuse, threaten, or harass another person." Annoy.com had allowed people to send anonymous and lewd electronic mail to public officials. Attorney William Bennett Turner argued in an appellant brief that the language of Section 223 unconstitutionally punishes indecent material under the Miller Test:

There is no conceivable government interest that could justify [Section] 223's content prohibition of "indecent" speech.... The government cannot even advance the interest in protecting children from exposure to "indecent" material — the interest that it unsuccessfully urged to support the other provisions of the Act held unconstitutional.... The provisions at issue here apply regardless of the age of the recipient, govern communications among adults, and have no safe harbor defenses.

Nevertheless, the Supreme Court refused to revisit its earlier decision. Internet pornography and the profitable business that surrounds it have created First Amendment issues because of photographic artists such as Barbara Nitke, who sued the government in 2001. She argued that community judgments about obscenity could empower the most restrictive community, which would affect the entire Internet. In *Nitke v. Gonzalez,* however, the government won. The court held:

There is insufficient evidence on the record to enable us to make a finding as to whether "the variation in community standards is substantial enough that the potential for inconsistent determinations of obscenity is greater than that faced by purveyors of traditional pornography, who can control the dissemination of their materials."

The Supreme Court affirmed without comment. In another case dealing with children's access to sexually explicit materials online, *Mainstream Loudon v. Board of Trustees of the Loudon County Library,* a federal judge enjoined enforcement of a Virginia library's policy to block public access to such Internet sites. While recognizing a compelling government interest in reducing illegal access to pornography, the court ruled that the library had adopted an overbroad policy to address speculative concerns with no evidence of illegal access or citizen complaints. The lawsuit against the library alleged that the policy violated the First Amendment and was an unconstitutional prior restraint. An earlier ruling declared: "The First Amendment applies to, and limits, the discretion of a public library to place content-based restrictions on access to constitutionally protected materials within its collection." The court held that receiving Internet information was consistent with the type of public forum the library routinely offered.

In another twist on the library issue, seven Minneapolis librarians claimed that the amount of pornography on Central Library computers created a "hostile, offensive, palpably unlawful working environment." Library patrons downloading pornographic images prompted at least two bills in Minnesota to require blocking or filtering software on all school and library computers. Ultimately, the library director apologized to the public and announced plans to require sign-ins at workstations, as well as limiting computer use to thirty minutes.

A three-judge panel of the Third Circuit in Philadelphia at first rejected the Children's Internet Protection Act, which requires filtering software on computers at libraries supported by federal funds. The court unanimously ruled the law unconstitutional. It said filters tend to overblock educational content:

While most libraries include in their physical collection copies of volumes such as *The Joy of Sex* and *The Joy of Gay Sex,* which contain quite explicit photographs and descriptions, filtering software blocks large quantities of other, comparable information about health and sexuality.... One teenager testified that the Internet access in a public library was the only venue in which she could obtain information important to her about her own sexuality. Another ... witness described using the Internet to research breast cancer and reconstructive surgery for his mother.... Even though some filtering programs contain exceptions for health and education, the exceptions do not solve the problem of overblocking constitutionally protected material ... not only information relating to health and sexuality that might be mistaken for pornography or erotica,

but also vast numbers of Web pages and sites that could not even arguably be construed as harmful.

Popular filtering software programs blocked non-pornographic sites. The court rejected the government's argument that technology is imperfect. The court accepted the plaintiff's argument against the government that libraries constitute a public forum subject to a strict scrutiny First Amendment analysis:

Because the filtering software mandated by CIPA will block access to substantial amounts of constitutionally protected speech whose suppression serves no legitimate government interest, we are persuaded that a public library's use of software filters is not narrowly tailored to further any of these interests. Moreover, less restrictive alternatives exist that further the government's legitimate interest in preventing the dissemination of obscenity, child pornography, and material harmful to minors, and in preventing patrons from being unwillingly exposed to patently offensive, sexually explicit content.

The court noted that there are less restrictive options such as enforcing library rules prohibiting access to pornography or providing unfiltered computers in restricted areas. Instead, the measure would have restricted funds to any library that did not keep minors from visual depictions of obscene content, child pornography or content generally harmful to minors.

Citing *FCC v. League of Women Voters of California* and other cases, the court concluded that the government has no right to restrict speech for content reasons: "By interfering with public libraries' discretion to make available to patrons as wide a range of constitutionally protected speech as possible, the federal government is arguably distorting the usual functioning of public libraries as places of freewheeling inquiry."

CIPA, which would have been enforced through FCC actions and the provisions of the Library Services Technology Act, was enjoined from going into effect while the Supreme Court considered an appeal. The Court was faced with a series of arguments that the ACLU outlined. It contended:

- The law violates the First Amendment.
- Web site blocking is erratic and ineffective.
- The law was passed against the advice of Congress' own experts.
- Web blocking is contrary to the mission of public libraries.
- The blocking will widen the digital divide.

Nevertheless, six justices agreed in *United States v. American Library Association* to reverse the lower court and uphold the law. The plurality opinion, written by Chief Justice William

Rehnquist, noted that Internet pornography has been a serious problem for public libraries: "Some patrons also expose others to pornographic images by leaving them displayed on Internet terminals or printed at library printers." The federal government provides two sources of funding to public libraries: (1) discounted rates for Internet access and (2) technology grants for equipment. The Court considered filtering "reasonably effective." Further, the law allows libraries to disable filters "to enable access for bona fide research or other lawful purposes." The plurality rejected the First Amendment issues that the lower court raised but noted library decision-making and the need for broad discretion. Rehnquist found instead that "the government has broad discretion to make content-based judgments in deciding what private speech to make available to the public."

Funding decisions typically use content-based criteria. In *American Library Association*, the Supreme Court held: "Public library staffs necessarily consider content in making collection decisions and enjoy broad discretion in making them." Thus, a public library is not a public forum: It "does not acquire Internet terminals in order to create a public forum for Web publishers to express themselves, any more than it collects books in order to provide a public forum for the authors of books to speak." Instead, the Court said library resources exist "to facilitate research, learning, and recreational pursuits by furnishing materials of requisite and appropriate quality." Because Chief Justice Rehnquist found a library is not a public forum, he refused to apply a strict scrutiny standard:

A library's need to exercise judgment in making collection decisions depends on its traditional role in identifying suitable and worthwhile material; it is no less entitled to play that role when it collects material from the Internet than when it collects material from any other source. Most libraries already exclude pornography from their print collections because they deem it inappropriate for inclusion. We do not subject these decisions to heightened scrutiny; it would make little sense to treat libraries' judgments to block online pornography any differently, when these judgments are made for the same reason.

The Court found no problem with the requirement that adults must ask librarians to unblock Web sites or disable filters because "the Constitution does not guarantee the right to acquire information at a public library without any risk of embarrassment." In a concurring opinion, Justice Stephen Breyer also rejected the strict scrutiny approach. "The statutory restriction in question," he wrote, "is, in essence, a kind of 'selection' restriction (a kind of editing)." This is especially true when there is a need to be "shielding" children from exposure.

In a dissenting opinion, Justice John Paul Stevens wrote that

CIPA "operates as a blunt nationwide restraint on adult access to 'an enormous amount of valuable information' that individual librarians cannot possibly review." He argued that government "may not suppress lawful speech" and reduce adult access to "only what is fit for children." He wrote:

Unless we assume that the statute is a mere symbolic gesture, we must conclude that it will create a significant prior restraint on adult access to protected speech. A law that prohibits reading without official consent, like a law that prohibits speaking without consent, "constitutes a dramatic departure from our national heritage and constitutional tradition."

Justice Stevens saw local library discretion as similar to academic freedom at a university, and penalizing funding violates the First Amendment: "An abridgment of speech by means of a threatened denial of benefits can be just as pernicious as an abridgment by means of a threatened penalty."

In a strident separate dissent, Justice David Souter, joined by Justice Ruth Bader Ginsburg, wrote that CIPA "says only that a library 'may' unblock, not that it must."

Children could be restricted to blocked terminals, leaving other unblocked terminals in areas restricted to adults and screened from casual glances. And, of course, the statute could simply have provided for unblocking at adult request, with no questions asked. The statute could, in other words, have protected children without blocking access for adults or subjecting adults to anything more than minimal inconvenience, just the way (the record shows) many librarians had been dealing with obscenity and indecency before the imposition of federal conditions.

Souter wrote that a local library could not impose adult restrictions and that the opinion ignored that, when a library does not have a book, a patron may use interlibrary loan:

[T]he Internet blocking here defies comparison to the process of acquisition. Whereas traditional scarcity of money and space require a library to make choices about what to acquire, and the choice to be made is whether or not to spend the money to acquire something, blocking is the subject of a choice made after the money for Internet access has been spent.... Thus, deciding against buying a book means there is no book (unless a loan can be obtained).... The proper analogy therefore is not passing up a book that might have been bought; it is either to buying a book and then keeping it from adults lacking an acceptable "purpose," or to buying an encyclopedia and then cutting out pages with anything thought to be unsuitable for all adults.

Souter argued that CIPA and the Court's support for it defied library history and reminded the Court that, by the time of McCarthyism, the American Library Association had explicitly opposed censorship in its own Bill of Rights. The American library tradition has favored adult access and adult inquiry:

Quite simply, we can smell a rat when a library blocks materials already in its control, just as we do when a library removes books from its shelves for reasons having nothing to do with wear and tear, obsolescence, or lack of demand. Content-based blocking and removal tell us something that mere absence from the shelves does not.

Souter concluded: "There is no good reason, then, to treat blocking of adult enquiry as anything different from the censorship it presumptively is."

The Court has become increasingly interested in Internet issues, especially when there is concern about children accessing obscene or pornographic content and when the pornography industry victimizes them. The question of whether computer-animated virtual child pornography can be restricted came before the Court in 2001. An appeals court held that the Child Pornography Prevention Act of 1996 was unconstitutional in prohibiting computer images that do not involve real children. At issue was whether there was a government interest beyond attempting to protect real victims of child pornography. In a 6-3 decision, the Supreme Court ruled in *Ashcroft v. Free Speech Coalition* that CPPA violated the First Amendment. It held that the statute's language was "overbroad and unconstitutional" because it defined images as "any visual depiction, including any photograph, film, video, picture, or computer-generated image or picture" that "is, or appears to be, a minor engaging in sexually explicit conduct." The Court rejected government arguments that pedophiles could use virtual pornography to seduce children. Justice Kennedy's opinion said the law went beyond law the Court set forth in its child pornography case, *New York v. Ferber*: "As a general rule, pornography can be banned only if obscene, but under *Ferber*, pornography showing minors can be proscribed whether or not the images are obscene under the definition set forth in *Miller*." However, restriction on computer-morphed images was found to be too sweeping. By quoting the First Amendment, Justice Kennedy and the Court's majority made it clear that they found CPPA to be a disturbing intrusion on First Amendment rights:

[A] law imposing criminal penalties on protected speech is a stark example of speech suppression. The CPPA's penalties are indeed severe. A first offender may be imprisoned for 15 years.... A repeat offender faces a prison sentence of not less than 5 years and not more than 30 years.... While minor pun-

ishments can chill speech, ... this case provides a textbook example of why we permit facial challenges to statutes that burden expression. With these severe penalties in force, few legitimate movie producers or book publishers, or few speakers in any capacity, would risk the distribution of images in or near the uncertain reach of this law. The Constitution gives significant protection from overbroad laws that chill speech within the First Amendment's vast and privileged sphere. Under this principle, the CPPA is unconstitutional on its face if it prohibits a substantial amount of protected expression.

The articulation of a "vast and privileged sphere" of First Amendment protection is expansive in terms of the type of speech under the umbrella of safety. Outside the safe zone are "defamation, incitement, obscenity, and pornography produced with real children." By contrast, the Court was concerned that CPPA might render illegal Shakespeare's *Romeo and Juliet* or the popular movie *American Beauty*. CPPA, the Court found, failed to distinguish isolated sexual scenes from the *Miller* requirement to evaluate the "work as a whole." It rejected the argument that because virtual child pornography and real child pornography might soon be impossible to distinguish, prosecution would become difficult:

The hypothesis is somewhat implausible. If virtual images were identical to illegal child pornography, the illegal images would be driven from the market by the indistinguishable substitutes. Few pornographers would risk prosecution by abusing real children if fictional, computer images would suffice.

In his concurrence, Justice Clarence Thomas wrote that the government failed to provide evidence of any case in which someone charged with production of illegal child pornography had raised reasonable doubt by contending the images were virtual and not of real children.

Justice Sandra Day O'Connor, joined by Chief Justice Rehnquist and Justice Scalia, offered a partial dissent. They disagreed that CPPA's virtual-child-pornography ban was overbroad: "Such images whet the appetites of child molesters, ... given the rapid pace of advances in computer-graphics technology, the Government's concern is reasonable." Rehnquist added in a separate dissent that the CPPA statute had clearly defined explicit content as sex that was genital-genital, oral-genital, anal-genital or oral-anal, bestiality, masturbation, sadistic or masochistic abuse, or "lascivious exhibition of the genitals or pubic area." Rehnquist and Scalia argued unsuccessfully that the definition relates only to hard-core child pornography and not to classic plays or movies.

Internet Libel

Portions of the Communications Decency Act not struck down by the *Reno v. ACLU* ruling have been used to protect Internet service providers from liability for libel. A federal district court, for example, protected America Online from a libel suit by a Clinton Administration official and his wife against the Drudge Report. The report, republished on AOL's site, said the husband had a history of spousal abuse. The court ruled that Section 230 of the act protects providers of interactive services from liability for third-party materials, even though AOL exercises some editorial control and is more than a passive carrier. Internet gossip columnist Matt Drudge, as a result, was left to defend himself in the libel suit. In the years since the case, much remains unsettled about defamation on the free-wheeling Internet. As was noted earlier in the discussion of Twitter, the lack of a definable mass audience makes it difficult to measure economic impact of statements that *may* damage individual reputation.

Beyond libel law, the changing nature of the social Internet also renders problematic content owner rights. The emergence of a sharing culture, promoted by sites that encourage users the share content with online friends or fans, introduces a new media model. Content owners, who benefit from advertising revenue generated by increased numbers of site visitors, must also try to protect property rights.

Copyright on the Internet

The Internet presents questions about protection of intellectual property rights. Copyright protects original material upon its creation, and the creator has exclusive rights to reproduce and distribute it, as well as the right to create other works derived from the original. Therefore, uploading a document or media file, copying an Internet posting and re-transmitting it without permission all could violate copyright and digital theft law. Even browsing through material on a computer, which causes a copy of the digital information to be held in temporary memory, could possibly constitute illegal copying. Alternately, such use might be interpreted as the digital form of reading a book in a library or a magazine at a newsstand, and not a copyright infringement.

The growth of Internet sites that link to or frame a small section of another site's content raised a new question of copyright infringement. In 1997, the *Washington Post* and five other news organizations charged a group of Internet news sites with copyright infringement for republishing and repackaging media Web pages for profit. The organizations charged that the news sites copied trademarks for use as links and republished copyrighted material with advertising that generated revenue for the pirates rather than the copyright holders. The suit was settled out of court when the news sites agreed to provide links but not to frame any content from the news organization's sites. The *Los Angeles Times* won its case against FreeRepublic.com, a Web site that reprinted full-text online news stories and invited caustic reader reaction.

Other copyright questions surround computer-generated material. To qualify for copyright protection, material must be fixed in a tangible medium and must be original. It remains to be determined whether material created and transmitted electronically is "fixed in a tangible medium." For example, a live broadcast is not fixed in a tangible medium and is not protected unless it is simultaneously put on videotape. In contrast, a document put on a hard drive disk, CD or DVD is fixed. Thus, is material created but not saved on a computer, and then sent over the Internet, fixed in a tangible medium and subject to copyright protection? One court has held that material in a computer's random access memory is sufficiently fixed to be protected.

In 1995 and again in 1998, Congress updated copyright laws in part to deal with such issues. It enacted the Digital Millennium Copyright Act of 1998 to eliminate an apparent loophole in the Digital Performance Rights in Sound Recordings Act that had permitted webcasters to digitally transmit recordings without copyright licenses or fees. The law grants webcasters a statutory license to transmit, with certain limitations, recordings at fees established voluntarily or by a Copyright Arbitration Royalty Panel. The fees ended many webcasts. For example, some college radio stations ended webcasts when forced to pay as much as $20,000 in music licensing fees.

In the meantime, the Supreme Court upheld the Sonny Bono Copyright Term Extension Act of 1998 as a constitutional exercise of congressional powers. The 7-2 decision in *Eldred v. Ashcroft* dismissed concerns about free expression. However, Justices Stevens and Breyer wrote dissenting opinions. Breyer wrote: "The Copyright Clause and the First Amendment seek related objectives — the creation and dissemination of information." In this view, the two should work together to promote free expression and dissemination of ideas. The law extended copyrights on, for example, Disney's Mickey Mouse for another twenty years to 2023. Many twentieth-century icons were kept out of the public domain. Also, the rock music band Metallica sued the Napster.com site in 2000 for copyright infringement and racketeering over its free software that allowed users to trade MP3 copies of music on an unrestricted basis. The digital music format allowed CD quality songs to be converted into a personal computer format, and this made possible the easy distribution of pirated copies over the Internet. The software made it so easy that thousands of music bootleggers clogged university campus network systems.

International distribution of illegal copies *via* the Internet is a problem for Internet service providers and computer users. A German judge ruled that ISPs may be held liable for their roles in distributing illegal copies. However, the Supreme Court has let stand a New York Court of Appeals ruling that ISPs are not liable for transmissions but are akin to telephone and telegraph companies that are accorded common law qualified privilege against liability. That ruling protected Prodigy from a defamation lawsuit. In the Metallica case, two of three universities — Yale and Indiana — blocked access to Napster.com in exchange for being dropped from the lawsuit. The band claimed large numbers of students were using campus computer systems to access the Napster site and trade pirated music. Metallica also identified 335,000 Napster screen names in 60,000 pages of documents. Napster ultimately yielded to legal pressures by removing 317,377 users, a move that did not prevent the traders of bootleg music from returning. At the same time, the company MP3.com settled its lawsuit by halting access to major label songs after a federal district court ruled its database of more than 80,000 songs was copyright infringement against Time Warner, Sony and others. MP3 agreed to pay licensing fees to music companies.

The Napster case, though, attracted much attention. "Napster has built a business based on large-scale piracy," the complaint alleged. The Recording Industry Association of America also sued over the distribution of MP3 music. A district court held that record companies and artists owned the music and issued an injunction prohibiting Napster from "engaging in, or facilitating ... copying, downloading, uploading, transmitting, or distributing ... copyrighted recordings." The Ninth U.S. Circuit Court of Appeals agreed, holding that Napster infringed on music reproduction and distribution rights and that its sharing software went beyond a fair use. It distinguished Internet file sharing from the Supreme Court's ruling in *Sony Corp. v. Universal Studios, Inc.* that video cassette recorders constituted a fair use. Following the decision, Napster was unable to reach an agreement with music companies to compensate them. Subsequently, federal District Court Judge Marilyn Patel in San Francisco ordered Napster to curb trading of copyrighted music. Napster went ahead with plans to develop a fee-based system, even though it had no initial agreement with record companies. At the same time, alternative services such as Gnutella, Aimster, Grokster and Kazaa prompted new legal challenges, as record companies struggled to develop their own pay sites. In 2002 four of five record companies suspended legal action against Napster in order to avoid inquiries into their copyright actions; Napster continued to be threatened with bankruptcy; and Bertelsmann ultimately agreed to pay $8 million for its assets.

The original Napster no longer exists, and Gnutella, Grokster, Madster, KaZaA and other services — after flourishing for awhile — faced various legal challenges, In 2003, the recording industry filed lawsuits against hundreds of people, including college students in campus housing and parents of teens who illegally shared music. However, it lost a case before the D.C. Circuit Court of Appeals. The copyright challenges forced Napster to eliminate illegal file swapping and create new software to monitor users' behavior. Thus, the one-time adversaries became partners.

The Supreme Court overturned the Ninth Circuit Court summary judgments that had insulated Grokster and Streamcast from copyright infringement liability. In *MGM v. Grokster*, the Court held that "one who distributes a device with the object of promoting its use to infringe copyright, as shown by clear expression ... is liable." The peer-to-peer networks featured the sharing of mostly copyrighted works, without any attempt to filter. The Court found that file sharing was not similar to VCR recording, which the 1984 *Sony* decision protected from liability. The number of downloads each day influenced the Court's decision, but the opinion stopped short of revisiting the earlier law: "It is enough to note that the Ninth Circuit's judgment rested on an erroneous understanding of *Sony* and to leave further consideration of the *Sony* rule for a day when that may be required." Digital video recording devices, such as TiVo, however, may hasten the day when the Court will reconsider whether the VCR recording protection afforded in the *Sony* case for the purpose of time-shifting program viewing will survive.

A 1995 committee report of the U.S. Patent and Trademark Office to consider copyright questions on the Internet failed to resolve the issues. While it suggested that computer transmissions should be considered "copies" similar to photocopies of a book page, it decided that existing copyright law was generally adequate to deal with the Internet.

Conditions changed quickly on the Web. If a subscriber uses a service to send copyrighted material, is the service as well as the user guilty of copyright violation? For example, a company could publish a magazine online. A user could copy a story and send it to millions of Internet users. Who is liable? Two courts have found ISPs liable for their subscribers' copyright infringements, and one has found to the contrary. A key factor was whether the provider had, or should have had, prior knowledge of the infringement. Online providers who electronically screen or preview material may be held accountable for copyright infringements, although providers who act as common carriers may not.

Google, by uploading copyrighted book material, has become involved in what is known as the Google Book Search Settlement. An administrator in the class-action lawsuit is creating a system to pay authors for use of their works.

A problem arose from the theft of wireless network signals from homes and business. People have broken into private networks in order to facilitate illegal file transfers. In 2005, for

THE MUSIC LABELS VERSUS FILE SHARING

Although the Recording Industry Association of America ceased filing lawsuits in 2008, the industry group continues to pursue previous cases against individuals using peer-to-peer sites to share copyrighted songs and video. In a Boston case, four labels — Sony BMG, Warner Bros., Arista and UMG — won a $675,000 civil jury award in 2009 against a graduate student who "willfully engaged in thousands of copyright infringements," but it was subsequently reduced in 2010 to $67,500, or $2,250 per infringement (one-third of a federal statute minimum $750) from thirty songs illegally shared. District Judge Nancy Gertner, in a sixty-two-page order, rejected both the recording industry desire to tie the case to billions of dollars in claimed losses and a Harvard legal team argument of much lower actual damages based upon the iTunes price of 99 cents per legal download (the industry receives seventy cents "wholesale price"). Instead, Judge Gertner found that a jury award was higher than she would have ordered and "unconstitutionally excessive" damages, in part, because those who had settled paid so much less:

> This award is far greater than necessary to serve the government's legitimate interests in compensating copyright owners and deterring infringement. In fact, it bears no meaningful relationship to these objectives.... I have merely reduced the award to the greatest amount that the Constitution will permit given the facts of this case. There is no question that this reduced award is still severe, even harsh. It not only adequately compensates the plaintiffs for the relatively minor harm that Tenenbaum caused them; it sends a strong message that those who exploit peer-to-peer networks to unlawfully download and distribute copyrighted works run the risk of incurring substantial damages awards. Tenenbaum's behavior, after all, was hardly exemplary. The jury found that he not only violated the law, but did so willfully.

The industry sent thousands of claims letters over several years to alleged violators and settled out of court with most for payments of less than $5,000. A handful of people refused to settle, and these cases continue to go forward. In Minnesota, for example, one woman was hit with a $1.9 million jury award, which was later reduced to $54,000 in a second trial. In the Boston case, the Digital Theft Deterrence Act of 1999 was used against a graduate student who admitted he had freely shared copyrighted music. In 1999, the record showed, Joel Tenenbaum had used Napster to download songs and place them in a shared folder. After Napster closed, he used Kazaa and other services, such as LimeWire, through 2007. Under federal procedure, Tenenbaum could have received a new trial, but his legal team raised a constitutional challenge. At issue is the constitutionally permissible size of punitive damages and the statutory range provided under the digital theft law. On appeal in the First Circuit, Tenenbaum's lawyer argued in 2011 that the jury verdict was excessive, unreasonable and in violation of due process. At oral arguments, judges seemed skeptical about the need to protect noncommercial copyright infringers.

Meanwhile, following a $105 million settlement with LimeWire, RIAA went after Box.Net copyright infringers. Using the Digital Millennium Copyright Act, Mashable.com reported that takedown notices were issued to copyright infringers. An attorney for plaintiffs pointed to congressional intent to punish willful conduct. Tennenbaum had been warned that what he was doing was wrong, and he persisted with the behavior on more than one site — even after one location was closed. The music industry said it needs to now stop noncommercial copies because Internet peer-to-peer technologies have a "viral nature" that empowers users to damage copyright holders: "Now, this technology turns home copiers into home distributors." The unprecedented nature of what the technology allows an individual to do, plaintiffs argued, forced music labels to protect their economic interests. Appellate judges, however, also heard that restrictive limits on noncommercial use also are harmful to libraries and archives.

Sources: Jonathan Saltzman, *Judge Slashes Downloading Penalty, Calls $675k Award in BU Student's Case "Excessive,"* Boston Globe, July 10, 2010, *available at* http://boston.com; Nancy Gohring, *Judge Cuts File-sharing Fine to $67,500,* It World, http://itworld.com/print/113554; Debbie Rosenbaum, *Gertner's Ruling on Damages,* Joel Fights Back, http://joelfightsback.com/; Sony BMG Music et al. v. Tenenbaum, 721 F. Supp. 2d 85 (D. Mass. 2010); Digital Theft Deterrence Act, 17 U.S.C. § 504(a), (c)(1) (1999); Brenna Erlich, *After LimeWire, the RIAA Cracks Down on Box.Net Infringers,* Mashable, http://mashable.com/2011/05/20/riaa-boxnet/.

example, St. Petersburg, Florida, police arrested a 41-year-old who had hacked into a home network by parking his SUV nearby and using a laptop computer.

Clearly, the convenience of wireless networking comes at a price — the availability of signals for potentially illegal activities and the possibility of invasion of privacy of legal and paying users. ISP liability continues to spawn new case law. For example, Craigslist — used by individuals to advertise — was found not liable for housing classifieds that discriminated in violation of federal law and also entitled to immunity from gun violence that may have resulted from a weapon purchased online. State attorneys general and lawmakers continued to target Craigslist and its inability to filter all illegal activities, including under-aged sex trafficking. Craigslist responded with changes — removing all adult advertising.

The Internet and Privacy Issues

Workers using the Internet for personal reasons could find that employers have access to everything. People using the Internet from home for banking, shopping and email could find they have less privacy protection than when engaging in such activities by mail or in person. Additionally, social networking sites allow users to set privacy settings, but new users may skirt them. In other developments:

- A police search of a smartphone by arresting officers without a warrant generally violates the Fourth Amendment (*Riley v. California*, 2014).
- Google apologized for Street View vehicles collecting personal data from open WiFi networks, and Facebook reported

conducting secret psychological content filtering experiments — a top company officer apologized that the routine product testing was "poorly communicated."

• Facebook won an $873 million judgment against a Canadian spammer who flooded more than four million users with sexually explicit messages promoting penis enlargement products and illegal drugs.

• YouTube banned videos intended to incite violence or encourage dangerous, illegal activities.

Carpenter v. United States
138 S.Ct. 2206 (2018)

Facts: In a series of 2011 robberies and arrests, Timothy Ivory Carpenter was placed near four robberies *via* cellphone location data. Carpenter moved to suppress evidence because there was no warrant or showing of probable cause.

Issues: Historical mobile data offer a picture of user movement, and this raises Fourth Amendment privacy concerns. Under *Katz v. United States, Riley v California* and *Kyllo v. United States*, technologies are subject to not only the Stored Communications Act, but also Fourth Amendment protection of "people, not places."

Decision/holding: Chief Justice John Roberts was joined by Justices Ruth Badar Ginsburg, Stephen Breyer, Sonia Sotomayor, and Elena Kagan to reverse and remand the case as an illegal search: "[W]e hold that an individual maintains a legitimate expectation of privacy in the record of his physical movements as captured through CSLI." The holding was narrow: "We do not express a view on matters not before us: real-time CSLI or 'tower dumps.'" Justices Kennedy, Thomas, Alito, and Gorsuch filed dissenting opinions. Kennedy thought location data were similar to business records, Alito found a distinction of physical searches, and Gorsuch desired to overturn *Katz* privacy dicta.

Reasoning: "But while the third-party doctrine applies to telephone and bank records, it is not clear whether its logic extends to the qualitatively different category of cell site records.... A person does not surrender all Fourth Amendment protection by venturing into the public sphere.... Moreover, the retrospective quality of the data gives police access to a category of information otherwise unknowable."

Justice Gorsuch, in his dissent, argued that before *Katz*, a Fourth Amendment claim did not turn on "a judge's personal sensibilities about the 'reasonableness' of ... expectations...."

There have been other issues.

Politwoops, a Web site that archived politicians' tweets, raised issues about the privacy rights of a user to delete content once published. The Open Foundation created the site at a 2010 meeting of computer hackers in the Netherlands. The Sunlight Foundation extended access to the United States in 2012. Because of legal issues, Politwoops faced closure in about thirty countries. Twitter disconnected access within the United States, citing Terms of Service violations.

Walmart sent Jeph Jaques, author and cartoonist, a cease-and-desist letter for the Walmart.horse Web site. It featured only the image of a horse pasted in front of a store photograph. Walmart did not accept simple fair use parody instead of trademark infringement. It then filed a complaint with the World In-

tellectual Property Organization under the Uniform Domain Name Dispute Resolution policy. Rather than litigate, the Web site was voluntarily removed.

New technologies also threatened to erode traditional common law views about the sanctity of privacy in one's own home. Privacy becomes a question when law enforcement authorities tap into computer transmissions. While a court order is required, it may be possible for computer users to encrypt transmissions. In 1993 the National Security Agency proposed a clipper chip to allow decoding.

Web-based telephone services, such as Vonage, posed an interesting privacy problem for regulators and the courts. The U.S. Court of Appeals for the D.C. Circuit, upheld the FCC decision that law enforcement agencies require wiretap compatibility. The court, though, exempted university and private computer networks, as well as instant messaging. The clarification of the scope of the Communications Assistance for Law Enforcement Act, CALEA, meant that Voice over Internet Protocol (VoIP) was not exempt from regulation under all circumstances.

PRIVACY AT WORK
Ontario v. Quon
560 U.S. 746 (2010)

The Supreme Court reversed the Ninth Circuit Court of Appeals in finding in favor of the Ontario, California, Police Department and its monitoring of on-duty officer text messages.

In 2001, the city had issued police officers pagers, which had limits on the amount of text sent and received each month. When some officers exceeded the limits, a review of two months found that SWAT team member Jeff Quon had many personal and sexual messages during work hours. After being disciplined, he and other officers alleged violation of privacy on Fourth Amendment grounds, as well as the Stored Communications Act.

A district court found that the city had conducted a reasonable audit of the text messages and that the officers' privacy had not been violated, but the appeals court reversed the decision. At issue was the nature of a reasonable expectation of privacy at work, the ability of employers to conduct legitimate investigations of work-related misconduct and the evolving nature of the technology.

In a narrow ruling, the Supreme Court found the police department's warrantless search was reasonable because it was motivated by a legitimate work-related purpose and was not excessive in scope. A city policy informed employees that all messages on city-owned equipment could be reviewed in connection with computer use, the Internet and email. The text messages, however, had been sent and received over radio frequencies. Still, police officers had been given verbal advance warning that the general policy applied to texting. A case-by-case precedent led Justice Anthony Kennedy to write: "The judiciary risks error by elaborating too fully on the Fourth Amendment implications of emerging technology before its role in society has become clear." Justice Antonin Scalia disagreed on that point: "The-times-they-are-a-changin' is a feeble excuse for disregard of duty."

Beyond the Internet and Future Regulatory Issues

Congress has proposed dozens of bills seeking to regulate various aspects of the Internet — pharmacy consumer protection, online investor protection, spam advertising limitations, email protection and e-commerce protection. One bill sought to limit sales of prescription drugs by requiring Web sites to include a page that lists licensed pharmacists. The mood to regulate was promoted by cases such as that of a Seattle doctor ordered to halt online prescribing of the sexual dysfunction drug Viagra after a 16-year-old boy and a woman posing as a man obtained prescriptions. The Food and Drug Administration raised concerns about the rampant online sale of prescription drugs. State attorneys general, meanwhile, maintained that licensing and monitoring of health care professionals should continue to be a matter of state regulation. Nevertheless, former Senate Democratic Leader Tom Daschle of South Dakota concluded that Congress had not kept pace with technological change. He stated: "Internet users are often promised basic privacy protection, only to have their expectations disappointed and their personal information put up for sale or disseminated in ways to which they never consented."

The global nature of telecommunications will pose new challenges. In the United Kingdom, for example, the government in 2000 planned for a spy center capable of tracking every email and Web site hit; but civil libertarians were outraged at the plan, even if its purpose was to crack down on cyber crime.

Social Media and the First Amendment

While *Reno v. ACLU* established a strong First Amendment right to use the Internet, the shift of communication to social media and social networking sites presents new issues for the courts. Facebook users, for example, agree to a terms-of-service agreement based upon a set of community standards. Most other sites and computer software also require user agreements.

EMERGING TECHNOLOGY ISSUES

The development of Internet and social media sites offered fertile ground for important developments to watch:

- Google removal of search results, such as revenge porn.
- Facebook content filtering and removal.
- Social media site responses to government data requests.
- Reduced Internet speeds based upon huge usage.
- Legislative response to the FCC Net neutrality elimination.
- Illegal videotaping of subjects without consent.
- Regulation of small drone video cameras.
- Photographer image rights.
- The European right-to-be-forgotten cases.

Source: AEJMC Law & Policy Division, Facebook group, https://www.facebook.com/groups/281106198661787/.

In an important social media case, *Packingham v. North Car-*

olina, the Supreme Court struck down a state statute that made it a felony for registered sex offenders to access social media. In 2002, Lester Gerard Packingham, then 21, had been convicted of having sex with a 13-year-old girl and became a registered sex offender. In 2010, he posted on Facebook under the identity "J.R. Gerrard" his joy at having a traffic ticket tossed out of court. In a sweeping First Amendment decision, the Supreme Court found that it "must exercise extreme caution before suggesting that the First Amendment provides scant protection for access to vast networks in that medium."

The Court continued:

North Carolina with one broad stroke bars access to what for many are the principal sources for knowing current events, checking ads for employment, speaking and listening in the modern public square, and otherwise exploring the vast realms of human thought and knowledge. These websites can provide perhaps the most powerful mechanisms available to a private citizen to make his or her voice heard.

They allow a person with an Internet connection to "become a town crier with a voice that resonates farther than it could from any soapbox."

In sum, to foreclose access to social media altogether is to prevent the user from engaging in the legitimate exercise of First Amendment rights. It is unsettling to suggest that only a limited set of Web sites can be used even by persons who have completed their sentences.

The Supreme Court found that North Carolina law was overbroad, but the state may pass "specific, narrowly tailored laws that prohibit a sex offender from engaging in conduct that often presages a sexual crime, like contacting a minor or using a website to gather information about a minor."

Taken together, *Reno, Elonis and Packingham* offer a glimpse into the long-term thinking of a majority of justices. When coupled with the Fourth Amendment mobile geo-location data privacy concerns expressed in *Carpenter v. United States*, it appears that the Supreme Court believes there are significant individual rights to use online communication as the modern-day public square. The Court views the Internet and social media sites as at the core of First Amendment political speech. It is unclear, however, whether the Court will extend this view beyond the reach of government state action within a criminal law context to civil litigation by private parties. As we learn in privacy chapter of this textbook, freedom of expression can be limited through this type of litigation.

A broader question is whether the Supreme Court will uphold National Labor Relations Board cases protecting employees from imposing broad company social media policies that reach into private page content. Corporations exercise their First

ELONIS v. UNITED STATES
575 U.S. 723 (2015)

The Supreme Court reversed and remanded the conviction of Anthony Elonis for making Facebook threats in violation of 18 U.S.C.S., Sec. 875(c), but the lower court a year later found "harmless error" in jury instructions. The Supreme Court denied a subsequent appeal.

Elonis' wife left him, and he used the pseudonym "Tone Dougie" on Facebook "to post self-styled rap lyrics containing graphically violent language and imagery concerning his wife, co-workers, a kindergarten class, and state and federal law enforcement." He used disclaimers that the posts were ficticious and an exercise of his First Amendment rights. Still, the targets of the alleged attacks — including his wife and former boss who fired him — sought protection orders. The FBI began monitoring the posts and later charged Elonis under the federal statute with a "threat... to injure the person of another."

At trial, Elonis sought a jury instruction that the government was required to prove that his intent was to communicate a "true threat." However, the judge instead instructed jurors that Elonis "could be found guilty if a reasonable person would forsee that his statements would be interpreted as a threat." Elonis was convicted on four of five counts, and he appealed. The Third Circuit U.S. Court of Appeals affirmed the conviction under the reasonable-person standard of a threat, and Elonis appealed this point of law to the Supreme Court.

Chief Justice John Roberts wrote the opinion that reversed the conviction. He first noted a 2010 "Halloween Haunt" post of a photograph in which Elonis held a toy knife to a co-worker's neck with a caption that said, "I wish" — leading to his firing and a new post:

Moles! Didn't I tell y'all I had several? Y'all sayin' I had access to keys for all the f***in' gates. That I have sinister plans for all my friends and must have taken home a couple. Y'all think it's too dark and foggy to secure your facility from a man as mad as me? You see, even without a paycheck, I'm still the main attraction. Whoever thought the Halloween Haunt could be so f***in' scary?

After the firing, Elonis adapted a sketch about killing the president and substituted his wife, explaining that while it is illegal to threaten to kill someone, it is not illegal to explain the law.

Hi, I'm Tone Elonis. Did you know that it's illegal for me to say I want to kill my wife? ... It's one of the only sentences that I'm not allowed to say.... Now it was okay for me to say it right then because I was just telling you that it's illegal for me to say I want to kill my wife.... Um, but what's interesting is that it's very illegal to say I really, really think someone out there should kill my wife.... But not illegal to say with a mortar launcher..... I also found out that it's incredibly illegal, extremely illegal to go on Facebook and say something like the best place to fire a mortar launcher at her house would be from the cornfield behind it because of easy access to a getaway road and you'd have a clear line of sight through the sun room.... Yet even more illegal to show an illustrated diagram. [diagram of the house].

Elonis went on to ask about the protection order, "Is it thick enough to stop a bullet?" Among his rap lyrics were "Pull my knife, flick my wrist, and slit her throat... Leave her Bleedin' from her jugular in the arms of her partner [laughter]." The Court, however, concluded from precedent that, "'the crucial element separating legal innocence from wrongful conduct' is the threatening nature of the communication... The mental state requirement must therefore apply to the fact that the communication contains a threat."

Justice Clarence Thomas dissented. He concluded that the Court overturned nine circuits but failed to replace the reasonable-person standard. In his view these were "true threats" that lacked First Amendment protection: "Nothing in the statute suggests that Congress departed from the 'conventional *mens rea* element' of general intent.... I would not impose a higher mental-state requirement here." He added that the "departure from our precedents" makes "threats one of the most protected categories of unprotected speech." Fighting-words doctrine, for example, has not "generally ... required a heightened mental state under the First Amendment."

In the end, the majority decision found error in a reasonable-person jury instruction. In 2016, however, the Third Circuit Court of Appeals found "harmless error" and reinstated Elonis' conviction because he posted a violent message after a FBI visit: "The evidence overwhelmingly demonstrates Elonis knew how the post would be interpreted. No rational juror could have found Elonis did not have the purpose of threatening FBI agents or did not know his posts about FBI agents would be regarded as a threat." United States of America v. Anthony Douglas Elonis, 841 F.3d 589, 601 (3d Cir. 2016). Elonis had already served his time and was released based upon the earlier eroneous negligence standard. In 2017, he continued to publicly post on Facebook, but nothing of a threatening nature (https://www.facebook.com/anthony.elonis). He later removed his public profile. The Supreme Court denied certiorari and further review of the Third Circuit conclusion. Elonis v. United States, 574 U.S. 723 (2017).

In *Counterman v. Colorado* (2023) the Court voted 7-2 that prosecutors must prove a defendant has some subjective understanding of the "threatening nature" of statements in true threat cases. In review of a state stalking statute, the Court developed a recklessness standard based upon First Amendment "breathing space." The *Counterman* decision clarifies *Elonis* by deciding that the state of Colorado must prove both its objective reasonable person standard, as well as an awareness of a subjectively threatening character to online posts. Criminal true threats involve a defendant understanding both his or her word content and how others would see these as threatening. By doing so, prosecutors may prove that the defendant was reckless in publishing threatening words.

Amendment rights when managing social media sites, but employees appear to have a right to communicate on social media about collective bargaining and broader union labor issues. Social media present a wide range of new legal questions:

- Will European Union antitrust fines against Google influence large social media company behavior?

• Will the U.K. idea that Facebook users have a right to delete posts made as teens spread to the United States?

• Does the First Amendment protect "liking" a racist Instagram post?

• What is the future of law enforcement mobile smart phone searches for people at public events?

• Will social media sites effectively limit revenge porn through filtering and blocking?

• How will Facebook Live and other streaming social media tools be regulated, if at all?

• Is there a First Amendment right to share fake news or other deceptive political content?

• Will Twitter's misinformation labels be sufficient self-regulation to keep the government out of its business?

• Will states succeed in imposing social media laws (such as Utah's parental approval for TikTok) that can survive constitutional First Amendment challenges?

• How will copyright, trademarks and patents be protected in an ever-changing online world of AI content synthesis?

• How will AI and robotics alter social, technologic and legal norms about human communication?

• Will AI technology replace media employment, assist employees, or spark unpredictable content innovation?

• Is it possible for social media platforms to survive as both common carriers and content creators and editors?

It is clear that the online social media space remains fluid in terms of law, regulation and policies. This has been the case for more than two decades. The First Amendment offered social media and other technology companies substantial freedom to innovate, grow and profit. Third party liability protection under Section 230 may or may not survive amid lawmakers growing angst over the concentration of power. The U.S. Supreme Court in 2023 balked at limiting Section 230 powers for Google (*Gonzalez v. Google*) and Twitter (*Twitter v. Taamneh*), and a partisan Congress appeared to be focused on the upcoming presidential election.

The success of social media coincided with the decline in local newspaper profits, and there is some interest in reviving the public interest concept within government regulation. At the same time, the Supreme Court appears to be on a path to protect Internet free expression when it causes no harm and breaks no laws. However, the balancing of interests continues to create conflicts and cases. For example, the courts recognize the right of schools to educate students without disruption. Likewise, commercial speech rights extend only to legal services and products, transparent disclosure of financial interests, and content that does not deceive reasonable consumers.

It was unclear how much new First Amendment law may be

spawned because of the rapid AI adoption during the past year. In one Georgia state court case, Open AI was sued for defamation by the Second Amendment Foundation and others. New media technologies always challenge the status quo.

Internet TV challenged the traditional government broadcast regulation model. Author Ken Auletta has observed that we live in a confusing time with respect to mass media: "I think we have to look at the world as a great paradox.... On the one hand, you've got growing concentration.... On the other hand, you've got this democratic instrument, this technology that basically challenges companies." Daschle's Electronic Rights for the Twenty-First Century Act was not given serious consideration.

SUMMARY

This chapter focused on legal and regulatory issues involving new communication technology — telephones, digital television and the Internet. The predicted convergence of online and wireless media is leading to new cases and conflicts set in motion amid online media disruption of traditional regulation. As Justice Thomas wrote, "[T]he principal legal difficulty that surrounds digital platforms" is that "applying old doctrines to new digital platforms is rarely straightforward." The struggle is to find legal and regulatory standards that will pass constitutional muster years after the technological developments are no longer new. As Lee Bolinger observed, the central problem is, "...to evolve global norms about these rights and to determine which global freedom of expression norms are essential for this interconnected world." In parts of the world, regulators are fighting what Shoshana Zuboff has called "surveillance capitalism" that uses data collection for profit. As we will learn in the next chapter, creators also face unique concerns because, as Nancy Whitmore observed, "...we live in a world awash in individual expression and user-generated content."

The COVID-19 coronavirus global pandemic raised the stakes for the importance of online behavior. For example, concerns about essential business tools, such as Zoom video conferencing, centered upon potential lack of data privacy and security in China, echoing historical concerns.

Changing social and political conditions created from the September 11, 2001, terrorist attacks also presented complex changes. New communication technologies may be used for good or evil, and regulators struggle to allow for advances without making it easier to harm people. Some social media sites warn users about data they collect on postings and user locations. As Facebook tells users, "Remember, when you post to another person's timeline, that person controls what audience can view the post. Additionally, anyone who gets tagged in a post may see it, along with their friends." User settings may limit public viewing, but data are saved for use by the company for advertising purposes and the government, if subpeoned.

The boundaries and limitations of communication and business in cyberspace remain unsettled. As one scholar has noted, digital and Internet technologies present a paradox: "Utopian and dystopian views about the future of the Internet describe two very different future scenarios." Faced with such uncertainty, we will likely see much action within the courts, as parties dispute the virtual landscape.

Competition between previously separate industries, such as is happening with cable and telephone companies, has created unfair situations that may force future government intervention. At the same time, advances in technology will continue to present new legal challenges to the First Amendment freedoms of speech and press. As Jacques Ellul observed decades ago, "The process of technological encroachment upon reality always consists in breaking up reality into malleable fragmentary units." The "mobile Internet" today is rapidly shifting new behaviors at the expense of old ones.

For more than two decades, online business has been eroding the economic power of brick and mortar retail stores, and the global pandemic favored Amazon's business model over physical experiences. At this writing, it is not known whether governments will move to limit the power of huge online commercial successes — Amazon, Apple, Google, and Facebook. In the future, there are likely to be numerous pressing issues, such as:

- Evolving terms of service social networking site user agreements and expectations about data privacy protection.
- Differing national legal standards and expectations within a global Internet government by international law.
- Interest by companies and governmental interests in creating social media user guidelines.
- Student and employee social media rights state laws.
- State biometrics and facial recognition laws.
- Artificial intelligence natural language and *generative* processing, chatbots, augmented reality, and Internet-connected devices.

The path ahead will be defined by discussion of online privacy, broadband access and privacy protection, big data and security, mobile speeds and prices, data retention rules, and promotion of new technologies.

Among the many newer cases and issues to watch in the year ahead are labor law limitations on employer social media policy restrictions, broader labor and employment law changes, and revenge porn and other potential content restrictions. The Facebook Cambridge Analytica data breach of seventy-one million U.S. accounts may redefine boundaries, as the FTC, SEC, FBI and Department of Justice were reported to be investigating.

The Internet and social media were two large waves of tech-

nological change, and artificial intelligence can be thought of as the third wave in our lifetimes. Jared Schroeder wrote in 2018 that "[w]hile individuals generally share less meaningful bonds with others in virtual spaces, individuals both intentially and unconsciously limit" engagement to agreeable sources and messages, "fragmented communities," and "echo-chambers filled with belief-affirming information." We enter a time in which it may be impossible to know if a chatbot posing as a friend is spreading false information filled with #deepfakes video.

The study of new communication technology law presents many challenges and opportunities. Within the broader context of communication and the law, regulation and court challenges are literally redefining the field. From algorithm filtering by media companies to surveillance and outright government censorship, new communication technology law will be increasingly complex, defined by new conflicts and cases, and evolving to chase rapid diffusion of new tools. As we will see in the next chapter, expression ownership demands a new level of interest and focus.

BIBLIOGRAPHY

Articles

Dorf, Michael C. & Sidney G. Tarrow. "Stings and Scams: 'Fake News,' the First Amendment, and the New Activist Journalism," 20 *Pennsylvania Journal of Constitutional Law* 1 (2017 October).

Federal Trade Commission, "Follow Up on March Letter to Instagram Influencers. 2017-01436," Sept. 6, 2017, https://www.ftc.gov/system/files/documents/foia_requests/all_of_the_signed_letters.pdf.

Murphy, Megan R. "Context, Content, and Intent: Social Media's Role in True Threat Prosecutions. 168 *University of Pennsylvania Law Review* 733 (February 2020).

Russ, Caroline. "Tweet Takers & Instagram Fakers: Social Media & Copyright Infringement," 22 *Tulane Journal of Technology & Intellectual Property* 205 (2020).

Schroeder, Jared. "Marketplace Theory in the Age of AI Communications," 17 *First Amendment Law Review* 22 (2018).

Wiener, Jason. "Social Media and the Message: Facebook, Forums, and First Amendment Follies," 55 *Wake Forest Law Review* 217 (2020).

Books

Bolinger, Lee C. & Callamard, Agnès (eds.) *Regardless of Frontiers, Global Freedom of Expression in a Troubled World.* New York: Columbia University Press, 2021.

Lipschultz, Jeremy H. *Social Media Law and Ethics.* New York:

Routledge, 2024.

Mills, Jon L. *Privacy in the New Media Age*. Gainesville: University Press of Florida, 2015.

Whitmore, Nancy J. *Creative Expression and the Law*. Lanham: Rowman & Littlefield, 2021.

Zuboff, Shoshana. *The Age of Surveillance Capitalism: The Fight for a Human Future at the New Frontier of Power*. New York: Public Affairs, 2019.

Cases

A&M Records, Inc. v. Napster, Inc., 239 F.3d 1004 (9th Cir. 2001).

Ashcroft v. ACLU, 542 U.S. 656 (2004).

Ashcroft v. ACLU, 535 U.S. 564 (2002).

Ashcroft v. Free Speech Coalition, 534 U.S. 234 (2002).

Biden v. Knight First Amendment Institute, 141 S. Ct. 1220 (2021), *vacating as moot & remanding,* Trump v. First Amendment Institute at Columbia University, 928 F.3d 226 (2d Cir. 2019).

Carpenter v. United States, 138 S. Ct. 2206 (2018).

Eldred v. Ashcroft, 537 U.S. 186 (2003).

Elonis v. United States, 575 U.S. 723 (2015).

FCC v. League of Women Voters, 468 U.S. 364 (1984).

FCC Memorandum and Order ("The Pulver Order") 04-27 (2014).

Free Speech Coalition v. Reno, 198 F.3d 1083 (9th Cir. 1999).

Gonzalez v. Google, 143 S. Ct. 1191 (2023).

Keefe v. Adams, 840 F.3d 523 (8th Circuit, 2016), *cert. denied,* 137 S.Ct. 1448 (2017).

Knight First Amendment Institute at Columbia University v. Trump, No. 18-1691-cv (2d Cir. July 9, 2019).

Mahanoy v. B.L., 141 S.Ct. 2938 (2021).

Mainstream Loudon v. Board of Trustees of the Loudon County Library, 24 F. Supp. 2d 552 (E.D. Va. 1998).

MGM v. Grokster, 545 U.S. 913 (2005).

Minnesota v. Tatro, 816 N.W.2d 509 (Minn. 2012).

Murphy v. Twitter, Inc., 30 Cal. App. 5th, 2021 Ca;. App. LEXIS 60 (2021).

NetChoice v. Paxton, 1:21-CV-840-RP (5th Cir. West Dist. Texas (Dec.1, 2021).

Nitke v. Gonzalez, 547 U.S. 1015 (2006).

Nunes v. Lizza, 12 F.4th 890 (8th Cir., 2021).

Packingham v. North Carolina, 137 S. Ct. 1730 (2017).

Riley v. California, 134 U.S. 2473 (2014).

Reno v. ACLU, 521 U.S. 844 (1997).

SBC v. FCC, 373 F.3d 32 (D.C. Cir. 2004).

Sony Corp. v. Universal Studios, Inc., 464 U.S. 417 (1984).

Twitter v. Taamneh, 143 S. Ct. 1206 (2023).

United States v. American Library Association, 539 U.S. 194 (2003).

United States Telecommunications Association v. FCC, 855 F.3d 381 (D.C. Cir. 2017).

Verizon v. FCC, 740 F.3d 623 (D.C. Cir. 2014).

Statutes, Rules and Regulation

Children's Online Privacy Protection Act, 16 CFR 312.10(a) (2003).

Children's Privacy Protection Act, 18 U.S.C. § 2556(8) (1996).

Digital Millennium Copyright Act, H.R. 2281 (105th Cong., 2d Sess. 1998).

Communications Decency Act, 47 U.S.C. § 223, 230 (1996).

Open Internet Order, 30 FCC Rcd. 5638 (2015).

Protecting and Promoting the Open Internet, 80 Fed. Reg. 19,738 (Apr. 13, 2015), 47 C.F.R. 1.

13

Intellectual Property

By Cayce Myers

☑ **Headnote Questions**

- What is the copyright duration of works created since 1978?
- How does intellectual property differ from other forms of personal property?
- What part of expression does copyright protect?
- What are the parts of the Fair Use Doctrine? Which part is most important?
- What exclusive rights does a copyright holder have?
- What is the public domain, and why is it important to the function of copyright?
- What types of information are not copyrightable?
- What two things must be established to prove copyright infringement?
- What is "poor man's copyright"?
- How long does a trademark last and under what circumstances may it be renewed?
- In what manner must all marks be used before they may be registered as trademarks?

The First Amendment and the constitutional protections afforded what has become known as "intellectual property" are two sides of the same coin, for their legal functions advance and balance the societal purpose of each other. While the First Amendment protects freedom of speech, the Constitution's protections of intellectual property — writing, video, music, and other artistic works — create the right to profit financially from one's creative abilities and resourcefulness. To help reach this end, Article I of the Constitution gives Congress the power "to promote the Progress of Science and useful Arts, by securing for limited Times to Authors and Inventors the exclusive Right to their respective Writings and Discoveries." In *Goldstein v. California* (1973), the U.S. Supreme Court interpreted the phrase "to promote" as meaning as "to encourage" and "to stimulate."

"Intellectual property" is an umbrella term that includes copyright, trademark, patents and trade secrets. Communication professionals, including journalists, typically confront issues of copyright and trademark. Because of that, this chapter focuses mainly on those two areas of intellectual property law. The Copyright Act of 1976 is the primary federal statutory application of this power over copyrights and protects original, created works. In the realm of trademarks and service marks, the Trademark Act of 1946, also known as the Lanham Act after its sponsor, Democratic Representative Frederick D. Lanham of Texas, is the principal implementation of the power and protects symbols and images that signify the authenticity of commercial goods or services.

COPYRIGHTS

The relationship between copyright law and the First Amendment is so strong and so essential to the role of communication in the United States (in both its political/democratic and economic/capitalistic aspects) that, in *Harper & Row Publishers v. Nation Enterprises* (1985), the Supreme Court labeled copyright "the engine of free expression" — though some have described it instead as an instrument of corporate censorship. As the Court explained in *Mazer v. Stein* (1954), "[T]he economic philosophy behind the clause empowering Congress to [protect] copy rights is the conviction that the encouragement of individual effort by personal gain is the best way to advance [the] public welfare through the talents of authors and inventors." This "encouragement," according to the Court in *Twentieth Century Music v. Aiken* (1975), takes the form of a guarantee of a fair return for one's creative labor as a means of promoting "the general public good," while advancement of the public welfare includes the "production of ... works of lasting benefit to the world, as the Court explained in *Washingtonian Publishing v. Pearson* (1939).

Because copyright limits free access to information and knowledge, it also fundamentally restricts access to all expression otherwise protected by the First Amendment. Copyright and the First Amendment constantly find themselves in opposition to each other.

There are competing and yet complementary philosophical foundations for the protection of created works — competing, in that works protected by copyright, as a result of the economic monopoly given the works' owners, are unavailable for unrestricted use by others; and complementary, in that the assumption is that works no longer protected by copyright serve as the basis for the creation of new copyrightable works. Thus, the twofold purpose of copyright is:

1. To protect creators' the rights financially benefit from while also controlling the use of their work, and
2. To preserve the public interest by guaranteeing eventual access to the work in the public domain.

As will be seen, the law has generally treated the first foundation/purpose as more important.

Though copyright law in Great Britain began in 1710 with the Statute of Anne as a way for government to track and censor printed material through the granting of a royal privilege and license to printers, copyright law in the United States has always aimed to encourage creativity by providing authors and artists with legal protection for their creative activities. The first federal copyright law, in 1790, adapted from the British statute, offered legal protection for fourteen years for books, maps and charts. Prints were added to this list in 1802; musical compositions in 1831; dramatic compositions and the public performance thereof in 1856; photographs in 1865; drawings, paintings, sculpture and designs and models for the creation of fine art in 1870; and the performance of musical compositions in 1897. The Copyright Act of 1909 provided for the protection of unpublished works designed for exhibition or performance, and, as technological innovation progressed through the twentieth century, resulting in the invention of the motion picture, the phonograph record, and radio and television broadcasts, all these various forms of communication were deemed copyrightable, to one degree or another. The Copyright Act of 1976 goes so far as to protect all "original works of authorship fixed in any tangible medium of expression, now known or later developed, from which they can be perceived, reproduced, or otherwise communicated, either directly or with the aid of a machine or device."

By continually expanding the subject matter of copyright, Congress attempted to encourage creativity and innovation. Works whose copyrights have expired are deemed to be in the "public domain," available for public use in further creativity and innovation — such as, for example, the many works published about Sherlock Holmes before January 1, 1926, and F. Scott Fitzgerald's classic novel, *The Great Gatsby* (1925), which entered the public domain on January 1, 2021. A perhaps more consequential event will occur when the Walt Disney film introducing Mickey Mouse and Minnie Mouse, *Steamboat Willie* (1928), loses its copyrighted status and enters the public domain on January 1, 2024. (It should be remembered that works that are not eligible for the legal protection of copyright have always been in the public domain.)

What's Copyrightable — and What's Not

Copyright law protects only the form or style — that is, the way something is described, which is embodied in the concept of "authorship" — in which an idea is expressed or communicated. The federal statute extends copyright protection to "original works of authorship," some of which are:

1. Literary work;
2. Musical works, including any accompanying words;
3. Dramatic works, including any accompanying music;
4. Pantomimes and choreographic works;
5. Pictorial, graphic and sculptural works;
6. Motion pictures and other audiovisual works;
7. Sound recordings;
8. Architectural works.

Copyright does not protect any of the elements inherent in, underlying or part of the manner in which an idea is expressed or communicated. This distinction is known as the "idea/expression dichotomy." Copyright thus protects the expression, not the idea itself. What this means is that copyright does not prohibit others from using the ideas or information found in copyrighted works. In 1879, the Supreme Court used this rule in *Baker v. Seldon* to distinguish between the copyrightability of a book (that is, the form of the expression of the idea) and the non-copyrightability of the "peculiar system [or method] of bookkeeping" explained in the book (that is, the idea itself), noting that "there is a clear distinction between the book, as such, and the art which it is intended to illustrate." The Court concluded: "The description of the art in a book, though entitled to the benefit of copyright, lays no foundation for an exclusive claim to the art itself. The object of the one is explanation; the object of the other is use."

As a result, copyright law does not protect news, facts, ideas or theories, procedures, concepts, processes, systems, methods of operation, principles, history, works produced by federal and state governments — including private images of state-owned property and privately annotated official state statutes[1] — standard calendars, height and weight charts, typography or blank forms, listings of ingredients or contents, formulas, compounds, recipes, titles, names, short phrases and slogans, other facts and works consisting entirely of information that is common property and contains no original authorship, useful articles and works of function or utility — including, clothing, whose design is generally one of style, product attributes that are more properly included in "trade dress," such as, color, smell, and taste — and anything not expressed in tangible form, such as narrated ideas. The best known examples of works "produced by" the federal government yet copyrightable are postage stamps. Another exception involves computer programming language which until recently most had understood to be a type of procedure, concept, process, system, or method unprotectable by copyright. In *Google v. Oracle America* (2021), the Supreme Court presumed that the copied lines of Java programming code are eligible to be copyrighted.[2]

The leading case that delineates the distinction between what is and is not copyrightable was handed down in 1991. The issue in *Feist Publications v. Rural Telephone Service* was whether the alphabetical listing of names in the white pages of telephone books may be copyrighted. Though facts themselves are not copyrightable, a compilation — or the form — in which facts appear generally is. Feist took the alphabetical listing of names in the Rural Telephone Service's telephone book after Rural refused to license the use of the names in a Feist-produced phone book. The question was: Did Feist violate Rural Telephone Service's copyright?

The Supreme Court said, no, and sided with Feist. Works protected by copyright must be "original to the author," though not necessarily "novel," generally defined as "new," "unusual," or "innovative." Originality, thus, has two components:

• Independent creation by the author (that is, not copied from another source), and
• Some minimal degree of creativity.

In *Burrow-Giles Lithographic v. Sarony* (1884), the Supreme Court ruled that even "the mere mechanical reproduction of the physical features" of a person in a photograph contained enough "selecting and arranging" as part of the posing of the subject to meet the required nominal originality standard.

Thus, facts may not be copyrighted because they are not and cannot be original. A collation or compilation of facts is copyrightable if it is original in its selection of facts or their arrangement, but legal protection is limited to the selection or arrangement. Copyright never extends to facts themselves. In addition, copyright law does not provide protection for *scènes à faire*, French for "scene to be made," which is a typical convention for any genre. For instance, a children's story may have genre conventions such as an evil queen, handsome prince, or fairly godmother. A spy novel may contain conventions such as gadgets, fast cars, secret compartments, or a villain. Computer codes can also fall into this *scènes à faire* category. The U.S. Court of Appeals for the Second Circuit analyzed in *Computer Associates International, Inc. v. Altai, Inc.* the level of protection non-literal aspects of a computer code receive. To analyze these situations the court developed the Abstraction-Filtration-Comparison test, which tests whether the non-literal aspects of a computer program have copyright protection.

Copyright Ownership

Ownership of a created work belongs to the work's creator (or joint creators). This is the general rule, according to the federal copyright statute. An author or artist may not own a work, however:

1. If it was created "within the scope" of one's employment,
2. If a specific contract provision exists between two parties to the contract stating the conditions and extent of ownership, or
3. If the work was created as a commissioned "work for hire."

First, because employers have the right to benefit economically from the work that employees produce as part of their jobs, a worker's legal rights are greatly limited when he or she accomplishes or creates something within the scope of the worker's employment. This precept is central to the law of agency. In such cases, the employer is legally the author of the work and owns the copyright. Second, any copyright owner may transfer ownership, either as a whole or in part, to another by means of a written contract or agreement or through the provisions of a will. Thus, an employer's ownership rights may be transferred back to the employee who first created the work for the employer, or to anyone else. Third, "a work specifically ordered or commissioned" may be deemed to be owned by the person or entity

---

[1] Recently, the Supreme Court determined that the copyright on licensed pictures of state-owned property — here, a shipwreck — was not enforceable by the photographer against state use. *See* Allen v. Cooper, 140 S. Ct. 994 (2020). The Supreme Court has also determined that privately developed annotations of official state statutes are not copyrightable. *See* Georgia v. Public.Resource.org, 140 S. Ct. 1498 (2020).

[2] 141 S. Ct. 1183 (2021). Based on its agreement with the Federal Circuit Court of Appeals that the copied lines are copyrightable — *see* Oracle America v. Google, 886 F.3d 1179 (Fed. Cir. 2018) — the Supreme Court concluded that Google's use of approximately 11,500 lines of Java programming code it used (about 0.4% of the total) for its Android platform for mobile computing devices without Oracle's permission was a "fair use."

which "ordered or commissioned" it.

This third situation served as the basis of the ownership claim in *Community for Creative Non-Violence v. Reid* (1989). In that case, a nonprofit group conceived the idea of a sculpture depicting homelessness in Washington, D.C. — and not just any sculpture but one whose attributes and characteristics the group extensively dictated to the artist it hired. After the artist had been fully paid for his efforts, the two sides disagreed on future plans for the sculpture and each claimed sole ownership, the sculptor on the grounds that he created the work and the group on the grounds that the sculptor's efforts were a "work for hire." The Supreme Court concluded that sculptor James Reid had been "an independent contractor," in that he had been paid by, but not controlled or assisted by, the nonprofit group in his artistic efforts, and that the sculpture did not fall within one of the copyright statute's nine, limited work-for-hire categories that would have allowed ownership by the group. Despite the degree of its involvement, the nonprofit group was thus not the "author" of the work and did not own its copyright.

Copyright thus belongs to the creator/author of the work, at least, initially. Yet, it is also important to note that "mere ownership" of an original work, much less a copy of an original work, does not mean that the possessor holds the copyright. A sale or transfer of the object may dispose of the artifact itself but does not include a sale or transfer of the copyright, without an express, written agreement to the contrary.

Copyright Notice and Registration

At the moment a work is created, that is, "fixed in any tangible medium" for the first time, it is automatically copyrighted, without the author having to do anything. As a result, official registration with the U.S. Copyright Office (USCO) — which in 2022 registered more than 484,589 claims and recorded 14,714 documents containing over 1.1 million works — is voluntary and not a legal requirement. Yet, because all claims of copyright infringement start with accusations of illegal copying, the initial defense is proof that one's work was created prior to the creation of an accuser's similar work. Thus, official registration is highly recommended. Registration establishes a public record of the copyright and is required of works of U.S. origin before a lawsuit for copyright infringement may be filed in federal court to allow the copyright owner the right to collect statutory damages and possibly attorneys' fees.

At the very least, every work should prominently feature a proper copyright notice, which includes three elements:

1. © (the letter "c" in a circle) or the word "Copyright" or the abbreviation "Copr.,"
2. The year of first publication,

3. The name of the copyright owner.

For example, then, a proper copyright notice could look something like this:

Copyright © 2022 Peter Panther

In addition, some authors have sought legal protection in what has been known as "poor man's copyright." In such situations, a copy of the created work is not officially registered, but rather sent to oneself through the mail — and keeping the package in one's possession, unopened — to establish its date of creation through the postmark on the package, in the expectation of saving the money spent on the registration fee while at the same time establishing authenticity of the work and protecting one's legal right to monetary damages in case of copyright infringement. However, "poor man's copyright" — the claim that mailing, receiving and storing a work in a sealed, stamped envelope is an inexpensive substitute for the copyright process — is a myth. As the Copyright Office states on its Web site: "There is no provision in the copyright law for any such type of protection, and it is not a substitute for registration." It is important to note that the Copyright Act of 1909 was highly technical and made formal requirements for registration. When determining ownership of older copyreights whether those copyrighted works are still protected sometimes depends on whether those formalities were met.

Legal Rights of Copyright Owners

Because intellectual property — such as a copyrighted work — is a form of personal property, yet property of a unique kind,[3] the legal rights of copyright owners differ from those of owners of all other types of property, which generally include the right to control and to exclude all others from the use of one's property, complete and unlimited ownership of the property itself, and the right to bequeath the property to one's heirs permanently and in

---

[3] In a classic definition of copyright as property, Justice Oliver Wendell Holmes wrote:

The notion of property starts ... from confirmed possession of a tangible object, and consists in the right to exclude others from interference with the more or less free doing with it as one wills. But, in copyright, property has reached a more abstract expression. The right to exclude is not directed to an object in possession or owned.... It restrains the spontaneity of men where, but for it, there would be nothing of any kind to hinder their doing as they saw fit. It is a prohibition of conduct remote from the persons or tangibles of the party having the right. It may be infringed a thousand miles from the owner and without his ever becoming aware of the wrong. It is a right which could not be recognized or endured for more than a limited time, and therefore ... it is one which hardly can be conceived except as a product of statute.

White-Smith Music Publ'g v. Apollo Co., 209 U.S. 1, 19 (1908) (Holmes, J., concurring).

perpetuity. However, the right to exclude is not essential to the enjoyment of intellectual property or its value to its owner.[4] In fact, others' use of the copyrighted work can actually enhance its overall worth.

Yet, the evolution of the Internet has brought with it the reality that the custody or ownership of content is questionable, or problematic at best, in cyberspace. Some believe the risk is that fewer and fewer original works will be produced, which will end "ownership," and harm the importance of and protections inherent in copyright.

As a means of protecting the value of created works, copyright owners enjoy six exclusive, legal rights that provide unique protections to intellectual property:

1. The right to reproduce the copyrighted work in copies and phono-records;
2. The right to prepare derivative works based upon the copyrighted work;
3. The right to distribute copies or phono-records of the copyrighted work to the public by sale or other transfer of ownership, or by rental, lease or lending;
4. The right to perform the copyrighted work publicly;
5. The right to display the copyrighted work publicly;
6. The right to perform the copyrighted work publicly by means of a digital transmission.

Thus, copyright is essentially the right to say no. However, several mitigating points should be noted. First, while the last four of these six rights are public rights, the first two may be violated either publicly or privately. Second, because federal law does not limit copyright infringement to commercial uses only, all uses of copyrighted material not approved by the copyright holder violate the copyright owner's rights, unless excused or mitigated by some defense or by other statutory limitation. Third, this list of far-reaching legal rights is not comprehensive. As an example of a legal right not listed yet also included in the Copyright Act of 1976, authors and artists who have transferred or sold their rights to others, may terminate those transfers — in effect, cancel the sale — and regain control over copyrighted works that they created thirty-five years after the date of the original transfer. For example, Victor Willis, lyricist of the disco group the Village People, has already had his termination rights upheld. Others are expected to follow his lead.

Of the six exclusive rights, the first is obviously the most fundamental and important. It allows copyright owners the right to prohibit all others from reproducing the work in the form of copies, recordings, adaptations and publishing. Thus, a copyrighted work would be infringed by reproducing it in whole or in any substantial part. For example, the well-known 2008 Barack Obama "HOPE" poster was created by the artist Shepard Fairey and subsequently licensed for use on clothing and other merchandise without permission from the original photograph's owner. Thus, the medium in which the work is reproduced makes no difference.

In *New York Times v. Tasini* (2001), the Supreme Court agreed with a group of freelance journalists that they had sold only first publication rights to the *New York Times* and that subsequent electronic reproduction first required an additional license from and another royalty payment to the writers. Yet, seven years later, in *Greenberg v. National Geographic* (2008), a federal appellate court found that "an exact, unrevised digital replica of 1,200 pre-existing collective works (that is, magazines)" on a CD-ROM was not a new anthology or collective work, but only a republication of a copyrighted collection. Almost two decades later, in *Reed Elsevier v. Muchnick* (2010), more than 2,500 journalists and free-lancers received $9 million in royalties for the unauthorized use of their copyrighted material.

When phono-recordings are involved, this exclusive right is limited by the statutory license available to anyone wishing to record his or her own version of a musical composition or song, without the copyright owner's consent. This is not the legal right to copy and sell the original but a compulsory license to "cover" the original, provided that proper licensing or royalty fees are paid. Royalty rates are published annually in Title 37 of the *Code of Federal Regulations*. Failure to obtain such a license before distribution is illegal copying and an infringement of copyright. Penalties can include a court-ordered injunction forbidding further distribution and a recall of any or all phono-records already shipped.

The second right gives copyright owners control over all subsequent uses of their works, including the creation of sequels.

As an example, Sylvester Stallone — movie star and screenplay author of *Rocky* (1976), *Rocky II* (1979) and *Rocky III* (1982) — took a thirty-one-page film treatment by Timothy Anderson, which incorporated characters initially created by Stallone, and made the movie *Rocky IV* (1985) that pitted Stallone's boxer, Rocky Balboa, against Ivan Drago, a "scientifically trained" Russian opponent. Stallone was not required to pay Anderson anything for tort claims of unjust enrichment, because Anderson's film treatment was an infringing derivative work, using characters so extensively developed that any subsequent use in any work automatically belongs to their creator, Sylvester Stallone. As another example, Castle Rock Entertainment — which owns the copyright to comedian Jerry Seinfeld's television series, *Seinfeld* — was able to stop publication of

---

[4] Randy Barnett, *All We Need Is "Love"?* ¶ 5, Mar. 6, 2007, VOLOKH CONSPIRACY, volokh.com/posts/1173221206.shtml. Professor Barnett explained the difference between tangible and intangible personal property this way: "With tangible property you control your stuff. With intangible property you control other people's stuff." *Id.*

The Seinfeld Aptitude Test by Beth Golub — a short book with trivia questions from the show — on the grounds that it was an unauthorized derivative work. Even though "Castle Rock ... evidenced little if any interest in exploiting this market for derivative works based on 'Seinfeld,' such as by creating and publishing 'Seinfeld' trivia books," the federal appellate court in *Castle Rock Entertainment v. Carol Publishing* (1998) ruled that the "law must respect that creative and economic choice."

This legal right to control derivative works even includes, for example, re-compiling and assembling new works, comprised of newly bound articles (assembled according to subject matter) from legally purchased copies of *National Geographic* magazine and Lucasfilm's recent attempts to control fan-filmed homages and unofficial sequels to its *Star Wars* series of films, as well as J.K. Rowling's right to halt a fan's Harry Potter lexicon and E.L. James' retelling of her *50 Shades of Gray* (2011) from the perspective of her male lead. However, there are cases where a derivative works falls under fair use because it is a parody (discussed later in this chapter). For example, the 2001 novel *The Wind Done Gone* by Alice Randall, which is an alternative version of Margaret Mitchell's 1936 novel *Gone With the Wind*, was found to be fair use and not an infringement by the U.S. Court of Appeals for the Eleventh Circuit in *Suntrust Bank Inc, v. Houghton Mifflin Co.* (2001).

The third right gives copyright owners the exclusive control over publication and distribution of their works, whether it be by sale, lease, lending or downloading. This right is also known as "The First Sale Doctrine," in that it guarantees the copyright owner the legal right to prohibit others from any and all distribution of the work, prior to its first sale. At that point, the new owner of the work may choose to display the work publicly or to sell the work to someone else; however, the owner does not have the right to do anything else with the work, including making additional copies of it or re-selling it in a different form, as the ownership rights involve only the mere possession of the work and not its copyright. In addition, this right specifically does not include any renting, leasing or lending of phono-records or computer software for commercial purposes by any owner after the first sale.

In 2013, the Supreme Court ruled in *Kirtsaeng v. John Wiley & Sons* that the First Sale Doctrine has "no geographic boundaries," meaning that copyright owners cannot ban resale of physical copies of their works inside the United States at a lower price than intended by the copyright owners. Textbook publishers criticized the decision as an economic loss for the United States, while others saw the decision as a necessary balance of legal rights and interests. What remains unsettled is the extent to which the First Sale Doctrine protects the resellers of electronic products, such as e-books and digital music files.

The remaining three exclusive rights give the copyright own-er the legal right to control the performance, display and digital transmission of copyrighted works, sometimes known as public performing rights. Prior to congressional enactment of the Copyright Act of 1976, the broadcast reception in a public fast- food restaurant of songs being played as part of a radio station's programming was not considered a public performance, since the shop keeper did nothing more than turn on the radio for his patrons to enjoy. Today, that act clearly is a public performance that must be licensed unless it is included in a list of statutory exemptions, which include face-to-face nonprofit educational activities and religious worship services. The performance:

1. Must involve no profit motive or private financial gain in that no one involved or responsible is paid any fee and
2. Must include no admission charge, either direct or indirect.

Other performances, displays and transmissions that require copyright permissions and licensing include: the online streaming to subscribers of freely available broadcast television programs, the renting of motion pictures in combination with rooms in which they may be viewed, the transmission of screen displays of a copyrighted work to subscribers, satellite antenna television reception in a local bar of National Football League games that are blacked out in a particular media market, Internet bulletin board displays of copyrighted *Playboy* photographs,[5] and the use of copyrighted songs by presidential candidates without permission of their copyright owners. In fact, they even include those copyrighted songs — such as, "Puff, the Magic Dragon" — that Girl Scouts sing around the campfire, and enforced by the Recording Industry Association of America; the American Society of Composers, Authors & Publishers; Broadcast Music, Inc., and the Society of European Stage Authors & Composers. (See Figure 1.) Each organization has licensing agents whose job it is to persuade every business everywhere to pay for the background music they use. And as the amount and dollar value of material re-posted online have grown, private companies have become involved by buying copyrights and then initiating their own lawsuits.

Copyright Duration

Copyright law in the United States has encouraged creativity by providing authors and artists ever-lengthening legal protection for their creative activities. The first federal copyright law, in 1790, offered legal protection for books, maps, and charts for

---

5 *See* ABC v. Aereo, Inc., 573 U.S. 431 (2014) (streaming); Columbia Pictures v. Aveco, Inc., 800 F.2d 59 (3d Cir. 1986) (renting movies); National Football League v. McBee & Bruno's, 792 F.2d 726 (8th Cir. 1986) (professional football games); On Command Video v. Columbia Pictures, 777 F. Supp. 787 (N.D. Cal. 1991) (screen displays); Playboy Enters. v. Webbworld, 991 F. Supp. 543 (N.D. Tex. 1997) (nude photographs).

fourteen years from the date of publication, with an option for a single fourteen-year renewal. The second federal statute, in 1831, extended this initial period of protection to twenty-eight years, with an option for a fourteen-year renewal period. The third statute, in 1909, extended the renewal term to twenty-eight years, and the fourth statute extended the term of protection for anything created before 1976 to forty-seven years, while providing anything created after 1976 copyright protection for the life of the author, plus an additional fifty years (depending upon certain formalities were previously met). With the passage of the Copyright Term Extension Act of 1998 — sometimes still known as the "Mickey Mouse Protection Act" — copyright protection became available for the life of the author, plus seventy years.

Figure 2 shows the current copyright terms for the different types of owners. But how long is too long? At what point does the continuing expansion of copyright term limits violate the "limited times" constraint of the Constitution's copyright clause? Don't repeated term extensions effectively create never-ending copyrights? In addition, it's one thing to extend protection for future works but quite another to apply these new limits to existing works and thereby reduce the amount of content in the public domain, which is also a crucial piece of the American system of copyright. This was the challenge to the Copyright Term Extension Act in *Eldred v. Ashcroft* in 2003. However, it proved to be a weak challenge. The Supreme Court ruled 7-2 that the federal statute was "a rational enactment" and concluded that the Court was "not at liberty to second-guess congressional determinations and policy judgments of this order, however debatable or arguably unwise they may be."

The Court dealt with a similarly difficult question nine years later when it heard the appeal in *Golan v. Holder*, which involved a challenge to the Uruguay Round Agreements Act of 1994, enacted to bring the United States into compliance with international treaty obligations by extending copyright protection to works that are still protected in their country of origin. Was Congress thus "free to restore copyright protection to works that had entered the public domain and become public property," including paintings by the Spanish artist Pablo Picasso, films by the Italian director Frederico Fellini, books by the British author C.S. Lewis, and symphonies by the Russian composer Igor Stravinsky? Did Congress have to act to remedy "past inequities of foreign authors who lost or never obtained copyrights in the United States," at the expense of American "orchestra conductors, educators, performers, publishers, film archivists, and motion picture distributors who have relied on artistic works in the public domain for their livelihoods"? Must there "be a 'bright line' drawn around the public domain" to protect free speech rights and the public interest in continuing creativity and innovation? Is there a "constitutional line" Congress

must not cross when it comes to delineating the public domain? The Court ruled that Congress could restore copyrighted status to works already in the American public domain when it determined that national interests — including, "ensuring exemplary compliance with our international obligations, securing greater protection for U.S. authors abroad, and remedying unequal treatment of foreign authors" — were "best served by our full participation in the dominant system of international copyright protection." Thus, there is no "constitutional significance to" or protection for "a work's public domain status," which appears to guarantee continued litigation over a work's copyright standing. After four years of litigation, courts have determined that the song "Happy Birthday to You" is no longer under copyright — it was first published in 1893 as "Good Morning to All." As a result, other copyrights are also being challenged, including those protecting the songs "We Shall Overcome" and "Kumbaya."

Proving Infringement

From the moment a work is "fixed in any tangible medium of expression" — published or unpublished, officially registered or not — it is constitutionally protected by federal law, which effectively preempts state regulation and means that copyright infringement claims must be filed in federal court. Lawsuits claiming infringement must be filed within three years of the alleged infringement, though the Court in *Petrella v. MGM* (2014) established some limited exceptions.

Infringement occurs when someone assumes, appropriates or usurps any of the exclusive rights granted copyright owners, without authorization. Infringement may be through the creation of an unauthorized derivative work. It may be the result of an unauthorized public display of copyrighted material. It may be a result of vicarious or indirect action, as when recorded music is performed publicly without a license or downloaded without payment. It may occur when a new work infringes on — in that it borrows from or copies portions of — another prior work, which is the most common form of copyright infringement.

It does not matter whether infringement is intentional. Legal liability for innocent — unknowing or non-deliberate or unconscious — plagiarism or copyright infringement is well recognized by the law.

Infringement claims are usually brought in federal court, typically in the U.S. District Court where the infringing party resides. However, in 2022 the U.S. Copyright Office sought to reduce the barrier for smaller infringement claims by creating the Copyright Claims Board (CCB), where infringement claims of less than $30,000 can be heard. Established by the Copyright Alternative in Small Claims Enforcement Act, the CCB has heard around 180 claims in the 2022 fiscal year. There are also state court jurisdiction over copyright infringement under state written by **NEIL STRAUSS**   illustrated by **BERNARD CHANG**

FIGURE 1

"Revenge of the Copyright Cops" by Neil Strauss / Copyright © 2003 Neil Strauss. Used with permission

TERMS OF COPYRIGHT PROTECTION
UNDER 1998 TERM EXTENSION ACT

DATE OF WORK	TERM OF PROTECTION
Created after January 1, 1978	Life of the author plus 70 years; 95 years from first publication or 120 years from creation, whichever is shorter, for works made for hire, anonymous, pseudonymous works or corporate authorship
Created but not published or registered before January 1, 1978	Life of the author plus 70 years or December 31, 2002, whichever is longer
Created before January 1, 1978, and published before December 31, 2002	Life of the author plus 70 years or December 31, 2047, whichever is longer
Pre-1978 works still in their original or renewal term of copyright	95 years from the date that copyright was originally secured

FIGURE 2

copyright laws, some of which pre-date federal copyright protection.

To prove copyright infringement, two essential conditions must be established.

First, the evidence must show proof of one's ownership of the copyrighted work. Without this there is no injury which can be remedied. This is the major benefit of official registration with the U.S. Copyright Office, which legally establishes both ownership and date of creation.

Second, the copyright owner must prove that the copyrighted work itself has been illegally copied. In some cases, this is not difficult — as with the use of boxer Mike Tyson's facial tattoo in the 2011 film *The Hangover Part II* (though this raises the harder question of whether tattoos on a human body or graffiti on buildings owned by someone other than the artist can be copyrighted). But because copying usually cannot be proven directly, courts allow it to be proven indirectly with evidence that:

1. The other person had access to the copyrighted work, and
2. The new work created or produced by the other person is substantially similar to the original, copyrighted work.

"Access," of course, may be defined as actually having seen or having had contact with an earlier work, having knowledge of, or having had the opportunity to see or have contact with the earlier work. The concept of "substantial similarity" is not as easily defined. For example, is the storyline of the 2012 movie *Premium Rush*, about a Manhattan bicycle messenger with a mysterious envelope being pursued throughout New York City by a corrupt police officer, too similar to that of a 1998 novel, *Ultimate Rush*, about a San Francisco messenger on in-line skates pursued by Chinese assassins after delivering an opened package containing illegal stock information?

Professor Melville Nimmer developed two sub-categories of the concept of "substantial similarity" to help with the definition:

1. "Comprehensive nonliteral similarity," and
2. "Fragmented literal similarity."

The first is an example of non-infringing, legally permissible similarity, and the second is an example of infringing, impermissible similarity. Others see the distinction between the two as the difference between "inspiration" and "imitation," still others as the difference between "homage" and "theft" (or "plagiarism"), or between the "new way" and the "old way" of creative expression, or as the point where copyright ends and cultural appropriation begins.

The first type of similarity could occur when two works share the same all-encompassing and central theme. For example, consider the narrative theme of star-crossed, unlucky lovers, cursed by destiny. William Shakespeare wrote *Romeo and Juliet* in 1597 based on this theme. But assuming for a moment that the play is still copyrighted today — which it is not — would

Robert Wise's 1961 film *West Side Story* violate Shakespeare's copyright? Does it matter that Shakespeare's "Juliet" character is named "Maria" in the film? What about Franco Zeffirelli's 1968 film *Romeo & Juliet*? What about James Cameron's 1997 film, *Titanic* — which is essentially *Romeo and Juliet* set on a big boat? What about Jonathan Levine's 2013 film, *Warm Bodies*, in which "R" — an unusual zombie with feelings — falls in love with the still-living Julie? What about the 2014 CW television series *Star Crossed*, in which an alien hero is attracted to a human heroine? Or what about Andrzej Bartkowiak's 2000 film *Romeo Must Die* — which does not include any character named "Romeo" anywhere in the movie?

Based on this hypothetical fact situation, the Zeffirelli film could not be made without Shakespeare's agreement; certainly, the names of the characters are the same, but the film also includes the same characters and the same narrative transferred onto the motion picture screen. However, neither the CW television series nor the Wise, Cameron, Levine or Bartkowiak films would violate Shakespeare's copyright. They have a "comprehensive nonliteral similarity" to the original *Romeo and Juliet* in the most general, broadest, non-infringing sense. They are all about doomed lovers, but they do not copy from the original.

On the other hand, Timothy Anderson's appreciation of Sylvester Stallone's *Rocky* films led him to write a film treatment for *Rocky IV* (1985), which copied characters and their characteristics, as well as Rocky Balboa's back story — all of which demonstrated his admiration for and acknowledgement of Stallone's original work. Anderson's only original contribution was what happened to whom and what Rocky did next. His work demonstrated a "fragmented literal similarity" to Stallone's already copyrighted work and thus infringed Stallone's copyright. Could Anderson have written his own story about some down-and-out athlete, even perhaps a boxer, who overcomes great obstacles to win a contest no one believes he can win? Yes, he could have, but he didn't. Could he have negotiated a license from/contract with Stallone for Anderson to write a *Rocky IV* film treatment for pay? Yes, he could have; but, again, he didn't.

A more complex example of a copyright infringement claim involved George Harrison — former member of the Beatles and himself an internationally known performing artist — and his 1970 hit song "My Sweet Lord." Harrison composed the song in 1969 with Billy Preston, though Harrison is credited as sole author. His music company, Harrisongs Music, held the copyright. In 1971, Bright Tunes Music, the owner of the copyright for the song "He's So Fine" — a 1963 hit for the Chiffons — sued him for plagiarism resulting in copyright infringement. Harrison lost. The federal district court concluded that "it is perfectly obvious to the listener that in musical terms, the two songs are virtually identical except for one phrase."

Bright Tunes was thus able to establish copyright infringe-

ment, first, by showing that it held the copyright to the song "He's So Fine," originally written by Ronald Mack. Second, it was able to prove copying by Harrison by establishing that he had access to the song and that the two songs were legally similar. "He's So Fine" had been on the top of the American music charts for five weeks in 1963 and had ranked in the top thirty in Great Britain for seven weeks. Harrison even conceded access, admitting that he "remembered hearing [the song] when it was popular." The substantial similarity between the two songs was discussed extensively and agreed upon — Harrison's own expert witness agreed with the court that he "had never come across this unique ... use of these materials," and Harrison himself "conceded ... that the two songs were 'strikingly similar' as played by a pianist during the ... trial." As a result, the trial court "concluded that the substantial similarity coupled with access constituted copyright infringement," even though the judge stated that he believed that the impermissible infringement was "subconsciously accomplished."

In 2010, the band Men at Work — whose 1982 hit song "Down Under" has served as the unofficial anthem for the country of Australia for thirty years — was found to have taken the song's distinctive flute solo from the 1932 children's campfire song "Kookaburra Sits in the Old Gum Tree." The group lost its last appeal in 2011, and the plagiarism cost it 5 percent of the royalties the song had earned during the past decade. That same year, the film documentary *The Agony and the Ecstasy of Phil Spector* included twenty-one of his greatest hits, without his permission, based on the contention that his music cannot be evaluated except as a whole. On the other hand, release of a documentary film about mostly anonymous studio musicians who actually recorded many of the biggest hits of the 1960s working as contract session labor for many different record labels, a group known as the Wrecking Crew, has been indefinitely delayed because the producer cannot afford to pay licensing fees for the 132 songs included in the film. And a movie about rock guitarist Jimi Hendrix may not include any of his music, a result of licensing disagreements between the filmmaker and the Hendrix estate.

An even more problematic legal situation arises when advertisers create "sound-alike tracks" — songs that "mimic" a group's musical style. Artists complain that such music represents a way for advertising agencies to get around licensing requirements and enable them to sell something the artist never intended to sell. Yet because artists generally can't copyright a style, mood or sound, it is very difficult to establish any actual violation of copyright laws.

The Fair Use Defense

The most important and far-reaching statutory limitation to the exclusive rights of copyright owners is the defense found in the Fair Use Doctrine.[6] The use of copyrighted works for "criticism, comment, news reporting, teaching (including multiple copies for classroom use), scholarship [and] research" is permitted by the rule, as is any other use which is determined to be a "fair use" as a result of the application of the rule's four factors:

1. The purpose and character of the use, including whether such use is of a commercial nature or is for nonprofit educational purposes;
2. The nature of the copyrighted work;
3. The amount and substantiality of the portion used in relation to the copyrighted work as a whole;
4. The effect of the use upon the potential market for or value of the copyrighted work.

The Supreme Court's ruling in *Harper & Row Publishers v. Nation Enterprises* (1985) demonstrates this analysis. Harper & Row had contracted with former President Gerald Ford to publish his memoirs, *A Time to Heal* (1979). The autobiography would focus on Ford's presidency, the political aftermath of the resignation of President Richard Nixon, accused of orchestrating the 1972 burglary of Democratic National Committee offices in the Watergate building, and Ford's pardon of him. Harper & Row had sold the rights to publish excerpts from the book to *Time* magazine, but even before the book was published, *The Nation* magazine scooped everyone and published an article using copyrighted material from the book. When *Time* magazine sought to get out of its contract with Harper & Row, the publisher sued *The Nation* for copyright infringement.

The magazine agreed in court that its exact copying of between 300 and 400 words of direct quotations from Ford's original 200,000-word manuscript, some 13 percent of the entire article, would violate copyright unless it was deemed to be "fair use." After analyzing and applying each of the four factors, the Supreme Court ruled in favor of Harper & Row.

First, the Court held, *The Nation* "went beyond simply reporting uncopyrightable information and actively sought to exploit the headline value of its infringement, making a 'news event' out of its unauthorized first publication of a noted figure's copyrighted expression." Thus, its intended purpose was commercial in that it intended to "supplant ... the copyright holder's commercially valuable right of first publication." Second, the Court noted, "[T]he fact that a work [was] unpublished [was] a critical

element of its 'nature,'" as pre-publication "confidentiality and creative control" were critical to the value and success of the project. As such, "The author's right to control the first public appearance of his expression weighs against [any] use of the work before its release." Third, without regard to any exact number of words that may be considered "substantial," the Court agreed with the trial-level court that *The Nation* took "essentially the heart of the book." The excerpts taken played "a key role in the infringing work." Finally — recognizing that the fourth factor "is undoubtedly the single most important element in fair use" — the Court concluded that Harper & Row had "established a *prima facie* case of actual damage that respondents failed to rebut," especially given the "extensive prepublication quotations from an unreleased manuscript without the copyright owner's consent [which pose] substantial potential for damage to the marketability of first serialization rights."

However, the Court reached a somewhat different conclusion in *Campbell v. Acuff-Rose Music* (1994). In that case, the rap music group, 2 Live Crew, parodied a well-known 1964 song, "Oh, Pretty Woman," written by Roy Orbison and William Dees, in express defiance of its owner's determination not to grant permission for the use. The 2 Live Crew 1989 version of the song, written by Luther Campbell, took the original song's opening snare drum beat and bass line but then created its own lyrical vision (or version) of a woman who is anything but attractive or feminine or faithful to her boyfriend. Because of its "fragmented literal similarity," if the use is not a "fair use," then the 2 Live Crew parody clearly infringes on the Acuff-Rose copyright.

In analyzing 2 Live Crew's use of the song, according to the Fair Use Doctrine's four factors, the Supreme Court acknowledged the commercial nature of the use up front but downplayed that first factor's determinative importance, saying only that the first "factor tends to weight against a finding of fair use." After essentially dismissing the relevance of the second factor — both songs, after all, had already been published — the Court found itself in agreement with the trial court in its analysis of the third, substantiality/amount, factor and determined that "2 Live Crew had not helped themselves overmuch," contrary to the appellate court's earlier conclusion that the parody had taken "the heart of the original and [made] it the heart of a new work." As the Supreme Court ruled in *Sony v. Universal City Studios* (1984), "[E]very commercial use of copyrighted material is presumptively an unfair exploitation of the monopoly privilege that belongs to the owner of the copyright."

So how much is too much? The answer to this question was also at the heart of the $7.3 million jury verdict awarded to the Marvin Gaye estate in 2015 on the grounds that Robin Thicke's "Blurred Lines" (2013) was substantially similar to Gaye's "Got to Give It Up" (1977). The similarity between the two songs ba

---

[6] Yet application of the Fair Use Doctrine to works not easily divisible or susceptible to partial use, such as artwork or poetry, is not easy. For example, if "fair use" "allows artists to borrow from other works so long as they give a new expression or meaning to the original work," at what exact, legally ascertainable point does such borrowing — or "mash-up" — become improper appropriation? *See* Michael Rips, *Fair Use, Art, Swiss Cheese & Me*, N.Y. Times, June 17, 2012, Week In Review, at 5.

sically amounted to "atmospheric and textual elements," bass phrasing and cowbell syncopation. Thus, according to the federal appellate court in *Williams v. Gaye* (2018), the song's authors were deemed guilty of stealing a "vibe." The issue, then, is not so much about chords as it is about "feel." But when, exactly, does "feel" rise to the level of copyright infringement?

In *Campbell*, the Supreme Court stated that "context is everything" and a "fair use" analysis "asks what else the parodist did besides go to the heart of the original." It found that "2 Live Crew not only copied the first line of the original, but thereafter departed markedly from the Orbison lyrics for its own ends." Finally, the Court warned against presuming economic harm in any analysis of the fourth, market, factor, as the appellate court had done. Rather, the Court ruled, "[A]s to parody pure and simple, it is more likely that the new work will not affect the market for the original ... by acting as a substitute for it."

Thus, the parody here targeted the original and transformed it into something entirely new and copyrightable — a separate, original work. Parody, the Court concluded, "[H]as an obvious claim to transformative value.... Like less ostensibly humorous forms of criticism, it can provide social benefit, by shedding light on an earlier work, and, in the process, creating a new one." Clearly, then, a transformative use is a "fair use."

But what is a transformative use? Paramount Pictures took a well-known 1991 picture of actress Demi Moore, eight months pregnant and partially nude, from the cover of *Vanity Fair* magazine, doctored it — by taking a similarly posed photograph of a semi-nude, pregnant model and super-imposing the head of actor Leslie Neilson on the body and then used the resulting photograph to promote its 1993 movie, *The Naked Gun 33 1/3: The Final Insult*. The photographer, Annie Leibovitz, sued but lost — because the movie poster was a parody of Leibovitz's earlier photograph.

Yet, the publication of a three-year-old nude photo of a TV news reporter participating in a wet T-shirt contest was not a transformative "fair use," according to the federal appellate court in *Balsley v. LFP* (2012), since, by publishing it "clearly for commercial purposes" in an unaltered form, "*Hustler* was selling a [copyrighted] picture, and not a [news] story." But could Dr. Seuss' *How the Grinch Stole Christmas* (1957) be retold as a raunchy, one-woman play — *Who's Holiday!* (2016) — from the viewpoint of the Grinch's spouse, the former Cindy Lou Who, who had just completed a prison term for his murder? Yes. Absolutely.

These cases suggest another unanswered question: Are there any other types of uses that qualify as transformative uses? Though only future court rulings can answer the question, it is at the heart of the many "Hitler Downfall" parodies now existing on YouTube, in which Adolph Hitler — in a scene from the 2004 German film, *Der Untergang* — rages and rants not about his approaching doom but about the end of the Robert Mueller investigation, about the delayed Brexit deal, about a pizza takeout order, about Donald Trump winning the 2016 presidential election, about working for minimum wage at McDonalds, about his interaction with an Indian call center, about the 2008 global financial crisis, and about the parodies themselves. There is even a YouTube channel — Hitler's Rants Parodies — devoted exclusively to such clips. Or what about Randy Moore's 2013 movie, *Escape from Tomorrow*, about a father going insane at Walt Disney World? Could the filmmaker use Disney's copyrighted images in his critique of Disney's concept of family entertainment? Whether such examples are transformative uses, and thus protected by copyright, is not clear.

So, what do all these rulings tell us about what uses of copyrighted works are "fair"?

First, the question of "whose dime" is a very important issue. For a commercial use to be fair, it must be transformative, as the Court found that it was in *Campbell*. Even when the use involves teaching, including multiple copies for classroom use, if students must pay for a supplemental course packet that includes photocopied excerpts from books and other periodicals for use in class, it is not a "fair use." This rule was established in *Basic Books v. Kinko's Graphics* (1991). One may argue that requiring students to purchase a large number of books in a given course makes the cost of higher education nearly prohibitive. Yet, because of the commercial interests involved — including the fact that Kinko's made a significant profit from the sales of these anthologies, which also themselves competed with the sale of the books from which the excerpts were taken — the company was guilty of copyright infringement in the making of unauthorized copies of copyrighted works. In 2023, the U.S. Supreme Court further analyzed the first element of fair use in *Andy Warhol Foundation for the Visual Arts, Inc. v. Goldsmith* (2023). That case involved the use of an Andy Warhol silkscreen painting, Orange Prince, that was a derivative of a 1984 photograph taken by Lynn Goldsmith of the pop singer Prince. The Warhol portrait was used by magazine *Vanity Fair* on a cover commemorating Prince. Goldsmith sued for infringement and the Supreme Court held that the derivative work of Warhol had to be weighed in context with commercialism. In effect, the court held that when evaluating the first prong of fair use courts have to evaluate the transformativeness of the fair use needs to provide a "different meaning or message than the original." The result of this decision may lead to increased infringement suits against artists and others who create derivative works from copyrighted materials, like Goldsmith's photo.

Second, unpublished works not only have a higher degree of copyright protection than published ones, but they also are further protected in that possession of the work does not give the owner the right to use it otherwise. For example:

• May the letters of the late author J.D. Salinger be published because they are available to researchers in publicly accessible libraries? No. Salinger's estate still owns and controls copyright in the unpublished letters.

• May the personal letters from George Steinbrenner, the late owner of the New York Yankees, written in 1949 to a female friend, be published by the recipient in a book she wants to write about their relationship? No. They may not be published although they may be sold.

• May students record and subsequently post a professor's lectures online? Although students have a right to the private possession of such recordings, making the recordings available to others by online posting would violate the intellectual property rights of the professor.

• May a journalist befriend acquaintances of the author Harper Lee and write a book based on such access? Yes. Despite Lee's public statement denying that she had authorized any such book or that she willingly participated in the project, such a book may be published as long as it is based on the journalist's own observations and does not include any material in which Harper Lee's estate has a copyright claim.

Possession may indeed be nine-tenths of the law, but not where the copyright owner's exclusive rights of copying and derivative works are concerned. Just ask Eva Gabrielsson, long-time partner of Swedish author Stieg Larsson. Despite having possession and ownership of the late writer's laptop computer containing an unpublished sequel to his Millennium series of novels featuring Lisbeth Salander — *The Girl with the Dragon Tattoo* (2005) — the copyright to the unpublished work (specifically, the right to publish a sequel as a derivative work) is owned by Larsson's family, since Gabrielsson and Larsson never married, and she did not qualify as his legal heir.

Third, the acceptable quantity of the portion used in relation to the whole, cannot be calculated as a specific percentage. There is no "20 percent rule" or "40-word rule." There is no exact amount; whatever it is, is a muddy swamp. How much constitutes "the heart" of a work is a question which cannot be answered in general terms, only on a case-by-case, contextual basis and then only in relation to the fourth part of the Fair Use Doctrine. As the Supreme Court concluded in *Campbell v. Acuff-Rose Music* (1994), "it is uncontested," that — had it not been legally excused as being transformative — 2 Live Crew's lifting of the opening snare drum beat and bass line of Roy Orbison's "Pretty Woman" would have been sufficient — because of the "fragmented literal similarity," however insignificant it was — to constitute illegal copying.

Fourth, unless a work is transformative, the copyright owner has the right not only to exploit the market for his or her work but also to choose what potential markets to exploit in the fu-

ture and which ones to avoid. It is solely the copyright owner's choice. In addition, it makes no difference whether the infringement is for or not for monetary gain. Castle Rock Entertainment, owner of the *Seinfeld* television series copyright, could choose for whatever reason not to publish any "Seinfeld" trivia book, such as *The Seinfeld Aptitude Test* (1994), and the law "must respect that creative and economic choice," according to the federal appellate court in *Castle Rock Entertainment v. Carol Publishing* (1998). Similarly, author J.D. Salinger could stop publication of an unauthorized sequel — John David California's *60 Years Later: Coming Through the Rye* (2009) — to his own ground-breaking coming-of-age novel, *Catcher in the Rye* (1951). Although a federal appellate court required Salinger to prove harm from the publication, it agreed that the Salinger estate's control over the markets for all derivative works based on his writings meant that the unauthorized sequel was an infringement of his copyright. More recently, a "mash-up" of verbal and visual imagery from the "Star Trek" television series (1966-1969) and Dr. Seuss' book, "Oh, the Places You'll Go!" (1990), resulting in the new book, "Oh, the Places You'll Boldly Go," was determined to violate copyright and not be a "fair use" because it was not transformative.

The challenge of "fair use," then, is to develop a centrist application of the doctrine, one that is not too narrow and restrictive and one that is not too broad and inclusive, yet one that is substantially more assertive and expansive than that which is regularly applied today.

Copyright's Digital Transformation

If the primary purpose of copyright law is to protect the copyright owner's right to make copies, then technological innovation has always been the enemy of copyright. For most of recorded history, copying was difficult. Yet, every invention since Johannes Gutenberg's printing press in 1436 has made it progressively easier to copy and, thus, has taken the physical ability to control one's creation ever further out of the hands of the copyright holder. Indeed, the printing press made texts easier to duplicate and easier to disseminate, with or without the acquiescence or approval of the original author.

As a result, copyright law has always viewed technological developments cautiously — whether the created expression takes the form of printed marks on a page or analog radio waves or digital bits of information. As innovations have developed and copyright owners have become increasingly aware of the profit potential in these new methods of "publication," there has at the same time developed a growing assumption of infringement, a belief by copyright holders that technological innovations will be used to their detriment. Today, the Internet enables the flouting of copyright in ways and on a scale unimaginable, even as recently as twenty years ago.

A century ago, the new, "disruptive" technology was the player piano, and the question before the Supreme Court was whether player piano rolls were copies of songs or something else. If they were copies, then player piano manufacturers should pay copyright owners for each copy produced; if they were something else, then the manufacturers could continue to do what they were doing — which was to purchase a single piece of copyrighted sheet music legally, have someone create the "recording" of the music, and sell these rolls to consumers without any further royalty payment on the manufacturers' part. In *White-Smith Music Publishing v. Apollo*, the Court ruled in 1908 that player piano rolls were mechanical reproductions and not copies of musical compositions — and, in fact, were not music at all, since most people could not read the perforations and/ or otherwise gather musical thoughts from the rolls themselves — and that no additional royalty payments were required, according to then current copyright law.

Contributory Infringement. Thus, it should have surprised no one when several film production companies, looking at the new Sony Betamax video tape recorder, concluded that the sale of each machine must be taxed to pay the film production companies for the royalties they would lose from all the copying (and copyright infringement) that would result from their use and misuse by consumers. The fear of infringement was so real that Jack Valenti, then head of the Motion Picture Association of America, said "the VCR is to the American film producer and the American public as the Boston strangler is to the woman home alone." In 1984, however, the Supreme Court held in *Sony v. Universal City Studios* that time-shifting — the viewing of a recorded program at a time other than when it was first broadcast — was a "fair use" of the new technology, in that it actually increases the value of the copyrighted work by increasing the size of its audience through the option of what might be considered a deferred purchase. Further, the Court held that manufacturers of video cassette recorders cannot be held legally responsible for contributing to copyright infringement as long as the machines are "capable of substantial non-infringing uses."

Twenty years later, Grokster, a peer-to-peer computer file-sharing service whose users downloaded copyrighted music files without permission, argued similarly that its software was also capable of innocent uses in that it could be used, for example, to download very large data files, such as the complete works of William Shakespeare. Was Grokster thus liable for the acts of those who used its software to download music illegally and violate copyright? In *MGM v. Grokster* (2005), the Supreme Court concluded that the file-sharing service was legally liable, because of its intent in the marketing and sales campaigns for its software was to encourage customers to infringe copyright.

Grokster shut down shortly thereafter as part of the settlement of the lawsuit.

The modern two-part test for contributory infringement thus seems to be:

1. Is the technology capable of substantial non-infringing uses? and
2. Is the manufacturer/seller's intent to encourage or induce others to violate copyright?

This focus on capability and intent is also evident in the position that the Digital Millennium Copyright Act of 1998 takes in immunizing Internet service providers and not holding them legally liable for any copyright violations by their users.

Digital Sampling and Mash-ups. The availability of almost all copyrighted works in digital format today is threatening the exclusive rights of copyright holders as never before, especially the right to reproduce a copyrighted work and the right to make derivative works from the original. This threat is particularly evident in the area of musical composition — unsurprising in view of the long tradition of "borrowing" — known as sampling, which may be loosely defined as the incorporation or re-purposing of a snippet, a recognizable portion of a song, into another song through some digital means. WhoSampled.com, the "ultimate database of sampled music, remixes, and cover songs," claims to have links to 99,000 songs by 39,000 artists. So many examples are now available that lists and smartphone apps of sampled songs abound.

An interesting example of video sampling is the short film *A Fair(y) Use Tale* (2007) by Professor Eric Faden. The ten-minute film uses snippets of dialogue from characters in Disney animated films to create a critical parody to explain copyright law and "fair use." The words and phrases, used sometimes *ad nauseum*, from twenty-seven Disney cartoon feature films — from *Snow White and the Seven Dwarfs* (1937) to *Bambi* (1942) to *Sleeping Beauty* (1959) to *The Little Mermaid* (1989) to *Toy Story* (1995) to *Finding Nemo* (2003) — to construct its educational narrative focus. Its transformative nature claim is based on the film's creative use of copyrighted Disney characters, despite Disney's well-known, highly restrictive attitude regarding the use of its characters by all others, including scholars engaged in the study of popular culture.

And, sometimes, whole albums are "mashed" together into something else entirely. A well-known example occurred when the hip-hop group Danger Mouse took *a cappella* samples from the 2003 *Black Album* by rapper Jay-Z and combined them with instrumental loops from the Beatles' 1968 *White Album*, creating a musical mixture known as *The Grey Album* (2004). Though legal problems quickly arose — Danger Mouse never sought copyright clearance for its use of the Beatles' songs, lawsuits were threatened, and nearly 200 Internet sites posted tracks from the bootleg album in support of Danger Mouse on what came to be known as Grey Tuesday — its release began the "mainstreaming of the mash-up," which continues today. A recent example was the artist Baauer's surprise viral Internet hit, "Do the Harlem Shake," which subsequently climbed the pop charts in 2013 and included the voices of several uncredited — and unpaid — artists. Yet, clearly, the delight of the mash-up lies in its inspired pairing of diametrically different artists and their creative expressions which would be unlikely to exist in reality, except as a mash-up. Despite the fact that the best mash-ups are always unauthorized, unlicensed ones, copyright law, of course, expects musicians and consumers to make appropriate payments for what they use to create new creative expression.

An early example of a mashed-up movie is Joe Dante's *The Movie Orgy* (1968), which is nothing more than discarded 16mm film footage, both amateur and professional, "creatively re-edited" into what Dave Kehr in the *New York Times* described in 2011 as

a hilarious meta-movie in which five or six stories seem to be going on at once (giant grasshoppers invade Chicago as flying saucers attack Washington), constantly interrupted by prom night do's and don'ts, stomach-churning commercials for laxative pills and disturbing excerpts from children's television shows (including a stuffed cat and mouse who perform "Jesus Loves Me" on piano and drums).

More recently, fans have taken full seasons of television series, downloaded them and re-edited them in an order different from that in which they were originally released. With the digital format of modern film, many believe that every form of creative expression that can be combined will be somewhere on the Internet. Our "mash-up culture" is an Internet creation.

The legal rule today, however, is still simple and straightforward: A license is required whenever you use any piece of another's copyrighted music or art or film or writing.

A license to sample may be "standard practice" in the music industry. Do not believe the so-called "fair use rule" in the music industry that says if it's four notes or less, then it's all right. That is wrong, as the 2005 ruling in *Bridgeport Music v. Dimension Films* demonstrates.

There, three notes lasting two seconds were sampled from the 1975 Funkadelic song "Get Off Your Ass and Jam" in the 1990 N.W.A. song "100 Miles and Runnin'," which was included as part of the 1998 film *I Got the Hook Up*. The three notes still were sufficient to constitute copyright infringement. The federal appellate court acknowledged that digital sampling is often

tionally common but said that the solution was to "get a license or do not sample.... Sampling is never accidental.... When you sample a sound recording, you know you are taking another's work product." The only exception is when short phrases or clichés are involved, since they lack the necessary degree of originality and creativity required by copyright. For example, the single exclamation, "Oh!," sampled forty-two times in the background of Jay-Z's 2009 single, "Run This Town," had no essential significance to the original recording of Eddie Bo's "Hook and Sling — Part I" (1969) and thus could not be the basis of a copyright infringement claim.

"Copyleft" and Future Challenges to Copyright. The ready availability (and easy manipulation) of digitized information on the Internet has destabilized the creative system copyright is meant to protect. This, in turn, has led to two results.

First, copyright enforcement has become too powerful, too nit-picky, too rigid. It protects more than ever and criminalizes more than ever, stifling creativity "with a vengeance and in such a manner as to stifle rather than advance ... 'Science and the useful Arts.'"[7] This part of the problem is further exacerbated and the positions of the different parties become even more inflexible and seemingly more confused when a corporate entity is involved.

Second, legal theorists — Professor Lawrence Lessig is one — are re-examining the very nature of intellectual property in non-physical cyberspace. The Internet, in Lessig's view in *The Future of Ideas* (2001), is a commons area and should be structured as "a common market of innovation," and its uses not structured, regulated or restricted as private property. Goods, such as intellectual property, in such common areas

[A]re a resource for decentralized innovation. They create the opportunity for individuals to draw upon resources without connections, permission, or access granted by others. They are environments that commit themselves to being open. Individuals and corporations draw upon the value created by this openness. They transform that value into other value ... [since] *the digital world is closer to the* [Jeffersonian] *world of ideas than to the world of things* (emphasis in original).

---

[7] Randy Barnett, *Reds in Suits*, REGULATION, at 65 (Fall 2002) (quoting U.S. CONST., art I, § 8, ¶ 8), notes:

[M]ore than a few view one person's use of his own physical property as "theft" of another's intangible property. Because of so-called intellectual property, the property owner cannot fully use what he reasonably thought was his; he cannot copy music from one of his CDs onto his computer and then move the files onto his MP3 player. He cannot make photocopies of a book that he owns, and then hand those copies to a friend or a class of students. He cannot use his own guitar to play particular notes or his voice to sing particular lyrics in public.

FIGURE 3

This philosophy has led to the development of the "copyleft" concept, a copyright licensing arrangement — sometimes known as a Creative Commons license — that gives all possessors and users of a work the same control over it as authors, including the right to copy and share it with others, and to modify and distribute derivative versions — rights exclusively reserved to copyright holders under copyright law. The "copyleft" symbol is a backwards "C" in a circle (see Figure 3) but has no legal significance or meaning. Though the concept obviously has potential application to other types of intellectual property, open source software development is the most common application of the concept today.

Clearly, some new interpretation of (or, failing that, intensive education regarding) copyright law and its myriad of applications to what are no more than various combinations of digital bits in cyberspace needs to be developed. Previously unheard-of problems are now being confronted. For example:

• Under what circumstances might a work created by a bot or by using artificial intelligence be protected by copyright? The law works created by humans, but the USCO has said some generative AI content does receive copyright protection if the work has substantial human involvement. What is the threshold of that involvement? How will generative AI change the nature of copyright infringement? Courts will be sorting out these issues for years to come.

• Who owns memes — those pictures, edited images, video clips and ideas that capture the Internet's imagination for a moment and are shared over and over and over again? Does the creation of memes violate copyright law? Yes, in all likelihood, since generally the creator of the original owns all progeny and subsequent modifications of it, too, though a claim of "fair use" might substantially mitigate monetary damages.

• Is every unauthorized inclusion (however small or brief) of copyrighted or trademarked images — such as artwork, sculpture, commercial products, or books or other writings — in movies or video games an illegal use requiring the awarding of damages? And how do we know what is copyrighted since works may not have been registered with the U.S. Copyright Office? For example, while dance routines are copyrightable, what about the brief victory dances in the videogame "Fortnite"? The Copyright Office has taken the position that the dance, sometimes called the "Carlton" or the "Floss," is not complex enough to be copyrightable. So, how complex is complex enough, and how simple is too simple?

• How can music best be made available to consumers, in a manner that properly credits and compensates copyright holders? In 2018, some 38 percent of consumers got their music by infringing others' copyrights. So, should artists charge for their music and thus limit their audience, or should they seek the widest possible audience, one that uses their music without permission or remuneration?

• Is using one's telephone to take pictures of housing diagrams, illustrations and pictures contained in a book available for purchase an infringement of a publisher's copyright? In all likelihood, yes, since such copying of a book is very similar to pirating music. A definitive result would of course depend on the outcome of a judicial analysis of the fact situation using the Fair Use Doctrine.

• In its effort to create "the universal library," did Google's book-scanning project create copyrighted works out of those already in the public domain or violate the rights of unknown owners of so-called "orphan works" or infringe on existing copyrights by digitizing them to make them easily accessible online? After all, the federal appellate court in *Authors Guild v. HathiTrust* (2014) determined that a searchable book database for the sight impaired was a copyrightable transformative use. Was Google's project, in the words of Siva Vaidhyanathan, "a single liquid fabric of interconnected words and ideas," or, was it really, as others believed, a bold attempt to control all the world's information and data? Publishers reached a settlement with Google in 2012, a lawsuit by authors was dismissed in 2013, and appeals were exhausted in 2016. So, what's permissible now?

• What level of copyright protection do short social media posts, such as tweets, receive? How much of a tweet may be used, according to the Fair Use Doctrine, when the entire "tweet" is limited to 280 characters or less?

• Do musical scores in the public domain and available for free online unfairly hurt publishers' sales of modern editions that may be copyrightable as a result of substantial changes to the music?

• May publishers electronically limit the readable "shelf life" of an electronic copy of a book in a public library's collection — an "e-book" — so it will "wear out" (and the library be forced to buy another copy for lending to patrons) at a rate similar to that of print versions of the book? If digital goods can be "loaned" at all, must ownership, specifically possession, be transferred?

• Does the Copyright Office have unilateral administrative power to permit copyright infringement of automobile or smart phone software to allow owners to use Internet applications (known as "apps") that have not been approved by the manufacturer — a practice known as "jail-breaking" — to recalibrate performance?

• Which is better legislatively, to hold Internet sites and services, such as Kim Dotcom's Megaupload service or Alexandra Elbakyan's file-sharing Sci-Hub Web site, responsible for theft and piracy by their users or to hold individual users liable for unauthorized downloads of music, films, books, and articles? A partial answer may be found in *Cobbler Nevada v. Gonzales* (2018), where the appellate court held that a user could not be held personally liable for others' copyright infringement just because he "failed to police" his connection to the BitTorrent peer-to-peer file-sharing network.

• As both professional and amateur sports organizers increasingly turn to claims of contractual copyright entitlements as a way of cornering the entertainment marketplace for themselves, how do the media and artists and others deal with the growing monopolies' control of larger and more diverse businesses that disseminate information about sporting events?

• Should the conversion of academic publishers' copyrighted works into Adobe's public document format and the posting of PDF files on university-controlled Internet sites for educational purposes — for students to read, download and copy, all without paying royalty fees — be considered copyright infringement? Whose dime must cover the costs, and to what degree must accessibility be restricted for this practice to qualify under the copyright statute as "teaching (including [the right to make] multiple copies for classroom use)" and be protected as a "fair use" of copyrighted works? In *Cambridge University Press v. Becker*, the federal appellate court has twice (2014, 2018) overturned trial court rulings (2012, 2016) that had essentially set mathematical, quantitative thresholds for "fair use" when it should have used a holistic, qualitative approach. Most recently, in 2020, the trial court determined that a majority (37 of 48) of the uses complained of were fair uses.

• Can YouTube be held legally liable for its own blindness to the uploading by some users of copyrighted videos, despite the safe harbor provisions of the Digital Millennium Copyright Act of 1998?

• How will three-dimensional "printing," which can reproduce objects by spraying layers of plastic or ceramics into the shape of an item, change the nature of manufacturing and challenge the legal concepts of ownership and copyright?

• Do online news aggregation Web sites that compile news stories without publishers' permission infringe copyright? Yes, according to the trial court in *Associated Press v. Meltwater News* (2013), especially if such sites resell the news stories they collect and repost.

• What implications do digital "reincarnations" or holograms have for copyright and the ownership of one's image? Must holograms be licensed to be used legally?

• Is a tweet embedded in an article in an online publication's Web site a violation of copyright? Yes, if this violates a copyright owner's exclusive right to distribute or display copyrighted images or material, the trial court ruled in *Goldman v. Breitbart News Network* (2018).

• Will non-fungible tokens (NFT's) ever serve as copyright alternatives? Since NFT's are digital marks of ownership usually recorded in a blockchain ledger, isn't that the same as copyright and might NFT's not supplant copyright at some future point? But if copyright is a legal system and not a technical one, doesn't that mean that the rights represented by copyright still belong to the creator of the work and that an NFT is essentially useless in demonstrating legal ownership and control? Are NFT's the future of legal protection or another opportunity for piracy? Or maybe NFT's are merely a passing fad?

As is clear, the evolving technological landscape that is known as cyberspace promises that more issues such as these will arise in the future. Siva Vaidhyanathan argues that "more than ever, the law restricts what individuals can do with the elements of their own culture. Generally, the exercise of copyright protection is so extreme these days that even the most innocent use of images or song lyrics ... can generate a legal threat," which will force everyone to get legal permission for every snippet of anything they use in any and every new creation of their own, which in turn will create a logistical logjam and financial nightmare. Others, including Scott Turow, a novelist and former president of the Authors Guild, fear that without a strong copyright law, the markets that copyright protects will be undermined by piracy, which is "a lucrative, innovative, global enterprise. Clusters of overseas [computer] servers can undermine much of the commercial basis for creative work around the world, offering users the speedy, secret transmission of stolen goods." They also warn:

[S]ince the Enlightenment, Western societies have been lulled into a belief that progress is inevitable. It never has been. It's the result of abiding by rules that were carefully constructed and practices that were begun by people living in the long shadow of the Dark Ages. We tamper with those rules at our peril.

Still others argue that we live in a "post-genius" world in which the ideas of "independent creation" and "originality" are cultural myths that have long outlived their legal usefulness. But, whether we like it or not, as we are reminded by Vaidhyanathan, "as the most pervasive regulation of speech and culture, the copyright system will help determine the richness and strength of democracy in the twenty-first century."

TRADEMARKS/SERVICE MARKS

If copyright is the "engine of free expression," as the Supreme Court concluded in *Harper & Row Publishers v. Nation Enterprises* (1985), then trademark law — along with the U.S. Constitution's Commerce Clause, which gives Congress the power to control trade among states — is the engine of economic expression and the means to protect the economic value of a company's brands, as well as its reputation. Specifically, a trademark "must show that the primary significance of the term in the minds of the consuming public is not the product but the producer." In the 1938 case *Kellogg v. National Biscuit*, the question was whether Kellogg could market a shredded wheat breakfast cereal in competition with a cereal manufactured by National Biscuit Co. The Supreme Court ruled that it could, that in the public's perception the trademark did not necessarily denote or designate the National Biscuit product as opposed to a similar product by any other company, according to Justice Louis Brandeis.

Thus, words, designs or phrases — or any combination of the three — that denote a specific product, service or company may be registered with the U.S. Patent and Trademark Office and protected by the Lanham Act of 1946, giving companies an exclusive right to use the mark in their commercial dealings with the consuming public. For example, the Amateur Sports Act of 1978 gives the International Olympic Committee exclusive control over the games' multicolored, interlocking rings, as well as, the words "Olympic" and "Olympiad." As a result, the Supreme Court, in *San Francisco Arts & Athletics v. U.S. Olympic Committee* (1987), upheld an injunction prohibiting the use of the word "Olympic" to promote the "Gay Olympic Games." This then explains why companies do everything they can to associate themselves with a trademarked product or event without overstepping their bounds and violating that trademark, such as the Atlanta Food Truck Park & Market did when it promoted its "Souper Bowl Village" at the same time the city of Atlanta was hosting the Super Bowl and its own "fan village" — "Super Bowl LIVE" — nearby.

A product's design or image, as part of its "trade dress," may also be registered as a trademark, if its elements in general:

1. Are nonfunctional,
2. Have secondary meaning, and
3. Are recognized by the public as an "unmistakable, certain, and primary means of identification," as the appellate court ruled in *In re Swift & Co.* (1955), which would lead to a likelihood of consumer confusion if misused by others. In fact, this statutory concept is so all-inclusive that "nothing ... shall prevent the registration of a mark ... which has become distinctive of [an] applicant's goods in commerce."

Examples of trade dress include the shape of the Coca-Cola soft drink bottle, the sewing design on the back pocket of Levi's jeans, the color of Owens-Corning fiberglass insulation, the sound of Harley-Davidson motorcycles, the green and yellow color combination on John Deere agriculture equipment, and the red soles on Christian Louboutin women's shoes.

The basic, federal requirement for a trademark or service mark is that it be distinctive. The Adidas three-stripe design is not sufficiently distinctive, for example, while the Nike "swoosh" is. As a result, disputes increasingly result from demands that trademarked words in apparent common usage — such as, emoji — be licensed, and lawsuits increasingly challenge tiny aspects of distinctiveness, such as whether the phrase "2.0" represents a unique product or service and may be trademarked. In 2019, a federal appellate court ruled that VersaTop Support Systems owns the "2.0" mark, as least as far as the "trade show pipe and drape" market is concerned, concluding that a likelihood of confusion existed where "the marks were identical, the goods were related, and the marketing channels overlapped."

Lawsuits over "distinctiveness" also many times involve claims of "trademark bullying" of small businesses by large corporations, in part, because there are a decreasing number of names that are available to be trademarked. They also involve novel questions, such as, can scents be trademarked? Importantly, the "distinctiveness" of trademarks should be market tested before their adoption, something RJ-Metrics failed to do before it introduced a new logo — an orange dodecahedron — that to some looked like a giant pair of men's underpants.

The requirement of distinctiveness in trademark law roughly corresponds to the originality requirement in copyright law. For example, the phrase "three-peat" — which means three consecutive sports championships — has been trademarked by National Basketball Association coach Pat Riley since 1988. Distinctiveness is also similar to the common law protection against unfair competition available in tort law. In *International News Service v. Associated Press* (1918), for example, the INS was re-distributing news stories the AP had reported, written, sold and disseminated. INS represented the stories as its own work. On the grounds that news stories are quasi-property, the Supreme Court held that the re-distribution — even if the INS rewrote the stories in a different format — created a likelihood of confusion, misleading INS customers, and denied the AP full value for its news-gathering efforts. The INS was "endeavoring to reap where it [had] not sown and ... appropriating to itself the harvest of those who [had] sown."

However, though trademarks must be distinctive, they may not:

• Consist of a flag or emblem or insignia of any country;
• Resemble a person's name, signature or likeness without consent;
• Resemble any other trade or service mark;
• Be merely descriptive of the product;
• Be primarily descriptive (or mis-descriptive) of the product's geographic origin; or
• Be a surname.

At one time trademarks were prohibited from being scandalous, immoral, deceptive, or disparaging of persons or groups. The prohibition was thrown out by the Supreme Court, however, in *Matal v. Tam* (2017) and *Iancu v. Brunetti* (2019);

In *Matal v. Tam*, the Supreme Court weighed the First Amendment's protection of offensive language against the Lanham Act's protection of the public from disparaging trademarks. The Asian-American rock band the Slants' so-called "right to offend" was unanimously determined to be more important. Thus, the government cannot forbid the expression of other viewpoints, even offensive ones, because the First Amendment forbids censorship by the government, even when dealing with trademarks.

This rule was expanded two years later in *Iancu v. Brunetti* to include immoral and scandalous marks, prohibiting the government from denying trademark protection to Erik Brunetti's "subversive" clothing brand he calls FUCT, for "Friends U Can't Trust" (the mark is "pronounced as four letters, one after the other: F-U-C-T"). Some believe it to be "the equivalent of the past participle form of the paradigmatic profane word in our culture." No matter. The government cannot promote any viewpoint by prohibiting others. Nor can it act as a public gatekeeper or morality enforcer when denying or canceling a trademark based on its potential offensiveness or immoral or scandalous nature.

Once a mark is registered with the U.S. Patent & Trademark Office, it is good for ten years and may be renewed for unlimited ten-year periods, as long as it is regularly and continually used "in commerce," — and not to protect one's right of publicity or

right to privacy — though a period of three consecutive years of non-use raises the legal presumption of abandonment. A registered trademark should be noted on the product by ® (the letter "R" in a circle is an indication of official registration). An unregistered mark may use ™ (for trademarks) or ℠ (for service marks) as a notice alerting the public of one's legal claim to the use of the mark.

Under the Trademark Revision Act of 1988, a mark no longer has to be in use before an application for registration is filed. An "intent to use" application gives the requestor at least six months to begin using the mark. The mark is not actually registered until it is placed "in use," but the "intent to use" rules protect it from infringement by someone who has never used the mark nor previously applied for its registration.

CONTINUUM OF TRADEMARK PROTECTION

MOST
Fanciful
 Arbitrary
  Suggestive
   Descriptive
    Generic
LEAST

FIGURE 4

Degrees of Protection

The degree of protection varies along a continuum, with fanciful or coined marks receiving the most protection, descriptive marks receiving the least, and generic marks receiving no protection whatsoever — first distinguished in *Abercrombie & Fitch v. Hunting World* (1976) — as Figure 4 illustrates.

Fanciful or coined marks are generally created words or designs with no dictionary meaning, such as "Exxon." Arbitrary marks are commonplace words or symbols that do not describe the product of company with which they are associated, such as "Apple" computers. Such "marks convey nothing about the nature of the product except through knowledge of the market," in the words of Arthur Miller and Michael Davis. Suggestive marks, on the other hand, are familiar words or phrases that are used to suggest what the product or service really is, such as the Lifetime television network, whose programming is primarily aimed at women, or the Spike television network, whose programming was primarily aimed at men. As might be surmised, descriptive marks actually describe the thing or company, such as *Money*, a personal finance magazine. Proof of some secondary or non-natural meaning is required before descriptive marks may be registered as trademarks.

Generic marks are the names of a product or service and cannot function as trademarks, such as "aspirin," an over-the-counter pain reliever, also known as acetyl salicylic acid. At one time, "aspirin" was a protected trademark, but it fell into common usage, no longer distinguishing the particular product of its manufacturer and was invalidated by a federal trial court in *Bayer v. United Drug* (1921). Similarly, "thermos" was the registered name for its vacuum-insulated containers, before it also began to be commonly used and thus was subsequently invalidated as a distinct trademark in *King-Seeley Thermos v. Aladdin Industries* (1963) And DuPont lost control over the trademark, "cellophane," when it was determined in *DuPont Cellophane v. Waxed Products* (1936) that everyone referred to all thin, plastic sheeting (waxed or not) by that name. Other former marks which fell into generic usage include trampoline, rollerblades, and escalator.

Corporations, therefore, are constantly on the lookout for public misuse of their trade and service marks to prevent what has been called "genericide" — the death of trademarks by common or generic use — and regularly place advertisements showing correct trademark usage and write letters to journalists and others who use trademarks incorrectly in the media.

The rule is simple: Trademarks and service marks are proper nouns, which should be capitalized, and not common nouns, verbs or adjectives. The correct usage for trademarks, for example, would be: Xerox® photo-copiers, Egg Beaters® egg substitute food product, Scotch® brand adhesive tape, Play-Doh® modeling compound, Johnson & Johnson's Kleenex® facial tissues, a Jeep Grand Cherokee® sport utility vehicle, Certs® breath freshening mints, Formica® laminated plastic surfaces, U-Haul® truck and automobile trailer rentals, Dow Chemical's Styrofoam® building insulation board, Wham-O's Frisbee® brand plastic flying disc, Duraflame® artificial fireplace logs. These companies have introduced new words into common usage through the marketing of their products and have made themselves a lot of money in the process — like Apple's iPad® tablet computer — but also constantly worry about the unintended consequences of "genericization" and "brand deterioration."

Threats to Trademarks

Because the primary purpose of trademarks is to identify and distinguish products and services, making money for their owners while at the same time generating valuable goodwill, trademark owners are very sensitive to any and all threats to their marks, including inadvertent product confusion they themselves may cause. The two most serious threats to trademarks are:

1. Likelihood of confusion, and
2. Dilution.

In 2013, for example, Tiffany's sued Costco for selling "Tiffany engagement rings," claiming that the term violated the jeweler's trademark. Costco's defense is that "Tiffany" is merely a descriptive term for a Tiffany-style (six-prong) diamond engagement ring setting. In 2020, a trial in the case was ordered, after the appellate court ruled that jurors might conclude that Costco customers could discern that Tiffany's rings were not available for sale at Costco. The case was settled out of court in 2021.

First and foremost, a mark's strength is of critical importance in assessing its likelihood of confusion with another mark. In addition, though there is no exact statutory checklist, courts generally consider the following factors:

• Similarity of the marks themselves;
• Similarity of the goods or services identified by the marks;
• Similarity of trade channels or marketing methods;
• Whether sales promoted by the marks are "impulse buys" or "considered purchases";
• Strength of the competing marks;
• Actual confusion;
• The number of similar marks or names on similar or related goods;
• Length of time of concurrent use of the marks without actual confusion;
• The variety (or range) of goods on which each mark is used.

No single factor is determinative of the likelihood of confusion. Each must be analyzed individually and also must be applied on a case-by-case basis.

In recent years, trademark disputes have been increasing. For example, Sears' sales of "Bagzilla" garbage bags, "monstrously strong bags," were held not to confuse consumers by suggesting any relation between the bags and Godzilla, the giant radioactive Japanese monster of movie fame. McDonald's Corp. has registered more than thirty trademarks with the prefix "Mc" combined with the name of a food item available at its stores. In U.S. courts, the company has prevented a variety of firms from using the prefix, from "McSleep" (denoting a hotel chain) to "McDental" (denoting a dental practice). But the New York Stock Exchange was not able to stop a gambling casino from using the name "New York $lot [Slot] Exchange" as its trademark, as the court concluded that the public was not likely to be confused. But how similar is too similar? Does the slogan for a New York coffee shop, Everyman Espresso — "I [coffee mug drawing] N.Y." — violate New York City's own trademarked slogan, "I ♥ N.Y."®? Does such trademark "bullying" really protect the value of the original mark?

Even parodies of trademarks may cause a likelihood of confusion and may be the basis of a lawsuit, even if created in jest. A diaper bag with the words "Gucci Goo," designed to look like the well-known Gucci brand while at the same time allegedly poking fun at it, was held to be infringing on the Gucci trademark, as was the use of the name "A.2." — supposedly used as a pun or play on words on Nabisco's famous "A.1." steak sauce trademark. Claims of parody are no defense, "where the purpose of the similarity is to capitalize on a famous mark's popularity for the defendant's own commercial gain," according to the trial court in *Hard Rock Café v. Pacific Graphics* (1991). Yet, Haute Diggity Dog, the owner and creator of "Chewy Vuiton" dog toys — and the maker of products for dogs, like "Chewnel #5," "Dog Perignon" and "Sniffany & Co." — won a 2006 lawsuit brought by Louis Vuitton, in part, because of a parody defense, as did the creator of a dog chew toy, named "Bad Spaniels" and shaped like a bottle of Jack Daniel's whiskey. Could this same reasoning be successfully applied in the dispute between Cheetos, the well-known cheese snack, and Peatos, an orange-colored snack made from peas and lentils?

Even when there is little likelihood of confusion, there is always the concern that the trademark will lose its power or strength to identify and distinguish the product or service it represents and, as a result, suffer dilution. Generally, this protection is only available to those marks that have acquired strength through prolonged and substantial use. A classic example of the potential for a trademark to be diluted was the sale of a poster with the words, "Enjoy Cocaine," in the flowing red and white type-script used by the Coca-Cola Company, which asked for and received a court order halting the sale of the poster in 1972. In 2014, Chik-fil-A sued a Vermont folk artist, claiming that his t-shirts with the slogan "Eat More Kale" infringed on the company's well-known promotional slogan, "Eat Mor Chikin." Walt Disney's use of Caterpillar construction machinery in the 2003 movie *George of the Jungle 2* resulted in a claim by Caterpillar that the villains' use of its equipment in the movie tarnished its trademark. A court disagreed, concluding that viewers could distinguish between the identity of the film's villains and the equipment they used. And in 2018-19 alone, for example, the Public Theatre in New York City sued the Public Hotel, the Atlanta Braves sued Braves Taxi company, the Girl Scouts sued the Boy Scouts, Tempur Sealy sued Mattress Firm, and — tired of its detectives being depicted as the bad guys — Pinkerton Consulting & Investigations threatened to sue Take-Two International Software, publishers of the hit videogame, "Red Dead Redemption II."

The doctrine of trademark dilution became federal law with the Trademark Dilution Act of 1995, which protected trademarks from other uses that blurred the distinctiveness of the mark, or tarnished or disparaged it. Its provisions were subse-

quently revised and clarified in the Trademark Dilution Revision Act of 2006. The statute provides for three exemptions from liability:

- Fair use by competitors in comparative advertising or promotion, criticism and parody;
- All forms of reporting and news commentary; and
- Any noncommercial use of a mark.

As an example of the third exemption, the late television actor Andy Griffith filed a trademark dilution lawsuit against a Wisconsin man who had changed his legal name to "Andy Griffith" prior to a try for election to the office of county sheriff that included a "Back to Mayberry" campaign slogan, which was available on clothing, yard signs, condoms and other merchandise. Griffith, the actor, lost on the grounds that the candidate's use of the "Andy Griffith" trademark name was a noncommercial use, "not to propose a commercial transaction but to seek elective office [which is] fundamental First Amendment protected speech," according to the federal trial court in 2007. Griffith, the candidate, came in third in the sheriffs race.

In a case involving Victoria's Secret and Victor's Little Secret — retailers whose only similarity was their names — the Supreme Court held that similarity alone is not sufficient to support a claim for trademark dilution. Actual economic harm, it ruled, must be proved, such as loss of sales or profits. The Court's conclusion that federal law required proof of "actual dilution, rather than a likelihood of dilution," in *Moseley v. V Secret Catalogue* (2003), led Congress to revise the statute by enacting the Trademark Dilution Revision Act of 2006, which lowered the statutory burden of proof required from actual harm to a likelihood of dilution and also defined "dilution by blurring" as impairment of the distinctiveness of the mark and "dilution by tarnishment" as reputational harm to the mark. A simpler solution would be to buy the competing brand name and its associated intellectual assets, as Hobby Lobby Stores did.

Increasingly, all trademarks should also have a substantive international component that aims to protect the mark in multinational settings and outside national borders, because — simply put — trademarks and logos and brand names are worth a lot of money. As there is currently no single way to register a trademark and have it legally enforceable worldwide, misappropriated uses of marks abound internationally. This can lead to benign misunderstandings or to serious situations, as when Apple, Inc., was forced to pay $60 million — down from an initial demand of $400 million — to a Chinese company to which it had already paid $55,000 for the worldwide rights to the name "iPad," after it was threatened with invalidation of its trademark in China on the grounds that it had not initially negotiated "in good faith."

Trademark's Digital Transformation

The Internet has become a battleground for trademarks, since "navigation around the globe's computer networks relies on the special system of domain names," James Gleick writes, like CO-CA-COLA.COM. Though these names are actually addresses, they are of critical importance to companies promoting their products and services, blending together, as they do, "features of trademarks, vanity license plates, postal codes, radio-station call letters, and graffiti." This problem takes on additional dimensions when companies' joint efforts are divided, as when NBC bought Microsoft's interests in MSNBC.com in 2012. The problem, of course, is how to make every name or mark uniquely identifiable using the system. This in itself can create a problem when a domain name, susceptible to misinterpretation, does not perfectly fit the product, as the Newark Nut Company — whose online products include bulk nuts and dried fruits — discovered when it bought NUTS.COM.

But the basic problem with Internet domain names is the difficulty of getting a distinctive name to identify a company or product clearly and specifically.[8] Too few words generally need to do too much work, in two senses.

First, many people bought domain names just because they could or because others had neglected to protect their rights. For example, McDonald's Corp. found that journalist Joshua Quittner had registered MCDONALDS.COM before it got around to doing so.

Second, others found that well-known businesses were trying to control names they thought were theirs. As an example, Anand Ramnth Mani (that is, A.R. Mani) of Vancouver, Canada, registered ARMANI.COM and discovered that the fashion empire of Giorgio Armani wanted it, too. From there it's only gotten more complicated. For example, Delta Airlines, Delta Faucets, Delta Financial and some 300 other companies all wanted DELTA.COM. Delta Financial of Woodbury, New York, had it first, though Delta Airlines finally won the "pure" dot-com address — dumping its own DELTA-AIR.COM Internet address — and Delta Faucets settled for DELTAFAUCET.COM. (Delta Financial is now bankrupt, a victim of the 2007 sub-prime mortgage crisis and recession.) A more emotional fight involving issues of law and cultural appropriation is now being conducted by eight South American nations surrounding the Amazon River basin against the online retail giant of the same name, another by activists against the Walt Disney Co. over its trademark of the Swahili phrase "hakuna matata" used in both *The Lion King* (1994) and in its live action/computer-generated imagery 2019 remake.

Unsurprisingly, the result of this demand for domain names has been "a land grab in trademarks," according to James Gleick. It has taken on additional historical tones when it became known as "cybersquatting," a reference to earlier land grabs during the periods surrounding settlement of the American West and gold and other mineral discoveries, when "squatters" attempted to wrest control of a claim from its rightful owner by moving in without permission and taking it over. In 2011, the Internet Corporation for Assigned Names and Numbers (known as ICANN) addressed this situation by creating more domain names through the introduction of new suffixes as alternatives to *.COM, *.ORG, *.INFO and *.NET — including *.XXX, *.BIZ, *.APP, *.SECURE, *.BLOG, and *.WEB. Nearly 1,000 new domains were added in 2014, including: *.TATTOO, *.CEO, *.SHOES, *.COFFEE, *.GUITARS, *.NINJA, and *.FLORIST. The question for trademark owners concerned about cybersquatting is whether the move has created a new, more flexible "domain name system revolution" or whether all the different suffixes have started, what some legal writers have termed, a "World War Web." Many trademark owners have already acted defensively, and sometimes at exorbitant cost, to register domain names they have no intention of using simply to protect their name and trademark from misuse, such as those purchasing domain names with their company's name associated with the word "sucks."

Some trademark owners have also successfully used the federal Trademark Dilution Revision Act of 2006, which largely supplanted the Trademark Dilution Act of 1995, to stop others from using their trademarks as Internet domain names.

Others have used the Anti-Cybersquatting Consumer Protection Act of 1999, which provides for remedies, including injunctions and monetary damages, to trademark owners who can show (1) the mark was distinctive or famous at the time the accused cyber-squatter registered the domain name and (2) the cyber-squatter acted with "a bad faith" intent to profit from the mark. The statute also lists the following nine factors to help courts determine intent:

• One's trademark or other intellectual property rights in the domain name itself;

• Whether the domain name contains the owner's legal name;

• The owner's prior use of the domain name in connection with the actual sale of goods or services;

• Any lawful, noncommercial use of the trademark in a domain name, such as in comparative advertising, criticism or comment, or parody;

• Intent to harm the trademark owner's goodwill which is represented by the mark;

---

[8] Recently the Supreme Court determined that two generic words — "booking" and ".com" — could be combined to create a mark recognized as a distinctive name by consumers and thus protectable as a trademark. *See* U.S.P.T.O. v. Booking.com, 140 S. Ct. 2298 (2020).

• Any offer to sell the domain name to another without having used (or intending to use) it in commerce;

• Intentionally providing misleading contact information when applying for domain name registration;

• The acquisition or holding of multiple domain names that are confusingly similar to well-known, distinctive marks; and

• The extent to which a mark incorporated into a domain name is distinctive or famous.

In the first appellate examination of the new law, *Sporty's Farm v. Sportsman's Market*, the federal appellate court, in 2000, found bad faith and a violation of the statute when "Competitor X of Company Y ... registered Y's trademark as a domain name and then transferred that name to Subsidiary Z, which operates a business wholly unrelated to Y."

Minimally, then, before any mark is used in commerce today, an online trademark search should be conducted to determine if a company in a similar line of business already uses a similar logo or company name or Internet uniform resource locater, sometimes known as a Web address. Failure to do so could lead to a lawsuit seeking to prevent the company from using the logo or mark or domain name in question, even though the mark is already in use by the company and is developing business and goodwill for the company — in addition to a possible tort claim for unfair competition. As an example, a federal trial court in 2013 forced Jian Yao to give sixteen Internet domain names through which he had sold counterfeit fragrances and accessories to Chanel, Inc., to stop using Chanel trademarks or "any confusingly similar" marks, and not to conduct any business on the Internet for five years.

SUMMARY

The Constitution's protections of intellectual property — video, music, books and other original, artistic works — create the right to profit financially from one's abilities and resourcefulness. To help reach this end, the Constitution gives Congress the power "to promote the Progress of Science and useful Arts, by securing for limited Times to Authors and Inventors the exclusive Right to their respective Writings and Discoveries." Intellectual property consists of copyright, trademarks and patents. Copyright law protects created works of authors and artists. Trademark law protects the symbols and images that signify the authenticity of commercial goods or services. (Patent law protects inventions and discoveries and is beyond the scope of this discussion.) The federal statute which implements the Constitution's grant of power over copyrights is the Copyright Act of 1976; the federal statute which implements the Constitution's grant of power over trademarks is the Trademark Act of 1946, also known as the Lanham Act

Copyright protects original works of authorship, but not the idea underlying the expression. Originality has two components: independent creation and creativity. Trademark law protects symbols that identify products and services in a distinctive manner. For a mark — including shapes, colors and sounds — to be valid, it must be used to promote the buying and selling of goods or services.

Copyright attaches to a work at the moment it is fixed in a tangible form and belongs to the creator, unless it was created as part of one's employment, as part of a contract or as a commissioned work-for-hire. Mere ownership of a work does not include the ownership of the copyright. In addition, any sale of the work does not necessarily include the sale of the copyright, without specific terms stating such in a contract. Registration with the U.S. Copyright Office is voluntary, and there is no such thing as "poor man's copyright."

Trademarks must be registered with the U.S. Patent & Trademark Office to be officially valid. They cannot be scandalous, immoral or deceptive; consist of a flag or emblem of a country; resemble any person's name or likeness without consent; resemble any other trademark; be merely descriptive of the product; be primarily descriptive of a product's geographic origins; or be a surname.

Copyrights on works created after January 1, 1978, last for the life of the author, plus seventy years. The Supreme Court upheld this rule in 2003 in *Eldred v. Ashcroft*. Once registered, a trademark is good for ten years and may be renewed for an unlimited number of ten-year periods, as long as it is used in commerce. Trademarks have different degrees of protection, depending upon whether they are fanciful, arbitrary, suggestive or descriptive with proof of secondary meaning. Generic marks have none.

A copyright owner has the exclusive right to copy the work, to create a derivative work, to distribute the work to the public, to perform the work in public, to display the work in public and to control the digital transmission performance of the work. In essence, copyright is the right to say, "no," though the First Sale Doctrine gives copyright owners the right to prohibit others from all distribution of the work prior to its first sale.

Copyright infringement occurs when someone other than the copyright holder appropriates any of the exclusive rights guaranteed copyright owners. Unauthorized copying is the most common form of infringement. It does not matter whether the infringement was intentional. To prove infringement, two elements must be established: ownership and copying. To prove copying, two conditions must be proven: the infringing party's access to the work and that the infringing party's new work is "substantially similar" to the original, copyrighted work, involving at least a "fragmented, literal similarity."

Trademark infringement occurs when someone creates an

other mark that results in a likelihood of confusion or dilutes the distinctiveness of the original mark.

The only defense to a claim of copyright infringement is found in the Fair Use Doctrine, which may be found in the Copyright Act of 1976. The use of copyrighted works for "criticism, comment, news reporting, teaching ... scholarship [and] research" is permitted by the rule, as is any other use that is determined to be "fair" as a result of the application of the rule's four factors applied on a case-by-case basis: (1) the purpose and character of the use; (2) the nature of the work; (3) the amount of the copyrighted work used; and (4) the use's effect on the market for the work. A parody which creates a transformative use is a "fair use," as determined by the Supreme Court in *Campbell v. Acuff-Rose Music.*

Parodies of trademarks may cause a likelihood of confusion and can be prohibited as a result. The Trademark Dilution Act of 1995 and the Trademark Dilution Revision Act of 2006 protect trademarks from other uses that lessen their distinctiveness and generally may take two forms: (1) dilution by blurring, and (2) dilution by tarnishment. There are three exemptions from liability: (1) "fair use" by competitors in comparative advertising (including parodies); (2) all forms of news reporting and commentary, and (3) any noncommercial use of a mark.

As the transformation of communication moves from printed marks on a page to analog radio waves to digital, binary bits of information, intellectual property law is struggling to keep up with technological innovation. Copyright law is faced with technology's liability for contributory infringement, the problem of the required licensing of digital sampling and mash-ups, the concept of "copyleft" and the new applications of copyright law in cyberspace, while trademark law struggles to distinctively identify entities in an Internet domain name address system that is unable to deal easily with confusingly similar names or those taken by cybersquatters.

Yet the law seems to presume the legal uses of new technology and does not presume technological innovation to be infringing as long as: (1) the technology is capable of substantial noninfringing uses, and (2) the seller's intent is not to induce others to violate the law.

Finally, to protect intellectual property, attorney David Lilenfeld recommends:

• Register your trademarks with the U.S. Patent & Trademark Office;
• Reserve your name and company name as domain names, as well as social media "handles" on Facebook, Twitter, LinkedIn, and other social media sites;
• Register written and other valuable materials with the U.S. Copyright Office; ... and
• Monitor your intellectual property for possible infringement.

BIBLIOGRAPHY

Articles

Bajaj, Vikas. "The Trouble with 'Sucks'," *N.Y. Times*, Apr. 13, 2015, https://nyti.ms/1H1aEw6.

Crouch, Dennis. "My New Mark: 'Trademark 2.0,'" *Patently-O.com*, Apr. 25, 2019, https://patentlyo.com/patent/2019/04/new-mark-trademark.html.

Darlington, Shasta. "Tech Giant and South American Nations Clash Over Right to Web Domain," *N.Y. Times*, Apr. 19, 2019, at A7.

Feuer, Alan. "Graffiti as Copyright Flash Point," *N.Y. Times*, July 18, 2018, at C1.

Ferguson, William. "The Mainstream Mash-Up," *N.Y. Times Magazine*, Dec. 12, 2004, https://www.nytimes.com/2004/12/12/magazine/12MAIN.html.

Flatow, Ira. "Digital Music Sampling: Creativity or Criminality," *NPR.org*, Jan. 28, 2011, https://www.npr.org/2011/01/28/133306353/Digital-Music-Sampling-Creativity-Or-Criminality.

Harris, Elizabeth. "The Carlton Dance Fails the Copyright Test," *N.Y. Times*, Feb. 16, 2019, at C3.

Kempner, Matt. "Super Bowl to Souper Bowl: Companies Tiptoe Around Trademark Law," *Atlanta Journal-Constitution*, Jan. 30, 2019, at S1.

Laird, Lorelei. "Opening Statements: Do Memes Violate Copyright Law?" *ABA Journal*, Sept. 1, 2016, *available at* https://www.abajournal.com/magazine/article/do_memes_violate_copyright_law/.

Lilenfeld, David. "Biz Voices: Guard Intellectual Property," *Atlanta Journal-Constitution*, Feb. 13, 2011, at D2.

Lisby, Gregory C. "Web Site Framing: Copyright Infringement through the Creation of an Unauthorized Derivative Work," 6 *Communication Law and Policy* 541 (2001).

Mielczarek, Natalia & W. Wat Hopkins. "Copyright, Transformativeness and Protection for Internet Memes," 98 *Journalism and Mass Communication Quarterly* 37-58 (2021).

Needleman, Sarah. "'Fortnite' Dance Move Spawns a Lawsuit from Rapper," *Wall Street Journal*, Dec. 17, 2018, at B4.

Needleman, Sarah. "Pinkerton Detectives Still Exist, and They're Tired of Being the Bad Guys," *Wall Street Journal*, Jan. 22, 2019, at A1.

Porter, Eduardo. "In a Ruling, the Legacy of Betamax," *N.Y. Times*, Mar. 27, 2013, at B1.

Rustad, Michael. "Copyrights in Cyberspace: A Roundup of Recent Cases," 12 *Suffolk University Law Review* 106 (2011).

Schwaback, Aaron. "Reclaiming Copyright from the Outside In: What the Downfall Hitler Meme Means for Transformative Works, Fair Use & Parody," 8 *Buffalo Intellectual Property Law Journal* 1 (2012).

Shenk, Joshua. "The End of 'Genius,'" *N.Y. Times*, July 20, 2014, Sunday Review section, at 6.

Vaidhyanathan, Siva. "Copyright Jungle," *Columbia Journalism Review*, September/October 2006, at 42.

Books

Aufderheide, Patricia & Peter Jaszi. *Reclaiming Fair Use: How to Put Balance Back in Copyright* (2d ed.). Chicago: University of Chicago Press, 2011.

Ginsburg, Jane C., Jessica Litman & Mary Kevlin. *Trademark & Unfair Competition Law: Cases & Materials* (6th ed.). New York: Foundation Press, 2017.

Gleick, James. *The Information: A History, A Theory, A Flood.* New York: Pantheon Books, 2011.

Gorman, Robert A., Jane C. Ginsburg & Anthony Reese. *Copyright: Cases & Materials* (9th ed.). New York: Foundation Press, 2017.

Kur, Annette & Vytautas Mizaras (eds.). *The Structure of Intellectual Property Law.* Cheltenham, United Kingdom: Edward Elgar Publishing, 2011.

LaFrance, Mary. *Copyright Law in a Nutshell* (3d ed.). St. Paul: West Group, 2017.

Lessig, Lawrence. *The Future of Ideas: The Fate of the Commons in a Connected World.* New York: Random House, 2001.

Lewinski, Silke von. *Copyright throughout the World.* New York: Thomson West, 2018.

Miller, Arthur R., & Michael H. Davis, *Intellectual Property in a Nutshell* (3d ed.). St. Paul: West Group, 2000.

Nimmer, Melville B., & David Nimmer. *Nimmer on Copyright: A Treatise on the Law of Literary, Musical & Artistic Property & the Protection of Ideas.* New York: Matthew Bender, 2018.

Patry, William F. *How to Fix Copyright.* New York: Oxford University Press, 2012.

Patry, William F. *Patry on Copyright.* New York: Thomson Reuters, 2018.

Patry, William F. *Patry on Fair Use.* New York: Thomson Reuters, 2018.

Cases

ABC v. Aereo, Inc., 573 U.S. 431 (2014).

Abercrombie & Fitch v. Hunting World, 537 F.2d 4 (2d Cir. 1976).

ABKCO Music v. Harrisongs Music, 722 F.2d 988 (2d Cir. 1983).

Allen v. Cooper, 140 S. Ct. 994 (2020).

Anderson v. Stallone, 11 U.S.P.Q. 2d 1161 (C.D. Calif. 1989).

Andy Griffith v. William Fenrick, n/k/a, Andrew Jackson Griffith, 486 F. Supp. 2d 848 (W.D. Wisc. 2007).

Andy Warhol Foundation for the Visual Arts, Inc. v. Goldsmith, 142 S.Ct. 1412 (2023).

Associated Press v. Meltwater News, 106 U.S.P.Q.2d (BNA) 1509 (S.D. N.Y. 2013).

Authors Guild v. HathiTrust, 755 F.3d 87 (2d Cir. 2014).

Baker v. Seldon, 101 U.S. 99 (1879)

Balsley v. LFP, Inc., 691 F.3d 747 (6th Cir. 2012).

Basic Books v. Kinko's Graphics, 758 F. Supp. 1522 (S.D. N.Y. 1991).

Bayer v. United Drug, 272 F. 505 (S.D. N.Y. 1921).

Bridgeman Art Library v. Corel Corp., 36 F. Supp. 2d 191 (S.D. N.Y. 1999).

Bridgeport Music v. Dimension Films, 410 F.3d 792 (6th Cir. 2005).

Bright Tunes Music v. Harrisongs Music, 420 F. Supp. 177 (S.D. N.Y. 1976).

Burrow-Giles Lithographic v. Sarony, 111 U.S. 53 (1884).

Cambridge University Press v. Becker, 446 F. Supp. 3d 1145 (N.D. Ga. 2020).

Campbell v. Acuff-Rose Music, 510 U.S. 569 (1994).

Castle Rock Entertainment v. Carol Publishing, 150 F.3d 132 (2d Cir. 1998).

Caterpillar v. Walt Disney Co., 287 F. Supp. 2d 913 (C.D. Ill. 2003).

Chanel Inc. v. Yao (No. 3:07-cv-30032-MAP), Order of Sanctions (D. Mass., Dec. 12, 2013), https://www.govinfo.gov/content/pkg/USCOURTS-mad-3_07-cv-30032/pdf/USCOURTS-mad-3_07-cv-30032-0.pdf.

Cobbler Nevada v. Gonzales, 901 F.3d 1142 (9th Cir. 2018).

Coca-Cola v. Gemini Rising, 346 F. Supp. 1183 (E.D. N.Y. 1972).

Columbia Pictures v. Aveco, Inc., 800 F.2d 59 (3d Cir. 1986).

Community for Creative Non-Violence v. Reid, 490 U.S. 730 (1989).

Computer Associates International, Inc. v. Altai, Inc., 982 F.2d 693 (2d. Cir. 1992).

Dr. Seuss Enterprises v. ComicMix, 983 F.3d 443 (S.D. Calif. 2020).

DuPont Cellophane v. Waxed Products, 85 F.2d 75 (2d Cir. 1936).

Eldred v. Ashcroft, 537 U.S. 186 (2003).

Feist Publications v. Rural Telephone Service, 499 U.S. 340 (1991).

Georgia v. Public.Resource.org, 140 S. Ct. 1498 (2020).

Golan v. Holder, 565 U.S. 302 (2012).

Goldman v. Breitbart News Network, 302 F.Supp.3d 585 (2018).

Goldstein v. California, 412 U.S. 546 (1973).

Google v. Oracle America, 141 S. Ct. 1183 (2021).

Greenberg v. National Geographic, 533 F.3d 1244 (11th Cir. 2008), *cert. denied*, 550 U.S. 1070 (2008).

Gucci Shops v. R.H. Macy & Co., 446 F. Supp. 838 (S.D. N.Y. 1977).

Hard Rock Café Licensing v. Pacific Graphics, 776 F. Supp. 1454 (W.D. Wash. 1991).

Harper & Row Publishers v. Nation Enterprises, 471 U.S. 539 (1985).

In re Swift & Co., 223 F.2d 950 (Cust. & Pat. App. 1955).

Iancu v. Brunetti, 139 S. Ct. 2294 (2019).

International News Service v. Associated Press, 248 U.S. 215 (1918).

Kellogg v. National Biscuit, 305 U.S. 111 (1938).

King-Seeley Thermos v. Aladdin Industries, 321 F.2d 577 (2d Cir. 1963).

Kirtsaeng v. John Wiley & Sons, 568 U.S. 519 (2013).

Leibovitz v. Paramount Pictures, 137 F.3d 109 (2d Cir. 1998).

Louis Vuitton Malletier v. Haute Diggity Dog, 464 F. Supp. 495 (E.D. Va. 2006).

Matal v. Tam, 137 S. Ct. 1744 (2017).

Mazer v. Stein, 347 U.S. 201 (1954).

McDonald's v. Druck & Gerner, DDS, d/b/a/ McDental, 814 F. Supp. 1127 (N.D. N.Y. 1993).

MGM v. Grokster, 545 U.S. 913 (2005).

Moseley v. V Secret Catalogue, 537 U.S. 418 (2003).

Nabisco Brands v. Kaye, 760 F. Supp. 25 (D. Conn. 1991).

Naruto v. Slater, 888 F.3d 418 (9th Cir. 2018).

National Football League v. McBee & Bruno's, 792 F.2d 726 (8th Cir. 1986).

New York Stock Exchange v. New York, New York Hotel, 69 F. Supp. 2d 479 (S.D. N.Y. 1999).

New York Times v. Tasini, 533 U.S. 483 (2001).

On Command Video v. Columbia Pictures, 777 F. Supp. 787 (N.D. Cal. 1991).

Playboy Enterprises v. Webbworld, 991 F. Supp. 543 (N.D. Tex. 1997).

Petrella v. MGM, 572 U.S. 663 (2014).

Princeton University Press v. Michigan Document Services, 99 F.3d 1381 (6th Cir. 1996).

Quality Inns v. McDonald's, 695 F. Supp. 198 (D. Md. 1988).

Reed Elsevier v. Muchnick, 559 U.S. 1237 (2010).

Salinger v. Random House, 811 F.2d 90 (2d Cir. 1987).

Salinger & Salinger v. Colting, 607 F.3d 68 (2d Cir. 2010).

San Francisco Arts & Athletics v. U.S. Olympic Committee, 483 U.S. 522 (1987).

Santa Clara County v. Southern Pacific Railroad, 118 U.S. 394 (1886).

Sony v. Universal City Studios, 464 U.S. 417 (1984).

Sporty's Farm v. Sportsman's Market, 202 F.3d 489 (2d Cir. 2000).

Star Athletica v. Varsity Brands, 137 S. Ct. 1002 (2017).

Suntrust Bank Inc, v. Houghton Mifflin Co., 268 F.3d 1257 (11th Cir. 2001).

Tiffany & Co. v. Costco Wholesale, 274 F. Supp. 3d 216 (S.D. N.Y. 2017), *reversed & remanded*, 971 F.3d 74 (2d Cir. 2020).

Toho v. Sears Roebuck, 645 F.2d 788 (9th Cir. 1981).

Twentieth Century Music v. Aiken, 422 U.S. 151 (1975).

U.S. Patent & Trademark Office v. Booking.com, 140 S. Ct. 2298 (2020).

VersaTop Support Systems v. Georgia Expo, 921 F.3d 1364 (Fed. Cir. 2019).

VIP Products v. Jack Daniel's Properties, 953 F.3d 1170 (9th Cir. 2020).

Washingtonian Publishing v. Pearson, 306 U.S. 30 (1939).

White-Smith Music Publishing v. Apollo, 209 U.S. 1 (1908).

Williams v. Gaye, 885 F.3d 1150 (9th Cir. 2018).

Web Sites

Compendium of the U.S. Copyright Office Practices (3d ed., 2017), https://copyright.gov/comp3/.

Copyright at Cornell Library: Copyright and the Public Domain, Cornell University Library, https://guides.library.cornell.edu/copyright/publicdomain.

U.S. Copyright Office, https://www.copyright.gov/.

U.S. Patent & Trademark Office, https://www.uspto.gov/.

WhoSampled.com (2021), https://www.whosampled.com/.

Other Sources

A Fair(y) Use Tale (2007). Stanford University Centre for Internet & Society, https://cyberlaw.stanford.edu/blog/2007/03/fairy-use-tale.

Hitler Rants Parodies (undated), YouTube.com, https://www.youtube.com/user/hitlerrantsparodies.

U.S. Code (undated), Legal Information Institute, Cornell Law School, https://www.law.cornell.edu/uscode/text#.

U.S. Code, Title 15, Chapter 22 – Trademarks (undated), Legal Information Institute, Cornell Law School, https://www.law.cornell.edu/uscode/text/15/chapter-22.

U.S. Code, Title 17 – Copyrights (undated), Legal Information Institute, Cornell Law School, available at https://www.law.cornell.edu/uscode/text/17.

14

Privacy Rights in an Open and Changing Society

By Samuel A. Terilli Jr., Sigman Splichal
and Kearston L. Wesner

☑ Headnote Questions

- What expectation of privacy do individuals have in American society?
- What kinds of information are private?
- What legal remedies are available for individuals who believe their privacy has been invaded?
- Are any legal remedies available to the news media when they report about private matters?
- Is a right of privacy recognized in the U.S. Constitution?
- Do students have any privacy rights?
- What special privacy issues or concerns do computers and digital technologies raise?

Privacy. American citizens often make social and legal claims that they have a fundamental right to privacy. Since 1928, when U.S. Supreme Court Justice Louis Brandeis characterized privacy as the "right to be let alone" in *Olmstead v. United States*, we have wrestled with key questions. Let alone by whom? The government, business, neighbors or the media? The answers to those questions, and our expectations of privacy, have changed over time.

New digital technology — from massive databases and social networks to sophisticated search engines, fitness trackers and surveillance cameras on streets and in buildings — and new fears ranging from identity theft to terrorist attacks, have combined to make privacy a major concern in today's world.

With the spread of COVID-19 in 2020 and the resulting medical and economic crises, new privacy concerns developed alongside the efforts to bring the virus under control. Several large technology companies, including Google and Apple, developed methods to use cell phones, apps and other devices to assist in the contact tracing and the tracking of individuals with the virus or exposed to those with it. Some companies and government agencies even used drones and surveillance cameras to assist in maintaining quarantines. While many lauded these efforts to use new digital tools and social media to aid these public health efforts, others understandably raised concerns about privacy and how this personally identifiable information might be used in the future.

Contact tracing, health checks, quarantines and cell phone tracking seemed simultaneously necessary and exceedingly dangerous given the privacy concerns raised by employees, customers, neighbors and patients. Arguably, smart pandemic management was on a inevitable collision course with traditional notions of personal privacy in western countries. While the pandemic seems to be subsiding, the privacy concerns are hardly resolved.

This lack of resolution is not surprising when one considers the fact that the privacy concerns related to digital communications, big data and social media are still playing themselves out in the courts and legislatures across the globe. The last few years were no exception.

Despite bipartisan and popular support for a federal privacy law, Congress has made no progress, in part due to entrenched special interests among the business and technology sectors and reform advocates seeking broad change. Instead, the focus has shifted to legislative action at the state level, notably California, Virginia and Colorado.

For example, the California Consumer Privacy Act went into effect in 2020, affecting mid- to large-sized companies. It gives new privacy rights to California residents and requires changes in the way businesses collect, use and transfer personal information. This law broadens the protection of privacy over time and looks to be a model for other states and possibly even the federal government.

While legislatures in other states have been responding to polls showing popular support for more control of data privacy, the resulting legislation may reflect compromise. The Florida Senate passed a bill in 2023 that gave consumers greater access to and control over the information businesses collect about them, including the ability to opt out of some data collection practices. Last-minute amendments to the bill, however, effectively limited most of its provisions to the largest companies and excluded most companies from requiring opt-outs.

Several states and municipal governments also began to tackle privacy issues related to police and private company use of facial recognition technology. This technology has raised many general privacy concerns as well as numerous specific objections regarding systemic errors and discrimination against minority communities. The latter concerns stem from how the databases underlying facial recognition technology are created, how the software is trained on those databases, and how police or private companies deploy the resulting technology in communities.

The U.S Supreme Court was also motivated by privacy concerns in *Americans for Prosperity Foundation v. Bonta* (2021), even though the case was not a traditional privacy case. In *Bonta*, the Court rejected a California law requiring charities to disclose their major donors to the state. In a 6-3 decision, the Court held that the state's interest in preventing fraud and self-dealing did not outweigh the right of free association the donors' desire for anonymity. Both the majority and dissenting opinions focused on the concern for donor privacy.

In recent years, the privacy issue has frequently arisen not only in the context of pandemics and government data collection, but in the context of news media reports related to the private lives of celebrities and others.

In 2016, for example, privacy rights, new media, new technologies and celebrity culture collided in court and in the headlines with the $140 million verdict against Gawker Media, in a case filed by Terry Bollea, better known as Hulk Hogan, over the airing of a brief, grainy sex tape of Hogan with the wife of one of his friends. Whatever one may think of Gawker's penchant for posting outrageous news and gossip, the notion that a celebrity who openly bragged about his sex life could convince a jury he was damaged to the tune of $115 million in compensatory damages plus another $25 million in punitive damages shocked many observers. Just a few months later, Gawker and its chief executive officer would file for bankruptcy, and Bollea later settled for a reported $31 million.

In 2018, another famous celebrity, Olivia De Havilland, met with less luck in her statutory right of privacy, misappropriation of her likeness, and false light privacy claims against the FX Network over a miniseries docudrama that featured — without her permission — an actress playing her for about seventeen minutes and some fictitious dialogue. An appellate court in California rejected the notion that the actress could use that state's privacy law to control nonfictional or fictional entertainment about her history.

There is no question documentaries, entertainment media, the Internet, social media and mobile telephones are affecting societal expectations and legal doctrines regarding privacy. Every year legislators and consumer advocates propose new laws and litigants file new lawsuits aimed at online services and social media giants and their data collection and sales practices.

In 2020, a federal appellate court in California breathed new life into a class action lawsuit against Facebook over its use of what is known as "third-party tracking plug-ins." While just about everyone who uses social media knows that sites collect information about the users, much of that information is used for commercial purposes, including the targeting of advertising to the user. What many did not know is that Facebook apparently uses these third-party plug-ins to track its users' browsing even when they are not logged into Facebook. The court allowed the case to go to trial under various privacy claims, California law and federal law.

The outrage over this practice reflects a growing concern about privacy on the Internet. In 2009, for example, more than 90 percent of people surveyed considered online privacy to be an important issue in society. In 2013 and to this day, the ubiquitous search engine Google has faced precedent-setting litigation in the United States over wiretapping allegations related to its Street View project, and in Europe over what has become known as the European "right to be forgotten." While many scholars agree that European countries protect privacy to a greater degree than the United States, researchers and some critics have found that even Europe's stricter standards for online publications have flaws.

The frontiers and legal battle lines over privacy continue to evolve, driven in large part by advances in technology. Privacy concerns have arisen in the context of cellular telephones, drones — both private and government ones — and continuing revelations about the activities of the National Security Agency. In 2018, the Supreme Court decided in *Carpenter v. United States* that police need a warrant to obtain cell phone location data absent certain compelling circumstances, and that cell phone users have a legitimate expectation of privacy in the information a telephone service provider maintains.

The privacy battle took on an increasingly political tone in 2017 when President Donald Trump essentially repealed new online privacy protections adopted by the Federal Communications Commission under the Barack Obama Administration. The repeal effectively allowed broadband providers such as Verizon and Comcast to collect and sell their users' online information with fewer restrictions (and without consent), though some providers, no doubt fearing a backlash, said they would not do so.

As the political winds shifted in 2021 and 2022, the relatively new Biden Administration appeared willing to address the actions during the Trump Administration and so far has started addressing some privacy concerns, including for example the use of artificial intelligence, algorithms, and social media and digital advertising targeting children. The general subject is in a state of flux, particularly given the growing importance of the so-called metaverse and the use of blockchains in what is becoming known as Web3.

Privacy is a social concept much older than our modern technologies, though. It motivated settlers seeking religious and political freedom in the seventeenth century and drove revolutionary patriots affronted by England's disregard for the autonomy of their businesses and the sanctity of their homes. The concept of privacy can be found in the liberal theories of Enlightenment philosophers, whose emphasis on individual liberties based on natural rights inspired the founders. Essential elements of privacy are woven into the nation's most hallowed documents.

While privacy as a social value was apparent during the nation's early years, it remained elusive as a *legal* right. Only in the last 100 years has it entered the legal mainstream, mainly due to changes in the way Americans live and think. To be understood in an information-driven society — both in social and legal contexts — privacy must be viewed as a value that changes as society tries to balance the rights of individuals with its needs and desires for information. Courts typically consider the customs, mores and conventions of the community.

This chapter looks, first, at the evolution of the concept of privacy. It then focuses on the development of privacy as a legal doctrine and on the four distinct privacy torts: (1) publication of embarrassing private facts, (2) physical and technological intrusion, (3) false light invasion of privacy and (4) commercialization. The chapter addresses related torts as well as constitutional and statutory privacy, both of which place limits on government use of personal information — limits that have important implications for journalists, especially in the era of databases, the Internet, social media and data journalism.

THE EVOLUTION OF A RIGHT TO PRIVACY

The general concept of privacy was not unknown in English common law, the dominant legal system in Colonial America. Cases dating to the Norman Conquest recognized a value resembling privacy in individuals' property rights. In 1741, the House of Lords, then England's highest court, invoked in *Pope v. Curl* a property-rights doctrine to protect contents of personal letters from unauthorized publication. The case is important in the development of privacy in American law because it acknowledged a property right not just in individuals' letters, but in the retention and control of the personal ideas and information in those letters sent to others.

John Locke, an English philosopher whose writings influ-

enced Thomas Jefferson and other founders, argued that government has a duty to protect fundamental rights such as life, liberty and property. These rights were described in the Declaration of Independence, the Constitution and the Bill of Rights. Almost 200 years later, the Supreme Court gleaned from the concept of liberty a constitutional right of privacy in *Griswold v. Connecticut* (1965).

In his book *Privacy in Colonial New England*, historian David H. Flaherty explored the precursors to modern privacy. He observed that although privacy as a legal doctrine evolved slowly, its underlying values were expressed in colonial customs. Courts, he said, protected privacy values indirectly by enforcing laws against trespass, limiting government searches and seizures, hearing defamation cases and recognizing privileged communications between wives and husbands. Ironically, as Flaherty pointed out, there was little physical privacy — in the modern sense — in most homes and public accommodations. Homes often lacked individual sleeping quarters, and families congregated in common beds. Communal sleeping arrangements also were common in public inns. Traces of the practice remained as late as 150 years ago: During his early career as a struggling, small-town lawyer, Abraham Lincoln shared a room and bed above his office with a law partner.

Flaherty noted that the concept of informational privacy was officially recognized during Benjamin Franklin's tenure as postmaster general before the American Revolution. Postmasters were required to swear an oath that they would not knowingly open any letters in their custody.

Values underlying privacy also were apparent as the American Revolution drew near, and they played a central role in the colonists' growing hostility toward British rule. In 1761, Boston lawyer James Otis spoke against the practice of general search warrants violating the sanctity of the home, declaring that a man's house is his castle. On the eve of the Revolution, each colony drew up a list of grievances against British authorities. On each list was concern about general warrants, which authorized government agents to search premises at will without first presenting evidence of a specific violation of the law. After the colonies won independence, James Madison, a main proponent of a bill of rights spelling out individual liberties, introduced a proposal at the Constitutional Convention to limit the scope of government searches. That proposal, which established "the right of the people to be secure ... against unreasonable search and seizures," was later adopted as the Fourth Amendment.

Values supporting privacy also found expression in the writings of nineteenth-century English philosopher John Stuart Mill. He argued in his influential *On Liberty* that the government should have no say in certain kinds of personal conduct, absent a compelling social interest and impact on others.

PRIVACY AS A LEGAL RIGHT

Legal claims related to privacy developed slowly during the nation's first century, in part because society was largely agrarian. Land was sparsely settled. This physical distance reduced unwanted contacts and intrusions.

The demographics of American society shifted dramatically with the Industrial Revolution. Technological developments such as the steam engine led to manufacturing-based cities populated by factory workers. Physical distance between people shrank as cities grew, and those in foreign lands began a new flow of immigration. In those crowded cities, the barriers of time and space common to rural settings no longer insulated individuals from unwanted contacts.

Dramatic technological developments in the nineteenth century began to threaten privacy. Alan F. Westin traced them in *Privacy and Freedom*, a comprehensive study of privacy issues. He noted that several technological developments in the late nineteenth century changed long-standing attitudes toward expression and surveillance. These innovations were the microphone and telephone in the late 1870s, the Kodak camera in the 1880s, and the dictograph recorder in the 1890s.

In 1877, the *New York Times* expressed concern about the effect of new technology on privacy. It called the telephone "a nefarious instrument" with "vast capabilities for mischief" that promised to rob individuals of their personal privacy. Responding to a decision by the city to allow telephone wires to be attached to city lamp posts, the *Times* cautioned:

Every confidential remark made to a lamp-post by a belated Democratic statesman could be reproduced by a telephone connected with any other lamp-post.... Men who had trusted to friendly lamp-posts, and embraced them with the utmost confidence in their silence and discretion, would find themselves shamelessly betrayed, and their unsuspecting philosophies literally reported to their indignant families.

While increased technology spurred the growth of industrial cities and the development of such privacy-altering inventions as the telephone, other innovations — high-speed newspaper presses and advanced photography — spawned an aggressive kind of journalism, a distant cousin to what was espoused by the colonial and revolutionary printers who catered to society's well-read and politically astute. New printing processes reproduced newspapers quickly and cheaply. As a result, a journalism developed that often directed its content at the swelling numbers of city dwellers. The "penny press" era of the mid-nineteenth century later yielded to "yellow journalism," sensationalistic news coverage designed to boost newspaper circulations that reached its peak toward century's end. Newspaper readers, not so interested in the complexities of politics and other public

issues, sought information about misdeeds and travails. This new readership, coupled with journalists armed with cameras intruding into new, heretofore private areas, sometimes brought newspaper practices and privacy concerns into conflict.

In 1890, two former law partners and Harvard Law School classmates took issue with newspaper practices and technologies of the day. Louis Brandeis and Samuel Warren, upper-crust Boston lawyers, wrote "The Right to Privacy" for the *Harvard Law Review*. The seminal article would steer the notion of a legal right of privacy toward the mainstream of American law. Attempting to document what they considered a climate of journalistic excess, the authors wrote: "Instantaneous photographs and newspaper enterprise have invaded the sacred precincts of private and domestic life; and numerous mechanical devices threaten to make good the prediction that 'what is whispered in the closet shall be proclaimed from the house-tops." Brandeis and Warren argued that individuals possess certain attributes, such as sentiments and intellect, over which they have rights akin to personal property rights.

While Brandeis and Warren nudged the issue of privacy onto the social and legal stages, the development of a unified legal theory remained elusive. In the ensuing decades, the legal contours of privacy developed piecemeal and with many variations. Seventy years after "The Right to Privacy" was published, torts expert William Prosser summarized the extent of the common law development of privacy in an article in the *California Law Review*. Titled simply "Privacy," it dealt with tort law and not with constitutional or statutory questions of privacy. After reviewing some 200 privacy-related cases, Prosser identified four separate torts: (1) disclosure of embarrassing private facts about individuals; (2) intrusion, the physical or technological violation of an individual's privacy; (3) false light, the intentional dissemination of highly offensive false publicity about another; and (4) appropriation, or the use of another person's likeness without permission.

THE PRIVACY TORTS

American law assumes members of society have certain duties toward one another. These duties — derived from customs, mores and values — are often recognized in common law cases and in various statutes; they form the basis of tort law. Under the theory of tort law, when a member of society violates a duty toward another person that results in an identifiable harm, the injured person may recover damages. One class of duties deals with privacy and the harm — usually mental — that results when it is violated. When the news media are involved, courts have balanced individual privacy with other interests, such as the free flow of information about matters of public concern. Since the nature of the harm is usually mental, privacy tort law protects only individuals, not businesses or corporations that exist merely as creatures of law. Businesses and corporations may, though, have claims related to the theft or disclosure of trade secrets and other confidential business information.

Tort law varies from state to state. Any generalizations are based on trends in cases from the various states. Actual application of law in privacy cases may vary from state to state.

Embarrassing Private Facts

Definition: The publication of private information that would be highly offensive to a reasonable person and is not a matter of legitimate public concern.

The common law acknowledges that some information about individuals should remain beyond the reach of neighbors — and the media — and that disclosure normally would lead to unwarranted embarrassment or humiliation. The embarrassing private facts tort rests on several questions, each of which a plaintiff must answer effectively to advance a privacy claim. As one considers these questions, consider also the facts of the Hulk Hogan dispute with Gawker and the 2016 verdict for $140 million over the sex tape introduced at the beginning of this chapter. Is a sex tape inherently private and its publication online inherently outrageous? Is there ever any possible news value that might protect the airing of such a tape?

What is publication? In libel law, "publication" has a specialized meaning. At a minimum, a libel plaintiff must prove a defamatory communication reached at least one person other than the plaintiff and defendant. Under the embarrassing private facts tort, however, "publication" means "publicity," that is, widespread communication. Publication in a newspaper, magazine or other print medium satisfies this requirement, as does dissemination by broadcast, cable and the Internet.

Is the information private? As a threshold, a plaintiff must establish that the information in question is, in fact, private. What happens in public, or appears in public records, normally is not considered private. In *Cox Broadcasting Co. v. Cohn* (1975), the Supreme Court held that the news media are not liable for publication of personal information already available to the public, even in this case where publication violated a state statute designed to protect rape victims. Thus, generally, a person involved in an car accident or who is the victim of a crime cannot claim invasion of privacy based on photographs of or stories about the accident. Likewise, a participant in a public rally or parade cannot claim privacy related to the event.

Even intimate personal information cannot normally be the basis for a privacy claim if it is already widely known, as Oliver Sipple learned after he thwarted an assassination attempt on President Gerald Ford in 1975. News accounts of his heroism disclosed that he was gay, a fact already well-known in his community in San Francisco.

Consent is also a factor in determining whether personal information is public or private. The question of consent will be addressed later in this chapter, but in general, a person ordinarily may not provide information knowingly to the news media and later claim an invasion of privacy, although in some instances consent effectively might be withdrawn. One can easily envision the relevance of disclosures made on social networking sites. A person who discloses previously private information on a widely accessible social network may be surrendering a degree of his or her privacy.

What kind of information might be considered highly offensive to a reasonable person? To be sufficiently offensive, a private disclosure must outrage the community's notions of decency. Some courts have added that the public's legitimate interest in personal information ends when a publication forgoes legitimate news values in favor of a morbid and sensational prying into private lives. Often, stories dealing with medical conditions, hospital stays or other intimate health matters present the most problems for journalists. As a rule, invasive stories or pictures that deal with physical or mental illness or expose the intimate parts of the body, require particular caution. *The Restatement (Second) of Torts* suggests several problem areas: sexual relations, humiliating illnesses, intimate personal letters, family disputes, details of home life, stolen photos or photos taken in private places, and information from individual tax returns.

A plaintiff must prove the *widespread publicity* of intimately private material that a *reasonable person* would find *highly offensive*, and that the information was *not* related to a *matter of public concern*. In many private-facts cases involving the news media, however, plaintiffs fail because most of what is printed or broadcast is chosen because it *is* newsworthy.

What constitutes a matter of public concern? Even if a plaintiff can establish that disclosure is highly offensive, the likelihood of winning a privacy suit is slim if the plaintiff has become part of a public event or controversy. Information related to traditional news values is likely to deal with matters of public concern. Information about politics, law enforcement, crime, domestic violence, suicide, medical advances and social trends falls within the realm of traditional news.

The 1982 case of Hilda Bridges, who became an unintended celebrity on a very public stage, dramatically underscores the dearth of privacy protection for individuals caught up in news events. She was dragged into a public matter when police officers — and members of the news media — surrounded her apartment when her estranged husband took her hostage and forced her to undress to prevent her from fleeing. During the standoff, he shot himself, and police rushed the apartment. Bridges fled naked and distraught into the street, clutching only a hand towel. *Today* newspaper in Cocoa Beach, Florida, published a revealing photograph, and she sued for invasion of privacy and infliction of emotional distress.

Satisfied that such publicity was unwarranted and highly offensive, a Florida jury awarded Bridges $10,000. An appellate court, however, unanimously set aside the award, ruling that the law had not been properly followed. The jury erred, the court reasoned, because the events happened in public and because crime was a matter of public concern. The judge noted that individual privacy at some point must yield to the public interest, even if embarrassing or distressful.

The result was essentially the same when a bystander at a public event thwarted an attempt to assassinate President Gerald Ford during his visit to San Francisco in 1975. As described earlier, Oliver Sipple's act of heroism drew him into the limelight, illuminating both his Vietnam War record as well as the fact that he was gay. Sipple, well known in San Francisco's gay community before the Ford episode, sued the *San Francisco Chronicle* and other newspapers for invasion of privacy. He argued that while his public actions were newsworthy, his private life was not, and that disclosure of his sexual orientation caused him embarrassment because this fact was not widely known. A California appellate court held that both his heroism and sexual orientation were newsworthy, noting that his heroic behavior cut against gay stereotypes.

While much of what is newsworthy deals with matters of social and political importance, anything out of the ordinary can lead to newsworthiness. If one commits a public act that results in police intervention, courts have held one cannot expect those acts to be private. Unusual occupations, hobbies, talents and other qualities that attract public attention are newsworthy. Furthermore, newsworthiness normally stands the test of time in privacy actions. Once one becomes the object of public attention due to a crime or other newsworthy action, one generally remains a matter of legitimate interest in the public's mind.

What about instances when news accounts reveal private information about public officials or public figures? As a rule, most activities of public persons are newsworthy by virtue of their public status. When the *Miami Herald* disclosed that Democratic presidential contender Gary Hart spent the night with a woman who was not his wife, for example, some critics raised questions about the proper bounds of reporting and the *Herald's* conduct, but no one seriously raised the legal question of privacy because Hart was a candidate for president

Private Facts and Constitutional Protections. The media have some protection under the First Amendment when they publish truthful, lawfully obtained information about matters of public concern. Several cases help define the scope of this protection.

In *Cox Broadcasting Corp. v. Cohn*, parents of a teenage girl who was raped and murdered sued an Atlanta television station for broadcasting the girl's name. The suit was based on a Georgia statute that forbade publication of names of alleged rape victims. WSB-TV had obtained the name from records provided at

an open court hearing. The Georgia Supreme Court upheld the parents' right to sue, but the U.S. Supreme Court reversed in 1975, focusing on the fact that judicial records revealed the information. It said the onus should be on government to ensure privacy by keeping certain information out of the public domain. The Court added that allegations of crime and the resulting proceedings are matters of legitimate public concern.

Similarly, the Supreme Court held in 1989 that the *Florida Star*, a small weekly newspaper, was protected when it published the name of a rape victim that it obtained from a routine police report posted on a public bulletin board at the Duval County Sheriff's Department. The rape victim sued the newspaper, claiming that it violated a state criminal statute barring publication of the names of alleged rape victims. She argued that this constituted evidence of breach of duty supporting an award of civil damages for invasion of privacy. A jury agreed and awarded her $100,000. The Supreme Court overturned the verdict, holding that the Constitution prevents states from punishing the news media — even by allowing civil damages — for publishing truthful, lawfully obtained information.

The Supreme Court reaffirmed the public nature of public records in *Doe v. Reed* (2010). Although the case was not a press case, it involved the public's right to information about individuals. Under Washington's Public Records Act, the names of people who sign petitions calling for a referendum to overturn a state law are available to the public. The petition in question called for a vote on Washington's new law extending some benefits to same-sex couples. The plaintiffs argued that disclosing their names would violate their First Amendment rights to free speech and association. The Supreme Court rejected this claim, noting that the law served sufficiently important government interests in discouraging fraud, fostering transparency and protecting the integrity of the state's electoral process. The case was not a privacy case, and while privacy interests were obviously close to the core of the plaintiffs' concerns, they were insufficient to strike down that provision of the state's public records law as a general matter.

Consent as a Defense. Consent can be a strong defense in a disclosure of private facts case. Ordinarily, individuals may not knowingly and willingly disclose personal information and then claim invasion of privacy. However, there are important considerations regarding consent. First, consent must come from someone with the authority or legal capacity to provide the information. A friend cannot give consent for the use of private information about a college roommate. A day-care operator cannot independently give consent for children under his or her care, nor can a hospital official give consent when the privacy of patients is involved. Minor children cannot give legal consent. Second, consent need not to be in writing, but written consent is almost always easier to prove in court than oral consent. Third, as a rule, the more intimate the information, the more important for the reporter to be sure consent was clearly given, either explicitly or implicitly. Consent is explicit when professional communicators ask for and receive permission to use personal information for publication.

Implied Consent. Reporters frequently talk to sources and use the information without specifically asking for permission. Members of the public generally understand the function of reporters. If journalists identify themselves and sources talk willingly, there should be no problem. Implied consent is problematic, however, if private information is obtained from someone who does not understand that it is likely to be published.

Withdrawing Consent. Whether a person who explicitly consented can later withdraw the consent is a tricky question. Some courts have ruled that a person cannot withdraw consent later, especially if the person providing information is a newsworthy adult and the journalist uses the private information for legitimate news purposes, but whether such forms of consent or similar agreements amount to enforceable contracts remains unclear.[1]

Intrusion

Definition: The invasion of a person's solitude, either physically or by use of technological devices.

The fundamental purpose of the tort of intrusion — to protect a person's solitude — can be traced to many of the nation's early values. But the notion of intrusion has gone beyond the traditional legal doctrine of trespass, or physical intrusion, to mechanical and electronic violations of private space. The means of intrusion have changed from the "instantaneous photography" that riled Brandeis and Warren to the miniature video cameras that, as explained later, left ABC's *Prime Time Live* reeling in 1996 from a $3.5 million verdict that cost the network dearly in terms of legal fees and credibility, even though the award was ultimately reduced to just $2. The tort of intrusion, whether physical or technological, deals with the *act of gathering information*, not the content of the information gathered.

Privacy in Public and Quasi-Public Places. Under the common law, people in public places have little expectation of privacy with regard to what they do. People engaging in public activities

must assume they might be photographed, filmed or recorded. The public sphere almost certainly includes widely accessible Web sites, including many social networks, as well as more traditional, physical spaces.

While people in public places do not forgo all rights to privacy, journalists encounter few problems when they photograph or report about what is reasonably considered public. Photographs taken from public streets or sidewalks typically record only what any passerby would see and thus rarely raise any privacy concerns. Courts have applied similar reasoning to individuals on private property that is customarily open to the public, such as malls, restaurants and businesses. The key issue is the presence or absence of any reasonable expectation of privacy.

Courts also have suggested that journalists may be persistent when encountering people in public without invading their privacy, so long as the behavior is not highly intrusive or overzealous. Journalistic behavior that is simply annoying is not necessarily an invasion of privacy, but behavior can become legally problematic when it is menacing or harassing, as has been the case with some paparazzi pursuing celebrities.

Trespass or Physical and Technological Intrusion. According to *The Restatement (Second) of Torts*, anyone who enters private property without consent of the owner or possessor commits a trespass. Everyone has seen "No Trespassing" signs posted to warn unwanted visitors. The common law and statutory law protect private property from intruders and define specific penalties for the crime. Entering private property without permission or staying on it after being asked to leave poses legal dangers for journalists, whose rights are normally no different from those of any other private citizen.

As a rule, a visitor on private property must obtain permission before entry. One must obtain permission from the possessor of the property, be it the owner or someone with contractual control over the property, such as a renter, caretaker or tenant.

Consent may be either explicit or implied. Explicit consent occurs when a visitor asks for and is granted permission. A reporter might request an interview at a residence or at a business office, for example. When the purpose of the visit is obscured, however, or when journalists simply lie about their intentions, the question of trespass is much less clear.

Journalists have an array of devices that enhance newsgathering, from telephoto lenses, to sensitive listening devices, to miniaturized video cameras. Technological intrusion is as old as the discussion of privacy. As noted earlier, in 1890, Brandeis and Warren were concerned about a new kind of "instantaneous" photography that no longer required willing subjects to remain perfectly still. Today, the culprit likely would be a mini video camera or even a smart phone. As a rule, the use of technology that enhances viewing or listening is legal as long as it does not effectively let the journalist hear or see what normally

---

[1] In a related, but factually different, context, the Supreme Court has limited the freedom of reporters to change reporter/source agreements that rise to the level of rudimentary contracts. In *Cohen v. Cowles Media*, it said a reporter's promise to keep a source's name private could be treated by states as an oral contract without violating the First Amendment rights of the journalist. Journalists had argued that the source's name was newsworthy and that the ultimate decision to use or not to use newsworthy information should reside with the news media. 501 U.S. 663 (1991).

could not be observed. If a device simply allows a journalist to see or hear what might be witnessed in public, there is no intrusion. People who go into public places — streets, parks and college campuses, for example — enjoy very little privacy, as long as they are not menaced or harassed. That is, the zone of privacy they enjoy is very small compared to the privacy they can expect in their homes or other private places.

Several cases involving the same television network demonstrate how troublesome the question of lawful access to private property and technological intrusion can be. In 1997, a North Carolina jury awarded the Food Lion grocery chain $3.5 million in damages after ABC's *Prime Time Live* carried a report, afforded by hidden video cameras, that Food Lion relabeled and restocked meat after its expiration date. The judge had allowed the jury to consider fraud and trespass charges against ABC without considering the veracity of the network's report on Food Lion's business practices. The jury based its award on the fact that *Prime Time Live* producers had committed a trespass by obtaining access to Food Lion facilities through fraudulent job applications. Even though an appellate court reduced the Food Lion judgment to $2 in 1999, the case illustrates the dangers reporters face in a society increasingly wary of certain reporting techniques. These techniques may be worthy of consideration depending on a review of local law and when the subject of the story clearly raises a strong public interest and there is no reasonable alternative means of reporting. Much will depend on the balance struck by a court between any reasonable expectation of privacy and the value of the story. In addition to evaluating the inherent intrusiveness, courts often will consider the actual necessity of the technologically enhanced means of reporting. Even the use of a shotgun microphone to eavesdrop on conversations may raise issues.

Courts also recognize that people have enhanced privacy expectations in certain spaces within public areas. For example, courts often distinguish between photographing or videotaping an accident victim in public generally versus doing it in a more private space such as an ambulance or a rescue helicopter.

Relatively new technologies have added to the possibilities and legal concerns. Cell phones that can be use to take and transmit photographs have raised new privacy concerns, prompting businesses — particularly health clubs — to ban them and many states to make illegal video voyeurism when there is a reasonable expectation of privacy. For example, President George W. Bush signed the federal Video Voyeurism Prevention Act of 2004, applicable to improper photographs, film and videotape taken on federal property when an individual has a reasonable privacy expectation.

Similar issues can arise in the context of the paparazzi who photograph celebrities with an intrusive telephoto lens or through trespass or other unlawful means. Google's Street View project and similar efforts have also raised privacy claims over both the collection of incidental information, such as email addresses. As if strangely outfitted cars were not enough to stir privacy advocates, drones, too, have become a relatively common sight in domestic skies. Whether drones are used by police or other government agencies, commercial or private ventures, or journalists, the risks to privacy are obvious, yielding increased demands for clear regulation and public oversight.

Custom and Usage. While explicit consent requires a request of a property owner or possessor, implied consent occurs in a number of ways under what is called the "custom and usage" doctrine. A degree of access is implied by custom or typical use of private and quasi-private property. It is customary to cross private property to ring someone's doorbell to solicit contributions or sell a product, absent a locked gate, a "No Trespassing" sign or other warning. It is also customary for shoppers and diners to enter stores and restaurants. This access assumes a visitor does not engage in unwanted activities and leaves when asked.

A reporter's entry into private property with government officials raises interesting and complex privacy concerns. Some courts have found this to be a customary and allowable practice, particularly when covering crimes or disasters, while other courts have rejected these arguments and allowed lawsuits at least against the government agents, if not the press.

In *Wilson v. Layne* (1999), the Supreme Court indicated that individuals can win lawsuits on privacy grounds when law enforcement officers take journalists into private homes. In this case, officers from Montgomery County, Maryland, sought to arrest Dominic Wilson for violating his probation. Believing that Dominic was staying with his parents, federal marshals and sheriff's deputies conducted an early-morning raid at the home of Charles and Geraldine Wilson. As part of "Operation Gunsmoke" — a program started in 1992 in which law enforcement agencies routinely invited journalists to accompany them in apprehending fugitives — a *Washington Post* reporter and photographer accompanied officers on the raid. The Wilsons sued the officers for violating their Fourth Amendment rights against unreasonable search and seizure by bringing into the home journalists who had no official role in the search.

Chief Justice William Rehnquist, writing for a unanimous Court, conceded that reporter ride-alongs were common at the time of the raid and that the law governing the practice was uncertain. Nevertheless, he concluded, the presence of third parties with no legitimate law enforcement roles during the execution of a search warrant violated the Fourth Amendment's core interest in residential privacy.

He rejected the argument that the presence of reporters during raids served a legitimate law enforcement purpose and also rejected the argument that the publicity resulting from ride-alongs significantly benefited the government by publicizing efforts to combat crime. The media play an important role by informing the public about law enforcement activities, he wrote, but Fourth Amendment concerns were paramount in the *Wilson* case, not good public relations for the police. Finally, Rehnquist rejected the argument that the presence of journalists could, in some instances, minimize abuse of suspects and protect the safety of officers.

Recording Conversations with Sources. Journalists often record conversations with their sources to create verbatim records of complicated information and lengthy direct quotes. In many states, this practice poses no legal problem because the law assumes that an exact account of a conversation can only benefit all parties involved. Parties to a conversation are legally allowed to recount a conversation to others, and the law simply extends this reasoning to allow taped conversations.[2] In some states, however, it is illegal to record a conversation without the consent of *all* parties. The reasoning assumes that if a person knows a conversation is being taped, the person might behave or respond differently. Perhaps the source would be more cautious or guarded in his or her comments or say nothing at all. At least twelve states require that all parties to a conversation know when the conversation is recorded. In cases involving personal contact, a journalist may ask for permission or may assume consent if a tape recorder is in full view and turned on. It is always a good idea to state before the conversation begins that it is being taped. This creates a record of consent. For telephone conversations, one should request consent before taping begins and restate it at the beginning of the conversation. These laws may be subject to challenges in some states, depending on the local law, if applied to all nonconsensual recordings illegal regardless of the absence of any privacy interest.

In *Bartnicki v. Vopper* (2001), the Supreme Court addressed the issue of whether the media would be liable for publishing or broadcasting illegal recordings made independently by third parties and given to journalists. Frederick Vopper, a public affairs radio commentator, broadcast parts of an illegally recorded telephone conversation that was sent to him anonymously. The chief negotiator for a teachers' union, who was a participant in the call, sued Vopper for violating Pennsylvania and U.S. wiretapping laws, which invoke civil and criminal penalties for unlawful interception.

The Supreme Court declined to apply the "general laws doctrine" it had applied previously in cases involving reporter's privilege, source confidentiality agreements and newsroom searches. Under this doctrine, journalists are bound by content-neutral laws that apply generally in society, as long as those

laws do not unduly burden the news media. Journalists receive no special immunity. In *Bartnicki*, however, the Court concluded that the privacy interests here were outweighed by the interest in publishing matters of public concern. It stressed that participation in public affairs often results in a loss of privacy. The Court held the news media would be blameless in publishing the recording as long as they had no role in creating the illegal recording, they obtained the recording legally, and the content of the recording involved a matter of public concern.

False Light

Definition: The widespread publication of facts that place a plaintiff in a false light that is highly offensive to a reasonable person and was published with actual malice (at least in stories of public concern).

Newsweek's cover on March 28, 1988, showed a young man, hands clasped behind his head, being frisked by police against a backdrop of flashing patrol-car lights. The headline read: "The Drug Gangs/Waging War on America's Cities/Anti-Drug Sweep in Los Angeles." On April 25, the photo reappeared on an inside page over the small headline "Correction." A caption explained that the man in the photo was released without being charged and that *Newsweek* did not mean to suggest that the man was being arrested. It is not known what transpired between *Newsweek* editors and the young man, but one might logically ask whether the magazine cover had cast him in a false light.

Had the *Newsweek* case resulted in a lawsuit for false light invasion of privacy, the plaintiff would have had some of the same burdens of proof as a libel plaintiff. Consequently, false-light cases are often filed in tandem with libel actions. A plaintiff must prove identification (not always a given in a fictionalization), falsity, and that the publisher was at fault — that material was published recklessly or with knowledge of falsity.

False-light plaintiffs, however, would not allege loss of reputation. They would argue that being cast in a highly offensive false light caused some other kind of harm. Also, unlike a libel plaintiff, a false-light plaintiff must prove widespread publication — publicity — not just legal publication. Some states have refused to recognize false-light claims, citing First Amendment concerns, the similarity to libel claims and even the doctrinal confusion over what false light really means.

False Light and Actual Malice. In the 1967 case of *Time, Inc. v. Hill*, the Supreme Court held that all false-light plaintiffs — not just public officials and public figures, as in libel actions — must prove actual malice if involved in matters of public concern. The *Hill* case began in 1952 when three escaped convicts entered the home of James Hill near Philadelphia and held his family hostage for a day. The ordeal received sensational newspaper coverage and was the inspiration for Joseph Hayes' novel

---

[2] Federal law permits a party to a conversation to record it, so long as the recording is not for criminal purposes. However, the Federal Communication Commission, under penalty of lost phone service, requires all parties to consent. *See* 18 U.S.C.A. § 2511 (West Supp. 1996).

The Desperate Hours. It was later the basis for a Broadway play and a film starring Humphrey Bogart. In 1955, *Life* magazine published a story titled "True Crime Inspires Tense Play" that purported to describe what actually happened. *Life* carried photos from the Philadelphia tryouts for the play, including one of the sons being mistreated by a "brutish convict." Another photo showed the daughter biting the hand of an abusive convict. Both photos were embellishments, since the real captors did not harass the family. Arguing that *Life* used the family's name and experience for trade purposes, the Hills sued for invasion of privacy. They won at trial in 1963, but the Supreme Court set aside the damages in a 5-4 vote, applying the new legal rule that false-light plaintiffs involved in matters of public concern must prove actual malice. (A point of interest: The Hills' lawyer was Richard Nixon, later U.S. president.)

Courts are most likely to find disclosures highly offensive in two ways:

1. Fictionalization, which is the embellishment or addition of information to an otherwise factual presentation, a device more common to television or stage dramatizations than to news coverage; and,

2. Distortion, which occurs when elements of a story are deceptively juxtaposed, or when information is omitted, presented out of context or presented in an improper context.

Fictionalizations. *Time v. Hill* suggests that when a drama or novel is modeled on real events, false-light problems can arise even when names and other facts are changed. Fictionalization also can pose problems when a real person's name is used, but use of a real name normally will not sustain a privacy action unless the person's identity is also appropriated. Both a name and facts are usually necessary for there to be legal problems. The fact that the name used in the publication is coincidentally the same as the name of a real person not intended by the publisher or otherwise related or even similar to the character in the published material will not support a false-light privacy claim. A plaintiff must adequately allege a strong resemblance to a fictional character for the claim to proceed in court. Novels, films and television programs often carry disclaimers, advising readers and viewers that their plots and characters are fictional and that any similarities to real people are coincidental. While disclaimers might prove helpful in marginal cases, they are not a fail-safe way to prevent false-light claims.

Fictionalization also can occur in simple news stories when a writer fabricates or exaggerates facts and quotes. While such distortions are deplorable as a matter of ethics, they also can result in legal problems. In *Cantrell v. Forest City Publishing* (1973), for example, the widow of an accident victim successfully sued the *Cleveland Plain Dealer* for invasion of privacy after a reporter wrote a story implying he had spoken to the woman at her home. She argued that the story held her and her family up for pity and ridicule, humiliated them and caused mental distress. The Supreme Court upheld the verdict, agreeing that the substantial misrepresentations in the publication knowingly cast the family in a false light.

To succeed, a false-light plaintiff must prove the alleged misrepresentations were significant. A plainly unbelievable story — one with facts that defy reason and logic — can be the basis of a successful false-light claim. Minor falsifications, as in libel cases, will not sustain a false-light privacy claim.

Distortions. Until the upsurge in so-called TV "docudramas" and "infotainment," news organizations were much more likely to find themselves defending false-light lawsuits over instances involving information out of context or inappropriately juxtaposed with other information. The *Newsweek* example presented at the beginning of the discussion on false light is illustrative. The subject, photographed in a public place in the course of a newsworthy event, would have had little recourse if a photo caption simply had said police frisked him during a drug sweep. However, the use of the photo with the various headlines and cutlines implied that the subject of the photo was a suspect in a drug sweep that was part of the war on drugs.

Courts will closely scrutinize the accuracy and context of any captions or descriptions of the photographs or other artwork appearing with text. The use of file photos and video street scenes is commonplace in most news organizations but can pose problems. Such practices should raise red flags when the subject matter is sensitive or individuals might be identified. Editors should take special care when selecting file photos or footage of auto accidents to illustrate stories on drunken driving or using street scenes for hard-to-illustrate stories on delicate, controversial or possibly embarrassing topics.

Appropriation

Definition: The use of a person's name, likeness or image, without permission, for commercial gain.

Appropriation was one of the first privacy torts to develop, in part, because it resembled property rights — an area of law familiar to nineteenth century courts. But it is also a tort with which courts initially had difficulty because it alleged a mental harm based on unwanted publicity. The field of psychology was not highly developed, and the notion that something as intangible as mental suffering could be quantified for the purpose of monetary damages troubled courts.

Though private people sometimes make claims of commercial appropriation, most claims involve a more modern legal development: celebrities trying to protect the commercial value of their names and likenesses.

A Right to Publicity. Courts consistently have balked at the notion that people who seek public attention could claim a mental harm based on public exposure. While courts are not likely to award public persons damages for mental harm in appropriation cases, they have recognized a property-like right when someone uses the name or likeness of a celebrity or other public person for financial gain without authorization. In some states, people can barter and inherit this right to publicity.

Most commercial appropriation cases involve advertising or related enterprises, where the defendant has attempted to capitalize on a celebrity's identity. For example, an enterprising portable toilet business borrowed the phrase "Here's Johnny," Ed McMahon's nightly introduction from *The Tonight Show With Johnny Carson,* to advertise its product. To capitalize on the link, the firm also advertised itself as "The World's Foremost Commodian." Even though neither his complete name nor likeness was used, Carson won his appropriation claim in 1983.

The use of celebrity look-alikes and sound-alikes is common practice in advertising and sometimes results in appropriation lawsuits. Courts typically ask if the impersonation pirated the celebrity's distinctive style or identity. The Ninth Circuit upheld a $2.5 million judgment for singer Tom Waits, whose raspy voice Frito-Lay corn chips imitated in an advertisement. The court said Waits had a property right "to control the use of his identity as embodied in his voice." Athletes have raised this issue in the context of videogames using virtual players who are nearly identical in many features to their real-life counterparts. While the results have been mixed in the courts, the key issue is whether the game developers failed to transform sufficiently each player's identity or likeness in creating the games.

News media do not violate the right of publicity by using an individual's name or likeness to report news or promote news content, but they must be careful not to imply, without permission, that the person somehow is endorsing the content or publication. A key consideration for courts in these cases is whether the so-called news article is a thinly veiled excuse to use the celebrity's photographs. That is, are the celebrity's photographs incidental to an article of actual news value? Or is the media simply publishing the celebrity's valuable or embarrassing photographs to obtain a commercial advantage?

The Supreme Court has only decided one appropriation case. In 1977, it held that a TV station could not successfully assert a news exemption after airing footage of Hugo Zacchini, the "Human Cannonball." The station broadcast on a news program his entire 15-second act — in which he was shot from a cannon onto a net. Zacchini sued the station for appropriation and won. In *Zacchini v. Scripps Howard Broadcasting*, the Court refused to block a jury trial on Zacchini's $25,000 damage claim despite the program's newsworthiness because broadcasting the entire act threatened the economic value of the performance.

The use of names and likenesses also can pose problems in literary works, films, television and other forms of communication. Obtaining permission is an important defense, and many studios and producers will do exactly that to avoid claims, in spite of the cost. Most problems are avoided by the use of signed releases or consent forms, but lawsuits still occur over, for example, the breadth or interpretation of those agreements.

Definition of Commercial. The potential breadth and definition of what is or is not a commercial use can be a hotly contested issue. Many courts limit these laws to the actual commercial sale or advertising of products or services, thus allowing some films and documentaries without triggering these laws.

INTENTIONAL INFLICTION OF EMOTIONAL DISTRESS

The wide berth the First Amendment affords professional communicators makes it difficult for people who feel harmed by the media to succeed in court. Libel law, discussed in Chapter 6, requires plaintiffs to prove that defamatory information is false, and that the publishers of alleged defamations were at fault — that publication resulted from either negligent or reckless practices or with outright knowledge of falsehood. False light invasion of privacy typically imposes similar burdens on plaintiffs, and plaintiffs under the embarrassing private facts tort have little chance of recovering damages when involved in matters of public concern. As a result, lawyers sometimes file other legal actions, often in tandem with libel or privacy suits, based on general legal doctrines that have largely developed outside the umbrella of First Amendment protections.

One such end-run approach is the tort of intentional infliction of emotional distress, based on something akin to the common law doctrine of malice or ill will. It allows recovery of damages for severe emotional harm or deliberate or reckless conduct that is deemed outrageous and extreme, a judgment normally determined by the sensibilities of the jury. Private individuals fare better in emotional distress cases.

The leading media case on intentional infliction of emotional distress unfolded in the 1980s after a dispute between pornography mogul Larry Flynt, the publisher of *Hustler* magazine, and the Rev. Jerry Falwell, a prominent Virginia-based TV evangelist. The case was the subject of the movie *The People v. Larry Flynt.* Falwell sued Flynt and *Hustler* for libel, invasion of privacy and intentional infliction of emotional distress after the magazine ran a crude take-off of "The first time ..." advertising campaign of Campari Liqueur. The campaign focused on celebrities who recalled their first experiences imbibing the upscale liqueur. Double-entendre in the interviews gave readers the impression — until the end of the ads — that the celebrities were discussing their first sexual experiences. *Hustler* cast Falwell in one of the "first-time" interviews, reporting that his first sexual encounter was with his mother in an outhouse.

Hustler published a disclaimer stating that the page was an advertising parody "not to be taken seriously." The Roanoke, Virginia, jury found in favor of *Hustler* on the libel claim, holding that no reasonable person would believe the parody to be true. The judge dismissed the privacy claim, because only appropriation is recognized as an invasion of privacy action in Virginia, and Falwell's identity had not been appropriated for commercial purposes. But the jury awarded Falwell $200,000 on the emotional distress claim. The U.S. Court of Appeals for the Fourth Circuit upheld the judgment, reasoning that the actual malice standard for public figures in libel cases did not apply to emotional distress. Flynt appealed to the Supreme Court.

The Court unanimously overturned the lower courts. Citing journalism's long history of social and political caricature, Chief Justice Rehnquist reasoned that allowing public figures to collect damages without proving actual malice would chill social and political discourse. He noted that the essence of political cartooning often focused on "unfortunate physical traits or politically embarrassing events — an exploration often calculated to injure the feelings of the subject of the portrayal. The art of the cartoonist is often not reasoned or evenhanded, but slashing and one-sided." The outrageousness requirement, he noted, was subjective and "would allow a jury to impose liability on the basis of the jurors' tastes or views, or perhaps on the basis of their dislike of a particular expression." To prevail, Rehnquist wrote, public figures and officials must prove that the communication was false and published with actual malice.

Courts typically will not allow plaintiffs to use emotional distress claims to evade the defenses applicable to defamation claims, particularly if the distress claim merely recasts a defamation claim. The Supreme Court confirmed this rule in a case involving the controversial Westboro Baptist Church of Topeka, Kansas, and its anti-gay protests and pickets at the funerals of U.S. soldiers killed in Iraq and Afghanistan. In 2009, a U.S. court of appeals reversed, on free speech grounds, a jury verdict in favor of the father of a fallen serviceman and his claims for invasion of privacy and intentional infliction of emotional distress. The Supreme Court affirmed in 2011. As in *Hustler Magazine v. Falwell*, it held in *Snyder v. Phelps* that the speech in question plainly related to matters of public, rather than private, concern, even if the context of the speech (the funeral, for example) was particularly hurtful to the family of the soldier. Consequently, the state could apply reasonable time, place or manner regulations[3] but could not under the First Amendment prohibit or punish the picketers on the basis of the content of the speech, even if the jury deemed the setting outrageous.

A variant of intentional infliction of emotional distress is the tort of outrage, which focuses exclusively on the behavior of the defendant. For example, in 1988, personnel from a Florida TV station went to a local police department after officials disclosed that skeletal remains found a year earlier were those of a 6-year-old boy reported missing three years before. A police officer removed the child's skull from a drawer in a laboratory. Images of the skull were broadcast as part of a report on crime. After the boy's family watched a newscast showing a dramatic close-up of the skull, they filed an invasion of privacy and outrage lawsuit. Trial testimony centered on callous comments made during the TV station's newsroom debate over whether to air the close-up footage. A Florida appellate court rejected the privacy claim but held that the newscast easily surpassed the outrageousness requirement.

Plaintiffs also have received damages in some jurisdictions for negligent infliction of emotional distress, which occurs when media behavior exposes individuals to dangers that the media should have reasonably foreseen. For example, a California court in 1975 held a radio station responsible after a young driver was killed trying to keep up with a disc jockey who traveled around awarding prizes. It said that the accident was a foreseeable consequence of the promotion, which encouraged prize-seekers to rush from place to place. Other courts, however, have been unwilling to hold the media accountable for unforeseeable consequences, such as copycat behavior.

CONSTITUTIONAL AND STATUTORY PRIVACY

The privacy torts do not present the only reasons for special caution when gathering and disseminating information. Constitutional concerns and privacy statutes, which place limits *on government*, have implications for journalists seeking information under government control. Limits on how the government uses personal information indirectly affect journalists. And such limits on government use of private information — in this information-soaked era with its headlines about government and private enterprise abuses — are politically attractive to politicians and other policy-makers and records custodians.

Constitutional privacy may prove indirectly relevant to newsgathering when individuals use these constitutional arguments to bolster privacy claims against the news media, potentially offsetting the presumption favoring publication of private facts about matters of public concern. Statutory privacy designed to protect individuals from government abuse also provides a rationale — sometimes unwarranted — for withholding information from the public and news media.

Constitutional Privacy

Over time, the Supreme Court has defined a range of constitu-

---

[3] For an interesting examination of such regulations, *see Phelps-Roper v. Koster*, 713 F.3d 942 (8th Cir. 2013) (holding state had a significant interest in protecting privacy of funeral attendees for a brief time and limited area, but striking statute to extent it burdened too much speech by defining covered "funerals" broadly to include processions and other activities).

tional privacy protections. Although the word "privacy" appears nowhere in the Constitution, the Court has nonetheless recognized a right to be free from unreasonable governmental intrusion and eavesdropping. For example:

• Reasoning that freedom from intrusion is based on a "zone of privacy" around a person, not a specific place, the Court ruled in *Katz v. United States* in 1967 that a government wiretap on a telephone booth was unconstitutional.

• In *NAACP v. Alabama*, the Court in 1958 struck down an Alabama law that required certain organizations, including civil rights groups, to turn over membership rolls to the state. The Court held the rule violated the associational rights of current and potential members of the NAACP, who might not exercise those rights out of fear of government retaliation.

However, a recent shift in the Court — particularly in its view of "penumbral" decisional privacy rights, which are rights implied in various amendments to the U.S. Constitution — suggests that its view of privacy has also shifted. The Court has actually begun to unwind some of the protections it recognized more than 50 years ago.

• In 1965, the Court fashioned a decisional privacy right in *Griswold v. Connecticut*, a case invalidating a state law criminalizing the dissemination of birth control information. This right was implied in the "penumbra" of various amendments to the Constitution.

Citing *Griswold* and related cases, the Supreme Court decided *Lawrence v. Texas* (2003), a 6-3 decision that struck down a state statute that criminalized consensual sodomy between adults of the same sex. Writing for the majority, Justice Anthony Kennedy articulated a rationale based on respect for the private lives and intimate choices of two Texas men who were arrested in an apartment:

Liberty protects the person from unwarranted government intrusions into a dwelling or other private places. In our tradition the state is not omnipresent in the home. And there are other spheres of our lives and existence, outside the home, where the state should not be a dominant presence. Freedom extends beyond spatial bounds. Liberty presumes an autonomy of self that includes freedom of thought, belief, expression, and certain intimate conduct. The instant case involves liberty of the person both in its spatial and more transcendent dimensions.

The decision overruled the Court's contrary 1986 holding in *Bowers v. Hardwick*, prompting a stinging dissent from Justice Antonin Scalia, who, with Chief Justice Rehnquist and Justice Clarence Thomas, questioned the existence of any fundamental constitutional right to engage in same-sex sexual acts. Thomas

added his own dissent in which he questioned the existence of any general constitutional right of privacy.

Griswold v. Connecticut also laid the foundation for the Court's 1967 decision in *Loving v. Virginia* and 2015 decision in *Obergefell v. Hodges*, which recognized interracial and same-sex marriage, respectively.

Griswold also paved the way for the Court's 1973 decision in *Roe v. Wade*, which guaranteed a constitutional right to abortion. In 2022, the Court decided *Dobbs v. Jackson Women's Health Organization*, which overturned *Roe*. According to the Court, the Constitution does not refer to abortion, and the right to abortion receives no implicit constitutional protection. The *Dobbs* decision has sparked discussion about its broader potential impact on privacy generally. *Dobbs* suggests that the Court interprets privacy as the right to shield information from disclosure, not to make personal decisions free from government interference.

Most importantly to media professionals, however, has been the recent willingness of the Supreme Court to recognize a constitutional right of informational privacy — the right of individuals to control information about themselves. This right of informational privacy does not seem to overlap with the Court's concerns raised in *Dobbs*. Concerns about privacy had been raised in several cases addressing government use of computers to gather, store and disseminate information about private individuals.

In 1976, Justice William Brennan expressed concerns about the effects of new information technologies on privacy. In *United States v. Miller*, the Court held that individuals retained no privacy interest in information voluntarily given to a bank. Cautioned Brennan: "Development of photocopying machines, electronic computers and other sophisticated instruments has accelerated the abilities of government to intrude into areas which a person normally chooses to exclude from prying eyes and inquisitive minds."

A year later, the Court acknowledged a right of informational privacy in upholding a New York state practice of compiling and storing in a computer prescription drug records on individuals. Such a practice did not violate individuals' constitutional right of privacy, Justice John Paul Stevens wrote, so long as strict security was in place to ensure the privacy of the information. He wrote the Court was not unaware of the threat to privacy implicit in the accumulation of vast amounts of personal information in computerized data banks or government files.

In *Department of Justice v. Reporters Committee for Freedom of the Press*, the Supreme Court reacted to a long-standing concern about the threat that computers pose to personal privacy; it articulated the practical obscurity doctrine in response to a news media request for information contained in a government database. In essence, the Court reasoned in 1989 that computers have obliterated traditional barriers of time and space that once afforded individuals a measure of "practical obscurity" — or distance — from their official past. Because of computers, the Court noted, individuals no longer can move to another place to escape past deeds or count on the passage of time to dim official memories. Following this reasoning, it suggested that information compiled in central government computers — even information gathered from various *public* records — regained a privacy interest when brought together in one place. In fact, the Court reasoned, if the information were indeed *public*, reporters should have no need to see a government database. Under the reasoning of the *Reporters Committee* case, public-record information about individuals can be shielded from disclosure simply because it exists in a computer database.[4]

The privacy issue is particularly thorny as to the types of information the government may collect and use with regard to teachers, police officers and other public employees.

The Freedom of Information Act

Since the Great Depression, government's appetite for information has grown steadily, hitting full stride with the Great Society programs of the 1960s that coincided with the growth of systems analysis — a management technique that depended on vast amounts of data. To balance governmental need for information, much of it personal, statutes were passed to ensure that the government gathered information only for specific purposes and that it be used only for those purposes. One of the first such statutes was the federal Freedom of Information Act, passed in 1966 to ensure maximum access to records of federal executive agencies. While the act espouses openness, it also attempts to balance access with competing values. The result was nine exemptions, several of which raise privacy concerns as grounds for withholding information. (The federal Freedom of Information Act is discussed in Chapter 17.)

Exemption 3 applies to records specifically exempted by other federal statutes. For a statute to qualify under the exemption, it must establish criteria or types of matters for withholding and allow no discretion by agency personnel. Laws governing numerous agencies, including the Internal Revenue Act, which handles personal income tax records, fall into this category. The exemption also covers the Census Bureau, the Consumer Products Safety Commission and the Federal Trade Commission.

Exemption 6, which applies to personnel, medical and similar files, shields information that would "constitute a clearly unwarranted" invasion of privacy. Implicit in this language is the understanding that a balancing process must occur to determine

whether withholding is warranted. The "similar files" wording has been applied to a range of information.

Exemption 7 covers disclosure of certain law enforcement records, including disclosures that would invade privacy. In the *Reporters Committee* case, the Court recognized privacy interests in certain compilations of criminal records — even records that were public at their original source. For example, if a record is contained in a central government database, such as an FBI computer, it might be considered private. The same record at a courthouse in the jurisdiction where the crime occurred would be public. The court said that since the privacy/access balance typically favors withholding records when they are contained in computer compilations, courts don't need to engage in case-by-case balancing with the public interest in disclosure. The simple determination that a record is in a computer compilation was sufficient to withhold it, the court reasoned.

In 2004, the Supreme Court heard *Favish v. Office of Independent Counsel*. The case raised privacy and FOIA issues, including the question of the privacy interests of family members of a dead person. It grew out of requests for photographs taken during the investigation into the death of Vince Foster, a former deputy counsel in the Clinton White House. In 1993, he was found dead in a park in Washington, D.C. The National Park Service, FBI, Office of Independent Counsel and House and Senate committees independently investigated. All concluded that his death was a suicide, but rumors lingered. The District of Columbia Court of Appeals, in 1999, denied the records request of Accuracy in Media, a media watchdog organization, which had requested the photographs from the National Park Service. Allan Favish, a lawyer who had participated in the litigation, renewed the request in California by serving it on the Office of Independent Counsel, seeking 150 photographs.

The office released more than 100 photos but withheld several for reasons at first not clearly articulated. Favish later dropped twenty-one photos from his request. Eventually the office relied upon the privacy language of Exemption 7. The district court ruled for Favish on one photo and certain issues regarding the quality of the photos but withheld ten to protect the privacy interests of Foster's family. The Ninth Circuit Court of Appeals reversed the district court's ruling and held that, though the privacy interests of the family were a valid consideration, they had to be weighed against the public interest in the investigation. Because the court of appeals did not have the photos in question, the case was remanded to the district court for further analysis and the required balancing of the privacy and access interests. On remand, the district court ordered the release of five photos and withheld, on privacy grounds, the other five. The Ninth Circuit affirmed. In 2004, the Supreme Court reversed the appellate court and held that under the FOIA surviving family members have a right to personal privacy regarding the photographic images of the scene of a close rel-

---

[4] *See* Bursac v. Souzzi, 37 Media L. Rep. (BNA) 1109 (N.Y. Sup. Ct. 2008) (applying the *Reporter's Committee* reasoning to New York's state public records law and ruling that a county official who posted the plaintiff's photograph on a "wall of shame" Web page following her arrest for driving while intoxicated must remove the posting even though the arrest was a matter of public record).

ative's death. The Court said such privacy interests outweighed, under the FOIA, the public's interest in disclosure.

In *FCC v. AT&T* (2011), the Court held 8-0 that while corporations are protected under the Fourth Amendment from unreasonable searches and seizures, they are not shielded under the personal privacy language of Exemption 7 (c) from FOIA requests for documents they provided to the government. Corporations do not have personal privacy rights, and the exemption protects only the privacy of individuals, not businesses.

The Privacy Act of 1974

The Privacy Act was meant to create a "Code of Fair Information Practices" to regulate government agencies. The Senate report on the legislation noted that one purpose of the act was "to promote government respect for the privacy of citizens" by ensuring that executive branch agencies follow certain rules regarding the gathering and disclosing of information. The Privacy Act is most likely to affect requests for information that is not clearly covered by the legislation. In such cases, custodians of records tend to be very cautious because the Privacy Act imposes penalties on custodians who release protected information. Withholding information that should be disclosed, on the other hand, may violate the federal Freedom of Information Act, but that legislation poses no penalties for wrongly withholding information.

Other Privacy Concerns

A number of other federal and state statutes raising privacy concerns can erect barriers to information gathered and kept by government and, in some cases, private institutions. A few key examples are discussed below.

Driver's Privacy Protection Act. Driver's license records have long been a source of information for journalists, more so in recent years with the growth of computer-assisted reporting. In 1991, for example, the *Miami Herald* used a computer analysis of state Division of Motor Vehicle records to show that many drunken drivers were allowed back on the road. In 1997, however, federal legislation limited access to such records. The law was partly in response to the slaying of California actress Rebecca Schaeffer by a fan who located her address through driver records obtained by a private investigator. The intent of the law is to inhibit stalkers and anyone else who might harm an individual after linking a name with an address. The federal legislation contains a provision that allows states to disclose such information if they enact a provision notifying drivers that they have an option to withhold personal information.

Several states challenged the law, arguing that Congress had overstepped its authority in attempting to regulate a state prac-

tice. The Seventh and Tenth Circuits of the U.S. Court of Appeals upheld the law. The Fourth Circuit, however, sided with South Carolina, which argued the law was unconstitutional because state driver's license information constituted internal state activity and lay beyond the scope of congressional jurisdiction. In *Condon v. Reno* (2000), the Supreme Court reversed the Fourth Circuit. Writing for a unanimous Court, Chief Justice Rehnquist held that the release or sale of drivers' license information constituted interstate commerce, thereby giving Congress regulatory authority.

The Buckley Amendment. Enacted as the Family Educational Rights and Privacy Act, or FERPA, the Buckley Amendment requires educational institutions receiving federal money to keep certain student records private. Directory information, such as names, addresses and majors, is not covered. Academic records, including non-criminal disciplinary records, are. Before 1992, the Department of Education advised institutions that campus crime records should be considered student disciplinary records — a position that frustrated many media organizations, particularly campus newspapers. A 1992 amendment, however, states that crime reports are not educational records and cannot be withheld as disciplinary records.

Rape Shield Laws. Whether to publish the name of a rape victim is a controversial topic, both legally and ethically. Rape shield laws were designed to encourage victims to come forward by preventing the additional trauma of publicity. Some courts have upheld such laws. In Florida, however, the state supreme court, in 1994, upheld a ruling that the state's law was unconstitutional in a case spawned by the William Kennedy Smith rape trial. The court relied heavily on *Florida Star v. B.J.F.*, which held the news media should not be punished for publishing truthful, lawfully obtained information about matters of public concern absent a state interest of the highest order.

Juror Shield Laws. Much has been said and written about protecting jurors' privacy, particularly since the Rodney King police brutality and the O.J. Simpson murder trials. Since the Supreme Court's 1984 ruling in *Press-Enterprise v. Superior Court*, jurors' selection and identity have been presumptively public matters. But after the King and Simpson cases, and the Timothy McVeigh trial in the Oklahoma City bombing, the tide began to change. Citing privacy, judges appear to be routinely impaneling anonymous juries, a practice once reserved for the trials of organized crime kingpins when juror safety was a factor; and some states have passed laws expressly allowing the practice.

Computer Privacy. Journalists continue to depend heavily on computer databases and online sources. Going online enables journalists to access a vast array of information quickly. Many significant news stories are based on an analysis of government databases. Most laws dealing with computer privacy are designed to place limits on government. The Computer Matching and Privacy Act of 1988, for example, limits the ability of government to routinely cross-reference information in various government databases. The Electronic Communications Privacy Act of 1986 made the interception of computer communications a crime, and the Computer Crime Act of 1986 made it unlawful to access or disclose certain records in computer form. Many of the laws, reflecting some of the constitutional and statutory concerns discussed previously, treat computerized information as more threatening to privacy than similar information in paper files. Such laws can be vague or over-inclusive in ways that inhibit legitimate journalists.

The computer/privacy debate also has begun to focus on private-sector information practices. In 2000, after conducting a series of Web site surveys, the FTC abandoned its long-standing policy supporting self-regulation. Instead, it announced support for federal legislation to protect online consumers, much to the dismay of the Online Privacy Alliance, an informal industry coalition that included some of the biggest online companies. FTC officials recommended that Congress establish standards regarding online information collection. More recent controversies have focused on the search information, email and personal identifiers retained by companies such as Google (including YouTube) and various cellular telephone providers.

In 2014, the Pew Research Center published a study that indicated most people are generally not worried about the collection of their search information and receipt of targeted advertising if that's the price for getting certain online services at no cost, though many also indicated some concerns about tracking geographic locations through mobile devices.

A growing privacy concern involves the posting of diary entries and other information by individuals on online social networking sites such as Facebook and LinkedIn. Many students and others have found that once information is posted and widely shared, the expectation of privacy lessens. Employers, government agencies and others have used these sites to gather information about individuals. In 2007, Facebook triggered substantial public criticism with its Beacon advertising program that transmitted users' online purchasing information to their friends on the social network. Facebook ultimately changed the program, added an opt-out feature, and apologized to its users.

Social media sites, search engines, business interests and individual consumers have increasingly engaged in online conduct that may erode or at least alter societal expectations and norms regarding personal privacy. Facebook's various privacy policies and controversies, Google's retention of search histories and user information, cell phone tracking capabilities, and even cable companies and other companies that can read, block or track certain types of messages all stand to change traditional notions

about what is private and what is not.

In 2012, Facebook entered into a $9.5 million settlement with a class of its members who had sued over the site's Beacon program (started in 2007) that effectively gathered and disseminated information about Facebook members' online activities without their consent. In addition to the payment, which went to attorney's fees and to set up a new foundation dedicated to user education and protection of online identities, Facebook agreed to end the Beacon program.

The conflict over what privacy rules or laws apply to the online collection of personal information by commercial sites is likely to continue as new government agencies enter this arena and as more people look for ways to control their own data.

In a reminder that the world is shrinking, Google in 2014 hit the so-called "right to be forgotten" wall in Europe when the European Court of Justice ruled that it must comply with local law and thus will have to remove, after a process, certain items from its search results. The results are potentially dramatic not only for the giant search engine's business model, but for fundamental notions of public access to information as well, showing once again that on privacy matters Europe and the United States are two related, but very different legal worlds.

Health Insurance Privacy. The privacy rules under the Health Insurance Portability and Accountability Act of 1996 took effect in 2003. They do not directly apply to the media, but they do affect many businesses, including hospitals. They probably are more likely to refuse to release information about patients or even to confirm that an accident victim has been admitted. In addition, the law may influence the tone and direction of future privacy legislation.

The HIPAA rules limit the use and disclosure of individuals' health information by doctors, hospitals, health-care clearinghouses, insurance plans, their business associates, and many employers who provide health care or coverage. For example, employers may not use the information to make personnel decisions, and any covered entity may only disclose the information for purposes related to treatment, payment and health care operations, unless the individual has provided a clear, voluntary authorization permitting disclosure. The rules also require that each covered business adopt privacy procedures and train a designated privacy official to assure compliance.

The rules do not provide for private lawsuits seeking enforcement but do provide for investigations by the Department of Health and Human Services, which can then seek civil and criminal penalties for violations. Examples of exceptions allowing disclosure, even without authorization by individuals, include public health investigations, law enforcement, emergencies and national security; but there is no exception for any reports to journalists — even for the release of limited information concerning admission and discharge dates of patients.

The law and its consequences took on new importance with the 2014 reporting on the Ebola story, causing journalists to attempt to balance patient privacy with needed reports to the public. Hospitals were typically advised that they could release general information without patient names in an effort to keep people informed about possible risks of exposure.

Privacy After September 11, 2001

The terrorist attacks of September 11, 2001, have had a far-reaching impact on society, laws and notions of privacy. These matters are still evolving. Interestingly, some government officials responsible for security matters have recently argued that privacy can no longer be equated with anonymity in terms of personal information and private communications. They contend that government must have greater access, particularly to certain telecommunications and financial information, to guard against terrorist and criminal acts and that the focus of privacy advocates should be on the creation of legal safeguards limiting the permissible uses of that information by government.

The USA PATRIOT Act increased federal authority in a number of ways. It relaxed restrictions on the sharing of information between law enforcement agencies and intelligence agencies, enhanced the government's subpoena power to obtain and inspect email records of suspected terrorists, expanded bank record-keeping requirements to track transactions and money laundering, and permitted roving wiretaps of suspected terrorists. More than 300 pages long, the law received virtually no debate or congressional oversight before its passage.

Not long after his reelection in 2004, President George W. Bush began urging renewal of PATRIOT Act provisions as well as expansion of certain government powers to obtain records without judicial approval. After months of negotiations with Congress and amid media reports of government wiretapping of international telephone calls, a compromise was reached in 2006. The act was renewed with a few modifications limiting some government powers to obtain routine library records and providing people served with terrorism-related subpoenas the right to challenge the nondisclosure and gag order requirements of the subpoenas. The renewal, though, made permanent most of the PATRIOT Act's provisions.

In 2008, President Bush and Congress squared off and then compromised over a major expansion of government power to conduct surveillance, including a significant revision of the thirty-year-old Foreign Intelligence Surveillance Act governing the liability of telecommunications companies that facilitated secret and possibly illegal government wiretaps after the 2001 terrorist attacks. As part of the compromise, Congress included in the new law immunity for the companies that had cooperated with the government in conducting warrantless wiretaps, a hotly contested issue that led to prompt but unsuccessful legal chal-

lenges. In 2011, President Obama signed a four-year extension of the PATRIOT Act as previously amended. But in 2015 the law and the practice of collecting in bulk data about the telecommunications of Americans hit a legislative and judicial snag as key provisions of the act were challenged and then expired for lack of a legislative deal on revisions and an extension.

During the coming years, the pressure to invest government with new powers and to use computer technology and the Internet to track and prevent terrorism will continue to be strong. The results may include not only a contraction of the privacy rights of individuals, but also a contraction of sources of information available to journalists. The controversies that arose in 2013 and 2014 as a result of Edward Snowden's disclosures of data-mining by the National Security Agency only made more obvious the potential impact of new technology on what once seemed to be settled notions of privacy. While many continue to debate the exact nature of the NSA's data collection and the impact of the Snowden revelations on national security, there is no doubt that the furor over the NSA will fuel privacy debates, new guidelines and a fresh look at government surveillance

SUMMARY

Despite assaults on their privacy from various quarters — and perhaps in part because of those assaults — Americans remain strong in their belief in the right to be let alone. Privacy concerns are manifested in constitutions, statutes and common law cases that attempt to balance individual rights with competing values, including the right of the news media to publish and the right of the public to be informed. It is to be expected that the rights of individuals and of a free and vigorous press often will clash. The balance has generally tilted toward the press because of the bedrock principle that a democratic society works best when information flows freely.

Journalistic excesses are not lost on the public, whose declining opinion of journalism has been reflected in some polls. The results of declining confidence can be seen in the outcome of some court cases. Lack of public confidence in the news media also can embolden politicians to pass laws limiting press freedoms in the name of privacy.

BIBLIOGRAPHY

Articles

Calo, M. Ryan. "The Drone as Privacy Catalyst," 64 *Stanford Law Review* 29 (2011).

Coleman, A.D. "Private Lives, Public Places: Street Photography Ethics," 2 *Journal of Mass Media Ethics* 60 (Spring /Summer 1997).

Editorial, "The Telephone Unmasked," *New York Times,* Oct. 12,

1877, at 4.

Hopkins, W. Wat. "*Snyder v. Phelps* and the Unfortunate Death of Intentional Infliction of Emotional Distress as a Speech-Based Tort," 3 *Journal of Media Law and Ethics* 1 (2012), https://law.ubalt.edu/academics/publications/medialaw/.

Prosser, William. "Privacy," 48 *California Law Review* 383 (1960).

Smith, Jeffery A. "Moral Guardians and the Origins of the Right to Privacy," 10 *Journalism and Communications Monographs* 63 (2008).

Warren, Samuel D. & Louis D. Brandeis. "The Right to Privacy," 4 *Harvard Law Review* 220 (1890).

Woo, Jisuk. "The Right Not to be Identified: Privacy and Anonymity in the Interactive Media Environment," 8 *New Media Society* 949 (2006).

Books

Ernst, Morris & Alan Schwartz. *Privacy, The Right To Be Let Alone,* London: MacGibbon & Kee, 1962.

Flaherty, David H. *Privacy in Colonial New England.* Charlottesville: University Press of Virginia, 1972.

Glasser, Charles, ed. *International Libel & Privacy Handbook.* New York: Bloomberg Press, 2006.

Hixson, Richard F. *Privacy in a Public Society: Human Rights in Conflict.* New York: Oxford University Press, 1987.

Pember, Don. *Privacy and the Press.* Seattle: University of Washington Press, 1972.

Restatement (Second) Torts, American Law Institute, 1977.

Rule, James B. *Privacy in Peril: How We Are Sacrificing a Fundamental Right in Exchange for Security and Convenience.* New York: Oxford University Press, 2007.

Westin, Alan F. *Privacy and Freedom.* New York: Atheneum, 1967.

Cases

Anderson v. Gannett Co., 994 So. 2d 1048 (Fla. 2008), *affirming* Gannett Co. v. Anderson, 947 So. 2d 1 (Fla. Ct. App. 2007).

Armstrong v. H&C Communications, Inc., 575 So. 2d 280, 282 (Fla. Ct. App. 1991).

Ayeni v. Mottola, 35 F.3d 680 (2d Cir. 1994).

Barber v. Time, Inc., 159 S.W.2d 291 (Mo. 1942).

Bartnicki v. Vopper, 532 U.S. 514 (2001).

Bisbee v. Conover, 452 A.2d 689 (N.J. 1982).

Briscoe v. Reader's Digest Association, 483 P.2d 34 (Cal. 1972).

Cantrell v. Forest City Publishing, 419 U.S. 245 (1973).

Cape Publications, Inc. v. Bridges, 423 So. 2d 426 (Fla. Ct. App. 1982).

Carpenter v. United States, 138 S. Ct. 2206 (2018).

Carson v. Here's Johnny Portable Toilets, Inc., 698 F.2d 831 (6th Cir. 1983).

Christoff v. Nestle USA, Inc., 47 Cal. 4th 468 (Cal. 2009).

City of Ontario v. Quon, 560 U.S. 746 (2010).

Cohen v. Cowles Media, 501 U.S. 663 (1991).

Condon v. Reno, 528 U.S. 141 (2000), *rev'g* 155 F.3d 453 (4th Cir. 1998).

Cox Broadcasting Co. v. Cohn, 420 U.S. 469 (1975).

Dahlstrom v. Sun-Times Media, 777 F.3d 937 (7th Cir. 2015).

De Havilland v. FX Networks, LLC, 21 Cal. App. 5th 845 (Ct. App. Cal. 2018).

Dempsey v. National Enquirer, Inc., 702 F. Supp. 927 (D. Maine 1988).

Denver Publishing Co. v. Bueno, 54 P.3d 893 (Colo. 2002).

Department of Justice v. Reporters Committee for Freedom of the Press, 489 U.S. 749 (1989).

Department of State v. Washington Post Co., 456 U.S. 595 (1982).

Desnick v. ABC, 44 F.3d 1345 (7th Cir. 1995).

Dobbs v. Jackson Women's Health Org., 142 S. Ct. 2228 (2022).

Elvis Presley Enterprises v. Elvis Tours, 14 Media L. Rep. (BNA) 1053 (6th Cir. 1987).

Factors, Inc., v. Pro Arts, Inc., 4 Media L. Rep. (BNA) 1144 (2d Cir. 1978).

Favish v. Office of Independent Counsel, 541 U.S. 157 (2004).

Florida Star v. B.J.F., 491 U.S. 524 (1989).

Florida v. Globe Communication Corp., 648 So. 2d 110 (Fla. 1994).

Food Lion v. Capital Cities/ABC, 194 F.3d 505 (4th Cir. 1999).

Forsher v. Bugliosi, 608 P.2d 716 (Cal. 1980).

Galella v. Onassis, 353 F. Supp. 196 (S.D.N.Y. 1972).

Geisler v. Petrocelli, 616 F.2d 636 (2d Cir. 1980).

Griswold v. Connecticut, 381 U.S. 479 (1965).

Hart v. Electronic Arts, Inc., 717 F.3d 141 (3d Cir. 2013).

Hustler Magazine v. Falwell, 485 U.S. 46, 55-56 (1988).

Jacova v. Southern Radio and Television Co., 83 So. 2d 34 (Fla. 1955).

Jews for Jesus, Inc. v. Rapp, 997 So. 2d 1098 (Fla. 2008).

John Doe v. Sam Reed, 561 U.S. 186 (2010).

Katz v. United States, 389 U.S. 347 (1967).

Keller v. Elec. Arts, Inc., 724 F.3d 1268 (9th Cir. 2013).

Kelley v. Post Publishing Co., 98 N.E.2d 286 (Mass. 1951).

Lane v. Facebook, Inc., 696 F.3d 811 (9th Cir. 2012).

Lawrence v. Texas, 539 U.S. 558 (2003).

Livingston v. Kentucky Post, 14 Media L. Rep. (BNA) 2076 (Ky. Cir. Ct. 1987).

Loving v. Virginia, 388 U.S. 1 (1967).

Lowe v. Hearst, 487 F.3d 246 (5th Cir. 2007).

Macon Telegraph Publishing Co. v. Tatum, 436 S.E.2d 655 (Ga. 1993).

Martin Luther King Jr., Ctr. for Soc. Change v. American Heritage Prod., Inc., 296 S.E.2d 697 (Ga. 1982).

McCall v. Courier Journal & Louisville Times, 623 S.W.2d 882 (Ky. 1981).

Medical Laboratory Management Consultants v. ABC, 306 F.3d 806 (9th Cir. 2002).

Moreno v. Hanford Sentinel, Inc. 172 Cal. App. 4th 1125 (Cal. Ct. App. 2009).

NAACP v. Alabama, 357 U.S. 449 (1958).

Obergefell v. Hodges, 576 U.S. 644 (2015).

Olmstead v. United States, 227 U.S. 438 (1928).

Pavesich v. New England Life, 50 S.E. 68 (Ga. 1905).

People for Ethical Treatment of Animals v. Berosini, 867 P.2d 1121 (Nev. 1994).

People v. Melongo, 6 N.E.3d 120 (Ill. 2014).

Phelps-Roper v. Koster, 713 F.3d 942 (8th Cir. 2013).

Pope v. Curl, 2 Atk. 342, 26 Eng. Rep. 608 (1741).

Prahl v. Brosamle, 295 N.W.2d 768 (Wis. 1980).

Rawlins v. Hutchinson Publishing Co., 543 P.2d 988, 996 (Kan. 1975).

Riley v. California, 573 U.S. 373 (2014).

Roberson v. Rochester Folding Box Co., 64 N.E. 442 (N.Y. 1902).

Sanders v. American Broadcasting Co., 978 P.2d 67 (Cal. 1999).

Schuyler v. Curtis, 42 N.E. 22 (N.Y. 1891).

Shulman v. Group W. Prod., 955 P.2d 469 (Cal. 1998).

Sidis v. F-R Publishing Co., 113 F.2d 806 (2d Cir. 1940).

Sipple v. Chronicle Publishing Co., 201 Cal.

Snyder v. Phelps, 562 U.S. 443 (2011), aff'g 580 F.3d 206 (4th Cir. 2009).

Stressman v. American Blackhawk Broadcasting Co., 416 N.W.2d 685 (Iowa 1987).

Time, Inc. v. Hill, 385 U.S. 374, 377 (1967).

Trump v. O'Brien, 958 A.2d 85 (N.J. Super. Ct. App. Div. 2008).

Tyne v. Time Warner Entertainment Co., 336 F.3d 1286 (11th Cir. 2003).

Tyne v. Time Warner Entertainment Co., 901 So. 2d 802 (Fla. 2005).

United States v. Miller, 425 U.S. 435, 451 (1976).

Virgil v. Sports Illustrated, 424 F. Supp. 1286 (S.D. Cal. 1984).

Virgil v. Time, Inc., 527 F.2d 1122 (9th Cir. 1975).

Waits v. Frito-Lay, Inc., 978 F.2d 1093, 1100 (9th Cir. 1992).

Weirum v. RKO General, Inc., 539 P.2d 36 (Cal. 1975).

Welling v. Weinfeld, 866 N.E.2d 1051 (Ohio 2007).

Whalen v. Roe, 429 U.S. 589, 605 (1977).

White v. Samsung Elec. of America, Inc., 971 F.2d 1395, 1399 (9th Cir. 1992).

Wilson v. Layne, 526 U.S. 603 (1999).

Wolfson v. Lewis, 924 F. Supp. 1413 (E.D. Pa. 1996).

Wood v. Fort Dodge Messenger, 13 Media L. Rep. (BNA) 1614 (Iowa Dist. Ct. 1986).

Zacchini v. Scripps Howard Broad., 433 U.S. 562, 575 (1977).

Statutes

Computer Fraud and Abuse Act of 1986, 18 U.S.C. 1030 (1986).

Computer Matching and Privacy Act of 1988, 5 U.S.C. Sec. 552a (1988).

Driver's Privacy Protection Act of 1994, 18 U.S.C.A. 2721 (1994).

Electronic Communications Privacy Act of 1986, 18 U.S.C. Sec 2510-2523 (1986).

Family Educational Rights and Privacy Act, 20 U.S.C.A. Sec. 1232g (1974).

Freedom of Information Act, 5 U.S.C. Sec. 522 (1966).

Health Insurance Portability and Accountability Act of 1996, 42 U.S.C.A. Sec. 1320d-4; 29U.S.C. Sec. 1181 et seq and 42 U.S.C. 1320d et seq. (1996).

Privacy Act of 1974, 5 U.S.C. Sec. 552a (1974).

Video Voyeurism Prevention Act of 2004, 18 U.S.C.A. 1801 (2004).

15

Confidential Sources and Information

By Anthony L. Fargo

✓ **Headnote Questions**

- How is the constitutional journalist's privilege limited?
- To what extent is a journalist's work product protected from disclosure?
- In what ways have recent cases cast doubt on the future of the constitutional privilege?
- What common characteristics do state shield laws have? How do they differ?
- What are the advantages and disadvantages of shield laws?
- What is the status of attempts to pass a federal shield law?
- What issues do digital technology raise in regard to the journalist's privilege?
- What are the potential legal ramifications of voluntarily revealing a confidential source?
- How did Congress respond to a Supreme Court decision on newsroom searches?

Some journalists go through their entire careers without using a confidential source, while others rely on such sources daily. Reporting on politics, national security and financial markets may require journalists to navigate complex relationships with sources who provide deep background information that cannot be published, or who agree to be quoted only anonymously or with pseudonyms.

The use of confidential sources carries significant ethical baggage. Journalists are supposed to tell their audiences the truth, but using a confidential source requires hiding part of the truth. They must be careful not to put such sources in danger by being careless with their identities, but they also must guard against being used for unsavory purposes by people to whom they have pledged confidentiality. The complexity of the ethical relationships between journalists and sources is reflected in the ethics code of the Society of Professional Journalists. It discourages journalists from relying on confidential sources, while admonishing them to keep their promises of confidentiality.

This same ambiguity is evident in the law regarding journalists and their sources. A journalist who receives a subpoena to appear before a grand jury or in a courtroom to name a confidential source faces being found in contempt of court and fined or jailed for refusing to cooperate. The extent to which a journalist is protected from that fate varies widely, based on whether the agency issuing the subpoena is federal or state and where it is located. The U.S. Supreme Court's sole attempt to clarify the law in 1972 backfired because of a sharp divide among the justices. Further complicating things are varying degrees of legal protection for journalists' non-confidential work product, such as unpublished photographs and unaired video images, and new challenges posed by digital technology.

Journalists who voluntarily reveal sources, meanwhile, may find they are liable for damages to their sources for breaking promises of confidentiality. They also have to be concerned that police may get search warrants allowing officers to rummage through files for evidence related to criminal acts.

The tension between journalists and those who seek their testimony and work product arises from conflicting views of journalists' duties. Reporters argue that if they reveal their sources, those and other potential sources will stop going to the press with important information. That, in turn, will harm the press's ability to act as a watchdog, or check, on government and corporations. Critics of a privilege for journalists argue that journalists are no different from other citizens who have a duty to testify when they have relevant and important information about a legal controversy. Journalists who refuse to obey valid orders to appear before grand juries or in court are putting themselves above the law, which no person has a right to do.

Faced with powerful challenges to what they see as a professional obligation to protect sources, journalists have turned to the First Amendment for shelter. That has not proved entirely successful, leading press organizations to seek statutory protection in most state legislatures and from Congress. The media have been successful in getting legislation approved in the states, but the statutes carry their own limitations.

CONSTITUTIONAL PRIVILEGE

Although the First Amendment was ratified in 1791, reporters did not claim that it protected them from revealing sources until the middle of the twentieth century. However, the first prominent case involving a reporter protecting the identity of a news source arose in 1848. A *New York Herald* reporter wrote a story about a treaty intended to be secret. The Senate held him in contempt when he refused to name his source and jailed him in the Capitol for ten days. When it became apparent he would not talk, he was released.

The standoff between the reporter and the Senate was typical of the occasional skirmishes that arose between journalists and authorities until the 1950s. A newspaper would publish a controversial story, leading authorities to issue a subpoena to the publisher or writer demanding to know the source. The journalist would refuse to cooperate, citing professional obligations. The reporter would be held in contempt, or authorities would give up, or the information would be revealed some other way.

It is not clear from the historical record why journalists did not seek protection under the First Amendment during the nineteenth and early twentieth centuries, but there are several possible explanations. Many of the cases involved state court proceedings, and the Supreme Court did not rule that the First Amendment restrained state abridgement of speech and press rights until the 1920s, in *Gitlow v. New York*. Also, it would be two more decades before opinions from the Supreme Court began laying the groundwork for a more robust protection for speech and press rights.

Furthermore, legal experts viewed privileges suspiciously — and perhaps none so suspiciously as the journalist's privilege. Although privileges protecting attorneys, medical doctors, mental health workers and pastors from testifying against clients, patients and congregants had existed through statutory or common law for many years, they were seen as impediments to the legal system's search for truth. John Henry Wigmore, a leading expert on evidence law in the early 1900s, who is still cited frequently, wrote that a privilege should only be recognized if a communication was conducted in confidence, confidentiality was essential to the relationship between the communicators, society considered the relationship important, and the harm of disclosing the communication outweighed the benefit. Wigmore found that most privileges, including the journalist's privilege,

lacked one or more of the four elements he described.

It was not until 1958 that a reporter claimed that the First Amendment protected her right to conceal her source. Marie Torre, an entertainment columnist for a New York newspaper, quoted a CBS executive as blaming singer and actress Judy Garland for delays in bringing a variety show starring Garland to television. Garland sued CBS for libel and breach of contract and demanded that Torre reveal her source. Torre refused, claiming the First Amendment press clause protected her. But in an opinion written by Judge Potter Stewart, who would soon join the Supreme Court, the Second U.S. Circuit Court of Appeals ruled against Torre. The court determined that while there might be circumstances in which journalists should have a right to conceal sources, Torre's information went to the heart of Garland's suit and had to be disclosed. Torre served ten days in jail for contempt but never revealed her source.

Conflicts between the press and authorities over sources remained rare until the late 1960s. One study showed that the number of subpoenas served on the media jumped from a total of about one or two per year nationwide to more than seventy per year. Sociologist Michael Schudson has argued that tensions grew between the press and government in the 1960s because journalists became less likely to take government pronouncements at face value after catching the government in lies about the Bay of Pigs invasion of Cuba and about the war in Vietnam. Younger journalists in particular were more open to nontraditional sources, such as the leaders of various social movements who often did not want to speak to the media on the record but wanted to get publicity for their causes. Law enforcement officials, frustrated that the news media seemed to know more about potentially dangerous organizations than they did, and no longer able to count on voluntary cooperation from journalists, began seeking subpoenas to force journalists to turn over source names, tapes, notes and other information about the groups and their members.

Branzburg v. Hayes

The Supreme Court agreed to weigh in on the growing controversy about confidential sources by consolidating four cases involving three reporters who had refused to cooperate with grand juries investigating alleged crimes linked to their sources. The Court issued its opinion in *Branzburg v. Hayes* in 1972.

Grand juries twice subpoenaed the first of the three reporters because of stories about drug traffic in Kentucky. Paul Branzburg of the *Courier-Journal* in Louisville wrote a story about two hashish dealers he called "Larry" and "Jack" who told him about their lives in the drug trade. He wrote another story that included interviews with several drug users in Frankfort, the state capital. The sources ranged from a 14-year-old student to a state employee. Both stories resulted in grand jury subpoenas seeking Branzburg's testimony about his sources, which he resisted, citing Kentucky's shield law for reporters.

In 1970, the Kentucky Court of Appeals, then the state's highest court, ruled 5-1 against Branzburg. It noted that Kentucky's shield law barred courts, grand juries and other government bodies from forcing a journalist to reveal the "source of any information" obtained in the course of his or her work. However, the court determined that Branzburg could not claim the statutory privilege's protection for what he saw because his personal observation, not his sources, was the "information." The court later denied a rehearing in the Louisville case and ruled against Branzburg in the Frankfort case.

The second reporter, Paul Pappas, worked for a Massachusetts TV station and covered an outbreak of apparently racially motivated violence in New Bedford. He recorded a man reading a statement outside a store that was also a Black Panthers headquarters. The Black Panthers told Pappas he could return later with his camera as long as he agreed not to report on anything except an anticipated police raid. Pappas returned and was allowed to enter, but the raid did not happen while he was there, and he filed no story.

Authorities learned he was in the headquarters building, however, and subpoenaed him to appear before a state grand jury. Pappas answered some questions before the grand jury but nothing about what or whom he saw. He moved to quash the subpoena, but a superior court judge denied the motion.

On appeal, the Massachusetts Supreme Judicial Court ruled against Pappas. Noting that Massachusetts had no statutory privilege, it held that to create one by constitutional or common law "would be engaging in judicial amendment of the Constitution or judicial legislation."

The third reporter, Earl Caldwell, was a correspondent for the *New York Times* in Oakland, California, and covered the Black Panthers. In a 1969 story, David Hilliard, the Black Panther Party's chief of staff, told him the party's goals included the "overthrow of the government by way of force and violence." Hilliard was being investigated for a speech before the story appeared in which he allegedly threatened President Richard Nixon's life. Caldwell was subpoenaed to appear before a federal grand jury to testify and surrender his interview notes.

A federal district court agreed that Caldwell could refuse to testify about his sources' identities but ruled that he had to enter the grand jury room and answer all other questions. Caldwell, fearing an appearance in the grand jury room would end his relationship with the Black Panthers, appealed to the Ninth U.S. Circuit Court of Appeals. In 1970, a Ninth Circuit panel ruled that he not only did not have to identify his confidential sources but also did not have to appear before the grand jury at all. It noted that Caldwell swore that he had no information for the grand jury beyond his published stories except that covered by the district court's protective order. In the narrow circum-

stances of this case, the court held, "[T]he public's First Amendment right to be informed" had to be balanced against any compelling interest the government could show for a witness's appearance before a grand jury. The court said it saw no real public interest in Caldwell's appearance given the probable damage to the First Amendment his appearance would cause.

Branzburg and Pappas appealed to the Supreme Court, as did the government in Caldwell's case. The consolidated cases gave the Court the chance to rule on privilege questions in a state with a shield law, in a state without a shield law, and in a federal proceeding.

Justice Byron White's opinion for the 5-4 majority in *Branzburg v. Hayes* began by asserting that the First Amendment needs to protect newsgathering. "[W]ithout some protection for seeking out the news, freedom of the press would be eviscerated," he wrote. But that protection did not exempt reporters from providing evidence to grand juries. The Court said that neither common law nor constitutional law favors the type of privilege the reporters were seeking, and most states at that time, as well as Congress, had declined to provide reporters with statutory protection.

The Court also found insufficient evidence for the claim that lack of a privilege would harm relationships between reporters and sources, for instances of reporters being forced to testify were rare and were unlikely to deter sources. It also noted that the press had flourished throughout American history without a common law or constitutional privilege, and it dismissed the concern that the number of subpoenas had increased in recent years, saying that such concerns were "treacherous grounds" on which to build a constitutional privilege.

Justices also were concerned by practical aspects of the reporters' claims to a First Amendment privilege. For one thing, how would lower courts determine who would be entitled to it? The "liberty of the press is the right of the lonely pamphleteer who uses carbon paper or a mimeograph just as much as the large metropolitan publisher who utilizes the latest photocomposition methods." Justice White wrote that press freedom is an individual right that does not belong just to the institutional press. The functions that reporters perform, he said, are "also performed by lecturers, political pollsters, novelists, academic researchers and dramatists." The majority also worried that the type of qualified privilege the reporters sought would force courts to engage in complicated calculations about whether government interests were compelling or evidence was relevant. Such issues not only would bog down the courts but raised serious questions about judges second-guessing legislatures about which crimes were most important.

Although the majority rejected a constitutional privilege that would protect journalists who witnessed crimes from testifying before grand juries, it noted that Congress and the state legislatures were free to create such a right by statute. Also, the majority said it had no power to prevent state courts from recognizing a privilege under the free-press guarantees in state constitutions. The Court concluded with a warning to prosecutors and judges that the decision did not mean that it was open season on journalists and their sources: "We do not expect courts will forget that grand juries must operate within the limits of the First Amendment as well as the Fifth."

In what proved to be a pivotal concurring opinion, Justice Lewis Powell, who had voted with the majority, said he wanted "to emphasize what seems to me to be the limited nature of the Court's holding." He favored a case-by-case balancing of the competing interests between law enforcement and journalists. Such balancing should occur, he wrote, when a journalist is called to provide testimony "bearing only a remote and tenuous relationship to the subject of the investigation," or if the journalist reasonably believed the testimony would not fulfill "a legitimate need of law enforcement."

In a strongly worded dissenting opinion, Justice William O. Douglas advocated an absolute privilege that would bar the government from subpoenaing a journalist unless the reporter was suspected of a crime, in which case the Fifth Amendment would protect the journalist from self-incrimination. Justice Douglas argued that a free press was essential to self-government and that the majority opinion would interfere with the public's right to know. "The press has a preferred position in our constitutional scheme, not to enable it to make money, not to set newsmen apart as a favored class, but to bring fulfillment to the public's right to know," he wrote.

Justice Potter Stewart, writing in dissent for himself and Justices William Brennan and Thurgood Marshall, complained that the majority had adopted a "crabbed view of the First Amendment." He wrote that the majority opinion would allow government officials "to undermine the historic independence of the press by attempting to annex the journalistic profession as an investigative arm of government." Also, he wrote, the majority opinion would interfere with "the broad societal interest in a full and free flow of information to the public."

"Simple logic," Justice Stewart wrote, showed that confidential sources were necessary to the press's proper functioning. Journalists could not gather news without informants, he wrote, and confidentiality was necessary to maintain relationships with informants. An unchecked government subpoena power, he added, not only would deter sources from talking to reporters but also would deter reporters from pursuing stories that likely would land them in front of grand juries.

Although Justice Stewart shared many of Justice Douglas's concerns about the impact of the majority opinion, he did not go so far as to advocate an absolute privilege. Instead, he argued that the government's subpoena power in regard to the press should be limited by requiring the government to show, before enforcing a subpoena, that

- There is probable cause to believe the reporter had "clearly relevant" information about a crime;
- The information could not be obtained elsewhere; and
- The government had a "compelling and overriding interest in the information."

Aftermath of Branzburg

One result of the Supreme Court's Branzburg ruling was a sharp increase in the number of subpoenas served on the news media. A series of surveys of news organizations conducted from the late 1980s through 2001 by the Reporters Committee for Freedom of the Press found that the responding news organizations reported between 820 and 4,500 subpoenas per year, depending upon how many media outlets responded to the survey. A more recent study by law professor RonNell Andersen Jones had similar findings, with news organizations reporting more than 3,000 subpoenas nationwide in one year.

However, only 3 to 5 percent of the subpoenas issued to news organizations sought the names of confidential sources, according to the RCFP studies. Most subpoenas sought copies of stories already published or aired.

There is no record to indicate that any of the reporters in the Branzburg case ever testified before a grand jury.

Caldwell predicted in a magazine article shortly after the Court issued its decision that it would mean the end of investigative reporting because no source could ever trust that a reporter would protect his identity. But soon afterward, the Watergate scandal that forced President Richard Nixon to resign in 1974 broke open with the help of Washington Post reporters Carl Bernstein and Bob Woodward and their confidential sources, to whom they dedicated their book All the President's Men. They were able to protect the identity of their most famous source, known as "Deep Throat," for more than thirty years before former FBI deputy director Mark Felt voluntarily identified himself.

While Watergate would seem to vindicate the Supreme Court majority's view that the press would continue to flourish without a constitutional privilege, something more complicated was actually going on. Lower federal courts began ruling, within months of the Branzburg decision, that the decision created, or allowed the creation of, a qualified constitutional or common law journalist's privilege. For example, the Second U.S. Circuit Court of Appeals ruled in 1972 that a journalist did not have to reveal his source for a story about shady real estate deals to one of the parties involved in a civil lawsuit over the deals. The appellate court in Baker v. F & F Investments determined that Branzburg was not directly controlling because it dealt with grand jury subpoenas rather than a civil dispute. The appellate panel wrote that the First Amendment did not allow either direct or indirect stifling of the press absent a "compelling concern" that did not exist in the case.

In an attempt to explain how *Branzburg* could be a victory for the press, First Amendment lawyer James Goodale wrote in 1975 that the Douglas and Stewart dissents and Justice Powell's call for a case-by-case balancing of interests, particularly if the information sought was irrelevant to an investigation, amounted to a plurality endorsement of a qualified journalist's privilege except in cases where grand juries sought eyewitness testimony about crime. Similarly, Justice Stewart, in a 1974 law school speech that was published as a law review article in 1975, suggested that the "enigmatic" Powell concurrence created a "four and a half to four and a half" decision, leaving *Branzburg's* interpretation open.

Another development in 1975 further complicated lower courts' attempts to determine journalists' rights to protect sources. Congress approved a new evidence code for the federal courts that included a rule about how courts should determine the legitimacy of a privilege claim by a prospective witness. Instead of specifically adopting most of the privileges commonly recognized by state laws, Congress instead instructed the federal courts to adhere to "the principles of the common law as they may be interpreted by the courts of the United States in the light of reason and experience." Rule 501 left the question of whether journalists had a privilege allowing them to protect sources up to the courts to decide on a circuit-by-circuit basis.

As a result, most federal appellate circuits have recognized a qualified privilege grounded in the First Amendment when journalists are subpoenaed to testify in civil or criminal cases. Federal courts generally have agreed, however, that there is no privilege when a journalist is subpoenaed by a properly convened grand jury investigating a specific crime. The Third Circuit has grounded the privilege its judges have recognized in common law rather than the First Amendment, and the Sixth has flatly rejected the existence of a constitutional privilege, saying that the Supreme Court in *Branzburg* foreclosed any recognition of such a privilege. The Seventh Circuit, in a 2003 case to be discussed in more detail later in this chapter, rejected a privilege for non-confidential information and expressed skepticism about a privilege for confidential material.

The development of the qualified constitutional privilege in federal appellate circuits has been uneven at best, but it is possible to identify some common questions that have arisen in litigation over reporters' rights. These questions deal with who may claim the privilege, how the privilege is qualified, in what types of proceedings the privilege applies, and what types of information are protected.

Who Is a Journalist?

Surprisingly, given the concern that the *Branzburg* court expressed about defining who would be protected by a journalist's

privilege, the issue has rarely arisen in federal appellate courts. To the extent that it has, the courts have developed a requirement that those claiming the privilege show that they gathered the information being subpoenaed for the purpose of disseminating it to the public and while engaged in investigative journalism. The federal circuits have found that the privilege could protect the sources and work of a nonfiction book author and a documentary filmmaker. The courts have rejected privilege claims by the host of a hotline about professional wrestling who admitted he was more entertainer than journalist and a woman who gathered information to help her partner's defense in a criminal trial before deciding to write a book.

The case of Julian Assange, founder of the controversial Web site Wikileaks, has spurred considerable debate about who is or is not a journalist. In 2019, he was indicted on seventeen counts of violating the Espionage Act by obtaining and publishing classified material leaked by a former Army intelligence analyst. Journalists disagree on whether Assange is a journalist, although he has worked with news organizations in the past. There was broader agreement that the prosecution could open the door to criminalizing the publishing of news based on leaked classified material — which journalists regularly do. A London court denied his latest appeal of his extradition in June 2023, but it was still pending at this writing.

How Is the Privilege Qualified?

Appellate courts generally have used Justice Stewart's three-part *Branzburg* test in balancing the interests of journalists and those seeking the names of confidential sources. It requires someone subpoenaing the press to show that the information is relevant to the legal question at hand, important to resolving the question and unavailable from other sources.

The third part of the test has led to disagreements among the circuits. The Second Circuit has indicated that a party seeking to unmask a confidential source must first exhaust all other sources for the information before seeking it from a reporter. The District of Columbia Circuit Court of Appeals, however, has said that a litigant must only exhaust all *reasonable* alternative sources. In a 2005 case, Wen Ho Lee, a former government scientist seeking the identities of federal employees who leaked information about him to the press, persuaded the D.C. Circuit to allow him to depose reporters who wrote about the espionage case against him. The court ruled for Lee even though he had only been able to depose twenty of the hundreds of possible sources for the stories about him. The court found that twenty was a reasonable number because many of the possible sources had claimed that national security or other considerations prevented them from testifying.

In What Types of Proceedings Does the Privilege Apply?

Federal appellate courts are more likely to find that a qualified constitutional privilege exists when journalists are subpoenaed to testify in civil instead of criminal cases. The Sixth Amendment guarantees criminal defendants the right to a fair trial, and the government's interest in protecting citizens against crime is a strong counter-argument to a journalist's desire to protect sources. While the Seventh Amendment protects the right to a jury trial in civil cases, its protection does not extend as far as the Sixth Amendment and does not set up the same type of conflict with the journalist's privilege.

The number of privilege cases heard since *Branzburg* varies widely from circuit to circuit. In some circuits an appellate court might never have been asked to decide if a privilege applied in a particular type of proceeding. Privilege has been recognized in civil cases by the First, Second, Third, Fourth, Fifth, Eighth, Ninth, Tenth, Eleventh, and District of Columbia circuits.

The Second, Third, Eleventh and District of Columbia circuit courts have recognized a constitutional privilege in criminal cases. One example is *United States v. Burke,* a 1983 case in which the Second Circuit, using the Stewart three-part test, determined that a criminal defendant had failed to show a need for documents from *Sports Illustrated* related to a story about his alleged part in a college basketball point-shaving scheme.

There is some disagreement among the circuits about whether a journalist may rely on the privilege in a libel suit if the journalist or the journalist's employer is the defendant. In 2000, the First Circuit held the plaintiff might have been able to prove actual malice because of the defendant's failure to reveal a source, but the question was moot because the jury determined that the plaintiff had not proven that the statements about him were false and defamatory. However, the Fourth Circuit, in 1986, applied the Stewart three-part test in a libel case against NBC and denied politician Lyndon LaRouche's subpoena for the names of sources the network used, finding he had not exhausted alternative ways to find the information.

Further complicating the law in regard to libel cases is *Herbert v. Lando,* a 1979 Supreme Court decision in which the justices held that libel defendants do not have a First Amendment right to refuse to testify about their state of mind or editorial process in the preparation of an allegedly defamatory story. A good rule of thumb would be to assume that a court will be reluctant to give defendants a major advantage by allowing them to conceal their sources for potentially libelous material.

What Types of Information Are Protected?

There is general consensus among most federal appellate circuits that journalists have the limited right to conceal confidential sources from civil litigants, criminal prosecutors, criminal defendants or all three. There is less consensus regarding non-confidential materials such as unpublished photographs, unaired television footage, and notes.

In 1988, in *United States v. LaRouche Campaign,* the First Circuit Court of Appeals ordered NBC to comply with a subpoena from a criminal defendant for outtakes of its interview with a leading witness in a pending criminal case. Although the court ruled against the network, it agreed that four of NBC's arguments for refusing to turn over non-confidential material were valid. NBC argued that disclosure would:

• Raise the threat of government interference in the news-gathering process;
• Make NBC appear to be an investigative arm of the court;
• Serve as a disincentive for networks to gather and maintain unaired material; and
• Place an undue burden on employees' time and resources.

The court acknowledged that there was a "lurking and subtle threat" to journalists if forced disclosure of their materials became the norm, but it determined that the defendant's due process and fair trial rights overcame NBC's objections.

NBC's arguments in *LaRouche v. NBC* neatly summarize the concerns journalists and their employers have raised in fighting disclosures of their work products. Federal appellate circuits have split almost evenly in determining whether the First Amendment protects non-confidential material from disclosure. The Second, Third and Ninth circuits agree that non-confidential material is protected, although to a lesser extent than confidential material. The Second Circuit is the only federal appellate court that has developed a specific test for determining whether non-confidential material must be disclosed. In *Gonzales v. NBC,* the court held that when non-confidential material is subpoenaed, a court should weigh whether the information is of likely relevance to the underlying case and is not reasonably obtainable elsewhere. This approach differs from the Stewart three-part test requiring a clear showing of relevance and the exhaustion of alternative means of obtaining the information, which the Second Circuit has adopted in cases involving confidential sources.

The Fifth and Seventh circuits have held that subpoenas for non-confidential information raise no First Amendment concerns in criminal cases. In a 1998 case, a Fifth Circuit panel rejected a television station's attempt to quash subpoenas from both the prosecution and defense for outtakes of interviews with an arson suspect, finding that there was no threat that sources would dry up if the material was disclosed.

The Fourth Circuit rejected reporters' arguments against disclosure in *In re Shain,* a criminal case involving a state senator accused of taking bribes who had given interviews to the reporters, finding that no legitimate First Amendment concerns were implicated. However, a Fourth Circuit panel one year later upheld a lower court's decision in a civil suit to quash a subpoena for reporters' notes from an interview with a named source.

Cracks in the Privilege

Since the early 2000s, journalists have lost several high-profile attempts to protect confidential source identities. The cause of the losing streak is debatable but most likely can be traced to a combination of bad facts and increasing judicial impatience with uncooperative journalists.

The first case involved a terrorism trial in Northern Ireland. Three reporters who had interviewed an American informant in the Real IRA group for newspaper stories and a potential book fought a subpoena for their interview tapes. Michael McKevitt, the leader of the Real IRA, was facing trial for his alleged role in a bombing that killed twenty-eight people, and the informant was expected to be the star witness against him. McKevitt's attorneys hoped that statements to reporters by the informant, whose identity had been published, would impeach his testimony at trial.

A U.S. district court judge in Chicago ordered the reporters to comply with the subpoena, and they subsequently lost their appeal to the Seventh Circuit. Judge Richard Posner wrote in the Seventh Circuit's 2003 opinion in *McKevitt v. Pallasch* that the reporters had no First Amendment interests to protect given that the source was known and did not object to the tapes being used at trial.

The opinion questioned the wisdom of recognizing any type of journalist's privilege under federal law in the wake of *Branzburg*. Judge Posner wrote that federal courts that had recognized a constitutional privilege for confidential sources had acted surprisingly and audaciously, given the ruling in *Branzburg*. Those that had extended the privilege to non-confidential material were, Posner wrote, "skating on thin ice."

A year later, Providence, R.I., TV station WJAR aired a tape allegedly showing a city official accepting a bribe. An undercover informant had recorded the tape, which was part of the federal government's evidence in an upcoming corruption trial involving the mayor and other officials. A special prosecutor subpoenaed reporter James Taricani to testify about his source for the tape, which was supposed to be sealed until the trial. Taricani refused to cooperate, was found in civil contempt and was ordered to pay $1,000 a day until he named the source.

The First Circuit Court of Appeals denied Taricani's appeal, determining that the special prosecutor's investigation into the leak was similar enough to a grand jury investigation that *Branzburg* precluded any privilege. The station continued paying the fine for nearly three months before the district court judge recalled Taricani for a hearing on whether he should be found in criminal contempt. While Taricani was awaiting the hearing, his source, an attorney for one of the corruption defendants, came forward and admitted supplying the tape to Taricani. Although the source's identity had become known, the judge still found Taricani guilty of criminal contempt and sentenced him to six months of house arrest.

The case that garnered the most attention in the post-McKevitt era involved *New York Times* reporter Judith Miller and *Time* magazine reporter Matthew Cooper. The case began after Joseph Wilson, a former American ambassador to Iraq, wrote an op-ed column in the *Times* saying the government had sent him to Africa to check out reports that Iraq was trying to obtain yellow cake uranium, an ingredient used to make nuclear weapons. Wilson wrote that he found no evidence to back up the reports, but the George W. Bush Administration nevertheless cited the reports in justifying the decision to invade Iraq in 2003.

After Wilson's column appeared, syndicated columnist Robert Novak wrote that two administration officials told him that Wilson was married to a CIA operative named Valerie Plame. The motive for the leak was not entirely clear, although Wilson claimed the administration ruined his wife's career at the CIA to get back at him for questioning the motives for the Iraq invasion. What was clear was that the leak of an undercover intelligence operative's name to the press was a possible violation of federal law. A special federal prosecutor was named to look into the leak, which went to other journalists besides Novak.

Miller, who never wrote about Plame, and Cooper were subpoenaed to testify about who gave them Plame's name, but they refused to cooperate. Eventually, a three-judge panel of the D.C. Circuit Court of Appeals ruled unanimously that no common-law privilege protected the two reporters from testifying, although the three judges differed on whether such a privilege might exist under other circumstances. The Supreme Court denied certiorari.

Cooper and Miller continued to refuse to testify, but on the day that they were to be sentenced to jail for contempt, *Time* editor Norman Pearlstine gave the court Cooper's notes and email messages regarding his source. Pearlstine had decided that it was futile to keep fighting after the Supreme Court refused to hear the case. Miller continued to resist, however, and served eighty-five days in jail before her source, I. Lewis "Scooter" Libby, chief of staff to Vice President Dick Cheney, released her from her promise not to name him. Libby was eventually convicted of lying to investigators about his role in the leak of Plame's identity, but President Bush commuted his prison sentence. Novak, who died in 2009, identified his sources to authorities as Deputy Secretary of State Richard Armitage and Karl Rove, a political adviser to President Bush. Neither was charged with a crime. The only person to serve jail time over the leak was Miller.

At about the same time that the Miller case was capturing headlines, the Wen Ho Lee case mentioned earlier in this chapter was playing out in the federal courts in Washington, D.C. After being cleared of espionage charges that he had sold nuclear secrets to China while working at the Los Alamos weapons laboratory in New Mexico, Lee sued the Departments of Justice and Energy for violating the Privacy Act of 1974 by leaking information about him to the press. After failing to get anyone at either agency to admit to being the source of the leaks, he subpoenaed reporters from several news organizations to learn the identities of their sources.

Five reporters were found in contempt of court and ordered to pay fines of $500 a day until they complied, with the imposition of the fines delayed while they appealed. In 2005, the District of Columbia U.S. Court of Appeals dismissed the contempt citation against Jeff Gerth of the *New York Times,* finding he had no relevant evidence, but upheld the citations against James Risen of the *Times,* Bob Drogin of the *Los Angeles Times,* Josef Hebert of the Associated Press and Pierre Thomas of ABC. The appellate court determined that Lee had exhausted all other reasonable sources for the information. A sixth reporter, Walter Pincus of the *Washington Post,* lost his challenge to a subpoena from Lee in a district court ruling after the other reporters' appeal had failed. However, Lee reached a financial settlement with the government and, in an unusual move, also with the news organizations employing the subpoenaed reporters, ending his need for the reporters' testimony.

Judith Miller was a player in another case involving government subpoenas. After someone in federal law enforcement told her and *Times* reporter Philip Shenon that the government was investigating several Islamic charities in the United States with suspected ties to terrorists, a federal prosecutor subpoenaed a telephone company for *Times* phone records to learn who Miller and Shenon had talked to. The *Times* challenged the subpoenas, but the Second Circuit Court of Appeals ruled in 2006 that the newspaper had no standing to challenge a subpoena to a phone company, at least in this situation.

Also in 2006, a freelance video journalist in San Francisco lost in his attempt to avoid jail time for contempt after he refused to comply with a federal grand jury subpoena for outtakes of footage he shot at a political protest. The grand jury hoped Joshua Wolf's unaired video would help identify protesters who injured a police officer and tried to set fire to a police car.

The Ninth Circuit Court of Appeals, in rejecting Wolf's appeal, sidestepped the question of whether he would qualify as a "journalist" under the constitutional privilege. Instead, the court noted that he was resisting a grand jury subpoena, which meant that he had no privilege under *Branzburg* and Ninth Circuit precedent. Wolf ended up serving the longest jail term for contempt of any reporter in history — nearly seven and a half months — before he and prosecutors reached a deal in which he would turn over his outtakes in exchange for not being forced to testify before the grand jury.

Two other Bay Area reporters fared somewhat better, but only because their source came forward. Mark Fainaru-Wada and Lance Williams had written about steroid use among baseball players for the *San Francisco Chronicle* and in a book. Part of their reporting, however, was based on grand jury testimony from a federal investigation into the Bay Area Laboratory Cooperative, or BALCO, an alleged source of illegal steroids. A special prosecutor subpoenaed the reporters to learn the source of the grand jury transcripts, which were supposed to remain secret. A district court judge in 2006 ruled against the reporters in their challenge to the subpoena, noting that no other persons could identify the leaker.

While the reporters' appeal to the Ninth Circuit was pending, the source of the grand jury transcript stepped forward — an attorney for one of the people indicted in the case against BALCO, who admitted he hoped the leak would cause a mistrial in his client's case. The reporters' testimony was no longer required, and the subpoenas were withdrawn.

In a case similar to that of Wen Ho Lee, a former reporter subpoenaed in another Privacy Act lawsuit briefly faced the possibility of financial ruin before a timely settlement was reached. Toni Locy, formerly of *USA Today,* refused to testify about her government sources for stories about Steven Hatfill, who was suing the government for leaking information about him to the press. Attorney General John Ashcroft publicly identified the scientist as a "person of interest" in the investigation into mailings of anthrax in 2001 to various politicians and journalists, resulting in five deaths. Hatfill was eventually cleared and sued the government for leaking information about him. After Locy refused to identify her sources for stories she wrote about the anthrax investigation, a federal judge ordered her to pay progressively higher fines that would total $45,000 in three weeks. Judge Reggie Walton, in an unusual twist, also ordered that she pay the fines personally rather than having her former employer do so. While Locy's appeal was pending, however, Hatfill and the government reached a multi-million-dollar settlement, ending the need for her testimony.

While the losses, jail sentences and threats of heavy fines greatly concerned journalists, the outcomes of the cases likely were affected by questionable behavior by the sources and the journalists involved. The sources in the Taricani and BALCO cases turned out to be attorneys who were under court order not to reveal evidence in pending cases. The sources in the Miller and Cooper case violated federal law, possibly for political revenge, in revealing the identity of an undercover intelligence officer. The sources who leaked information to reporters about the Lee and Hatfill investigations did considerable damage to each man's reputation while hiding their own identities.

Also, it should be noted that several of the cases involved grand jury or special prosecutor subpoenas, which fall under the holding in *Branzburg.* In the Lee and Hatfill cases, judges used the Stewart three-part test to weigh the competing interests, and while the test often favors journalists subpoenaed in civil cases, it is not a guarantee of victory.

National Security and the Privilege

National security issues were involved in several of the cases mentioned in the previous section, including the two involving Judith Miller. It should come as no surprise that national security issues have become particularly sensitive since the terrorist attacks of September 11, 2001, making it harder for journalists to fight subpoenas for sources of classified information.

In 2012, Attorney General Eric Holder announced that he was naming two federal prosecutors to look into leaks of classified information to the press about the death of terrorist leader Osama bin Laden and other clandestine operations. The *New York Times* noted that the Obama Administration had in three years already prosecuted more government employees for leaking information to the media than all previous administrations combined. In 2013, former CIA operative John Kiriakou became the first representative of that agency to go to jail for leaking information to a reporter.

So far, only one journalist has been subpoenaed in relation to the leak prosecutions. James Risen, a *New York Times* reporter and author of the book *State of War,* was subpoenaed to testify in the trial of former CIA employee Jeffrey Sterling, who was suspected of being a source for Risen's book chapter about an unsuccessful clandestine operation to sabotage Iran's suspected nuclear weapons development. Risen fought the subpoena, but the Fourth U.S. Circuit Court of Appeals ruled that there was no privilege when a reporter witnessed criminal activity (in this case, revealing classified information), citing *Branzburg.* The Supreme Court denied certiorari. Holder told reporters after the Fourth Circuit decision that "no reporter who is doing his job is going to jail" while Holder was in office. The government and the defense later dropped attempts to force Risen to testify about his sources at Sterling's trial. Sterling was convicted of disclosing classified information and sentenced to forty-two months in prison.

The fact that more reporters were not subpoenaed in the Obama leak investigations is somewhat surprising because journalists are often the most direct witnesses to leaks. Some press advocates fear that the relative lack of journalists being subpoenaed in recent years only means that the government no longer needs to subpoena them. Lucy Dalglish, then executive director of the Reporters Committee for Freedom of the Press, told an interviewer in 2012 that she believed the government had honed its ability to track emails, phone calls and other communications and thus no longer needed to subpoena reporters in leak investigations because it could find out to whom they were talking without their testimony. Later revelations by Edward Snowden about the National Security Agency's widespread ability to tap the phone calls and Internet traffic of citizens seemed to bear out those concerns.

In 2013, the Associated Press learned that federal investigators had secretly examined the records of twenty phone lines used by reporters and editors at the news agency, apparently in response to a story about the CIA's successful operation to stop a terrorist attack on an airliner. The Associated Press said the seizure of the phone records was a "serious interference with A.P.'s constitutional rights to gather and report the news."

At about the same time, Fox News expressed outrage that Justice Department investigators had conducted expansive surveillance of Fox reporter James Rosen and had named him as a possible leak co-conspirator in the affidavit it used in court to request access to email records of Rosen and his alleged source. The affidavit noted that Rosen and a source in the State Department allegedly giving him information about North Korea's nuclear program often entered and left the source's office building about the same time.

President Donald Trump and Attorney General Jeff Sessions publicly stated early in the Trump Administration that they planned to be tough on people who leaked classified information to the press. Early in Trump's presidency, former NSA contractor Reality Winner was charged with revealing classified information after *The Intercept*, an online publication, reported that the NSA had discovered that Russian military intelligence had launched a cyber attack against an American voting-software supplier. Winner pleaded guilty to a single charge in 2018 and was sentenced to sixty-three months in prison, an unusually long sentence for a leaker.

Also in 2018, James A. Wolfe, a former security director for the Senate Select Intelligence Committee, was indicted for allegedly lying to investigators about his contacts with reporters. To support their case, investigators cited phone and e-mail records of Wolfe and several reporters, including Ali Watkins of the *New York Times*, with whom Wolfe once had a personal relationship. Authorities also cited messages Wolfe sent to reporters through encrypted messaging apps. The information Wolfe allegedly passed along included the names of witnesses the committee was interviewing privately about alleged Trump campaign officials' ties to Russia. He pleaded guilty in 2018 to one count of lying to the Federal Bureau of Investigation and was sentenced to two months in prison.

Press and human rights organizations are becoming increasingly concerned about the ability and willingness of governments worldwide to identify journalists' sources through electronic surveillance. A UNESCO report in 2017 warned that protections for journalists and their sources were eroding because of national security fears and mass surveillance. In the United States, the Stored Communication Act allows federal investigators to access email, cloud storage and other records through court-issued or administrative warrants or subpoenas. Additionally, an agency seeking such records can issue a notice preclusion order that bars the service provider served with the warrant from notifying its customers that their records are being seized. Additionally, federal law allows the FBI to issue administrative subpoenas called national security letters to service providers to seize electronic records, also without notice to the provider's affected customers.

In 2021, the Biden administration revealed that the Justice Department under former President Trump had seized phone and e-mail records of journalists working for the *Washington Post*, *New York Times*, and CNN without notifying the media outlets. President Joe Biden, who succeeded Trump in 2021, condemned the seizures of reporters' records. The seizures were apparently tied to several leak investigations.

To combat the concerns about surveillance, some news organizations are encouraging sources to use encrypted messaging apps like Signal and WhatsApp to communicate with journalists. As the Wolfe case demonstrates, however, those apps are also vulnerable if users fail to take precautions to hide their activity or if they allow the apps to automatically upload and archive their messages to the cloud. Some news organizations have created links on their Web sites to software called SecureDrop, which hides the identities of people uploading sensitive files not only from investigators but from reporters on the receiving end. Early adopters have so far found no major vulnerabilities associated with SecureDrop, but it is somewhat complicated to install and use and can be expensive.

The bottom line is that technology has made it easier for authorities to uncover confidential sources without alerting journalists but has also made it easier to conceal sources.

State Common Law and Constitutional Privileges

Eight states have no statutory privileges, but state appellate court rulings in all but Mississippi and Wyoming have found that there is a qualified journalist's privilege based on the courts' interpretations of the First Amendment, state constitutions, common law or some combination of the three.

Courts in Iowa and New Hampshire have stated that the qualified privilege in those states was rooted in the free press guarantees of their state constitutions. Missouri and Virginia courts have based their findings on the First Amendment. The Idaho Supreme Court found support for the privilege in both the federal and state constitutions, while the Massachusetts privilege is based on the Supreme Judicial Court's interpretation of state common law.

STATUTORY PRIVILEGE

Because the U.S. Constitution is the supreme law of the land,

one who asserts a right to do or not do something would naturally prefer to have that right enshrined as constitutional. The supremacy of the Constitution accounts to some extent for the continued insistence of journalists that their right to refuse to comply with subpoenas is protected by the Constitution despite the holding in *Branzburg*.

If a right has no constitutional basis or an unsettled one, the next best solution is often a statute. For journalists, seeking legislation that gives them a right to protect their sources and work product has a long tradition. Maryland passed the first state shield law in 1896, and while other states were slow to follow suit, the *Branzburg* decision and later controversies such as the Judith Miller cases have led thirty-nine states and the District of Columbia to follow Maryland's lead. Additionally, two states, New Mexico and Utah, have established the same protection through the adoption of formal court rules. New Mexico's courts did so after the state supreme court declared the state's statutory shield unconstitutional. Hawaii is the most recent state whose legislature has approved a shield statute, which Gov. Josh Green signed in June 2023. Wyoming's legislature considered a shield law in 2021 and 2023, but it did not pass. There also have been numerous efforts over the years to pass a federal shield law, all unsuccessful.

Shield laws have both advantages and disadvantages in relation to constitutional privileges.

Advantages:

• Legislatures can define classes of persons — such as journalists — to favor, as long as by doing so they do not strip others of their constitutional rights.

• Courts can often take years, even decades, to fully develop the parameters of constitutional rights. Legislatures can move much more quickly, if they choose to do so.

• Legislatures can amend shield laws to take account of new technologies or controversies more quickly than the courts can react to the same issues.

Disadvantages:

• Courts tend to interpret shield laws narrowly because they conflict with the need to present all relevant information in trials and other legal proceedings. This makes it unlikely that a court will protect a journalist in a way that the legislature did not clearly anticipate when it wrote the statute.

• The ability of legislatures to amend shield laws quickly could also work against journalists if lawmakers come under pressure from police or other citizens to limit journalists' rights for some reason.

• A statutory privilege generally will give way to a conflicting constitutional right, such as the Sixth Amendment right to a fair trial for a criminal defendant, instead of being balanced on a case-by-case basis.

State shield laws vary widely, as might be expected, but all of them share three basic characteristics. They define:

• Whom the laws protect;

• What the laws protect, such as confidential source identities and unpublished non-confidential information; and

• How the protection is qualified, sometimes by omission.

JURISDICTIONS WITH SHIELD LAWS

Alabama   Alaska   Arizona   Arkansas   California Colorado   Connecticut   Delaware   District of Columbia   Florida Georgia   Hawaii   Illinois   Indiana   Kansas   Kentucky   Louisiana   Maine   Maryland   Michigan   Minnesota   Montana   Nebraska   Nevada   New Jersey   New Mexico   New York   North Carolina   North Dakota   Ohio   Oklahoma   Oregon   Pennsylvania   Rhode Island   South Carolina   South Dakota Tennessee   Texas   Utah   Vermont   Washington   West Virginia Wisconsin

Who Is Protected? Shield laws generally define "journalist" or similar terms by what the covered person does, what type of entity the person works for, or both. Some states are not specific about who is protected. For example, Michigan's shield law defines a covered person as a "reporter or other person who is involved in the gathering or preparation of news for broadcast or publication." Connecticut, on the other hand, defines a covered person as someone working for

any newspaper, magazine or other periodical, book publisher, news agency, wire service, radio or television station or network, cable or satellite or other transmission system or carrier, or channel or programming service for such station, network, system or carrier, or audio or audiovisual production company that disseminates information to the public, whether by print, broadcast, photographic, mechanical, electronic or any other means or medium.

The shield laws in Delaware, Florida, Indiana, Texas and West Virginia require that the person claiming protection must be earning income from journalism. The Indiana statute, for example, states that a covered person is someone "who receives or has received income" from engaging in journalistic activity. Such a requirement could make it difficult for bloggers, freelancers and student journalists to claim protection under the statute. By contrast, Maryland's legislature recently changed that state's shield law to protect student journalists specifically. West Virginia's relatively new law has an exception to its income requirement for student reporters who meet all other qual-

ifications for the statute's definition of "reporter."

How a shield statute defines who is protected can be problematic if the definition is too narrow, which may explain why some states define "journalist" broadly and others very specifically. As new media emerge, broad definitions may give courts more leeway in deciding who qualifies. A specific definition can avoid courts defining the covered person too narrowly, however, as long as the list of eligible media employees is inclusive.

The narrowness of some statutory definitions of covered persons has led to bizarre outcomes. In 1986, the Michigan Court of Appeals ruled that a television reporter was not protected by the shield law as then written (it was later amended) because it referred only to print media reporters. More recently, the Eleventh U.S. Circuit Court of Appeals, in a diversity jurisdiction case, ruled that a writer for *Sports Illustrated* was not protected by the Alabama shield law because the law did not specifically mention magazines.

In 2022, a unique issue arose when Las Vegas *Review-Journal* investigative reporter Jeff German was found stabbed to death outside his home. Police seized all of his computers, phones, and other electronic devices as evidence, leading his employer to move to block investigators from searching the devices out of fear that confidential sources German used would be revealed, including police officers. The case raised the question of whether the state's strong shield law protected the sources of a deceased journalist. After months of legal haggling, the newspaper and the defendant — a county official who was the target of a German investigation — agreed in May 2023 to the appointment of a special master to examine German's devices to determine what was relevant to the criminal case.

What Is Protected? Twelve of the forty-three shield laws refer only to confidential sources or information in the statutory language. Those twelve are in Alabama, Alaska, Arizona, Arkansas, Illinois, Indiana, Kentucky, Maine, New Mexico, Ohio, Pennsylvania and Rhode Island. Fairly typical is the Kentucky shield law, which states that "[n]o person shall be compelled to disclose ... the source of any information procured or obtained" through journalistic work.

In the other states and the District of Columbia, journalists are protected not only from having to disclose the names of confidential sources but also from having to disclose other information obtained through newsgathering activities. Again, the definitions vary widely from the broad to the specific. The Tennessee statute, for example, simply states that a journalist does not have to disclose any information. At the other extreme, the Colorado shield law defines protected "news information" as "any knowledge, observation, notes, documents, photographs, films, recordings, videotapes, audiotapes, and reports, and the contents and sources thereof." However, the Colorado statute excludes information gathered at a news conference, published or broadcast, or based on a journalist's personal observation of the commission of a crime. Like the Colorado statute, most shield laws either explicitly or implicitly exclude published or broadcast materials from protection.

Journalists fighting subpoenas in state courts raise most of the same concerns mentioned earlier in regard to federal courts. However, news organizations and amici curiae raised a relatively novel argument in 2020: that subpoenas for unpublished images from a Seattle civil-rights protest could put journalists in danger at future protests. Seattle police sought unaired footage and unpublished photographs from five news organizations after a racial-justice protest turned violent. The news organizations argued that being forced to provide evidence to the police would make journalists appear to be in collusion with law enforcement, which could lead protesters to attack photographers at future protests to avoid being identified. A superior court judge rejected the media's motion to quash the subpoena, but the police withdrew the subpoena after the Washington Supreme Court indicated it would hear the media's appeal.

How Is the Protection Limited? About a quarter of the shield laws are written in such a way that they could be read as absolute prohibitions on forcing journalists to reveal sources or other information. Statutes in Alabama, Arizona, California, Indiana, Kentucky, Montana, Nebraska, Nevada, New York (for confidential material only), Oregon, Pennsylvania, South Dakota, Texas (for civil cases only) and Vermont (for confidential material only) have no qualifying language.

However, the fact that a shield law does not have qualifying language does not mean reporters will never be ordered to testify or turn over information they have gathered. Even absolute shield laws can be balanced against other statutes or constitutional rights. In California, for example, the state supreme court in 1990 ruled that a reporter and photographer who witnessed an arrest had to testify for the defense at the subsequent trial. Although California is the only state in which the shield law is also part of the state constitution, the court held that in this case the defendant's Sixth Amendment rights outweighed the reporters' rights. In the same year, however, the California Supreme Court ruled that reporters had an absolute right to refuse to testify or provide evidence in a civil case.

Most states with shield laws and court rules protecting reporters use some variation of the Stewart three-part test to provide exceptions to the right to protect sources and work product. Arkansas, however, protects reporters unless it is shown that information from the source was published "in bad faith, with malice, and not in the interest of the public welfare." Alaska's shield law says the privilege can be overcome if it is shown that withholding the information would "result in a miscarriage of justice or the denial of a fair trial" or would "be contrary to the public interest."

Several shield laws have provisions that make it difficult for a journalist to protect a source while relying on information from that source as a defense in a defamation case. Shield laws in Colorado, Louisiana, Minnesota, Oklahoma, Oregon and Tennessee say that a journalist may not simultaneously claim that the journalist got defamatory information from a reliable source and then refuse to identify that source.

In Massachusetts, which does not have a shield law, a judge entered a default judgment against the *Boston Globe* in a defamation and invasion of privacy suit when the paper refused to reveal its confidential sources to the plaintiff. The Massachusetts Supreme Judicial Court affirmed the $2.1 million award to a doctor implicated by the paper in the chemotherapy overdose death of a *Globe* columnist.

Are Bloggers Journalists? One question that has arisen is whether non-traditional communicators, such as bloggers and people who publish online magazines, or e-zines, may claim the same rights as mainstream journalists, including rights conveyed by shield laws. The answer is still unclear, in part because not many courts have dealt with the question.

In 2006, the California Court of Appeals ruled that the publishers of an online news magazine devoted to Apple electronic products did not have to comply with subpoenas from Apple seeking the identities of people who leaked information to the e-zines about upcoming products. The court, in *O'Grady v. Superior Court,* found there was no "theoretical basis" for treating e-zine publishers differently than print media publishers protected by the state shield law. The New Hampshire Supreme Court came to a similar conclusion in regard to its state constitutional privilege, finding that a Web site that monitored mortgage lenders was a "reporter" for the purpose of the privilege. In Illinois, a judge in a case similar to the facts of *O'Grady* initially ruled that a Web site could not protect its source for images of an upcoming smart phone before reversing himself and finding that the site was eligible for shield-law protection.

However, courts in New Jersey and Oregon have found that bloggers who claimed protection under shield laws in those states did not qualify as news media or journalists under the statutes' definitions.

The New Jersey Supreme Court determined that a blogger being sued for libel over allegations of illegal activity by a company that provided services to pornographers did not have a sufficient journalism background or affiliation to claim protection under the state shield law. In a similar case, a federal district court judge in Oregon found that a blogger who was sued for defamation by a financial services company and one of its employees was not affiliated with the types of media covered in the shield law. Also, the court noted that the shield law specifically barred journalists from its protection when they were defendants in a libel case. The Ninth Circuit reversed and remanded parts of the lower court decision dealing with libel privileges but not the shield law ruling.

Cases like the ones in California, Illinois, New Jersey and Oregon, as well as the Julian Assange controversy mentioned earlier, are real-world examples of a philosophical debate about what constitutes "journalism" in a rapidly changing media landscape and who qualifies as a journalist and may claim privilege protection. One concern among commentators is that extending protections designed for traditional media employees to bloggers and other citizen journalists would make the privilege so broad that courts and legislators would be tempted to limit or eliminate it. Commentators have responded to the concern by either recommending that the privilege be limited to those who fit a somewhat narrow definition of "journalist" or extended to all of those who inform the public about important issues, including bloggers and other nontraditional journalists.

Anonymous Comments. A related debate has arisen about whether people who post anonymous comments on news organization Web sites should be protected by shield laws. The question has come up in a number of cases since 2008 in which potential libel plaintiffs, prosecutors and defense attorneys subpoenaed media Web sites for identifying information about people who commented on online stories.

Newspapers, like Web site operators, are considered "interactive service providers" protected from liability for their users' actions under Section 230 of the Communications Decency Act. Courts have developed tests to determine when ISPs must provide identifying information about their anonymous users, such as the Internet Protocol numbers of their computers or subscriber information. The tests that are most often cited were developed in *Doe v. Cahill* in Delaware and *Dendrite International v. Doe* in New Jersey. Both tests require someone wishing to force an ISP to unmask an anonymous user to notify the user that his or her identity is being sought and show that the libel case being considered is viable. Additionally, courts are expected to weigh a plaintiff's need for the information against the user's First Amendment right to engage in anonymous speech.

In cases that arose starting in 2008 in Florida, Illinois, Indiana, Montana, North Carolina and Texas, however, newspapers subpoenaed by libel plaintiffs, prosecutors and criminal defense attorneys claimed their state shield laws protected their users' identities. For the most part, courts agreed that newspaper users' identities were protected under the statutes or that the newspaper employees subpoenaed were "journalists" as defined by the shield laws.

However, a trial judge in Illinois determined that the shield law in that state probably did not apply to the identities of five commenters who responded to a story about the slaying of a child. Despite the judge's doubts, however, he determined that the *Alton Telegraph* would have to identify only two of the com-

menters, who appeared from their comments to have direct knowledge about the crime's suspect that prosecutors had a right to ask them about.

In the first case decided by a state appellate court, the Indiana Court of Appeals ruled that the state shield law did not apply to the identities of anonymous commenters. However, it said the trial judge in the libel case, in which the *Indianapolis Star* was not a party, should have used the Dendrite Test before ordering the paper to identify a commenter.

Critics of this use of the shield law argue, similar to critics of extending shield law protection to bloggers, that extending the definition of confidential source to include readers who comment on stories invites harsh reactions from legislators. Other critics, including some journalists and media attorneys, argue that it is wrong to equate the often uninformed or crude comments of readers with the type of information provided by confidential sources for investigative stories. It probably is also ethically unnecessary because most Web site user agreements warn comment posters that the Web site operator will not protect them from legal consequences of their posts. The counterargument is that journalists who value the First Amendment should not be in the business of withholding its protections from people they invite to their sites to enhance the public forum. At the least, some have argued that news organizations should protect the identities of posters whose comments have contributed materially to the reporting of a story, while directing other posters to the protection offered by the Dendrite Test.

A Federal Shield Law?

Because of the inconsistencies among federal appellate circuits about the level of protection journalists enjoy under the constitutional privilege, Congress has considered shield law bills a number of times. Legislative efforts picked up steam in the years immediately following *Branzburg*, when dozens of bills were introduced. However, disagreements among senators, representatives and journalists over the scope of the privilege and whether it was necessary derailed the efforts.

Interest in passing a shield law also increased in the wake of the Judith Miller and similar cases. In the 111th Congress, a bill that would have created a qualified journalist's privilege passed in the House by a wide margin. However, the Wikileaks Web site's disclosure of classified military and diplomatic communications raised fears that the shield law could protect sites like Wikileaks, leading to calls to amend the Senate version of the bill to exclude such sites from protection. Although Senate sponsors promised to amend the bill to allay administration concerns, it died without a vote. Under congressional rules, a bill that is not passed by both houses during a two-year session of Congress must start the legislative process from scratch in the next session.

A new version of the House bill was introduced in the 112th Congress but never got to a subcommittee vote. After news reports about the government's seizure of Associated Press phone records and about the surveillance of a Fox News reporter, mentioned earlier in this chapter, versions of a federal shield law bill were introduced in the House and Senate in 2013. The House bill would have protected persons who earned some portion of their incomes from gathering and reporting news. It would have exempted from protection anyone who possessed information that would threaten national security, reveal a trade secret or private information about a person, or that was needed to prevent serious injury or death. The Senate version would not have required someone to earn income from journalistic activity but contained fewer exemptions, although it also exempted persons with information about credible threats to national security or information that could prevent death or serious injury. Both versions of the bill would also have protected journalists from subpoenas for their phone and Internet use records. Neither version passed during the 113th Congress.

A House bill was introduced in the 115th Congress in 2017 that was identical to earlier successful House bills, but it did not pass, and no Senate companion bill was introduced. Identical bills were introduced in the House and Senate in the 117th Congress in 2021 and, notably, focused more on protecting journalists and sources from subpoenas for their electronic communication records than past versions. The House version passed unanimously in that chamber in 2022 but never came to a vote in the Senate. Senators and representatives from both major political parties announced in June 2023 that they were sponsoring the same bills for consideration in the 118th Congress.

Other Sources of Protection

Journalists, like all other persons, are protected under federal law from abusive or unreasonable subpoenas. Federal Rule of Criminal Procedure 17 (c), for example, allows courts to quash subpoenas if compliance would be "unreasonable or oppressive." Federal Rule of Civil Procedure 26 (c) allows federal courts to issue protective orders for witnesses if compliance with a subpoena would cause them "annoyance, embarrassment, oppression, or undue burden or expense." These and similar rules in the states can protect journalists even if the courts rule that the First Amendment does not.

In addition, the U.S. Department of Justice adopted guidelines in 1970 that are designed to make it harder for the department to subpoena journalists. The rule requires department attorneys to exhaust other sources before turning to the media and requires the attorney general's approval before a member of the news media is subpoenaed. The guidelines were amended in 2014 after media uproar over the AP phone records and Rosen incidents to make it harder for government attorneys to sub-

poena journalists and to require that the attorney general approve more of the subpoenas to journalists rather than lower-level Department of Justice officials.

The Biden administration has not followed the Obama and Trump administrations in aggressively prosecuting leakers of classified documents, and in 2022 Attorney General Merrick Garland announced another revision to the guidelines that would bar federal investigators from seizing reporters' communication records except in narrow emergency situations. The announcement came after President Biden condemned the Trump administration for secretly accessing records of reporters at the *New York Times, Washington Post,* and CNN.

LIABILITY FOR REVEALING A SOURCE

As we have seen, journalists often fight hard to avoid being forced to reveal confidential sources, even going to jail. But what happens when the opposite scenario occurs and journalists voluntarily reveal their sources after promising not to?

In *Cohen v. Cowles Media Co.,* the Supreme Court ruled in 1991 that the First Amendment did not bar sources from suing news organizations for revealing their identities.

The source in the case, Dan Cohen, was a public relations professional working for a candidate for lieutenant governor in Minnesota. After he gave reporters documents revealing that the opposing candidate had been arrested twice, reporters at the two major newspapers in the Twin Cities determined that the charges were minor and had been expunged from the candidate's record. Editors at the *Minneapolis Star-Tribune* and the *St. Paul Pioneer Press* then ordered the reporters to shift the focus of the story to Cohen's attempt to smear the candidate on the eve of the election and to name him as the source. Cohen was fired from his job after the stories appeared. He sued the newspapers for fraudulent misrepresentation and breach of contract and won $700,000 in damages. However, the Minnesota Court of Appeals and Minnesota Supreme Court reversed the trial court judgment. The Minnesota Supreme Court also speculated on whether Cohen could have prevailed on a legal theory known as *promissory estoppel* but also rejected that idea, finding that the First Amendment would bar holding the press liable for an editorial judgment as to what it should print.[1]

The U.S. Supreme Court reversed. While the newspapers argued that a judgment against them would violate the protections for publishing lawfully acquired, truthful information, the Court said it had doubts about whether Cohen's identity was lawfully obtained because the newspapers broke their promises

---

[1] Promissory estoppel is "[t]he principle that a promise made without consideration may nonetheless be enforced to prevent injustice if the promisor should have reasonably expected the promisee to rely on the promise and the promisee did actually rely on the promise to his or her detriment." BLACK'S LAW DICTIONARY 692-93 (11th ed. 2019).

of confidentiality. It also noted that the First Amendment does not immunize the press from "the incidental, and constitutionally insignificant" burdens associated with enforcing generally applicable laws, such as fraud and breach of contract.

Perhaps because breaking a promise of confidentiality raises serious ethical as well as legal issues, there have not been a large number of similar cases. In 1993, relying on *Cohen,* the Eighth U.S. Circuit Court of Appeals reinstated a lawsuit against a magazine publisher over a broken promise to a source. In *Ruzicka v. Conde Nast Publications, Inc.,* a woman sued after a writer promised to protect her identity if she agreed to be interviewed for a story about patients sexually abused by their therapists. Although her name was not used, she argued that she was still recognizable because of details the writer included in the story. In Georgia, a state appellate court upheld a judgment against a TV station in 1994 after it promised to digitally alter an AIDS victim's appearance in a story about the disease but failed to do so adequately to hide his identity. More recently, an online publication, *The Intercept,* volunteered to pay the legal expenses of Reality Winner, a former National Security Agency contractor, after journalists accidentally identified her to NSA employees while verifying information in docments she mailed anonymously. She was sentenced to 66 months in prison for leaking documents about a Russian attempt to hack into U.S. voting machines in 2016. She was released to a halfway house in 2021 and is now on probation.

Although the issue has apparently never been litigated, it would seem unlikely that a journalist could be sued successfully for identifying a source under court order and threat of a contempt citation.

SEARCH WARRANTS

While journalists regard subpoenas demanding that they reveal their sources or turn over unpublished information to be nuisances at best and threats to the First Amendment at worst, subpoenas generally provide enough time for challenges in court. Search warrants are more ominous. If a police officer arrives at the door with a valid search warrant, the warrant usually gives the officer the right to search physical and digital files immediately. Journalists fear that search warrants might be used for fishing expeditions through their files in search of source information.

In 1978, the Supreme Court ruled that nothing in either the First Amendment or the Fourth Amendment, which protects citizens against unreasonable searches and seizures, protects the news media from valid warrants. In *Zurcher v. Stanford Daily,* police in California served a search warrant at the Stanford University student newspaper looking for photographs and negatives from its coverage of a violent protest at the university that injured several police officers. The paper sued the police,

arguing that the search violated the First and Fourth Amendments, especially in light of the fact that no one at the paper was suspected of being involved in the protest. But the Supreme Court rejected the arguments, finding that the Fourth Amendment does not bar searches of places unassociated with criminal suspects if police reasonably believe evidence is there. That includes newsrooms, the First Amendment notwithstanding.

Alarmed, press groups lobbied Congress to pass a law barring law enforcement agencies from searching newsrooms. Congress responded by passing the Privacy Protection Act of 1980, which generally bars law enforcement agencies from searching or seizing the possessions of someone engaged in "public communication." The law limits the power of authorities to search or seize work products, defined as impressions, conclusions, opinions or theories of the communicators, and documentary material, which includes notes, photographs, film, negatives, videotapes, audio tapes and computer records.

There are exceptions, however. Police are allowed to search and seize work product and documentary materials if

- The communicator is suspected of a crime;
- The material is needed immediately to prevent serious injury or death;
- There is reason to believe that the material in question would be destroyed, altered or hidden in response to a subpoena; or
- A subpoena has been issued, all appeals have been exhausted and any further delay would interfere with the interests of justice.

Not surprisingly, it is rare to hear of a newsroom being the subject of a police search.

However, in 2019, police in San Francisco used a sledge hammer to open the front gate of freelance journalist Bryan Carmody's home. They handcuffed Carmody for more than five hours while they searched his home and seized his phones and computers. Carmody had obtained a copy of a police report about the death of a former public defender and sold it to local news organizations. Police also got search warrants for his phone records. San Francisco's police chief later apologized for the raid and admitted it was probably illegal under California law, even though two judges had signed off on the warrants. The San Francisco Board of Supervisors agreed to a $369,000 settlement with Carmody.

PRACTICAL TIPS

How can journalists navigate the complicated legal and ethical terrain associated with the use of confidential sources? Here are a few tips:

• Become familiar with the federal and state law in your region regarding the protection of journalists from forced disclosure of their sources and work product.

• Make sure you are aware of your employer's policies regarding the use of confidential sources and anonymous quotations.

• Get an editor's or news director's approval, if possible, before agreeing to keep a source's identity secret.

• Never enter into a confidentiality agreement with a source unless you are clear on the source's motives for providing information.

• When possible, persuade a source to go on the record or direct you to a document or someone who will agree to be quoted by name.

• Find out whether the source would be willing to be identified if you face jail time or heavy fines for protecting the source's identity.

• Never voluntarily provide anyone with the name of a confidential source without that source's permission, preferably in writing.

• For sources who work in highly sensitive government or private sector jobs, avoid using cell phones, emails and other electronic communication if possible. Meet in person and communicate by paper. If that is not possible, use encrypted apps such as Signal or WhatsApp or invest in SecureDrop.

SUMMARY

There have been confidential sources nearly as long as there have been reporters. These sources often provide valuable information to journalists, but there are ethical and legal risks to entering into confidential relationships. The sources may be engaging in illegal or unethical behavior by talking to the press, and quoting them anonymously requires reporters to hide part of the truth of a story from the audience.

Despite the ethical concerns, journalists have continued to use confidential sources. On occasion, grand juries have sought the identities of sources, and journalists often resist those demands. They fear that identifying sources will discourage those and other sources from going to the media with information the public should know. Also, professional codes admonish journalists not to break promises to their sources.

It was not until the 1950s that journalists began arguing that the press clause of the First Amendment should be interpreted as protecting their right to conceal sources from discovery. As the number of subpoenas rose in the late 1960s and early 1970s, the Supreme Court accepted the cases of three reporters who had resisted efforts to get them to name their sources to grand juries investigating crimes.

The Supreme Court's 1972 decision in *Branzburg v. Hayes* held that the First Amendment did not give journalists a right to refuse to testify to grand juries when the reporters had direct evidence of criminal activity involving their sources. The Court expressed concern that recognizing such a privilege would create considerable trouble for the lower courts. For example, how would courts define who was protected by the privilege, given that anyone can claim to be a journalist? Also, the justices were concerned that the privilege would bog down the courts in determining which subpoenas were proper and which were not.

Four justices dissented. Justice Douglas called for an absolute privilege protecting journalists from answering all subpoenas. The other three justices, led by Justice Stewart, advocated the recognition of a qualified privilege, which would protect journalists from testifying unless the government could show that the information it sought was important to the case, relevant to the case and unavailable elsewhere.

The pivotal opinion in the *Branzburg* case turned out to be Justice Powell's concurrence, which emphasized the limited nature of the majority opinion and also seemed to agree with some parts of Justice Stewart's dissent. Because Justice Powell was the fifth vote for a 5-4 majority, his confusing concurrence left lower courts somewhat baffled about how to interpret the decision. The Supreme Court has accepted no other journalist's privilege case to resolve the confusion.

As a result, the federal appellate circuits have developed a qualified constitutional privilege along the lines suggested by Justice Stewart. The privilege varies from circuit to circuit, however, with most circuits adopting a privilege that protects journalists in some cases from being forced to testify in civil cases. Several circuits also protect journalists from being forced to disclose sources in criminal cases.

Three circuits have extended protection to non-confidential work products, such as unpublished photographs, unaired video or notes, on the theory that forcing journalists to disclose those materials also interferes with their rights under the First Amendment. Non-confidential information gets less protection than confidential material, however. Three other circuits have expressly refused to protect journalists from disclosing non-confidential information in criminal cases.

After a 2003 decision in the Seventh Circuit cast doubt on whether other circuits had been right to recognize a privilege, journalists lost a series of high-profile cases in which special prosecutors, grand juries and civil litigants sought the names of their sources. The losses led journalists and members of Congress to call for the passage of a federal shield law, which would give journalists limited protection from subpoenas in federal courts, but so far Congress has been unable to pass such a law.

Shield laws are much more common in the states. Forty-two states and the District of Columbia have statutes or formal state court rules that give widely varying degrees of protection to journalists. About a fourth of the shield laws protect only confidential sources or confidential information, but the rest also protect non-confidential work product.

State shield laws vary widely in how they define who is protected, what is protected and to what extent. Eleven laws are written in absolute terms, and three others protect some information absolutely, but state courts have ruled that even absolute statutory privileges must give way if the journalist's statutory right conflicts with someone else's constitutional right.

In recent years, there has been much debate about whether shield laws should protect bloggers and other nontraditional journalists as well as mainstream media employees. Courts have been divided on the question, and the small number of cases so far does not provide a clear answer. Likewise, the jury is still out on whether shield laws protect the identities of people who post anonymous comments on news organization Web sites. Several state trial courts have said yes; but there have been few cases, and the first case decided by a state appellate court ruled against the newspaper on the shield law question. Digital technology has also made it harder to protect sources from electronic surveillance, but it also provides apps and software that allow journalists and sources to communicate more securely — although no system is foolproof.

In addition to finding their way through the unsettled nature of privilege law, journalists must also be aware that voluntarily identifying their sources may make them liable for damages if the disclosure harms a source. And, in rare situations, journalists may find themselves on the receiving end of search warrants, although an act of Congress limits the government's power to use that device on newsrooms.

Given the ethical and legal issues in regard to confidential sources, the best advice for a journalist might be to avoid using such sources whenever possible. If you do enter into an agreement with a source to protect their identity, however, be prepared to keep that promise, even if it means jail or fines. If a story is not worth that price, do not make the promise.

BIBLIOGRAPHY

Articles

Alexander, Laurence B. "Looking Out for the Watchdogs: A Legislative Proposal Limiting the Newsgathering Privilege to Journalists in the Greatest Need of Protection for Sources and Information," 20 *Yale Law & Policy Review* 97 (2002).

Alonzo, Joseph S. "Note: Restoring the Ideal Marketplace: How Recognizing Bloggers as Journalists Can Save the Press," 9 *New York University Journal of Legislation & Public Policy* 751 (2005/2006).

Bates, Stephen. "*Garland v. Torre* and the Birth of Reporter's Privilege," 15 *Communication Law & Policy* 91 (2010).

Berger, Linda L. "Shielding the Unmedia: Using the Process of Journalism to Protect the Journalist's Privilege in an Infinite Universe of Publication," 39 *Houston Law Review* 1371 (2003).

Boylan, Peter. "Green Signs Bill Protecting the Work of Journalists," (Honolulu) *Star-Advertiser*, June 25, 2023, https://www.staradvertiser.com/2023/06/25/hawaii-news/green-signs-bill-protecting-the-work-of-journalists/

Buchanan, Kelly. "Freedom of Expression and International Criminal Law: An Analysis of the Decision to Create a Testimonial Privilege for Journalists," 35 *Victoria University of Wellington Law Review* 609 (2004).

Caldwell, Earl. "Ask Me. I Know. I Was the Test Case," *Saturday Review*, Aug. 5, 1972, at 5.

Carter, Edward L. "'Not to Disclose Information Sources': Journalistic Privilege Under Article 19 of ICCPR," 22 *Communication Law and Policy* 399 (2017).

Eliason, Randall D. "Leakers, Bloggers and Fourth Estate Inmates: The Misguided Pursuit of a Reporter's Privilege," 24 *Cardozo Arts & Entertainment Law Journal* 385 (2006).

Goodale, James C. "*Branzburg v. Hayes* and the Developing Qualified Privilege for Newsmen," 26 *Hastings Law Journal* 709 (1975).

Gutierrez, Gabe, Erik Ortiz & Kayla McCormick. "Reality Winner, Imprisoned for Leaking Classified Report, Calls Case Against Trump 'Incredibly Ironic,'" NBC.com, Sept. 14, 2022, https://www.nbcnews.com/politics/donald-trump/reality-winner-imprisoned-leaking-classified-report-calls-case-trump-i-rcna 46683.

Jones, RonNell Andersen. "Avalanche or Undue Alarm: An Empirical Study of Subpoenas Received by the News Media," 93 *Minnesota Law Review* 585 (2008).

Jones, RonNell Andersen. "Media Subpoenas: Impact, Perception, and Legal Protection in the Changing World of American Journalism," 84 *Washington Law Review* 317 (2009).

Jones, RonNell Andersen. "Rethinking Reporter's Privilege," 111 *Michigan Law Review* 1221 (2013).

Kielbowicz, Richard B. "The Role of News Leaks in Governance and the Law of Journalists' Confidentiality, 1795-2005," 43 *San Diego Law Review* 425 (Summer 2006).

Kimball, Michele Bush. "The Intent Behind the Cryptic Concurrence That Provided a Reporter's Privilege," 13 *Communication Law and Policy* 379 (2008).

Kirtley, Jane E. "Mask, Shield and Sword: Should the Journalist's Privilege Protect the Identity of Anonymous Posters to News Media Websites?," 94 *Minnesota Law Review* 1478 (2009/2010).

Kissinger, Ashley I., & Katharine Larson. "Shielding Jane and John Doe: Can the Media Protect Anonymous Online Speech?" *Communications Law*, July 2009, at 4.

Koningisor, Christina. "The De Facto Reporter's Privilege," 127 *Yale Law Journal* 1176 (2018).

Lee, William E. "A Revisionist View of Journalist's Privilege:

Justice Powell, Branzburg and the 'Proper Balance,'" 34 *Cardozo Arts & Entertainment Law Journal* 113 (2016).

Martin, Jason A., Mark Caramanica & Anthony L. Fargo. "Anonymous Speakers and Confidential Sources: Using Shield Laws When They Overlap Online," 16 *Communication Law and Policy* 89 (2011).

Martin, Jason A., & Anthony L. Fargo. "Rebooting Shield Laws: Updating Journalist's Privilege to Reflect the Realities of Digital Newsgathering," 24 *University of Florida Journal of Law & Public Policy* 47 (2013).

Mehra, Achal. "Newsmen's Privilege: An Empirical Study," 59 *Journalism Quarterly* 560 (1982).

Newberg, Katelyn. "Murder Suspect Supports RJ's Plan to Search Slain Reporter's Phone," (Las Vegas) *Review-Journal*, May 1, 2023, https://www.reviewjournal.com/crime/courts/murder-suspect-supports-rjs-plan-to-search-slain-reporters-phone-2770772/.

Packer, Cathy. "The Politics of Power: A Social Architecture Analysis of the 2005-2008 Federal Shield Law Debate in Congress," 31 *Hastings Communication/Entertainment Law Journal* 395 (2009).

Papandrea, Mary-Rose. "Citizen Journalism and the Reporter's Privilege," 91 *Minnesota Law Review* 515 (2007).

Rebaza, Claudia & Lauren Said-Moorhouse. "Julian Assange Loses Latest Appeal against Extradition to the US," CNN, June 9, 2023, https://www.cnn.com/2023/06/09/uk/julian-assange-extradition-appeal-intl-gbr/index.html

Savage, Charlie. "Holder Hints Reporter May Be Spared Jail in Leak," *New York Times*, May 28, 2014, at A13.

Savage, Charlie & Leslie Kaufman. "Phone Records of Journalists Seized by U.S.," *New York Times*, May 24, 2013, at A1.

Shepard, Jason M. "After the First Amendment Fails: The Newsmen's Privilege Hearings of the 1970s," 14 *Communication Law and Policy* 373 (2009).

Sherwood, Margaret. "Comment: The Newsman's Privilege: Government Investigations, Criminal Prosecutions and Private Litigation," 58 *California Law Review* 1198 (1970).

Smith, Dean C. "*Price v. Time* Revisited: The Need for Medium-Neutral Shield Laws in an Age of Strict Construction," 14 *Communication Law and Policy* 235 (2009).

Smith, Dean C. "The Real Story Behind the Nation's First Shield Law: Maryland, 1894-1897," 19 *Communication Law and Policy* 3 (2014).

Ugland, Erik. "Demarcating the Right to Gather News: A Sequential Interpretation of the First Amendment," 3 *Duke Journal of Constitutional Law & Public Policy* 113 (2008).

Uncredited. "Seattle Police Department Subpoenas Five News Outlets for Protest Photos, Video," Press Freedom Tracker, June 18, 2020, https://pressfreedomtracker.us/all-incidents/seattle-police-department-subpoenas-five-news-outlets-protest-photos-videos/.

Youm, Kyu Ho. "International and Comparative Law on the Journalist's Privilege: The Randal Case as a Lesson for the American Press," 1 *Journal of International Media & Entertainment Law* 1 (2006).

Books

Bernstein, Carl & Bob Woodward. *All the President's Men*. New York: Simon & Schuster, 1974.

Berret, Charles. *Guide to SecureDrop*. New York: Tow Center for Digital Journalism, 2017.

Gordon, Aaron David. *Protection of News Sources: The History and Legal Status of the Newsman's Privilege* (2 vols.) (1971) (unpublished dissertation, University of Wisconsin) (copy on file at Indiana University Herman B. Wells Library).

Posetti, Julie. *Protecting Journalism Sources in the Digital Age*. Paris: UNESCO Publishing, 2017.

Reporters Committee for Freedom of the Press. *Agents of Discovery: A Report on the Incidence of Subpoenas Served on the News Media in 2001*. Arlington, Va.: RCFP, 2003.

Risen, James. *State of War: The Secret History of the CIA and the Bush Administration*. New York: Simon & Schuster, 2006.

Schudson, Michael. *The Sociology of News* (2d ed.). New York: W.W. Norton & Co., 2011.

Wigmore, John Henry. *Evidence in Trials at Common Law*, vol. 8 (McNaughton rev.). Boston: Little, Brown & Co., 1961.

Cases

Alton Telegraph v. Illinois, No. 08-MR-548 (Ill. Cir. Ct. May 15, 2009).

Ammerman v. Hubbard B'Casting, Inc., 551 P.2d 1354 (N.M. 1976).

Ayash v. Dana-Farber Cancer Institute, 822 N.E.2d 667 (Mass. 2005).

Baker v. F & F Investments, 470 F.2d 778 (2d Cir. 1972).

Branzburg v. Hayes, 408 U.S. 665 (1972).

Branzburg v. Meigs, 503 S.W.2d 748 (Ky. 1971).

Branzburg v. Pound, 461 S.W.2d 345 (Ky. 1970).

Bridges v. California, 314 U.S. 252 (1941).

Brown v. Commonwealth, 204 S.E.2d 429 (Va. 1974).

Cahill v. Doe, 884 A.2d 451 (Del. 2005).

Caldwell v. United States, 434 F.2d 1081 (9th Cir. 1970).

Church of Scientology International v. Daniels, 992 F.2d 1329 (4th Cir. 1993).

Cohen v. Cowles Media Co., 501 U.S. 663 (1991).

Delaney v. Superior Court, 789 P.2d 934 (Cal. 1990).

Dendrite International Inc. v. John Doe No. 3, 775 A.2d 756 (N.J. Super. Ct. App. Div. 2001).

Garland v. Torre, 259 F.2d 545 (2d Cir. 1958).

Gitlow v. New York, 268 U.S. 652 (1925).

Gray v. St. Martin's Press, 221 F.3d 243 (1st Cir. 2000).

Hatfill v. Mukasey, 539 F. Supp. 2d 96 (D.D.C. 2008).

Herbert v. Lando, 441 U.S. 153 (1979).

In re Caldwell, 311 F. Supp. 358 (N.D. Cal. 1970).

In re Contempt of Stone, 397 N.W.2d 244 (Mich. Ct. App. 1986).

In re Contempt of Wright, 700 P.2d 40 (Idaho 1985).

In re Grand Jury Subpoena (Storer Communications, Inc.), 810 F.2d 580 (6th Cir. 1987).

In re Grand Jury Subpoena, Joshua Wolf, 201 Fed. Appx. 430 (9th Cir. 2006) (unpublished).

In re Grand Jury Subpoena, Judith Miller, 397 F.3d 964 (D.C. Cir. 2005); *cert denied,* Cooper v. United States, 545 U.S. 1150 (2005); Miller v. United States, 545 U.S. 1150 (2005).

In re Grand Jury Subpoenas to Fainaru-Wada and Williams, 438 F. Supp. 2d 1111 (N.D. Cal. 2006).

In re Indiana Newspapers, Inc., 963 N.E.2d 534 (Ind. Ct. App. 2012).

In re Madden, 151 F.3d 125 (3d Cir. 1998).

In re Pappas, 266 N.E.2d 297 (Mass. 1971).

In re Petroleum Products Antitrust Litigation, 680 F.2d 5 (2d Cir. 1982).

In re Shain, 978 F.2d 850 (4th Cir. 1992).

In re Special Proceedings, 373 F.3d 37 (1st Cir. 2004).

In re Special Proceedings, C.A. No. 01-47 (D.R.I. Dec. 9, 2004).

Johns-Byrne Co. v. TechnoBuffalo LLC, No. 2011 L 009161 (Ill. Cir. Ct. July 13, 2012).

LaRouche v. NBC, 780 F.2d 1134 (4th Cir. 1986).

Lee v. U.S. Department of Justice, 287 F. Supp. 2d 15 (D.D.C. 2003).

Lee v. U.S. Department of Justice, 401 F. Supp. 2d 123 (D.D.C. 2005).

Lee v. U.S. Department of Justice, 413 F.3d 53 (D.C. Cir. 2005).

McKevitt v. Pallasch, 339 F.3d 530 (7th Cir. 2003).

Mortgage Specialists, Inc. v. Implode-Explode Heavy Industries, Inc., 999 A.2d 184 (N.H. 2010).

Multimedia WMAZ, Inc. v. Kubach, 443 S.E.2d 491 (Ga. Ct. App. 1994).

NBC v. Gonzales, 194 F.3d 29 (2d Cir. 1999).

NBC v. LaRouche Campaign, 841 F.2d 1176 (1st Cir. 1988).

New York Times Co. v. Superior Court, 796 P.2d 811 (Cal. 1990).

New York Times v. Gonzales, 459 F.3d 160 (2d Cir. 2006).

O'Grady v. Superior Court, 139 Cal. App. 4th 1423 (Cal. Ct. App. 2006).

Obsidian Finance Group LLC v. Cox, 740 F.3d 1284 (9th Cir. 2014).

Obsidian Finance Group, LLC v. Cox, 2011 U.S. Dist. LEXIS 137548 (D. Or. Nov. 30, 2011).

Opinion of the Justices, 373 A.2d 644 (N.H. 1977).

Price v. Time, Inc., 416 F.3d 1327 (11th Cir. 2005).

Riley v. City of Chester, 612 F.2d 708 (3d. Cir. 1979).

Ruzicka v. Conde Nast, 999 F.2d 1319 (8th Cir. 1993).

Shoen v. Shoen, 5 F.3d 1298 (9th Cir. 1993).

Silkwood v. Kerr-McGee Corp., 563 F.2d 433 (10th Cir. 1977).

Sinnott v. Boston Retirement Board, 524 N.E.2d 100 (Mass. 1988).

State ex. rel. Classic III, Inc. v. Ely, 954 S.W.2d 650 (Mo. Ct. App. 1997).

Too Much Media LLC v. Hale, 20 A.3d 364 (N.J. 2011).

United States v. Burke, 700 F.2d 70 (2d Cir. 1983).

United States v. Smith, 135 F.3d 963 (5th Cir. 1998).

United States v. Sterling, 724 F.3d 482 (4th Cir. 2013); cert. denied, Risen v. United States, 134 S. Ct. 1361 (2014).

von Bulow v. von Bulow, 811 F.2d 136 (2d Cir. 1987).

Winegard v. Oxberger, 258 N.W.2d 847 (Iowa 1977).

Zerilli v. Smith, 656 F.2d 705 (D.C. Cir. 1981).

Zurcher v. Stanford Daily, 436 U.S. 547 (1978).

Web Sites

Reporters Committee for Freedom of the Press, "The Reporter's Privilege," http://www.rcfp.org/reporters-privilege (last visited May 31, 2023).

Society of Professional Journalists, Code of Ethics, available at https://www.spj.org/ethicscode.asp (last visited June 1, 2023).

Other Sources

155 Congressional Record H4209 (daily ed. Mar. 31, 2009) (reporting voice vote on H.R. 985).

Alaska Stat. art. 3 § 09.25.310 et seq. (LexisNexis 2023).

Ark. Code Ann. § 16-85-510 (LexisNexis 2023).

Attorney General's Guidelines on Subpoenas to Reporters, 28 C.F.R. § 50.10 (2023).

Calif. Const. art. I, § 2.

Colo. Rev. Stat. § 13-90-119 (LexisNexis 2023).

Conn. Gen. Stat. § 52-146t (LexisNexis 2023).

Espionage Act of 1917, 18 U.S.C.S. § 793 et seq. (LexisNexis 2023).

Federal Rules of Civil Procedure § 26 (c) (2023).

Federal Rules of Criminal Procedure § 17 (c) (2023).

Federal Rules of Evidence § 501 (2023).

Free Flow of Information Act, H.R. 2932, 112th Cong., 1st Sess. (2011).

Free Flow of Information Act, S. 987, 113th Cong., 1st Sess. (2013).

Free Flow of Information Act, H.R. 1962, 113th Cong., 1st Sess. (2013).

Free Flow of Information Act, H.R. 4382, 115th Cong., 1st Sess. (2017).

Ind. Code Ann. § 34-46-4-1 (LexisNexis 2023).

Intelligence Identities Protection Act of 1982, 50 U.S.C.S. § 3121 (LexisNexis 2023).

Ky. Rev. Stat. § 421.100 (LexisNexis 2023).

Md. Cts. & Jud. Proc. Code Ann. § 9-112 (LexisNexis 2023).

Mich. Comp. Laws § 767.5a (LexisNexis 2023).

Nev. Rev. Stat. § 49.275 (LexisNexis 2023)

Privacy Act of 1974, 5 U.S.C.S. § 552a (LexisNexis 2023).

Privacy Protection Act of 1980, 42 U.S.C.S. § 2000aa (LexisNexis 2023).

Protection for Private Blocking and Screening of Offensive Material, 47 U.S.C.S. § 230 (LexisNexis 2023).

Protect Reporters from Excessive State Suppression Act, H.R. 4330, 117th Cong., 1st Sess. (2022).

Protect Reporters from Excessive State Suppression Act, S. 2457, 117th Cong., 1st Sess. (2022).

S.D. Codified Laws § 19-2-15 (LexisNexis 2023)

Stored Communication Act, 18 U.S.C.S. § 2701 et seq. (LexisNexis 2023).

Tenn. Code Ann. § 24-1-208 (LexisNexis 2023).

W.Va. Code § 57-3-10 (LexisNexis 2023).

16

Access to Courts

By Dean Smith

☑ **Headnote Questions**

- How might coverage of a criminal case interfere with a defendant's right to a fair trial?
- Under what circumstances may a judge impose a gag order on the media?
- When may a court proceeding be closed to the public and the press?
- Does the First Amendment require judges to allow cameras in courtrooms?

Millions of viewers nationwide tuned in while Derek Chauvin faced a jury of his peers for his role in the 2020 death of George Floyd. The killing of an unarmed African-American man by a white police officer set off months of protests and riots that left thirty-five people dead and $2 billion in property damage. Video of Floyd's death shocked the world, and court proceedings in 2021 became the latest "trial of the century."

After Chauvin's conviction, a question remained: Should cameras in courts become the rule rather than an exception? "The time is right to consider whether requirements ... should be amended to accommodate broader public access," Minnesota Supreme Court Chief Justice Lorie Gildea wrote in an order to the state's Advisory Committee on Rules of Criminal Procedure. An expert panel convened in 2022 to explore the issue.

Ramsey County Judge Richard Kyle Jr. said livestreaming the trial added transparency without disruption. "We were able to protect the jurors, we were able to protect the child witnesses, and the public saw really what happens in a trial," he told the press. Others, like District Attorney Dominick Matthews, voiced concern. "We could always say in the past that the courtroom is a safe place," he said, but cameras "will have a very damaging effect on our ability to do justice."

That debate encapsulates an argument that has been raging among journalists and legal professionals for more than a century: the so-called "free press-fair trial debate." When must the public's right to know be set aside for the sake of someone's right to a fair trial?

The news media are filled with stories related to the judicial system. Whether it's a celebrity charged with murder, charges of rape against a sports star, or a hearing for a suspected terror-ist, the courts generate news that grips the public. However, coverage of sensational investigations and court cases often leads to concern about the effects of coverage on trial fairness and allegations of "trial by media."

The free press-fair trial issue presents a conflict between rights guaranteed by two amendments to the Constitution: the First Amendment right of freedom of the press and the Sixth Amendment right to a fair and speedy trial. Some argue that unrestrained coverage of crimes, arrests, pretrial proceedings and trials threatens Sixth Amendment rights and restrictions must be placed on the media to ensure the proper administration of justice. Others contend that the First Amendment cannot be subordinated to the Sixth Amendment, that a free press plays a critical role as a watchdog to ensure a fair trial.

The U.S. Supreme Court has adopted a balancing approach in dealing with free press-fair trial conflicts, consistently instructing trial judges to take steps to protect the rights of defendants without harming the rights of journalists to attend court proceedings. In general, the Court has held that restrictions on the media may be imposed only as the last resort. This does not mean that judges do not still attempt to restrict the media and trial participants, seal records or close courtrooms. In 2012, the Colorado judge in the James Holmes case issued a gag order barring reporters from discussing certain aspects of the case and initially sealed all of the documents related to the case. Holmes was charged with the 2012 shootings at the Aurora theater. In 2014, however, the same judge wrote an eloquent opinion championing journalists' role in the proper functioning of the judicial system.

THE NATURE OF THE PROBLEM

While recent developments in the use of social media by jurors and reporters have complicated issues, the free press-fair trial conflict manifests in three basic ways:

(1) *Pretrial publicity* may make it difficult to find impartial jurors who have not made up their minds about the defendant's guilt or innocence before the trial begins.

(2) *During-trial publicity* may taint a sitting jury, causing jurors to base a verdict on what they read, see or hear in the media, rather than solely on the evidence presented at trial.

(3) *The presence of journalists* in the courtroom may cause physical and/or psychological distraction and disruption.

Pretrial Publicity

Jurors are supposed to arrive at a verdict based on evidence presented in court. Rules of evidence prevent certain types of information from being presented to the jury. Anyone who has watched a courtroom drama on TV — real or fictional — knows that hearsay and opinions are not allowed. But the media don't follow court rules of evidence in deciding what to publish or broadcast. Thus, considerable information that will never reach the jury in the courtroom could reach potential jurors as they watch TV or read news accounts.

The Supreme Court, in *Murphy v. Florida*, ruled that jurors need not be "totally ignorant of the facts and issues involved" to be considered impartial. Exposure to "information about a ... defendant's prior convictions or to news accounts of the crime with which he is charged" is not alone enough to disqualify a potential juror. The Supreme Court held that so long as a juror does not have "strong and deep impressions which will close the mind against the testimony that may be offered in opposition to them," the juror can be considered impartial.

The trick is to determine what types of publicity can result in "strong and deep impressions." Numerous court decisions, especially those in which criminal convictions have been overturned on appeal, have discussed types of news stories that can cause prejudice. In addition, the American Bar Association and voluntary bench-press-bar committees in several states have developed guidelines to help identify potentially prejudicial material. Most of the guidelines recognize that reporting the following types of information can create a danger.

Prior Criminal Records. Prior charges and convictions are part of the public record, and journalists may believe it important to inform the public of a defendant's past. But a criminal record is not normally admitted as evidence since the jury is supposed to base its verdict on evidence relating to the *current* charge only. Keeping information about a defendant's record from jurors may be fruitless if they have been informed of it by the media.

Note, however, that the Supreme Court has said that knowledge of a defendant's prior criminal record *alone* is not enough to disqualify a potential juror.

Confessions or Other Admissions. Defendants sometimes make statements to police that are declared inadmissible because of Fifth Amendment protection against self-incrimination or some other reason, such as law enforcement failing to inform a suspect of constitutional rights. As with criminal records, jurors who have seen media reports of a confession, or even references to the existence of a confession, may have a hard time forgetting those reports.

Results of Investigative Procedures or Tests. Admissibility of test results can be the basis for a battle in a criminal case, and such information is often kept from a jury. Reporting that the accused refused to submit to a test or procedure could leave the impression that the defendant had something to hide.

Opinions on Character, Guilt or Innocence. As numerous cases have shown, the media attach derogatory nicknames to suspects, report alleged character flaws or suspicious behavior, or conduct on-the-street interviews. These so-called "trials by media" can result in perceptions of guilt regardless of evidence introduced at trial.

Speculation on Evidence or Witnesses. Prospective witnesses who tell journalists what they intend to say in court may change their minds or be prevented from making certain statements before the jury. Police officers and lawyers may often be the source of leaks about potential evidence or witnesses, adding a ring of authority to the speculation.

In addition to these categories, any sensational coverage of a crime is potentially prejudicial. Three important cases in which the Court considered claims that pretrial publicity robbed defendants of their rights to impartial juries provide examples of prejudicial coverage, as well as the types of publicity that may constitute grounds to overturn a conviction.

Irvin v. Dowd, decided in 1961, marked the first time the Court overturned a state criminal conviction because of prejudicial publicity. Leslie "Mad Dog" Irvin, as he was dubbed, was charged with the murder of Whitney Wesley Kerr, one of six victims in a series of murders near Evansville, Indiana. Irvin was tried for only one murder, but the police, prosecutors and media all intimated they believed he was responsible for all six. The Court described the publicity surrounding the trial as "a barrage of newspaper headlines, articles, cartoons and pictures." News stories revealed Irvin's juvenile record, his prior convictions for arson and burglary, and his court-martial on AWOL charges during World War II. The media also reported that he had confessed to the six murders and offered to plead guilty if promised a ninety-nine-year sentence. One report characterized Irvin as remorseless and without a conscience.

The effects of publicity were evident during jury selection. The court excused 268 of 430 prospective jurors for having already formed opinions. Of the twelve chosen, eight said they thought Irvin was guilty but could be fair and impartial.

In reversing Irvin's conviction and death sentence, the Court found: "With his life at stake, it is not requiring too much that [Irvin] be tried in an atmosphere undisturbed by so huge a wave of public passion and by a jury other than one in which two-thirds of the members admit, before hearing any testimony, to possessing a belief in his guilt." Irvin was retried, again found guilty, and sentenced to life in prison.

In *Rideau v. Louisiana*, in 1963, the Court again reversed a conviction, here based on the pretrial broadcasting of a confession. Wilbert Rideau was charged with bank robbery, kidnapping and murder. Without being informed of his right to remain silent and have an attorney, he confessed on camera. A twenty-minute interview with Rideau, during which he was "flanked by the sheriff and two state troopers," was broadcast for three consecutive days to estimated audiences of 24,000, 29,000 and 53,000 in Calcasieu Parish, Louisiana, with a population of about 150,000. Rideau's motion for a change of venue was denied, and the trial was held with a jury that included three people who said they had seen the televised confession. Rideau was convicted and sentenced to death.

The Supreme Court ruled that the judge's refusal to move the trial to a community in which Rideau's confession had not been televised violated the defendant's due process rights. On retrial, Rideau was once again convicted, and the Louisiana Supreme Court upheld that second conviction.

In *Sheppard v. Maxwell*, in 1966, the Court issued a ruling that has become synonymous with prejudicial publicity. The Court's reversal of Samuel Sheppard's conviction was based on all three problems listed earlier, but the focus here would be on the nature and extent of the pretrial coverage.

In the early morning of July 4, 1954, Marilyn Sheppard was beaten to death in her home in a suburb of Cleveland, Ohio. Her husband, Samuel, a surgeon and member of a prominent family, said he was asleep on the couch downstairs and was awakened by his wife's cries. Sheppard testified that when he ran upstairs, he saw what he called "a form" by his wife's bed and was struck and knocked unconscious. After he came to, he said, he went downstairs, saw someone run out the door and pursued the person to the lake behind his home, where a struggle ensued and he was again knocked out. When he awoke and returned to the house, he determined his wife was dead. He then called a neighbor, who called the police.

The pretrial publicity was relentless and, according to the Supreme Court, virulent. Within days of the murder, Cleveland newspapers focused on Sheppard's alleged lack of cooperation — which the Court later indicated was untrue — and his refusal to take a lie detector test or be injected with truth serum. Front-page editorials charged "Somebody's Getting Away with Murder" and demanded an inquest. The inquest called the next day was held in a school gymnasium and broadcast live. During and after, news stories emphasized incriminating evidence, much of which was never presented at trial. The media also focused on Sheppard's personal life, especially his admitted affair with one woman and alleged — but never admitted or proven — affairs with others. A few days after the inquest, a front-page editorial asked, "Why Isn't Sam Sheppard in Jail?" At about 10 p.m. the day the editorial appeared, Sheppard was arrested and charged with murder.

Between July 5, when the murder was first reported in the media, and July 30, the day Sheppard was arrested, the *Cleveland Plain Dealer* ran a page-one story about the case twenty-five of the twenty-six days. The *Cleveland Press* ran a page-one story each of the twenty-three days it published during that period and printed three page-one editorials.

In its opinion overturning Sheppard's conviction — eleven years after the jury verdict — the Court listed numerous examples of prejudicial coverage. Before jury selection, all three Cleveland papers published the names and addresses of the jurors. "As a consequence, anonymous letters and telephone calls, as well as calls from friends, regarding the impending prosecution were received by all of the prospective jurors," the Court wrote. Despite this, Judge Edward Blythin, running for re-election, refused to move the location or delay the start of the trial, despite the fact that all but one of the jurors admitted reading about the case.

Despite prejudicial pretrial coverage, the Court said that alone did not constitute a denial of due process. Instead, the Court said its reversal of Sheppard's conviction was based on the "totality of the circumstances," including juror exposure to publicity during the trial and disruptions the media caused. (Recent scholarship has suggested that the Court at the time and scholars later might have exaggerated press disruption in this endlessly debated case.)

In addition to these three important cases, the Court, in *Skilling v. United States*, a 2010 case, laid out a number of factors that must be considered before publicity can be deemed prejudicial. First, the Court wrote, it is important to consider "the size and characteristics of the community in which the crime occurred." In large, diverse communities, it is highly unlikely that unbiased jurors would not be available. Second, the Court held that to be prejudicial, stories must contain a confession or some other blatantly prejudicial information "of the type readers or viewers could not reasonably be expected to shut from sight." Third, courts should consider the amount of time that passed between the reported crime and the trial. Finally, the Court said it is important to consider whether a jury provided an "overwhelming victory" for the prosecution. The Court concluded this consideration was of "prime significance" for proving prejudicial effects on the jury.

During-Trial Publicity

The same types of stories that could prejudice potential jurors before a trial can also taint a sitting jury. The Court said, in *Marshall v. United States*, in 1959, that the effect of prejudicial information "may indeed be greater" when it reaches jurors through the media rather than through testimony in court "for it is then not tempered by protective procedures."

The Supreme Court has considered several cases involving prejudicial during-trial coverage. In *Marshall,* it reversed the conviction of Howard R. Marshall, charged with illegally dispensing drugs to an undercover Food and Drug Administration inspector. During the trial, two potentially damaging newspaper articles appeared. One reported Marshall had two prior felony convictions, had written prescriptions for dangerous drugs, and, while serving a forgery sentence in Oklahoma, had told a legislative committee he practiced medicine with a $25 mail-order diploma. The article said Marshall acted as a physician and prescribed drugs for Hank Williams before the singer's death. The second article said Marshall was arrested with his wife, who was convicted on drug charges and went to jail.

The judge refused to admit as evidence much of the information published in the articles because of its highly prejudicial nature. After the articles were published, the judge questioned each juror and learned that seven had seen at least one story. The jurors said they could be impartial, however, and the judge denied Marshall's motion for a mistrial. The jury brought in a conviction, which the Supreme Court overturned because of the jurors' exposure to the prejudicial information.

Publicity during trial also played a role in the reversal of Sam Sheppard's conviction. The jury was not sequestered until it began deliberations, and the judge failed to give adequate instructions about exposure to the media. Sheppard's attorney requested several times that the judge question jurors about exposure to prejudicial media. The judge refused all but once. That one instance resulted from a television and radio broadcast in which Walter Winchell reported that a woman arrested in New York for robbery said she was Sheppard's mistress and mother of his child. Two jurors admitted hearing the broadcast — despite the judge's instructions. After jurors assured him the broadcast would not affect their decisions, the judge "merely asked the jury to 'pay no attention whatever to that type of scavenging.... Let's confine ourselves to this courtroom, if you please.'" The Supreme Court considered such admonitions insufficient to protect the jury.

The Effects of Publicity

While there is widespread agreement about the types of publicity that are prejudicial, there is less agreement about the actual *effects* on jurors. The Sixth Amendment does not guarantee a defendant freedom from inflammatory publicity; it guarantees a trial by an "impartial jury." The key question is whether news coverage of a case — either pretrial or during trial — actually affects jurors' impartiality. Opinions and evidence are mixed. In all of the cases discussed previously, the jurors told the judges that, despite publicity, they could be impartial. However, Justice Tom Clark, who wrote the Court's opinion in *Irvin v. Dowd*, was skeptical: "No doubt each juror was sincere when he said that he would be fair and impartial," but "[w]here so many, so many times, admitted prejudice, such a statement of impartiality can be given little weight."

Numerous efforts to measure the effects of publicity on jurors during the past six decades have proved inconclusive. As one study concluded in 2010, "[A]fter 50 years of scientific research on juries and juror decision making, there are still many gaps in understanding how factors such as pretrial publicity ... influence juries." A key problem with empirical studies is that they generally involve mock trials and juries, rather than real jurors and real cases. Real juror deliberations are conducted behind closed doors, and courts fear that allowing researchers to tape deliberations might improperly influence jurors. Jurors in experiments are often exposed to news stories after which the trial immediately begins. This ignores the fact that, in real life, exposure to prejudicial coverage may go on for months before the trial starts. Real jurors have time to either forget what they saw or, perhaps because of repeated references, they become convinced of its accuracy. In experiments, jurors are exposed to the same news stories, an unrealistic circumstance that may affect the studies' results.

Despite their drawbacks, experimental research and studies of public reaction to news stories are the main sources of data for lawyers, judges and scholars. An article in the *Stanford Law Review* summarized the results of empirical studies:

> Experiments to date indicate that for the most part juries are able and willing to put aside extraneous information and base their decisions on the evidence. The results show that when ordinary citizens become jurors, they assume a special role in which they apply different standards of proof, more vigorous reasoning and greater detachment.

In the landmark 1966 study *The American Jury* by Harry Kalven and Hans Zeisel, not one of 555 judges who had presided over 3,576 criminal cases mentioned publicity as a factor. That's largely due to the fact that most criminal cases receive little publicity. While trials that are particularly scandalous or involve famous defendants such as O.J. Simpson may receive a great deal of media attention, these trials can make us lose sight of the fact that prejudicial publicity is often only a factor in rare cases. A 1999 study reported that of 134 federal, first-degree murder cases, 65 percent received little or no newspaper coverage. The study found no significant relationship between the amount of publicity a case received and the verdict. Conviction rates in cases that generated publicity were virtually identical to those in cases involving no publicity. Thus, although some research has found potential jurors are more affected by television coverage of sensational crimes than they are by print coverage, most cases warrant little or no coverage at all by either print or broadcast journalists.

Disruption in the Courtroom

Publishing or broadcasting prejudicial material isn't the only way the media might hamper a fair trial. The presence of journalists and equipment in court could disrupt the proceedings, perhaps distracting jurors and trial participants or creating an atmosphere inconsistent with calm deliberation. Some people, including Supreme Court justices, have argued that the presence of cameras in courtrooms causes psychological disruption sufficient to violate a defendant's rights.

The trial of Bruno Hauptmann in 1935 for kidnapping Charles and Anne Morrow Lindbergh's 18-month-old son is often cited as an example of journalists disrupting the judicial process and the reason the American Bar Association recommended in 1937 that cameras be banned in courtrooms.

Because of the international popularity of Charles Lindbergh, the first person to fly solo across the Atlantic Ocean, journalists from around the world crowded into the small town of Flemington, New Jersey, where the trial was held. Estimates of the number of media members ranged from 200 to nearly 1,000. While the Hauptmann trial may have been the impetus for the camera ban, the evidence indicates most journalists obeyed the judge's ban on photographing while court was in session. And, while the case has been cited as evidence of press misbehavior, various accounts seem to indicate that court officials and the public contributed to the lack of decorum as much as the media. Regardless of who was to blame, the trial became a prominent example of media interference with the judicial process.

By the 1960s, when Texas financier Billie Sol Estes went on trial for swindling, only two states — Colorado and Texas — permitted televising trials. Estes' attorney objected to broadcasting the proceedings, but the judge allowed both radio and television to broadcast the pretrial hearing live. According to the Supreme Court, twelve cameramen moved around the courtroom; cables and wires were "snaked across" the floor; three microphones were set up on the judge's bench; and "others were beamed at the jury box and the counsel table."

Four cameras — one for each of the three major networks and one for a local station — and camera operators were confined to a booth specially constructed at the rear of the courtroom and painted to blend into the walls. Only the state's opening and closing arguments and the delivery of the jury's verdict were broadcast live with sound. Other portions were filmed, without sound and broadcast during regular newscasts.

The Court's opinion in *Estes v. Texas* was 5-4 to overturn Estes' conviction, saying he had been deprived of "that judicial serenity and calm to which [he] was entitled." Justice Tom Clark wrote that televising trials caused both physical and psychological disruptions and could negatively impact the jury, judge, witnesses and defendant.

The *Sheppard v. Maxwell* case still provides the classic example of disruptions resulting from media presence. Journalists filled most of the seats in the 26-by-48-foot room. The judge allowed about twenty newspaper and wire service reporters to sit at a temporary table inside the bar directly behind Sheppard and his attorney, making "confidential talk [between them] ... almost impossible.... They frequently had to leave the courtroom to obtain privacy." The journalists' frequent movement in and out "caused so much confusion that, despite the loud-speaker system installed in the courtroom, it was difficult for the witnesses and counsel to be heard." The media were permitted to install private telephone lines and telegraphic equipment in all of the rooms on the floor where the courtroom was located. A radio station set up broadcasting facilities in a room next to the jury room. Cameras were not permitted in the courtroom, but "[i]n the corridors outside the courtroom there was a host of photographers and television personnel with flash cameras, portable lights and motion picture cameras."

The Supreme Court summarized the situation this way: "The fact is that bedlam reigned ... during the trial and newsmen took over practically the entire courtroom, hounding most of the participants in the trial, especially Sheppard." This "carnival atmosphere," coupled with prejudicial publicity that saturated the community before and during the trial, led the Court to reverse Sheppard's conviction. When retried a few months later, he was found not guilty.

Despite changes in technology that have reduced the intrusive nature of cameras, allowing cameras and smart phones that would allow journalists to tweet from the courtroom continues to be a contentious issue.

COMPENSATING FOR PREJUDICIAL PUBLICITY

There are two broad categories of remedies designed to deal with problems created by media coverage of trials:

1. Those designed to compensate for prejudicial publicity.
2. Those designed to prevent prejudicial publicity and control

the presence and/or activities of journalists in court.

The key difference between the remedies is that the first seeks to mitigate or lessen the *effects* of media coverage without restricting it. Therefore, use of the first category of remedies does not raise First Amendment concerns because it does not hinder the press. In contrast, remedies in the second category are designed to control journalists, prevent access to proceedings and limit coverage, thus raising serious concerns.

The Supreme Court has repeatedly declared that the trial judge has the responsibility to protect a defendant's right to a fair trial. In *Sheppard*, *Estes*, *Rideau* and *Irvin* – although the Court indicated its disapproval of the press' performance – it focused on what the judges should have done to safeguard the defendants' rights. Here we will focus on the traditional tools that judges use to compensate for the effects of publicity without restricting access or publication.

Change of Venue

When a trial is moved to a new location, it's called a "change of venue." The new location is one in which the publicity has not been as intense and potential jurors are less likely to have been influenced. Change of venue requires, however, that a defendant give up another Sixth Amendment right — the right to be tried in the "district wherein the crime shall have been committed." Generally, this presents no problem since the motion for a venue change comes from the defense.

Whether a change of venue will be effective in mitigating the impact of publicity depends on several factors, one being how far the trial is moved. In *Irvin v. Dowd*, the judge agreed to move the trial from Vanderburgh County, Indiana, to neighboring Gibson County. Considering that 90 percent of prospective jurors questioned said they believed Irvin was guilty, it would appear that moving the trial such a short distance did little to protect his right to an impartial jury.

If a case is subject to nationwide publicity, it's unlikely that moving it anywhere would make a difference. Defense lawyers tried to get the trial of Enron executives Kenneth Lay and Jeffrey Skilling moved from Houston, citing a pretrial survey showing more than 80 percent of potential jurors believed they were guilty. But U.S. District Court Judge Sim Lake refused, saying adequate safeguards existed. On appeal, the Supreme Court in *Skilling v. United States* created a test to determine when a change of venue is warranted.

While a change of venue may make it easier to find unbiased jurors, it also increases costs and inconveniences. A major objection to moving the 1995 trial of Oklahoma City bombers Terry Nichols and Timothy McVeigh was the hardship caused for survivors and victims' families who wanted to attend. In response, Congress passed the Antiterrorism and Effective Death Penalty

Act of 1999, requiring closed-circuit televising of a federal trial when it is moved from its original location out of the state and more than 350 miles away.

Change of Venire

"Venire" refers to the pool of potential jurors from which a trial jury will be selected. To change the venire is to import jurors from another community. The tool is much less common than change of venue. A change of venire only works if the publicity has been confined to the place where the crime occurred. It also can be an expensive since it requires transporting, housing and feeding jurors during the trial.

Continuance

To continue a trial is to delay it. Delaying requires a defendant to sacrifice his right to a speedy trial in hopes of enhancing juror fairness. Delaying may be effective if publicity surrounding an arrest and trial can reasonably be expected to diminish over time. Studies have shown that people forget much of what they read in newspapers or saw on television news; and, especially in large cities, a continuance may mean another crime will have taken over the headlines by the time the trial begins. Of course, there's always the possibility that publicity will flare up again once a trial starts. In addition, for defendants who are not granted bail or are unable to pay it, delaying a trial means they must remain in jail longer awaiting trial.

Voir Dire

"*Voir dire*" is the term for the process at the beginning of a trial when potential jurors are questioned to determine if they can be impartial. It is a crucial part of the trial and, in highly publicized trials, it can take weeks, with hundreds of jurors questioned. In the murder trial of O.J. Simpson, 304 prospective jurors were questioned over eleven weeks. In the trial of Jeffrey Skilling, the court sent a seventy-seven-question, fourteen-page document to each of 400 perspective jurors asking about news sources, exposure to Enron-related stories and opinions regarding the defendants. Jury selection for the Aurora theater shooting case was also long and complex. The court summoned 9,000 potential jurors, 403 of whom were asked face-to-face questions over thirty-eight days.

Both the prosecution and defense may challenge an unlimited number of jurors for cause. The judge then determines if there is sufficient reason to believe a potential juror is biased or otherwise unsuited to sit on the jury. Attorneys for both sides also can dismiss a limited number of jurors with peremptory challenges and need not cite reasons. The number of peremptory challenges available to each side differs depending on the type of case and jurisdiction.

Judges, including Supreme Court justices, have placed great faith in the *voir dire* process and believe that it can effectively weed out biased jurors. Critics note that potential jurors can and do hide the truth, whether consciously or unconsciously.

Admonitions to the Jury

A judge may order jurors not to read, watch or listen to coverage of a trial, not to discuss it with anyone except other jurors and then only when deliberations begin, and not to use the Internet or other means to research a case. These admonitions are meant to underscore jurors' responsibility to decide the case based solely on the law and evidence. Failure to follow orders can result in removal from a jury, citation for contempt or both. In the Aurora theater shooting case, the judge released three jurors because one had discussed media coverage of the trial with the other two. Whether admonitions actually prevent juror exposure to media coverage is uncertain, but, as with *voir dire*, most judges say they believe that admonitions are effective in most cases.

Sequestration

Sequestration is the most extreme, costly and seldom-used remedy to shelter jurors from publicity. Sequestration means isolating the jury for the duration of the trial. It entails housing the jurors in a hotel, screening their phone calls and monitoring their use of media to ensure they do not see or hear media coverage. While sequestration can be effective, it has many drawbacks. It adds significantly to the cost of the trial because the state must transport, house, feed and guard the jurors. More important, sequestration creates significant disruptions to jurors' lives and eliminates from juries people who cannot leave their families or jobs for weeks or even months. In addition, keeping jurors away from family, friends and normal routines for an extended period may have unintended psychological effects, causing jurors to resent the defendant and blame him or her for disrupting their lives.

PREVENTING OR DIMINISHING PUBLICITY

Trial judges sometimes try to control what information journalists have access to or prevent the media from publishing or broadcasting information. These efforts raise significant First Amendment issues, and during the past twenty years, the Supreme Court has severely limited their use. Remedies aimed at eliminating or reducing prejudicial publicity fall into six categories: (1) restrictive orders (also called "gag orders") aimed at the media, (2) restrictions on trial participants, (3) post-publication sanctions, (4) court closures, (5) denials of access to court records, and (6) bans or limits on the use of cameras.

Gag Orders on the Media

While in *Sheppard v. Maxwell* the Supreme Court provided a list of tools trial judges could use to protect defendants' rights, it never suggested judges issue restrictive orders prohibiting the media from publishing information. Yet that's exactly what some judges did in the wake of that decision.

In 1976, the Supreme Court put a halt to the indiscriminate use of press gag orders. The landmark case *Nebraska Press Association v. Stuart* began on October 18, 1975, when police arrived at the Henry Kellie home in Sutherland, Nebraska, a town of 850 people, to find six family members with shotgun wounds to their heads. Five were already dead, and the sixth died later. The next day Erwin Charles Simants, a neighbor, was arrested and charged. He admitted to police that he had killed the Kellies and was arraigned. Reporters learned of his confession and publicized the information, along with speculation — later confirmed by autopsies — that Simants had sexually assaulted some of the victims after killing them.

Both geography and Nebraska law complicated protecting Simants' right to a fair trial. The court in which Simants was to be tried was in North Platte, population 19,000, just twenty miles east of Sutherland in Lincoln County. Publicity had been as widespread in North Platte, the largest city in southwest Nebraska, as in Sutherland. Nebraska law restricted the use of continuance and change of venue by requiring the accused be brought to trial within six months and that change of venue be to an adjoining county, all of which were smaller.

The county attorney proposed a solution to Judge Ronald Ruff: a gag order barring publication of potentially prejudicial material. Judge Ruff barred coverage of testimony and evidence during a preliminary hearing. He also ordered journalists to abide by the Nebraska Bar-Press Guidelines, a set of recommendations for minimizing prejudicial publicity.

The media immediately appealed to District Court Judge Hugh Stuart. Finding that there was a "clear and present danger that pre-trial publicity could harm the defendant's right to a fair trial," Judge Stuart vacated Judge Ruff's order and entered his own, which also incorporated the bar-press guidelines and prohibited publication of specific information — including the existence and contents of Simants' confession and information relating to the sexual assaults — until after a jury had been impaneled. His order also prohibited the media from reporting on the exact nature of the gag order itself.

Although the Supreme Court granted *certiorari*, it denied a motion to expedite review or stay the order during the trial. It was not until five months after Simants was tried, convicted and sentenced to death that a unanimous Court held that Stuart's gag order was a prior restraint that violated the First

Amendment. Incidentally, Simants' conviction was eventually overturned on the ground that a sheriff had tried to influence the sequestered jury. On retrial, Simants was found not guilty by reason of insanity, which was his original plea.

In *Nebraska Press Association,* all nine justices agreed that the gag order was unconstitutional, but they did not agree on the reasons. Chief Justice Warren Burger, joined by four other justices, took a balancing approach, using a variation of the clear and present danger test, developed in the context of sedition cases. After acknowledging that prior restraints "are the most serious and the least tolerable infringement on First Amendment rights," Burger wrote that the constitutionality of a gag order had to be determined by looking at the circumstances of a particular case. He said three factors must be considered:

(1) the nature and extent of pretrial news coverage,

(2) whether other measures would be likely to mitigate the effects of unrestrained publicity, and

(3) how effectively a restraining order would actually be.

Burger wrote that Judge Stuart was correct in concluding there would be pervasive pretrial publicity, but he failed to consider whether alternative measures might have protected Simants' rights. Burger voiced doubts about the effectiveness of the gag order. Noting the crimes took place in a community of 850 people, he wrote: "It is reasonable to assume that, without any news accounts being printed or broadcast, rumors would travel swiftly by word of mouth. One can only speculate on the accuracy of such reports, given the general propensities of rumors; they could well be more damaging than reasonably accurate news accounts." Thus, Stuart's order failed Burger's balancing test and was unconstitutional.

Three justices — William Brennan, Thurgood Marshall and Potter Stewart — were willing to go further, finding that gag orders on the press would always be unconstitutional. Two other justices — Byron White and John Paul Stevens — indicated they might agree to an absolute ban at a later date.

A year after *Nebraska Press Association,* the Supreme Court struck down an order prohibiting publication of the name and picture of an 11-year-old charged with murder. The juvenile court judge had allowed journalists to attend the detention hearing but then banned publication of the child's name and a photo. By the time the judge issued the gag order, the boy's name and picture had already been widely published and broadcast. In *Oklahoma Publishing Co. v. District Court,* the Supreme Court said that once the judge permitted journalists to attend the hearing, he could not prohibit them from publishing the information they gathered while in attendance.

Nebraska Press Association and *Oklahoma Publishing Co.* have made it extremely difficult for a trial judge to justify gagging the press. Appellate courts have struck down gag orders prohibiting publication of jurors' names, evidence presented in open court but outside the presence of the jury, videotapes made during the government's investigation of alleged drug trafficking, the identities of juvenile offenders and victims, and defendants' prior criminal records and nicknames, such as "Quapaw Quarter rapist" and "Sugarhouse rapist."

Docudramas based on sensational crimes have led a number of defendants to seek to prevent such broadcasts. One example involved an attempt by Lyle and Erik Menendez to prevent the broadcast in Los Angeles County of *Honor Thy Father and Mother: The True Story of the Menendez Murders* while they awaited retrial on charges of murdering their parents. The brothers, who ultimately were convicted, claimed that airing the program in the county would make it impossible to find an unbiased jury. Applying the Nebraska Press Association Test in *Menendez v. Fox Broadcasting,* a California federal district court disagreed, holding that the trial judge could adequately protect the defendants' rights by implementing *voir dire* and jury instructions.

In 1996, the Sixth U.S. Circuit Court of Appeals declared unconstitutional a gag order in a civil case involving Procter & Gamble Co. and Bankers Trust Co. An attorney who represented Bankers Trust provided a *Business Week* reporter with copies of documents relating to the lawsuit that had been sealed by the trial judge. Hours before the story based on the documents was to go to press and without holding a hearing or giving *Business Week* a chance to protest, the judge issued a gag order barring publication. A few weeks later, Judge John Feikens unsealed the documents on which the story was based. Yet he still refused to rescind his order barring the magazine from publishing its article. The Sixth Circuit Court of Appeals called this a "classic case of a prior restraint" in violation of the First Amendment. The trial judge failed to demonstrate that publication would cause irreparable harm to a substantial government interest and had not provided McGraw-Hill the opportunity to argue the merits of the gag order.

Since *Nebraska Press Association,* only a few gag orders on the media have been upheld on appeal. In 2004, the Colorado Supreme Court affirmed in part a gag order in the Kobe Bryant rape case. Eventually, the charge against the NBA star was dropped. Before that, however, the trial judge issued a gag order prohibiting seven media outlets from publishing information from transcripts of closed proceedings they had received erroneously.

Because of the massive media interest in the case, the trial court set up an email list to disseminate public proceeding transcripts. Inadvertently, the court reporter e-mailed transcripts of closed hearings held to determine the admissibility of evidence relating to the accuser's prior and subsequent sexual conduct. The trial judge ordered anyone who had received the transcripts to delete them and not reveal their contents. Holding that preventing public disclosure of irrelevant information about the accuser's sexual history was a compelling interest, the Colorado

Supreme Court narrowed the order by striking the requirement that recipients must delete all copies and limiting the ban on disclosure to just those portions deemed "not relevant and material."

In 1990, the Eleventh Circuit Court refused to lift a temporary gag order prohibiting CNN from disseminating the contents of tape recordings of conversations between deposed Panamanian dictator Manuel Noriega, who was in jail in Miami awaiting trial on federal drug charges, and his lawyers. Jail officials had allegedly made the tapes, and CNN had obtained them legally. On a motion from Noriega's attorneys, a U.S. district judge issued a temporary restraining order prohibiting CNN from broadcasting the tapes and ordered the network to submit the tapes to him so he could decide whether their dissemination would present a "clear, immediate, and irreparable danger" to Noriega's rights and should be banned. The next day, the judge limited his order to material that was privileged. CNN appealed the order but also disobeyed it by continuing to air the excerpts from the tapes it had broadcast prior to the gag order.

The court of appeals refused to lift the district court's order, saying CNN's failure to allow the judge to inspect the tapes had made it impossible for the court to balance the network's First Amendment rights against Noriega's Sixth Amendment rights. The Supreme Court denied *certiorari*, despite vigorous dissent from Justices Marshall and Sandra Day O'Connor, who said the trial judge's order could not be reconciled with *Nebraska Press Association* and the Pentagon Papers case. CNN eventually turned the tapes over to the district judge, who concluded that broadcast of the remaining unaired portions would not violate Noriega's rights.

Despite the fact that the gag order was ultimately lifted, CNN was found in contempt of court for airing portions of the tapes while the restraining order was in force. CNN was given the choice of paying a large fine or airing an apology and paying a smaller fine. CNN chose to pay an $85,000 fine and broadcast an apology. This case illustrates an important point journalists

must keep in mind: Even if a court order is declared unconstitutional, a person who violates the order while it is in effect can be found guilty of contempt of court and subject to fines and/or imprisonment. This is known as the "collateral bar rule," which states that a person who disobeys a court order may not collaterally challenge the constitutionality of the order as a defense to the contempt of court charge. The reasoning behind the rule is simple: The effectiveness of the entire judicial system would be severely hampered if individuals were free to make their own decisions as to which court orders to obey and which to ignore. Under many circumstances, waiting for appellate review of a court order imposes little or no hardship on the individual subject to the order. But the situation changes when gag orders are imposed on the media since timeliness is the essence of news, and waiting for an appellate court ruling could change news into history.

A 1972 case in the U.S. Court of Appeals for the Fifth Circuit illustrates the strict application of the collateral bar rule. In *United States v. Dickinson*, two Baton Rouge, Louisiana, reporters were held in contempt and fined $300 each for disobeying a federal judge's order not to report on what took place during a hearing that was open to the public. The hearing was held to investigate the state's motives in prosecuting a federal volunteer worker charged with conspiring to murder the Baton Rouge mayor. The volunteer said the charges were brought to harass him because of his civil rights activities. Because the volunteer might later be tried on the criminal charges, the U.S. district judge ordered there be no media coverage of what occurred at the hearing. On appeal, the Fifth Circuit struck down the gag order as unconstitutional but sustained the contempt convictions of the reporters. The court wrote:

We begin with the well-established principle in proceedings for criminal contempt that an injunction ... *must be obeyed*, irrespective of the ultimate validity of the order. Invalidity is no defense to criminal contempt. ... "People simply cannot have the luxury of knowing that they have a right to contest the correctness of the judge's order in deciding whether to willfully disobey it.... Court orders have to be obeyed until they are reversed or set aside in an orderly fashion."

While the court recognized that "[t]imeliness of publication is the hallmark of 'news,'" it added, "But newsmen are citizens, too.... They too may sometimes have to wait."

More than a decade later, the First Circuit adopted a more flexible approach, ruling that a "transparently invalid" gag order could be violated with impunity as long as the publisher first made "a good faith effort" to have an appellate court reverse the order. The case resulted from the *Providence Journal*'s violation of a judge's order prohibiting publication of information the paper had received from the FBI. The information, which the FBI had gathered through illegal wiretaps in the 1960s, related to reputed organized crime leader Raymond L.S. Patriarca, who had died in 1985. In 1976, the *Journal* had sought access to transcripts of the wiretaps under the federal Freedom of Information Act. The FBI denied the request, and a federal court upheld the denial, ruling that release of the transcripts would violate Patriarca's privacy. However, after his death, the FBI released the transcripts to the *Journal* and other news outlets. After a Providence radio station aired some of the information from the transcripts, Patriarca's son sued to prevent further publication, claiming dissemination of the information would violate his privacy.

On November 13, 1985, Judge Francis Boyle issued an order barring publication of the wiretap information. The next day, the *Journal* published an article in direct disobedience of the order. Though Judge Boyle vacated his order on November 19, acknowledging that it was likely unconstitutional, in 1986, he found the *Journal* and editor Charles Hauser in contempt, fining the paper $100,000, giving Hauser an eighteen-month suspended sentence and ordering him to perform 200 hours of community service. The *Journal* appealed, and a three-judge panel of the First Circuit reversed the convictions. While it recognized that the collateral bar rule is the "general rule," it emphasized that the case involved a prior restraint on speech, which, it said, represents "an unusual class of orders because they are presumptively unconstitutional." It held that the Nebraska Press Association Test was the standard that applied to evaluating the constitutionality of Boyle's gag order and that it was "patently clear" the order did not meet that test. Boyle had failed even to consider two prongs of the test. The court noted that the purpose of a temporary restraining order, such as Boyle issued, is to preserve the status quo while the court considers the case. However, for newspapers, the court said, the status quo "is to publish news promptly that editors decide to publish. A restraining order disturbs the status quo and impinges on the exercise of editorial discretion."

A few months later, the First Circuit reheard the case *en banc*, affirmed the three-judge panel's ruling but modified it. It said that in the future a publisher had to "make a good faith effort to seek emergency relief from the appellate courts" before violating an invalid gag order. The Supreme Court declined to reconcile the apparent conflict between the Fifth and First circuits when it dismissed the government's appeal in the *Providence Journal* case on procedural grounds.

In trying to understand these two cases, it's important to keep in mind that *Dickinson* is binding precedent only in the Fifth Circuit and *In re Providence Journal* only in the First Circuit. Both cases are federal cases, and individual states are free to devise their own rules regarding application of the collateral bar rule when state court judges issue gag orders. Some courts have chosen to follow the First Circuit's lead. In 1998, the Mis-

sissippi Supreme Court unanimously overturned the contempt conviction of a *Delta Democrat Times* reporter who had disobeyed a trial judge's order not to report on a criminal defendant's juvenile record, which was discussed in open court. The state high court noted that the trial judge did not consider the Nebraska Press Association Test.

In contrast, in 2002, a New Jersey trial judge held four *Philadelphia Inquirer* reporters in contempt and fined them $1,000 each for printing the name of a juror in a high-profile murder trial even though two months earlier the New Jersey Supreme Court had struck down the order prohibiting publication of jurors' names. Thus, despite some successes in challenging contempt convictions resulting from disobeying gag orders, many attorneys advise journalists to obey such orders until they are reversed on appeal or, at the least, to make a sincere effort to obtain appellate review before disobeying an order.

VIOLATING COURT ORDERS & CONTEMPT OF COURT

The *Collateral Bar* Rule:
A journalist must obey a court order, even an obviously unconstitutional gag order, until an appellate court overturns it.

The *Providence Journal* Rule:
The press may violate a "patently invalid" gag order after a "good faith effort" to get an appellate court to overturn it.

Restrictions on Trial Participants

While *Nebraska Press Association* made it very difficult for judges to gag the media, it is easier for them to restrict the flow of information to the media by issuing gag orders aimed at trial participants, especially attorneys. Generally, courts view gag orders on trial participants as less distasteful under the First Amendment because they do not prevent the media from disseminating information but simply make it more difficult for journalists to obtain it. Courts also have greater power over trial participants, especially lawyers, than they do over non-participant journalists. However, newsgathering does receive some First Amendment protection, and trial participants have their own First Amendment rights to speak. Thus, there are limits on judges' gag powers. Before considering how those limits apply to the typical gag orders aimed at attorneys, witnesses, defendants and jurors, a somewhat unusual situation — a gag order aimed at newspapers that were themselves participants in the case — will be addressed.

In *Seattle Times Co. v. Rhinehart*, the Supreme Court said the strict Nebraska Press Association Test did not apply when the media themselves were parties to the litigation and had obtained information through the pretrial discovery process. The *Seattle Times* and *Walla Walla Union-Bulletin* were defendants in a libel and invasion of privacy lawsuit brought by Keith Rhinehart, head of the Aquarian Foundation, a religious group. The newspapers wanted information on the foundation's members and donors, but the foundation refused, arguing that publication of such information would violate the members' and donors' First Amendment rights. A Washington state trial judge ordered the group to release the information but issued an order prohibiting the newspapers from publishing what they learned as parties to the lawsuit.

The Supreme Court unanimously upheld the judge's order, saying it was not a classic prior restraint requiring strict First Amendment scrutiny. Preventing abuse of the discovery process was a substantial governmental interest sufficient to justify the order, the Court said, but the papers could publish the same information if they obtained it through some other way.

Seattle Times v. Rhinehart was an unusual case. Usually restrictive orders prohibit attorneys or witnesses from making statements that might prejudice the outcome of a trial. These rules are important to know, as attorneys and jurors can be great sources for legal reporters.

Attorneys. The American Bar Association's Model Rules of Professional Conduct provide that an attorney should not make public statements that "have a substantial likelihood of materially prejudicing" a pending case. While not expressly prohibiting any particular type of comment, the rules list certain subjects likely to cause prejudice, including statements about the character, credibility, reputation or criminal record of a party, suspect or witness; the existence or contents of a confession or a suspect's refusal to make a statement; the results of examinations or tests or the refusal of a suspect to take a test; opinions as to a defendant's guilt or innocence; or even that "a defendant has been charged with a crime, unless there is included therein a statement explaining that the defendant is presumed innocent until and unless proven guilty."

In 1994, amidst the massive publicity surrounding the O.J. Simpson murder trial, the ABA amended its rules to add a right-of-reply for defense lawyers. The provision says that an attorney "may make a statement that a reasonable lawyer would believe is required to protect a client from the substantial undue prejudicial effect of recent publicity not initiated by the lawyer or the lawyer's client." At the same time, the ABA added language directing prosecutors to "refrain from making extrajudicial comments that have a substantial likelihood of heightening public condemnation of the accused."

About forty states have adopted rules governing attorney statements. Most follow the ABA's model, allowing an attorney to be disciplined for making prejudicial statements even if the judge hasn't issued an order limiting extrajudicial statements.

In *Gentile v. State Bar of Nevada*, Nevada's rules were challenged by a lawyer disciplined for holding a press conference in which he declared his client innocent and questioned the integrity of grand jury witnesses. In 1991, the Supreme Court ruled that the "substantial likelihood of material prejudice" standard did not violate the First Amendment. Chief Justice William Rehnquist, noting that lawyers are "officers of the Court," justified applying a different standard to attorneys than to the media and general public. "Because lawyers have special access to information through discovery and client communications," he wrote, "their extrajudicial statements pose a threat to the fairness of a pending proceeding since lawyers' statements are likely to be received as especially authoritative."

Whether a state has adopted specific rules limiting attorneys' statements, a trial judge has the power to issue gag orders aimed at attorneys. One of the key criticisms of Judge Lance Ito's conduct of the O.J. Simpson murder trial was his failure to regulate the attorneys' out-of-court comments. Ito justified his approach by noting that California had not adopted a rule limiting attorney speech. But most commentators agreed that Ito as judge did not need a bar association or state supreme court rule to give him the power to prohibit lawyers' prejudicial statements. In fact, during the subsequent civil lawsuit brought against Simpson by the families of the victims, Judge Hiroshi Fujisaki imposed a wide-ranging gag order on all trial participants, including the lawyers.

If an attorney violates a gag order, the result can be a contempt of court conviction. In 1995, the Second U.S. Circuit Court of Appeals upheld the criminal contempt conviction of Bruce Cutler, attorney for alleged organized crime boss John Gotti, because he violated a trial court order prohibiting extrajudicial statements by attorneys if there was a "reasonable likelihood" that statements would interfere with a fair trial. The trial court found that Cutler knowingly and willfully violated its order by repeatedly speaking to journalists.

Gag orders on lawyers have been struck down when they were overbroad or when the trial judge failed to consider alternative measures. In a case resulting from the trial of the people accused of bombing the World Trade Center in 1993, the Second Circuit vacated a gag order prohibiting the attorneys from publicly discussing any aspect of the case. The trial judge had issued the blanket order without considering whether less restrictive means were possible. In 1986, a New York appeals court overturned as "vague and overbroad" an order prohibiting attorneys from "any discussion of this case with the news media," even telling reporters what time court would convene.

Witnesses. Judges sometimes issue gag orders aimed at witnesses. Such orders will be upheld if they are necessary to protect a defendant's right to a fair trial and alternative measures are not available. In 1984, a U.S. district judge in North Carolina issued an order prohibiting all potential witnesses in a murder trial from making "any extrajudicial statement relating to the testimony in this case that such potential witnesses may give, or relating to any of the parties or issues such potential witnesses expect or should reasonably expect to be involved in this case, or relating to the events leading up to and culminating" in the crime. The order specifically forbade potential witnesses from giving interviews to the press. The case involved the trial of Ku Klux Klan and Nazi party members for the shooting deaths of five people in Greensboro, North Carolina. In upholding the gag order, the Fourth Circuit noted that there had already been tremendous publicity and that many of the potential witnesses were relatives of the victims. The appellate court agreed with the trial judge that alternative remedies, such as change of venue, jury admonitions or sequestration, would be ineffective or impractical.

In 1990, the Supreme Court upheld the right of a grand jury witness to publish his own testimony after the jury term ended. A grand jury investigates but does not decide a person's guilt or innocence. Instead, it determines if there is sufficient evidence to formally charge someone with a crime. Grand juries meet in secret, and grand jurors are prohibited from revealing what goes on during the proceedings. Florida law took the traditional grand jury secrecy even further, though, by prohibiting witnesses from disclosing their own testimony.

Because of articles he had written, Michael Smith, a reporter for the *Charlotte* (Florida) *Herald-News*, was called to testify before a grand jury investigating alleged wrongdoing in the State Attorney's Office and Sheriff's Department in Charlotte County. After the grand jury term ended, he wanted to use his testimony in his writing and claimed he had a First Amendment right to do so. Noting the information related to government misconduct and constituted "speech which has traditionally been recognized as lying at the core of the First Amendment," the Supreme Court unanimously held the Florida law unconstitutional in the case of *Butterworth v. Smith*. Its opinion was narrow, however, restricted solely to a witness publishing his *own* testimony *after* the grand jury term ended.

Defendants. Occasionally judges try to gag defendants, with mixed results. Some appellate courts have struck down such gag orders using the same test applied to the media in *Nebraska Press Association* while others have upheld restrictions on defendants' speech by applying the *Gentile* standard. Saying it saw no "legitimate reasons" for treating "individuals, including defendants" differently than the press, the Sixth Circuit used the Nebraska Press Association Test to strike down a gag order that barred a congressman, on trial for mail and bank fraud, from commenting publicly on his own case outside Congress.

In contrast, the Fifth Circuit upheld a sweeping gag order in a high profile, federal corruption and racketeering case in-

volving former Louisiana Governor Edwin W. Edwards and others. The trial court had prohibited parties, lawyers and witnesses from giving "any extrajudicial statement or interview" to "any public communications media" that "could interfere with a fair trial or prejudice any defendant, the government, or the administration of justice," including statements "intended to influence public opinion regarding the merits of the case."

One defendant appealed the gag order to the Fifth Circuit, which upheld it, saying that if a trial court

determines that there is a "substantial likelihood" (or perhaps even merely a 'reasonable likelihood,' a matter we do not reach) that extrajudicial commentary by trial participants will undermine a fair trial, then it may impose a gag order on the participants, as long as the order is also narrowly tailored and the least restrictive means available.

A few weeks later, former Governor Edwards was fined $1,700 — $100 per word — for violating a similar gag order in a related case by discussing allegedly exculpatory evidence with reporters outside court.

Jurors. Jurors are always prohibited from discussing the trial in which they are involved while it is going on, just as they are barred from reading, viewing or listening to news about the trial. Recently, courts have had to deal with jurors posting updates on social media sites such as Facebook and Twitter during a trial or jury deliberation or using Google to research cases, activities which are also not allowed. Such during-trial restrictions on jurors are considered essential to preserving the integrity of the process. But concerns arise when judges impose restrictions on post-verdict juror speech. The two most common reasons for post-verdict restraints are to protect jurors' privacy and to ensure the secrecy of deliberations.

The Supreme Court has never ruled on the constitutionality of restrictions on post-verdict juror interviews, but a number of lower courts have upheld narrowly tailored restrictions. For example, the New Jersey Supreme Court upheld a ban on contacting jurors who had been dismissed after failing to reach a verdict until after a new trial was held.

If the ban on juror interviews is overly broad, it is unlikely to survive. In 1991, the Ohio Supreme Court declared unconstitutional an order prohibiting anyone, including journalists, from discussing a highly publicized murder case with jurors. More than a decade earlier, the U.S. Court of Appeals for the Ninth Circuit struck down a similar order requiring everyone, including the media, to "stay away from the jurors."

Sometimes restrictions on juror interviews will be modified or upheld in part by appellate courts in an attempt to balance the interests at stake. In 1994, the Third Circuit upheld a trial judge's order informing jurors that they were under no obligation to speak to journalists and banning journalists from asking a juror about the votes or statements of other jurors.

In 1995, two federal district courts in California declared unconstitutional state laws designed to prevent jurors and witnesses from selling their stories to the media. California's legislature had enacted the laws in response to publicity surrounding the O.J. Simpson trial. One law made it a misdemeanor for a juror or ex-juror to accept a benefit of more than $50 to talk or write about his or her jury service until ninety days after the trial concluded. It also prohibited anyone from paying a juror or ex-juror more than $50. The other law barred crime witnesses from accepting payment for their stories until one year after the crime had occurred or, if a criminal prosecution had begun, until a final verdict was reached.

Michael Knox, an original juror in the Simpson case who was dismissed part way through the trial, challenged the juror gag law. He wanted to write a book about his experiences, and the Los Angeles district attorney informed him and his publisher they would be prosecuted if they entered into a publishing agreement in violation of the California law. The federal court ruled that the law was a content-based prior restraint and was not narrowly tailored to serve a compelling government interest. Furthermore, it said the law was unconstitutionally overbroad and vague. In the other case, a coalition of media organizations challenged the witness gag law as unconstitutional. The court agreed, holding that it violated both the U.S. and California constitutions.

Post-Publication Sanctions

Just as the Supreme Court established constitutional limits on gagging the media, it also set up First Amendment barriers to post-publication punishment for reporting about the operation of the judicial system. Post-publication sanctions can be divided into two categories: contempt of court citations issued by judges and criminal penalties imposed by statutes for the publication of certain types of information.

Contempt of Court. Judges have the power to find people in contempt if they disobey court orders, show disrespect for the court or otherwise engage in conduct that interferes with the administration of justice. A contempt of court citation can result in a fine, imprisonment or both. Judges have the power to punish someone for any act of disobedience or disrespect, and some judges have used their powers to punish criticism of and commentary about their own actions and the judicial process. In the 1940s, however, the Supreme Court effectively put an end to judges' use of contempt of court to punish critics. It ruled that out-of-court commentary could not be punished as contempt unless it presented a clear and present danger of interfering with the fair administration of justice.

The first such case to reach the Supreme Court joined two appeals, *Bridges v. California* and *Times Mirror Co. v. Superior Court*. In one case, labor leader Harry Bridges was held in contempt after he publicly called a judge's ruling in a labor dispute outrageous and threatened to tie up the docks on the Pacific coast if the judicial order was enforced. In the second case, the *Los Angeles Times* was held in contempt for a series of anti-union editorials, which, the trial court said, were aimed at influencing decisions in pending labor disputes. Ironically, the Supreme Court used the same opinion to strike down the contempt convictions of both militant labor leader Bridges and the anti-union *Los Angeles Times*.

Writing for a five-member majority, Justice Hugo Black dismissed the argument that contempt powers held by judges were an appropriate tool for preserving public respect for courts. "The assumption that respect for the judiciary can be won by shielding judges from published criticism wrongly appraises the character of American public opinion," he wrote. "[A]n enforced silence ... would probably engender resentment, suspicion, and contempt more than it would enhance respect." Resurrecting the old clear and present danger test, which the Court had first used in World War I sedition cases, Black wrote that judges could punish commentary on pending cases only if such publications presented an imminent and extremely serious threat to the fair administration of justice.

Bridges and subsequent cases have virtually eliminated the ability of judges to punish criticism or general commentary on the judicial system. It's important to remember, however, that none of those cases involved efforts to influence jury decisions, disobedience of court orders, in-courtroom disruptions of judicial proceedings or disrespectful behavior. Judges can and do continue to use their contempt powers to punish such conduct, whether the perpetrator is a journalist or not.

State Statutes. It is not unusual for state laws to declare certain information relating to the justice system — such as juvenile offender, adoption and involuntary commitment records — confidential. Such laws generally bar officials from releasing the information to unauthorized individuals, including journalists. Some states have tried to go further in protecting confidentiality by enacting laws that penalize the media for publishing certain information relating to the courts. In two cases in the 1970s, the Supreme Court ruled such state laws unconstitutional, holding that government could not punish the publication of truthful information that had been lawfully obtained unless there was a compelling need to do so.

In the first case, the *Virginian Pilot* was fined $500 for violating a statute that made it a crime to publish information about confidential proceedings of the Virginia Judicial Inquiry and Review Commission, which heard complaints about judges' misconduct or disabilities and conducted its proceedings in secret to encourage the public to file complaints and to protect judges from the reputational harm from unwarranted complaints. The *Virginian Pilot* identified a judge who was being investigated and reported that the commission had not filed a formal complaint against him. Acknowledging that the commission could meet in secret and keep its records confidential, a unanimous Supreme Court held in *Landmark Communications v. Virginia* that imposing criminal sanctions on the publication of such information, which "lies near the core of the First Amendment," was unconstitutional.

The following year, the Court struck down a West Virginia law that made it a crime for newspapers to publish the names of youths charged as juvenile offenders unless they first obtained written approval from the juvenile court. Two Charleston papers were indicted for identifying a 14-year-old who had shot and killed a classmate. His name was obtained in interviews with witnesses, police and an assistant prosecuting attorney. Again the Supreme Court unanimously ruled in favor of the press. The press argued that the statute imposed a prior restraint since it required a judge's permission. In *Smith v. Daily Mail Publishing Co.*, the Court said it didn't matter whether the law was labeled a prior restraint since, "First Amendment protection reaches beyond prior restraints."

Relying on its decision the previous year in *Landmark Communications*, the Court found that publication of lawfully obtained, truthful information could be punished only to further a compelling state interest. While protecting the anonymity of juvenile offenders to enhance their chances of rehabilitation was an important interest, the Court held it was not sufficient to justify the infringement of First Amendment rights caused by imposing criminal sanctions for the publication of true information. It noted that while every state had a law providing for the confidentiality of juvenile proceedings, only five states "impose criminal penalties on nonparties for publication of the identity of the juvenile." Finally, the Court said the statute didn't even accomplish its goal since it only punished newspaper publication of juveniles' names. Radio stations in the area had broadcast the youth's name but were not indicted.

Court Closures

As noted, the Supreme Court in *Sheppard v. Maxwell* did not suggest that gag orders on the press be used as a remedy for prejudicial publicity. Nor did it suggest closing the courtroom to the press and public. In fact, in *Sheppard* the Court specifically reiterated its antipathy toward judicial secrecy. But, like gag orders, court closures became popular with judges seeking to avoid the problems they believed trial coverage caused.

Criminal Trials. In 1980, the Supreme Court began limiting judges' ability to close access to their courtrooms by ruling in *Rich-*

mond Newspapers v. Virginia that the press and public have a First Amendment right to attend criminal trials. It may seem odd that the Court used the First Amendment's guarantee of freedom of the press as a source of access rights, especially since the Sixth Amendment specifically provides for public trials. But the Court had earlier ruled that the Sixth Amendment's guarantee of a public trial was a *defendant's* right. If the defendant agreed to give up his constitutional right to a public trial, then the press or members of the public could not claim a Sixth Amendment violation.

In 1978, John Paul Stevenson, charged with murdering a hotel manager, waived his right to a public trial. The prosecutor had no objections. So Circuit Court Judge Richard Taylor agreed to conduct the trial behind closed doors. It's easy to understand why. This was to be Stevenson's fourth trial on the same charge. The Virginia Supreme Court had overturned his 1976 conviction because of the use of inadmissible evidence. A second trial ended in a mistrial when one of the jurors had to be excused for illness and no alternate was available. A third trial, which Judge Taylor also agreed to close, ended in a mistrial when one prospective juror told others about Stevenson's previous trials.

After Judge Taylor ordered the fourth trial closed, the Richmond Newspapers Company protested and asked for a hearing, which Taylor conducted in secret. At its conclusion, he stuck by his decision that the extraordinary circumstances justified a closed trial. The next day he dismissed the jury, ruled the state had not presented sufficient evidence to justify a guilty verdict and declared Stevenson not guilty. The decision was reported in a two-sentence order, and because the trial had been conducted behind closed doors, there was no way for the public to determine if Taylor's conclusion was justified.

Richmond Newspapers appealed the closure to the Virginia Supreme Court, which refused to overturn Taylor's decision. The U.S. Supreme Court, however, ruled 7-1 that the closure was unconstitutional. (Justice Lewis Powell, a Virginian, did not participate because he was acquainted with people involved.) As in *Nebraska Press Association*, the justices in *Richmond Newspapers* were divided on reasoning. The majority of seven produced six different opinions, with no opinion garnering the endorsement of more than three justices.

Chief Justice Warren Burger, joined by Justices Byron White and John Paul Stevens, rested his opinion on the history of open trials in the Anglo-American justice system. Contending that trials had been open "to all who care to observe" since before the Norman Conquest, Burger wrote open trials discouraged perjury and official misconduct, inspired public confidence in the justice system, and have "significant community therapeutic value," helping to defuse community outrage over crime. Although the First Amendment contains no express language regarding access to criminal proceedings, Burger wrote that the guarantees of freedom of speech and press and the rights to assemble and petition the government all "share a common core purpose of assuring freedom of communication on matters relating to the functioning of government. Plainly it would be difficult to single out any aspect of government of higher concern and importance to the people than the manner in which criminal trials are conducted." The public right of access to a criminal trial can be overcome only by "an overriding interest," Chief Justice Burger concluded, and only if the trial judge finds that "alternative solutions" are inadequate to ensure fairness. Burger expressly declined to provide examples of overriding interests that might justify closure, writing that Judge Taylor had "made no findings to support closure [and] no inquiry ... as to whether alternative solutions would have met the need to ensure fairness."

In a concurring opinion, which later became influential in shaping a test for determining when courts could be closed, Justice William Brennan, joined by Justice Thurgood Marshall, stressed the structural value of open courts: the role openness plays in self-government. "[P]ublic access to trials acts as an important check, akin in purpose to the other checks and balances that infuse our system of government," Brennan wrote. Open trials, he wrote, "play a fundamental role" in ensuring defendants receive fair trials and assuring the public that "procedural rights are respected, and that justice is afforded equally. Closed trials breed suspicion of prejudice and arbitrariness, which in turn spawns disrespect for law."

Two years after *Richmond Newspapers*, the Supreme Court ruled 6-3 that a blanket rule requiring courtroom closure during the testimony of minor victims in sex crime cases violated the First Amendment. A trial judge in Norfolk County, Massachusetts, had closed the trial of a man charged with raping three girls, two 16-year-olds and one 17-year-old. The judge interpreted a state statute as *mandating* closure of the entire trial. On appeal, the Supreme Judicial Court of Massachusetts interpreted the statute more narrowly, holding that it only required closure during the testimony of minor sex crime victims. The *Boston Globe* appealed to the Supreme Court.

In *Globe Newspaper Co. v. Superior Court*, Justice Brennan, for the majority, wrote that closure of criminal trials had to be determined case by case on the basis of a "compelling governmental interest" and had to be "narrowly tailored to serve that interest." While Brennan conceded that protecting "minor victims of sex crimes from further trauma and embarrassment" was a compelling interest, it did not justify a *mandatory* closure law since such a measure was not narrowly tailored. Case-by-case findings were needed to consider such factors as "the minor victim's age, psychological maturity and understanding, the nature of the crime, the desires of the victim, and the interests of parents and relatives." Brennan questioned the state's second justification for the law — that closure encouraged minor victims to come testify — because there was no empirical evidence to support the claim.

Continuing the trend of opening courtrooms to the press and public, the Supreme Court ruled in 1984 that jury selection is an integral part of a criminal trial and, therefore, is subject to the First Amendment presumption of access. *Press-Enterprise Co. v. Riverside County Superior Court* (which is known as *Press-Enterprise I* to distinguish it from a later case of the same name) began when a California judge closed almost six weeks of jury selection in a rape and murder trial involving a teenage victim. After the defendant was convicted and sentenced to death, the judge refused to release the transcript of the *voir dire*, saying, "[S]ome of the jurors had some special experiences in sensitive areas that do not appear to be appropriate for public discussion." After failing to obtain relief from the California appellate courts, the *Press-Enterprise* petitioned the Supreme Court to grant *certiorari*, which it did.

The Court unanimously ruled that closure of the *voir dire* violated the First Amendment. Chief Justice Burger, writing for the Court, used both the historical arguments he had articulated in *Richmond Newspapers* and Justice Brennan's structural /functional arguments. The "historical evidence," he wrote, indicates that, "since the development of trial by jury, the process of selection of jurors has presumptively been a public process with exceptions only for good cause shown." As for the functional argument, he wrote: "The open trial thus plays as important a role in the administration of justice today as it did for centuries before our separation from England.... Openness ... enhances both the basic fairness of the criminal trial and the appearance of fairness so essential to public confidence in the system."

Just as Justice Brennan had held in *Globe Newspaper Co.*, Chief Justice Burger in *Press-Enterprise I* said the presumption of open *voir dire* proceedings "may be overcome only by an overriding interest based on findings that closure is essential to preserve higher values and is narrowly tailored to serve that interest." The trial judge must present specific, written findings to justify closure and demonstrate that alternatives are not available. In this case, the trial judge failed to present findings to show that closure was necessary for a fair trial. The judge also "failed to consider whether alternatives were available to protect the interests of the prospective jurors."

Despite these rulings, judges still sometimes attempt to close jury selection. In 2010, Judge Warren Wilbert ruled that jury selection in the trial of Scott Roeder, accused of murdering a late-term abortion provider in Kansas, would be closed. "[T]he dissemination of information from the juror selection process," he reasoned, "would create a real and present danger of the defendant's ability to receive a fair trial." When several media outlets sued, the Kansas Supreme Court, in *Wichita Eagle v. Wilbert*, ordered Judge Wilbert to reconsider his ruling and held that court closures must balance the defendant's right to a fair trial and the public's right of access.

In 2014, the Colorado judge in the trial of James Holmes for the 2012 shooting at the premier of *The Dark Knight Rises* wrote a memorable opinion explaining why it was important to keep *voir dire* open. Holmes's attorneys moved to close jury selection to preserve their client's right to a fair trial. At a hearing on the motion, the prosecution partially joined the motion, arguing for closed introductory jury selection sessions and closed individual *voir dire*. However, a group of media organizations filed an objection opposing any closure.

Citing the experience and logic test, Justice Brennan's concurrence in *Nebraska Press Association*, and *Press-Enterprise I*, Judge Carlos A. Samour Jr. denied the parties' request for closure, reasoning that the presence of the press would ensure a fair trial. The final two sentences of Samour's opinion in *People of the State of Colorado v. James Eagan Holmes* sums up what many believe to be true:

> Contrary to the parties' speculation, openness and public pressure will ensure that suspicions of potential juror misconduct are publicized and will discourage those inclined to abuse the system. Hence, the presence of the public and the watchful eye of the media will enhance the fairness and effectiveness of the jury selection process.

Other Criminal Proceedings. In 1986, the Supreme Court extended the First Amendment presumption of openness to a criminal pretrial proceeding, specifically a preliminary hearing. In some states a preliminary hearing is known as a "show-cause" hearing; it is designed to determine if the government has sufficient evidence to bind a defendant over for trial. *Press-Enterprise v. Riverside County Superior Court*, known as *Press-Enterprise II*, resulted from the closure of a forty-one-day preliminary hearing in the case of Robert Diaz, a nurse accused of murdering twelve patients by administering massive doses of a heart drug.

As he had in *Press-Enterprise I*, Chief Justice Burger, writing for the majority, combined the historical justifications he relied on in *Richmond Newspapers* with Justice Brennan's concern for the structural value of openness to establish a two-pronged test for deciding when a constitutional right of access applies to a particular type of proceeding. The preliminary hearing at issue in *Press-Enterprise II* passed the so-called test "of experience and logic." First, the Court said, "[T]here has been a tradition of accessibility to preliminary hearings of the type conducted in California," and second, "preliminary hearings are sufficiently like a trial" to justify the conclusion that openness was necessary for the proper functioning of the process. The chief justice noted that the preliminary hearing was often the "final and most important" criminal proceeding since so few cases proceed to trial and often presented the only opportunity for the public to observe the criminal justice system. Furthermore, the absence of a jury at a preliminary hearing made public and press

attendance even more important to protect "'against the corrupt or overzealous prosecutor and against the compliant, biased, or eccentric judge.'"

Deciding that a First Amendment right of access attached to the preliminary hearing was only the first step in the analysis, however. The Court had noted in earlier cases that the right of access was qualified and could be overcome by an overriding or compelling interest. Therefore, before closing a proceeding, a trial judge must provide "specific, on the record findings" that "'closure is essential to preserve higher values and is narrowly tailored to serve that interest.'" The Court further held that, if the overriding interest to be served by closure was the defendant's right to a fair trial, a judge had to find that there was "a substantial probability" of prejudice resulting from an open proceeding, that closure would prevent the harm and that reasonable alternatives to closure would be unable to protect the defendant's rights.

WHEN MAY A JUDICIAL PROCEEDING BE CLOSED?

A judge must follow a specific path to determine whether a judicial proceeding may be closed:

First, the judge must determine whether a First Amendment right of access attaches to the particular type of proceeding. The Supreme Court has said there is a right of access to criminal trials and preliminary hearings, but if a judge is evaluating a closure motion for a different type of proceeding, the judge must consider the following:

- whether this type of proceeding has historically been open to the public (the experience test), and
- whether public access plays a significant positive role in the functioning of the proceeding in question (the logic test).

Second, if the judge decides a right of access exists, the judge must determine whether that right can be overcome by a compelling interest. To close the court, the judge must issue specific, written findings that

- closure is essential to preserve higher values, such as the defendant's fair trial rights or jurors' or victims' privacy rights; and
- the closure is narrowly tailored, that is, as brief as possible to serve the interest.

Third, if the overriding interest justifying closure is the defendant's right to a fair trial, the judge must find that

- there is a substantial probability that an open proceeding will interfere with that right,
- closure will be effective in protecting the right, and
- there are no reasonable alternatives to closure.

Although more complicated, the closure test articulated by the Court in *Press-Enterprise II* is similar to the gag order test used in *Nebraska Press Association*. Both emphasize a judge's responsibility to evaluate the effectiveness of the order and to try other alternatives before infringing First Amendment rights. In the years since *Press-Enterprise II*, lower courts have applied the closure test to a variety of proceedings.

In a high-profile case called *Seattle Times v. United States District Court*, the Ninth Circuit ruled in 1988 that closing a pretrial detention hearing violated the First Amendment. Stella Nickell was charged with murdering her husband and a woman she did not know by placing poison in Excedrin capsules on store shelves to make her husband's death appear to be a random product-tampering case. The hearing was to determine whether she would be released pending trial.

Applying the first portion of the *Press-Enterprise II* test, the Ninth Circuit noted that pretrial detention hearings were relatively new and there was no history of access. However, it said the arguments in favor of openness were sufficient to support a constitutional right of access to them. It concluded that there was inadequate evidence that an open detention hearing would prejudice Nickell's right to a fair trial and that the trial judge had not sufficiently considered alternatives.

Based on a First Amendment right of access and a state constitutional provision guaranteeing open courts, a North Carolina trial court in 1994 refused to close pretrial evidence suppression hearings in the case resulting from the murder of Michael Jordan's father. Evidence-suppression hearings present special problems since their sole purpose is to determine whether certain evidence will ever be presented to a jury. If evidence, such as an allegedly coerced confession, is declared inadmissible during a public hearing, the media are free to report on its existence. The fear, then, is that potential jurors will learn about the evidence, remember it and perhaps be influenced by it even though it was never used in court.

On the other hand, evidentiary hearings are often crucial to the outcome of a criminal trial because they can determine the strength of the prosecution's case. If a judge refuses to suppress a damaging piece of evidence, such as a confession or the results of laboratory tests, the case against the defendant may be so strong that he or she decides to plead guilty and no trial is ever held. Furthermore, evidentiary hearings often deal with allegations of police and prosecutorial misconduct, which are important to bring to public attention.

In 1979, the Supreme Court held that the Sixth Amendment did not provide the public with a right to attend pretrial evidence hearings. That case preceded *Richmond Newspapers*, however, and was not based on the First Amendment. Since the Court began articulating a First Amendment right of access to proceedings, many lower courts have reached the same conclusion, as did the North Carolina judge in the murder trial of James Jordan, Michael Jordan's father, and have recognized a right of access to pretrial evidentiary hearings.

Courts have also held that a constitutional right of access attaches to numerous other types of criminal proceedings, including plea and sentencing hearings, bail hearings, post-trial examinations of jurors about potential misconduct, hearings on a motion to compel a defendant to give a blood sample for an HIV test, hearings on a criminal defendant's recusal motion (asking the judge to remove himself from the case), and contempt-of-court hearings for a juror accused of disobeying a court order. However, some types of criminal proceedings, notably grand jury proceedings, have historically been held behind closed doors, and courts continue to rule that the First Amendment presumption of openness does not apply. The D.C. Court of Appeals underscored this point in 1998 when it ruled that the media did not have a right of access to court proceedings and documents related to the grand jury investigation of the Monica Lewinsky-President Bill Clinton affair.

Juvenile Proceedings. Juvenile proceedings historically were closed to the public. The primary goal of the juvenile justice system was considered rehabilitation rather than punishment. State laws often provided for closed hearings and confidential records to avoid stigmatizing minors by making their identities and crimes known to the public. Prompted by a rash of high profile, serious crimes by juveniles during the 1990s, however, many states have now opened their juvenile proceedings and records to the public and press, especially when the crimes involved would be felonies if committed by adults.

The Supreme Court has not ruled on whether the First Amendment right of access applies to juvenile proceedings. However, because there is a history of secrecy associated with juvenile proceedings and because many people who work with juvenile offenders believe confidentiality plays an important role in rehabilitation, several courts have held that the First Amendment right of access does not apply to such proceedings. For example, in 1981, the Vermont Supreme Court flatly declared, "[A] juvenile proceeding is so unlike a criminal prosecution that the limited right of access described in *Richmond Newspapers* does not govern."

On the other hand, some courts have found a constitutional right of access to juvenile proceedings — either based on the First Amendment or on state constitutions. The Tennessee Supreme Court ruled the public has a qualified First Amendment right to attend hearings at which juvenile court judges determine whether youths charged with crimes will transfer to adult court for trial. Supreme Courts in Oregon and South Carolina have interpreted their state constitutions to provide a qualified right of access to juvenile proceedings.

State statutes have become important as a source of access as more state legislatures have enacted laws declaring juvenile proceedings open to the public. Some states provide that a judge can close a proceeding only "when the public interest and the welfare of the child are best served by so doing" or "the best interest of the child or of the community" requires it. About one-third now require public proceedings when minors are charged with crimes that would constitute felonies by adults or with certain serious, violent crimes, such as street gang activity, murder, rape, kidnapping and arson.

A few states base openness on the age of the juvenile. Illinois has a unique provision declaring juvenile hearings closed "except for the news media and the crime victim." The law also says the court may prohibit anyone in attendance at a hearing from disclosing the juvenile's identity. Despite the trend toward openness, about a quarter of the states still keep juvenile proceedings closed or permit judges to exclude the press and public at their discretion.

Because the law is not uniform across jurisdictions, journalists who wish to report on juvenile proceedings should acquaint themselves with the law on the topic in the state or federal district in which they work.

Civil Proceedings. Although the Supreme Court has not ruled that civil trials are subject to the same First Amendment right of access as criminal proceedings, numerous lower courts have held that the press and public enjoy a right of access to such proceedings. In 2011, the Judicial Conference of the United States, which sets policy for federal courts, adopted a national policy that encourages federal courts to limit instances in which they seal entire civil case files. The conference, a body comprised of senior circuit court judges, concluded that federal judges should seal civil case files only when statutory law requires or extraordinary circumstances justify sealing.

Some courts have based this right of access on the First Amendment, following the Supreme Court reasoning in *Richmond Newspapers*. Others have found a common law or state constitutional basis for access. Still others have used a combination of constitutional and common law.

One of the most frequently cited cases involving access to civil proceedings is *Publicker Industries v. Cohen*, decided by the U.S. Court of Appeals for the Third Circuit in 1984. Reporters for the *Philadelphia Inquirer* and *Wall Street Journal* appealed when denied access to hearings in a lawsuit resulting from a corporate proxy fight. The Third Circuit recognized both constitutional and common law rights of access to civil proceedings, saying that "the public's right of access to civil trials and records is as well established as that of criminal proceedings and records." Other courts have followed the Third Circuit in finding a right of access to many civil proceedings.

Not every type of civil proceeding is open to the press and public. Like grand jury and juvenile proceedings, some civil hearings traditionally have been closed and remain closed under state statutes. Involuntary commitment and adoption proceedings are two of the most commonly closed civil proceedings. Just as with criminal proceedings, judges sometimes find that even when a right of access exists for a particular type of civil proceeding, a compelling interest can overcome that right as long as the closure is narrowly tailored. Two of the most com-

mon interests used to justify closure are preventing the disclosure of trade secrets and protecting individual privacy, especially if the litigation involves a child.

Civil discovery proceedings have generated a number of access lawsuits. Discovery is the pretrial phase of a lawsuit during which the litigants attempt to collect the information they need from one another and from third-party witnesses. Traditionally, discovery in civil litigation has not been open to the press and public. In fact, it is usually conducted in attorneys' offices rather than in public courthouses. Because there is no history of public access and because so much of the information gathered during discovery never becomes part of the official court record, judges often rule that there is no right of access to discovery proceedings. There have been exceptions, however. In one case, a federal district court held that representatives of the media should be allowed to attend sessions when depositions from the New York mayor and a former police commissioner were being taken in a lawsuit against the city. During the antitrust suit the federal government filed against Microsoft in 1998, the D.C. Court of Appeals ruled that journalists were entitled to attend the depositions from several Microsoft employees, including CEO Bill Gates. It based its decision on a little-known 1913 statute, which provided that depositions taken as part of Sherman Antitrust Act lawsuits "shall be open to the public as freely as are the trials in open court." As will be discussed later, some courts *have* ruled there is a right of access to discovery documents.

Denials of Access to Court Records

Since *Richmond Newspapers*, many lower courts have presumed that the First Amendment right of access to court proceedings extends to the documents filed in connection with those proceedings. The Supreme Court in deciding *Press Enterprise I* and *II* didn't distinguish between access to a judicial proceeding itself and access to at least one type of court record: the transcript of the proceeding. In *Press Enterprise II*, Chief Justice Burger wrote, "Denying the transcript of a 41-day preliminary hearing would frustrate what we characterized as the 'community therapeutic value' of openness."

The Constitution is not the only source of a right of access to court records. Many states have access statutes. In addition, both state and federal courts have long recognized a common law right of access. Two years before it decided *Richmond Newspapers*, the Supreme Court, in *Nixon v. Warner Communications, Inc.*, acknowledged that the common law created a "presumption ... of access to judicial records."

Courts have ruled that this general right of access applies to an array of criminal and civil court records. In 2012, the District of Columbia Court of Appeals ruled the First Amendment right of access to jury selection established in *Press-Enterprise* extended to questionnaires filled out by the sixteen jurors and alternates impaneled in the murder trial of the man who was convicted of killing former congressional intern Chandra Levy. This followed a similar decision to release the questionnaires of jurors administered during the trial of baseball player Barry Bonds for perjury and obstruction of justice.

In 1983, the Ninth U.S. Circuit Court of Appeals ruled that pretrial motions and documents filed in the John DeLorean drug prosecution had to be made public. "There is no reason to distinguish between pretrial proceedings and the documents filed in regard to them," the court wrote in finding a constitutional right of access. The same court held that there is a right of access to post-conviction records, including pre-sentencing reports and post-sentencing documents filed in connection with a motion to reduce a sentence. In civil cases, courts have found a right of access to pleadings, documents filed in connection with pretrial motions, summary judgment papers, and settlement agreements.

Some types of court records are not generally available to the press and public. Grand jury proceedings are closed, as are most grand jury records, including transcripts and evidence. However, when a grand jury hands down an indictment, it becomes a public record even though sometimes a court may seal an indictment until an arrest has been made. Adoption and involuntary commitment records are additional types of documents that are often declared confidential by state law and, therefore, unavailable to the press and public.

Research suggests that patent trials are another area where documents are routinely filed under seal. This is often done with little oversight, and many of the filings do not contain trade secrets or information that need to be protected. As one court noted in a high profile patent case, the result is that "many patent trials ... contain mountains of sealed exhibits."

Juvenile Records. Just as access to juvenile proceedings has increased in recent years, so has access to juvenile court records. While most states still consider most juvenile records confidential, some permit access to records of cases involving felonies or specific serious, violent offenses. In addition, several courts have recognized at least a qualified right of access to juvenile records. Sometimes judges allow the press access to redacted versions of records. For example, in a case involving the Federal Juvenile Delinquency Act, the judge prohibited access to proceedings but did permit release of records that had been edited to hide the identities of the defendants.

Discovery Documents. As previously indicated, access to civil discovery is sometimes an area of controversy. Journalists not only have sought to be present during the actual taking of depositions but also have tried to obtain access to deposition transcripts and documents obtained as part of discovery. They have enjoyed the most success when seeking access to discovery documents that have been filed with a court but are less likely to be granted access to unfiled materials.

A 1988 D.C. Court of Appeals case, *Mokhiber v. Davis*, illustrates this distinction. Russell Mokhiber, an investigative reporter, sought access to discovery documents from a civil lawsuit settled four years earlier. The court held that Mokhiber had no right to see materials that had never been submitted to the court but did have a right of access to papers submitted to the court, including those obtained *via* discovery. Likewise, in an antitrust case, a federal district court in California held that a common-law right of access attaches to documents in both civil and criminal cases as soon as they are filed.

In 2009, the Connecticut Supreme Court issued a detailed ruling involving sealed documents filed in twenty-three actions alleging sexual abuse by Roman Catholic clergymen. The Court ruled that there was a presumptive right of public access to "judicial documents" or "any document filed that a court reasonably may rely on in support of its adjudicatory function." Although the cases had been settled and withdrawn in 2001, four newspapers filed motions in 2002 seeking an order vacating the sealing of the documents. Although the court recognized there was a split as to whether discovery related documents should be considered public, the court concluded that because discovery can have an impact on the outcome of a case, those documents should be public in order to advance the public interest in judicial monitoring.

In other instances, courts have ruled that there is no right of access to discovery materials until the trial has begun or the documents have been introduced into evidence. Additionally, some courts have agreed to seal certain discovery documents to protect personal privacy. The Sixth Circuit ruled that protecting the associational privacy rights of non-parties was sufficient cause to justify sealing a list of Ku Klux Klan members obtained as part of discovery in a civil lawsuit resulting from the fire-bombing of a Black couple's home.

Other reasons frequently given for denying access to discovery materials filed with a court are to protect trade secrets and to ensure the efficient functioning of the judicial process. A 2001 case involving discovery documents filed in a lawsuit against Bridgestone/Firestone, Inc. after the death of an 18-year-old football player from West Virginia University provides an example of a court protecting trade secrets. When media companies sued to unseal nine discovery documents and ten pages excerpted from legal briefs, the Eleventh Circuit ruled that under the "good cause" standard, Bridgestone/Firestone's interest in keeping trade secrets confidential had to be balanced against the press' contention that disclosure would serve the public's interest in health and safety.

An example of a court protecting the functioning of the legal system is a decision of the U.S. District Court for Arizona, which denied access to unfiled discovery materials in a class action suit resulting from savings and loan association failures. The court said access would impede the progress of the case and create administrative burdens for the court and parties.

While most courts have refused to recognize a right of access to unfiled discovery documents, a few judges have ruled in favor of openness and declined to seal discovery materials except upon a showing of good cause. For example, a Minnesota trial court, in 1992, denied a motion from a St. Paul City Council member who was a defendant in a civil lawsuit to seal all discovery materials on the grounds that disclosure would cause her public humiliation and reputational harm. The court said there was a common law and statutory presumption of openness and rejected the closure request as overbroad. However, it did agree to temporarily seal unfiled materials relating to medical, financial and psychological records.

Courts have traditionally been reluctant to make records obtained as a result of the criminal discovery process open to the public. The discovery process involves the exchange of materials the prosecution will use to secure a conviction and materials the defense will use to achieve an acquittal. Prosecutors are not required to turn over all evidence gathered in an investigation, but prosecutors must share with the defense evidence that may exonerate the defendant. This material may or may not eventually be submitted as evidence at trial.

Like civil courts, criminal courts typically make a distinction between material that is filed with the court and material that is not, with most courts unwilling to find a common law or First Amendment right of access to unfilled material. A 2010 study found no examples of a federal court attaching a First Amendment or common law right of access to material disclosed during criminal discovery unless the material was later filed with the court. The same study concluded that Florida is the only state to specifically allow access to all criminal discovery records by state statute, while Rhode Island is the only state to specifically allow some access to criminal records through a judicial opinion. Under Florida public-records law, records provided to a defendant in a criminal case are accessible, although a court may order specific information be kept confidential. In 1985, in *State v. Cianci*, the Rhode Island Supreme Court developed a four-part test based on the Supreme Court judicial access decisions to determine when closure of discovery materials was justified.

Audio-Visual Records. As the use of audio-visual materials in court has increased, so too have efforts by journalists, especially broadcasters, to obtain copies of them. Sometimes the parties to litigation and judges are reluctant to allow broadcasters to copy audio-visual records because they fear the airing of such tapes will invade privacy, interfere with a fair trial, implicate innocent third parties and/or sensationalize and distort the judicial process. Some judges have argued that the right of access to court records is met by simply allowing journalists to see or hear audio-visual evidence or by providing reporters written transcripts. Broadcasters who want to air portions of tapes are seldom satisfied with such limited access and claim a right to copy as well as to see and hear.

The Supreme Court addressed the issue in 1978 when it denied media requests to copy former President Richard Nixon's Watergate audiotapes. In *Nixon v. Warner Communications*, the Court recognized a common law presumption of access. Justice Lewis Powell, however, writing for the Court, noted that "the right to inspect and copy judicial records is not absolute." In this case, the Presidential Recordings and Materials Preservation Act, passed by Congress within weeks of President Gerald Ford's pardon of Nixon for his part in the Watergate scandal, superseded the common law presumption of access. That act gave the Administrator of General Services the responsibility for overseeing public access to the tapes.

Since *Richmond Newspapers*, lower courts have recognized either a constitutional or common law right to inspect and copy audio-visual records, but that right is not absolute and can be outweighed by other interests. Several good examples of how courts balance the interests for and against access came in the early 1980s, when two FBI sting operations, known as ABSCAM and BRILAB, resulted in four different access-to-tapes lawsuits. During ABSCAM, the FBI videotaped government officials allegedly accepting bribes from undercover agents. In BRILAB, the tapes were of Texas officials allegedly accepting bribes in the awarding of state employee insurance contracts. Broadcasters wanted copies of the tapes.

In the first case, resulting from the trial of former Congressman Michael Myers, the Second U.S. Circuit Court of Appeals allowed the media to copy the tapes. Once the evidence was introduced in court, it reasoned, "[I]t would take the most extraordinary circumstances to justify restrictions on the opportunity of those not physically in attendance at the courtroom to see and hear the evidence, when it is in a form that readily permits sight and sound reproduction." The court considered the impact that copying of tapes might have on the fair trial rights of Myers and future ABSCAM defendants but concluded that the risks were not sufficient to justify "curtailing the public's right of access to courtroom evidence." It added: "Defendants, as well as the news media, frequently overestimate the extent of the public's awareness of news."

In the other two ABSCAM cases, the Third and D.C. Circuits also granted broadcasters the right to copy the tapes despite claims that airing the tapes would interfere with the defendants' fair trial rights and invade the privacy of unindicted third parties. The D.C. Circuit, however, told the trial judge that he could edit the tapes before releasing them to eliminate portions that might harm innocent third parties.

In contrast, in the BRILAB case, the Fifth Circuit upheld the trial court's refusal to allow copying of the FBI tapes. First, it said the media's right of access was satisfied when journalists were allowed to view the tapes as they were played in open court and were given transcripts. While the court acknowledged there was a common law right of access to the tapes, it said the fair trial rights of a defendant who had not yet been tried outweighed the access right.

Media have continued to try to obtain copies of audio-visual materials used in court. For example, in 1996, the Eighth Circuit followed the approach taken by the Fifth Circuit in the BRILAB case and denied media access to the videotape of President Bill Clinton's testimony in the Whitewater-related fraud trial of James McDougal. The tape had been played in open court, and transcripts were released to the public. The court said the press and public "were given access to the information contained in the videotape," and this met First Amendment requirements. In 2013, in a case involving the trial of a former police officer convicted of rape and indecent assault on a minor, the Massachusetts Supreme Court ruled that documentary filmmaker Steve Audette did not have a First Amendment or common law right of access to an audiotape "room recording" of trial proceedings made by a court reporter because the recording was "not the official record of the trial" and was never filed with the court. The court further held that Audette's right of access was satisfied by the typed transcript of the proceedings, which is a public document.

Terrorism-Related Secrecy

After the September 11, 2001, attacks on the World Trade Center and Pentagon, disputes arose as the government sought to close proceedings and seal records in cases with ties to terrorism. The first controversy began ten days after the attacks when Chief Immigration Judge Michael J. Creppy issued a directive mandating closure of all "special interest" immigration hearings. "Special interest" cases are those in which sensitive or national security information may be presented, including information related to terrorism. In December, a Michigan immigration judge held a closed hearing to decide if Rabih Haddad, who had overstayed his tourist visa and was suspected of having connections to al-Qaeda, could be deported. Several media organizations, along with members of Haddad's family and the public, sued, contending the closed proceeding was unconstitutional. Both a federal trial court and the U.S. Court of Appeals for the Sixth Circuit agreed that the First Amendment right of access established in *Richmond Newspapers* applied, even though the immigration hearings were not actually court proceedings but administrative, quasi-judicial proceedings. The courts held that the Creppy directive requiring blanket closure of all "special interest" hearings was unconstitutional.

A few months later, in a case involving closed deportation hearings in Newark, the Third Circuit issued a contradictory decision, ruling 2-1 that there was no constitutional right of access to such proceedings. In 2003, the Supreme Court refused to hear an appeal in the case, thereby failing to resolve the conflict between the two circuits.

The proceedings involving convicted 9/11 conspirator Zacarias Moussaoui included instances of secrecy. U.S. District Judge Leonie Brinkema barred the release of jurors' names in the sentencing hearing due to "the intense media and public interest in this case," blocked release of a Justice Department report on the FBI's handling of intelligence about the 9/11 attacks, and allowed scores of documents to be filed under seal or heavily redacted. Even at the appellate court level, portions of oral arguments were closed and documents sealed.

The basis for most of the secrecy in the Moussaoui proceedings was the Classified Information Procedures Act, which sets procedures for the handling of classified information in criminal cases. CIPA provides that if the U.S. attorney general certifies that an open hearing will result in the disclosure of classified information, the hearing must be closed and records sealed. In one of several appeals during the Moussaoui case, the Fourth Circuit acknowledged, "There can be no question that the First Amendment guarantees a right of access by the public to oral arguments [before] this court." However, the court also recognized the requirements of CIPA and declared that "the Government's interest in the security of classified information is a compelling one" sufficient to overcome the right of access. The court bifurcated the oral argument into open and closed portions and gave the government five days to edit a transcript of the closed portion for public release.

In 2004, the Supreme Court denied *certiorari* in another terrorism case in which every document, including dockets, was sealed, and all parties and attorneys were gagged. Mohamed Kamel Bellahouel, an Algerian married to a U.S. citizen, was detained in Florida in 2001, initially for overstaying his student visa. He was held for five months, during which time he was transported to Virginia to testify before the grand jury that indicted Moussaoui. Bellahouel filed a *habeas corpus* petition challenging his deportation proceedings with a U.S. district court in Florida. The court kept the case off the public docket, sealed all records and prohibited the parties and their attorneys from speaking publicly. Bellahouel appealed to the Eleventh Circuit Court of Appeals, where a clerk briefly and inadvertently listed the case on the public oral argument calendar, prompting news coverage of the extreme secrecy surrounding the case. The court of appeals upheld the secret proceedings, and Bellahouel appealed to the Supreme Court, which on its docket used only the initials M.K.B. to identify him. It released a heavily redacted version of Bellahouel's petition for *certiorari* but kept the government's brief in opposition secret.

Although journalists had been allowed to cover previous hearings at Guantánamo Bay, those involving fourteen "high value" detainees, including confessed 9/11 mastermind Khalid Sheikh Mohammed, were conducted in secret beginning in 2007. Known as Combatant Status Review Tribunals, they were to determine if detainees qualified as enemy combatants and could be tried by the military. The government refused to release the audiotape of Mohammed's hearing, at which he confessed to involvement in thirty-one terrorist plots including 9/11. A censored transcript was made public.

The Supreme Court's 2008 ruling that foreign detainees at Guantánamo Bay have the right to challenge their imprisonment in civilian courts opened the door for more battles. In more than 100 cases brought as a result of the ruling, the Justice Department filed unclassified documents under seal, restricting access to judges, lawyers and government officials. Secrecy was necessary, they said, because some unclassified documents mistakenly contained classified information. In 2009, a federal district judge ruled the sealing of unclassified documents violated the public's First Amendment and common law right of access to judicial records. "Public interest in Guantanamo Bay generally and these proceedings specifically has been unwavering. The public's understanding of the proceedings, however, is incomplete without the factual returns. Publicly disclosing the factual returns would enlighten the citizenry and improve perceptions of the proceedings' fairness," Judge Thomas Hogan wrote. He gave the government two months to make public the unclassified documents or request continued

secrecy for specific words or lines with an explanation of why the material should be protected.

U.S. District Judge Gladys Kessler held the Department of Defense in contempt because it disobeyed a court order to videotape the release hearing of a Guantanamo Bay detainee, Mohammed Al-Adahi. Kessler previously had ruled that while the hearing could be conducted in secret to protect national security information, the government was to videotape the testimony and make it available later. Then, in 2010, Chief Judge David Sentelle of the U.S. Court of Appeals for the District of Columbia abruptly closed the courtroom during a *habeas corpus* hearing for detainee Adham Awad despite the fact that both his lawyer and the Justice Department had consented to a public hearing.

Although the Pentagon received praise in 2010 from news organizations when the Department of Defense revised its rules for reporters covering military trials at Guantánamo, these incidents raise numerous important questions about the balance of power between the government, the people and the press. Indeed, continued uncertainty about these issues was evident in 2017, when the Court of Appeals for the D.C. Circuit disagreed with a lower court and said, no, the public does not have a right to view videotape of Guantánamo guards force-feeding a prisoner who was on a hunger strike.

CAMERAS IN COURTROOMS

In 1976, only two states — Texas and Colorado — allowed cameras in courtrooms; in 2010, every state allowed at least some camera coverage. A key reason for the shift was technological advances that eliminated the need for obtrusive flashes, bulky cameras and electrical cords. Also important were changing public and judicial attitudes. At the same time courts were recognizing the importance of allowing public and press access to the judicial process, video cameras were becoming part of everyday life for most Americans. Today, many people videotape seemingly mundane events in their life and post them on social media.

The situation was significantly different in the twentieth century, when cameras were intrusive and their presence in court was viewed as inconsistent with judicial dignity and decorum. The first official bans on cameras in the courtroom followed the 1935 trial of Bruno Hauptmann for the kidnapping of the Lindbergh baby. In 1937, the American Bar Association adopted Canon 35 as part of its Canons of Professional and Judicial Ethics. The canon, which declared that cameras "detract from the essential dignity of the proceedings, degrade the court and create misconceptions with respect thereto in the mind of the public," recommended that cameras be banned in all courtrooms. That recommendation, which was amended in 1952 to specifically include television cameras, was followed by most states for more than four decades.

When the Supreme Court heard its first cameras-in-the-courtroom case, *Estes v. Texas*, it agreed with the ABA that TV cameras intruded upon "the solemn decorum of court procedure." Justice Tom Clark, writing for the Court, said jurors could be distracted by equipment and the mere knowledge the trial was being televised. "Not only will the juror's eyes be fixed on the camera," he wrote, "but also his mind will be preoccupied with the telecasting rather than with the testimony." Witnesses, he wrote, "may be demoralized and frightened, some cocky and given to overstatement; memories may falter, as with anyone speaking publicly, and accuracy of statement may be severely undermined. Embarrassment may impede the search for truth, as may a natural tendency toward over-dramatization." Finally, for the defendant, the presence of TV cameras "is a form of mental — if not physical — harassment, resembling a police line-up or the third degree," Clark wrote.

Justice John Marshall Harlan wrote a concurring opinion in which he shared his colleagues' fears about disruption caused by cameras. However, he speculated that someday television might become "so commonplace ... in the daily life of the average person" that its disruptive influence would disappear.

By the 1980s, Harlan's prediction had nearly come true. In its second cameras-in-the-courtroom case, *Chandler v. Florida*, the Supreme Court in 1981 held that "no one has been able to present empirical data sufficient to establish that the mere presence of the broadcast media inherently has an adverse effect on that process." Florida was one of several states that began experimenting with cameras in courts in the 1970s. In *Chandler*, which involved two Miami Beach police officers charged with burglarizing a restaurant, the judge allowed a television camera in despite the defendants' objections. While only about three minutes of the trial were broadcast, the officers appealed their conviction, claiming that the televising of trials was "inherently a denial of due process."

Writing for a unanimous Court, Chief Justice Burger — who throughout his tenure as chief justice steadfastly opposed the introduction of cameras into federal courts — declared that the mere presence of cameras did not automatically deprive a defendant of a fair trial. He wrote that broadcast coverage might, in some cases, violate a defendant's constitutional rights, but the mere possibility of prejudice did not justify a ban on televising trials. Instead, a defendant would have to prove that "the presence of cameras impaired the ability of the jurors to decide" the specific case.

While *Chandler v. Florida* permits states to open their courtrooms to cameras, it does not require them to do so. The Supreme Court did *not* say that photographers have a First Amendment right to take their equipment into courtrooms. It said that states were free to experiment with television coverage. This point was underscored two years later in a case out of Miami. U.S. District Judge Alcee Hastings, who was charged with accepting a bribe, asked to have his trial televised and was joined by news media organizations in challenging the ban on cameras in federal courts. After the trial court denied the motion, the media appealed to the Eleventh U.S. Circuit Court of Appeals, which upheld the lower court ruling, saying there was no constitutional right, under either the First or Sixth Amendment, to bring cameras into court.

The Federal Rules of Criminal Procedure have prohibited televising of federal criminal trials for more than fifty years. In 1983, in *United States v. Hastings*, the United States Court of Appeals for the Eleventh Circuit affirmed that Federal Rule 53 did not violate the First Amendment. Several media organizations and the defendant in the Hastings case wanted the trial court to televise proceedings. Discussing *Globe Newspapers*, the court concluded the right to attend criminal trials could not be extended to the right to televise, record or broadcast.

Although cameras are still banned in most federal courts, there have been multiple attempts to experiment with cameras in federal courts. In the early 1990s, limited television coverage of civil proceedings was tried under an experimental program authorized by the Judicial Conference of the United States, which sets policy for the federal courts. An evaluation of the program by the Federal Judicial Center found that judges became more favorable toward cameras in the courts after the experiment began. Judges and court personnel believed the guidelines governing the program were workable and that journalists were generally cooperative. Judges and attorneys reported minimal or no effects of cameras in the courtrooms. Despite such favorable reactions, the Judicial Conference, in 1994, voted 19-6 to terminate the program.

In 2010, the Supreme Court barred a federal district court from broadcasting a non-jury trial in a case involving Proposition 8, which amended the California Constitution to include a section providing that the state would only recognize marriage between a man and a woman as valid. *Hollingsworth v. Perry* began when the Ninth Circuit Judicial Council decided to begin a pilot program allowing the limited use of cameras in federal district courts in the circuit. Cases would be selected for participation by the chief judge of the district court in consultation with the chief circuit judge. Judge Vaughn R. Walker of the District Court for the Northern District of California announced that under the pilot program the lawsuit involving a challenge to California's Proposition 8 would be streamed live to courthouses in other cities and recorded for broadcast on the Internet. Wishing to block the recording and broadcasting of their testimony, supporters of the proposition filed an application for a stay of the decision with the Supreme Court. In a *per curiam* opinion, the Court held that, while it was not "expressing any views on the propriety of broadcasting court proceedings generally," the district court had not properly amended its local rules to allow for broadcasting of the trial in accordance with federal law. Thus, although the trial was recorded, it was never broadcast or streamed via the Internet.

In 2011, the Judicial Conference decided to conduct a three-year pilot program to evaluate the effects of cameras in federal courts. Under the program, cameras controlled by judges were placed in fourteen volunteer federal district courts. Only civil proceedings are recorded, and both parties and the judge must consent to the recording, with the proceedings being available on a Web site at a later time. The presiding judge also is allowed to terminate recordings for any reason the judge considers "necessary or appropriate."

Although federal courts themselves have not always been open to broadcasting their proceedings, during the past few years Congress has repeatedly considered legislation to permit federal judges, both trial and appellate, to open their courtrooms to cameras. In 2011, a Senate judiciary subcommittee met to hear testimony over a bill, the Cameras in the Courtroom Act of 2011, that would have required the Supreme Court to televise its public proceedings. The hearing included testimony from a witness who offered numerous quotes from past and present justices who have opposed allowing cameras into the Court. The bill was sent to the House, where it was referred to committee. The bill was reintroduced in both houses in 2017, but no action was ever taken.

While the Supreme Court has also been reluctant to allow cameras, in 2000, in *Bush v. Gore*, for the first time it released audiotapes of oral arguments immediately after they were completed. Since *Bush*, the Court has occasionally released expedited audio of oral arguments in high profile cases at the request of media. In 2012, it declined media organizations' requests to tape arguments in three cases challenging the Patient Protection and Affordable Care Act (better known as "Obamacare") but agreed to release same-day audio recordings of the arguments, which lasted nearly six hours over three days.

All fifty states allow some camera coverage. However, the extent of coverage permitted differs greatly among the states, and journalists are well advised to study their individual state rules regarding trial and appellate proceedings before taking a camera, tape recorder or Smartphone into a courtroom. The best sources for information about cameras-in-the-courtroom rules in the fifty states is the Web site of the Radio-Television News Directors Association.

At one end of the spectrum is Florida, the site of the Casey Anthony trial, where there is a presumption of camera access that can be overcome only by a finding that electronic coverage of a trial would have a "qualitatively different" effect than other types of media. In California, broadcasting is permitted by written order of the judge, though recording jurors, jury selection, and conferences between participants is barred. At the other end of the spectrum are Alabama and South Dakota, where the

consent of all parties and attorneys is needed.

Like California, many states require consent of the presiding judge, and many place restrictions on the photographing of jurors and certain trial participants, such as juveniles. Most states limit the number of cameras allowed and specify where cameras may be placed. State rules often require pooling agreements among various media.

Despite some recent trials receiving gavel-to-gavel coverage, cameras in the courts continue to be a contentious issue. In 2004, a California trial judge prohibited camera coverage of the murder trial of Scott Peterson, accused of killing his wife, Laci, and their unborn child. A year later, another California judge banned cameras during the child molestation trial of pop star Michael Jackson. In contrast, on the other side of the country in North Carolina, another Peterson — this one Michael, a novelist and former newspaper columnist and mayoral candidate — was convicted of murdering his wife in a trial broadcast live on Court TV.

PORTABLE ELECTRONIC DEVICES AND SOCIAL MEDIA

Recently, judges have had to consider to what extent they will allow trial observers to engage in blogging from the courtroom. Most federal courts have not addressed the issue, but some have begun to confront it — with differing results. In 2009, U.S. District Judge J. Thomas Marten granted Ron Sylvester, a reporter for the *Wichita* (Kansas) *Eagle*, permission to use a Blackberry to update his Twitter account while covering a federal racketeering trial. While Sylvester had been tweeting from the courtroom since 2007, Marten's decision was the first official order from a federal judge allowing this form of coverage. Not long after Marten's order, however, U.S. District Judge Clay Land wrote that Rule 53 of the Federal Rules of Criminal Procedure should be interpreted as banning tweeting. According to Judge Land, the rule's prohibition on the "broadcasting of judicial proceedings" included "sending electronic messages from a courtroom that contemporaneously describe the trial proceedings and are instantaneously available for public viewing."

To date, the U.S. Circuit Courts of Appeals have remained silent on the issue of tweeting or using wireless communication devices. In addition, many states have yet to consider the question of whether updating a Twitter feed is "broadcasting." However, even states that have traditionally been camera friendly may have trouble adjusting to new media such as Twitter. For example, in Florida, as mentioned above, electronic media and still photography coverage of proceedings is allowed. In early 2010, however, the Standing Committee on Rules of Practices and Procedures considered a statewide ban on electronic devices in courthouses, although the proposal was voted down.

In 2013, Utah's rules about electronic coverage of courtroom proceedings underwent drastic changes to allow more coverage.

While Utah's prior rules had only allowed cameras in appellate courts under tight restrictions and banned them in trial courts, under new rules cameras, live streaming, live blogging and tweeting are allowed in all courts unless a judge provides a specific compelling reason to deny coverage. In 2014, however, Utah revised its rules regarding video, reversing the presumption that recording is allowed and, instead, letting individual judges use a large number of factors to determine when taping is allowed. Portable electronic devices may be used inside courtrooms, but may not be used to record or transmit images or sound of court proceedings.

While some courts are allowing Twitter, others have banned it — particularly in high profile cases. In 2012, Judge Charles Burns of Illinois banned all spectators, including journalists, from tweeting during the trial of William Balfour, who was charged with the murder of singer Jennifer Hudson's mother. The same year, Judge John Cleland banned all "electronic-based communications" from the courtroom during the trial of former Pennsylvania State University football coach Jerry Sandusky for sex abuse. Like federal judges who have interpreted Rule 53 to prohibit tweeting, Cleland interpreted Pennsylvania state court laws that ban broadcasting of court proceedings to prohibit tweeting from the trial. Although Cleland originally interpreted the rule to only prohibit the tweeting of direct quotes, when members of the media including the Associated Press and ESPN filed a motion seeking clarification, he modified his ruling to ban all tweeting from the trial.

Most courts appear to be taking an ad hoc approach, and there is no consensus on whether to let journalists use portable devices to do live updates during trails, with many jurisdictions considering the issue on a case-by-case basis. Even when cameras are allowed in courtrooms or media organizations are allowed to broadcast video from closed circuit cameras, judges still sometimes ban the use of portable electronic devices in a courtroom. A study conducted by the Reporter's Committee for Freedom of the Press concluded that different jurisdictions are adopting various rules and no preferred approach has emerged. Therefore, tweeting from a judge's courtroom, journalists should check the court's standing orders and see if the court's electronic device policy is posted. If it's unclear how the court will apply rules designed to deal with traditional electronic media to live-blogging, journalists should contact the court's public information officer.

SUMMARY

While concern about press coverage of the justice system has persisted for years, debate over the free press-fair trial issue escalated during the 1960s when the Supreme Court overturned several murder convictions on the grounds that publicity had deprived defendants of their Sixth Amendment right to a fair

trial. Sensational coverage of the O.J. Simpson trial in 1995 again brought the controversy into focus, and high-profile twenty-first century cases, such as the highly publicized Casey Anthony and George Zimmerman trials in Florida, have kept the debate going. The perceived conflict between the First and Sixth Amendments can occur in three ways: Pretrial publicity can make it difficult to find impartial jurors; during-trial publicity can influence a sitting jury; and the presence of journalists and/or their equipment in the courtroom can cause physical or psychological disruption.

Two broad categories of remedies are available to judges. First are the traditional remedies designed to compensate for — but not eliminate — publicity. The most commonly used remedies are change of venue, continuance, rigorous *voir dire* and jury admonitions. The second category consists of remedies aimed at reducing or eliminating publicity. They are more problematic since they directly affect the media's ability to obtain and report information related to the judicial system. Beginning in the 1970s, the Supreme Court began placing First Amendment restrictions on the use of these remedies.

In 1976, in *Nebraska Press Association v. Stuart*, the Supreme Court held that gag orders constitute prior restraint and could be used only if (1) there was pervasive publicity likely to interfere with a fair trial, (2) an order would effectively remedy that, and (3) no other remedies were available. This test made it difficult to justify gagging the media and greatly reduced the number of gag orders issued and upheld on appeal. However, journalists must remember that if a judge issues a gag order, violating it can result in a contempt of court citation even if the order is struck down later. While some appellate courts have said journalists can violate a patently invalid gag order if timely appeal is not available, others have enforced the collateral bar rule, which requires that a person obey a judicial order and then challenge its constitutionality as a defense to contempt of court.

Gag orders aimed at trial participants generally are not subject to the same rigorous test of constitutionality as gag orders aimed at the media. In *Gentile v. State Bar of Nevada*, the Supreme Court said it was permissible to punish an attorney who made extrajudicial statements that posed a "substantial likelihood" of interfering with a fair trial. While judges have greater leeway in restricting the speech of lawyers and other trial participants, there are First Amendment limits. A gag order cannot be overbroad and cannot be issued unless necessary to protect a defendant's right to a fair trial, and no other alternative measures are available.

In addition to restricting the use of prior restraints on media coverage of the courts, the Supreme Court has also applied the First Amendment to limit the use of post-publication sanctions. In the 1940s, it ruled that judges could not use their contempt of court powers to punish coverage of the judicial process unless such publications presented a clear and present danger of inter-

fering with the fair administration of justice. This stringent
standard has virtually eliminated the practice of judges citing
for contempt journalists and others who criticize the courts.
Three decades later, the Court strengthened the media's protection against post-publication punishments when it ruled that
the media could not be punished for publishing lawfully obtained, truthful information unless necessary to serve a compelling governmental interest.

In a series of cases in the 1980s, the Supreme Court also put
a halt to the use of court closures as a means of controlling publicity when it held that the press and public have a First
Amendment right of access to criminal proceedings. The Court
established a multi-part test for determining when a hearing
could be closed, which requires a judge to issue written findings
that closure is essential to serve higher values and is as narrowly tailored as possible. While the Supreme Court has not
ruled directly on whether a constitutional right of access exists
to civil proceedings, lower courts have found a qualified First
Amendment right of access and have used the same test the
Court mandated for closing criminal proceedings.

Many lower courts also have found that a First Amendment
access right extends to judicial records. Even if they recognize a
constitutional right of access, courts are unanimous that the
common law provides both the press and public the right to inspect certain judicial records. Increasing online access to judicial records is generating concerns about misuse of public information and privacy, prompting some efforts to restrict electronic access. Media attempts to gain access to some types of
records — especially juvenile records, discovery materials and
audio-visual records — have caused conflicts, and courts have
disagreed about the extent of access rights.

One of the major free press-fair trial battles has involved
cameras in courtrooms. In 1965, the Supreme Court overturned
a criminal conviction on the grounds that TV cameras caused
physical and psychological disruptions inconsistent with the
Sixth Amendment's guarantee of a fair trial. In the decades that
followed, as cameras became less obtrusive and television became more ubiquitous, some states began to allow video coverage of judicial proceedings, ultimately leading the Court to revise its position. In *Chandler v. Florida* in 1981, it ruled that
the mere presence of cameras did not automatically deny a defendant a fair trial. While there is no constitutional right to
bring cameras into courts, the Court said, states are free to do
so. By 2009, all fifty states allowed some form of camera coverage of courts. Most federal courts continue to ban cameras, despite generally favorable responses to a limited experiment with
camera coverage in the 1990s.

Conflicts between the press and the judiciary are inevitable
since each is committed to advancing a different interest and
those interests often appear to be at odds. Judges and attorneys
see their primary responsibility as ensuring fair trials and the
proper functioning of the judicial system. Their key concern is
protecting the rights of litigants, witnesses and jurors. Journalists see their primary responsibility as informing the public and
serving as a watchdog over government, including the judicial
branch. Their key concern is protecting freedom of the press
and the public's right to know.

The Supreme Court has made it clear that the First and
Sixth Amendments are of equal importance. Neither takes precedence over the other. The press has broad First Amendment
rights to observe on the judicial process, and the judiciary must
find ways to respect those rights while at the same time ensuring that trials are fair, jurors are unbiased and the process operates smoothly, effectively and openly.

BIBLIOGRAPHY

Articles

Ardia, David. "Court Transparency and the First Amendment," 38 *Cardozo Law Review* 385 (2017).
Hengstler, Gary A. "Pressing Engagements: Courting Better Re-lationships Between Judges and Journalists," 56 *Syracuse Law Review* 419 (2006).
Hopkins, W. Wat. "*Sheppard v. Maxwell* Revisited: A 'Roman Holiday,' a 'Carnival' or 'Decorum Comparable with the Best'?" 7 *Journal of Media Law & Ethics* 4 (2020).
Levine, Raleigh Hannah. "Toward a New Public Access Doc-trine," 27 *Cardozo Law Review* 1739 (2006).
Powers, Christopher. "Textual Misconduct: What Juror Texting Means for Courts," 67 *Syracuse Law Review* 303 (2017).
Silver, Derigan. "Media Censorship and Access to Terrorism Trials: A Social Architecture Analysis." 25 *Notre Dame Jour-nal of Law, Ethics, and Public Policy* 143 (2011).

Books

Alexander, S.L. *Covering the Courts: A Handbook for Journal-ists.* Rowman & Littlefield, 2004, https://www.myilibrary.com.
Bunker, Matthew D. *Justice and the Media: Reconciling Fair Trials and a Free Press.* Mahwah, N.J.: Lawrence Erlbaum Associates, 1997.
Snyder, Robert W., ed. *Covering the Courts: Free Press, Fair Trials & Journalistic Performance.* New Brunswick, N.J.: Transaction, 1999.

Cases

Al-Adahi v. Obama, 672 F. Supp. 2d 114 (D.C. Cir. 2010).
Amato v. Richmond, 157 F.R.D. 26 (E.D. Va. 1994).
Arkansas Democrat-Gazette v. Zimmerman, 20 S.W.3d 301 (Ark. 2000).

Associated Press v. United States Dist. Court, 705 F.2d 1143 (9th Cir. 1983).

Baloga v. Maccabee, 20 Media L. Rep. (BNA) 2201 (Minn. Dist. Ct. 1992).

Belo Broad. Corp. v. Clark, 654 F.2d 423 (5th Cir. 1981).

Boumediene v. Bush, 553 U.S. 723 (2008).

Brady v. Maryland, 373 U.S. 83 (1963).

Bush v. Gore, 531 U.S. 98 (2000).

Butterworth v. Smith, 494 U.S. 624 (1990).

Calif. First Amendment Coalition v. Lungren, No. C 95-0440-FMS, 1995 U.S. Dist. LEXIS 11655 (N.D. Cal., Aug. 9, 1995).

Capital Cities Media v. Toole, 463 U.S. 1303 (Brennan, Circuit Justice) (1983).

CBS v. District Court, 727 F.2d 1174 (9th Cir. 1984).

Chandler v. Florida, 449 U.S. 560 (1981).

Chicago Tribune Co. v. Bridgestone/Firestone, Inc., 263 F.2d 1304 (11th Cir. 2001).

Commonwealth v. Winfield, 985 N.E.2d 86 (Mass. 2013).

Connecticut Magazine v. Moraghan, 676 F. Supp. 38 (D. Conn. 1987).

Courier-Journal v. Marshall, 828 F.2d 361 (6th Cir. 1987).

Detroit Free Press v. Ashcroft, 195 F. Supp. 2d 948 (E.D. Mich. 2002), *aff'd*, 303 F.3d 681 (6th Cir. 2002).

Dhiab v. Trump, 852 F.3d 1087 (D.C. Cir. 2017).

Doe v. Santa Fe Independent School District, 933 F. Supp. 647 (S.D. Tex. 1996).

Dove Audio v. Lungren, No. CV 95-2570 RG (JRX), 1995 WL 432631 (C.D. Cal., June 14, 1995).

Estate of Rosenbaum v. New York City, 21 Media L. Rep. (BNA) 1987 (E.D.N.Y. 1993).

Estes v. Texas, 381 U.S. 532 (1965).

Florida *ex rel.* Miami Herald Publishing Co. v. McIntosh, 340 So. 2d 904 (Fla. 1976).

Florida v. Green, 395 So. 2d 532 (Fla. 1981).

Gannett Co., Inc. v. DePasquale, 443 U.S. 368 (1979).

Gentile v. State Bar of Nevada, 501 U.S. 1030 (1991).

Globe Newspaper Co. v. Superior Court, 457 U.S. 596 (1982).

Hollingsworth v. Perry, 558 U.S. 183 (2010)(per curiam).

In re Am. Continental Corp./Lincoln Savings & Loan Securities Litigation, 18 Media L. Rep. (BNA) 2303 (D. Ariz. 1991).

In re Cable News Network, Inc., 917 F.2d 1543 (11th Cir. 1990), denying cert. 498 U.S. 976 (1990).

In re J.S., 438 A.2d 1125 (Vt. 1981).

In re Providence Journal, 820 F.2d 1342 (1st Cir. 1986), *modified*, 820 F.2d 1354 (1st Cir. 1987) (en banc).

In re Russell, 726 F.2d 1007 (4th Cir. 1984).

In re Wall Street Journal, 601 Fed. Appx. 215 (4th Cir. 2015).

Irvin v. Dowd, 366 U.S. 717 (1961).

Jeffries v. Mississippi, 724 So. 2d 897 (Miss. 1998).

KUTV v. Conder, 668 P.2d 513 (Utah 1983).

Landmark Communications v. Virginia, 435 U.S. 829 (1978).

M.K.B. v. Warden, 540 U.S. 1213 (2004).

Makhiber v. Davis, 14 Media L. Rep. (BNA) 2313 (D.C. Cir. 1988).

Marshall v. United States, 360 U.S. 310 (1959).

Menendez v. Fox Broad. Co., 22 Media L. Rep. (BNA) 1702 (C.D. Cal. 1994).

Murphy v. Florida, 421 U.S. 794 (1975).

NBC v. Cooperman, 501 N.Y.S.2d 405 (App. Div. 1986).

Nebraska Press Association v. Stuart, 427 U.S. 539 (1976).

Nixon v. Warner Communications, 435 U.S. 589 (1978).

North Jersey Media Group v. Ashcroft, 308 F.3d 198 (3d Cir. 2002), *cert denied* North Jersey Media Group, Inc. v. Ashcroft, 538 U.S. 1056 (2003).

Ohio ex rel. Cincinnati Post v. Court of Common Pleas, 570 N.E.2d 1101 (Ohio 1991).

Oklahoma Publishing Co. v. District Court, 430 U.S. 308 (1977).

Oregonian Publishing v. Deiz, 613 P.2d 23 (Or. 1980).

People of the State of Colorado v. James Eagan Holmes, No. 12CR1522, Order In Regards to Defendant's Request to Close Jury Selection to the Public (D-154-a2, Jun. 11, 2014).

People v. Bryant, 94 P.3d 624 (Colo. 2004), *stay denied sub nom.* United States v. District Court, 542 U.S. 1301 (Breyer, Circuit Justice 2004).

Press-Enterprise Co. v. Riverside County Superior Court, 464 U.S. 501 (1984).

Press-Enterprise Co. v. Riverside County Superior Court, 478 U.S. 1 (1986).

Procter & Gamble Co. v. Bankers Trust Co., 78 F.3d 219 (6th Cir. 1996).

Publicker Industries v. Cohen, 733 F.2d 1059 (3d Cir. 1984).

Richmond Newspapers v. Virginia, 448 U.S. 555 (1980).

Rideau v. Louisiana, 373 U.S. 723 (1963).

Rosado et al. v. Bridgeport Roman Catholic Diocesan Corp., 970 A.2d 656, 682 (Conn. 2009).

Schenck v. United States, 249 U.S. 47 (1919).

Seattle Times v. Rhinehart, 467 U.S. 20 (1984).

Seattle Times v. United States District Court, 845 F.2d 1513 (9th Cir. 1988).

Sheppard v. Maxwell, 384 U.S. 333 (1966).

Skilling v. U.S., 561 U.S. 358 (2010).

Smith v. Daily Mail Publishing Co., 443 U.S. 97 (1979).

State v. Neulander, 801 A.2d 255 (N.J. 2002).

Tennessee v. James, 902 S.W.2d 911 (Tenn. 1995).

Times Mirror C. v. Superior Court, 314 U.S. 252 (1941).

United States v. Antar, 38 F.3d 1348 (3d Cir. 1994).

United States v. Brown, 218 F.3d 415 (5th Cir. 2000).

United States v. Burr, 25 F. Cas. 49 (D. Va. 1807).

United States v. CNN, 865 F. Supp. 1549 (S.D. Fla. 1994).

United States v. Cutler, 58 F.3d 825, 828 (2d Cir. 1995).

United States v. Dickinson, 465 F.2d 496 (5th Cir. 1972).

United States v. Ford, 830 F.2d 596 (6th Cir. 1987).

United States v. Hastings, 461 U.S. 499 (1983).

United States v. Hastings, 695 F.2d 1278 (11th Cir. 1983).

United States v. McDougal, 103 F.3d 651 (8th Cir. 1996).

United States v. Microsoft Corp., 165 F.3d 952 (D.C. Cir. 1999).

United States v. Moussaoui, 65 Fed. App'x 881 (4th Cir., 2003).

United States v. Myers, 635 F.2d 945 (2d Cir. 1981).

United States v. Noriega, 752 F. Supp. 1032 (S.D. Fla.), aff'd sub nom. In re CNN, Inc., 917 F.2d 1543 (11th Cir.).

United States v. Salameh, 992 F.2d 445 (2d Cir. 1993).

United States v. Shelnutt, 2009 U.S. Dist. LEXIS 101427 (M.D. Ga., Nov. 2, 2009).

United States v. Sherman, 581 F.2d 1358 (9th Cir. 1978).

United States v. Three Juveniles, 862 F. Supp. 651 (D. Mass. 1994), aff'd, 61 F.3d 86 (1st Cir. 1995).

Wichita Eagle v. Wilbert, No. 103,666 (Kan. Jan. 12, 201.

Woven Elec. Corp. v. Advance Group, Inc., 19 Media L. Rep. (BNA) 1019 (4th Cir. 1991).

Access to Public Documents and Meetings

By Michele Kimball

☑ **Headnote Questions**

- Why is access to government information important?
- What legal provisions provide a right for access to government records and meetings?
- How are open government provisions balanced with other rights, like privacy or protection of national security?
- How do these laws work, and how can people use them?
- What obstacles to access to government information exist?

Access to government information provides a balance of power to citizens. It's the capacity to understand how government works and what it is doing. Consider access to government information the window through which we can watch our representatives serve the people. Without it, citizens are completely in the dark — making it possible for corruption to flourish. With knowledge of the government's actions, citizens can evaluate whether their governmental representatives are working in their best interests. Some examples of how information gathered through open government provisions shed light on government function:

- An analysis of thousands of documents from the Department of Defense showed the reality of civilian casualties, including children, in war. The *New York Times* investigation was awarded the 2022 Pulitzer Prize for International Reporting.
- Disparities emerged in the effects of the COVID-19 pandemic among race, ethnicity and socioeconomic lines. Tracking a year of medical examiner's data through public records requests allowed one community to determine the hardest hit among them.
- Unclassified documents reporters requested from the Department of Homeland Security in 2020 showed that the agency compiled intelligence reports about journalists in an effort to track leaks. After the revelation became public, the practice ceased.
- After the raid of a reporter's home in San Francisco, docu-

ments requested through a public records request showed that law enforcement officers were told not to use body-worn cameras because footage could be compromising. Another document request regarding the same incident showed that the reporter was improperly questioned by authorities. The search warrants in the case were later deemed unlawful, and the city paid a settlement to the reporter for $369,000.

These are just a few examples. By one researcher's count, one in five print stories and one in ten broadcast stories relied on public records. FOIA scholar Margaret Kwoka said the numbers could be higher as journalists don't always reveal their reporting techniques in their stories.

There are two categories of open government provisions: federal and state. The federal Freedom of Information Act and Government in the Sunshine Act cover most federal agencies, except for the president, the Congress and the federal judiciary.

Citizens can watch government in action by looking at documents or sitting in on meetings. It may seem like a simple transaction — taking a seat at a meeting or looking in a government file — but it is worth much more. And there is a long history of legal provisions that give us the right to do it.

OPEN GOVERNMENT AND THE LAW

The reasons open government provisions exist have everything to do with keeping our democracy strong. Scholar Alexander Meiklejohn introduced the concept of self-governance, meaning that a strong citizenry is one that uses the power of knowledge of the inner workings of government to direct elected officials in how to better represent their constituents. Meiklejohn described this as a social compact for citizens to remain vigilant over their government. Scholar Vincent Blasi also recognized the importance of the ability to oversee the performance of government officials' duties to ensure they are in the best interests of the citizenry — a public with a keen understanding of what its representatives are doing is a checking power on government corruption. An open government is a source for providing citizens the power to hold government accountable and encourage a strong, healthy democracy that functions in their best interests.

Value of Openness

However, while our modern perspectives might assume that the founders of our country agreed with the value of open government, that was not necessarily the case. The road to open government had its bumps, even at the very beginning. The members of the Continental Congress, gathering in Philadelphia in May of 1775 to plan out a new government, agreed "that the members consider themselves under the strongest obligations of honor to keep the proceedings secret, until the majority shall direct them to be made public," according to a scribe's notes. The group again renewed that vow of secrecy in November of the same year in a formal resolution.

A Brief History

About fourteen years later, as our nascent government began presiding as an actual bicameral Congress, the conflict existed between government officials who recognized the need for openness but weren't sure they actually wanted it. The founders recognized the necessity of press observations of government function to document the development of a democracy guided by the will of the people. However, that recognition did not yield an automatic sense of openness, and the adversarial relationship between government officials and the press was part of the fabric of the development of the early republic. Not twenty-four hours after submitting for ratification an amendment to the U.S. Constitution guaranteeing the right to a free press, the framers argued about whether to bar the press from the floor of the House of Representatives.

It was James Madison who reminded his colleagues that while the press may distort what was happening on the floor, it would be far more unwieldy to have to try to report one's position and statements without the help of the press. The motion to bar the press was withdrawn, as were others who attempted to establish control over press coverage, instead ending the debate with a caution that printers should be more accurate and impartial in the future.

Meanwhile, the Senate held a more circumspect view of the press, and it was unwilling to provide access to its proceedings. The congressional division between barring and providing access to the press took on a political edge. The Federalist majority saw press coverage of Congress as a source of civil unrest among the citizenry, while the Republican minority viewed the press as a weapon to wield against the majority. The Republicans used this division to fight for openness in Senate proceedings and worked against restrictions of the press in the House in an effort to preserve liberty — specifically by ensuring that citizens knew what their representatives were doing and saying on their behalf. Eventually, the Senate opened its doors to press and public view in December 1794. Following the House procedure, the Senate did not hire stenographers to record its proceedings, but instead relied on newspaper reporters' chronicles.

More than thirty years after those arguments, Madison again extolled the importance of an educated, knowledgeable citizenry in a Democratic society. He wrote in an 1822 letter about the educational system in Kentucky:

Nothing could be more irrational than to give people power, and to withhold from them information with which power is abused. A people who mean to be their own governors must arm themselves with power which knowledge gives. A popular government without popular information or the means of acquiring it is but a prologue to a farce or a tragedy, or perhaps both.

Access to State and Federal Information

The U.S. Supreme Court has recognized the value of public access to information to maintain an informed citizenry. In *New York Times Co. v. Sullivan*, the Court declared that the "central meaning" of the First Amendment is that it protects discussion about government and officials. Without guarantees of free speech, self-governance is an unobtainable goal. But the Court has been reluctant to extend that guarantee to access to the government information necessary to give content to that speech.

Only in the context of criminal trials has the Court fully considered the access issue. First in *Richmond Newspapers v. Virginia* and then in *Press-Enterprise Co. v. Superior Court* (II),[1] it held that the acquisition of newsworthy information was entitled to First Amendment protection. It took pains, however, to limit its holding to a particular kind of access — that of criminal trials. Indeed, at least two justices emphasized this narrow focus in concurring opinions.

But the logic of the case can't be confined to criminal-justice

---

[1] The case has the designation (II) to distinguish it from an earlier case with the same name.

proceedings. The Court based its decision, first, on the premise that access to criminal trials contributes to the self-governing function and promotes the democratic process. It added that criminal trials are historically open. Whether this latter observation is an independent test or merely evidence of the truth of the first part is unclear, but several lower federal courts have seized on the language to allow access based on the First Amendment.

Despite the aforementioned legal support for openness, all levels of government have a lengthy history of blocking public scrutiny of records and meetings. Upon signing the Freedom of Information Act in 1966, President Lyndon B. Johnson highlighted the friction between access and government secrecy. In fact, his statement focused more about blocking access to information than providing it. He said:

> This legislation springs from one of our most essential principles: a democracy works best when the people have all the information that the security of the nation will permit. At the same time, the welfare of the nation or the rights of individuals may require that some documents not be made available.

Nevertheless, the law stood, providing the nation with the right to federal information. This right is not absolute, and there are exemptions to what must be provided. In fact, the tensions President Johnson discussed between open government and the need to protect personal privacy and national security still exist.

Open Government at the State Level

Every state in the country and the District of Columbia have some form of open government provisions allowing access to records or meetings, but they vary greatly. State access laws apply to state, county, and municipal records and meetings. The legal provisions that shape access rights at the state level come in four forms, listed from most binding to least: state constitutions, state laws, common law, and attorneys general opinions. Not every state will use all four forms, but that is where to look to evaluate a state's open government laws.

State Constitutions

Six state constitutions provide access rights to government information: Florida, California, New Hampshire, North Dakota, Louisiana and Montana. The Montana Constitution, for example, provides that "[n]o person shall be deprived of the right to examine documents or to observe the deliberations of all public bodies or agencies ... except in cases in which the demand of individual privacy clearly exceed the merits of public disclosure." Montana's is unusually explicit, but most state constitutions

have provisions paralleling the First Amendment that can be employed in the right circumstances. Florida's reads,

> Every person has the right to inspect or copy any public record made or received in connection with the official business of any public body, officer, or employee of the state, or persons acting on their behalf, except with respect to records exempted pursuant to this section or specifically made confidential by this Constitution. This section specifically includes the legislative, executive, and judicial branches of government and each agency or department created thereunder; counties, municipalities, and districts; and each constitutional officer, board, and commission, or entity created pursuant to law or this Constitution.

It also includes provisions for access to meetings, as well as a requirement that any exemption to the public records or open meetings laws in the state pass by no less than a two-thirds vote in the Florida legislature.

Common Law

Under the common law of England — the traditional, judge-made law passed from generation to generation — access to public information was limited. The doors of legislative bodies were usually closed to the public, and citizens were allowed to inspect or copy public records only if they were able to show what was called a "proper interest." Just what formed a "proper interest" was uncertain for citizens then and historians now.

Virtually all early reported judicial decisions describe controversies over records, not meetings. Evidently there was no right of access to meetings. After the American Revolution, meetings of legislative bodies on both sides of the Atlantic became much more open, without judicial prodding. The outcomes in the great majority of these older common law cases turned on whether an interest — a need to see the record — was so important that the record would be available in a lawsuit. If a citizen, say, wanted to see all the town's utility bills out of personal curiosity, his interest wasn't proper. If, on the other hand, access to the record was essential to proving that he had paid his own bill, then the interest was proper and access was granted.

These cases have long captured the attention of scholars and litigants. But largely forgotten are those cases in which citizens sought access, not to serve a personal or private interest, but to serve the general or public welfare. It may be surprising to learn that those who claimed to represent the public interest were often successful.

In a leading case, the Michigan Supreme Court concluded in 1928 in *Nowack v. Fuller*, "If there is any rule of English common law that denied the public the right of access to public records, it is repugnant to the spirit of our democratic institutions.

332   COMMUNICATION AND THE LAW

Ours is a government of the people."

Despite its limitations, the common law can be a highly effective access tool. In one case, for example, a common-law-based suit forced a government official to create a record that did not exist, something a statute never does. A sheriff had negotiated a settlement with a discharged deputy but kept no documents relating to the settlement. He said the law did not require any. A newspaper filed suit under the state freedom of information act and under the common law. The state supreme court ruled that no statute obligated the sheriff to create or maintain records of the settlement agreement. As a result, there was no record to be demanded under the state's right-to-know law.

But the common law claim fared better. In *Daily Gazette Co. v. Withrow*, the court held that the common law required a record to be made:

Whenever a written record of the transaction of a public officer, in his office, is a convenient and appropriate mode of discharging the duties of his office, it is not only his right but his duty to keep that memorial, whether expressly required to do so or not; and when it is kept it becomes a public document.

The common law required the sheriff first to create a record that he then was ordered to disclose.

Access to records not available otherwise may be possible through requests based on a common-law theory. Legislative bodies, for example, typically exclude themselves from the reach of right-to-know statues. In *Schwartz v. Department of Justice*, however, a federal district court noted that all three branches of government are subject to the common law right of access, and it ordered the release of records of Peter A. Rodino Jr., then chairman of the House Judiciary Committee. These decisions, of course, are binding only in jurisdictions where the rulings were made, but they represent some creative or last-resort uses to which the common law can be put.

The use of common law is limited, however. Its answer to the question of what is a public record is narrow — generally confined to documents that memorialize some official transaction such as a deed or minutes of a meeting. Even when a document is clearly a public record and the requester's purpose proper, a custodian may withhold it if disclosure is outweighed by some other interest, such as personal privacy.

In the everyday world, a demand based on the common law is so unusual that it is likely to be met by an official with a puzzled or blank look. Requesters are likely to use common law to leverage access when there are no better options, meaning there is not specific language in an existing state statute that helps. An additional obstacle is that using a common law argument is more effective in a lawsuit, which is time-consuming, expensive, and the outcome may be unpredictable. Still, given the right cir-

cumstances, the common law can be used to fill the cracks left by constitutions and statutes.

State Statutes

Every state in the country has developed some form of open government statutes. However, they vary in strength and functionality. Additionally, access to records and meetings is generally granted by government employees who are interpreting the law, which has produced further inconsistency in application. States laws are usually structured one of two ways: they provide overarching access to records and meetings unless there is a specific exemption listed in the law, or they exempt categories of information, and access can be granted if the requisite information falls outside that block.

Attorneys General Opinions

Absent any other available legal provisions, an attorney general's opinion can be used to provide insight into the application of open government provisions. These are nonbinding opinions from a state attorney general intended to help shed light on how the law should be applied. They do not carry the weight of a judicial opinion or a statute — they are more analogous to legal advice from the office of the attorney general to explain what the existing law says. They do not change law or create new law. In the context of open government, another government official or office might request an interpretation of whether the law should apply to a particular request, or how the office should apply a provision in the law.

PRACTICAL APPLICATIONS OF OPEN GOVERNMENT PROVISIONS

Although every state in the country has open government provisions, the system does not always work perfectly. Understanding and using the law is one of the best ways to ensure that these provisions remain intact. Citizens are routinely blocked from accessing public records. For example, a Pennsylvania access professional refused to give a prison inmate a copy of the state constitution, saying it was not a public record. Government agencies have withheld access to information from one new organization to encourage other competing outlets to provide more favorable coverage. Records custodians have hidden government information in desk drawers to avoid making it available to requesters.

If records custodians are gatekeepers to government information, they don't always open the gate. Government agencies' preferences for secrecy has specific roots.

First, finding and copying public records require time and labor, and providing facilities for public meetings is inconvenient and expensive. Limited resources can best be directed at whatever a particular government agency regards as its primary function, perhaps issuing drivers' licenses or collecting garbage.

Second, opening meetings and records chills creativity and effectiveness in government. If the casual suggestions and give-and-take of frank, brainstorming discussions are open to public examination, and perhaps ridicule, innovators and risk-takers in government won't make bold or daring proposals. The quality of decision-making will suffer.

Third, some interests — national security and personal privacy, for example — are more important than the public interest in access to government information.

And, finally, secrecy prevents disclosure of government waste, incompetence, unfairness and criminal activity.

To these specific objections, advocates of public access respond that providing information is not just an annoying appendage to the duties of government and officials; rather, it is a primary function of government. The public has a need to know what its government is doing if democracy is to work. They also argue that members of the public have good ideas. By excluding them from the early stages of decision-making, government is deprived of a fertile source of imaginative suggestions. And by denying the public access during the formative stages of a proposal, it is being excluded at the very time its input can be most effective. Moreover, access to ideas that are rejected can sometimes be as telling about the governmental processes as those that are accepted.

While most right-to-know advocates concede that there are times when a specific interest, such as protecting military movements or an ongoing law enforcement investigation, will override a generalized interest in disclosure, they argue that any exceptions must be specific. Officials may attempt to use a narrow, reasonable exception to a general policy of disclosure as a catch-all to hide information that ought to be available.

Understanding one's rights in accordance to open government laws is essential to effective access to information. Additionally, there are best practices to requesting information that will also assist in a successful outcome.

FREEDOM OF INFORMATION ACT

In general, the Federal Freedom of Information Act requires federal government agencies to make their records available for inspection and copying unless the records fall into one of nine categories. The act does not apply to Congress, the courts, the president or the president's staff, or the vice president.

Although the FOIA does not apply to the president, the executive sets the expectations for the administration's openness. For example, In the early days of President Joe Biden's term, the administration communicated a commitment to transparency and released on the White House's Web site financial disclosures, ethics pledge waivers, visitor logs and tax returns. In 2022, the Biden administration committed in the Fifth Open Government National Action Plan to more public feedback while requesting or accessing data and increased opportunities to participate in the development of open government regulations. They also plan to address the needs of socioeconomic groups and underserved communities in ensuring equitable access to data and information.

When President Barrack Obama took office, one of his earliest acts was to publish an Open Government Memorandum, calling for an expansion of the records available online, bringing thousands of data sets to Data.gov for public information. The administration was not perfect — it is also remembered for long response times to FOIA requests — but it made more governmental transparency possible across agencies.

The Trump Administration was less likely to embrace the philosophy of transparency than its predecessors. It removed data from public disclosure, refused to allow government officials to relay information, and removed specific topics and issues from government Internet sites. It removed data sets from Open.WhiteHouse.gov, and it closed the Open.gov site created by the previous administration. Members of the press filed more FOIA cases to force governmental transparency during the Trump administration than were filed during the Bush and Obama administrations combined.

However, the greatest obstacles to access to federal records are backlogs to responses to requests. According to the Government Accountability Office, FOIA backlogs increased by 97 percent from 2021 to 2022 during the Biden administration.

While an agency must respond to a request for information within twenty days, that is merely recognizing receipt of the request. It often takes much longer to actually fill the request. For example, in response to a request for information about how the FDA licensed a COVID-19 vaccine, the agency said that it would need fifty-five years to review the necessary records. A federal court ordered that the FDA expedite the release.

The FOIA is relatively simple in its construction, but its effects can be far-reaching. The law applies to "any executive department, military department, government corporation, government-controlled corporation or other establishment in the executive branch of the government."

Some information must be published by an agency — statements of its organization, functions, procedures and rules, for example, and steps one must take to obtain information, including copies of decisions. Other agency records must be specifically requested. The FOIA does not define "agency record," but judicial interpretations are so broad as to include almost anything containing information, so long as it was created by and is under control of the agency. Audio tapes and computer disks, as well as written materials, are agency records. Some records appointment books, calendars and telephone logs, for example

— may exist only for the convenience of individual employees. They aren't agency records. And the FOIA does not require an agency to create a document that does not exist.

In a key FOIA case, *Department of Justice v. Reporters Committee for Freedom of the Press*, Justice John Paul Stevens wrote for the majority:

[T]he basic purpose of the Freedom of Information Act [is] to open agency action to the light of public scrutiny.... Official information that sheds light on an agency's performance of its statutory duties fall squarely within that statutory purpose. That purpose, however, is not fostered by disclosure of information about private citizens that is accumulated in various government files but that reveals little or nothing about an agency's own conduct.

For many, this view is unsupported by the language of the statute. Justice Ruth Bader Ginsburg observed in *Department of Defense v. Federal Labor Relations Authority* that the "'core purpose' limitation is not found in FOIA's language. A FOIA requester need not show that ... disclosure would serve any public purpose, let alone a 'core purpose' of 'opening agency action to the light of public scrutiny' or advancing 'public understanding of the operations of activities of the government.'"

Advocates of an expansive interpretation of the FOIA argue that the law's purpose is the discovery of truth. The more restrictive view is often based on the argument that the purpose of the FOIA is only to disclose the final actions of government. The law itself contains no statement of purpose, leaving plenty of room for interpretation.

In an effort to eliminate this confusion and strengthen FOIA, Congress passed the OPEN FOIA Act of 2009. The law requires Congress to state clearly and explicitly its intention to create statutory exemptions, and it acts as a safeguard against an inclination to increase exemptions. The FOIA Improvement Act of 2016 required the creation of a consolidated online request portal, created a Chief FOIA Officers Council, and strengthened the federal FOIA ombudsman, the Office of Government Information Services.

In a memorandum to the heads of executive departments and agencies in 2022, Attorney General Merrick Garland reminded them that requests should be treated with a presumption of openness and that information should be disclosed unless an agency can foresee harm to one of the nine exemptions. He also encouraged "proactive disclosures," which encourage agencies make information available ahead of requests, such as posting online categories of previously released documents that are likely to be requested again. The federal FOIA Advisory Committee has also recommended that Congress invest in emerging technology that would assist agencies in searching for records and filling requests more quickly and efficiently.

Exemptions

There are nine exemption categories in the FOIA. Agencies may withhold access to information only if that information falls into one or more of these categories. The law does not require that the information be kept confidential if it falls within these categories, however. Agencies have the discretion to release information if it so chooses, meaning that secrecy is not required.

Exemption 1: National Security. This exemption authorizes the president to make and enforce rules to keep information secret in the interest of national defense or foreign policy. The rules are established by executive order without congressional involvement. While the president has leeway to decide what documents should be protected, the order must make plain both the procedures for classifying and declassifying and the underlying criteria for determining whether a specific document should be classified.

Administrations since that of George Washington have withheld information because of national security concerns. Even the most outspoken advocates of public access concede that the release of certain information would be devastating for the country. But critics claim that national security has also been used to shield misconduct or incompetence from public view.

The national security exemption was used to block access to photographs and video of Osama bin Laden's death in 2011. According to a federal district court ruling in *Judicial Watch v. U.S. Department of Defense*; "A picture may be worth a thousand words. And perhaps moving pictures bear an even higher value. Yet, in this case, verbal descriptions of the deal and burial of Osama Bin Laden will have to suffice."

As originally enacted, the exemption gave the executive branch virtually blanket authority to classify information in the interest of national security or foreign policy. For example, in the 1973 case *Environmental Protection Agency v. Mink*, the Supreme Court held that the mere fact that the administration had classified a document was enough to justify withholding the document. The FOIA, it ruled, just did not allow a national security classification to be challenged. Partly in response to that decision, Exemption 1 was amended in 1974 to permit a court to examine a document in private to determine whether it should be released. The amendment also allowed courts to order the release of non-classified portions of otherwise properly classified documents, that is, segregating portions of a document.

The exemption has become one of the most important weapons in the war on terrorism because the federal government has instituted rules and presidents have issued executive orders classifying large amounts of information in the name of national security. Some critics have argued that the orders cover more than national security matters. For instance, many people do not associate national security with trade agreements, but under a 2003 executive order, any document received from a foreign government "is presumed to cause damage to the national security" and is not subject to release.

A uniquely frustrating response within the national security exemption is what is known as a "Glomar response" or "Glomar denial." This is a response in which the federal government can't acknowledge the existence of a requested record on the grounds that a simple admission can be a harm to national security. The concept originated from a 1976 case, *Phillipi v. CIA*, in which a reporter sought information about the Glomar Explorer, a massive salvage ship built by the CIA to raise a sunken Russian nuclear submarine during the Cold War. If the CIA were to respond to the reporter's request for information, it would be in effect, confirming the existence of the clandestine vessel. As it did in the original case, the denial often states that the agency can neither confirm nor deny that it has any records matching the request.

Courts today scrutinize agency actions closely to see whether the government follows its own procedures to classify documents. But they remain reluctant to overrule government experts as to whether the release of a particular document would threaten national security. Given the potential consequences of a mistake, the line between information that is safe and information that is harmful may be too fine for courts to draw with confidence.

Exemption 2: Administrative Documents. This exempts from required disclosure routine and insignificant matters that are "related solely to the internal personnel rules and practices of an agency." The exemption protects routine administrative documents, such as rules about lunch hours or sick leave, because it's considered burdensome for an agency to have to assemble and maintain the material for public inspection, and the public wouldn't reasonably be expected to have an interest. And, though the decisions of lower courts are not uniform, the exemption also protects agency manuals and rules — such as law enforcement manuals — if their release would help people dodge the law. (Materials like these are often also exempt under Exemption 7, law enforcement records, which will be explained later in this chapter.)

Federal agencies often use this exemption to prevent the release of documents they consider sensitive. However, in *Milner v. Department of the Navy*, the Supreme Court overruled thirty years of case law that agencies had used to deny access using this exemption and significantly narrowed its scope.

Exemption 3: Other Laws. This exempts records that are "specifically exempted from disclosure by statute ... provided that such statute (a) requires that matter be withheld from the public in such a manner as to leave no discretion on the issue, or (b) establishes particular criteria for withholding or refers to particu-

lar types of matters to be withheld." An example is 50 U.S.C 403(g), under which the Central Intelligence Agency is not required to disclose its organization, functions, names, official titles, salaries or number of personnel employed. There are probably hundreds of statutes that authorize withholding information from disclosure.

The exemption applies only to statutes and not to agency rules and regulations. Thus, an agency can't exempt itself; only Congress can do that. Similarly, an agency can't invoke the exemption because a state law may protect certain records. A federal appellate court held in *McDonnell v. United States* that state juvenile records in possession of federal authorities could not be withheld under this exemption because the federal law protected only federal juvenile delinquency proceedings from disclosure. A record exempt from disclosure under state law may be available under the FOIA. The opposite may also be true.

In recent years, a number of educational institutions have invoked student privacy rights as grounds for withholding records under FOIA's Exemption 3. The Family Education and Rights Protection Act helps protect students' right to privacy in their educational records. However, many schools around the country have used this law to deny access to information on criminal activities on campus, the use of influence and political clout in the admissions process, and athletic program misconduct.

Exemption 4: Trade Secrets. This exemption protects "trade secrets and commercial or financial information" that individuals and businesses supply to the government. For Exemption 4 to apply, the information must be commercially valuable, actually used in a trade or business and maintained in secret.

The idea is to protect the competitive positions of those who submit confidential information to the government. If companies that voluntarily submit information cannot depend upon it being held in confidence, they may refuse to cooperate, impairing the government's ability to get information. When the government compels production of the information, the rationale becomes strained; and this exemption would seem not to apply.

This distinction was muddied, however, by a 1992 case, *Energy Project v. NRC*, in which the Court of Appeals for the District of Columbia held that when a company submits information voluntarily, even if the government could have compelled disclosure, the information enjoys exempt status. This decision has been criticized, for it seems to invite collusion between an agency and a business when neither wants the information to be made public. An agency and a business simply agree to voluntary submission, undermining a line of cases that refused to recognize an agency's pledge of confidentiality as a substitute for meeting the standards of Exemption 4. Whether the other circuits will follow this court's lead is unknown. But because of the number of FOIA cases it decides due to its location in the District of Columbia, and the expertise it has developed in this area, the FOIA decisions of the D.C. Circuit merit special attention. They are highly influential.

More recently, the Supreme Court's decision in *Food Marketing Institute v. Argus Media Leader* provided a broadened interpretation of confidentiality in favor of protecting businesses and potential trade secrets. The exemption applies when disclosure of the information would cause "substantial competitive harm." The Court held that the information can be exempted when it is "customarily and actually treated as private by its owner and provided to the government under an assurance of privacy." The determination does not weigh whether the release would cause genuine harm. This new perspective may restrict the ability for the public to track how much tax money goes to private companies. Almost immediately, members of the Senate filed legislation to clarify the substantial competitive harm standard.

Businesses themselves sometimes try to protect their interests in secrecy through "reverse FOIA" suits. In these, a business that has provided information to the government sues the government to stop it from making the information public. Reverse FOIA suits involve only information that falls into an exempt category, usually Exemption 4, and that the government has the discretion to release. These suits challenge the release as an abuse of discretion.

Exemption 5: Inter- and Intra-Agency Memoranda. The use of this exemption to deny access to information has skyrocketed in recent years. Designed to allow employees to candidly express their ideas and positions, this exemption is intended to protect the deliberative process an agency embarks upon before adopting a policy. Exemption 5 is both a complex and important exemption: More than 95 percent of all documents are inter- or intra-agency memoranda.

The distinction between accessible and closed can be fine, according to the 2021 Supreme Court case *United States Fish & Wildlife Service v. Sierra Club, Inc.* The Sierra Club had attempted to gain access to government reports of the impact of updated regulations on industrial facilities and structures that had potential to harm aquatic life. The documents several agencies used to explore the issue were shielded from disclosure due to deliberative process privilege, which allows that information generated in forming an ultimate decision is considered deliberative, and therefore not accessible. However, information developed before the final decision on the matter that helps explain the policy can be considered predecisional and subject to FOIA.

In deciding whether the privilege is applicable, courts, as in *Coastal States Gas Corporation. v. Department of Energy*, examine whether a particular predecisional document is "so candid and personal in nature that public disclosure is likely in the future to stifle honest and frank communication within the agency," whether it is in the form of a recommendation or a draft and whether it considers the "pros and cons ... of one viewpoint or another."

The Supreme Court decided an important FOIA case involving Exemption 5 in 2001. In *Department of the Interior v. Klamath Water Users Protective Association*, it unanimously ruled in favor of public disclosure of correspondence between Native American tribes and the Department of the Interior. The case involved a dispute over water rights in the Klamath River Basin in Oregon and California.

Water users, competing with a handful of Native American tribes for water-use rights, filed FOIA requests for documents the tribes had turned over to the Bureau of Indian Affairs in the Interior Department. The government denied the request, saying the papers were inter-agency memoranda and should be withheld from the public under Exemption 5. The Court reiterated several of its earlier FOIA rulings, stating that the "limited exemptions do not obscure the basic policy that disclosure, not secrecy, is the dominant objective of the Act." It also pointed out that FOIA mandates a "general philosophy of full agency disclosure," which would "help ensure an informed citizenry, vital to the functioning of a democratic society."

In addition to executive privilege, Exemption 5 incorporates several other common law privileges, including attorney-client confidences and a lawyer's work product — documents prepared by attorneys as part of their representation. But courts also have cited lesser-known privileges, including, for example, one that protects commercial information created by government itself if its disclosure would put the government at a competitive disadvantage, for example in contract negotiations.

Exemption 6: Personal Privacy. This exemption protects "personnel and medical files and similar files the disclosure of which would constitute a clearly unwarranted invasion of personal privacy." Congress enacted the exemption to protect intimate and personal details in government files. No specific kinds of files are categorically exempt, though some are more likely to contain the sort of information the exemption is designed to protect. The court deliberations in these cases shows the balancing tests that take place between providing access to government information and the need to protect personal privacy.

The term "similar files" in the language in the exemption has been interpreted broadly. An appellate court in *New York Times Co. v. NASA* held that the voice recordings of the crew in the space shuttle Challenger was a "similar file" because the tape revealed personal information about particular individuals. The tapes contained the final radio transmissions before the shuttle exploded, killing everyone on board. Although NASA had released written transcripts of the recordings, the *New York Times* had requested access to the recordings themselves. The court refused, holding that the privacy interests being protected are the families of those who died in the explosion. It decided that the pain the families would experience in hearing the sounds of their loved ones' voices as they died was a privacy interest that weighed more than any information that could be gleaned from hearing the other sounds in the recordings.

Other decisions, however, have hardly concerned the sort of items usually associated with medical and personnel records. In *Department of Defense v. Federal Labor Relations Authority*, two unions sought certain federal employees' home addresses. The privacy interest at stake was that of individuals not wanting to be bothered at home with work-related matters.

The Supreme Court reversed a lower court that had ordered release of the addresses. It balanced the competing interests and found that if the privacy interest of the employees was slight, the weight on the public interest side of the judicial balance beam was even slighter. Disclosure of home addresses would not shed appreciable light on government operations or activities. With this case, the Court has instructed lower courts to consider only the broad purpose of the FOIA in striking a balance — to what extent does disclosure enlighten the public about the operations of government? The particular purpose of the requester is irrelevant.

In a 2011 decision, *FCC v. AT&T*, the Supreme Court ruled that corporations have no right of personal privacy under this exemption. In rejecting AT&T's claim that corporations should be defined as "persons," Chief Justice John Roberts wrote, "We trust that AT&T won't take it personally."

Exemption 7: Law Enforcement Records. The purpose of this exemption is to protect law enforcement records and other information whose disclosure would jeopardize federal investigations. The exemption can apply to the details of a specific investigation or of general investigative techniques or policies. The exemption also protects the physical safety of officials, informants and others in the criminal justice system.

As originally enacted, the exemption applied to "investigatory files compiled for law enforcement purposes." Courts interpreted that to give a blanket exemption to any file that met the threshold test of being "investigatory." In one case, a court ruled that, even though there was no on-going or contemplated law enforcement proceeding, an analysis of the bullet that killed President John F. Kennedy was exempt because it remained part of an investigatory file.

Congress narrowed the exemption in 1976 to avoid results like that. First, it limited withholding only to situations where release would cause any of several specific kinds of harm, such as the disclosure of the identity of a confidential source. Second, it allowed only the withholding of certain records, not entire files. Authorities had often withheld an entire file even if only one record in it contained exempt material. One result of this amendment was to give historians and others access to a wealth

of important material, like the files related to executed spies Julius and Ethel Rosenberg — that had remained sealed for decades as an "investigatory file." Agencies complained that the amendment went too far in the other direction and no longer gave adequate protection to some sensitive law enforcement information, particularly training manuals and other non-investigatory materials. So the exemption was again amended in 1986.

For a record to be exempt from required disclosure, a two-part test must be met. First, it must be determined that the records or information were compiled for "law enforcement purposes." This includes more than investigatory records; training manuals, for example, are exempt.

The Supreme Court answered one crucial question in 1989: Could an agency invoke Exemption 7 to deny access to information that was originally compiled for a purpose other than law enforcement but was later assembled for a criminal investigation? A majority of the Court in *John Doe Agency v. John Doe Corp.* said it could, for the statute's language did not require the original purpose of the information to be considered. Justice Antonin Scalia dissented, arguing that the majority focused too tightly on the words of the law. He complained that the decision allows the policy behind the exemption to be "readily evaded (or [made] illusory) if it requires nothing more than gathering up documents the government does not wish to disclose, with a plausible law-enforcement purpose in mind. This is a hole one can drive a truck through."

Whether the information is compiled for law enforcement purposes is only the first part of the test. For the exemption to apply, it must also be shown that release of the information "could reasonably be expected to cause" one of six specific kinds of harm. It exempts from disclosure information that would:

7(A): Interfere with law enforcement investigations,
7(B): Deny a person a right to a fair trial or impartial adjudication,
7(C): Constitute an unwarranted invasion of privacy,
7(D): Reveal the identity of a confidential source,
7(E): Disclose law enforcement techniques, guidelines and procedures "if such disclosure could reasonably be expected to risk circumvention" of the law, and
7(F): Endanger the life or physical safety of an individual.

Four are noncontroversial and have received little judicial attention, but exemptions 7A and 7C have produced not only confusion but litigation. Exemption 7A allows withholding if disclosure could "interfere with enforcement proceedings." If enforcement proceedings are over, however, or if none are on the horizon, this exemption shouldn't apply. Nonetheless, some agencies claim the exemption on the basis that a case may arise or be reopened.

Exemption 7C allows records to be withheld if their release

could "reasonably be expected to constitute an unwarranted invasion of personal privacy." This exemption is similar to Exemption 6 in that a balancing of the privacy interest and the public interest is required. A comparison of the wording of the two exemptions suggests that privacy interests should receive greater weight here. Before the privacy interest prevails in Exemption 6, the intrusion must be "clearly unwarranted." Here it must only be "unwarranted."

In a key case that shaped the concept of this privacy exemption, in *Department of Justice v. Reporters Committee for Freedom of the Press*, the Court held that a request for information about a person's criminal history was unwarranted because it shed little light on "public understanding of the operations or activities of government."

The case is important, not just for an explanation of the substantive test to be used, but for the insights it provides about the Court's attitude toward electronic data. Most of the records the Reporters Committee sought were available in one place or another in the form of accessible, traditional, paper records. Getting them would require a lot of legwork. The federal government had them all in one place — a computer. But the Court said the records, in electronic form, were qualitatively different; the power of the computer to assemble and manipulate the data held vastly greater potential to violate personal privacy.

In 2004, the Supreme Court decided another important FOIA case involving the conflict between access and privacy and ruled in favor of "survivor privacy" in *National Archives and Records Administration v. Favish*. California attorney Allan Favish sued for access to photos taken at the death scene of Vince Foster, former top aide to President Bill Clinton. The Court held exemption 7(C) allowed the government to withhold documents that "could reasonably be expected to constitute an unwarranted invasion of personal privacy." It ruled that survivors of a deceased person could assert a privacy interest in "their own piece of mind and tranquility."

Exemption 8: Records of Financial Institutions. This exemption applies to records related to government supervision of financial institutions such as banks and savings and loans. The purpose is to protect the security and integrity of financial institutions. To withhold information under Exemption 8 the information must meet three requirements: (1) the information must pertain to a financial institution, (2) the exempting agency must have some kind of responsibility over the financial institution in question, and (3) the information being withheld must relate to reports about examinations, operations, or conditions of the institution.

In 2020, the James Madison Project filed a FOIA request with the Department of the Treasury asking for records pertaining to accusations that Wells Fargo bank had accounts for people without permission. The Department of the Treasury invoked Exemption 8, and the issue ended up in court. Recognizing that Exemption 8 is interpreted broadly, the judge hearing the case concluded that the information being requested should be released because the information did not reveal specifically exempted information like examinations, deliberations or recommendations, and much of it was already in the public domain in the form of a magazine article.

Exemption 9: Geophysical Data. An exemption to "geological and geophysical information and data, including maps, concerning wells," it protects oil well data. The original intent was to protect information provided to the government by oil companies so that speculators could not use the information to their advantage if it were released publicly. It is similar to Exemption 4 in that it protects against the release of confidential commercial information. It is considered one of the least used exemptions, and therefore there is little information available about how it is interpreted in federal courts.

Electronic Freedom of Information Act

The access guaranteed by the FOIA did not keep pace with the electronic revolution. Some government agencies used their conversion to computerized record-keeping as a way not to release information. They argued that the new formats make reproducing information too expensive or unwieldy, or that the FOIA did not require releasing electronic data. In addition, agencies under pressure to raise revenue began charging fees for data that would have been free in paper form.

To solve some of these problems, Congress passed the Electronic Freedom of Information Act Amendments in 1996. The EFOIA guarantees that records maintained in computer databases are as accessible as paper records. It requires that agencies make regulations, opinions, policy statements and similar information available electronically, and it requires agencies to provide information in the format requested whenever possible. Under the EFOIA, agencies must make reasonable efforts to search for requested records in electronic form, except when a search would significantly interfere with agency information.

The legislative history surrounding the law may ultimately provide broader access to governmental information and limit the Supreme Court's problematic ruling in *Department of Justice v. Reporters Committee*, in which the Court limited access to governmental records that revealed information relevant to the agency's "core purpose." Access advocates, including those in Congress, disagreed with the Court's decision. Congressional leaders indicated they crafted the EFOIA amendments to address this restrictive view of access to public records.

Using electronic government information encourages more inclusivity in access and more creative and effective uses of government information. Research has shown that countries that promote and support electronic access to government information yield proactive citizens who have an increased trust in their governments. As technology advances, so does the potential for citizen engagement. In measuring the effectiveness of e-government efforts, the top priorities that emerged were: security, usability, applicable content, relevant services, and citizen engagement.

While using the FOIA and EFOIA takes patience and persistence, many important stories, including numerous Pulitzer Prize winners, have come from government documents accessed through the FOIA. Such stories have focused on human rights violations, official corruption, workplace and aircraft accidents, bridge safety, cocaine trafficking, unsafe consumer products, serious health hazards and questionable research programs on humans.

FEDERAL MEETINGS

The Government in the Sunshine Act, enacted in 1976, extends to the meetings of the agencies covered by FOIA. For the law to apply, the agency must be headed by a body of two or more members. Meetings that are subject to the act must be announced at least one week in advance, including information about the time, location and subject of the meeting. It prohibits informal discussions and decision-making to precede the meeting in an effort to ensure that government action is conducted in public view.

Like FOIA, there is a series of exemptions to what must be discussed publicly. However, analogous to redaction, the act allows (but does not require) that portions of meetings be closed if the subject under discussion falls into an exempted category. If an exemption applies, the agency must balance the public interest in openness against the particular interest the exemption is designed to protect before closing a meeting.

Seven of the Sunshine Act's ten exemptions parallel those of the FOIA. The act has nothing like FOIA Exemption 5 (inter- and intra-agency memoranda) or Exemption 9 (geological or geophysical data). Instead, the act's Exemption 5 protects agency discussions that "involve accusing any person of a crime, or formally censuring any person." A general discussion doesn't qualify. It must focus on a specific person and, if it concerns a crime, a specific charge.

Exemption 9 shields two kinds of discussions: those that might jeopardize the stability of a financial institution or might trigger significant speculation in financial instruments, and those that might "significantly frustrate implementation of a proposed agency action." One court has limited the exemption to matters whose disclosure would allow someone to profit at government expense or allow an agency regulation to be evaded. Exemption 10 of the Sunshine Act permits closure when discussions concern a subpoena or participation in a civil action or proceeding, such as arbitration or adjudication.

BEST PRACTICES FOR ACCESSING FEDERAL RECORDS

Putting open government provisions into action is important for maintaining the strengths of the laws. It is by using them that citizens constantly remind government agencies of their value. For example, during the COVID-19 pandemic, the uncertainty even affected access to information, which only came to light from use of the provisions.

Changes in processing requests during the COVID-19 pandemic were inconsistent. The Federal Bureau of Investigation said it would take only mailed requests, while the Centers for Disease Control and Prevention said it would not take mailed requests. Meanwhile, responding to federal records requests while employees were working offsite due to quarantines caused increased delay and confusion. Some agencies allowed expedited requests for information that would pose an imminent threat to health and safety if it were not released.

At the local level, however, gathering information received special protections in many locations' public health emergency policies. Agencies recognized the importance of press coverage to inform the public, and they provided exemptions to allow for the dissemination of news.

The FOIA requires that a record be "reasonably described" by a requester so it can be located. An agency can charge reasonable search and copying fees. There are standard fee schedules, but individual requirements vary, so a requester needs to ask for an estimate of costs. The law authorizes waivers for educational and non-commercial scientific institutions and for the news media when the requested information will "contribute significantly to public understanding of the operation or activities of Government." To qualify for consideration, a requester will have to explain the purpose of the request, something not otherwise required.

Though the FOIA requires a quick response to a request, substantive compliance — the production of the record or specific grounds for denial — can take months or even years. Some federal agencies are overwhelmed by requests. FOIA.gov, the federal government's centralized open government website, provides a backlog search function to follow agencies' unfilled FOIA requests. Some of them are many years old.

Filing Requests. Anyone may file FOIA requests — U.S. citizenry is not required. While members of the press often use FOIA in their work, most records requests are from people asking for information about themselves, such as medical information, immigration information, and law enforcement reports. There are many templates and letter generators online to help re- questers write a request for information under FOIA. The request must be made in writing. It should describe the records being re-

WHO IS A 'REPRESENTATIVE OF THE MEDIA'?

1. Gathers information of potential interest → 2. to a segment of the public; → 3. uses its editorial skills to turn the raw materials into a distinct work; and → 4. distributes the work → 5. to an audience

quested, and it should follow the specific agency's regulations. At a minimum, a FOIA request should include contact information for the requester, a reasonable description of the records being requested, the format being requested, and any requests for fee waivers or expedited processing.

A government agency cannot develop an uncommunicated policy to deny requests unless they are submitted in a particular form. The CIA had a blanket policy requiring that any emailed requests for information must have a specific "to" and "from" field, as well as a subject matter and a time frame. Without those four pieces of information, the CIA would refuse to process the request. However, the CIA did not show how those four pieces of information were necessary, and a D.C. district court held the policy was unlawful.

Time Limits. It is natural to want information to be provided immediately, but that is not the norm when managing FOIA requests. They can take months or years to process. An agency must respond to a request within twenty business days. That does not mean it must fill that request — it must make a determination on the request. An agency's determination will tell the requester which records will be released and which may be withheld.

An agency may extend the deadline for an additional ten days if some kind of "unusual circumstances" exist. That may be defined as a request that would yield a voluminous amount of records, the records are stored far away, or the request requires a consultation among agencies.

In certain circumstances, agencies can provide expedited processing to a request if it determines there is a "compelling need." FOIA defines compelling need as an imminent threat to life or physical safety or urgency to inform the public about government activity.

Fee Structures. Those who are trying to access federal records through FOIA can be charged for three processes that may be necessary to fill the request: searching, reviewing, copying. Searching is the process by which the agency looks for the rec-

ords being requested. Then agencies need to review the record to see what is in there, and whether any of it is exempt from disclosure or needing redaction. Once that is complete, the agency will need to duplicate the records to provide them to the requester.

The nature of the requester will also determine what may be charged. Certain kinds of requests can get some of the fees waived. Commercial requesters, or those who are using the information for commercial, trade or for-profit ventures, pay all fees. Educational institutions, noncommercial scientific institutions and representatives of the media do not pay search or review fees, and they receive the first 100 pages of copies free. Students and teachers fall into this category.

"Representatives of the Media." More attention has been given to interpreting the meaning of "representatives of the media." The FOIA statute itself defines it as "any person or entity that gathers information of potential interest to a segment of the public, uses its editorial skills to turn the raw materials into distinct work, and distributed that work to an audience."

In the 2015 case, *Cause of Action v. FTC*, the D.C. Circuit Court provided more insight into how this would be determined. It said that to fit this category, the criteria above would be considered five segments that must be applied to the requester, not the nature of the information being requested. If the requesters establish that they are members of the media generally, then it doesn't matter what they are requesting. The figure "Who Is a 'Representative of the Media'?" shows how the circuit court segmented the requirement.

Those who do not fit the commercial use definition, and who are not representative of the media, educational or scientific institutions, are in the "other requesters" category. These are requesters who will use the information for personal use, or are representatives of nonprofit organizations or public interest groups. Requesters in this category receive two hours of search time and the first 100 pages of copies free, and do not have to pay for the time it takes an agency to review the request.

Challenges to Denials. If requesters do not receive the information they are seeking, and they would like to challenge the denial, they must file an administrative appeal within ninety days. An administrative appeal is like asking the agency to take another look at the request and reconsider the denial. If the agency still denies access, and the requester still wants to challenge the denial, then the next step is a federal lawsuit. The legal burden of justifying secrecy is on the agency. A court can — but is not required to — order the government to pay attorneys' fees if a requester "substantially prevails."

Statutes and case law provide the framework for FOIA and the application of exemptions. Equally important is the commitment to openness by the governmental officials who establish and enforce agency rules regarding access.

STATE OPEN-GOVERNMENT LAWS

Every state has its own legal provisions to allow access to state and local information, and each right-to-know law is unique. Each differs, not only in its language, but in its political setting and judicial arena. It is essential to become well acquainted with the state law.

The practical applications of the state open government laws share similarities. They generally declare that all records and meetings are open to the public unless exemptions apply. Some states follow the federal lead and exempt only a few broad categories. This broad approach makes for a tidy-looking statute but probably causes more litigation because of the case-by-case balancing that inevitably goes with it.

Other states opt for specific, narrow exemptions, and, over the years, many have built a rather lengthy list. Florida has more than 1,100 exemptions, and Virginia exempts more than 100 types of records. Because of the length and apparent complexity, this narrow, specific approach results in an ugly law, but one that often works surprisingly well day-to-day because of its precision in describing what is accessible and what is not.

Many policy and legal issues are common to the federal FOIA and state right-to-know statutes. The decisions of federal courts in interpreting the FOIA, of course, are in no way binding on state courts interpreting their own laws. But the experience of federal courts in freedom of information issues may provide persuasive reasoning for states. So a careful review of the federal FOIA is not a bad place to acquire a background to understand local law.

However, unlike the federal FOIA, some states will only fill requests from state residents. Virginia's provision restricting requests to residents was upheld by the Supreme Court in 2013. It said, in *McBurney v. Young*, that because there is no constitutional right to access information through open-government laws, it is within a state's purview to limit access as it sees fit. Other states with similar limitations are Arkansas, Delaware,

Missouri, New Hampshire, and Tennessee.

The way the statute is written, as well as the language used within it, is very important to how the law will apply.

Public Records Defined

Public records laws will usually define the physical form of what is considered a record. It may read like Georgia's, "all documents, papers, letters, maps, books, tapes, photographs, computer based or generated information, data, data fields, or similar material," or Alaska's, "books, papers, files, accounts, writings, including drafts and memorializations of conversations, and other items, regardless of format or physical characteristics." Those two phrases, "similar material" and "regardless of format or physical characteristics," are extremely helpful when considering forms that may not yet be used or even invented.

Such was the issue with electronic records. Right-to-know laws were passed in an era of paper, folders and filing cabinets. Today many records are kept in electronic databases, accessible only through computers. Many states have amended their laws to accommodate this change, broadening the definition of "record" to include digitized ones. Electronic records raise special issues that courts and legislatures are struggling to deal with.

Local, state, and national governments are conducting an extraordinary amount of business *via* the computer and through emails, Twitter and text messages. While states may not explicitly include email in their open records statutes, most email communication regarding government business is considered a public record.

Even if email is not directly addressed in the open record statutes of most states, their definitions of records could include email. Oklahoma, for example, includes in its definition of a public record "data files created by or used with computer software, computer tape, disk ... or other material regardless of physical form or characteristic."

Some states have included text messages in their open government statutes. Texas states:

[T]he general forms in which the media containing public information exists include a book, paper, letter, document, email, Internet posting, text message, instant message, other electronic communication, printout, photograph, film, tape, microfiche, microfilm, Photostat, sound recording, map, and drawing and a voice, data, or video representation held in computer memory.

But even if text messages are not expressly included in the language, broad statutory descriptions may include all forms of communication or correspondence during which public business is being conducted.

Fee Provisions and Response Times

State and local government agencies can charge fees for searches, review and duplication. Critics of the fee provisions say that charging fees for something that is already being subsidized by taxpayers' money is unfair. Additionally, charging exorbitant fees have been used as a tactic by government agencies who want requesters to go away and serves as a barrier to those who can't afford to pay. Advocates for the fees would argue that government agencies are not meant to carry the time-consuming burden of gathering and copying voluminous public records requests.

Regardless of one's stance, determining how much in fees is warranted can be complicated if the statute is unclear. State laws can be disparate on the guidelines provided. Some fee provisions, like those in Utah's open government law, are very specific and explain that fees must be calculated for specific duties and based on the actual cost of duplication and the staff time for the lowest paid employee with the skills to complete the task. While other states, like Ohio, merely say that records should be made available "at cost."

Similar to the confusion surrounding fees, limitations on how long it should take to receive a response to a request can be challenging to interpret. Florida's statute only requires that the request receive a response in a "reasonable time." Virginia has a relatively specific statute, which requires that requesters will receive an initial response within five working days. If records custodians need more time, they can get an extension of seven working days.

Attending State or Local Meetings

All states allow access to certain government meetings. While documents may provide a paper trail of government action, attending meetings allows you to watch government function play out in real time. And like accessing public records, it is imperative to understand how each state law defines meetings.

Many statues define meetings as gatherings of public bodies at which public business is addressed. The meeting exists due to the congregation of participants and the topic under discussion. They are rarely focused on a physical form or location for a meeting. In Missouri, it is any meeting of a public governmental body at which public business is discussed. In New York, it is the gathering of a quorum of a public body to discuss public business. Some states include the requirement that a simple majority be present.

The language that defines a meeting is important to understand because the use of technology can also trigger open meetings statutes. Online forums or group emails and text messages may fit the definition of a meeting that should be publicly accessible. For example, the attorney general in Kansas opined that an online discussion board could be considered a public meeting, while the Florida attorney general said it would not.

This can be especially important during times of crisis. If city leadership must come together for swift decision-making that affects residents, the communication form that determines a meeting must be clear in order to allow public access. For example, during the social distancing requirements of the COVID-19 pandemic, determining how to provide public access to meetings required to be open by law became complicated.

Government agencies then had to revisit how their laws defined a meeting or a quorum of members, and then to devise plans for technologically distanced meetings that could still be open to the public. Florida's attorney general determined that if the statute allowed an agency to reach a quorum without being in person, then technological meetings like teleconferencing were permissible. However, if the state statute required an in-person quorum, then the attorney general approved of the suspension of the requirement during a state of emergency.

Key to the open meeting process is providing notice. Public bodies must provide notice in advance of the meeting to ensure the public is aware of it and can attend. The notice can be defined, as it is in Rhode Island, to include date, times and locations of meetings to be provided at least forty-eight hours in advance. Official minutes are taken during the meetings, and they then become a public record.

Due to the increase in meetings conducted electronically, notice should also include the technology being used as well as adjustments to accessibility for those who cannot use or do not possess the technology. For example, if the meeting is being livestreamed online, then a phone number should be available for those who cannot join online but who may want to call in.

However, members of the public should not be shuttled off to a different location to watch a live-stream when a public meeting is happening in person. Virginia's Supreme Court held that the public cannot be barred from entering the physical meeting room as a matter of course. (A school district had been forcing members of the public to watch a live feed of board meetings from a separate room.) While live feeds of meetings were helpful during the Covid-19 pandemic, in some jurisdictions they cannot be used permanently to replace face-to-face meetings attended by the public. The Virginia Supreme Court also held that once the Covid state of emergency ended, then board meetings had to return to being in person, rather than electronic.

Public meetings are not only important for the public to see what government is up to, but they also encourage a more active citizenry. The public becomes actively engaged in the government process by attending meetings. Open meetings can directly advance the core principles of representation government by requiring elected officials to be accountable to their constituents and deliberate out in the open.

BEST PRACTICES FOR ACCESSING STATE INFORMATION

A tension exists between officials who do not want to release information and those who request access to information, and some of the primary obstacles for requesters are delays from government agencies or no responses at all, inaccurate reasons for denying access, and charging unreasonable fees. Therefore, it is important for records requesters to prepare to ask for information by understanding what the laws in their states allow.

The first step is to read the state law. It should be easily accessible through an Internet search, or a check of each state attorney's Web site. The Reporter's Committee for Freedom of the Press has a user-friendly Open Government Guide that explains the law clearly for every state in the country.

Make sure the law allows access to the records being sought. It is often helpful to bring a copy of the law to the government office or meeting, just in case. If it is a document or file, check online to see if the government agency provides this information online. Some information that is clearly public or often requested will be made available online for ease of retrieval.

If it isn't available online, the next step is to either send a written request or to visit the office in person to request it. Written requests should include:

• The requester's contact information,
• A description, as specific as possible, of the records being sought. (But don't include why the information is necessary.)
• An explanation that the request is in accordance with a state statute,
• A request for an explanation for a denial, if one is warranted,
• A request for an estimate of fees, especially if costs will rise above a certain amount.

There is no definitive rule about which is better: sending a written request or showing up to ask for it in person. However, having the request in writing provides substantiation if there is some kind of disagreement during the process. And for those who go in person, having a written request as a backup when visiting in person can be an efficient practice.

While not every interaction with records custodians will be adversarial, it is better to be prepared. Access professionals believe in open government laws and their importance. But when it comes to practical application, obstacles get in the way. Access professionals are relatively consistent in the advice they wish they could impart to requesters. Some top advice from access professionals:[2]

• Be as specific as possible in your request; explain what you are trying to find. Sometimes this won't be possible, but when it is, try to be clear.
• Research before you ask — make sure you are asking the appropriate agency for information that the law allows to be released.
• Allow time for the request to be processed. It won't always be an immediate exchange, so be ready for a possible delay. Be realistic about what you are trying to get.
• Request a manageable amount of information. Large or voluminous requests are more difficult to fill, take more time to process, and may cost more.
• Anticipate fees for making copies or responding to large requests. Agencies can charge fees for making copies of records or for the amount of time it takes to fill requests.
• Be polite and empathetic to those filling requests.

If all of that preparation, knowledge of the law, and politesse does not work, there are still options. Access to public records and meetings may rest on the statutory enforcement provisions. Despite the statutory directive to open their processes to public scrutiny, agencies often try to hide behind exemptions for records and meetings.

If access to what should be an open record or a public meeting is blocked, there are a few options for recourse. First, go to the person in charge of the governing body or agency right away, explaining that access should be granted. If that doesn't work, get in touch with an open government advocacy group in your state or local area. It may have someone who can help. If all else fails, the next step would be to appeal to the district attorney's office or petition the court for a remedy.

Some states vest enforcement power with the local prosecutor, who has the power to investigate and file charges against public officials for violating open government laws. Florida law, for example, authorizes state prosecutors to file civil or criminal complaints against public officials who knowingly violate the public records law. Those officials can be removed from office and face criminal penalties of up to a year in jail and $1,000 fines. In fact, in 1999, for the first time in Florida's history, a public official who was convicted of a criminal violation of the state's public records law was actually sent to jail. A school board member spent seven days in jail before being released, pending an appeal. A jury convicted her of knowingly violating the law. The judge sentenced her to eleven months and fifteen days in jail. The governor also suspended her from office. Then, in 2003, a former Florida Speaker of the House, W.D. Childers, was sentenced to sixty days in jail for violating the state's open meetings part of its Sunshine Law.

In most cases, however, officials who violate the law face no penalties. Even where state statutes allow private citizens to file civil suits to enforce the law, the high costs of litigation discourage many people. Citizens, who make far more complaints about open government than the news media, know that fighting City Hall can be an expensive, time-consuming process. As a result, major media organizations have historically borne the burden of filing lawsuits to enforce the law. One study showed that the number of FOIA lawsuits brought by reporters and media companies has increased substantially, as has the backlog of suits waiting to be decided.

SUMMARY

The benefits of guaranteeing access to government information generally parallel those associated with protecting speech. That is, access to information promotes the discovery of truth, self-government, orderly change and self-fulfillment.

The federal Constitution and some state constitutions provide limited access to information. The common law can supplement other access tools, mainly statutes. The elastic quality of the common law, one of its historic weaknesses, is an asset to exploit when a tool must be found to reach information inaccessible by other means.

Federal and state statutes are the front-line means of access. Federal laws include the Freedom of Information Act and the Sunshine Act, which is the federal meetings law. Access to federal electronic records is covered in the Electronic Freedom of Information Act. Each state has its own counterpart to the federal laws, and many states are including access to electronic records, as well. As a group, these laws give each citizen the right to inspect and copy government documents or attend government meetings.

Some agencies and, in fact, entire branches of government are exempt. Each statute also identifies kinds of records or subjects of meetings that are exempt from required disclosure. In most, but not all of these exempt categories, secrecy is not required — meaning that it is up to the discretion of the agency to provide information within an exempted category. The government may open the record or meeting if the public interest in access outweighs the competing interest of the exception.

Access to government records and meetings is essential to meaningful participation in government. As vital and as obvious as that axiom is, only recently has there been a widespread and sustained effort to guarantee citizen access to governmental information. The United States ranks sixty-nine of 124 countries in the Global Right to Information Rating, dropping twenty-five places since 2015. The law is not perfect, but those who need it and use it must remain vigilant that it continues to function in the best interests of the electorate.

Access to government information enables the press to perform its watchdog function, however these are also citizens' rights. Open government provisions are like muscles that need to be exercised. Without using them, and without understanding their importance to the health of a democracy, they will fade away.

BIBLIOGRAPHY

Articles and Documents

Annals of Congress. 1st Cong. 1st Session, (1789), 951, 952, 955.

Associated Press. "School Board Member Free," *Palm Beach Post*, May 22, 1999, at A24.

Blanton, Thomas (ed.). "Freedom of Information at 40: LBJ Refused Ceremony, Undercut Bill with Signing Statement," The National Archives, July 4, 2006, https://nsarchive2.gwu.edu/NSAEBB/NSAEBB194/index.htm.

Blasi, Vincent. "The Checking Value in First Amendment Theory," 2 *American Bar Foundation Research Journal* 521 (1977).

Chance, Sandra F. & Christina Locke. "The Government-in-the-Sunshine Law Then and Now: A Model for Implementing New Technologies Consistent with Florida's Position as a Leader in Open Government," 35 *Florida State University Law Review* 245 (2008).

Congressional Research Service. "Freedom of Information Act (FOIA) Processing Changes Due to COVID-19: In Brief," Mar. 27, 2020, https://crsreports.congress.gov/product/pdf/R/R46292.

Conza, Sarina. "San Francisco Police Memo: Officers Told Not to Use Body Cams During Raid of Journalist's Home," *Reporters Committee for Freedom of the Press*, June 17, 2020, https://www.rcfp.org/carmody-bodycam-sfpd-memo/.

Cortez, Nathan. "Information Mischief Under the Trump Administration," 94 *Chicago-Kent Law Review* 315 (2019).

Ferguson, Kate. "Compliance Conundrum: The Use of Punitive Damage Provisions in State Freedom of Information Statutes," 46 *Columbia Human Rights Law Review* 371 (Fall 2014).

"Fewer Watchdogs, Uncooperative Public Officials Are Biggest Challenges to Open Government Today, According to Open Government Survey," *National Freedom of Information Coalition*, March 13, 2020), https://www.nfoic.org/blogs/news-release-biennial-open-government-survey-reveals-big-challenges/.

FOIA Project Staff. "When FOIA Goes to Court: 20 years of Freedom of Information Act Litigation by News Organizations and Reporters," *The FOIA Project*, January 13, 2021, http://foiaproject.org/2021/01/13/foialitigators2020/.

Government Accountability Office, "Freedom of Information Act: Selected agencies adapted to COVID-19 challenges, but actions needed to reduce backlogs," GAO-22-105845, March 29, 2022.

Halperin, T.D. "The Special Relationship: The Senate and the States, 1789-1801," in *The House and Senate in the 1790s,*

Kenneth Bowling & Donald Kennon (eds.). Athens, Ohio: Ohio University Press, 2002.

Kimball, M.B. "Law Enforcement Records Custodians' Decision-Making Behaviors in Response to Florida's Public Records Law," 8 *Communication Law and Policy* 313 (2003).

Kimball, M. B. "Mandated State-Level Open Government Training Programs," 28 *Government Information Quarterly* 481 (2011).

Kimball, M.B. "Shining the Light from the Inside: Access Professionals' Perceptions of Government Transparency," 17 *Communication Law and Policy* 299 (2012).

Lee, Ta Ho. "Public Records Fees Hidden in the Law: A Study of Conflicting Judicial Approaches to the Determination of the Scope of Imposable Public Records Fees," 21 *Communication Law and Policy* 251 (2016).

Memorandum from the Office of the Attorney General to heads of executive departments and agencies (March 15, 2022).

Mehta, Christine. "Annual Report: FOIA Lawsuits Reach Record Highs in FY 2018," *The FOIA Project*, Nov. 12, 2018), http://foiaproject.org/2018/11/12/annual-report-foia-lawsuits-reach-record-highs-in-fy-2018/.

Manoharan, A.P., J. Melitski & Holzer, M. "Digital Governance: An Assessment of Performance and Best Practices," 23 *Public Organization Review* 265 (2023).

Moon, M. J. "The evolution of e-government among municipalities: Rhetoric or reality? 63 *Public Administration Review* 424 (2002).

Powell, William, Jordan Murav-Goodman & Lindsay Wajert. "Special Analysis: Explicit Press Protections in State and Territorial Emergency Laws," *Reporters Committee for Freedom of the Press*, April 16, 2020, https://www.rcfp.org/emergency-laws -press-protections/.

Reporters' Committee for Freedom of the Press. "Press Freedom and Government Transparency During COVID-19," Spring 2020, https://www.rcfp.org/resources/covid-19/.

Roeder, Cassandra. "Transparency Trumps Technology: Reconciling Open Meetings Laws with Modern Technology," 55 *William and Mary Law Review* 2287 (2014).

Tinling, M. "Thomas Lloyd's Reports of the First Federal Congress," 18 *William and Mary Quarterly* 521 (October 1961).

Vera, Helen. "Regardless of Physical Form: Legal and Practical Considerations Regarding the Application of State Open-Records Laws to Public Business Conducted by Text Message," 32 *Communication Lawyer* 24 (Spring 2017).

"White House Releases Fifth Open Government National Action Plan to Advance a More Inclusive, Responsive, and Accountable Government," The White House (Dec. 28, 2022), https://www.whitehouse.gov/ostp/news-updates/2022/12/28/white-house-releases-fifth-open-government-national-action-plan-to-advance-a-more-inclusive-responsive-and-accountable-government/.

Books

Hopkins, W. Wat., ed. *The U.S. Freedom of Information Act at 50,* New York: Routledge, 2018.

Kwoka, Margaret, *Saving the Freedom of Information Act,* Cambridge, England: Cambridge University Press, 2021.

Meiklejohn, Alexander. *Free Speech and its Relation to Self-Government.* New York: Harper, 1948.

Mott, F. L. *Jefferson and the Press.* Baton Rouge: Louisiana State University Press, 1943.

Ritchie, D. A., *Press: Gallery: Congress and the Washington Correspondents.* Cambridge, Mass.: Harvard University Press, 1991.

Legal Provisions

Alaska Public Records Act, 2 AAC 96.900(4)(1994).

Berliner, Zisser, Walter & Gallegos, P.C. v. Security Exchange Commission, 962 F. Supp. 1348 (D. Colo. 1997).

Berry v. Board of Supervisors, 884 S.E.2d 515 (Va. 2023).

California Constitution, art. I, § 3(b)(1)(2014).

Cause of Action v. F.T.C., 799 F.3d 1108 (D.C. Cir. 2015).

Coastal States Gas Corp. v. Department of Energy, 644 F.2d 854 (D.C. Cir. 1980).

Common Cause v. NRC, 674 F.2d 921 (D.C. Cir. 1982).

Daily Gazette Co. v. Withrow, 350 S.E.2d 738, 747 (W.Va. 1986).

Department of Defense v. Federal Labor Relations Authority, 510 U.S. 487, 507 (1994).

Department of the Interior v. Klamath Water Users Protective Association, 532 U.S. 1 (2001).

Department of Justice v. Reporters Committee for Freedom of the Press, 489 U.S. 749 (1989).

Energy Project v. NRC, 975 F.2d 871 (D.C. Cir. 1992) (en banc).

Environmental Protection Agency v. Mink, 410 U.S. 73 (1973).

Executive Order No. 13,292, 68 C.F.R. 15,315 (2003).

Family Education and Rights Protection Act, 20 U.S. C. §1231g(b)(1) (2006).

FCC v. AT&T, 562 U.S. 397, 409 (2011).

Florida Attorney General Opinion, AGO 2020-03 (Mar. 19, 2020).

Florida Constitution, art. I, § 24(1992).

Florida Statute chapter 119.02(1909).

Food Marketing Institute v. Argus Media Leader, 588 U.S. (2019).

Freedom of Information Act, 5 U.S.C. § 552(1966).

Georgia Open Records Act, O.C.G.A. § 50-18-70(b)(2)(2012).

Government in the Sunshine Act, 5 U.S.C. § 552(b)(1996).

James Madison Project v. Dept. of Treasury, 478 F. Supp. 3d 8 (D.D.C. 2020).

John Doe Agency v. John Doe Corp., 492 U.S. 146 (1989).

Judicial Watch v. U.S. Department of Defense, 857 F. Supp. 2d

44 (D.C. Cir. 2012).

Louisiana Constitution, art. XII, § 3(1974).

McBurney v. Young, 569 U.S. 221 (2013).

McDonnell v. United States, 4 F.3d 1227 (3rd Cir. 1994).

Milner v. Department of the Navy, 562 U.S. 562 (2011).

Missouri Rev. Stat. § 610.010(5)(2004).

Montana Constitution, art II, § 9(1972).

Muckrock, LLC v. Cent. Intelligence Agency, 300 F. Supp. 3d 108 (D.D.C. 2018).

National Archives and Records Administration v. Favish, 541 U.S. 157 (2004).

New Hampshire Constitution, Part I, art. 8(1976).

New York Pub. Off. Law § 102(1)(2000).

New York Times Co. v. Sullivan, 376 U.S. 254 (1964).

North Dakota Constitution, art. XI, § 5(1974).

Nowack v. Fuller, 219 N.W. 749, 750 (Mich. 1928).

Ohio Rev. Code Ann. § 149.43(B)(1)(2019).

Oklahoma Statute tit. 51, § 24A.3(2004).

Open and Responsive Government Act, S. 2220, 116th Congress (July 23, 2019).

Opinion of the Florida Attorney General 2007 WL 1054632 (2007).

Opinion of the Kansas Attorney General No. 98-49 (1998).

Phillippi v. CIA, 546 F.2d 1009 (D.C. Cir. 1976).

Press-Enterprise Co. v. Superior Court (II), 478 U.S. 1 (1986).

Public Health and Medical Professionals for Transparency v. Food and Drug Administration, No. 4:21-cv-1058-P (N.D. Tex., 2022).

R.I. General Laws § 42-46-6 (2017).

Richmond Newspapers v. Virginia, 448 U.S. 555 (1980).

Schwartz v. Department of Justice, 435 F. Supp. 1203 (D.C. 1977), aff'd 595 F.2d 889 (D.C. Cir. 1979).

Suffolk City School Board v. Wahlstrom, 886 S.E.2d 244 (Va. 2023).

Tex. Gov't Code Ann. § 552.002(c) (2019).

United States Fish and Wildlife Service v. Sierra Club, Inc., 141 S. Ct. 777 (2021).

Utah Code Ann. § 63G-2-203(2016).

Va. Code Ann. § 2.2-3704(B)(4)(2017).

Wiesberg v. Department of Justice, 489 F.2d 1195 (D.C. Cir. 1973).

18

Newsgathering

By Charles N. Davis

☑ **Headnote Questions**

- To what extent does the First Amendment protect the right to gather news?
- What restrictions can constitutionally be placed on journalists covering newsworthy events in public places?
- Where has the battle to gather news in public places been most successfully fought?
- Do reporters have a First Amendment right to interview prisoners, view executions and gather news at schools or private businesses?
- Do reporters have a First Amendment right to enter private property to gather news?
- Does the First Amendment protect journalists who violate the law?

Information is the lifeblood of news. Journalists report on what happens in city halls and in the halls of Congress, in local courthouses and in the U.S. Supreme Court, in statehouses and in the White House. Their reports help broaden the public's understanding and help citizens make decisions vital to maintaining a democracy. To get the information they need, reporters must have access to meetings, to places and to government documents at the federal, state and local levels.

The Supreme Court has steadfastly ruled that the First Amendment protects the right to disseminate information, news and opinions. And in *Branzburg v. Hayes*, it recognized the press' First Amendment right to gather information because, "without some protection for seeking out the news, freedom of the press could be eviscerated." But the level of First Amendment protection for newsgathering activities is unclear. In that same *Branzburg* decision, the Court held that "the First Amendment does not guarantee the press a constitutional right of access to information not available to the public generally."

While the Court has acknowledged that the First Amendment protects newsgathering, the extent of that protection remains uncertain. The September 11, 2001, terrorist attacks renewed the age-old debate over the media's ability to gather news of military conflict abroad and at home; and that debate continues whenever competing interests vie for legal supremacy.

NEWSGATHERING IN PUBLIC PLACES

Newsworthy events most often occur in public, and journalists

are free to gather news from any places where anyone passing by activities could observe them. As one court held, once an individual is exposed to public observation, the person is not entitled to the same degree of privacy that he or she would enjoy within the confines of his or her own home. If news breaks on a public street, reporters may cover it.

Streets, sidewalks, parks and similar places are known as "traditional public forums," and the public and the press enjoy a general right of access to them and activities that occur there. In addition, the government often makes other property available for public use. Those places are known as "dedicated public forums." In most circumstances, the government may not limit or deny access to traditional or dedicated public forums, but may impose reasonable time, place and manner restrictions on activities that go on there.

The 2020 protests in the wake of the killing of George Floyd offered students of media law a living lesson in newsgathering in public places. The Press Freedom Tracker offers dozens of examples of journalists detained, arrested and assaulted — all merely for covering protests. It's a reminder that even where First Amendment law is quite clear, authorities can fail to live up to what they should know is legal. When journalists are obstructed from lawful newsgathering, so is the public's right to be informed and hold power to account.

Reporters, like other citizens, do not have free rein to go wherever they want whenever they want. Access to people and places — sometimes even seemingly public places — is often restricted. There are restrictions, for example, on how and when reporters may gather news in prisons, at disaster scenes, on military installations, at crash sites and in other public locations.

Judicial Proceedings

The battle over the First Amendment right to gather news in public places has been most successfully fought in the area of access to judicial proceedings. In 1980, the Supreme Court acknowledged a First Amendment right of public access to judicial proceedings. In *Richmond Newspapers v. Virginia*, it held that the First Amendment provides the public and the press with a right to attend trials. That watershed decision laid the groundwork for the evolving First Amendment right of access to other judicial proceedings, as well as to other governmental activities. Access to courts is covered in depth in Chapter 16.

Disaster, Accident and Crime Scenes

When a train derails or a school bus wrecks, cameras and news crews are not far behind. And, while reporters have a clear right to gather news so long as they break no laws in obtaining access, officials have, in the interest of safety or administrative efficiency, the authority to restrict access to public property when a disaster occurs. Indeed, the Supreme Court noted in *Branzburg*, "newsmen have no constitutional right of access to the scenes of crime or disaster when the general public is excluded." So, if a crime or disaster occurs on private property or a police or fire department restricts admittance to the scene, generally there is no First Amendment right of access. Journalists occasionally have been detained and even arrested for refusing to obey officials' orders to leave disaster scenes.

Some courts, however, have acknowledged a First Amendment right for journalists to cover news at accident scenes, so long as there is no interference with emergency activities. In addition, at least three states — California, Ohio and Virginia — have statutes that specifically recognize a right of press access to emergency and disaster scenes. "Members of the news media must be afforded special access to disaster sites in order that they may properly perform their function of informing the public," a California appeals court held. But even in California, authorities may curtail access where law enforcement officials are investigating a crime or securing an accident scene. The reasoning is that such sites pose dangers that emergency workers are uniquely qualified to evaluate before broad public access can be granted.

In addition to state laws allowing access to disaster scenes, access might be granted through the common law doctrines of implied consent and custom and usage. In one Florida case, reporters entered a fire-ravaged house without permission and photographed a silhouette left on the floor after a victim's body was removed. The victim's mother, who was out of town at the time of the fire and learned of her daughter's death from the news report, was outraged and sued the paper.

The Florida Supreme Court ruled that there was a "longstanding custom and practice throughout the country" that protected the media in such situations. It ruled that it was customary for journalists to accompany officials onto private property and that the photographer was asked to take photographs for the fire officials; therefore, the journalists were protected. Other courts across the country, however, generally have not adopted that reasoning.

NEWSGATHERING ON PUBLIC PROPERTY

While journalists are generally free to gather and report on news that occurs in public forums, newsgathering activities can be restricted on government property not open for general public use, that is, in nonpublic forums.

Prisons

The Supreme Court outlined some of the limitations of the First Amendment right of access to prisons and prisoners in three cases in the 1970s. In *Pell v. Procunier, Saxbe v. Washington Post* and *Houchins v. KQED*, it declared that the First Amendment does not guarantee the press access to correctional facilities or to specifically identified prisoners.

In *Pell*, the Court upheld California's rules that restricted media representatives' ability to interview specific prisoners. While the First Amendment prohibits the government from interfering with a free press, the Court held, the Constitution doesn't guarantee the press more access to correctional facilities than the average citizen has. In *Saxbe*, decided the same year, the Court upheld the constitutionality of a federal regulation that, like the California rule, prohibited interviews with specific prisoners. Finally, in *Houchins*, four years later, it held that, because the First Amendment does not require the release of information within the control of government, it does not require a sheriff to grant journalists access to a county jail.

In this triad of cases, the Court balanced the responsibility of prison officials to maintain order and provide a secure environment against journalists' right to gather news in volatile environments, and it ruled in favor of the government. The decisions gave officials considerable latitude in restricting access to prisons and prisoners. Some argue that the decisions gave too much latitude to correctional officials, who have grown increasingly restrictive over the years. According to a study the Society of Professional Journalists sponsored, many state correctional systems have seized upon the Court's rulings to restrict inmates' access to the outside world. Some regulations include bans on face-to-face interviews, others discriminate between so-called "legitimate" and "entertainment media," and still others ban the use of electronic equipment within a prison. The restrictions at issue in *Pell* pale in comparison to such bans.

California, responding to complaints from officials about an overwhelming number of requests from reporters to interview so-called "celebrity" prisoners, such as Charles Manson and the Menendez brothers, was the first state to embrace new, more restrictive policies designed to prevent high-profile criminals from becoming celebrities. These restrictions quickly spread to include all prisoners regardless of notoriety, however, and spread from state to state. The restrictions, which prohibit face-to-face interviews, make it almost impossible for reporters to cover other important prison-related stories, such as allegations of beatings, rapes and administrative abuses. Prisoners have even been punished in California for contacting the news media to report possible abuses.

Executions

Executions usually occur in prisons. So access to these events, particularly by broadcasters and photographers, is also subject to government fiat. Governments at the state and federal level tightly control access to executions.

In 1994, talk show host Phil Donahue tried unsuccessfully to get permission to televise the execution of a convicted murderer in North Carolina. The prison warden refused, and the state's supreme court ruled that the First Amendment did not require officials to allow taping of executions.

In 2001, two Internet companies lost a lawsuit in which they sought the right to stream the execution of Oklahoma City bomber Timothy McVeigh. A federal judge in Terre Haute, Indiana, said there is no First Amendment right to broadcast an execution from within a prison.

In addition, a federal appeals court ruled that California officials may bar the public and press during the preparation of inmates for execution. The court acknowledged that executions are unquestionably matters of great public importance and reasoned that more information leads to a better informed public, but it ruled that officials were justified in barring public access out of concern for the anonymity of execution team members. The ruling overturned a federal judge's decision that the public and press have a First Amendment right to attend executions.

Military Bases, Operations and War Zones

Neither military bases nor battlefields are public forums, and access to both is subject to all sorts of regulations. During the 1960s and 1970s, the press enjoyed broad access to battlefields. In fact, media reports on the Vietnam War are often credited with changing Americans' feelings about the war. During the 1983 invasion of Grenada, however, the military controlled the press much more. Reporters whom military escorts accompanied

on battlefields complained of attempts to censor their reports. As a result, an inquiry by a special panel of the Joint Chiefs of Staff concluded that "it is essential that the U.S. news media cover U.S. military operations to the maximum degree possible consistent with mission security and the safety of U.S. forces."

Despite the military's position on providing access to the media following Grenada, eight years later journalists again complained about restrictions during Operation Desert Storm. A group of journalists maintained in a special report to the Department of Defense that the military restrictions "made it impossible for reporters and photographers to tell the public the full story of the war in a timely fashion." In a report to the Defense Department, executives representing seventeen of the country's major news organizations — including ABC, CBS, NBC, CNN, the *Washington Post* and the *New York Times* — formally protested the pool system that limited the number of journalists allowed to cover certain stories and the long delays in getting copy to newsrooms in the United States. They also charged that reporters' copy was altered during military security reviews. Ultimately the Defense Department, key press associations and representatives from twenty news organizations agreed that "open and independent reporting" will be the "principle means" by which U.S. wars are covered.

Access debates and tight controls on battlefield journalists also marked the conflict in Afghanistan, which was precipitated by the terrorist attacks of September 11, 2001. The escalation of U.S. forces before the October 7, 2001, attacks on al-Qaeda and the Taliban generally occurred without a media presence; and press restrictions early in the conflict constrained coverage so severely that American reporters learned second-hand about the fall of Mazar-e-Sharif, a strategic gateway to U.S. troops based in nearby Uzbekistan.

Defense officials have described the war in Afghanistan as a different kind of war, one that required restrictions on journalists so that military operations and soldiers' lives would not be endangered. The compromises reached after the Gulf War did not hold, and journalists struggled to provide full coverage. Subsequent conflicts likewise have been less traditional, and more counterinsurgency operations means less access for journalists.

Strained relations between the military and reporters have been a staple of the war on terror. *Washington Post* reporter Doug Struck claimed that a U.S. soldier, whom he did not identify, threatened to shoot him if he went near the scene of a U.S. Hellfire missile strike in 2002. The military denied that a troop leader would knowingly threaten an American citizen, a response that Struck asserted was "an amazing lie." In February 2002 — when the war was more than four months old — the Pentagon began allowing journalists to accompany ground troops in combat, but only after the reporters agreed to delay filing their reports until military officials gave them permission.

Journalists can do little more than negotiate with the Defense Department and complain when access to military operations limits the amount of independent reporting that the press can do. Legal challenges to restrictions on press access to military operations have been unsuccessful.

The beginning of hostilities in Iraq in 2003 ushered in a new form of reporting, and with it a new word in the lexicon: embedding. Responding to the criticism of the first Gulf War conflict, the Pentagon launched an embedding policy that placed journalists within military units in the field. Reporters traveled, ate and slept alongside soldiers, in a carefully planned system that resulted in compelling images of live firefights and U.S. bombing runs as well as its share of criticism for tight controls on the movements of reporters.

Polling Places

Newsgathering near polling places has become controversial in recent years, to which anyone who has witnessed presidential elections can attest. Critics of exit polls claim they interfere with the election process, influencing undecided voters and discouraging potential voters from casting their ballots. Pollsters, however, assert that political speech about the electoral process is core First Amendment speech and must be protected.

Although the Supreme Court has not ruled on the issue of exit polling, a federal appellate court has. In 1988, the Ninth U.S. Circuit Court of Appeals struck down as unconstitutional a Washington law prohibiting exit polling within 300 feet of polling places. It said the law was a content-based restriction on voters' First Amendment rights to discuss their political views and the press' right to gather news. It acknowledged the state's compelling interest in preserving peace, order and decorum at polling places; but as one judge wrote, the law unduly restricts the media's right of access to information crucial to the political process. For that reason, the court ruled that it violated the principles embodied in the First Amendment.

Though not ruling on exit polling, the Supreme Court has upheld a law restricting campaign activities near polling places. In *Burson v. Freeman*, it upheld a Tennessee law prohibiting solicitation of votes and regulating the display and distribution of campaign material within 100 feet of a polling place. The Court acknowledged that the law regulated core political speech but found that it satisfied the strict scrutiny test, because the restricted zone is necessary in order to serve the state's compelling interest in preventing voter intimidation and election fraud.

Schools

Taxpayers own public schools. When school business is being conducted, however, schools are usually not open to the public. Journalists who want to gather news on school property, there-

fore, generally need permission from school officials. In addition, reporters and photographers need to be aware that minors cannot legally waive their rights. Thus, they cannot legally consent to interviews or be photographed. Many schools send standard photograph releases home, asking parents to give permission for their children to be photographed while at school.

The First Amendment, however, protects the right of reporters and photographers to cover events on school property from adjacent public property, such as sidewalks and streets.

NEWSGATHERING ON PRIVATE PROPERTY

When owners of private property and journalists clash over journalists' efforts to gather news on that property, courts frequently focus on whether the journalists had consent to enter the property. Reporters and photographers often don't have permission. Sometimes they enter over the objections of property owners; other times, a property owner is not present to grant permission.

Some states recognize a common law right for journalists to enter private property to gather news. In other states, entry without an owner's permission is trespassing, and both criminal and civil penalties could attach. In any event, remaining on private property after being ordered to leave by a property owner or a custodian of the property is almost always considered trespassing.

Ride-Alongs

A popular genre of TV shows involves journalists accompanying and recording the activities of law enforcement officers and emergency personnel. Police agencies sometimes encourage these so-called "ride-alongs" because they tend to put officers in a human, and sometimes heroic, light. And journalists argue that the practice serves a significant public interest by enabling public oversight of law enforcement, deterring crime and danger to police, and curbing potential police misconduct. All that may be true, but the practice still has come under increased scrutiny.

It has also been threatened by legal action. In 1999, the Supreme Court, in two unanimous opinions, struck a blow against ride-alongs. In both cases, the targets of searches sued law enforcement officials, claiming that, by inviting the press to accompany them on raids, the officials violated Fourth Amendment rights against unreasonable searches. The Court agreed, ruling in *Hanlon v. Berger* and *Wilson v. Layne* that police may be sued for allowing journalists to accompany them onto private property.

In *Wilson*, U.S. marshals and county sheriff's deputies allowed a reporter and photographer from the *Washington Post* to join their early-morning raid of a home where they expected to find a fugitive. He was not there, but his parents were rousted from bed in full view of the journalists. The photographs, one showing Charles Wilson in his underwear with an officer's gun to his head, were never published, but the couple, claiming an invasion of privacy, sued the officials.

In *Hanlon*, CNN crews accompanied U.S. Fish and Wildlife agents onto a Montana ranch in search of eagles that may have been poisoned by pesticides. The ranch owners sued the agents who had invited the journalists along.

Writing for the Court, Chief Justice William Rehnquist held that the public interest benefit of ride-alongs did not justify the Fourth Amendment violation. "Surely the possibility of good public relations for the police is simply not enough, standing alone, to justify the ride-along intrusion into a private home," he wrote. "And even the need for accurate reporting on police issues in general bears no direct relation to the constitutional justification for the police intrusion into a home in order to execute a ... warrant."

After nearly twenty years, the legal liability for members of the news media who accompany police on ride-alongs remains unclear.

Private Businesses Open to the Public

Reporters and photographers often face access problems when they cover events in places that are privately owned but open to the public, like restaurants and shopping malls. In 1968, the Supreme Court held that a shopping mall is the modern equivalent of a downtown business district. It retreated from that position in 1972, however, when it ruled that property does not lose its private character simply because the public is generally invited to use it.

So the First Amendment does not require owners of private businesses, including malls, to allow reporters to gather news on their property. But some states protect free speech rights on such property. California's constitution, for example, protects the rights to speak, write and publish; and the state's supreme court has interpreted these rights to apply to activities at malls. The Supreme Court affirmed that interpretation.

Restricting Paparazzi

In 1997, Princess Diana of England was killed in an automobile accident. Reports of the accident indicate that it might have been caused, in part, because Diana's driver was attempting to elude cars driven by celebrity photographers — called "paparazzi." As a result of the accident, an outcry arose for laws restricting the activities of paparazzi. Lawmakers responded to the outcry.

California, for example, adopted legislation that severely limits the use of telephoto lenses and other electronic equipment to gather news. The law creates a civil cause of action against pho-

tographers who trespass on private property to obtain photographs or who "technologically trespass" by employing enhancement devices, including telephoto lenses or high-powered microphones. The law establishes liability when a person

attempts to capture, in a manner that is offensive to a reasonable person, any type of visual image, sound recording, or other physical impression of the plaintiff engaging in a personal or familial activity under circumstances in which the plaintiff had a reasonable expectation of privacy, through the use of a visual or auditory enhancing device, regardless of whether there is a physical trespass, if this image, sound recording, or other physical impression could not have been achieved without a trespass unless the visual or auditory enhancing device was used.

In the wake of Princess Diana's death, Congress considered three separate bills — the so-called "paparazzi bills" — that would provide punishment for harassment by photojournalists. After several hearings, at which some celebrities testified about their lack of privacy, the bills died.

The controversy was rekindled in 2005 when a photographer rammed his minivan into Disney star Lindsay Lohan's Mercedes Benz. Spurred by Justin Timberlake, Cameron Diaz and others, Los Angeles police and prosecutors opened a criminal investigation into what they describe as a hyper-aggressive new breed of paparazzi willing to go to almost any lengths to get photographs. California lawmakers responded by toughening the previous law, greatly increasing the amount of damages possible when an individual commits an assault while trying to get a photograph or video.

LEGAL AND ILLEGAL NEWSGATHERING TECHNIQUES

How far may a journalist go to gather news? What behavior constitutes a newsgathering tort? Does the First Amendment protect a journalist from misleading a source? Can he use stolen documents? Can she conduct ambush interviews? Can a journalist secretly tape conversations?

The answers to these questions, and others like them, have, in recent years, driven the discussion about newsgathering, about how much journalists can push beyond traditional boundaries and about the use of new technologies. The Supreme Court has never ruled on a reporter's liability for publishing information from illegally obtained documents. In general, if a reporter lawfully acquires information about matters of public concern, states may not punish publication of the information absent a compelling interest. But a reporter, of course, may be punished for illegal activities.

In 1998, a reporter for the *Cincinnati Enquirer* learned this lesson the hard way. Michael Gallagher admitted to gaining access illegally to Chiquita Brands International's corporate voice-mail system. The newspaper fired him, and the state prosecuted him on multiple counts of violating Ohio's electronic communication privacy law and for unauthorized access to a computer. He pleaded guilty to two counts and was sentenced to five years of probation and 200 hours of community service work. Chiquita also sued him for defamation and for breaking into its voice mail system. Gallagher settled that lawsuit in 1999, and the terms were not released.

The *Cincinnati Enquirer* also suffered from the experience. It renounced the stories about Chiquita's business practices, apologized and paid more than $10 million to the company to avoid a lawsuit. A former lawyer for Chiquita — the reporter's source for the original story — unsuccessfully sued the newspaper, which he accused of breach of contract, fraud and negligence for breaking a promise by identifying him. In a unanimous, unsigned opinion, a three-judge panel of the U.S. Court of Appeals, Sixth Circuit held that the newspaper could not be held liable for the disclosures of a former employee. Nevertheless, the Supreme Court has held that liability can be found when journalists break promises to sources. The *Cincinnati Enquirer* has called the entire episode "one of the most unfortunate, and embarrassing, failures of modern investigative journalism."

Another hotbed of controversy in newsgathering involves tape-recorded conversations. In a highly anticipated 2001 decision, the Supreme Court held that the First Amendment protects the release of illegally tape-recorded conversations when neither the source nor the reporter plays a role in the unlawful interception. In a 6-3 decision, it held in *Bartnicki v. Vopper* that the First Amendment rights of the media outweigh a federal wiretapping statute designed to prevent interception of private conversations.

The case involved the dissemination of an illegal tape recording of a cell phone conversation between Gloria Bartnicki, the chief negotiator for a teacher's union in Wyoming Valley West School District in Pennsylvania, and Anthony Kane, the union's president. The tape included Bartnicki's complaints about the school board's reluctance to approve a proposal for a 3 percent pay raise and a discussion about blowing up the front porches of uncooperative school board members. An unknown person gave a copy of the tape to Jack Yocum, the leader of the group opposed to the union's wage proposals. Yocum passed a copy of the tape to Frederick Vopper, a radio talk show host, who played it repeatedly on his show.

Justice John Paul Stevens, writing for the majority, held that although the privacy of communications and the minimization of harm to those whose communications were illegally intercepted represented strong government interests, these interests did not outweigh the First Amendment right to publish matters of public concern.

Although they signed on to the majority's opinion, Justices

Stephen Breyer and Sandra Day O'Connor concurred in a narrower opinion, written by Breyer, stating that the publication was protected because the recording was of public interest and the speakers were public figures. Breyer and O'Connor were swayed by the fact that the federal statutes were broader than necessary to deter the relevant bad conduct and that the publication concerned a potential threat to public safety, decreasing the speaker's legitimate interest in maintaining the privacy of the communication.

Chief Justice Rehnquist, joined by Justices Antonin Scalia and Clarence Thomas, dissented, citing concern for privacy in electronic communications.

Journalists have also been successfully sued for breaching a duty of loyalty. In 1997, Food Lion sued Capital Cities/ABC, Inc., for an undercover report on the grocery store's food-handling policies. Reporters assumed false identities to get the jobs at Food Lion stores and used hidden cameras to expose practices in the grocer's delicatessens. Food Lion claimed intentional misrepresentation, deceit, fraud, negligent supervision, trespass, breach of fiduciary duty, civil conspiracy, violation of federal wiretap statutes, unfair and deceptive trade practices and violations of the Racketeer Influenced and Corrupt Organizations Act. A jury awarded Food Lion $1,500 in compensatory damages and $5.5 million in punitive damages, which the trial court reduced to $315,000. ABC appealed the decision, and the Fourth U.S. Circuit Court of Appeals cut the verdict to $2: $1 for trespass and $1 for breach of loyalty.

While some lower courts have allowed lawsuits against the media for engaging in fraud to obtain stories or footage, courts typically dismiss fraud claims where the claim is an alternative to a libel claim.

SUMMARY

The Supreme Court has noted that the First Amendment protects newsgathering. Specifically, both the First Amendment and the common law provide for the right of journalists to gather news from traditional public forums. In addition, the Court has interpreted the First Amendment to ensure a right of access to criminal judicial proceedings.

But the Court has also said that the First Amendment does not guarantee an unrestricted right to gather news on all public property and in all public places. Not all government-owned properties are public forums. Military bases and public schools are two examples. In addition, activity around polling places — including newsgathering — may be restricted. Legislative bodies also have passed laws restricting some newsgathering activities of paparazzi.

In 1999, the Supreme Court ruled on two cases involving journalists accompanying police on raids, known as "ride-alongs." It unanimously held that law enforcement officials violate the Fourth Amendment protections against unreasonable searches by allowing television crews and other journalists to accompany them.

The First Amendment does not require private businesses, including shopping malls and restaurants, to allow reporters unfettered access to their property. As a result, reporters do not have a right to remain on private property after being told to leave, and in some jurisdictions it may be illegal to enter the property at all without first gaining the permission of the property owner. Shopping malls and restaurants are considered private property.

While successful journalists have to be imaginative and persistent, sometimes gaining access to information and people in unconventional ways, they must remember that the First Amendment will not protect them when they commit crimes, such as trespassing. The media have also been held liable for fraud, breach of promise of confidentiality and breach of duty of loyalty to employers when reporters pose as employees to gain access to nonpublic areas.

BIBLIOGRAPHY

Articles

Alexander, Marc C. "Attention, Shoppers: The First Amendment in the Modern Shopping Mall," 41 *Arizona Law Review* 927 (1992).

Carney, Damian. "Self-regulation of Unlawful Newsgathering Techniques," 13 *Communications Law: Journal of Computer, Media and Telecommunications Law* 767 (2008).

Cate, Hugh C. "Military and Media Relations," *in* Wm. David Sloan & Emily Erickson Hoff, *Contemporary Media Issues.* Northport, Ala.: Vision Press, 1998.

Davis, Charles N. "Access to Prisons," *Quill,* May 1988, at 14.

DeParles, Jane. "17 News Executives Criticize U.S. for 'Censorship' of Gulf Coverage," *New York Times,* July 3, 1991, at A4.

Dyk, Timothy B. "Newsgathering, Press Access, and the First Amendment," 44 *Stanford Law Review* 927 (1992).

Jones, Merrit. "First Amendment Protection for Newsgathering: Applying the Actual Malice Standard to Recovery of Damages for Intrusion," 27 *Hastings Constitutional Law Quarterly* 539 (2000).

Kaufman, Ben. "Former Chiquita Lawyer Sues Paper," *Cincinnati Enquirer,* Sept. 28, 1999, at B2.

Kurtz, Howard & Barton Gellman. "Guidelines Set for News Coverage of Wars," *Washington Post,* May 22, 1992, at A23.

LeBel, Paul A. "Symposium: Undercover Newsgathering Techniques: Issues and Concerns. The Constitutional Interest in Getting the News: Toward a First Amendment Protection from Tort Liability for Surreptitious Newsgathering," 4 *William & Mary Bill of Rights Law Journal* 1145 (1996).

Lee, W. E. "Probing Secrets: The Press and Inchoate Liability for Newsgathering Crimes," 36 *American Journal of Criminal Law* 129 (2009).

Sager, Kelli L. & Karen N. Frederiksen. "Televising the Judicial Branch: In Furtherance of the Public's First Amendment Rights," 69 *Southern California Law Review* 1519 (1996).

Sharkey, Jacqueline E. "The Television War," *American Journalism Review,* May 2003, at 18.

Books

Chairmen of the Joint Chiefs of Staff Media-Military Relations Panel (1984).

Levine, Lee & C. Thomas Dienes. *Newsgathering and the Law.* New Providence, N.J.: LexisNexis/Matthew Bender, 2011.

Millar, Gavin. *Newsgathering: Law, Regulation and the Public Interest.* New York: Oxford University Press, 2016.

Reporters Committee for Freedom of the Press. *Homefront Confidential: How the War on Terrorism Affects Access to Information and the Public's Right to Know,* 6th ed. Arlington, Va.: Reporters Committee for Freedom of the Press, 2005.

Cases

Amalgamated Food Employees Union Local 590 v. Logan Valley Plaza, Inc., 391 U.S. 308 (1968).

Bartnici v. Vopper, 532 U.S. 514 (2001).

Branzburg v. Hayes, 408 U.S. 665 (1972).

Burson v. Freeman, 504 U.S. 191 (1992).

California First Amendment Coalition v. Calderon, 150 F.3d 976 (9th Cir. 1998).

City of Oak Cree v. King, 436 N.W.2d 285 (Wis. 1989).

Cohen v. Cowles Media Co., 501 U.S. 663 (1991).

Daily Herald Co. v. Munro, 838 F.2d 30 (9th Cir. 1988).

Entertainment Network v. Lappin, 134 F. Supp. 2d 1002 (S.D. Ind. (2001).

Florida Publishing v. Fletcher, 340 So. 2d 914 (Fla. 1976).

Florida Star v. B.J.F., 491 U.S. 524 (1989).

Food Lion v. Cap Cities/ABC Inc., 7 F. Supp. 8811 (M.D.N.C. 1995).

Forster v. Manchester, 19 A.2d 147 (Pa. 1963).

Houchins v. KQED, 438 U.S. 1 (1978).

Lawson v. Dixon, 446 S.E.2d 799 (N.C. 1994).

Lloyd Corp. Ltd. V. Tanner, 407 U.S. 551 (1972).

Pell v. Pecunier, 417 U.S. 817 (1974).

Pruneyard Shopping Center v. Robins, 447 U.S. 74 (1980).

Richmond Newspapers v. Virginia, 488 U.S. 555 (1980).

United States v. Albertini, 472 U.S. 675 (1985).

Wilson v. Layne, 526 U.S. 808 (1999).

Statutes

California Civil Code Section 1708.8(b) (2018).
California Penal Code Section 409.5(a) (2018).

Ohio Rev. Code Ann. Section 2917.13(B) (2018).
Personal Privacy Protection Act, S. 1203, 105th Cong. (1988).
Privacy Protection Act of 198, H.R. 3224, 105th Cong. (1988).
Virginia Code Section 15.2-17.14 and 27-15.5 (2018).

The Constitution of the United States of America*

We the People of the United States, in Order to form a more perfect Union, establish Justice, insure domestic Tranquility, provide for the common defence, promote the general Welfare, and secure the Blessings of Liberty to ourselves and our Posterity, do ordain and establish this Constitution for the United States of America.

Article I

Section 1

All legislative Powers herein granted shall be vested in a Congress of the United States, which shall consist of a Senate and House of Representatives.

Section 2

The House of Representatives shall be composed of Members chosen every second Year by the People of the several States, and the Electors in each State shall have the Qualifications requisite for Electors of the most numerous Branch of the State Legislature.

No Person shall be a Representative who shall not have attained to the Age of twenty five Years, and been seven Years a Citizen of the United States, and who shall not, when elected, be an Inhabitant of that State in which he shall be chosen.

[Representatives and direct Taxes shall be apportioned among the several States which may be included within this Union, according to their respective Numbers, which shall be determined by adding to the whole Number of free Persons, including those bound to Service for a Term of Years, and excluding Indians not taxed, three fifths of all other Persons.][1] The actual Enumeration shall be made within three Years after the first Meeting of the Congress of the United States, and within every subsequent Term of ten Years, in such Manner as they shall by Law direct. The Number of Representatives shall not exceed one for every thirty Thousand, but each State shall have at Least one Representative; and until such enumeration shall be made, the State of New Hampshire shall be entitled to chuse three, Massachusetts eight, Rhode-Island and Providence Plantations one, Connecticut five, New-York six, New Jersey four, Pennsylvania eight, Delaware one, Maryland six, Virginia ten, North Carolina five, South Carolina five, and Georgia three.

When vacancies happen in the Representation from any State, the Executive Authority thereof shall issue Writs of Election to fill such Vacancies.

The House of Representatives shall chuse their Speaker and other Officers; and shall have the sole Power of Impeachment.

Section 3

The Senate of the United States shall be composed of two Senators from each State, [chosen by the Legislature thereof,][2] for six Years; and each Senator shall have one Vote.

Immediately after they shall be assembled in Consequence of the first Election, they shall be divided as equally as may be into three Classes. The Seats of the Senators of the first Class shall be vacated at the Expiration of the second Year, of the second Class at the Expiration of the fourth Year, and of the third Class at the Expiration of the sixth Year, so that one third may be chosen every second Year; [and if Vacancies happen by Resignation, or otherwise, during the Recess of the Legislature of any State, the Executive thereof may make temporary Appointments until the next Meeting of the Legislature, which shall then fill such Vacancies.][3]

No Person shall be a Senator who shall not have attained to the Age of thirty Years, and been nine Years a Citizen of the United States, and who shall not, when elected, be an Inhabitant of that State for which he shall be chosen.

The Vice President of the United States shall be President of the Senate, but shall have no Vote, unless they be equally divided.

The Senate shall chuse their other Officers, and also a President pro tempore, in the Absence of the Vice President, or when

---

*The Constitution was adopted in 1788.
[1] Changed by section 2 of the Fourteenth Amendment.
[2] Changed by the Seventeenth Amendment to elections by the people of each state.
[3] Changed by the Seventeenth Amendment to an election process.

he shall exercise the Office of President of the United States.

The Senate shall have the sole Power to try all Impeachments. When sitting for that Purpose, they shall be on Oath or Affirmation. When the President of the United States is tried, the Chief Justice shall preside: And no Person shall be convicted without the Concurrence of two thirds of the Members present.

Judgment in Cases of Impeachment shall not extend further than to removal from Office, and disqualification to hold and enjoy any Office of honor, Trust or Profit under the United States: but the Party convicted shall nevertheless be liable and subject to Indictment, Trial, Judgment and Punishment, according to Law.

Section 4

The Times, Places and Manner of holding Elections for Senators and Representatives, shall be prescribed in each State by the Legislature thereof; but the Congress may at any time by Law make or alter such Regulations, except as to the Places of chusing Senators.

The Congress shall assemble at least once in every Year, and such Meeting shall be on [the first Monday in December,][4] unless they shall by Law appoint a different Day.

Section 5

Each House shall be the Judge of the Elections, Returns and Qualifications of its own Members, and a Majority of each shall constitute a Quorum to do Business; but a smaller Number may adjourn from day to day, and may be authorized to compel the Attendance of absent Members, in such Manner, and under such Penalties as each House may provide.

Each House may determine the Rules of its Proceedings, punish its Members for disorderly Behaviour, and, with the Concurrence of two thirds, expel a Member.

Each House shall keep a Journal of its Proceedings, and from time to time publish the same, excepting such Parts as may in their Judgment require Secrecy; and the Yeas and Nays of the Members of either House on any question shall, at the Desire of one fifth of those Present, be entered on the Journal.

Neither House, during the Session of Congress, shall, without the Consent of the other, adjourn for more than three days, nor to any other Place than that in which the two Houses shall be sitting.

Section 6

The Senators and Representatives shall receive a Compensation for their Services, to be ascertained by Law, and paid out of the Treasury of the United States. They shall in all Cases, except Treason, Felony and Breach of the Peace, be privileged from Arrest during their Attendance at the Session of their re-

spective Houses, and in going to and returning from the same; and for any Speech or Debate in either House, they shall not be questioned in any other Place.

No Senator or Representative shall, during the Time for which he was elected, be appointed to any civil Office under the Authority of the United States, which shall have been created, or the Emoluments whereof shall have been encreased during such time; and no Person holding any Office under the United States, shall be a Member of either House during his Continuance in Office.

Section 7

All Bills for raising Revenue shall originate in the House of Representatives; but the Senate may propose or concur with Amendments as on other Bills.

Every Bill which shall have passed the House of Representatives and the Senate, shall, before it become a Law, be presented to the President of the United States; If he approve he shall sign it, but if not he shall return it, with his Objections to that House in which it shall have originated, who shall enter the Objections at large on their Journal, and proceed to reconsider it. If after such Reconsideration two thirds of that House shall agree to pass the Bill, it shall be sent, together with the Objections, to the other House, by which it shall likewise be reconsidered, and if approved by two thirds of that House, it shall become a Law. But in all such Cases the Votes of both Houses shall be determined by yeas and Nays, and the Names of the Persons voting for and against the Bill shall be entered on the Journal of each House respectively. If any Bill shall not be returned by the President within ten Days (Sundays excepted) after it shall have been presented to him, the Same shall be a Law, in like Manner as if he had signed it, unless the Congress by their Adjournment prevent its Return, in which Case it shall not be a Law.

Every Order, Resolution, or Vote to which the Concurrence of the Senate and House of Representatives may be necessary (except on a question of Adjournment) shall be presented to the President of the United States; and before the Same shall take Effect, shall be approved by him, or being disapproved by him, shall be repassed by two thirds of the Senate and House of Representatives, according to the Rules and Limitations prescribed in the Case of a Bill.

Section 8

The Congress shall have Power To lay and collect Taxes, Duties, Imposts and Excises, to pay the Debts and provide for the common Defence and general Welfare of the United States; but all Duties, Imposts and Excises shall be uniform throughout the United States;

To borrow Money on the credit of the United States;

To regulate Commerce with foreign Nations, and among the several States, and with the Indian Tribes;

---

[4] Changed by section 2 of the Twentieth Amendment to January 3.

To establish an uniform Rule of Naturalization, and uniform Laws on the subject of Bankruptcies throughout the United States;

To coin Money, regulate the Value thereof, and of foreign Coin, and fix the Standard of Weights and Measures;

To provide for the Punishment of counterfeiting the Securities and current Coin of the United States;

To establish Post Offices and post Roads;

To promote the Progress of Science and useful Arts, by securing for limited Times to Authors and Inventors the exclusive Right to their respective Writings and Discoveries;

To constitute Tribunals inferior to the supreme Court;

To define and punish Piracies and Felonies committed on the high Seas, and Offences against the Law of Nations;

To declare War, grant Letters of Marque and Reprisal, and make Rules concerning Captures on Land and Water;

To raise and support Armies, but no Appropriation of Money to that Use shall be for a longer Term than two Years;

To provide and maintain a Navy;

To make Rules for the Government and Regulation of the land and naval Forces;

To provide for calling forth the Militia to execute the Laws of the Union, suppress Insurrections and repel Invasions;

To provide for organizing, arming, and disciplining, the Militia, and for governing such Part of them as may be employed in the Service of the United States, reserving to the States respectively, the Appointment of the Officers, and the Authority of training the Militia according to the discipline prescribed by Congress;

To exercise exclusive Legislation in all Cases whatsoever, over such District (not exceeding ten Miles square) as may, by Cession of particular States, and the Acceptance of Congress, become the Seat of the Government of the United States, and to exercise like Authority over all Places purchased by the Consent of the Legislature of the State in which the Same shall be, for the Erection of Forts, Magazines, Arsenals, dock-Yards, and other needful Buildings;—And

To make all Laws which shall be necessary and proper for carrying into Execution the foregoing Powers, and all other Powers vested by this Constitution in the Government of the United States, or in any Department or Officer thereof.

Section 9

The Migration or Importation of such Persons as any of the States now existing shall think proper to admit, shall not be prohibited by the Congress prior to the Year one thousand eight hundred and eight, but a Tax or duty may be imposed on such Importation, not exceeding ten dollars for each Person.

The Privilege of the Writ of Habeas Corpus shall not be suspended, unless in Cases of Rebellion or Invasion the public Safety may require it.

No Bill of Attainder or ex post facto Law shall be passed.

No Capitation, or other direct, Tax shall be laid, unless in Proportion to the Census or Enumeration herein before directed to be taken.[5]

No Tax or Duty shall be laid on Articles exported from any State.

No Preference shall be given by any Regulation of Commerce or Revenue to the Ports of one State over those of another: nor shall Vessels bound to, or from, one State, be obliged to enter, clear, or pay Duties in another.

No Money shall be drawn from the Treasury, but in Consequence of Appropriations made by Law; and a regular Statement and Account of the Receipts and Expenditures of all public Money shall be published from time to time.

No Title of Nobility shall be granted by the United States: And no Person holding any Office of Profit or Trust under them, shall, without the Consent of the Congress, accept of any present, Emolument, Office, or Title, of any kind whatever, from any King, Prince, or foreign State.

Section 10

No State shall enter into any Treaty, Alliance, or Confederation; grant Letters of Marque and Reprisal; coin Money; emit Bills of Credit; make any Thing but gold and silver Coin a Tender in Payment of Debts; pass any Bill of Attainder, ex post facto Law, or Law impairing the Obligation of Contracts, or grant any Title of Nobility.

No State shall, without the Consent of the Congress, lay any Imposts or Duties on Imports or Exports, except what may be absolutely necessary for executing its inspection Laws: and the net Produce of all Duties and Imposts, laid by any State on Imports or Exports, shall be for the Use of the Treasury of the United States; and all such Laws shall be subject to the Revision and Controul of the Congress.

No State shall, without the Consent of Congress, lay any Duty of Tonnage, keep Troops, or Ships of War in time of Peace, enter into any Agreement or Compact with another State, or with a foreign Power, or engage in War, unless actually invaded, or in such imminent Danger as will not admit of delay.

Article II

Section 1

The executive Power shall be vested in a President of the United States of America. He shall hold his Office during the Term of four Years, and, together with the Vice President, chosen for the same Term, be elected, as follows

Each State shall appoint, in such Manner as the Legislature thereof may direct, a Number of Electors, equal to the whole Number of Senators and Representatives to which the State may be entitled in the Congress: but no Senator or Representa-

---

[5] But the sixteenth Amendment allowed for the collection of income taxes.

tive, or Person holding an Office of Trust or Profit under the United States, shall be appointed an Elector.

[The Electors shall meet in their respective States, and vote by Ballot for two Persons, of whom one at least shall not be an Inhabitant of the same State with themselves. And they shall make a List of all the Persons voted for, and of the Number of Votes for each; which List they shall sign and certify, and transmit sealed to the Seat of the Government of the United States, directed to the President of the Senate. The President of the Senate shall, in the Presence of the Senate and House of Representatives, open all the Certificates, and the Votes shall then be counted. The Person having the greatest Number of Votes shall be the President, if such Number be a Majority of the whole Number of Electors appointed; and if there be more than one who have such Majority, and have an equal Number of Votes, then the House of Representatives shall immediately chuse by Ballot one of them for President; and if no Person have a Majority, then from the five highest on the List the said House shall in like Manner chuse the President. But in chusing the President, the Votes shall be taken by States, the Representation from each State having one Vote; A quorum for this Purpose shall consist of a Member or Members from two thirds of the States, and a Majority of all the States shall be necessary to a Choice. In every Case, after the Choice of the President, the Person having the greatest Number of Votes of the Electors shall be the Vice President. But if there should remain two or more who have equal Votes, the Senate shall chuse from them by Ballot the Vice President.][6]

The Congress may determine the Time of chusing the Electors, and the Day on which they shall give their Votes; which Day shall be the same throughout the United States.

No Person except a natural born Citizen, or a Citizen of the United States, at the time of the Adoption of this Constitution, shall be eligible to the Office of President; neither shall any Person be eligible to that Office who shall not have attained to the Age of thirty five Years, and been fourteen Years a Resident within the United States.

[In Case of the Removal of the President from Office, or of his Death, Resignation, or Inability to discharge the Powers and Duties of the said Office, the Same shall devolve on the Vice President, and the Congress may by Law provide for the Case of Removal, Death, Resignation or Inability, both of the President and Vice President, declaring what Officer shall then act as President, and such Officer shall act accordingly, until the Disability be removed, or a President shall be elected.][7]

The President shall, at stated Times, receive for his Services, a Compensation, which shall neither be increased nor diminished during the Period for which he shall have been elected, and he shall not receive within that Period any other Emolument from the United States, or any of them.

Before he enter on the Execution of his Office, he shall take the following Oath or Affirmation:— "I do solemnly swear (or affirm) that I will faithfully execute the Office of President of the United States, and will to the best of my Ability, preserve, protect and defend the Constitution of the United States."

Section 2

The President shall be Commander in Chief of the Army and Navy of the United States, and of the Militia of the several States, when called into the actual Service of the United States; he may require the Opinion, in writing, of the principal Officer in each of the executive Departments, upon any Subject relating to the Duties of their respective Offices, and he shall have Power to grant Reprieves and Pardons for Offences against the United States, except in Cases of Impeachment.

He shall have Power, by and with the Advice and Consent of the Senate, to make Treaties, provided two thirds of the Senators present concur; and he shall nominate, and by and with the Advice and Consent of the Senate, shall appoint Ambassadors, other public Ministers and Consuls, Judges of the supreme Court, and all other Officers of the United States, whose Appointments are not herein otherwise provided for, and which shall be established by Law: but the Congress may by Law vest the Appointment of such inferior Officers, as they think proper, in the President alone, in the Courts of Law, or in the Heads of Departments.

The President shall have Power to fill up all Vacancies that may happen during the Recess of the Senate, by granting Commissions which shall expire at the End of their next Session.

Section 3

He shall from time to time give to the Congress Information of the State of the Union, and recommend to their Consideration such Measures as he shall judge necessary and expedient; he may, on extraordinary Occasions, convene both Houses, or either of them, and in Case of Disagreement between them, with Respect to the Time of Adjournment, he may adjourn them to such Time as he shall think proper; he shall receive Ambassadors and other public Ministers; he shall take Care that the Laws be faithfully executed, and shall Commission all the Officers of the United States.

Section 4

The President, Vice President and all civil Officers of the United States, shall be removed from Office on Impeachment for, and Conviction of, Treason, Bribery, or other high Crimes and Misdemeanors.

---

[6] Changed by the Twelfth Amendment.

[7] Changed by the Twenty-Fifth Amendment.

Article III

Section 1

The judicial Power of the United States, shall be vested in one supreme Court, and in such inferior Courts as the Congress may from time to time ordain and establish. The Judges, both of the supreme and inferior Courts, shall hold their Offices during good Behaviour, and shall, at stated Times, receive for their Services, a Compensation, which shall not be diminished during their Continuance in Office.

Section 2

The judicial Power shall extend to all Cases, in Law and Equity, arising under this Constitution, the Laws of the United States, and Treaties made, or which shall be made, under their Authority; — to all Cases affecting Ambassadors, other public Ministers and Consuls; — to all Cases of admiralty and maritime Jurisdiction; — to Controversies to which the United States shall be a Party; — to Controversies between two or more States; [— between a State and Citizens of another State;]8 — between Citizens of different States, — between Citizens of the same State claiming Lands under Grants of different States, [and between a State, or the Citizens thereof, and foreign States, Citizens or Subjects.]9

In all Cases affecting Ambassadors, other public Ministers and Consuls, and those in which a State shall be Party, the supreme Court shall have original Jurisdiction. In all the other Cases before mentioned, the supreme Court shall have appellate Jurisdiction, both as to Law and Fact, with such Exceptions, and under such Regulations as the Congress shall make.

The Trial of all Crimes, except in Cases of Impeachment, shall be by Jury; and such Trial shall be held in the State where the said Crimes shall have been committed; but when not committed within any State, the Trial shall be at such Place or Places as the Congress may by Law have directed.

Section 3

Treason against the United States, shall consist only in levying War against them, or in adhering to their Enemies, giving them Aid and Comfort. No Person shall be convicted of Treason unless on the Testimony of two Witnesses to the same overt Act, or on Confession in open Court.

The Congress shall have Power to declare the Punishment of Treason, but no Attainder of Treason shall work Corruption of Blood, or Forfeiture except during the Life of the Person attainted.

Article IV

Section 1

Full Faith and Credit shall be given in each State to the public Acts, Records, and judicial Proceedings of every other State. And the Congress may by general Laws prescribe the Manner in which such Acts, Records and Proceedings shall be proved, and the Effect thereof.

Section 2

The Citizens of each State shall be entitled to all Privileges and Immunities of Citizens in the several States.

A Person charged in any State with Treason, Felony, or other Crime, who shall flee from Justice, and be found in another State, shall on Demand of the executive Authority of the State from which he fled, be delivered up, to be removed to the State having Jurisdiction of the Crime.

[No Person held to Service or Labour in one State, under the Laws thereof, escaping into another, shall, in Consequence of any Law or Regulation therein, be discharged from such Service or Labour, but shall be delivered up on Claim of the Party to whom such Service or Labour may be due.]10

Section 3

New States may be admitted by the Congress into this Union; but no new State shall be formed or erected within the Jurisdiction of any other State; nor any State be formed by the Junction of two or more States, or Parts of States, without the Consent of the Legislatures of the States concerned as well as of the Congress.

The Congress shall have Power to dispose of and make all needful Rules and Regulations respecting the Territory or other Property belonging to the United States; and nothing in this Constitution shall be so construed as to Prejudice any Claims of the United States, or of any particular State.

Section 4

The United States shall guarantee to every State in this Union a Republican Form of Government, and shall protect each of them against Invasion; and on Application of the Legislature, or of the Executive (when the Legislature cannot be convened) against domestic Violence.

Article V

The Congress, whenever two thirds of both Houses shall deem it necessary, shall propose Amendments to this Constitution, or, on the Application of the Legislatures of two thirds of the several States, shall call a Convention for proposing Amendments, which, in either Case, shall be valid to all Intents and Purposes, as Part of this Constitution, when ratified by the

---

8 Changed by the Eleventh Amendment.
9 Changed by the Eleventh Amendment.

10 Changed by the Thirteenth Amendment.

Legislatures of three fourths of the several States, or by Conventions in three fourths thereof, as the one or the other Mode of Ratification may be proposed by the Congress; Provided that no Amendment which may be made prior to the Year One thousand eight hundred and eight shall in any Manner affect the first and fourth Clauses in the Ninth Section of the first Article; and that no State, without its Consent, shall be deprived of its equal Suffrage in the Senate.

Article VI

All Debts contracted and Engagements entered into, before the Adoption of this Constitution, shall be as valid against the United States under this Constitution, as under the Confederation.

This Constitution, and the Laws of the United States which shall be made in Pursuance thereof; and all Treaties made, or which shall be made, under the Authority of the United States, shall be the supreme Law of the Land; and the Judges in every State shall be bound thereby, any Thing in the Constitution or Laws of any State to the Contrary notwithstanding.

The Senators and Representatives before mentioned, and the Members of the several State Legislatures, and all executive and judicial Officers, both of the United States and of the several States, shall be bound by Oath or Affirmation, to support this Constitution; but no religious Test shall ever be required as a Qualification to any Office or public Trust under the United States.

Article VII

The Ratification of the Conventions of nine States, shall be sufficient for the Establishment of this Constitution between the States so ratifying the Same. Done in Convention by the Unanimous Consent of the States present the Seventeenth Day of September in the Year of our Lord one thousand seven hundred and Eighty seven and of the Independence of the United States of America the Twelfth In witness whereof We have hereunto subscribed our Names.... [The names of signers follow.]

The Bill of Rights*

Amendment I

Congress shall make no law respecting an establishment of religion, or prohibiting the free exercise thereof; or abridging the freedom of speech, or of the press; or the right of the people peaceably to assemble, and to petition the government for a redress of grievances.

Amendment II

A well regulated militia, being necessary to the security of a free state, the right of the people to keep and bear arms, shall not be infringed.

Amendment III

No soldier shall, in time of peace be quartered in any house, without the consent of the owner, nor in time of war, but in a manner to be prescribed by law.

Amendment IV

The right of the people to be secure in their persons, houses, papers, and effects, against unreasonable searches and seizures, shall not be violated, and no warrants shall issue, but upon probable cause, supported by oath or affirmation, and particularly describing the place to be searched, and the per-

sons or things to be seized.

Amendment V

No person shall be held to answer for a capital, or otherwise infamous crime, unless on a presentment or indictment of a grand jury, except in cases arising in the land or naval forces, or in the militia, when in actual service in time of war or public danger; nor shall any person be subject for the same offense to be twice put in jeopardy of life or limb; nor shall be compelled in any criminal case to be a witness against himself, nor be deprived of life, liberty, or property, without due process of law; nor shall private property be taken for public use, without just compensation.

Amendment VI

In all criminal prosecutions, the accused shall enjoy the right to a speedy and public trial, by an impartial jury of the state and district wherein the crime shall have been committed, which district shall have been previously ascertained by law, and to be informed of the nature and cause of the accusation; to be confronted with the witnesses against him; to have compulsory process for obtaining witnesses in his favor, and to have the assistance of counsel for his defense.

Amendment VII

In suits at common law, where the value in controversy shall

---

* The first ten amendments to the Constitution were ratified effective December 15, 1791.

exceed twenty dollars, the right of trial by jury shall be pre-served, and no fact tried by a jury, shall be otherwise reex-amined in any court of the United States, than according to the rules of the common law.

Amendment VIII

Excessive bail shall not be required, nor excessive fines im-posed, nor cruel and unusual punishments inflicted.

Amendment IX

The enumeration in the Constitution, of certain rights, shall not be construed to deny or disparage others retained by the people.

Amendment X

The powers not delegated to the United States by the Consti-tution, nor prohibited by it to the states, are reserved to the states respectively, or to the people.

A Short Glossary of Legal Terms

absolute privilege – an immunity from DEFAMATION* suits that attaches to government officials protecting those officials from actions based on speech or writings made within their official capacities.

absolutism – the belief that the First Amendment pronouncement that no law should be made restricting free speech or a free press is absolute and, therefore, that there may be no restrictions on expression.

acquit – in criminal law, to find a defendant not guilty; in contract law, to release from an obligation.

act – STATUTORY LAW; used interchangeably with "law."

actionable – giving rise to a CAUSE OF ACTION.

actual damages – a monetary award in a lawsuit for actual injury or loss, such as harm to reputation, emotional distress or mental suffering; also called COMPENSATORY DAMAGES.

actual malice – knowledge of falsity or reckless disregard for whether material is true or false; this standard, sometimes called "*New York Times* actual malice," which all public officials and public figures must prove in order to prevail in libel actions, was first enunciated by the U.S. Supreme Court in *New York Times Co. v. Sullivan.*

adjudication – giving or pronouncing a judgment or decree; also, the judgment itself.

advance sheet – a pamphlet form of a decision issued at the time the decision is delivered.

allegation – a charge or declaration made in a lawsuit which the plaintiff is required to prove.

all-purpose public figure – in a libel or privacy action, a person of widespread fame or notoriety; a person of special prominence within society or of pervasive power and influence; a "household name."

amicus curiae – literally, "friend of the court"; a person, organization, company or government that provides information to a court — in the form of a BRIEF or argument — who is not a party in the case being litigated.

appeal – a plea to a higher court to alter or overturn a judgment of a lower court because of errors of law.

appellant – the party who appeals a court's decision, requesting that a higher court review the ruling or rulings of the lower court.

appellate court – a court that has jurisdiction to hear cases on appeal.

appellee – the party against whom an appeal is taken; that is, the party who won the case in the lower court.

appropriation – in privacy law, the use of a person's name, image or likeness without permission for trade purposes.

arraignment – a judicial proceeding at which a criminal defendant is formally informed of the charges against him or her and to which the defendant enters a plea.

Articles of Confederation – the first constitution of the United States; it was replaced by the constitution of 1787, which is still in force.

---

* Terms appearing in SMALL CAPITAL LETTERS appear as separate entries in the glossary.

B

bad tendency test – a judicial test that allows restrictions on expression when a court finds that the speech might have even the slightest tendency to cause harm.

bail – money or property that will be forfeited if a criminal defendant does not appear at a judicial proceeding.

bail bond (or bond) – a signed obligation with collateral attached to assure the appearance in court of an individual.

bait-and-switch – a sales technique whereby an item is advertised at a very low price, but shoppers are pressured to buy a more expensive item; in some cases, the low-priced item is not available or is available only on a very limited basis.

balancing – a court's weighing of competing interests guaranteed by law to determine which rights must give way.

Bill of Rights – the first ten amendments to the U.S. Constitution.

black letter law – an informal term indicating the basic principles of law generally accepted by the courts and/or embodied in the STATUTES of a particular jurisdiction.

Bluebook – the popular name of *A Uniform System of Citation,* the standard reference work for legal writing; it was originally developed by the *Harvard Law Review,* but, now in its 18th edition, is produced by the law reviews at Harvard, Columbia, Yale and the University of Pennsylvania.

bootstrapping – an attempt by a media libel defendant to elevate a plaintiff to PUBLIC FIGURE status as a result of the attention brought to the plaintiff by the defendant's coverage of the lawsuit.

brief – a written argument prepared by attorneys involved in an appeal, supporting the attorneys' positions. It contains a summary of the facts, the pertinent law and an argument of how the law applies to the facts. Briefs are prepared by counsel for both sides, but often *AMICUS CURIAE* briefs will also be filed. A BRIEF should not be confused with a CASE BRIEF, which is a synopsis of an opinion.

burden of proof – the elements a plaintiff must prove in order to prevail in a CIVIL ACTION, or that a prosecutor must prove in order to successfully convict a criminal DEFENDANT.

C

case brief – a synopsis of an opinion, generally only one or two pages long, highlighting the facts, question, holding and rationale of the opinion.

CATV – community antenna television; the early name for cable television, reflecting the perception that cable was a regional service designed to expand the reach of broadcast television.

cause of action – those facts which give rise to a right to sue.

censorship – the halting of expression at its source by the government; also called PRIOR RESTRAINT.

certiorari – the name of a WRIT issued by the U.S. Supreme Court when it agrees to review a case; it is an order to the lower court to send up the records. Some state supreme courts also use the term.

change of venire – the transfer of a jury pool from a distant jurisdiction to a location in which a crime was committed in order to seat jurors who have not been biased by publicity about the case.

change of venue – the moving of a trial to a location other than that in which the crime was committed in order to seat jurors who have not been biased by publicity about the case.

child pornography – material containing depictions of children in sexually explicit situations; it is not protected by the First Amendment; also called "kiddie porn."

citation – a notation indicating the location of legal authority. Also called a "cite."

civil action – a lawsuit alleging a private wrong, as opposed to a criminal wrong.

clear and present danger test – a test first enunciated by Justice Oliver Wendell Holmes in 1919 allowing restrictions on speech and press when the expression would cause substantive, immediate harm.

code – a classified arrangement of public laws in effect. Also called "compiled statutes" or "revised statutes."

collateral bar rule – the rule that a person who disobeys a court order may not challenge the constitutionality of the order as a defense to a CONTEMPT OF COURT charge.

colloquium – a libel plaintiff's proof of special circumstances in establishing that a defamatory statement is about or understood to be about the plaintiff.

commercial speech – communication intended to promote a business or service or sell a product.

common carrier – the regulatory category traditionally applied to service providers - like telephone services - that must provide universal, nondiscriminatory service to all on a first-come-first-served basis and may not control the messages they carry.

common law – court-created law; in modern usage, case law as opposed to statutory law; in theory, the common law was "discovered" rather than created by historical Anglo-Saxon courts. The discovery was based on the common customs of the times, thus the term "common." "Common" law was also distinguished from "ecclesiastical" or church law.

common law malice – ill will, hatred or spite.

compelling government interest – an overriding interest advocated by the government that must be proved in order for a regulation aimed at suppressing expression to be found constitutional. In such cases - which require STRICT SCRUTINY - the government must also prove that the regulation is narrowly tailored.

compensatory damages – a monetary award in a lawsuit for actual injury or loss, such as harm to reputation, emotional distress or mental suffering; also called ACTUAL DAMAGES.

complainant – the person bringing a legal complaint; the PLAINTIFF.

complaint – the first legal argument filed by a plaintiff.

constitution – a document outlining the organization of a government, specifying the rights, responsibilities and limits of that government.

contempt of court – willful disobedience of a lawful order of a court or any act calculated to embarrass, hinder or obstruct a court in the administration of justice.

content neutral restrictions – restrictions that are not related to the content of expression, but on circumstances related to the TIME, PLACE OR MANNER of the expression.

continuance – a judicial order that a criminal or civil action be delayed.

copyright – protection for the ownership of an original work that has been fixed in a tangible medium of expression.

copyright infringement – copying the form or expression of an idea without permission; punishable by a civil or criminal action or both.

criminal libel – a malicious publication that exposes or tends to expose a

living person or the memory of a deceased person to hatred, contempt ridicule or obloquy in violation of a statute; a prosecutor brings the criminal charges against the publisher of the publication.

cross-ownership – an array of FCC rules and statutory provisions aimed to protect diversity of ownership and content by preventing consolidation of media ownership.

D

damages – compensation recovered by a PLAINTIFF from a DEFENDANT.

DBS – direct broadcast satellites; they operate in GEOSYNCHRONOUS ORBITS to create a stable broadcast imprint or coverage area for transmission of messages and programming to receiving dishes 18 to 24 inches in diameter.

de novo – a second time; totally new.

defamation – communication that injures another's reputation, that is, that holds one up to scorn, ridicule or spite; SLANDER is oral defamation; LIBEL is written defamation.

defendant – the party against whom a lawsuit is brought.

demurrer – an allegation by a defendant that even if the facts alleged by a plaintiff are true, they do not state a sufficient CAUSE OF ACTION.

deposition – a formal interview by an attorney of a witness who answers questions under oath, but not in open court; also, the transcript of the interview.

deregulation – a policy of eliminating laws and regulations in favor of market pressures.

dictum – technically *obiter dictum,* this is an incidental comment in an opinion; a comment not necessary to the determination of the issue at hand; it is not binding precedent. The plural is *"dicta."*

digital sampling – converting sounds from existing songs to digital bits and then manipulating and combining notes to create a new song.

discovery – a proceeding through which parties in a case are informed of facts known by the adversarial parties.

diversity of citizenship action – a civil action in which the parties are residents of different states; the U.S. Constitution allows federal district courts to hear such cases, even if the subject matter of the suit is one of state law, as long as the amount in the controversy exceeds $75,000.

docket number – the numerical designation assigned to each case by a court; it is used to identify the case as it progresses through the judicial system.

DTH – direct-to-home; the services send video signals to home dishes or receivers in the United States, including the relatively high-power DBS systems and lower-power HSD systems.

DTV – *see* HDTV.

due process – a term used to describe the proper operation of legal proceedings according to the rules and principles that have been established to protect the rights of individuals.

E

effective competition – the standard that allows cable systems to operate without rate regulation; it exists when substantial overlap of services offered by cable and other providers exists.

en banc – a session in which the entire court — rather than a panel — hears and participates in the determination of a case.

enjoin – to require, by a judicial action, an individual to perform or refrain from performing some act.

equity – justice administered according to fairness as contrasted with the strict, formulated rules of COMMON LAW; it renders the administration of justice more complete, by affording relief where courts of law are incompetent to give it or enforce it.

erotica – sexually explicit material; generally "erotica" is a neutral term

that refers to material that can be distinguished from PORNOGRAPHY or OB-
SCENITY; erotica is protected by the First Amendment.

exemplary damages – a monetary award designed to punish a defendant
in a lawsuit for some action; the same as PUNITIVE DAMAGES.

ex parte – by, for or on behalf of one party.

F

fair comment and criticism – a COMMON LAW defense against a defamation
claim in which the defendant avows a right to express an opinion, based on
well-known or truthfully stated facts, without COMMON LAW MALICE against
a person who has entered the public sphere.

fair use – a provision in copyright law that allows copying of protected
material for use in certain specific circumstances.

false light – the privacy tort which protects individuals from the publication of material that is not necessarily defamatory but is false and offensive.

fault – culpability; it must be proved in order for an individual to prevail
in a libel action; the most common types of fault are NEGLIGENCE and ACTU-
AL MALICE.

felony – a serious crime punishable by imprisonment in a penitentiary, or
more serious punishment.

fighting words – language that is likely to cause an immediate, violent response; it lies outside First Amendment protection.

first sale – the doctrine that permits a copyright owner to collect royalties
the first time each copy of a work is sold. The purchaser may then rent or
resell that copy without permission, but may not make derivative works,
reproduce or publicly perform the work.

franchise agreement – the contract between local authorities and cable
operators that imposes conditions on cable systems in exchange for permission for them to string their cables along public rights-of-way.

G

gag order – an order by a court not to speak or write about matters before
the court.

geosynchronous orbit – an orbit that enables a satellite to maintain its position relative to the earth.

grand jury – an investigatory panel; a panel whose duty is to hear the
state's evidence in a criminal case and determine whether there is probable
cause to believe a crime has been committed and whether the accused
should stand trial; the grand jury does not determine guilt or innocence.

group libel – a DEFAMATION aimed at a group rather than an individual; if
the group is large, members of the group are precluded from bringing libel
actions because they are not sufficiently identified.

H

habeas corpus – literally, "you have the body"; a WRIT through which a
person can be brought before a court to determine whether the person has
been denied liberty without DUE PROCESS of law.

HDTV – high definition television or digital television (DTV); it uses digital
technology and a new transmission standard to improve picture and sound
quality and to provide an image area shaped more like a movie theater
screen than a traditional television screen.

headend – the control center of a cable system, where the cable operator
brings together programming from diverse sources before distributing it to
subscribers.

headnote – a summary of legal principles in a case, printed immediately
before the text of the opinion in a REPORTER; a case may be preceded by a
number of headnotes, depending upon the findings of the court.

holding – the declaration in an OPINION of the conclusion of law reached

by a court.

HSD – home satellite dish services; they are more properly called "fixed satellite services" and require a receiving dish approximately four to eight feet
in diameter to receive their low-power signals.

I

implied consent – consent that is not explicit, but may be available based
on the facts of the case.

in camera – in private; in a judge's chambers.

incorporation – in constitutional law, the process by which portions of the
BILL OF RIGHTS, including the First Amendment, have been applied to the
states *via* the Fourteenth Amendment's due process clause.

indict/indictment – a written accusation by a GRAND JURY charging a person with a crime.

inducement – a libel plaintiff's allegation that extrinsic facts make a statement defamatory although it is not defamatory on its face.

infra – a signal indicating that further information appears later in the text
or footnotes.

injunction – a court order halting some activity or commanding someone
to undo a wrong.

inter alia – literally "among other things."

interconnection rules – the rules that govern the ability of communication
service providers to link up with and use the network facilities of a competitor.

Internet – an international network created by high-speed, broadband
connections and satellite links.

interrogatory – a list of written questions posed by a party in a lawsuit to
the opposing party.

J

judgment – the HOLDING of a court in a case.

judgment n.o.v. – a judgment rendered in favor of one party in a case,
notwithstanding a verdict in favor of the opposing party; that is, the overruling of a jury verdict by a judge.

jurisdiction – the area over which a court has authority; the power and authority of a court to hear and determine a judicial proceeding; the area may
be geographic or based on the subject matter of the case. If a court does not
have jurisdiction, it may not render a legal decision in the matter.

K

Key Number – a permanent number assigned to a specific point of law in a
case, as developed by the West Publishing Company, to aid in the discovery
of material on the same topic of law in other cases.

L

leased-access channels – channels provided by cable systems for commercial lease, which, when not leased, cable operators may use to carry cable programming.

liable – responsible or answerable for some action.

libel – written communication that damages a person's reputation, that is,
that holds a person up to hatred, ridicule or scorn; a type of DEFAMATION.

libertarianism – a governmental theory allowing absolute and unrestricted
liberty, especially of thought and speech.

licensing – a governmental policy under which express permission must be
granted before material may be published.

likelihood of confusion – grounds for legal action to protect a TRADEMARK
from being confused with another trademark; courts compare the two
marks on a variety of factors to determine whether consumers are likely to
be confused as to the source, sponsorship or approval of a product.

limited-purpose public figure – in libel law, a person who voluntarily injects himself or herself into a public controversy in order to influence the outcome; also known as a "vortex public figure."

lock boxes – television set-top devices that can be programmed to eliminate certain channels or content.

M

malice – *see* COMMON LAW MALICE, ACTUAL MALICE.

mandamus – an order by a court directing a lower court or government official to do something.

marketplace of ideas theory – the theory that the government should exercise minimal control on speech, based on the notion that when all ideas are allowed to be expressed - that is, are allowed in the "marketplace of ideas" - truth will prevail.

misdemeanor – a criminal offense that is not serious enough to warrant a prison sentence; penalties are usually fines and community service or a sentence to a local jail.

moot – the absence of a genuine controversy or contention of law. Courts will rarely decide "moot" points of law unless there is an indication that the point of law is likely to recur in another case.

MSO – multiple system operator; a person who runs cable systems in several geographically dispersed locations.

multiplexing – a technology that enables the transmission of up to four television signals on one channel.

must-carry rules – a series of FCC rules requiring cable systems to carry all local broadcast signals.

N

negligence – a standard of FAULT in TORT law; an act or omission that a reasonably careful person would not take; in libel law, it is acting other than in a manner in which a reasonably careful or ordinarily prudent person would act or failure to follow accepted professional practices or standards.

network nonduplication rules – rules that allow television stations affiliated with a broadcast network to demand that a cable system black out network programming being carried on an imported station.

nonsuit – termination of an action without adjudicating the issues on the merits.

O

obscenity – pornographic material that has been determined by a court to meet the Supreme Court's test for obscene material articulated in *Miller v. California* and, therefore, lies outside First Amendment protection.

opinion – an explanation of the rationale for a judicial decision, that is, the holding of a court and the rationale for that holding; in libel law, a communication that cannot be proved to be true or false and, therefore, cannot be the subject of a successful libel action.

overbroad/overbreadth – a term used to refer to a law that prohibits or punishes legal as well as illegal conduct or speech.

P

parallel citation – a citation reference to the same case printed in a different REPORTER. (See definition of "reporter.")

PEG channels – cable television channels reserved by law for public, educational and government access.

per curiam – an opinion "by the court"; that is, an unsigned opinion.

peremptory challenges – rights by which an attorney may dismiss potential jurors without providing a reason; the number is generally limited based on the nature of the trial.

petit jury – a panel whose function it is to decide the facts of a case, that is, to determine guilt or innocence in a criminal suit and the party that prevails in a civil suit.

petitioner – the party who starts an EQUITY proceeding or the party who appeals a judgment to a higher court.

plaintiff – the party who brings a lawsuit.

pleading – a legal argument, filed in writing, outlining the contentions of a party in a lawsuit.

pocket supplement – also called a "pocket part," a supplement found in the back of a legal source book, updating the information contained within the book.

pornography – sexually explicit material that is in some way demeaning; it is protected by the First Amendment.

precedent – legal authority that must be followed, absent a sound legal basis for variance; previous cases on the same point of law.

preliminary injunction – a temporary order, generally to stop a person from doing something.

preponderance of evidence – the standard of proof in a civil action, determined by balancing the evidence and determining which allegations or contentions are more likely to be true.

prima facie case – a case that unless contradicted would likely prevail before a reasonable jury.

primary authority – mandatory legal authority; that is, judicial precedent or legislative enactment; authority that must be followed or contended with.

prior restraint – the prohibition of expression at its source by the government; also called CENSORSHIP.

promissory estoppel – a legal doctrine similar to contract law that holds that when a clear promise is intended to and does induce a specific action, that promise is binding if injustice can be avoided only by enforcing it.

publication – in libel law, the exposure of material to a third party.

public domain – material no longer protected by COPYRIGHT falls into the public domain, meaning that it is available for anyone to use without authorization.

public figure – *see* ALL-PURPOSE PUBLIC FIGURE and LIMITED-PURPOSE PUBLIC FIGURE.

public official – a government employee who has or appears to have substantial responsibility for or control over the conduct of government affairs.

punitive damages – a monetary award designed to punish a defendant in a lawsuit for some action; the same as EXEMPLARY DAMAGES. The U.S. Supreme Court has said that libel plaintiffs must prove ACTUAL MALICE in order to recover punitive damages.

Q

qualified privilege – a privilege to report information that appears in absolutely privileged *fora,* if certain conditions or qualifications are met, that is, if the report is accurate, fair and made without COMMON LAW MALICE.

quash – to vacate, abate or annul.

R

ratio decidendi – the rationale of a decision; that is, the legal point in the case which leads to the result.

reckless disregard – extreme indifference as to the truth or falsity of a defamatory statement; indifference that is tantamount to conscious, deliberate or intentional ignoring of the truth or falsity of a statement.

remand – to send back to a lower court for further proceedings, usually based upon the findings of a higher court.

report – to publish a decision of a court.

reporter – one in a series of books in which legal decisions are published; to publish the decisions.

reporter's privilege – the right of a journalist to keep the identities of sources or other information confidential.

respondent – in an EQUITY case, the party who answers the PETITIONER'S bill of particulars; in appellate practice, the party who contests or opposes an APPEAL.

retraction – a published statement acknowledging that a publication was in error; "taking back" an incorrect statement.

S

scienter – guilty knowledge; prior knowledge.

scope note – a short note identifying and limiting the content of a topic; it appears immediately after the topic's heading in a legal reference work.

search warrant – an order issued by a magistrate or other officer of the court authorizing law enforcement officials to search for and seize evidence of a crime.

secondary authority – persuasive but not mandatory (PRIMARY) authority; supporting material; it may include legal encyclopedias, treatises, law journal articles or text books.

sedition – attacks on the government punishable by law because they could cause unrest.

seditious libel – harsh criticism of the government.

sequestration – the isolation of members of a jury during the taking of evidence and/or the deliberations on the facts of a case.

service mark – any word, name, symbol or device, or any combination thereof, adopted and used by a manufacturer or merchant to identify its services and distinguish them from services provided by others.

session laws – published laws of a state, as enacted by each assembly in each session; laws listed in chronological, rather than topical, order.

Sheparding – to use a *Shepard's* citator index to locate all subsequent references to or uses of a case or other legal authority.

shield law – a statute providing journalists a testimonial privilege.

slamming – the illegal practice of switching a person's long-distance service provider without permission.

slander – oral communication that damages someone's reputation, that is, that would tend to hold a person up to scorn, ridicule or hatred; a type of DEFAMATION.

SMATV – also known as "private cable," a cable system within a single apartment building or bloc of buildings that does not use public rights-of-way; the system collects local television signals through antennas and satellite signals through receiving dishes and transmits them through the buildings.

special damages – a monetary award for financial or pecuniary loss.

standing – the right to bring a legal action.

star paging – a pagination scheme in reprint editions of court reporters, showing on its pages where the pages of the official text begin and end.

stare decisis – literally, "let the decision stand"; the legal doctrine of precedent; the tendency to follow, rather than overrule, precedent, i.e., the doctrine that a court will follow the principle established by a previous court when the facts of the cases are substantially the same.

statute of limitations – the time period in which a civil or criminal action must be brought.

statute/statutory law – law adopted by legislative bodies.

stay – a court order stopping some judicial action or order.

strict liability – the doctrine that a person is LIABLE for an act even if that action was unintentional and without FAULT.

strict scrutiny – a test to determine whether a regulation is constitutional; the test is used when the regulation is directed at the suppression of expression; under the test, the regulation is constitutional if it meets a COMPELLING GOVERNMENT INTEREST and is narrowly tailored.

subpoena – a command to appear in court at a certain time to testify about a certain matter; a **subpoena duces tecum** requires that the subpoenaed party bring certain documents or other materials to the hearing.

summary judgment – a ruling by a judge that there is no dispute of material fact between the two parties in a case, and that one party should win the case as a matter of law.

supra – a signal indicating that further information on a point or case is provided earlier in the text or footnotes.

syllabus – a summary of the case and the court's holding, prepared by the publisher of a REPORTER.

syndicated exclusivity – an FCC rule that prohibits cable companies from importing syndicated programs to which television stations possess exclusive contracts.

T

temporary restraining order – a court order to temporarily prevent an action.

time, place and manner restrictions – restrictions on expression based on the circumstances surrounding the expression rather than the content of the expression.

tort – a civil wrong by one person against another.

trade name – any name used by a person to identify his or her business or vocation.

trademark – a word, name, symbol or device or any combination thereof used to identify goods and distinguish them from those manufactured or sold by others.

trademark dilution – using a famous trademark in ways that blur its distinctiveness or tarnish or disparage it.

transformative – among the factors used to determine whether a use of copyrighted material is a FAIR USE or a COPYRIGHT INFRINGEMENT; courts examine whether the secondary use added value to the original copyrighted work.

V

vagueness – a rationale for finding a law unconstitutional because the law is not specific enough to give fair warning as to the parameters of the law.

venire – the potential jurors in a trial.

venue – the place in which a trial occurs.

voir dire – literally "to see, to say"; the process through which attorneys and a judge question potential jurors to determine whether they are qualified to serve.

W

wireless cable – a system licensed and regulated by the FCC that includes multi-point distribution services and multi-channel distribution services. It sends up to thirty-three channels by microwave signals to small antennas on subscribers' homes but does not cross public rights-of-way, so it does not require a local franchise.

work made for hire – intellectual property created as part of one's employment so that the employer, rather than the creator of the work, owns the COPYRIGHT; two types are (1) work done by an employee for an employer within the scope of employment; (2) a work specially commissioned or ordered for inclusion in a collective work if a work-for-hire agreement is signed.

writ – an order by a court requiring some action or giving authority and commission to that act.

The Authors

Stuart Brotman is the Alvin and Sally Beaman Professor of Journalism and Media Law Enterprise and Leadership at the University of Tennessee, Knoxville. He also serves as a Distinguished Fellow at The Media Institute. His email address is sbrotman@ utk.edu

Charles N. Davis is the dean of the Henry W. Grady College of Journalism and Mass Communication at the University of Georgia. He worked as a journalist in Georgia, Florida and Ireland for nearly ten years after graduating from North Georgia College. He received a master's degree from the University of Georgia and a Ph.D. degree from the University of Florida, where he assisted reporters and others with freedom of information questions for the Brechner Center for Freedom of Information. He taught at Georgia Southern University and was department chair at Southern Methodist University before joining the faculty at the University of Missouri. He edited *Access Denied: Freedom of Information in the Information Age* for Iowa University Press. His e-mail address is cndavis@uga.edu.

Anthony L. Fargo is an associate professor in The Media School at Indiana University and director of the Center for International Media Law and Policy Studies. He holds a bachelor's degree in English and journalism from Morehead State University and master's and doctorate degrees in mass communication from the University of Florida. He has taught at the University of Nevada, Las Vegas and the University of Rhode Island. His research has been published in *Communication Law and Policy, Free Speech Yearbook, Cardozo Arts & Entertainment Law Journal, Newspaper Research Journal, Journal of Broadcasting and Electronic Media, William & Mary Bill of Rights Journal, the William Mitchell Law Review, University of Arkansas Little Rock Law Review, Harvard Journal of Law & Public Policy, Journalism and Mass Communication Monographs, Journal of Media Law* (UK), *University of Florida Journal of Law & Public Policy, North Carolina Journal of Law and Technology, In Medias Res* (Hungary), and the *Journal of International Media and Entertainment Law*. He is on the board of the Indiana Coalition for Open Government. He is the faculty adviser for the IU student chapter of Reporters Without Borders. He is an adjunct faculty member in the Maurer School of Law and is on the advisory board for the IU Center for Law, Society, and Culture. His email address is alfargo@indiana.edu.

Mark Goodman is professor emeritus in the School of Media and Journalism at Kent State University, where he was the Knight Chair in Scholastic Journalism. Before that he was executive director of the Student Press Law Center. He has a degree in journalism from the University of Missouri and a law degree from Duke University. He has received more than two dozen national awards for his work in support of student journalism including awards from the Reporters Committee for Freedom of the Press, the Society of Professional Journalists and the National Council of Teachers of English. He also won the Gerald M. Sass Award for Distinguished Service to Journalism and Mass Communication from the Association of Schools of Journalism and Mass Communication. His email address is mgoodm10@kent.edu.

Karla K. Gower is director of the Plank Center for Leadership in Public Relations and a professor in the Advertising and Public Relations Department of the College of Communication and Information Sciences at the University of Alabama, where she teaches public relations courses. She has published a biography of Betsy Plank, a book on the relationship between journalism and public relations since World War II and two books on communication law topics. In addition, her articles have appeared in *Journalism and Mass Communication Quarterly, Journalism History, Communication Law and Policy* and other journals. Her research focuses on legal issues affecting corporate communication and the history of public relations. She received her bachelor's and law degrees from Western University, Canada, her master's degree from Arizona State University and her doctorate from the University of North Carolina at Chapel Hill. Her e-mail is gower@apr.ua.edu.

Steven Helle is a professor emeritus and former head of the Department of Journalism at the University of Illinois in Urbana-Champaign. He is co-author of *Last Rights: Revisiting Four Theories of the Press* and has published numerous articles on communication law in, among others, *Duke Law Journal, Journalism and Mass Communication Quarterly, Villanova Law Review, University of Illinois Law Review, Iowa Law Review, Illinois Bar Journal, Journalism and Mass Communication Educator* and *DePaul Law Review*. A former head of the Law Division of the Association for Education in Journalism and Mass Communication, he has served on the editorial boards of the *Illinois Bar Journal, Journalism Monographs* and *Communication Law and Policy*. He is past chair of the Media Law Committee and the Human Rights Section Council of the Illinois State Bar Association. He is the only person to receive the Campus Award for Excellence in Undergraduate Teaching at the University of Illinois on three occasions, most recently in 2010. He was also selected Freedom Forum Journalism Teacher of the Year in 1998. His J.D. and M.A. degrees are from the University of Iowa. His e-mail address is steveh@illinois.edu.

W. Wat Hopkins is emeritus professor of communication at Virginia Tech, where he teaches journalism and communication law courses. He has published three books and a number of articles on First Amendment topics and is editor of *Communication Law and Policy*, the research journal of the Law Division of the Association for Education in Journalism and Mass Communication. He is a past head of the Law Division and is also past president of the Virginia Coalition for Open Government. He was a founding member of Virginia's first Freedom of Information Advisory Council, an advisory and educational group established by the Virginia General Assembly. He was the Roy H. Park Distinguished Visiting Professor in the School of Journalism and Mass Communication at the University of North Carolina at Chapel Hill for the spring 2010 semester. He also received the 2022 Distinguished Service Award from the AEJMC Law and Policy Division. He received his bachelor's degree from Western Carolina University and his master's and Ph.D. degrees from UNC-CH. His e-mail address is whopkins@vt.edu.

Matt Jackson is an associate professor and head of the telecommunications department in the College of Communications at Pennsylvania State University. He teaches telecommunications regulation and policy, programming, management and communication law. He has published articles in *Journal of Broadcasting & Electronic Media, Federal Communications Law Journal, Communications Law and Policy, Hastings Communication and Entertainment Law Journal* and other journals. His research focuses on the evolution of intellectual property law and its impact on communication networks and free speech. He received his bachelor's and master's degrees from the University of Florida and his doctorate from Indiana University at Bloomington. His e-mail address is mattj@psu.edu.

Robert Kerr is a professor in the College of Journalism and Mass Communication at the University of Oklahoma. He is also a member of the affiliated faculty of OU's Institute for the American Constitutional Heritage. He teaches undergraduate and graduate courses in media law and history, and students have twice voted him recipient of his college's annual teaching award. His research focuses on First Amendment issues involving corporate political media spending and commercial speech, and on sports media. His 2019 article, "From Holmes to Zuckerberg: Keeping Marketplace-of-Ideas Theory Viable in the Age of Algorithms," in *Communication Law and Policy*, won the Stonecipher Award for Outstanding Scholarship in Media Law and Policy by the Association for Education in Journalism and Mass Communication's Law and Policy Division in 2020. His book *The Corporate Free-Speech Movement* (2008) foreshadowed the 2010 Supreme Court ruling in *Citizens United v. FEC* as well as the late 2000s economic crisis in global markets and economies. His articles have appeared in *Journalism and Communication Monographs, Journalism and Mass Communication Quarterly, Communication Law and Policy, The International Review for the Sociology of Sport, The First Amendment Law Review, American Journalism, The Journal of Sports Media* and *The Journal of Media Law and Ethics.*. He is a past winner of the National Communication Association's Franklyn S. Haiman Award for Distinguished Scholarship in Freedom of Expression. He received his bachelor's degree from Southern Arkansas University, his master's degree from the University of Oklahoma, and his doctorate from the University of North Carolina at Chapel Hill. He worked as a journalist for twenty years in Memphis, Las Vegas, and Texarkana. His email address is rkerr@ou.edu.

Michele Kimball's body of legal research focuses on government transparency and access to government information. She uses mixed research methods to evaluate the real-life applications of media law statutes and policies. Her research has appeared in *Communication Law and Policy, Government information Quarterly, Journal of Media Law and Ethics,* and *Newspaper Research Journal.* She teaches media law at The George Washington University in Washington, D.C. Her e-mail address is kimballshelley@gmail.com.

Jeremy Harris Lipschultz is Peter Kiewit Distinguished Professor in the School of Communication, University of Nebraska at Omaha. He leads the UNO Social Media Lab for Research and Engagement and is book review editor for *Journalism and Mass Communication Educator*. He is author of *Social Media Law and Ethics* (2022), *Social Media Communication*, fourth edition (2023) and other books about media and the First Amendment. He is @JeremyHL on Twitter and Instagram, and also is active on Facebook and LinkedIn. His email address is jeremy.lipschultz@gmail.com.

Cayce Myers is an associate professor and Director of Graduate Studies at Virginia Tech's School of Communication where he teaches public relations and communication law. He holds a Ph.D. and M.A. in mass communication from the Henry W. Grady College of Journalism and Mass Communication at the University of Georgia, a LL.M. focusing on media law from the

University of Georgia School of Law, a J.D. from Mercer University School of Law, and B.A. from Emory University. He is the co-author of the 4th and 5th editions of *Mass Communication Law in Virginia* and author of *Money in Politics: Campaign Fundraising in the 2020 Presidential Election* and *Public Relations History: Theory, Practice, and Profession*. He has also published in several scholarly journals and trade press on laws that affect public relations practice. His email is mcmyers@vt.edu.

Erica Salkin is a professor of communication studies and associate dean of the College of Arts and Sciences at Whitworth University in Spokane, Washington. Her research focuses on freedom of expression in academic settings, and she is the author of several articles and books on student media and student speech rights, including *Private Schools and Student Media: Supporting Mission, Students, and Community* from Lexington Books. She teaches courses in media writing, digital media, public relations and free speech as well as advises the student newspaper, *The Whitworthian*. Her email address is esalkin@whitworth.edu.

Jared Schroeder is an associate professor in the University of Missouri School of Journalism. His research focuses on First Amendment theory, particularly as it applies to freedom of expression and emerging technologies. He is the author of *The Press Clause and Digital Technology's Fourth Wave* and co-author of *Emma Goldman's No-Conscription League and the First Amendment*. He won the 2021 Harry W. Stonecipher Award for Distinguished Research on Media Law and Policy for his article "Fixing False Truths: Rethinking Truth Assumptions and Free-Expression Rationales in the Networked Era." His research has appeared in numerous peer-reviewed journals and law reviews. He regularly contributes to popular and industry publications. His email address is jcschroeder@missouri.edu.

Dean Smith is an assistant professor in the Nido R. Qubein School of Communication at High Point University, where he teaches media law and First Amendment history. He holds a master's degree from Yale Law School and a Ph.D. from the University of North Carolina at Chapel Hill. He is the 2012 winner of the Nafziger-White-Salwen Dissertation Award from the AEJMC and is author of *A Theory of Shield Laws*.

Sigman L. Splichal is a retired associate professor from the School of Communication at the University of Miami. He began his journalism career in 1971 and was a newspaper writer and editor in Georgia, Florida and Virginia. He received his bachelor's, master's and Ph.D. degrees from the University of Florida. He is co-editor of *Access Denied: Freedom of Information in the Information Age* and is author of numerous law and academic journal articles on legal and ethical topics. His e-mail address is nip@miami.edu.

Samuel A. Terilli is a retired assistant professor in the School of Communication at the University of Miami. He is also a practicing attorney and has represented and advised a variety of media organizations for twenty-two years. He received his bachelor's degree from the State University of New York at Albany and his juris doctorate from the University of Michigan. His e-mail address is sterilli@Miami.edu.

John C. Watson is an associate professor at the American University School of Communication in Washington, D.C. He holds a J.D. from the Rutgers School of Law and a Ph.D. from the University of North Carolina at Chapel Hill. He is the author of *Journalism Ethics by Court Decree: The Supreme Court on the Proper Practice of Journalism*. His research and commentary have been published in *Communication Law and Policy, Journal of Mass Media Ethics, Journalism History, Rutgers Race and the Law Review, Thomas M. Cooley Law Review* and other refereed, scholarly journals. He is the author of book chapters and encyclopedia entries on communication law. He has 21 years of experience as a daily newspaper reporter and city editor. He has been interviewed on communication and law issues by correspondents for NPR, NBC, CBS, CNN, ABC, BET, KBS (Korean Broadcasting System) and Fox News networks as well as *The New York Times, Washington Post* and *The Christian Science Monitor*. His e-mail address is jwatson@american.edu.

Kearston Wesner is an associate professor of media studies in the School of Communications at Quinnipiac University. In addition to teaching undergraduate courses in communications law and policy, media industries and trends, and media history, she teaches senior seminars in celebrity culture and popular music. Her research, which has appeared in *Communication Law and Policy, Journal of Law, Technology & the Internet, Ohio State Technology Law Journal, The Journal of Civic Information* and other journals, focuses primarily on privacy, technology and the First Amendment. She received her Ph.D. in mass communications with a specialization in media law from the University of Florida, her M.A. in linguistics from the University of Texas at Austin, and her J.D. from Cornell Law School. She previously served as the head of the AEJMC Law Division. Her email is kearston.wesner@quinnipiac.edu.

Kyu Ho Youm is a professor and Jonathan Marshall First Amendment Chair in the School of Journalism and Communication at the University of Oregon. He has published scholarly articles on communication law subjects in major U.S. and foreign academic journals, including *Journalism & Mass Communication Quarterly, Hastings Communication/Entertainment (COMM/ENT) Law Journal* and *International and Comparative Law Quarterly* of London. His articles have been cited by American and English courts, including the House of the Lords (the United Kingdom equivalent of the Supreme Court) and the High Court of Australia. A former head of the AEJMC Law Division and a former chair of the Communication Law and Policy Group of the International Communication Association, he serves on editorial boards of thirteen communication law journals in the United States and England. He has also served as the president of AEJMC. He received his bachelor's degree in South Korea and his master's and doctoral degrees from Southern Illinois University. He holds master of law degrees from the Yale Law School and Oxford University. His e-mail address is youm@uoregon.edu.

AUTHORS EMERETI

Dorothy Bowles was a professor at the University of Tennessee, has taught communications law at the graduate and undergraduate levels for thirty years. She is the author of *Kansas Media Law Guide* and *Media Law in Tennessee*, as well as numerous journal articles. She is an emeritus member of the board of directors of the Student Press Law Center and has held several offices in the Association for Education in Journalism and Mass Communications. She has worked as a newspaper reporter and editor and is co-author of one of the leading editing textbooks. In 2005, she received The Jefferson Prize, a top faculty award at the University of Tennessee. Her Ph.D. from the University of Wisconsin.

Sandra F. Chance is McClatchy Professor in Freedom of Information at the University of Florida,. She is also Executive Director of the Brechner Center for Freedom of Information. She teaches law of mass communication at the undergraduate and graduate levels and was named the Scripps-Howard National Journalism Teacher of the Year in 2005. She practiced media law with one of the country's largest law firms before joining the faculty at Florida. She has published articles in *Communication Law and Policy, Journal of Broadcasting & Electronic Media, Journalism & Mass Communication Quarterly, Journal of Law and Public Policy, UALR Law Review, Quill, Editor & Publisher* and other journals. She is on the board of directors of the First Amendment Foundation and is Sunshine Chair for the Society of Professional Journalists.

Thomas Eveslage was a professor of journalism in Temple University's School of Communications and Theater. He has directed the Master of Journalism program and chaired the Department of Journalism, Public Relations and Advertising. He holds a Ph.D. in journalism from Southern Illinois University at Carbondale. He has served on the board of directors of the Student Press Law Center, the Pennsylvania School Press Association and Quill and Scroll Society. He has written a column on student press law issues for more than ten years and has received the Lawrence Campbell Research Award three times from the Scholastic Journalism Division of the Association for Education in Journalism and Mass Communication. A member of Temple University's Teaching Academy, he was named Journalism Teacher of the Year in 2003 by AEJMC's Scholastic Journalism Division. He is a former copy editor and university news director.

F. Dennis Hale was an emeritus professor and former director of the School of Mass Communication at Bowling Green State University at the time of his death in 2008. He had published more than eighty book

chapters, convention papers and journal articles, many about mass media law. He was a former head of the Law Division of the Association for Education in Journalism in Mass Communication and had received research grants from the U.S. Justice Department and the Newspaper Research Council. His Ph.D. degree was from Southern Illinois University.

Louise Williams Hermanson was a professor in the Department of Communication at the University of South Alabama, until her death in 2001. She taught law, ethics, print journalism and media history. Her research interests focused on alternative dispute resolution in conflicts between media and the public. She had published numerous journal articles and book chapters. Her Ph.D. was from the University of Minnesota. She had worked as a professional journalist in South Carolina.

Robert L. Hughes was an attorney in Richmond. He taught law for nineteen years at the Virginia Commonwealth University School of Mass Communications. Before that, he was a reporter and editorial writer for newspapers in Charlotte and West Palm Beach. He has a B.A. degree from Davidson College, an M.J. degree from the University of Missouri and a J.D. degree from the University of Florida.

Paul E. Kostyu is a senior outreach and education specialist for the Office of the Ohio Consumers' Counsel, a state agency that advocates on behalf of residential users of public utilities. He is a former Ohio statehouse bureau chief and business writer for newspapers in Ohio, Michigan and North Carolina and at *National Geographic* magazine. He is also an adjunct associate professor of journalism at Ohio Wesleyan University, where he has taught courses in reporting, editing, journalism history and communication law. His Ph.D. degree is from Bowling Green State University. In 2005 he was a Kiplinger Fellow in Public Affairs Journalism at Ohio State University. He has published in *Communication and the Law, American Journalism, Journal of Mass Media Ethics* and *News Photographer* magazine.

Arati R. Korwar has taught courses in media law, visual communication and online journalism, most recently Louisiana State University. Her research in communication law and First Amendment issues has been published in *Communication Law and Policy, Journalism and Mass Communication Monographs* and other journals, and by the Freedom Forum First Amendment Center. As an American Society for Newspaper Editors fellow, she worked at *The New York Times on the Web*. She also worked at *The Times of India* as a reporter and copyeditor. She received a Ph.D. from the University of North Carolina at Chapel Hill.

Dan V. Kozlowski is an associate professor in the Department of Communication at Saint Louis University, where he teaches free expression, journalism and media courses. He also holds a secondary appointment in SLU's law school. His research has appeared in *Communication Law and Policy, Journalism & Mass Communication Quarterly, Journal of Media Law & Ethics, Free Speech Yearbook, The International Encyclopedia of Communication* and other places. His research interests include student speech rights, judicial decision-making, comparative law, and journalism and culture. He has twice won the Laurence R. Campbell Research Award from the Scholastic Journalism Division of AEJMC for the top faculty paper at the annual conference. He received Ph.D. from the University of North Carolina at Chapel Hill. He is former newspaper copy editor and page designer and has been a sports producer for WNBC-TV in New York City.

Greg Lisby is an emeritus professor of communication at Georgia State University, where he taught mass communication law and policy, and communication ethics. In addition to serving as a member of the editorial board of *Communication Law and Policy*, he has had articles published in *Journalism Monographs, Communication Law and Policy, Communications and the Law, Journalism Quarterly, Journal of Communication Inquiry, Newspaper Research Journal* and *Georgia Historical Quarterly*. The sixth edition of his book *Mass Communication Law in Georgia* was published in 2011. He was executive producer of a PBS documentary on film censorship in 2000. He is past head of the Law Division of the Association for Education in Journalism and Mass Communication and a past member of the editorial board of *American Journalism*. He was the 2003 recipient of the American Journalism Historians Association's book of the year award, the 2000 recipient of the *Georgia Historical Quarterly's* article of the year award, and the 1990 recipient of the Henry W. Grady Prize for Research in Journalism History. He received his Ph.D. from the University of Tennessee and his law degree from Georgia State University. He is a member of the State Bar of Georgia.

Mike McGregor is a professor of telecommunications and adjunct professor of law at Indiana University, where he teaches electronic media law and policy courses and introductory telecommunications courses. His research, which focuses on telecommunications policy making, the effects of policy decisions and e-government, has been published in *Communication Law and Policy, Journalism and Communication Monographs, Federal Communications Law Journal, COMM/ENT, Journalism Quarterly, Journal of Broadcasting and Electronic Media* and *Telecommunications Policy*. He has been a staff attorney at the Cable Television Information Center of the Urban Institute and has been an attorney/advisor in the Mass Media Bureau of the Federal Communications Commission. He received his bachelor's degree in history from Purdue University and his J.D. from Georgetown University Law Center.

Kathleen K. Olson is a professor in the Department of Journalism and Communication at Lehigh University. She has a Ph.D. in mass communication from the University of North Carolina at Chapel Hill and a law degree from the University of Virginia. She practiced law in Washington, D.C., and helped start the online version of the *Austin American-Statesman* in Austin, Texas. She co-authored *Mass Communication Law in Pennsylvania* and has published in *Communication Law and Policy, Journalism and Communication Monographs, Free Speech Yearbook* and other journals. Her research interests include intellectual property issues and the First Amendment.

Cathy Packer was the W. Horace Carter Distinguished Professor in the School of Journalism and Mass Communication at the University of North Carolina at Chapel Hill. She is also co-director of the UNC Center for Media Law and Policy. She teaches media law and Internet law and is the author of *Freedom of Expression in the American Military: A Communication Modeling Analysis*. A former newspaper reporter, she is co-editor of *The North Carolina Media Law Handbook*, to which she contributes the chapter on access to state and local records. She has published articles in *Journalism & Mass Communication Quarterly, Mass Comm Review, Carozo Arts & Entertainment Law Journal, Communication Law and Policy* and *Hastings Communications and Entertainment Law Journal*. She received her doctoral degree from the University of Minnesota.

Michael Perkins was chair of the Department of Communication at Brigham Young University until 2003 when he was killed in a kayaking accident. He had also taught at Drake University and the University of Costa Rica. His research, which focused on mass communication law internationally as well as in the United States, has been published in *Journalism and Mass Communication Quarterly, Communication Law and Policy, Journal of Mass Media Ethics, Gazette* and *Newspaper Research Journal*. He was the head of the AEJMC Law Division at the time of his death.

Milagros (Millie) Rivera-Sanchez teaches telecommunication courses at the National University of Singapore. She has published articles in *Journalism and Mass Communication Monographs, Journalism and Mass Communication Quarterly, Journalism History, The Federal Communications Law Journal, Communications and the Law, Hastings Communications* and *Entertainment Law Journal* and other journals. She holds a Ph.D. from the University of Florida. She spent the summer of 1999 in Chile as a Fulbright Scholar.

Susan Dente Ross is an associate professor at Washington State University. She teaches media law, First Amendment theory, access to public records and journalism skills courses. In addition to conducting research on the regulation of emerging communication technologies, she examines the application of the First Amendment to speech and studies how media coverage frames marginalized groups and affects social change.

Joseph Russomanno is an associate professor at Arizona State University. His articles have appeared in a variety of journals. He worked as a television news journalist – primarily as a producer and executive producer – for ten years. He received his Ph.D. from the University of Colorado.

Thomas A. Schwartz recently retired from School of Journalism and Communication at Ohio State University where he taught reporting, mass communication law and legal research. He is a former newspaper and magazine editor, reporter and photographer. His recent research emphasizes the U.S. Supreme Court and the First Amendment and South African freedom of expression. He is past editor of the journal *Communication Law and Policy*.

Robert Trager teaches at the University of Colorado at Boulder. He holds a Ph.D. in journalism and mass communication from the University of Minnesota and a J.D. from the Stanford Law School. He has practiced law in Washington, D.C., and with Time Warner Cable. He is also the founding editor of *Communication Law and Policy*.

Ruth Walden is an emeritus at the University of North Carolina at Chapel Hill. She has held academic positions in Utah and Wisconsin-Madison and was a newspaper reporter in Wisconsin and Illinois. She was also assistant director of judicial education for the Wisconsin Supreme Court. She is the author of *Insult Laws: An Insult to Press Freedom* and *Mass Communication Law in North Carolina* and has published a number of articles on media law and First Amendment theory. A former head of the Law Division of the Association for Education in Journalism and Mass Communication, she serves on the editorial boards of *Journalism & Mass Communication Quarterly* and *Communication Law and Policy*.

Case Index

Subject Index

Mapplethorpe, Robert, 72
Marconi Wireless Company, 157
Marconi, Guglielmo, 157
marketplace of ideas, 24, 28-30, 31, 180
Marshall, Howard, 304
Marshall, Thurgood, 60, 74, 130, 284, 308, 309, 315
Marten, J. Thomas, 324
Mary Washington, University of, 209
Maryland courts, 78, 113
mash-ups, *see* copyright and digital sampling/file
    sharing
Massachusetts courts, 107, 108, 109, 283, 315, 321,
    283, 315, 321
Mathison, David, 211
Matthews, Dominick, 301
"Max Hardcore," 67
Maynard, George, 44
Mazar-e-Sharif, 349
McConnell, Mitch, 16-17
McDougal, James B., 321, 321
McGraw-Hill, 60-61, 62, 308, 308
McKevitt, Michael, 287
McKinley, William, 23
McMahon, Ed, 271
McVeigh, Timothy, 275, 306, 349
Media Law Resource Center, 86, 112
Meese, Edwin, 69
meetings, state and local, 242
    see also Sunshine Act
Meiklejohn, Alexander, 24, 28, 93, 103, 329-30
Memmel, Scott, 213
Memoirs of a Woman of Pleasure, 70
Memoirs Test, *see* Roth/Memoirs Test
Memphis Press-Scimitar, 89
Men at Work, 244
Menendez, Erik and Lyle, 308
Merritt, Gilbert S., 61
Miami Herald, 159 266, 275
Michael, Robert T., 74
Michigan courts, 331
Mickey Mouse, 226
Miers, Harriet, 16
Mill, John Stuart, 25, 263
Miller Test, 71-73, 74, 77, 221
    See also obscenity
Miller, Darlene, 70
Miller, Judith, 287, 288, 289, 290, 293
Miller, Marvin, 71
Milton, John, 24, 25, 48-49, 51, 53, 58, 65
Minneapolis Star and Tribune, 294
Minnesota courts, 41, 54, 90, 107, 294, 301
Minnesota, University of, 122
Mississippi courts, 310
Mobil Oil Co., 95
Mohammed, Khalid Sheikh, 322
Mokhiber, Russell, 319
Montana courts, 101
Moore, Demi, 246
Moore, Randy, 246
Mother Earth magazine, 23
Motion Picture Association of America (MPAA), 79,
    248
Moussaoui, Zacarias, 321, 322
Movie Orgy, The, 249
movie ratings, *see* ratings
Mueller, Robert, 246
multichannel multipoint distribution service (MDS),
    219
Musk, Elon, 29, 137, 208
must-carry rules, *see* cable television and must car-

ry rules
"My Sweet Lord," 244
Myers, Michael, 321

N
NAACP, 273
Nabisco, 255
    See also National Biscuit Co.
Naked Gun 33 1 /3, 246
NASA, 336
Nation, The, 245
National Advertising Division, 141
National Advertising Review Board, 141
National Anthem, 39
National Association of Theater Owners, 79
National Biscuit Co., 252
    See also Nabisco
National Cable and Telecommunications Associa-
    tion, 183
National Enquirer, 95
National Football League, 240
National Jewish Democratic Council, 107
National Labor Relations Board, 150-51, 230
National Security Agency (NSA), 63, 208, 229, 262,
    289, 295
National Security Council, 62
National Television and Information Administra-
    tion, 163
National Television System Committee, 219
Native Americans, 174, 336
Nazis, 41, 312
NBC, 286
Near, Jay M., 54
Nebraska Press Association test, 310, 312
Nebraska Press Association, 57, 308
negligence, 97
Neilson, Leslie, 246
Netflix, 149
network neutrality, 193-94, 196, 211-12
neutral reporting, *see* defamation and neutral re-
    porting
New Hampshire courts, 111, 292
New Jersey courts, 87, 92, 98, 105, 184, 292, 310
New Mexico courts, 97
New York courts, 79, 92, 95, 101, 108, 109, 113, 311
New York Herald, 282
New York Times Co., 93
New York Times rule, *see* actual malice
New York Times, 55, 57, 93, 95, 104, 239, 264, 283,
    287, 288, 289, 329, 336
New Yorker, The, 108
newsgathering
    accident and disaster scenes, 348
    and executions, 349
    and the military, 349-50
    and polling places, 350
    and prisons, 348
    in private places, 350-51
    in public places, 347-48
    and schools, 350
    See also ride-alongs
newsroom searches, *see* searches/search warrants
Newsweek, 269, 270
Newton, Isaac, 24
NFL, 38-39
Nichols, Ruth A., 89
Nichols, Terry, 306
Nickell, Stella, 317
Nimmer, Melville, 243
Nitke, Barbara, 221

Nixon, Richard, 69, 245, 270, 284, 320
nondisclosure agreements, 62
Noriega, Manuel, 59-60, 309
Norman Conquest, 263, 314
North Carolina courts, 109
North Pauling High School (Georgia), 119
Novak, Robert, 104
Novick, Sheldon M., 57
Nuccio, Richard, 99
nude dancing, 40, 70

O
O'Brien Test, 38-39, 40, 45
O'Brien, David Paul, 37, 38-39
O'Connor, Sandra Day, 16, 40, 42, 60, 189, 225, 309
Obama, Barack, 16, 113, 188, 203, 211, 216, 239,
    262, 277, 289, 294, 333
Obmacare, 324
obscenity
    defined, 69
    See also indecency, Miller Test, pornography,
        Roth/Memoirs test
"Oh, Pretty Woman," 245
Ohio courts, 78, 89, 108, 111
Ollman Test, 104
    See also defamation and opinion
Olympics, 121
On Liberty, 263
Online Privacy Alliance, 276
Ontario courts, 113
Open Foundation, 229
Open Government Guide, 343
Open Internet Order, 194-95, 196, 210, 212
Openness Promotes Effectiveness in our National
    (Open) Government Act, 334
Operation Desert Storm, 349
Orbison, Roy, 24-46, 247
Oregon courts, 75, 317
Osborne, Clyde, 77
Otis, James, 263
Oxford University, 2

P
Pacifica Foundation, 169
Packingham, Lester G., 230
Pai, Ajit, 195, 212
pandering, 78
paparazzi, 351
Papish, Barbara, 122
Pappas, Paul, 283
Paramount Pictures, 91, 246
Patel, Marilyn, 227
Patient Protection and Affordable Care Act, *see*
    Obamacare
Patriarca, Raymond L.S., 310
Patriot Act, *see* USA PATRIOT Act
Patriot II, *see* Domestic Security Enhancement Act
Paul, Alice, 22
Pearlstine, Norman, 287
peer-to-peer file sharing, *see* copyright digital sam-
    pling/file sharing
Pence, Mike, 39, 44
Pennsylvania courts, 40
penny press, 264
Pentagon Papers case, 55, 57, 59, 61, 65, 309
Penthouse, 72, 73
People v. Larry Flynt, The, 271
Peterson, Laci, 324
Peterson, Michael, 324
Peterson, Scott, 324

Made in the USA
Monee, IL
20 July 2024

61546584R00216